Additional copies of *Instrument Pilot FAA Written Exam* are available from

Gleim Publications, Inc.
P.O. Box 12848
University Station
Gainesville, Florida 32604
(352) 375-0772 / (800) 87-GLEIM/(800) 874-5346
FAX: (352) 375-6940
Internet: www.gleim.com | E-mail: admin@gleim.com

The price is $18.95 (subject to change without notice). Orders must be prepaid. Use the order form on page 488. Shipping and handling charges will be added to telephone orders. Add applicable sales tax to shipments within Florida.

Gleim Publications, Inc. guarantees the immediate refund of all resalable materials returned in 30 days. Shipping and handling charges are nonrefundable.

REVIEWERS AND CONTRIBUTORS

Karen A. Hom, B.A., University of Florida, provided production assistance throughout the project.

Barry A. Jones, ATP, CFII, MEI, B.S. in Air Commerce/Flight Technology, Florida Institute of Technology, drafted material in previous editions and for this edition, and provided technical assistance throughout the project.

Joshua B. Moore, CFI, B.A., University of Florida, is our aviation technical research assistant and a flight instructor with Gulf Atlantic Airways in Gainesville, Florida. Mr. Moore researched questions, edited answer explanations, and incorporated revisions into the text.

John F. Rebstock, B.S., Fisher School of Accounting, University of Florida, reviewed portions of the text and composed the page layout.

Jan M. Strickland is our book production assistant. Ms. Strickland reviewed the manuscript and provided production assistance.

The CFIs who have worked with me throughout the years to develop and improve my pilot training materials.

The many FAA employees who helped, in person or by telephone, primarily in Gainesville, Orlando, Oklahoma City, and Washington, DC.

The many pilots and student pilots who have provided comments and suggestions about *Instrument Pilot Flight Maneuvers and Practical Test Prep* and *Instrument Pilot FAA Written Exam* during the past 10 years.

A PERSONAL THANKS

This manual would not have been possible without the extraordinary efforts and dedication of Jim Collis and Terry Hall, who typed the entire manuscript and all revisions, as well as prepared the camera-ready pages.

The author also appreciates the proofreading and production assistance of Melissa Gruebel, Kevin Jordan, Jessica Medina, and Shane Rapp.

Finally, I appreciate the encouragement, support, and tolerance of my family throughout this project.

Groundwood Paper and Highlighters -- This book is printed on high quality groundwood paper. It is lightweight and easy-to-recycle. We recommend that you purchase a highlighter specifically designed to be non-bleed-through (e.g., Avery *Glidestick*™) at your local office supply store.

SEVENTH EDITION

INSTRUMENT PILOT

FAA WRITTEN EXAM

for the FAA Computer-Based Pilot Knowledge Tests:

Instrument Rating - Airplane
Flight Instructor - Instrument - Airplane
Instrument Ground Instructor

Instrument Rating - Foreign Pilot
Flight Instructor - Instrument - Airplane Added Rating

by Irvin N. Gleim, Ph.D., CFII

ABOUT THE AUTHOR

Irvin N. Gleim earned his private pilot certificate in 1965 from the Institute of Aviation at the University of Illinois, where he subsequently received his Ph.D. He is a commercial pilot and flight instructor (instrument) with multiengine and seaplane ratings, and is a member of the Aircraft Owners and Pilots Association, American Bonanza Society, Civil Air Patrol, Experimental Aircraft Association, and Seaplane Pilots Association. He is also author of Practical Test Prep and Flight Maneuvers books for the private, instrument, commercial, and flight instructor certificates/ratings, and study guides for the private/recreational, instrument, commercial, flight/ground instructor, fundamentals of instructing, airline transport pilot, and flight engineer FAA knowledge tests. Three additional pilot training books are *Pilot Handbook*, *Aviation Weather and Weather Services*, and *FAR/AIM*.

Dr. Gleim has also written articles for professional accounting and business law journals, and is the author of widely used review manuals for the CIA exam (Certified Internal Auditor), the CMA exam (Certified Management Accountant), the CFM exam (Certified in Financial Management), the CPA exam (Certified Public Accountant), and the EA exam (IRS Enrolled Agent). He is Professor Emeritus, Fisher School of Accounting, University of Florida, and is a CFM, CIA, CMA, and CPA.

Gleim Publications, Inc.
P.O. Box 12848
University Station
Gainesville, Florida 32604

(352) 375-0772
(800) 87-GLEIM or (800) 874-5346
FAX: (352) 375-6940

Internet: www.gleim.com
E-mail: admin@gleim.com

ISSN 1092-1133

ISBN 1-58194-072-6

Sixth Printing: November 2001

This is the sixth printing of the seventh edition of *Instrument Pilot FAA Written Exam*. Please e-mail update@gleim.com with IPWE 7-6 in the subject or text. You will receive our current update as a reply.

EXAMPLE:

To: update@gleim.com
From: your e-mail address
Subject: IPWE 7-6

SOURCES USED IN INSTRUMENT PILOT FAA WRITTEN EXAM

The first lines of the answer explanations contain citations to authoritative sources of the answers. These publications can be obtained from the FAA, the Government Printing Office, and aviation bookstores. These citations are abbreviated as provided below:

AC	Advisory Circular		
ACL	Aeronautical Chart Legend	Fl Comp	Flight Computer
A/FD	Airport/Facility Directory	FTH	Flight Training Handbook
AFNA	Aerodynamics for Naval Aviators	IFH	Instrument Flying Handbook
AIM	Aeronautical Information Manual	MHP	Medical Handbook for Pilots
AvW	Aviation Weather	NTSB	National Transportation Safety Board Regulations
AWS	Aviation Weather Services	P/C Glossary	Pilot/Controller Glossary (AIM)
FAA-P-8740-50	On Landings, Part III	PHAK	Pilot's Handbook of Aeronautical Knowledge
FAR	Federal Aviation Regulations		

HELP !!

This is the Seventh Edition designed specifically for private pilots who aspire to the instrument rating. Please send any corrections and suggestions for subsequent editions to the author, c/o Gleim Publications, Inc. The last page in this book has been reserved for you to make comments and suggestions. It can be torn out and mailed to us.

Instrument Pilot FAA Written Exam is one of four related books contained in Gleim's Instrument Pilot Kit for obtaining an instrument rating. The other three are Gleim's *Instrument Pilot Flight Maneuvers and Practical Test Prep*, *Instrument Pilot Syllabus*, and *Aviation Weather and Weather Services*.

Save time, money, and frustration -- order these books today! See the order form on page 488. Please bring these books to the attention of flight instructors, fixed-base operators, and others with a potential interest in instrument flying. Wide distribution of these books and increased interest in flying depend on your assistance, good word, etc. Thank you.

NOTE: ANSWER DISCREPANCIES and UPDATES

Our answers have been carefully researched and reviewed. Inevitably, there will be differences with competitors' books and even the FAA. Send e-mail to update@gleim.com as described at the top right of this page, and visit our Internet site for the latest updates and information on all of our products. To continue providing our customers with first-rate service, we request that questions about our books and software be sent to us via <u>mail</u>, <u>e-mail</u>, or <u>fax</u>. The appropriate staff member will give each question thorough consideration and a prompt response. Questions concerning orders, prices, shipments, or payments will be handled via telephone by our competent and courteous customer service staff.

TABLE OF CONTENTS

[Call (800) 87-GLEIM to order your FAA Test Prep software]

SIXTH PRINTING (11/01) CHANGES

1. Pages 13-17. Updated description of FAA Test Prep software.

2. The FAA made revisions to or added the following questions:

Chapter 1:	Q. 17, 18a (new)
Chapter 3:	Q. 50a (new), 85 (new), 86 (new), 87 (new)
Chapter 4:	Q. 25, 56, 71a (new)
Chapter 5:	Q. 12a (new), 12b (new), 12c (new), 12d (new), 91a (new)
Chapter 6:	Q. 3a (new)
Chapter 10:	Q. 27a (new)
Chapter 11:	Q. 43a (new), 53a (new)

3. Pages 457-459. Updated the FAA Subject Matter Knowledge Code listing.

4. Pages 460-466. Numerous changes to the Subject Matter Knowledge Codes.

This printing reflects these changes.

PREFACE

The primary purpose of this book is to provide you with the easiest, fastest, and least expensive means of passing the FAA instrument rating (airplane) knowledge test. We have

1. Reproduced the actual FAA airplane test questions which can appear on your FAA knowledge test (airplane).

2. Reordered the questions into 91 logical topics.

3. Organized the 91 topics into 11 chapters.

4. Explained the answer immediately to the right of each question.

5. Provided an easy-to-study outline of exactly what you need to know (and no more) at the beginning of each chapter.

Accordingly, you can thoroughly prepare for the FAA knowledge test by

1. Studying the brief outlines at the beginning of each chapter.

2. Answering the questions on the left side of each page while covering up the answer explanations on the right side of each page.

3. Reading the answer explanation for each question that you answer incorrectly or with which you have difficulty.

4. Using Gleim's *FAA Test Prep* software which facilitates this process. See pages 12 through 16.

The secondary purpose of this book is to introduce *Instrument Pilot Flight Maneuvers and Practical Test Prep* and *Pilot Handbook*.

Instrument Pilot Flight Maneuvers and Practical Test Prep is designed to help prepare pilots for their flight training and the FAA instrument rating practical test. Each task, objective, concept, and requirement is explained, analyzed, illustrated, and interpreted so pilots will be totally conversant with all aspects of the instrument pilot practical test.

Pilot Handbook is a textbook of aeronautical knowledge presented in easy-to-use outline format. While this book contains only the material needed to pass the FAA knowledge test, *Pilot Handbook* contains the textbook knowledge required to be a safe and proficient pilot.

Most books create additional work for the user. In contrast, my books facilitate your effort. They are easy to use. The outline format, type styles, and spacing are designed to improve readability. Concepts are often presented as phrases rather than as complete sentences.

Read the introductory chapter, Introduction: The FAA Knowledge Test, carefully. Also, recognize that this study manual is concerned with **airplane** flight training, not helicopter training. I am confident this manual will facilitate speedy completion of your knowledge test. I also wish you the very best in completing your instrument rating, in subsequent flying, and in obtaining additional ratings and certificates.

Enjoy Flying -- Safely!

Irvin N. Gleim

November 2001

INTRODUCTION
THE FAA KNOWLEDGE TEST

This introduction explains how to obtain an instrument rating, and explains the content and procedure of the Federal Aviation Administration (FAA) knowledge test, including how to take the test at a computer testing center. The remainder of this chapter discusses and illustrates Gleim's *FAA Test Prep* software. Achieving an instrument rating is fun. Begin today!

Instrument Pilot FAA Written Exam is one of four books contained in Gleim's Instrument Pilot Kit. The other three books are

1. *Instrument Pilot Flight Maneuvers and Practical Test Prep*
2. *Instrument Pilot Syllabus*
3. *Aviation Weather and Weather Services*

Instrument Pilot Flight Maneuvers and Practical Test Prep presents each flight maneuver you will perform in outline/illustration format so you will know what to expect and what to do before each flight lesson. This book will thoroughly prepare you to complete your FAA practical (flight) test confidently and successfully.

Instrument Pilot Syllabus is a step-by-step syllabus of ground and flight training lesson plans for your instrument rating training.

Gleim's *Aviation Weather and Weather Services* combines all of the information from the FAA's *Aviation Weather* (AC 00-6A), *Aviation Weather Services* (AC 00-45E), and numerous FAA publications into one easy-to-understand book. It will help you study all aspects of aviation weather and provide you with a single reference book.

While the following books are not included in the Instrument Pilot Kit, you may want to purchase them if you do not already have them:

Pilot Handbook is a complete pilot reference book, which combines over 100 FAA books and documents including *AIM*, FARs, ACs, and much more.

Gleim's *FAR/AIM* is an easy-to-read reference book containing all of the Federal Aviation Regulations (FARs) applicable to general aviation flying, plus the full text of the FAA's *Aeronautical Information Manual* (*AIM*).

WHAT IS AN INSTRUMENT RATING?

An instrument rating is added to your private or commercial pilot certificate. A new certificate will be issued to you by the FAA upon satisfactory completion of your training program, an FAA knowledge test, and a practical test. A sample private pilot certificate with an instrument rating is reproduced below.

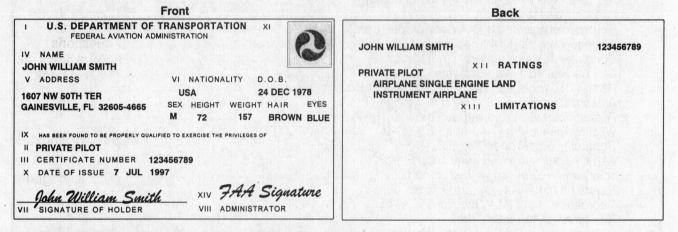

REQUIREMENTS TO OBTAIN AN INSTRUMENT RATING

1. Hold at least a private pilot certificate.

2. Be able to read, write, and converse fluently in English (certificates with operating limitations may be available for medically related deficiencies).

3. Hold a current FAA medical certificate.

    a. You must undergo a routine medical examination, which may be administered only by FAA-designated doctors called aviation medical examiners (AME).

    b. Even if you have a physical handicap, medical certificates can be issued in many cases. Operating limitations may be imposed depending upon the nature of the disability.

    c. Your certificated flight instructor-instrument (CFII) or fixed-base operator (FBO) will be able to recommend an AME.

        1) CFII is a flight instructor who has an instrument rating on his/her flight instructor certificate and is authorized to provide instruction for the instrument rating.

        2) An FBO is an airport business that gives flight lessons, sells aviation fuel, repairs airplanes, etc.

        3) Also, the FAA publishes a directory that lists all authorized AMEs by name and address. Copies of this directory are kept at all FAA offices, ATC facilities, and Flight Service Stations (FSS). Alternatively, go to the Gleim website at www.gleim.com/Aviation/AMESearch.html.

4. Receive and log ground training or complete a home-study course (such as using this book, *Instrument Pilot Flight Maneuvers and Practical Test Prep*, and *Aviation Weather and Weather Services*) to learn

    a. *Federal Aviation Regulations . . . that apply to flight operations under IFR*

    b. *Appropriate information that applies to flight operations under IFR in the Aeronautical Information Manual*

    c. *Air traffic control system and procedures for instrument flight operations*

    d. *IFR navigation and approaches by use of navigation systems*

    e. *Use of IFR en route and instrument approach procedure charts*

    f. *Procurement and use of aviation weather reports and forecasts and the elements of forecasting weather trends based on that information and personal observation of weather conditions*

    g. *Safe and efficient operation of aircraft under instrument flight rules and conditions*

    h. *Recognition of critical weather situations and windshear avoidance*

    i. *Aeronautical decision making and judgment*

    j. *Crew resource management, including crew communication and coordination*

5. Pass the instrument rating knowledge test with a score of 70% or better. All FAA tests are administered at FAA-designated computer testing centers. The instrument rating test consists of 60 multiple-choice questions selected from the airplane-related questions among the questions in the FAA's instrument rating test bank; the remaining questions are for helicopters. Each of the FAA's airplane-related questions is reproduced in this book with complete explanations to the right of each question.

6. Accumulate flight experience (FAR 61.65).

    a. 50 hr. of cross-country flight time as pilot in command, of which at least 10 hr. must be in airplanes

        1) The 50 hr. includes solo cross-country time as a student pilot, which is logged as pilot-in-command time.

        2) Each cross-country must have a landing at an airport that was at least a straight-line distance of more than 50 NM from the original departure point.

    b. A total of 40 hr. of actual or simulated instrument time in the areas of operations listed in 7. below, including

        1) 15 hr. of instrument flight training from a CFII

        2) 3 hr. of instrument training from a CFII in preparation for the practical test within 60 days preceding the practical test

        3) Cross-country flight procedures that include at least one cross-country flight in an airplane that is performed under IFR and consists of

            a) A distance of at least 250 NM along airways or ATC-directed routing
            b) An instrument approach at each airport
            c) Three different kinds of approaches with the use of navigation systems

    c. If the instrument training was provided by an authorized instructor, a maximum of 20 hr. permitted in an approved flight simulator or flight training device

7. Demonstrate flight proficiency (FAR 61.65). You must receive and log training, and obtain a logbook sign-off (endorsement) by your CFII on the following areas of operations:

    a. *Preflight preparation*
    b. *Preflight procedures*
    c. *Air traffic control clearances and procedures*
    d. *Flight by reference to instruments*
    e. *Navigation systems*
    f. *Instrument approach procedures*
    g. *Emergency operations*
    h. *Postflight procedures*

8. Alternatively, enroll in an FAA-certificated pilot school or training center that has an approved instrument rating course (airplane).

    a. These are known as Part 141 schools or Part 142 training centers because they are authorized by Part 141 or Part 142 of the FARs.

        1) All other regulations concerning the certification of pilots are found in Part 61 of the FARs.

9.   Successfully complete a practical test which will be given as a final exam by an FAA inspector or designated pilot examiner. The practical test will be conducted as specified in the FAA's Instrument Rating Practical Test Standards [FAA-S-8081-4C, dated October 1998, with Change 1 (December 1998) and Change 2 (March 1999)].

   a.   FAA inspectors are FAA employees and do not charge for their services.

   b.   FAA-designated pilot examiners are proficient, experienced flight instructors and pilots who are authorized by the FAA to conduct flight tests. They do charge a fee.

   c.   The FAA's Instrument Rating Practical Test Standards are outlined and reprinted in Gleim's *Instrument Pilot Flight Maneuvers and Practical Test Prep*.

FAA KNOWLEDGE TEST

1.   This book can be used in your preparation for the following FAA knowledge tests:

   a.   Instrument Rating - Airplane (IRA), which consists of 60 questions and has a time limit of 2 hr. 30 min.

   b.   Flight Instructor - Instrument - Airplane (FII), which consists of 50 questions and has a time limit of 2 hr. 30 min.

   c.   Instrument Ground Instructor (IGI), which consists of 50 questions and has a time limit of 2 hr. 30 min.

      1)   This test may include some helicopter-related questions. Just read the question carefully and, if you do not know the answer, take a guess. You need only 35 right out of 50 to pass the test.

   d.   Instrument Rating - Foreign Pilot (IFP), which consists of 50 questions and has a time limit of 2 hr. 30 min.

      1)   This test emphasizes FARs and weather more than the instrument rating (IRA) knowledge test.

   e.   Flight Instructor - Instrument - Airplane - Added Rating (AIF), which consists of 20 questions and has a time limit of 1 hr.

      1)   This test is for a CFII (helicopter) who wants to add an airplane rating to his/her CFII certificate.

NON-AIRPLANE TESTS

If you are using this book to study for a non-airplane pilot knowledge test, you should skip all of the obviously-airplane-related questions. Then, go to www.gleim.com/Aviation/nonairplane/ for the appropriate non-airplane questions.

---

2.   In an effort to develop better test questions, the **FAA frequently pretests questions** on pilot knowledge tests by adding up to 5 "pretest" questions. Thus, rather than the number of questions listed above, you may be required to answer up to 5 extra pretest questions. The pretest questions will not be graded. You will NOT know which questions are "real" and which are "pretest." Accordingly, you must attempt to answer all questions correctly.

3.   All of the questions in the FAA's instrument rating test bank that are applicable to airplanes have been grouped into the following 11 categories, which are the titles of Chapters 1 through 11:

   Chapter 1: Airplane Instruments
   Chapter 2: Attitude Instrument Flying and Aerodynamics
   Chapter 3: Navigation Systems
   Chapter 4: Federal Aviation Regulations
   Chapter 5: Airports, Air Traffic Control, and Airspace
   Chapter 6: Holding and Instrument Approaches

Chapter 7: Aeromedical Factors
Chapter 8: Aviation Weather
Chapter 9: Aviation Weather Services
Chapter 10: IFR En Route
Chapter 11: IFR Flights

Note that the FAA's questions are **not** grouped together by topic. We have unscrambled them for you in this book.

4. Within each of the chapters listed, questions relating to the same subtopic (e.g., missed approaches, holding patterns, turn rates, etc.) are grouped together to facilitate your study program. Each subtopic is called a module.

5. To the right of each question are

   a. The correct answer

   b. The FAA question number (See page 11 for information regarding the June 2001 FAA question numbering change.)

   c. A reference for the answer explanation

      1) EXAMPLE: *IFH Chap V* means *Instrument Flying Handbook*, Chapter V.
      2) See page iv for a listing of abbreviations used for authoritative sources.

6. Each chapter begins with an outline of the material tested on the FAA knowledge test. The outlines in this part of the book are very brief and have only one purpose: to help you pass the FAA instrument rating knowledge test.

   a. **CAUTION:** The **sole purpose** of this book is to expedite your passing the FAA instrument rating knowledge test. Accordingly, all extraneous material (i.e., not directly tested on the FAA knowledge test) is omitted even though much more information and knowledge are necessary to fly safely. This additional material is presented in Gleim's *Instrument Pilot Flight Maneuvers and Practical Test Prep*, *Aviation Weather and Weather Services*, *Pilot Handbook*, and *FAR/AIM*.

Follow the suggestions given throughout this chapter and you will have no trouble passing the pilot knowledge test the first time you take it.

HOW TO PREPARE FOR THE FAA KNOWLEDGE TEST

1. Begin by carefully reading the rest of this chapter. You need to have a complete understanding of the examination process prior to beginning to study for it. This knowledge will make your studying more efficient.

2. After you have spent an hour studying this chapter, set up a study schedule, including a target date for taking your knowledge test.

   a. Do not let the study process drag on because it will be discouraging, i.e., the quicker the better.

   b. Consider enrolling in an organized ground school course at your local FBO, community college, etc.

   c. Determine where and when you are going to take your FAA knowledge test.

3. Work through each of Chapters 1 through 11.

   a. Each chapter begins with a list of its module titles. The number in parentheses after each title is the number of FAA questions that cover the information in that module. The two numbers following the parentheses are the page numbers on which the outline and the questions for that particular module begin, respectively.

   b. Begin by studying the outlines slowly and carefully.

   c. Next, answer the multiple-choice questions under exam conditions. Cover the answer explanations on the right side of each page with the Gleim bookmark provided at the back of your book while you answer the multiple-choice questions.

1) Remember, it is very important to the learning (and understanding) process that you honestly commit yourself to an answer. If you are wrong, your memory will be reinforced by having discovered your error. Therefore, it is crucial to cover up the answer and make an honest attempt to answer the question before reading the answer.

2) Study the answer explanation for each question that you answer incorrectly, do not understand, or have difficulty with.

3) Use our *FAA Test Prep* software to assure that you do not refer to answers before committing to an answer AND to simulate actual computer testing center exam conditions.

4. Note that this test book (in contrast to most other question and answer books) contains the FAA questions grouped by topic. Thus, some questions may appear repetitive, while others may be duplicates or near-duplicates. Accordingly, do not work question after question (i.e., waste time and effort) if you are already conversant with a topic and the type of questions asked.

5. As you move from module to module and chapter to chapter, you may need further explanation or clarification of certain topics. You may wish to obtain and use the following Gleim books described on page 1.

   a. *Instrument Pilot Flight Maneuvers and Practical Test Prep*
   b. *Aviation Weather and Weather Services*
   c. *Pilot Handbook*
   d. *FAR/AIM*

6. Keep track of your work!!! As you complete a module in Chapters 1 through 11, grade yourself with an A, B, C, or ? (use a ? if you need help on the subject) next to the module title at the front of the respective chapter.

   a. The A, B, C, or ? is your self-evaluation of your comprehension of the material in that module and your ability to answer the questions.

      A   means a good understanding.
      B   means a fair understanding.
      C   means a shaky understanding.
      ?   means to ask your CFII or others about the material and/or questions and read the pertinent sections in *Instrument Pilot Flight Maneuvers and Practical Test Prep*, *Aviation Weather and Weather Services*, *Pilot Handbook*, and/or *FAR/AIM*.

   b. This procedure will provide you with the ability to see quickly (by looking at the first page of Chapters 1 through 11) how much studying you have done (and how much remains) and how well you have done.

   c. This procedure will also facilitate review. You can spend more time on the modules with which you had difficulty.

   d. *FAA Test Prep* software provides you with your historical performance data.

WHEN TO TAKE THE FAA KNOWLEDGE TEST

1. You must be at least 15 years of age to take the instrument rating knowledge test.

2. You must prepare for the test by successfully completing a ground instruction course under the supervision of your CFII, i.e., by studying this book.

   a. See "Authorization to Take the FAA Knowledge Test" on page 8.

3. Take the instrument rating knowledge test within the next 30 days.

   a. Get your knowledge test behind you.

4. Your practical test must follow within 24 months.

   a. Or you will have to retake your instrument rating knowledge test.

COMPUTER TESTING CENTERS

The FAA has contracted with several computer testing services to administer FAA knowledge tests. Each of these computer testing services has testing centers throughout the country. You register by calling an 800 number. Call the following testing services for information regarding the location of testing centers most convenient to you and the time allowed and cost to take the instrument rating (airplane) knowledge test.

CATS	(800) 947-4228, (650) 259-8559
LaserGrade	(800) 211-2754, (360) 896-9111

Also, about twenty Part 141 schools use the AvTEST computer testing system, which is very similar to the computer testing services described above.

GLEIM'S *FAA TEST PREP* SOFTWARE

Computer testing is consistent with aviation's use of computers (e.g., DUATS, flight simulators, computerized cockpits, etc.). All FAA knowledge tests are administered by computer.

Computer testing is natural after computer study. Computer-assisted instruction is a very efficient and effective method of study. Gleim's *FAA Test Prep* software is designed to prepare you for computer testing. *FAA Test Prep* software contains all of the questions in this book, context-sensitive outline material, and on-screen charts and figures. You choose either STUDY MODE or TEST MODE.

In STUDY MODE, the software provides you with an explanation of each answer you choose (correct or incorrect). You design each study session:

Topic(s) you wish to cover	Questions marked from last session -- test, study, or both
Number of questions	Questions missed from last session -- test, study, or both
Order of questions -- FAA, Gleim, or random	Questions missed from all sessions -- test, study, or both
Order of answers to each question -- FAA or random	Questions never answered correctly

In TEST MODE, you decide the format -- CATS, LaserGrade, AvTEST, or Gleim. When you finish your test, you can study the questions missed and access answer explanations. The software emulates the operation of the FAA-approved computer testing companies. Thus, you have a complete understanding of how to take an FAA knowledge test and know exactly what to expect before you go to a computer testing center.

For more information on Gleim's *FAA Test Prep* software, see page 12.

PART 141 SCHOOLS WITH FAA KNOWLEDGE TEST EXAMINING AUTHORITY

The FAA permits some FAR Part 141 schools to develop, administer, and grade their own knowledge tests as long as they use the FAA knowledge test questions, i.e., the same questions as in this book. The FAA does not provide the correct answers to the Part 141 schools, and the FAA only reviews the Part 141 school test question selection sheets. Thus, some of the answers used by Part 141 test examiners may not agree with the FAA or those in this book. The latter is not a problem but may explain why you may miss a question on a Part 141 knowledge test using an answer presented in this book.

AUTHORIZATION TO TAKE THE FAA KNOWLEDGE TEST

Before taking the instrument rating-airplane knowledge test, you must receive an endorsement from an authorized instructor who conducted the ground training or reviewed your home study in the required aeronautical knowledge areas, which are listed under item 4. of "Requirements to Obtain an Instrument Rating" on page 2.

For your convenience, a standard authorization form for the instrument rating-airplane knowledge test is reproduced on page 473. It can be easily completed, signed by a flight or ground instructor, torn out, and taken to the computer test site.

An instructor endorsement is not required for any instructor knowledge test or the instrument rating-foreign pilot knowledge test.

FORMAT OF THE FAA KNOWLEDGE TEST

The FAA's instrument rating knowledge test for airplanes consists of 60 multiple-choice questions selected from the questions that appear in the next 11 chapters.

Note that the FAA test will be taken from exactly the same questions that are reproduced in this book. If you study the next 11 chapters, including all the questions and answers, **you should be assured of passing your FAA instrument rating knowledge test.**

Additionally, all of the FAA legends and figures are contained in a book titled *Computer Testing Supplement for Instrument Rating*, which you will be given for your use at the time of your test. All of the airplane-related figures and most of the legends are reproduced in this book. We did not reproduce Legends 1 through 8, the *Airport/Facility Directory* Legend, and Legend 29, Temperature Conversion Chart because they are not needed to answer the test questions.

We need your help identifying which questions the FAA is pretesting (but not grading - see page 4). After you take your exam, please e-mail, fax, or mail us a description of these questions so we can anticipate their future use by the FAA.

WHAT TO TAKE TO THE FAA KNOWLEDGE TEST

1. The same flight computer that you use to solve the test questions in this book, i.e., one you are familiar with and have used before
2. A pocket calculator you are familiar with and have used before (no instructional material for the calculator allowed)
3. Authorization to take the knowledge test (see page 473)
4. Picture identification of yourself

NOTE: Paper and pencils are supplied at the examination site.

COMPUTER TEST PROCEDURES

To register for the pilot knowledge test by computer, you should call one of the computer testing services listed under "Computer Testing Centers" on page 7, or you may call one of their testing centers. These testing centers and telephone numbers are listed in Gleim's *FAA Test Prep* software under Vendors in the main menu. When you register, you will pay the fee with a credit card.

When you arrive at the computer testing center, you will be required to provide positive proof of identification and documentary evidence of your age. The identification presented must include your photograph, signature, and actual residential address, if different from the mailing address. This information may be presented in more than one form of identification. Next, you sign in on the testing center's daily log. Your signature on the logsheet certifies that, if this is a retest, you meet the applicable requirements (see "Failure on the FAA Knowledge Test" on page 11) and that you have not passed this test in the past 2 years. Finally, you will present your logbook endorsement or authorization form from your instructor, which authorizes you to take the test. A standard authorization form is provided on page 473 for your use.

Next, you will be taken into the testing room and seated at a computer terminal. A person from the testing center will assist you in logging on the system, and you will be asked to confirm your personal data (e.g., name, Social Security number, etc.). Then you will be prompted and given an online introduction to the computer testing system and you will take a sample test. If you have used our *FAA Test Prep* software, you will be conversant with the computer testing methodology and environment, and you will probably want to skip the sample test and begin the actual test immediately. You will be allowed approximately 2.5 hours to complete the actual test. This is 2.5 minutes per question. Confirm the time permitted when you call the testing center to register to take the test by computer. When you have completed your test, an Airman Knowledge Test Report will be printed out, validated (usually with an embossed seal), and given to you by a person from the testing center. Before you leave, you will be required to sign out on the testing center's daily log.

Each testing center has certain idiosyncrasies in its paperwork, scheduling, and telephone procedures, as well as in its software. It is for this reason that our *FAA Test Prep* software emulates each of these FAA-approved computer testing companies.

FAA QUESTIONS WITH TYPOGRAPHICAL ERRORS

Occasionally, FAA test questions contain typographical errors such that there is no correct answer. The FAA test development process involves many steps and people, and as you would expect, glitches occur in the system that are beyond the control of any one person. We indicate "best" rather than correct answers for some questions. Use these best answers for the indicated questions.

Note that the FAA corrects (rewrites) defective questions as they are discovered; these changes are explained in our updates -- see page iv. However, problems due to faulty or out-of-date figures printed in FAA Computer Testing Supplements are expensive to correct. Thus, it is important to carefully study questions that are noted to have a best answer in this book. Even though the best answer may not be completely correct, you should select it when taking your test.

YOUR AIRMAN KNOWLEDGE TEST REPORT

1. You will receive your Airman Knowledge Test Report upon completion of the test. An example knowledge test report is reproduced below.

    a. Note that you will receive only one grade as illustrated.

    b. The expiration date is the date by which you must take your FAA practical test.

    c. The report lists the FAA subject matter knowledge codes of the questions you missed, so you can review the topics you missed prior to your practical test.

Federal Aviation Administration
Airman Computer Test Report

EXAM TITLE: Instrument Rating Airplane

NAME: Jones David John

ID NUMBER: 123456789   TAKE: 1

DATE: 08/14/01   SCORE: 82   GRADE: Pass

Knowledge area codes in which questions were answered incorrectly. See appropriate knowledge test guide. A code may represent more than one incorrect response.

A20 B10 I05 J14 J33 J40

EXPIRATION DATE: 08/31/03

DO NOT LOSE THIS REPORT

Authorized instructor's statement. (If Applicable)

I have given Mr./Ms. _____ additional instruction in each subject area shown to be deficient and consider the applicant competent to pass the test.

Last _____ Initial _____ Cert. No. _____ Type _____
(Print Clearly)

Signature _____

CTD's Embossed Seal

---

2. Use the FAA's list of subject matter knowledge codes on pages 457 to 459 to determine which topics you had difficulty with.

    a. Look them over and review them with your CFII so (s)he can certify that (s)he reviewed the deficient areas and found you competent in them when you take your practical test.

3. Keep your Airman Knowledge Test Report in a safe place, as you must submit it to the FAA examiner when you take your practical test.

FAILURE ON THE FAA KNOWLEDGE TEST

1. If you fail (less than 70%) the knowledge test (virtually impossible if you follow our instructions on how to prepare, beginning on page 5), you may retake it after your CFII or ground instructor endorses the bottom of your Airman Knowledge Test Report certifying that you have received the necessary ground training to retake the test.

2. Upon retaking the test, you will find that the procedure is the same except that you must also submit your Airman Knowledge Test Report indicating the previous failure to the computer testing center.

3. Note that the pass rate on the instrument rating knowledge test is over 90%; i.e., less than 1 out of 10 fail the test initially. Reasons for failure include

   a. Failure to study the material tested (contained in the outlines at the beginning of Chapters 1 through 11 of this book);

   b. Failure to practice working the FAA exam questions under test conditions (all of the FAA questions on airplanes appear in Chapters 1 through 11 of this book); and

   c. Poor examination technique, such as misreading questions and not understanding the requirements.

REORGANIZATION OF FAA QUESTIONS

1. The questions in the FAA instrument rating test bank are numbered 4001 to 4942. The FAA questions appear to be presented randomly.

   a. We have reorganized the FAA questions into chapters and modules.

   b. The FAA question number is presented in the middle of the first line of the explanation of each answer.

2. Pages 462 through 468 contain a list of the FAA questions numbers 4001 to 4942 with cross-references to (1) the FAA's subject knowledge codes and (2) the chapters and question numbers in this book.

   a. For example, we have coded FAA question number 4002 as A24 and 4-19, which means it is covered under the FAA subject knowledge code, "FAR Part 61, Commercial Pilots," and is found in Chapter 4 as question 19 in this book.

   b. Note that, although 4001 to 4942 implies more questions than those in this book, we include only those that apply to airplanes.

      1) The remaining questions relate to helicopters and have been omitted from this book.

         a) These questions are indicated as NA in our cross-reference table.

   c. In June 2001, the FAA test bank was released without the familiar four-digit FAA question numbers. We identified all of the new questions and added them to the end of our cross-reference chart using our own question numbering system.

      1) The first four digits of this code refer to the month and year the question first appeared. The remaining digits identify the question number used in that particular FAA test bank release.

         a) For example, 0601-614 refers to the 614th question in the FAA's June 2001 test bank. It is found in Gleim Chapter 11 as question 84a.

With this overview of exam requirements, you are ready to begin the easy-to-study outlines and rearranged questions with answers to build your knowledge and confidence and PASS THE FAA's INSTRUMENT RATING KNOWLEDGE TEST.

Although no quantifiable data have been collected, the feedback we receive from users of our books and software indicates that they reduce anxiety, improve FAA test scores, and build knowledge. Studying for each test becomes a useful step toward advanced certificates and ratings.

SIMULATED FAA PRACTICE TEST

Appendix A, Instrument Rating Practice Test, beginning on page 448, allows you to practice taking the FAA knowledge test without the answers next to the questions. This test has 60 questions that have been randomly selected from the airplane-related questions in the FAA's instrument rating test bank. Topical coverage in this practice test is similar to that of the FAA Instrument Rating--Airplane test.

It is very important that you answer all 60 questions at one sitting. You should not consult the answers, especially when being referred to figures (charts, tables, etc.) throughout this book where the questions are answered and explained. Analyze your performance based on the answer key which follows the practice test in Appendix A.

Also rely on Gleim's *FAA Test Prep* software to simulate actual computer testing conditions including the screen layouts, instructions, etc., for CATS, LaserGrade, and AvTEST.

INSTRUCTIONS FOR THE *FAA TEST PREP* SOFTWARE

To install *FAA Test Prep*, put your CD-ROM in your CD-ROM drive. If an autoplay window appears after you insert the CD, follow the Setup Wizard. If no screen appears after you have inserted the CD, click on the Windows Start button, and select "Run" from a list of options. Type x:\setup.exe (if x is the drive letter of your CD-ROM), and click "OK." Follow the on-screen instructions to finalize the installation.

Gleim Publications requires all *FAA Test Prep* users to register their software for unlimited use, free updates, and technical support. To register, simply use the Personal Registration Number and Library Passkey(s) that were shipped with your CD-ROM, call (800) 87-GLEIM, or register online at (http://www.gleim.com/license.html).

Once you have installed *FAA Test Prep* onto your system, you can begin studying at any time by clicking on the icon placed on your desktop or the Windows Start Menu. Use the Tutorial in the HELP menu to go step by step through the study process, or start studying right away by clicking on Create Session. *FAA Test Prep* allows you to customize your study process using several different options.

Study Session

Study Sessions give you immediate feedback on why your answer selection for a particular FAA question is correct or incorrect and allow you to access the context-sensitive outline material that helps to explain concepts related to the question. Choose from several different question sources: all questions available for that library, questions from a certain topic (chapters and modules from Gleim books), questions that you missed or marked in the last session you created, questions that you have never answered correctly, questions from certain FAA subject codes, etc. You can mix up the questions by selecting to randomize the question and/or answer order so that you do not memorize answer letters.

You may then grade your study sessions and track your study progress using the performance analysis charts and graphs. The Performance Analysis information helps you to focus on areas where you need the most improvement, saving you time in the overall study process. You may then want to go back and study questions that you missed in a previous session, or you may want to create a study session of questions that you marked in the previous session, and all of these options are made easy with *FAA Test Prep*'s Study Sessions.

After studying the outlines and questions in a Study, you can switch to a Test Session. In a Test Session, you will not know which questions you have answered correctly until the session is graded. You can further test your skills with a Standard Test Session, which gives you the option of taking your pilot knowledge test under actual testing conditions using one of the emulations of the major testing centers.

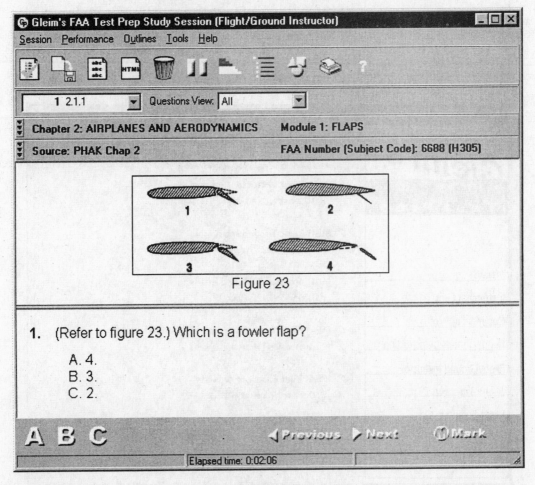

Standard Test Session

Take an exam in the actual testing environment of any of the major testing centers: CATS, AvTest, or Lasergrade. *FAA Test Prep* emulates the testing formats of these testing centers making it easy for you to study FAA questions under actual exam conditions. After studying with *FAA Test Prep*, you will know exactly what to expect when you go in to take your pilot knowledge test.

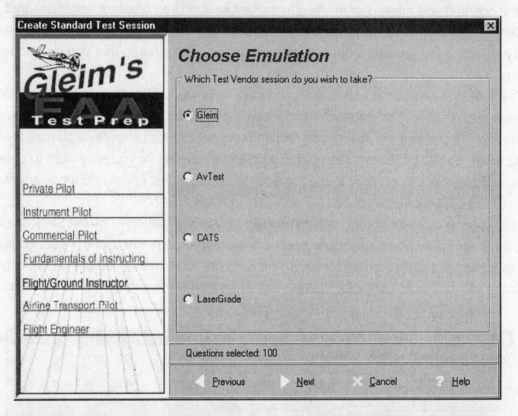

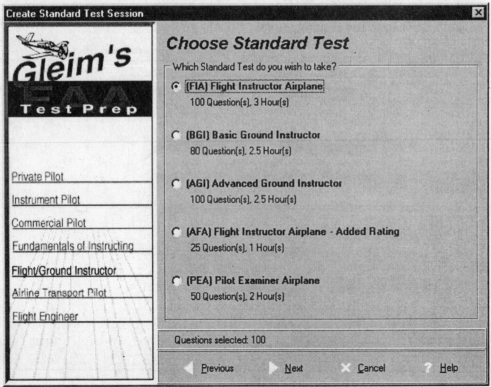

On-Screen Charts and Figures

One of the most convenient features of *FAA Test Prep* is the easily accessible on-screen charts and figures. Several of the FAA questions refer to drawings, maps, charts, and other pictures that provide information to help answer the question. In *FAA Test Prep*, you can pull up any of these figures with the click of a button. You can increase or decrease the size of the images, and you may also use our drawing feature to calculate the true course between two given points (required only on the private pilot knowledge test).

Instructor Print Options

FAA Test Prep is also a useful tool for instructors who want to create quizzes and assignments for their students. An instructor may mark questions in a session and then choose to print marked questions to create a quiz or test. (S)he may select to print an answer sheet, a blank answer sheet, and a renumbered printout of questions marked and any instructions that go along with the quiz or test.

INSTRUCTOR SIGN-OFF SHEETS

FAA Test Prep is capable of generating an instructor sign-off for FAA knowledge tests that require one. This sign-off has been approved by the FAA, and can be presented at the computer testing center as authorization to take your test—you do NOT need an additional endorsement from your instructor.

In order to obtain the instructor sign-off sheet for your test, you must first answer all questions in *FAA Test Prep* correctly. Then, select "Instructor Sign-Off Sheets" under the PERFORMANCE menu and select the appropriate test acronym using the index tabs (test acronyms are explained on page 4). If you have answered all of the required questions, the instructor sign-off sheet will appear for you to print. If you have not yet answered all required questions, a list of the unanswered questions, along with their location, will appear.

FAA Test Prep also contains a listing by state of all major testing center locations for CATS, AvTest, and LaserGrade. Gleim's *FAA Test Prep* is an all-in-one program designed to help anyone with a computer, Internet access, and an interest in flying to pass the pilot knowledge tests.

FREE Updates and Technical Support

Gleim offers FREE technical support to all registered users. Call (800) 87-GLEIM, send e-mail to support@gleim.com, or fill out the technical support request form online (www.gleim.com/techform.html). Gleim's new Online Updates feature makes updating your software and libraries even easier than before. Simply connect to the Internet, start the Gleim software, select Online Updates from the Test Prep Tools screen, and follow the on-screen instructions. Downloadable library updates will also be available online (www.gleim.com/updates.html) free to registered users of our CD-ROM software. For more information on our update service by e-mail, turn to page 472.

Obtain your copy of *FAA Test Prep* today. Order online at http://www.gleim.com/Aviation/IndivOrderForm.html or call 800 87-GLEIM.

If this Gleim test book saves you time and frustration in preparing for the FAA instrument rating knowledge test, you should use Gleim's *Instrument Pilot Flight Maneuvers and Practical Test Prep* to prepare for the FAA practical (flight) test. *Instrument Pilot Flight Maneuvers and Practical Test Prep* will assist you in developing the competence and confidence to pass your FAA practical test, just as this book organizes and explains the knowledge needed to pass your FAA instrument rating knowledge test.

Also, flight maneuvers are quickly perfected when you understand exactly what to expect before you get into an airplane to practice the flight maneuvers. You must be ahead of (not behind) your CFII and your airplane. Gleim's flight maneuvers books explain and illustrate all flight maneuvers so the maneuvers and their execution are intuitively appealing to you.

INSTRUMENT AND COMMERCIAL PILOT KITS

Due to customer feedback and requests, we have created kits for pilots with an interest in the instrument rating and commercial certificate. Gleim kits contain everything necessary to prepare for their FAA knowledge test, each flight lesson, and their FAA practical test (assuming previous purchase of **FAR/AIM** and **Pilot Handbook**). Our state-of-the-art **FAA Test Prep** software on CD-ROM is standard with each kit. Gleim kits are available at leading FBOs, flight schools, and aviation retailers or directly from Gleim.

Instrument Pilot Kit -- $114.95 (save 30%)

Includes: *Instrument Pilot Syllabus*
             Instrument Pilot Flight Maneuvers and Practical Test Prep
             Instrument Pilot FAA Written Exam
             Aviation Weather and Weather Services
             FAA Test Prep CD-ROM for Instrument Pilot
             Gleim Flight Bag

Commercial Pilot Kit -- $94.95 (save 30%)

Includes: *Commercial Pilot Syllabus*
             Commercial Pilot Flight Maneuvers and Practical Test Prep
             Commercial Pilot FAA Written Exam
             FAA Test Prep CD-ROM for Commercial Pilot
             Gleim Flight Bag

END OF INTRODUCTION

CHAPTER ONE
AIRPLANE INSTRUMENTS

This chapter contains outlines of major concepts tested, all FAA test questions and answers regarding airplane flight instruments, and an explanation of each answer. Each module, or subtopic, within this chapter is listed above with the number of questions from the FAA pilot knowledge test pertaining to that particular module. For each module, the first number following the parentheses is the page number on which the outline begins, and the next number is the page number on which the questions begin.

There are 68 questions in this chapter. We separate and organize the FAA questions into meaningful study units, i.e., chapters and modules. As an analogy, it is easier to deal with the "trees" if you understand the "forest." In this context, "trees" are individual FAA questions, and the "forest" is the instrument rating knowledge test. The organizational units between the overall instrument rating knowledge test and the individual instrument rating test questions are chapters and modules in this book.

CAUTION: The **sole purpose** of this book is to expedite your passing the FAA instrument rating knowledge test. Accordingly, all extraneous material (i.e., topics or regulations not directly tested on the FAA knowledge test) is omitted, even though much more information and knowledge are necessary to fly safely. This additional material is presented in *Instrument Pilot Flight Maneuvers and Practical Test Prep*, *Pilot Handbook*, *Aviation Weather and Weather Services*, and *FAR/AIM*, available from Gleim Publications, Inc. See the order form on page 488.

1.1 COMPASS ERRORS (Questions 1-11)

1. During taxi, you should check your compass to see that it is swinging freely and indicating known headings.

2. The difference between direction indicated by a magnetic compass not installed in an airplane and one installed in an airplane is called **compass deviation**.

   a. Magnetic fields produced by metals and electrical accessories in an airplane disturb the compass needle.

3. Magnetic compasses can be considered accurate only during straight-and-level flight at constant airspeed.

   a. When turning and accelerating/decelerating, the fluid level and compass card do not remain level, and magnetic force pulls "down" as well as toward the pole.

   b. These are known as the magnetic dip characteristics.

4. In the Northern Hemisphere, **acceleration/deceleration error** occurs when an airplane is on an easterly or westerly heading.

   a. A magnetic compass will indicate a turn toward the north during acceleration on an easterly or westerly heading.

   b. A magnetic compass will indicate a turn toward the south during deceleration on an easterly or westerly heading.

   c. Acceleration/deceleration error does not occur on a northerly or southerly heading.

5. In the Northern Hemisphere, **compass turning error** occurs when turning from a northerly or southerly heading.

   a. A magnetic compass will lag (and at the start of a turn indicate a turn in the opposite direction) when turning from a northerly heading.

      1) If turning to the east (right), the compass will initially indicate a turn to the west and then lag behind the actual heading until your airplane is headed east (at which point there is no error).

      2) If turning to the west (left), the compass will initially indicate a turn to the east and then lag behind the actual heading until your airplane is headed west (at which point there is no error).

   b. A magnetic compass will lead or precede the turn when turning from a southerly heading.

   c. Turning errors do not occur when turning from or through an easterly or westerly heading; i.e., turning errors are minimized at 90° and 270° headings.

6. These magnetic dip errors diminish as acceleration/deceleration or turns are completed.

1.2 PITOT-STATIC SYSTEM (Questions 12-21)

1. When both the airspeed indicator pitot tube and the drain hole are blocked, the airspeed indicator acts as an altimeter.

   a. At a given altitude, airspeed changes would not change the indicated airspeed.

   b. During climbs, the indicated airspeed will increase.

   c. During descents, the indicated airspeed will decrease.

   d. These changes occur as a result of the differential between the pressure of the air locked in the pitot tube and the static air vent pressure.

2. If an alternate static source is vented inside an unpressurized airplane, the static pressure is usually lower than outside pressure due to the Venturi effect of the outside air flowing over the cockpit.

    a. The airspeed indicator will indicate a faster-than-actual airspeed.
    b. The vertical speed indicator (VSI) will momentarily show a climb.
    c. The altimeter will read higher-than-actual altitude.

3. If the pitot tube becomes clogged with ice during flight, only the airspeed indicator will be affected.

    a. The altimeter and vertical speed indicator depend upon the static air vents.

    b. If the static ports are iced over, the vertical speed indicator will not reflect climbs and descents because the change in air pressure cannot be detected by the VSI.

4. If the vertical speed indicator is not calibrated correctly (e.g., continually indicates a descent or climb), it can still be used for IFR flight by adjusting for the error when interpreting the indications.

    a. The VSI is not a required instrument for IFR flight. (Nonetheless, the FAA requires you to report the inability to climb/descend at least 500 fpm and the FAA Instrument Rating PTS requires constant rate climbs/descents.)

5. The Mach meter or Mach indicator shows the ratio of aircraft true airspeed to the speed of sound at flight altitude by means of the pressure differential between static and impact sources, with correction for temperature and altitude.

6. If the outside air temperature increases during a flight at constant power and a constant indicated altitude, true airspeed (TAS) and true altitude will increase.

1.3 ALTIMETER (Questions 22-46)

1. The altimeter indicates the true altitude at the field elevation if the local altimeter setting is used in an accurate altimeter.

    a. Thus the altimeter indicates altitude in relation to the pressure level set in the barometric window.

2. Altimeters have three "hands" (like a clock's hour, minute, and second hands).

3. The three hands on the altimeter are generally arranged as follows:

    a. 10,000-ft. interval (thin needle with a flared triangular tip)
    b. 1,000-ft. interval (short, fat needle)
    c. 100-ft. interval (long, medium-thickness needle)

4. Altimeters are numbered 0 through 9.

5. To read an altimeter,

    a. First, determine whether the thin needle with the flared triangular tip rests between 0 and 1 (for 1-10,000 ft.), 1 and 2 (10,000-20,000 ft.), or 2 and 3 (20,000-30,000 ft.).

    b. Second, determine whether the shortest needle is between 0 and 1 (0-1,000 ft.), 1 and 2 (1,000-2,000), etc.

    c. Third, determine at which number the medium needle is pointing, e.g., 1 for 100 ft., 2 for 200 ft., etc.

6. Atmospheric pressure decreases about 1 in. Hg for every 1,000 ft. of altitude gained.

7.   The altimeter setting dial allows adjustment for nonstandard pressure.

   a.   A window in the face of the altimeter shows a barometric scale that can be rotated.

   b.   Rotating the altimeter setting dial changes the scale and the altimeter hands simultaneously in the same direction by 1,000 ft. per 1 in. Hg.

   c.   For example, changing from 29.92 in. to 30.92 in. increases indicated altitude by 1,000 ft., or from 30.15 in. to 30.25 in. increases indicated altitude by 100 ft.

8.   Prior to takeoff, the altimeter should be set to the current local altimeter setting.

   a.   With the current altimeter setting, the indicated altitude of the airplane on the ground should be within 75 ft. of the actual elevation of the airport for acceptable accuracy.

   b.   If the current local altimeter setting is not available, use the departure airport elevation.

   c.   The local altimeter setting should be used by all pilots in a particular area, primarily to provide for better vertical separation of aircraft.

   d.   During an IFR flight in Class E airspace below 18,000 ft. MSL, ATC will periodically provide the current altimeter setting.

9.   The standard temperature and pressure at sea level are 15°C and 29.92 in. Hg.

   a.   Pressure altitude is the indicated altitude when the altimeter setting is adjusted to 29.92 in. Hg, i.e., the height above the standard datum plane.

   b.   Pressure altitude is used in computations of density altitude, true altitude, and true airspeed.

   c.   Pressure altitude will equal true altitude when standard atmospheric conditions exist.

   d.   Pressure altitude and density altitude are the same at standard temperature.

10.   The altimeter must be set to pressure altitude when flying at or above 18,000 ft. MSL.

   a.   This setting guarantees vertical separation of airplanes above 18,000 ft. MSL.

11.   Since altimeter readings are adjusted for changes in barometric pressure but not for temperature changes, an airplane will be at lower-than-indicated altitude when flying in colder-than-standard air.

   a.   On warm days, you will be at a higher altitude (i.e., true altitude) than your altimeter indicates.

12.   When pressure lowers en route, your altimeter will register higher-than-actual altitude until you adjust the altimeter for the new altimeter setting.

1.4 GYROSCOPES (Questions 47-48)

1.   Listen to your electric gyroscopes for unusual noises after the battery is turned on but before the engine is started.

2.   One of the characteristics of a gyro is that it is resistant to deflection of the spinning wheel, which is based on two of Newton's laws of motion.

   a.   A body at rest will continue at rest and a body in motion will continue in motion in a straight line until acted upon by an outside force.

   b.   Deflection of a moving body is proportional to the deflective force applied and inversely proportional to the body's weight and speed.

1.5 HEADING INDICATOR (Questions 49-52)

1. The heading indicator (HI) should be set to the correct magnetic heading 5 min. after the engine is started.

    a. Prior to takeoff, check the heading indicator to determine that it continues to maintain the correct heading after taxi turns.

2. The remote indicating compass (RIC) combines the functions of the magnetic compass and the heading indicator. One component of the RIC is the slaving control and compensator unit, as shown in Fig. 143 on page 38.

    a. This unit contains a slaving meter needle which indicates the difference between the displayed heading and the actual magnetic heading.

        1) A right deflection (+) indicates a clockwise (right) error in the heading indicator compass card (i.e., the correct magnetic heading is to the right of the indicated heading).

            a) Depressing the right (counterclockwise) heading drive button will move the heading indicator compass card to the left, thus increasing (+) the indicated heading toward the correct value (i.e., from 180° to 190°).

        2) A left deflection (−) indicates a counterclockwise (left) error in the heading indicator compass card (i.e., the correct magnetic heading is to the left of the indicated heading).

            a) Depressing the left (clockwise) heading drive button will move the heading indicator compass card to the right, thus decreasing (−) the indicated heading toward the correct value (i.e., from 190° to 180°).

    b. To make corrections to the RIC, the system must be placed in the free gyro mode.

        1) After corrections are made, the system is returned to the slaved mode, which is the normal mode of operation.

1.6 ATTITUDE INDICATOR (Questions 53-61)

1. Prior to IFR flight, you should check the horizon bar, which should be erect and stable within 5 min. of engine warm-up.

    a. The horizon bar should not tilt more than 5° when making taxi turns.

    b. Remember that you can adjust the position of the miniature airplane, but it is the horizon bar that moves to indicate attitude in flight.

        1) The horizon bar remains parallel to the horizon as the airplane's attitude changes.

2. **Precession errors** (both pitch and bank) on attitude indicators are greatest when rolling out of a 180° steep turn in either direction.

    a. As the airplane returns to straight-and-level coordinated flight, the miniature aircraft will show a slight climb and a turn in the direction opposite to the turn just made.

        1) If you indicate straight-and-level, you will be descending and turning in the direction of the turn just made.

    b. These precession errors during turns (including coordinated turns) are caused by centrifugal force acting on the pendulous vanes (erection mechanism in the attitude indicator). It results in the precession of the gyro toward the inside of the turn.

3. Attitude indicators also reflect an error during skidding turns which precesses the gyro toward the inside of the turn.

    a. As the airplane returns to straight-and-level coordinated flight, the miniature aircraft shows a turn in the direction opposite to the skid. Pitch indication is not affected.

4. Deceleration precession makes some attitude indicators incorrectly indicate a descent.

    a. Conversely, acceleration through precession may result in attitude indicators incorrectly indicating a climb.

1.7 TURN-AND-SLIP INDICATOR (Questions 62-63)

1. Prior to engine start, the turn-and-slip indicator should indicate the needle centered, the tube full of fluid, and the ball approximately centered.

2. During taxi turns, the needle should deflect in the direction of the turn, and the ball should move freely opposite the turn due to centrifugal force.

1.8 TURN COORDINATOR (Questions 64-68)

1. The turn coordinator indicates rate of roll and rate of turn.

    a. When the bank is changing, the rate of roll is indicated.
    b. When the bank is constant, the rate of turn is indicated.
    c. Thus, the angle of bank is only indirectly indicated.

2. On taxi turns, the miniature aircraft indicates a turn in the direction of the taxiing turn, and the ball moves to the outside of the turn due to centrifugal force.

QUESTIONS AND ANSWER EXPLANATIONS

All the FAA questions from the instrument rating knowledge test relating to airplane flight instruments and the material outlined previously are reproduced on the following pages in the same modules as the outlines. To the immediate right of each question are the correct answer and answer explanation. You should cover these answers and answer explanations with your hand or a piece of paper while responding to the questions. Refer to the general discussion in the Introduction on how to take the FAA knowledge test.

Remember that the questions from the FAA instrument rating knowledge test bank have been reordered by topic, and the topics have been organized into a meaningful sequence. Accordingly, the first line of the answer explanation gives the FAA question number and the citation of the authoritative source for the answer.

1.1 Compass Errors

1.
4834. On the taxi check, the magnetic compass should

A— swing opposite to the direction of turn when turning from north.
B— exhibit the same number of degrees of dip as the latitude.
C— swing freely and indicate known headings.

Answer (C) is correct (4834). *(IFH Chap IV)*
When taxiing, the magnetic compass should be checked to make sure that the compass card is swinging freely and indicating known headings.
Answer (A) is incorrect because the compass exhibits turning errors only when the airplane is airborne and in a bank. Answer (B) is incorrect because compass turning errors occur in flight as a result of magnetic dip.

2.
4877. What should be the indication on the magnetic compass as you roll into a standard-rate turn to the left from an east heading in the Northern Hemisphere?

A— The compass will initially indicate a turn to the right.
B— The compass will remain on east for a short time, then gradually catch up to the magnetic heading of the aircraft.
C— The compass will indicate the approximate correct magnetic heading if the roll into the turn is smooth.

Answer (C) is correct (4877). *(IFH Chap IV)*
If you roll into a smooth, coordinated, standard-rate turn to the left or right from an east or west heading, the compass will indicate the approximate correct magnetic heading. There are no turning errors on turns from east or west headings.
Answer (A) is incorrect because the compass will initially indicate a turn in the opposite direction of a bank only when the airplane is turning from a north heading. Answer (B) is incorrect because when the airplane is turning from an east heading, the compass will immediately indicate a turn, if the roll into the turn is smooth.

3.
4886. What should be the indication on the magnetic compass as you roll into a standard rate turn to the right from an easterly heading in the Northern Hemisphere?

A— The compass will initially indicate a turn to the left.
B— The compass will remain on east for a short time, then gradually catch up to the magnetic heading of the aircraft.
C— The compass will indicate the approximate correct magnetic heading if the roll into the turn is smooth.

Answer (C) is correct (4886). *(IFH Chap IV)*
If you roll into a smooth, coordinated, standard-rate turn to the left or right from an east or west heading, the compass will normally indicate the approximate correct magnetic heading. Acceleration, not turning, errors are found in east or west headings in the Northern Hemisphere.
Answer (A) is incorrect because the compass will initially indicate a turn in the opposite direction of a bank only when turning from a north heading. Answer (B) is incorrect because, when turning from an east heading, the compass will immediately indicate a turn if the roll into the turn is smooth.

4.
4887. What should be the indication on the magnetic compass as you roll into a standard rate turn to the right from a south heading in the Northern Hemisphere?

A— The compass will indicate a turn to the right, but at a faster rate than is actually occurring.
B— The compass will initially indicate a turn to the left.
C— The compass will remain on south for a short time, then gradually catch up to the magnetic heading of the aircraft.

Answer (A) is correct (4887). *(IFH Chap IV)*
In turns from a southerly heading in the Northern Hemisphere, the compass leads the turn. That is, it indicates a turn in the proper direction but at a faster rate than is actually occurring.
Answer (B) is incorrect because the compass will initially indicate a turn in the opposite direction if the turn is made from a north, not south, heading. Answer (C) is incorrect because it describes a shallower-than-standard turn from a north, not south, heading.

5.
4888. On what headings will the magnetic compass read most accurately during a level 360° turn, with a bank of approximately 15°?

A— 135° through 225°.
B— 90° and 270°.
C— 180° and 0°.

Answer (B) is correct (4888). *(IFH Chap IV)*
In a turn through north or south, the compass indication will usually be incorrect. But in a turn through east or west, the compass indication is usually accurate. Therefore, the compass should be indicating properly when passing through 90° and 270°. This holds true for only medium to shallow bank turns, e.g., 15-30°.
Answer (A) is incorrect because the compass leads the heading in a turn through south. Answer (C) is incorrect because compass turning errors are greatest at north and south headings.

6.

4889. What causes the northerly turning error in a magnetic compass?

A— Coriolis force at the mid-latitudes.
B— Centrifugal force acting on the compass card.
C— The magnetic dip characteristic.

Answer (C) is correct (4889). *(IFH Chap IV)*
   Magnetic dip causes a compass needle to point both down toward the earth and to the magnetic pole. This characteristic causes turning errors.
   Answer (A) is incorrect because the Coriolis force of the spinning Earth affects winds rather than compass indications. Answer (B) is incorrect because centrifugal force is not related to compass turning errors.

7.

4890. What should be the indication on the magnetic compass when you roll into a standard rate turn to the left from a south heading in the Northern Hemisphere?

A— The compass will indicate a turn to the left, but at a faster rate than is actually occurring.
B— The compass will initially indicate a turn to the right.
C— The compass will remain on south for a short time, then gradually catch up to the magnetic heading of the aircraft.

Answer (A) is correct (4890). *(IFH Chap IV)*
   In turns from a southerly heading in the Northern Hemisphere, the compass leads the turn. That is, it indicates a turn in the proper direction but at a rate faster than the actual rate.
   Answer (B) is incorrect because the compass will initially indicate a turn in the opposite direction if the turn is made from a north, not south, heading. Answer (C) is incorrect because it describes a shallower-than-standard turn from a north, not south, heading.

8.

4891. What should be the indication on the magnetic compass as you roll into a standard rate turn to the right from a westerly heading in the Northern Hemisphere?

A— The compass will initially show a turn in the opposite direction, then turn to a northerly indication but lagging behind the actual heading of the aircraft.
B— The compass will remain on a westerly heading for a short time, then gradually catch up to the actual heading of the aircraft.
C— The compass will indicate the approximate correct magnetic heading if the roll into the turn is smooth.

Answer (C) is correct (4891). *(IFH Chap IV)*
   If you roll into a smooth, coordinated, standard-rate turn to the left or right from an east or west heading, the compass will indicate the approximate correct magnetic heading. There are no turning errors on turns from east or west headings.
   Answer (A) is incorrect because the compass will initially indicate a turn in the opposite direction of a bank only when turning from a north heading. Answer (B) is incorrect because when turning from a westerly heading, the compass will immediately indicate a turn if the roll into the turn is smooth.

9.

4892. What should be the indication on the magnetic compass as you roll into a standard rate turn to the right from a northerly heading in the Northern Hemisphere?

A— The compass will indicate a turn to the right, but at a faster rate than is actually occurring.
B— The compass will initially indicate a turn to the left.
C— The compass will remain on north for a short time, then gradually catch up to the magnetic heading of the aircraft.

Answer (B) is correct (4892). *(IFH Chap IV)*
   In turns from a northerly heading in the Northern Hemisphere, the compass will initially indicate a turn to the opposite direction. Then the compass heading will lag behind the actual heading until the airplane approaches an east or west heading.
   Answer (A) is incorrect because it describes a turn to the right from a southerly heading. Answer (C) is incorrect because it describes a shallower-than-standard turn from north.

10.

4893. What should be the indication on the magnetic compass as you roll into a standard rate turn to the left from a west heading in the Northern Hemisphere?

A— The compass will initially indicate a turn to the right.
B— The compass will remain on west for a short time, then gradually catch up to the magnetic heading of the aircraft.
C— The compass will indicate the approximate correct magnetic heading if the roll into the turn is smooth.

Answer (C) is correct (4893). *(IFH Chap IV)*
   If you roll into a smooth, coordinated, standard-rate turn to the left or right from an east or west heading, the compass will indicate the approximate correct magnetic heading. Turning errors appear on turns from north or south headings, not east or west.
   Answer (A) is incorrect because the compass will initially indicate a turn in the opposite direction of a bank only in a turn from a north heading. Answer (B) is incorrect because in a turn from an east heading, the compass will immediately indicate a turn if the roll into the turn is smooth.

11.
4894. What should be the indication on the magnetic compass as you roll into a standard rate turn to the left from a north heading in the Northern Hemisphere?

A— The compass will indicate a turn to the left, but at a faster rate than is actually occurring.
B— The compass will initially indicate a turn to the right.
C— The compass will remain on north for a short time, then gradually catch up to the magnetic heading of the aircraft.

1.2 Pitot-Static System

12.
4909. During flight, if the pitot tube becomes clogged with ice, which of the following instruments would be affected?

A— The airspeed indicator only.
B— The airspeed indicator and the altimeter.
C— The airspeed indicator, altimeter, and Vertical Speed Indicator.

13.
4830. If both the ram air input and the drain hole of the pitot system are blocked, what reaction should you observe on the airspeed indicator when power is applied and a climb is initiated out of severe icing conditions?

A— The indicated airspeed would show a continuous deceleration while climbing.
B— The airspeed would drop to, and remain at, zero.
C— No change until an actual climb rate is established, then indicated airspeed will increase.

14.
4854. What indication should a pilot observe if an airspeed indicator ram air input and drain hole are blocked?

A— The airspeed indicator will react as an altimeter.
B— The airspeed indicator will show a decrease with an increase in altitude.
C— No airspeed indicator change will occur during climbs or descents.

Answer (B) is correct (4894). *(IFH Chap IV)*
In turns from a northerly heading in the Northern Hemisphere, the compass will initially indicate a turn to the opposite direction, and the compass heading will lag behind actual until the airplane approaches an east or west heading.
Answer (A) is incorrect because it describes a turn to the left from a southerly heading. Answer (C) is incorrect because it describes a shallower-than-standard turn from north.

Answer (A) is correct (4909). *(IFH Chap IV)*
The pitot-static system is a source of pressure for the altimeter, vertical speed indicator, and airspeed indicator. The pitot tube is connected directly to the airspeed indicator, and the static vents are connected directly to all three. The pressure of air coming into the pitot tube (impact air pressure) is compared with the air pressure at the static system vents to determine airspeed.
Answer (B) is incorrect because the pitot tube is connected only to the airspeed indicator, not the altimeter. Answer (C) is incorrect because the pitot tube is connected only to the airspeed indicator, not the altimeter or vertical speed indicator.

Answer (C) is correct (4830). *(AC 91-43)*
When the airspeed indicator pitot tube and drain hole are blocked, the airspeed indicator will react as an altimeter. There will be a constant pressure within the pitot tube, and as the pressure from the static source decreases during a climb, the indicated airspeed on the altimeter will increase.
Answer (A) is incorrect because, as there is an increase in altitude, the airspeed indicator will show an increase in airspeed as the air pressure within the pitot tube is relatively greater than that of the static air. Answer (B) is incorrect because this reaction would occur if the ram air input, but not the drain hole, were blocked.

Answer (A) is correct (4854). *(IFH Chap IV)*
When the airspeed indicator pitot tube and drain hole are blocked, the airspeed indicator will react as an altimeter. There will be a constant pressure within the pitot tube, and as the pressure from the static source decreases during a climb, the indicated airspeed on the altimeter will increase.
Answer (B) is incorrect because indicated airspeed will increase, not decrease, with increases in altitude. Answer (C) is incorrect because differential pressure between the pitot tube and static air source changes, and so does indicated airspeed.

15.
4821. If both the ram air input and drain hole of the pitot system are blocked, what airspeed indication can be expected?

A— No variation of indicated airspeed in level flight even if large power changes are made.
B— Decrease of indicated airspeed during a climb.
C— Constant indicated airspeed during a descent.

16.
4913. If the outside air temperature increases during a flight at constant power and at a constant indicated altitude, the true airspeed will

A— decrease and true altitude will increase.
B— increase and true altitude will decrease.
C— increase and true altitude will increase.

17.
4908. If, while in level flight, it becomes necessary to use an alternate source of static pressure vented inside the airplane, which of the following should the pilot expect?

A— The vertical speed to show a climb.
B— The vertical speed to momentarily show a descent.
C— The altimeter to read higher than normal.

18.
4930. If, while in level flight, it becomes necessary to use an alternate source of static pressure vented inside the airplane, which of the following variations in instrument indications should the pilot expect?

A— The altimeter will read lower than normal, airspeed lower than normal, and the VSI will momentarily show a descent.
B— The altimeter will read higher than normal, airspeed greater than normal, and the VSI will momentarily show a climb.
C— The altimeter will read lower than normal, airspeed greater than normal, and the VSI will momentarily show a climb and then a descent.

18a.
0601-964. If, while in level flight, it becomes necessary to use an alternate source of static pressure vented inside the airplane, which of the following should the pilot expect?

A— The vertical speed to momentarily show a climb.
B— The gyroscopic instruments to become inoperative.
C— The altimeter and airspeed indicator to become inoperative.

Answer (A) is correct (4821). *(IFH Chap IV)*
If both the pitot tube input and the drain hole on the pitot system are blocked, the airspeed indication will be constant at any given altitude.
Answer (B) is incorrect because, during a climb, the airspeed indicator will indicate an increase, not decrease, due to the stronger differential pressure in the blocked pitot tube relative to the static vents. Answer (C) is incorrect because indicated airspeed would change with changes in altitude.

Answer (C) is correct (4913). *(IFH Chap III)*
As temperature increases, pressure levels rise farther above sea level and true altitude increases given a constant indicated altitude. As altitude increases with constant power, true airspeed increases.
Answer (A) is incorrect because TAS increases, not decreases. Answer (B) is incorrect because true altitude increases, not decreases.

Answer (C) is correct (4908). *(IFH Chap IV)*
Most aircraft equipped with a pitot-static system are provided with an alternate source of static pressure for emergency use. This source is usually vented inside the cabin. The pressure within an unpressurized cockpit is slightly lower than the pressure outside the airplane because of the Venturi effect of the air moving past the outside of the cockpit. When the alternate static source is used, the altimeter and airspeed indicator will read higher than actual, and the vertical speed indicator will momentarily show a climb.
Answer (A) is incorrect because the VSI will show only a momentary, not a steady-state, climb. Answer (B) is incorrect because the VSI indication will be a momentary climb, not a descent.

Answer (B) is correct (4930). *(IFH Chap IV)*
Most aircraft equipped with a pitot-static system are provided with an alternate source of static pressure for emergency use. This source is usually vented inside the cabin. The pressure within an unpressurized cockpit is slightly lower than the pressure outside the airplane because of the Venturi effect of the air moving past the outside of the cockpit. When the alternate static source is used, the altimeter will read higher than actual, and the vertical speed indicator will momentarily show a climb.
Answer (A) is incorrect because the altimeter and airspeed indicators will read higher, not lower, than normal, and the vertical speed indicator will momentarily show a climb, not a descent. Answer (C) is incorrect because the altimeter will read higher, not lower, than normal, and the vertical speed indicator will show level flight, not a descent, after the momentary climb.

Answer (A) is correct (0601-964). *(IFH Chap IV)*
Most aircraft equipped with a pitot-static system are provided with an alternate source of static pressure for emergency use. This source is usually vented inside the cabin. The pressure within an unpressurized cockpit is slightly lower than the pressure outside the airplane because of the Venturi effect of the air moving past the outside of the cockpit. When the alternate static source is used, the altimeter and airspeed indicator will read higher than actual, and the vertical speed indicator will momentarily show a climb.
Answer (B) is incorrect because the gyroscopic instruments are not affected by changes in the pitot-static system. Answer (C) is incorrect because the altimeter and airspeed indicator will read higher than actual, not become inoperative.

19.
4879. What would be the indication on the VSI during entry into a 500 FPM actual descent from level flight if the static ports were iced over?

A— The indication would be in reverse of the actual rate of descent (500 FPM climb).
B— The initial indication would be a climb, then descent at a rate in excess of 500 FPM.
C— The VSI pointer would remain at zero regardless of the actual rate of descent.

20.
4056. You check the flight instruments while taxiing and find the vertical speed indicator (VSI) indicates a descent of 100 feet per minute. In this case, you

A— must return to the parking area and have the instrument corrected by an authorized instrument repairman.
B— may take off and use 100 feet descent as the zero indication.
C— may not take off until the instrument is corrected by either the pilot or a mechanic.

21.
4864. What information does a Mach meter present?

A— The ratio of aircraft true airspeed to the speed of sound.
B— The ratio of aircraft indicated airspeed to the speed of sound.
C— The ratio of aircraft equivalent airspeed, corrected for installation error, to the speed of sound.

1.3 Altimeter

22.
4402. How should you preflight check the altimeter prior to an IFR flight?

A— Set the altimeter to 29.92" Hg. With current temperature and the altimeter indication, determine the true altitude to compare with the field elevation.
B— Set the altimeter first with 29.92" Hg and then the current altimeter setting. The change in altitude should correspond to the change in setting.
C— Set the altimeter to the current altimeter setting. The indication should be within 75 feet of the actual elevation for acceptable accuracy.

Answer (C) is correct (4879). *(IFH Chap IV)*
The vertical speed indicator operates from the static pressure source and indicates change in pressure. Thus, if the static pressure ports became iced over, there would be no change in the static pressure, and there would be no indication of descent or climb.
Answer (A) is incorrect because, with no change in pressure, the indication would be level flight, not a climb. Answer (B) is incorrect because, with no change in pressure, the indication would be level flight, not a climb or descent.

Answer (B) is correct (4056). *(IFH Chap IV)*
The needle of the vertical speed indicator (VSI) should indicate zero when the aircraft is on the ground or is maintaining a constant pressure level in flight. If it does not indicate zero, you must allow for the error when interpreting the indications in flight. Since the VSI is not a required instrument, you may fly when it is out of adjustment.
Answer (A) is incorrect because the VSI can be used by making allowances in flight. Answer (C) is incorrect because the VSI can be used by making allowances in flight.

Answer (A) is correct (4864). *(IFH Chap IV)*
The Mach meter indicates the ratio of aircraft true airspeed to the speed of sound at flight altitude. It uses the pressure differential between the impact and static air sources and corrects automatically for temperature and altitude.
Answer (B) is incorrect because the Mach meter uses true airspeed, not indicated airspeed. Answer (C) is incorrect because equivalent airspeed is the calibrated airspeed of an aircraft corrected for compressibility flow at a particular altitude. The Mach meter uses true airspeed.

Answer (C) is correct (4402). *(IFH Chap IV)*
Set the altimeter to the local altimeter setting before taking off, and verify that the indication is within 75 ft. of the actual elevation. If the difference is greater than 75 ft., you should consult an instrument repair shop.
Answer (A) is incorrect because setting the altimeter to 29.92 and adjusting for temperature gives density altitude, not true altitude. Answer (B) is incorrect because only indicated altitude, not change in altitude, is checked.

23.

4880. How should you preflight check the altimeter prior to an IFR flight?

A— Set the altimeter to the current temperature. With current temperature and the altimeter indication, determine the calibrated altitude to compare with the field elevation.

B— Set the altimeter first with 29.92" Hg and then the current altimeter setting. The change in altitude should correspond to the change in setting.

C— Set the altimeter to the current altimeter setting. The indication should be within 75 feet of the actual elevation for acceptable accuracy.

Answer (C) is correct (4880). *(IFH Chap IV)*
Set the altimeter to the local altimeter setting before taking off, and verify that the indication is within 75 ft. of the actual elevation. If the difference is greater than 75 ft., you should consult an instrument repair shop.
Answer (A) is incorrect because an altimeter can be adjusted for nonstandard pressure, not temperature. Answer (B) is incorrect because only indicated altitude, not change in altitude, is checked.

24.

4923. Pressure altitude is the altitude read on your altimeter when the instrument is adjusted to indicate height above

A— sea level.
B— the standard datum plane.
C— ground level.

Answer (B) is correct (4923). *(FTH Chap IV)*
Pressure altitude is the altitude read on your altimeter when the instrument is adjusted to indicate height above the standard datum plane, i.e., an altimeter setting of 29.92 in. The standard datum plane is a theoretical level where the weight of the atmosphere is 29.92 in. of Hg.
Answer (A) is incorrect because indicated altitude, not pressure altitude, is the altitude read on your altimeter (when set to the correct altimeter setting) to indicate the approximate height above mean sea level. Answer (C) is incorrect because the height above ground (absolute altitude) may be indicated directly on a radar altimeter, not by adjusting a pressure altimeter to 29.92 in.

25.

4910. The local altimeter setting should be used by all pilots in a particular area, primarily to provide for

A— the cancellation of altimeter error due to nonstandard temperatures aloft.
B— better vertical separation of aircraft.
C— more accurate terrain clearance in mountainous areas.

Answer (B) is correct (4910). *(IFH Chap IV)*
Because the altimeter in each airplane is equally affected by temperature and pressure variation errors, use of the local altimeter setting in a given area provides for better vertical separation of aircraft.
Answer (A) is incorrect because the altimeter setting does not compensate for nonstandard temperatures aloft. Rather, all altimeters in the area will reflect the same uncompensated amount. Answer (C) is incorrect because temperatures aloft must also be considered to assure terrain clearance.

26.
4484. (Refer to figure 84 below.) Which altimeter depicts 8,000 feet?

A— 1.
B— 2.
C— 3.

Answer (B) is correct (4484). *(IFH Chap IV)*
    When indicating 8,000 ft., an altimeter has the short hand (1,000-ft. intervals) on 8, the long hand (100-ft. intervals) on zero, and the thin hand with flared tip (10,000-ft. intervals) just below 1, as shown in altimeter 2.
    Answer (A) is incorrect because, in altimeter 1, both the thin hand and the short hand are on 8, which would indicate something in the vicinity of 88,000 ft. Answer (C) is incorrect because, while the short hand is pointing to 8 and the long hand is pointing to 0 (i.e., 8,000), the long thin needle with the flared tip (10,000-ft. indicator) is on 0, not on the fourth tick mark from the 0 toward the 1. Altimeter 3 is either broken or indicating 108,000 ft.

FIGURE 84.—Altimeter/8,000 Feet.

32   *Chapter 1: Airplane Instruments*

27.
4483. (Refer to figure 83 below.) Which altimeter depicts 12,000 feet?

A— 2.
B— 3.
C— 4.

Answer (C) is correct (4483). *(IFH Chap IV)*
When indicating 12,000 ft., an altimeter has the long hand (100-ft. intervals) on 0, the short hand (1,000-ft. intervals) on 2, and the thin hand with flared tip (10,000-ft. intervals) just over 1, as shown in altimeter 4.
Answer (A) is incorrect because, in altimeter 2, the thin hand is above 2 and the short hand is on 1, indicating 21,000 ft. Answer (B) is incorrect because, in altimeter 3, the short hand is on 1, the long hand is on 2, and the thin hand is above 1, indicating about 11,200 ft.

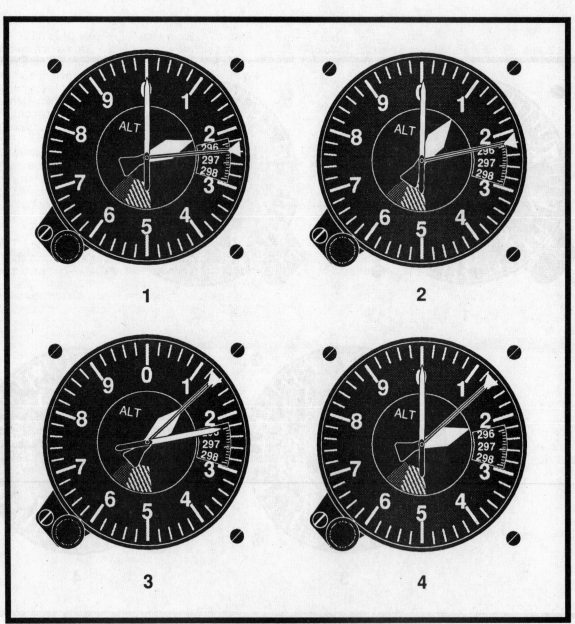

FIGURE 83.—Altimeter/12,000 Feet.

28.
4922. Altimeter setting is the value to which the scale of the pressure altimeter is set so the altimeter indicates

A— pressure altitude at sea level.
B— true altitude at field elevation.
C— pressure altitude at field elevation.

29.
4111. Altimeter setting is the value to which the scale of the pressure altimeter is set so the altimeter indicates

A— true altitude at field elevation.
B— pressure altitude at field elevation.
C— pressure altitude at sea level.

30.
4480. If you are departing from an airport where you cannot obtain an altimeter setting, you should set your altimeter

A— on 29.92" Hg.
B— on the current airport barometric pressure, if known.
C— to the airport elevation.

31.
4479. Which altitude is indicated when the altimeter is set to 29.92" Hg?

A— Density.
B— Pressure.
C— Standard.

Answer (B) is correct (4922). *(PHAK Chap 3)*
The altimeter setting is the value which permits the altimeter to indicate the true altitude at field elevation. Within the vicinity of a particular airport, the altimeter setting provides an accurate means of separating traffic vertically and also provides obstruction clearance. Note that the use of the word "true" here is not completely accurate because the altimeter setting does not correct for nonstandard temperature.
Answer (A) is incorrect because the altimeter setting causes the altimeter to indicate true altitude, not pressure altitude, at field elevation, not sea level. Answer (C) is incorrect because the altimeter setting causes the altimeter to indicate true altitude, not pressure altitude.

Answer (A) is correct (4111). *(IFH Chap IV)*
The altimeter setting is the value which permits the altimeter to indicate the true altitude at field elevation. Within the vicinity of a particular airport, the altimeter setting provides an accurate means of separating traffic vertically and also provides obstruction clearance. Note that the use of the word "true" here is not completely accurate because the altimeter setting does not correct for nonstandard temperature.
Answer (B) is incorrect because the altimeter setting causes the altimeter to indicate true altitude, not pressure altitude. Answer (C) is incorrect because the altimeter setting causes the altimeter to indicate true altitude, not pressure altitude, at field elevation, not sea level.

Answer (C) is correct (4480). *(IFH Chap IV)*
If you cannot obtain an altimeter setting at an airport, adjust your altimeter so it reads the current airport elevation.
Answer (A) is incorrect because setting the altimeter to 29.92 would provide only pressure altitude. Answer (B) is incorrect because the altimeter setting is the current barometric pressure adjusted to sea level.

Answer (B) is correct (4479). *(PHAK Chap 3)*
Pressure altitude is indicated when the altimeter is set to 29.92.
Answer (A) is incorrect because density altitude is pressure altitude corrected for nonstandard temperature. Answer (C) is incorrect because standard altitude is a nonsense concept in this context.

32.
4912. The pressure altitude at a given location is indicated on the altimeter after the altimeter is set to

A— the field elevation.
B— 29.92" Hg.
C— the current altimeter setting.

33.
4478. How can you determine the pressure altitude on an airport without a tower or FSS?

A— Set the altimeter to 29.92" Hg and read the altitude indicated.
B— Set the altimeter to the current altimeter setting of a station within 100 miles and correct this indicated altitude with local temperature.
C— Use your computer and correct the field elevation for temperature.

34.
4477. How can you obtain the pressure altitude on flights below 18,000 feet?

A— Set your altimeter to 29.92" Hg.
B— Use your computer to change the indicated altitude to pressure altitude.
C— Contact an FSS and ask for the pressure altitude.

35.
4911. At an altitude of 6,500 feet MSL, the current altimeter setting is 30.42" Hg. The pressure altitude would be approximately

A— 7,500 feet.
B— 6,000 feet.
C— 6,500 feet.

Answer (B) is correct (4912). *(PHAK Chap 3)*
Pressure altitude by definition is indicated altitude when the altimeter setting is 29.92. This is true regardless of area or true altitude.
Answer (A) is incorrect because you set the altimeter to a barometric pressure, not an elevation. Answer (C) is incorrect because the altitude indicated on the altimeter after it is set to the current altimeter setting is the indicated altitude, not pressure altitude.

Answer (A) is correct (4478). *(PHAK Chap 3)*
The pressure altitude is determined by setting your altimeter to 29.92 and reading the altitude indicated. No matter what altitude or location, the altimeter reads pressure altitude when the barometric window is set to 29.92" Hg.
Answer (B) is incorrect because it describes true altitude. Answer (C) is incorrect because correcting field elevation for temperature is a nonsense concept.

Answer (A) is correct (4477). *(PHAK Chap 3)*
Pressure altitude can be determined anywhere by setting the altimeter to 29.92.
Answer (B) is incorrect because it is much easier to just change the altimeter to 29.92. Answer (C) is incorrect because pressure altitude is determined by setting your altimeter to 29.92, not by contacting an FSS.

Answer (B) is correct (4911). *(IFH Chap IV)*
Rotating the altimeter's setting knob to a higher (or lower) barometric setting moves the hands to higher (or lower) indicated altitude at the rate of 1" Hg to 1,000 ft. of altitude. Given the current altimeter setting of 30.42 and the indicated altitude of 6,500 ft., resetting the window to 29.92 would lower indicated altitude by 500 ft. (30.42 – 29.92 = 0.5" Hg = 500 ft.). The new indicated altitude would be 6,000 ft. MSL, which would be pressure altitude.
Answer (A) is incorrect because a pressure change of 0.5" Hg results in an altitude change of 500 ft., not 1,000 ft. Answer (C) is incorrect because pressure altitude is equal to actual altitude only when the current altimeter setting is 29.92.

36.
4482. How does a pilot normally obtain the current altimeter setting during an IFR flight in Class E airspace below 18,000 feet?

A— The pilot should contact ARTCC at least every 100 NM and request the altimeter setting.
B— FSS's along the route broadcast the weather information at 15 minutes past the hour.
C— ATC periodically advises the pilot of the proper altimeter setting.

37.
4110. Which of the following defines the type of altitude used when maintaining FL 210?

A— Indicated.
B— Pressure.
C— Calibrated.

38.
4444. What is the procedure for setting the altimeter when assigned an IFR altitude of 18,000 feet or higher on a direct flight off airways?

A— Set the altimeter to 29.92" Hg before takeoff.
B— Set the altimeter to the current altimeter setting until reaching the assigned altitude, then set to 29.92" Hg.
C— Set the altimeter to the current reported setting for climb-out and 29.92" Hg upon reaching 18,000 feet.

39.
4446. While you are flying at FL 250, you hear ATC give an altimeter setting of 28.92" Hg in your area. At what pressure altitude are you flying?

A— 24,000 feet.
B— 25,000 feet.
C— 26,000 feet.

Answer (C) is correct (4482). *(IFH Chap IV)*
During IFR flight in Class E airspace below 18,000 ft. MSL, ATC periodically provides altimeter settings. Thus, you will continually hear the altimeter settings given to other pilots as you monitor ATC.
Answer (A) is incorrect because ATC provides the altimeter setting without being asked. Answer (B) is incorrect because FSSs do not broadcast the altimeter setting at 15 min. past the hour.

Answer (B) is correct (4110). *(IFH Chap IV)*
Above 18,000 ft. MSL (FL 180), pressure altitude is used to separate traffic. Pressure altitude is the altitude indicated on an altimeter when it is set to 29.92.
Answer (A) is incorrect because indicated altitude is the altitude shown on the altimeter after it is set to the current altimeter setting. Pressure altitude, not indicated altitude, is used at or above 18,000 ft. MSL. Answer (C) is incorrect because all altimeters are calibrated.

Answer (C) is correct (4444). *(FAR 91.121)*
When you are at an altitude of 18,000 ft. MSL (FL 180) or higher, the altimeter should be set to 29.92, which is pressure altitude. It does not matter whether you are on an airway.
Answer (A) is incorrect because indicated altitude (using local altimeter settings) should be used up to FL 180. Answer (B) is incorrect because you should set the altimeter to 29.92 upon reaching FL 180, not upon reaching your assigned altitude.

Answer (B) is correct (4446). *(IFH Chap IV)*
The pressure altitude is 25,000 ft. in your area because at FL 250 your altimeter should be set at 29.92. A flight level (FL) by definition means a pressure altitude.
Answer (A) is incorrect because FL 250 by definition means a pressure altitude of 25,000 ft., not 24,000 ft. Answer (C) is incorrect because FL 250 by definition means a pressure altitude of 25,000 ft., not 26,000 ft.

40.

4445. En route at FL 290, the altimeter is set correctly, but not reset to the local altimeter setting of 30.57" Hg during descent. If the field elevation is 650 feet and the altimeter is functioning properly, what is the approximate indication upon landing?

A— 715 feet.
B— 1,300 feet.
C— Sea level.

Answer (C) is correct (4445). *(IFH Chap IV)*
One in. of pressure equals approximately 1,000 ft. of altitude. If an altimeter should be set to 30.57 but is set to 29.92, it is set .65" Hg too low and thus will indicate 650 ft. (1,000 ft. x .65) less than actual altitude. Thus, if the airplane lands at an airport with a field elevation of 650 ft., the altimeter will indicate sea level, i.e., 650 ft. elevation minus the 650 ft. altimeter setting error.
Answer (A) is incorrect because 715 ft. is obtained by adding 65 ft. rather than subtracting 650 ft. Answer (B) is incorrect because 1,300 ft. is obtained by adding 650 ft. rather than subtracting 650 ft.

41.

4481. En route at FL 290, your altimeter is set correctly, but you fail to reset it to the local altimeter setting of 30.26" Hg during descent. If the field elevation is 134 feet and your altimeter is functioning properly, what will it indicate after landing?

A— 100 feet MSL.
B— 474 feet MSL.
C— 206 feet below MSL.

Answer (C) is correct (4481). *(IFH Chap IV)*
One in. of pressure equals approximately 1,000 ft. of altitude. If an altimeter should be set to 30.26 but is set to 29.92, it is set .34" Hg too low and thus will indicate 340 ft. (1,000 ft. x .34) less than actual altitude. Thus, if the airplane lands at an airport with a field elevation of 134 ft., the altimeter will indicate 206 ft. below sea level (134 ft. airport elevation – 340 ft. altimeter setting error).
Answer (A) is incorrect because 100 ft. is obtained by subtracting 34 ft. rather than subtracting 340 ft. Answer (B) is incorrect because 474 ft. is obtained by adding 340 ft. rather than subtracting 340 ft.

42.

4090. Under which condition will pressure altitude be equal to true altitude?

A— When the atmospheric pressure is 29.92" Hg.
B— When standard atmospheric conditions exist.
C— When indicated altitude is equal to the pressure altitude.

Answer (B) is correct (4090). *(IFH Chap IV)*
Pressure altitude will equal true altitude when standard atmospheric conditions exist at the current altitude, i.e, 29.92" Hg and 15°C at sea level.
Answer (A) is incorrect because, to get true altitude from an altimeter, both temperature and pressure must be standard. Answer (C) is incorrect because nonstandard temperatures will make indicated altitude deviate from true altitude.

43.

4089. Under what condition is pressure altitude and density altitude the same value?

A— At standard temperature.
B— When the altimeter setting is 29.92" Hg.
C— When indicated, and pressure altitudes are the same value on the altimeter.

Answer (A) is correct (4089). *(IFH Chap IV)*
Density altitude, by definition, is pressure altitude adjusted for nonstandard temperature. Accordingly, pressure altitude will equal density altitude at standard temperature.
Answer (B) is incorrect because pressure altitude has not been adjusted for nonstandard temperature. Answer (C) is incorrect because neither indicated nor pressure altitude is adjusted for nonstandard temperature.

44.
4109. Under what condition will true altitude be lower than indicated altitude with an altimeter setting of 29.92" Hg?

A— In warmer than standard air temperature.
B— In colder than standard air temperature.
C— When density altitude is higher than indicated altitude.

Answer (B) is correct (4109). *(IFH Chap IV)*
When temperature lowers en route, you are lower than your altimeter indicates. Similarly, when you are in colder-than-standard air temperatures, true altitude is lower than pressure altitude.
Answer (A) is incorrect because, when you are in warmer-than-standard air, the true altitude is above pressure altitude. Answer (C) is incorrect because, assuming an altimeter setting of 29.92, if density altitude is higher than indicated altitude, the air is thinner and thus warmer. When you are in warmer-than-standard air, the true altitude is above indicated altitude.

45.
4093. When an altimeter is changed from 30.11" Hg to 29.96" Hg, in which direction will the indicated altitude change and by what value?

A— Altimeter will indicate 15 feet lower.
B— Altimeter will indicate 150 feet lower.
C— Altimeter will indicate 150 feet higher.

Answer (B) is correct (4093). *(IFH Chap IV)*
Altimeter settings vary approximately 1" Hg for each 1,000 ft. of altitude. When the altimeter setting is changed from 30.11 to 29.96, it is lower by .15" Hg. Thus, the altimeter will indicate 150 ft. lower (1,000 ft. x .15). Remember that the indicated altitude and altimeter setting vary directly; i.e., when the altimeter setting is adjusted up, indicated altitude increases and vice versa.
Answer (A) is incorrect because .15" Hg is equal to 150 ft., not 15 ft. Answer (C) is incorrect because, when the altimeter setting is lowered, indicated altitude decreases, not increases.

46.
4091. Which condition would cause the altimeter to indicate a lower altitude than actually flown (true altitude)?

A— Air temperature lower than standard.
B— Atmospheric pressure lower than standard.
C— Air temperature warmer than standard.

Answer (C) is correct (4091). *(IFH Chap IV)*
When temperatures are warmer than standard, the pressure levels are raised. That is, the altimeter will indicate an altitude lower than that at which the aircraft is actually flying.
Answer (A) is incorrect because in colder-than-standard air, pressure levels drop. Thus, the altimeter reads higher, not lower, than true altitude. Answer (B) is incorrect because using the correct altimeter setting adjusts for nonstandard pressure.

1.4 Gyroscopes

47.
4881. Which practical test should be made on the electric gyro instruments prior to starting an engine?

A— Check that the electrical connections are secure on the back of the instruments.
B— Check that the attitude of the miniature aircraft is wings level before turning on electrical power.
C— Turn on the electrical power and listen for any unusual or irregular mechanical noise.

Answer (C) is correct (4881). *(IFH Chap V)*
Electric gyro instruments can be checked for irregular noises by listening to them after the battery is turned on but before the engine is started. You should notice any bearing clatters, clicks, or other unusual noises. Additionally, you can look at the instruments to see if they are in their expected positions. There are additional tests to pursue after the engine is started.
Answer (A) is incorrect because pilots should not be handling or touching electrical connections behind the instrument panel. Answer (B) is incorrect because, due to the construction of the turn coordinator, the miniature aircraft will be wings level before turning on the electrical power. Thus, this indication would not be a practical test for the electric gyro.

48.

4902. One characteristic that a properly functioning gyro depends upon for operation is the

A— ability to resist precession 90° to any applied force.
B— resistance to deflection of the spinning wheel or disc.
C— deflecting force developed from the angular velocity of the spinning wheel.

Answer (B) is correct (4902). *(IFH Chap IV)*

Newton's second law of motion states that the deflection of a moving body is proportional to the deflective force applied and is inversely proportional to its weight and speed. For a gyro, the resistance to deflection is proportional to the deflective force. This property is used by the attitude indicator.

Answer (A) is incorrect because precession is the name for the reaction to deflection. The gyro uses precession, not resists it. Answer (C) is incorrect because the deflective force is applied to, not developed by, the gyro.

1.5 Heading Indicator

49.

4885. What pre-takeoff check should be made of a vacuum-driven heading indicator in preparation for an IFR flight?

A— After 5 minutes, set the indicator to the magnetic heading of the aircraft and check for proper alignment after taxi turns.
B— After 5 minutes, check that the heading indicator card aligns itself with the magnetic heading of the aircraft.
C— Determine that the heading indicator does not precess more than 2° in 5 minutes of ground operation.

Answer (A) is correct (4885). *(IFH Chap V)*

Vacuum-driven gyros take several minutes to get up to speed. After about 5 min., set the heading indicator to the correct magnetic heading. After taxiing to the runup area, verify that the heading indicator still indicates the correct magnetic heading.

Answer (B) is incorrect because non-slaved heading indicators must be manually set to the correct magnetic heading. Answer (C) is incorrect because a precession error of no more than 3° in 15 min., not 2° in 5 min., is acceptable for normal operations.

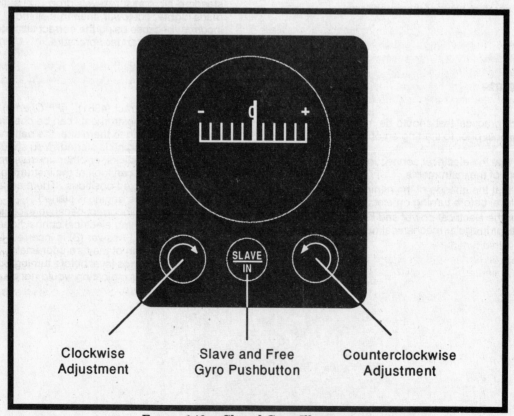

Figure 143.—Slaved Gyro Illustration.

50.
4827. (Refer to figure 143 on page 38.) The heading on a remote indicating compass is 120° and the magnetic compass indicates 110°. What action is required to correctly align the heading indicator with the magnetic compass?

A— Select the free gyro mode and depress the counter-clockwise heading drive button.
B— Select the slaved gyro mode and depress the clockwise heading drive button.
C— Select the free gyro mode and depress the clockwise heading drive button.

51.
4828. (Refer to figure 143 on page 38.) When the system is in the free gyro mode, depressing the clockwise manual heading drive button will rotate the remote indicating compass card to the

A— right to eliminate left compass card error.
B— right to eliminate right compass card error.
C— left to eliminate left compass card error.

52.
4829. (Refer to figure 143 on page 38.) The heading on a remote indicating compass is 5° to the left of that desired. What action is required to move the desired heading under the heading reference?

A— Select the free gyro mode and depress the clockwise heading drive button.
B— Select the slaved gyro mode and depress the clockwise heading drive button.
C— Select the free gyro mode and depress the counter-clockwise heading drive button.

1.6 Attitude Indicator

53.
4842. What pre-takeoff check should be made of the attitude indicator in preparation for an IFR flight?

A— The horizon bar does not vibrate during warmup.
B— The miniature airplane should erect and become stable within 5 minutes.
C— The horizon bar should erect and become stable within 5 minutes.

Answer (C) is correct (4827). *(IFH Chap IV)*
Some remote indicating compasses (RIC) have a separate slaving control and compensator unit with a deviation meter. The instrument shows any difference between the displayed heading and the magnetic heading. It also provides the controls shown in Fig. 143 to correct any errors. To correct from 120° indicated on the RIC to the magnetic heading of 110°, select the free gyro mode and depress the clockwise heading drive button until 110° heading on RIC is indicated **and** the deviation meter is centered.
Answer (A) is incorrect because using the counter-clockwise drive button would increase the indicated headings, e.g., from 120° to 130° indicated. Answer (B) is incorrect because the RIC must be in the free gyro mode to use the heading drive button.

Answer (A) is correct (4828). *(IFH Chap IV)*
A left compass card error means that the card has rotated too far to the left; i.e., it reads too high a heading. The clockwise adjustment rotates the indicating compass card to the right to eliminate left compass card error. For example, this would change a 120° heading to 110°.
Answer (B) is incorrect because you adjust to the right for left, not right, error. Answer (C) is incorrect because the clockwise manual heading drive button rotates the compass card to the right, not left.

Answer (C) is correct (4829). *(IFH Chap IV)*
If the heading on the compass is left of that desired, the compass has rotated too far to the right, which is a right compass error. Thus, the slaving control must be placed in the free mode, and the counterclockwise drive button must be depressed.
Answer (A) is incorrect because the clockwise heading drive button would correct a left, not a right, card error. Answer (B) is incorrect because the RIC must be in the free gyro mode to use the heading drive button and the counterclockwise heading drive button should be depressed.

Answer (C) is correct (4842). *(IFH Chap V)*
The pretakeoff check for attitude indicators is that, within the 5-min. warm-up, the horizon bar should erect to the horizontal position and remain at the correct position. It should remain stable during straight taxiing and taxi turns.
Answer (A) is incorrect because the horizon bar usually vibrates during warm-up as the gyro gets up to speed. Answer (B) is incorrect because the miniature airplane can be adjusted manually but otherwise remains stationary. It is the horizon bar that moves within the instrument face.

54.
4835. Which condition during taxi is an indication that an attitude indicator is unreliable?

A— The horizon bar tilts more than 5° while making taxi turns.
B— The horizon bar vibrates during warmup.
C— The horizon bar does not align itself with the miniature airplane after warmup.

55.
4861. During coordinated turns, which force moves the pendulous vanes of a vacuum-driven attitude indicator resulting in precession of the gyro toward the inside of the turn?

A— Acceleration.
B— Deceleration.
C— Centrifugal.

56.
4901. If a 180° steep turn is made to the right and the aircraft is rolled out to straight-and-level flight by visual references, the attitude indicator

A— should immediately show straight-and-level flight.
B— may show a slight climb and turn.
C— show a slight skid and climb to the right.

57.
4860. During normal coordinated turns, what error due to precession should you observe when rolling out to straight-and-level flight from a 180° steep turn to the right?

A— A straight-and-level coordinated flight indication.
B— The miniature aircraft would show a slight turn indication to the left.
C— The miniature aircraft would show a slight descent and wings-level attitude.

58.
4857. During normal operation of a vacuum-driven attitude indicator, what attitude indication should you see when rolling out from a 180° skidding turn to straight-and-level coordinated flight?

A— A straight-and-level coordinated flight indication.
B— A nose-high indication relative to level flight.
C— The miniature aircraft shows a turn in the direction opposite the skid.

Answer (A) is correct (4835). *(IFH Chap V)*
The horizon bar in an attitude indicator should not tilt more than 5° during a taxi turn. If it does, it is unreliable and should not be used for IFR flight.
Answer (B) is incorrect because the horizon bar will vibrate as the gyros get up to speed during warm-up. Answer (C) is incorrect because the horizon bar aligns itself with the center of the dial, indicating level flight. Then the miniature airplane must be adjusted to align with the horizon bar from the pilot's perspective.

Answer (C) is correct (4861). *(IFH Chap IV)*
The attitude indicator normally erects itself by discharging air equally through four exhaust ports, each of which is partially covered by a pendulous vane. During coordinated (and skidding) turns, centrifugal force moves the vanes from their vertical position, precessing the gyro toward the inside of the turn.
Answer (A) is incorrect because acceleration is a force that induces climb/descent errors in the attitude indicator. Answer (B) is incorrect because deceleration is a force that induces climb/descent errors in the attitude indicator.

Answer (B) is correct (4901). *(IFH Chap IV)*
In 180° coordinated steep turns, when the airplane is rolled out to straight-and-level flight, the attitude indicator will indicate a turn to the opposite direction along with a slight climb.
Answer (A) is incorrect because, when the airplane is rolled out of a coordinated 180° steep turn to straight-and-level flight, the attitude indicator will indicate a turn to the opposite direction with a slight climb; it will not immediately show straight-and-level flight. Answer (C) is incorrect because evidence of a skid error cannot be read from the attitude indicator, and the turn error would be to the left, not to the right.

Answer (B) is correct (4860). *(IFH Chap IV)*
In 180° coordinated steep turns, when the airplane is rolled out to straight-and-level flight, the attitude indicator will indicate a turn to the opposite direction along with a slight climb. Thus, the indicated turn would be to the left if the steep turn were made to the right.
Answer (A) is incorrect because the attitude indicator will show a slight climb to the left, not straight-and-level flight, and it does not indicate coordinated flight. Answer (C) is incorrect because it will indicate a slight climb, not a descent, and it will indicate a turning error.

Answer (C) is correct (4857). *(IFH Chap IV)*
Similarly to coordinated turns, the attitude indicator will show a bank in the opposite direction when the aircraft is rolled out of a skidding turn. However, there will be no nose-up indication.
Answer (A) is incorrect because the attitude indicator will show a slight turn in the opposite direction, not straight-and-level flight, and it does not indicate coordinated flight. Answer (B) is incorrect because a nose-high indication will result only when the aircraft is rolling out of a coordinated turn.

59.
4900. Errors in both pitch and bank indication on an attitude indicator are usually at a maximum as the aircraft rolls out of a

A— 180° turn.
B— 270° turn.
C— 360° turn.

Answer (A) is correct (4900). *(IFH Chap IV)*
Errors for both pitch and bank indication on an attitude indicator are greatest when rolling out of a 180° turn. This precession error, normally between 3° and 5°, is self-correcting by the part of the heading indicator called the erecting mechanism.
Answer (B) is incorrect because pitch and bank errors are usually the greatest after 180°, not 270°, of turn. Answer (C) is incorrect because pitch and bank errors are usually the greatest after 180°, not 360°, of turn.

60.
4919. When an aircraft is decelerated, some attitude indicators will precess and incorrectly indicate a

A— left turn.
B— climb.
C— descent.

Answer (C) is correct (4919). *(IFH Chap IV)*
Deceleration affects some attitude indicators through precession to incorrectly indicate a descent.
Answer (A) is incorrect because acceleration and deceleration result in erroneous pitch readings, not turning errors. Answer (B) is incorrect because acceleration, not deceleration, may result in precession-related errors indicating a climb.

61.
4918. When an aircraft is accelerated, some attitude indicators will precess and incorrectly indicate a

A— climb.
B— descent.
C— right turn.

Answer (A) is correct (4918). *(IFH Chap IV)*
Acceleration affects some attitude indicators through precession to incorrectly indicate a climb.
Answer (B) is incorrect because deceleration, not acceleration, may result in precession-related errors indicating a descent. Answer (C) is incorrect because acceleration and deceleration result in erroneous pitch readings, not turning errors.

1.7 Turn-and-Slip Indicator

62.
4882. Prior to starting an engine, you should check the turn-and-slip indicator to determine if the

A— needle indication properly corresponds to the angle of the wings or rotors with the horizon.
B— needle is approximately centered and the tube is full of fluid.
C— ball will move freely from one end of the tube to the other when the aircraft is rocked.

Answer (B) is correct (4882). *(IFH Chap V)*
Prior to starting an engine, you should determine that the needle of the turn-and-slip indicator is approximately centered and that the tube is full of fluid with the ball also approximately centered if the airplane is on a level surface.
Answer (A) is incorrect because the needle corresponds to rate and direction of turn, not wing or rotor angle. Answer (C) is incorrect because rocking the aircraft is not necessary. Freedom of movement of the ball is checked during taxi.

63.
4883. What indications should you observe on the turn-and-slip indicator during taxi?

A— The ball moves freely opposite the turn, and the needle deflects in the direction of the turn.
B— The needle deflects in the direction of the turn, but the ball remains centered.
C— The ball deflects opposite the turn, but the needle remains centered.

Answer (A) is correct (4883). *(IFH Chap V)*
During taxi, the turn-and-slip indicator ball should move freely opposite the direction of any turn since centrifugal force forces the ball to the outside. Also, the rate of turn indicator should indicate a turn in the proper direction.
Answer (B) is incorrect because the ball will deflect opposite to the direction of the turn. Answer (C) is incorrect because the needle deflects in the direction of the turn.

1.8 Turn Coordinator

64.
4847. What indications are displayed by the miniature aircraft of a turn coordinator?

A— Rate of roll and rate of turn.
B— Direct indication of bank angle and pitch attitude.
C— Indirect indication of bank angle and pitch attitude.

Answer (A) is correct (4847). *(IFH Chap IV)*
The turn coordinator indicates rate of roll and rate of turn. When the bank is constant, the rate of turn is indicated. When the bank is changing, the rate of roll is also indicated.
Answer (B) is incorrect because the turn coordinator only indirectly indicates bank angle and has no relationship to pitch attitude. Answer (C) is incorrect because the turn coordinator has no relationship to pitch attitude.

65.
4839. What does the miniature aircraft of the turn coordinator directly display?

A— Rate of roll and rate of turn.
B— Angle of bank and rate of turn.
C— Angle of bank.

Answer (A) is correct (4839). *(IFH Chap IV)*
The turn coordinator indicates rate of roll and rate of turn. When the bank is constant, the rate of turn is indicated. When the bank is changing, the rate of roll is also indicated.
Answer (B) is incorrect because the angle of bank is not directly indicated by the turn coordinator. Answer (C) is incorrect because the angle of bank is not directly indicated by the turn coordinator.

66.
4856. What indication is presented by the miniature aircraft of the turn coordinator?

A— Indirect indication of the bank attitude.
B— Direct indication of the bank attitude and the quality of the turn.
C— Quality of the turn.

Answer (A) is correct (4856). *(IFH Chap IV)*
The miniature aircraft of the turn coordinator indicates the rate of roll when bank is changing. When the rotation around the longitudinal axis is zero, the instrument indicates the rate of turn. Thus, it provides only an indirect indication of the angle of bank.
Answer (B) is incorrect because the turn coordinator does NOT provide a direct indication of bank. Answer (C) is incorrect because the ball in the turn coordinator, not the miniature aircraft, provides information on the quality of the turn.

67.
4921. The displacement of a turn coordinator during a coordinated turn will

A— indicate the angle of bank.
B— remain constant for a given bank regardless of airspeed.
C— increase as angle of bank increases.

Answer (C) is correct (4921). *(IFH Chap IV)*
The displacement of a turn coordinator increases as angle of bank (in coordinated flight) increases because the turn coordinator shows rate of turn, which increases as angle of bank increases.
Answer (A) is incorrect because the angle of bank is only indirectly indicated. Answer (B) is incorrect because, when the rate of roll is zero, the turn coordinator provides information concerning the rate of turn, which in turn changes as airspeed changes given a constant bank.

68.
4831. What indication should be observed on a turn coordinator during a left turn while taxiing?

A— The miniature aircraft will show a turn to the left and the ball remains centered.
B— The miniature aircraft will show a turn to the left and the ball moves to the right.
C— Both the miniature aircraft and the ball will remain centered.

Answer (B) is correct (4831). *(IFH Chap V)*
On a taxiing turn to the left, the turn coordinator shows a turn to the left, and the ball moves to the right. The centrifugal force of the turn, which is not offset by bank when taxiing, forces the ball opposite to the turn.
Answer (A) is incorrect because the ball moves to the outside of the turn due to centrifugal force. Answer (C) is incorrect because the miniature aircraft reacts to yaw and shows a turn to the left, and the ball reacts to centrifugal force by moving right.

END OF CHAPTER

CHAPTER TWO
ATTITUDE INSTRUMENT FLYING AND AERODYNAMICS

This chapter contains outlines of major concepts tested, all FAA test questions and answers regarding attitude instrument flying and aerodynamics, and an explanation of each answer. Each module, or subtopic, within this chapter is listed above with the number of questions from the FAA knowledge test pertaining to that particular module. For each module, the first number following the parentheses is the page number on which the outline begins, and the next number is the page number on which the questions begin.

There are 69 questions in this chapter. We separate and organize the FAA questions into meaningful study units, i.e., chapters and modules. As an analogy, it is easier to deal with the "trees" if you understand the "forest." In this context, "trees" are individual FAA questions, and the "forest" is the instrument rating knowledge test. The organizational units between the overall instrument rating knowledge test and the individual instrument rating test questions are chapters and modules in this book.

CAUTION: The **sole purpose** of this book is to expedite your passing the FAA instrument rating knowledge test. Accordingly, all extraneous material (i.e., topics or regulations not directly tested on the FAA knowledge test) is omitted, even though much more information and knowledge are necessary to fly safely. This additional material is presented in *Instrument Pilot Flight Maneuvers and Practical Test Prep*, *Pilot Handbook*, *Aviation Weather and Weather Services*, and *FAR/AIM*, available from Gleim Publications, Inc. See the order form on page 488.

2.1 TURNS (Questions 1-12a)

1. An airplane requires a sideward force to make it turn.

    a. When the airplane is banked, lift (which acts perpendicular to the wingspan) acts not only upward but horizontally as well.

    b. The vertical component acts upward to oppose weight.

    c. The horizontal component acts sideward to turn the airplane, opposing centrifugal force.

    d. The rate of turn (at a given airspeed) depends on the magnitude of the horizontal lift component, which is determined by bank angle.

2. A turn is said to be coordinated when the horizontal lift component equals centrifugal force (the ball is centered).

    a. Centrifugal force is greater than horizontal lift in skidding turns (the ball is on the outside of the turn).

    b. Centrifugal force is less than horizontal lift in slipping turns (the ball is on the inside of the turn).

3. To coordinate a turn, you should center the ball on the turn-and-slip indicator or the turn coordinator.

    a. Center the ball by applying rudder pressure on the side where the ball is (e.g., if the ball is on the left, use left rudder).

4. A standard-rate turn is indicated when the needle is on the "doghouse" (i.e., standard rate) mark on the turn-and-slip indicator.

5. The angle of attack must be increased in turns to maintain altitude because additional lift is required to maintain a constant amount of vertical lift.

    a. Thus, load factor always increases in turns (assuming level flight).

6. If airspeed is increased in a turn, the angle of bank must be increased and/or the angle of attack decreased to maintain level flight.

    a. Conversely, if airspeed is decreased in a turn, the angle of bank must be decreased and/or the angle of attack must be increased to maintain level flight.

2.2 TURN RATES (Questions 13-20)

1. The standard-rate turn is 360° in 2 min., i.e., 3°/sec.

    a. A half-standard-rate turn is 360° in 4 min., i.e., 1.5°/sec.

    b. EXAMPLE: A 150° heading change using a standard-rate turn would take 50 sec. (150° ÷ 3°/sec. = 50 sec.)

2. At a constant bank, an increase in airspeed decreases the rate of turn and increases the radius of the turn.

    a. The rate of turn can be increased and the radius of turn decreased by decreasing airspeed and/or increasing the bank.

2.3 CLIMBS AND DESCENTS (Questions 21-30)

1. Conditions that determine the pitch attitude required to maintain level flight are

    a. Airspeed
    b. Air density
    c. Wing design
    d. Angle of attack

2. When leveling off from a climb or descent to a specific altitude, you must start the level-off before reaching the desired altitude.

    a. Throughout the transition to level flight, the aircraft will continue to climb or descend at a decreasing rate.

    b. An effective practice is to lead the altitude by 10% of the indicated vertical speed.

        1) Since the last 1,000 ft. of a climb or descent should be made at 500 fpm, you will generally use a lead of 50 ft.

    c. To level off from a descent at a higher airspeed than descent speed, begin adding power 100 to 150 ft. above the desired altitude, assuming a descent rate of 500 fpm.

3. The pitch instruments are the attitude indicator, the altimeter, the vertical speed indicator, and the airspeed indicator.

    a. The attitude indicator should be used to make a pitch correction when you have deviated from your altitude; then the altimeter and vertical speed indicator are used to monitor the result.

    b. Altitude corrections of less than 100 ft. should be corrected by using a half-bar-width (i.e., less than a full-bar-width) correction on the attitude indicator.

4. To enter a constant-airspeed descent from level cruise and maintain cruise airspeed, simultaneously reduce power and adjust the pitch using the attitude indicator as a reference to maintain cruise airspeed.

5. To enter a constant-airspeed climb from level cruise, increase the pitch such that the artificial horizon indicates an approximate nose-high attitude appropriate for the desired climb speed.

    a. Then apply the desired climb power setting.

2.4 FUNDAMENTAL INSTRUMENT SKILLS (Questions 31-34)

1. The three fundamental skills for attitude instrument flying are (in order)

    a. **Instrument cross-check** -- the continuous and logical observation of instruments for attitude and performance information

    b. **Instrument interpretation** -- the understanding of each instrument's construction, operating principle, and relationship to the performance of the airplane

    c. **Airplane control** -- includes the following elements:

        1) Pitch control
        2) Bank control
        3) Power control

2.5 APPROPRIATE INSTRUMENTS FOR IFR (Questions 35-53)

1. Flight instruments are divided into the following three categories:

    a. Pitch instruments

        1) Attitude indicator (AI)
        2) Altimeter (ALT)
        3) Airspeed indicator (ASI)
        4) Vertical speed indicator (VSI)

    b. Bank instruments

        1) Attitude indicator (AI)
        2) Heading indicator (HI)
        3) Turn coordinator (TC) or turn-and-slip indicator (T&SI)
        4) Magnetic compass

    c. Power instruments

        1) Manifold pressure gauge (MP)
        2) Tachometer (RPM)
        3) Airspeed indicator (ASI)

2. For any maneuver or condition of flight, the pitch, bank, and power control requirements are most clearly indicated by certain key instruments. Those instruments which provide the most pertinent and essential information will be referred to as primary instruments. Supporting instruments back up and supplement the information shown on the primary instruments.

		PITCH	BANK	POWER
a.	Straight and level			
	Primary	ALT	HI	ASI
	Supporting	AI, VSI	AI, TC	MP and/or RPM
b.	Airspeed changes in straight and level			
	Primary	ALT	HI	MP and/or RPM initially
	Supporting	AI, VSI	AI, TC	ASI as desired airspeed is approached
c.	Establishing a level standard-rate turn			
	Primary	ALT	AI	ASI
	Supporting	AI, VSI	TC	MP and/or RPM
d.	Stabilized standard-rate turn			
	Primary	ALT	TC	ASI
	Supporting	AI, VSI	AI	MP and/or RPM
e.	Change of airspeed in level turn			
	Primary	ALT	TC	MP and/or RPM
	Supporting	AI, VSI	AI	ASI
f.	Transitioning from straight and level to constant airspeed climb			
	Primary	AI	HI	MP and/or RPM
	Supporting	ASI, VSI	AI, TC	ASI
g.	Straight constant airspeed climb			
	Primary	ASI	HI	MP and/or RPM
	Supporting	AI, VSI	AI, TC	ASI
h.	As power is increased to enter a straight, constant-rate climb			
	Primary	AI	HI	MP and/or RPM
	Supporting	ASI, VSI	AI, TC	--
i.	Straight, constant-rate, stabilized climb			
	Primary	VSI	HI	ASI
	Supporting	AI	AI, TC	MP and/or RPM

3. For straight-and-level flight, the magnetic compass replaces the HI as the primary bank instrument if the HI is inoperative.

4. The ball of the turn coordinator or turn-and-slip instrument indicates the quality of the turn.

2.6 UNUSUAL ATTITUDES (Questions 54-59)

1. For recovery from nose-low unusual attitudes (negative VSI, increasing airspeed, decreasing altitude, airplane below horizon on attitude indicator):

    a. Reduce power to prevent excess airspeed and loss of altitude.
    b. Level the wings with coordinated rudder and aileron.
    c. Gently raise the nose to level flight attitude.

2. For recovery from nose-high unusual attitudes (positive VSI, decreasing airspeed, increasing altitude, airplane above horizon on attitude indicator):

    a. Add power.
    b. Lower the nose.
    c. Level the wings.
    d. Return to the original altitude and heading.

3. When recovering without the aid of the attitude indicator, level flight attitude is reached when the altimeter and the airspeed indicator stop prior to reversing their direction of movement and the vertical speed indicator reverses trend.

4. If the attitude indicator has exceeded its limits in an unusual attitude, nose-low or nose-high attitude can be determined by the airspeed indicator and the altimeter.

    a. The vertical speed indicator is also useful but is not as reliable in turbulent air.

2.7 INOPERATIVE INSTRUMENTS (Questions 60-64)

1. To determine an inoperative instrument, analyze each instrument to determine what it is indicating, and determine which instrument is in conflict with the others.

2. Also, consider grouping the instruments by the systems which power them.

    a. The heading indicator and the attitude indicator are vacuum-driven.
    b. The turn coordinator is usually electric.
    c. The airspeed indicator, altimeter, and VSI rely on the static source.

        1) The airspeed indicator also relies on the pitot tube.

            a) Remember that, if the pitot tube's ram air and drain hole are clogged, the airspeed indicator acts as an altimeter; i.e., lower altitudes result in lower airspeeds and vice versa.

            b) Also remember that, if only the ram air hole is clogged, the pressure in the line will vent out the drain hole, causing the airspeed indication to drop to zero.

2.8 TURBULENCE AND WIND SHEAR (Questions 65-67)

1. In severe turbulence, set power for the design maneuvering speed (V_A), and maintain a level flight attitude.

    a. Attempting to turn or maintain altitude or airspeed may impose excessive load on the wings.

2. Flight at or below V_A means the airplane will stall before excessive loads can be imposed on the wings.

3. When climbing or descending through an inversion or wind-shear zone, you should be alert for any sudden change in airspeed.

QUESTIONS AND ANSWER EXPLANATIONS

All the FAA questions from the instrument rating knowledge test relating to attitude instrument flying and aerodynamics and the material outlined previously are reproduced on the following pages in the same modules as the outlines. To the immediate right of each question are the correct answer and answer explanation. You should cover these answers and answer explanations with your hand or a piece of paper while responding to the questions. Refer to the general discussion in the Introduction on how to take the FAA knowledge test.

Remember that the questions from the FAA instrument rating knowledge test bank have been reordered by topic, and the topics have been organized into a meaningful sequence. Accordingly, the first line of the answer explanation gives the FAA question number and the citation of the authoritative source for the answer.

2.1 Turns

1.
4870. What force causes an airplane to turn?

A— Rudder pressure or force around the vertical axis.
B— Vertical lift component.
C— Horizontal lift component.

Answer (C) is correct (4870). *(IFH Chap III)*
An airplane, like any object, requires a sideward force to make it turn. This force is supplied by banking the airplane so that lift is separated into two components at right angles to each other. The lift acting upward and opposing weight is the vertical lift component, and the lift acting horizontally and opposing centrifugal force is the horizontal lift component. The horizontal lift component is the sideward force that causes an airplane to turn.
Answer (A) is incorrect because the rudder pressure coordinates flight only when the airplane is banked. Answer (B) is incorrect because the vertical component of lift counteracts weight and thus affects altitude.

2.
4843. The rate of turn at any airspeed is dependent upon

A— the horizontal lift component.
B— the vertical lift component.
C— centrifugal force.

Answer (A) is correct (4843). *(IFH Chap III)*
At a given airspeed, the rate at which an airplane turns depends upon the amount of the horizontal component of lift.
Answer (B) is incorrect because the vertical component of lift determines altitude and change in altitude. Answer (C) is incorrect because centrifugal force acts against the horizontal lift component, thus acting against turning the airplane.

3.
4868. What is the relationship between centrifugal force and the horizontal lift component in a coordinated turn?

A— Horizontal lift exceeds centrifugal force.
B— Horizontal lift and centrifugal force are equal.
C— Centrifugal force exceeds horizontal lift.

Answer (B) is correct (4868). *(IFH Chap III)*
When a turn is coordinated, horizontal lift equals centrifugal force. This is indicated when the ball on the turn coordinator or turn-and-slip indicator is centered.
Answer (A) is incorrect because, when horizontal lift exceeds centrifugal force, there is a slipping turn. Answer (C) is incorrect because, when centrifugal force exceeds horizontal lift, there is a skidding turn.

4.
4915. The primary reason the angle of attack must be increased, to maintain a constant altitude during a coordinated turn, is because the

A— thrust is acting in a different direction, causing a reduction in airspeed and loss of lift.
B— vertical component of lift has decreased as the result of the bank.
C— use of ailerons has increased the drag.

Answer (B) is correct (4915). *(IFH Chap III)*
In comparison to level flight, a bank results in the division of lift between vertical and horizontal components. To provide a vertical component of lift sufficient to maintain altitude in a level turn, an increase in the angle of attack is required.
Answer (A) is incorrect because thrust is always a forward-acting force. The reduction in airspeed (assuming constant power) is due to an increase in angle of attack to compensate for the loss of vertical lift in a turn, i.e., to maintain altitude. Answer (C) is incorrect because in a coordinated turn the ailerons are streamlined and no aileron drag exists. When entering or recovering from turns, you can counteract the adverse yaw caused by aileron drag by use of the rudder.

5.
4931. (Refer to figure 144 below.) What changes in control displacement should be made so that "2" would result in a coordinated standard-rate turn?

A— Increase left rudder and increase rate of turn.
B— Increase left rudder and decrease rate of turn.
C— Decrease left rudder and decrease angle of bank.

Answer (A) is correct (4931). *(IFH Chap IV)*
Illustration 2 in Fig. 144 indicates a slip, in which the rate of turn is too slow for the angle of bank, and the lack of centrifugal force causes the ball to move to the inside of the turn. To return to a coordinated standard-rate turn, you should increase left rudder (i.e., step on the ball) and increase the rate of turn. A standard-rate turn is indicated when the needle is on the "doghouse" (i.e., standard rate) mark. It is presently indicating a half-standard-rate turn.
Answer (B) is incorrect because the rate of turn must be increased, not decreased, to establish a standard-rate turn. Answer (C) is incorrect because left rudder pressure must be increased, not decreased, in a slip to the left.

6.
4932. (Refer to figure 144 below.) Which illustration indicates a coordinated turn?

A— 3.
B— 1.
C— 2.

Answer (A) is correct (4932). *(IFH Chap IV)*
A coordinated turn is one in which the ball is centered as indicated in illustration 3. The horizontal component of lift equals centrifugal force.
Answer (B) is incorrect because illustration 1 shows a skidding turn, in which centrifugal force exceeds the horizontal component of lift. Answer (C) is incorrect because illustration 2 shows a slipping turn, in which centrifugal force is less than the horizontal component of lift.

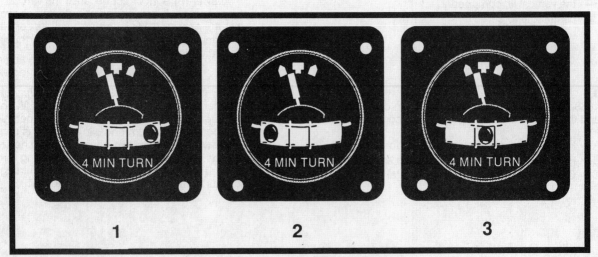

FIGURE 144.—Turn-and-Slip Indicator.

7.
4934. (Refer to figure 144 on page 50.) What changes in control displacement should be made so that "1" would result in a coordinated standard rate turn?

A— Increase right rudder and decrease rate of turn.
B— Increase right rudder and increase rate of turn.
C— Decrease right rudder and increase angle of bank.

Answer (B) is correct (4934). *(IFH Chap IV)*
Illustration 1 in Fig. 144 indicates a skid, in which the rate of turn is too great for the angle of bank, and excessive centrifugal force causes the ball to move to the outside of the turn. To return to coordinated flight, you should increase right rudder (i.e., step on the ball) to center the ball. A standard-rate turn is indicated when the needle is on the doghouse mark. Thus, the rate of turn must be increased to result in a standard-rate turn.
Answer (A) is incorrect because the rate of turn must be increased, not decreased. Answer (C) is incorrect because right rudder must be increased, not decreased.

8.
4933. (Refer to figure 144 on page 50.) Which illustration indicates a skidding turn?

A— 2.
B— 1.
C— 3.

Answer (B) is correct (4933). *(IFH Chap IV)*
A skidding turn occurs when centrifugal force is greater than horizontal lift. As shown by illustration 1, the ball is outside the turn.
Answer (A) is incorrect because illustration 2 shows a slipping turn. Answer (C) is incorrect because illustration 3 shows a coordinated turn.

9.
4935. (Refer to figure 144 on page 50.) Which illustration indicates a slipping turn?

A— 1.
B— 3.
C— 2.

Answer (C) is correct (4935). *(IFH Chap IV)*
A slipping turn is one in which the centrifugal force is less than horizontal lift. As shown by illustration 2, the ball is inside the turn.
Answer (A) is incorrect because illustration 1 shows a skidding turn. Answer (B) is incorrect because illustration 3 shows a coordinated turn.

10.
4844. During a skidding turn to the right, what is the relationship between the component of lift, centrifugal force, and load factor?

A— Centrifugal force is less than horizontal lift and the load factor is increased.
B— Centrifugal force is greater than horizontal lift and the load factor is increased.
C— Centrifugal force and horizontal lift are equal and the load factor is decreased.

Answer (B) is correct (4844). *(IFH Chap III)*
In skidding turns, centrifugal force is greater than horizontal lift. The load factor increases in level turns.
Answer (A) is incorrect because a slipping, not skidding, turn occurs when centrifugal force is less than horizontal lift. Answer (C) is incorrect because centrifugal force and horizontal lift are equal in a coordinated, not skidding, turn, and in a level turn the load factor is increased, not decreased.

11.
4878. When airspeed is increased in a turn, what must be done to maintain a constant altitude?

A— Decrease the angle of bank.
B— Increase the angle of bank and/or decrease the angle of attack.
C— Decrease the angle of attack.

Answer (B) is correct (4878). *(IFH Chap III)*
To compensate for added lift, which would result if airspeed were increased during a turn, the angle of attack must be decreased and the angle of bank increased if a constant altitude is to be maintained.
Answer (A) is incorrect because the angle of bank must be increased, not decreased. Answer (C) is incorrect because, as an alternative, the angle of bank can be increased.

12.
4833. When airspeed is decreased in a turn, what must be done to maintain level flight?

A— Decrease the angle of bank and/or increase the angle of attack.
B— Increase the angle of bank and/or decrease the angle of attack.
C— Increase the angle of attack.

12a.
0601-851. When airspeed is decreased in a turn, what must be done to maintain level flight?

A— Increase the pitch attitude and/or increase the angle of bank.
B— Increase the angle of bank and/or decrease the pitch attitude.
C— Decrease the angle of bank and/or increase the pitch attitude.

2.2 Turn Rates

13.
4904. If a standard-rate turn is maintained, how much time would be required to turn to the left from a heading of 090° to a heading of 300°?

A— 30 seconds.
B— 40 seconds.
C— 50 seconds.

14.
4905. If a half-standard-rate turn is maintained, how long would it take to turn 135°?

A— 1 minute.
B— 1 minute 20 seconds.
C— 1 minute 30 seconds.

15.
4895. If a half-standard-rate turn is maintained, how long would it take to turn 360°?

A— 1 minute.
B— 2 minutes.
C— 4 minutes.

Answer (A) is correct (4833). *(IFH Chap III)*
To compensate for the decreased lift resulting from decreased airspeed during a turn, the angle of bank must be decreased and/or the angle of attack increased.
Answer (B) is incorrect because the increased vertical lift required must be obtained by a decrease, not an increase, in angle of bank and/or an increase, not a decrease, in angle of attack. Answer (C) is incorrect because the angle of bank can be decreased as well as the angle of attack increased.

Answer (C) is correct (0601-851). *(IFH Chap III)*
To compensate for the decreased lift resulting from decreased airspeed during a turn, the angle of bank must be decreased and/or the angle of attack increased by increasing the pitch attitude.
Answer (A) is incorrect because the increased vertical lift required must be obtained by an increase in the pitch attitude and/or a decrease, not an increase, in the angle of bank. Answer (B) is incorrect because the increased vertical lift required must be obtained by a decrease, not an increase, in the angle of bank and/or an increase, not a decrease, in the pitch attitude.

Answer (C) is correct (4904). *(IFH Chap IV)*
A standard-rate turn means an airplane is turning at a rate of 3°/sec. A left turn from 090° to 300° is a total of 150° (90° to north and another 60° to 300°). Thus, at standard rate, it would take 50 sec. (150° ÷ 3°/sec.).
Answer (A) is incorrect because, at standard rate of turn, an airplane would turn left 90° to a heading of 360°, not 300°, in 30 sec. Answer (B) is incorrect because, at standard rate of turn, an airplane would turn left 120° to a heading of 330°, not 300°, in 40 sec.

Answer (C) is correct (4905). *(IFH Chap IV)*
A standard-rate turn means an airplane is turning at a rate of 3°/sec. Thus, a half-standard rate is a turn at the rate of 1.5°/sec. To turn 135° at half-standard rate would take 90 sec. (135° ÷ 1.5°/sec.) or 1 min. 30 sec.
Answer (A) is incorrect because an airplane would turn 90°, not 135°, in 1 min. at half-standard rate. Answer (B) is incorrect because an airplane would turn 120°, not 135°, in 1 min. 20 sec. at half-standard rate.

Answer (C) is correct (4895). *(IFH Chap IV)*
A standard-rate turn (3°/sec) takes 2 min. for 360°. A half-standard-rate turn (1.5°/sec.) would thus take 4 min. for 360°.
Answer (A) is incorrect because a half-standard-rate turn would take 1 min. to turn 90°, not 360°. Answer (B) is incorrect because a standard-rate, not half-standard-rate, turn completes 360° in 2 min.

16.
4896. If a standard-rate turn is maintained, how long
would it take to turn 180°?

A— 1 minute.
B— 2 minutes.
C— 3 minutes.

17.
4897. If a half-standard rate turn is maintained, how
much time would be required to turn clockwise from a
heading of 090° to a heading of 180°?

A— 30 seconds.
B— 1 minute.
C— 1 minute 30 seconds.

18.
4898. During a constant-bank level turn, what effect
would an increase in airspeed have on the rate and
radius of turn?

A— Rate of turn would increase, and radius of turn would
increase.
B— Rate of turn would decrease, and radius of turn
would decrease.
C— Rate of turn would decrease, and radius of turn
would increase.

19.
4914. Rate of turn can be increased and radius of turn
decreased by

A— decreasing airspeed and shallowing the bank.
B— decreasing airspeed and increasing the bank.
C— increasing airspeed and increasing the bank.

20.
4903. If a standard-rate turn is maintained, how much
time would be required to turn to the right from a heading
of 090° to a heading of 270°?

A— 1 minute.
B— 2 minutes.
C— 3 minutes.

Answer (A) is correct (4896). *(IFH Chap IV)*
A standard-rate turn means an airplane is turning at a
rate of 3°/sec. To turn 180° at a standard rate would take
60 sec. (180° ÷ 3°/sec.), or 1 min.
Answer (B) is incorrect because an airplane would
turn 180° in 2 min. at a half-standard-rate, not standard-
rate, turn. Answer (C) is incorrect because an airplane
would turn 540° in 3 min. at a standard rate (3°/sec.)

Answer (B) is correct (4897). *(IFH Chap III)*
A half-standard-rate turn means an airplane is turning
at a rate of 1.5°/sec. A turn clockwise from 090° to 180°
is a total of 90°. Thus, at a half-standard rate, it would
take 60 sec. (90° ÷ 1.5°/sec.).
Answer (A) is incorrect because it would take 30 sec.
to turn 90° at a standard, not half-standard, rate of turn.
Answer (C) is incorrect because an airplane would turn
135°, not 90°, in 1 min. 30 sec. at a half-standard rate of
turn.

Answer (C) is correct (4898). *(IFH Chap III)*
The radius of turn at a constant-bank level turn varies
directly with the airspeed, while the rate of turn at a
constant-bank level turn also varies with airspeed. If
airspeed is increased during a constant-bank level turn,
the radius of turn will increase, and rate of turn will
decrease.
Answer (A) is incorrect because the rate of turn
decreases, not increases. Answer (B) is incorrect
because the radius of the turn increases, not decreases.

Answer (B) is correct (4914). *(IFH Chap III)*
To increase the rate and decrease the radius of turn,
you should decrease airspeed and increase the bank
angle.
Answer (A) is incorrect because decreasing (shallowing) the bank decreases, not increases, the rate of turn.
Answer (C) is incorrect because the airspeed should be
decreased, not increased, to increase the rate of turn.

Answer (A) is correct (4903). *(IFH Chap IV)*
A standard-rate turn means an airplane is turning at
the rate of 3°/sec. A turn to the right (or left) from 090° to
270° is a total of 180°. Thus, at standard rate, it would
take 60 sec. (180° ÷ 3°/sec.), or 1 min.
Answer (B) is incorrect because it would take 2 min. to
turn 180° at a half-standard, not standard, rate of turn.
Answer (C) is incorrect because it would take 3 min. to
turn 270°, not 180°, at a half-standard, not standard, rate
of turn.

2.3 Climbs and Descents

21.
4899. Conditions that determine pitch attitude required to maintain level flight are

A— flightpath, wind velocity, and angle of attack.
B— airspeed, air density, wing design, and angle of attack.
C— relative wind, pressure altitude, and vertical lift component.

Answer (B) is correct (4899). *(IFH Chap III)*
Conditions that determine the pitch attitude required to maintain level flight are airspeed, air density, wing design, and angle of attack. At a constant angle of attack, any change in airspeed will vary the lift. Lift varies directly with changes in air density. An airplane's wing has lift characteristics that are suited to its intended uses. Lift increases with any increase in the angle of attack (up to the critical angle).
Answer (A) is incorrect because flight path is the direction of travel of the airplane, which in this case is level flight. Wind velocity is not considered in maintaining level flight. Angle of attack is the resultant pitch attitude to maintain level flight. Answer (C) is incorrect because relative wind is the direction of airflow produced by an airplane in flight, and the vertical lift component is an aerodynamic force that acts perpendicular to the relative wind. The density, not pressure, altitude is one condition which determines the pitch attitude required to maintain level flight.

22.
4906. Approximately what percent of the indicated vertical speed should be used to determine the number of feet to lead the level-off from a climb to a specific altitude?

A— 10 percent.
B— 20 percent.
C— 25 percent.

Answer (A) is correct (4906). *(IFH Chap V)*
To level off from a climb and maintain a specific altitude, you should start the level-off before reaching the desired altitude. If your airplane is climbing at 500 fpm, it will continue to climb at a decreasing rate throughout the transition to level flight. An effective practice is to lead the altitude by 10% of the indicated vertical speed (i.e., at 500 fpm, use a 50-ft. lead).
Answer (B) is incorrect because you should begin to level off from a climb at approximately 10%, not 20%, of the indicated vertical speed. Answer (C) is incorrect because you should begin to level off from a climb at approximately 10%, not 25%, of the indicated vertical speed.

23.
4907. To level off from a descent to a specific altitude, the pilot should lead the level-off by approximately

A— 10 percent of the vertical speed.
B— 30 percent of the vertical speed.
C— 50 percent of the vertical speed.

Answer (A) is correct (4907). *(IFH Chap V)*
To level off from a descent to a specific altitude, you should start the level-off before reaching the desired altitude. If your airplane is descending at 500 fpm, it will continue to descend at a decreasing rate throughout the transition to level flight. An effective practice is to lead the desired altitude by 10% of the indicated vertical speed (i.e., at 500 fpm, use a 50-ft. lead).
Answer (B) is incorrect because you should begin to level off from a descent at approximately 10%, not 30%, of the indicated vertical speed. Answer (C) is incorrect because you should begin to level off from a descent at approximately 10%, not 50%, of the indicated vertical speed.

23a.
0601-836. As a rule of thumb, altitude corrections of less than 100 feet should be corrected by using

A— two bar widths on the attitude indicator.
B— less than a full bar width on the attitude indicator.
C— less than a half bar width on the attitude indicator.

Answer (B) is correct (0601-836). *(IFH Chap V)*
As a general rule, altitude corrections of less than 100 ft. should be corrected by using a half-bar-width (i.e., less than a full-bar-width) correction on the attitude indicator.
Answer (A) is incorrect because altitude corrections of less than 100 ft. should be corrected by using a half-bar-, not a two-bar-, width correction on the attitude indicator. Answer (C) is incorrect because altitude corrections of less than 100 ft. should be corrected by using a half-bar-width correction on the attitude indicator, not less than a half-bar-width.

24.
4876. Which instruments should be used to make a pitch correction when you have deviated from your assigned altitude?

A— Altimeter and VSI.
B— Manifold pressure gauge and VSI.
C— Attitude indicator, altimeter, and VSI.

Answer (C) is correct (4876). *(IFH Chap V)*
The pitch instruments are the attitude indicator, the altimeter, the vertical speed indicator, and the airspeed indicator. The attitude indicator gives you a direct indication of changes in pitch attitude when correcting for altitude variations. The rate and direction of the altimeter and vertical speed indicator confirm the correct pitch adjustment was made, and the altimeter is used to determine when you have reached your assigned altitude.
Answer (A) is incorrect because the question implies that you have all instruments available. Without an attitude indicator, you would use the altimeter and vertical speed indicator to make pitch corrections. Answer (B) is incorrect because the manifold pressure gauge is a power, not pitch, instrument.

25.
4820. As a rule of thumb, altitude corrections of less than 100 feet should be corrected by using a

A— full bar width on the attitude indicator.
B— half bar width on the attitude indicator.
C— two bar width on the attitude indicator.

Answer (B) is correct (4820). *(IFH Chap V)*
As a general rule, altitude corrections of less than 100 ft. should be corrected by using a half-bar-width correction on the attitude indicator.
Answer (A) is incorrect because as a general rule, altitude corrections in excess of, not less than, 100 ft. should be corrected by an initial full-bar-width correction on the attitude indicator. Answer (C) is incorrect because altitude corrections of less than 100 ft. should be corrected by using a half-bar-, not a two-bar-, width correction on the attitude indicator.

26.
4924. To enter a constant-airspeed descent from level-cruising flight, and maintain cruising airspeed, the pilot should

A— first adjust the pitch attitude to a descent using the attitude indicator as a reference, then adjust the power to maintain the cruising airspeed.
B— first reduce power, then adjust the pitch using the attitude indicator as a reference to establish a specific rate on the VSI.
C— simultaneously reduce power and adjust the pitch using the attitude indicator as a reference to maintain the cruising airspeed.

Answer (C) is correct (4924). *(IFH Chap V)*
To enter a constant-airspeed descent from level cruising flight and maintain cruising airspeed, you should simultaneously reduce the power smoothly to the desired setting and reduce the pitch attitude slightly by using the attitude indicator as a reference to maintain the cruising airspeed.
Answer (A) is incorrect because airspeed will increase if you adjust the pitch attitude first. Answer (B) is incorrect because airspeed will decrease if you first reduce power. You use the airspeed, not vertical speed, indicator to maintain a constant airspeed.

27.
4925. To level off at an airspeed higher than the descent speed, the addition of power should be made, assuming a 500 FPM rate of descent, at approximately

A— 50 to 100 feet above the desired altitude.
B— 100 to 150 feet above the desired altitude.
C— 150 to 200 feet above the desired altitude.

Answer (B) is correct (4925). *(IFH Chap V)*
To level off from a descent at an airspeed higher than the descent speed, it is necessary to start the level-off before reaching the desired altitude. At 500 fpm, an effective practice is to lead the desired altitude by approximately 100 to 150 ft. above the desired altitude. At this point, add power to the appropriate level flight cruise setting.
Answer (A) is incorrect because, to level off at descent airspeed, not a higher airspeed, lead the desired altitude by approximately 50 to 100 ft. Answer (C) is incorrect because 150 to 200 ft. above the desired altitude is not a lead point when descending at 500 fpm.

28.
4926. To level off from a descent maintaining the descending airspeed, the pilot should lead the desired altitude by approximately

A— 20 feet.
B— 50 feet.
C— 60 feet.

Answer (B) is correct (4926). *(IFH Chap V)*
To level off from a descent at descent airspeed, lead the desired altitude by approximately 50 ft., simultaneously adjusting the pitch attitude to level flight and adding power to a setting that will hold airspeed constant. Trim off the control pressures and continue with the normal straight-and-level flight cross-check.
Answer (A) is incorrect because you should lead the desired altitude by approximately 50 ft., not 20 ft., when leveling off from a descent at descent airspeed.
Answer (C) is incorrect because you should lead the desired altitude by approximately 50 ft., not 60 ft., when leveling off from a descent at descent airspeed.

29.
4928. While cruising at 160 knots, you wish to establish a climb at 130 knots. When entering the climb (full panel), it is proper to make the initial pitch change by increasing back elevator pressure until the

A— attitude indicator, airspeed, and vertical speed indicate a climb.
B— vertical speed indication reaches the predetermined rate of climb.
C— attitude indicator shows the approximate pitch attitude appropriate for the 130-knot climb.

Answer (C) is correct (4928). *(IFH Chap V)*
To enter a constant-airspeed climb from cruising airspeed, raise the miniature aircraft in the attitude indicator to the approximate nose-high indication appropriate to the predetermined climb speed. The attitude will vary according to the type of airplane you are flying. Apply light elevator back pressure to initiate and maintain the climb attitude. The amount of back pressure will increase as the airplane decelerates.
Answer (A) is incorrect because, for the predetermined climb speed, the adjustment should be to the climb attitude, not just a climb indication on the instruments. Answer (B) is incorrect because the airspeed is predetermined, i.e., constant climb speed, not constant climb rate.

30.
4929. While cruising at 190 knots, you wish to establish a climb at 160 knots. When entering the climb (full panel), it would be proper to make the initial pitch change by increasing back elevator pressure until the

A— attitude indicator shows the approximate pitch attitude appropriate for the 160-knot climb.
B— attitude indicator, airspeed, and vertical speed indicate a climb.
C— airspeed indication reaches 160 knots.

Answer (A) is correct (4929). *(IFH Chap V)*
To enter a constant-airspeed climb from cruising airspeed, raise the miniature aircraft in the attitude indicator to the approximate nose-high indication appropriate to the predetermined climb speed. The attitude will vary according to the type of airplane you are flying. Apply light elevator back pressure to initiate and maintain the climb attitude. The required back pressure will increase as the airplane decelerates.
Answer (B) is incorrect because, for the predetermined climb speed, you make the adjustment to the climb attitude, not just a climb indication on the instruments. Answer (C) is incorrect because you make an initial pitch adjustment, not an increasing adjustment; i.e., airspeed will decrease gradually.

2.4 Fundamental Instrument Skills

31.
4862. What is the first fundamental skill in attitude instrument flying?

A— Aircraft control.
B— Instrument cross-check.
C— Instrument interpretation.

Answer (B) is correct (4862). *(IFH Chap V)*
The first fundamental skill in attitude instrument flying is instrument cross-check. Cross-checking is the continuous and logical observation of instruments for attitude and performance information.
Answer (A) is incorrect because the third, not first, fundamental skill in attitude instrument flying is aircraft control. Aircraft control is composed of three components: pitch, bank, and power control.
Answer (C) is incorrect because the second, not first, fundamental skill in attitude instrument flying is instrument interpretation. For each maneuver, you must know the performance to expect and the combination of instruments that you must interpret in order to control airplane attitude during the maneuver.

32.
4855. What are the three fundamental skills involved in attitude instrument flying?

A— Instrument interpretation, trim application, and aircraft control.
B— Cross-check, instrument interpretation, and aircraft control.
C— Cross-check, emphasis, and aircraft control.

33.
4859. What is the third fundamental skill in attitude instrument flying?

A— Instrument cross-check.
B— Power control.
C— Aircraft control.

34.
4840. What is the correct sequence in which to use the three skills used in instrument flying?

A— Aircraft control, cross-check, and instrument interpretation.
B— Instrument interpretation, cross-check, and aircraft control.
C— Cross-check, instrument interpretation, and aircraft control.

2.5 Appropriate Instruments for IFR

35.
4863. As power is reduced to change airspeed from high to low cruise in level flight, which instruments are primary for pitch, bank, and power, respectively?

A— Attitude indicator, heading indicator, and manifold pressure gauge or tachometer.
B— Altimeter, attitude indicator, and airspeed indicator.
C— Altimeter, heading indicator, and manifold pressure gauge or tachometer.

Answer (B) is correct (4855). *(IFH Chap V)*
The three fundamental skills involved in all instrument flight maneuvers are instrument cross-check, instrument interpretation, and aircraft control. Cross-checking is the continuous and logical observation of the instruments for attitude and performance information. Instrument interpretation requires you to understand each instrument's construction, operating principle, and relationship to the performance of your airplane. Aircraft control requires you to substitute instruments for outside references.
Answer (A) is incorrect because trim application is only one aspect of aircraft control. Answer (C) is incorrect because emphasis (along with fixation and omission) are common errors in instrument cross-checking.

Answer (C) is correct (4859). *(IFH Chap V)*
The third fundamental skill in instrument flying is aircraft control. It consists of pitch, bank, and power control.
Answer (A) is incorrect because instrument cross-check is the first, not third, fundamental skill in attitude instrument flying. Cross-checking is the continuous and logical observation of instruments for attitude and per-formance information. Answer (B) is incorrect because power control is only one component of aircraft control.

Answer (C) is correct (4840). *(IFH Chap V)*
The correct sequence in which to use the three fundamental skills of instrument flying is cross-check, instrument interpretation, and aircraft control. Although you learn these skills separately and in deliberate sequence, a measure of your proficiency in precision flying will be your ability to integrate these skills into unified, smooth, positive control responses to maintain any desired flight path.
Answer (A) is incorrect because aircraft control is the third, not first, skill used in instrument flying. Answer (B) is incorrect because instrument interpretation is the second, not first, skill and cross-check is the first, not second, skill used in instrument flying.

Answer (C) is correct (4863). *(IFH Chap V)*
In straight-and-level flight, when reducing airspeed from high to low cruise, the primary instrument for pitch is the altimeter; the primary instrument for bank is the heading indicator; and the primary instrument for power is the manifold pressure gauge or tachometer.
Answer (A) is incorrect because the primary pitch instrument is the altimeter, not attitude indicator. Answer (B) is incorrect because the primary bank instru-ment is the heading indicator, not attitude indicator; and the primary power instrument is the manifold pressure gauge or tachometer, not airspeed indicator.

36.

4836. What instruments are considered supporting bank instruments during a straight, stabilized climb at a constant rate?

A— Attitude indicator and turn coordinator.
B— Heading indicator and attitude indicator.
C— Heading indicator and turn coordinator.

Answer (A) is correct (4836). *(IFH Chap V)*
During a straight, stabilized climb at a constant rate, the heading indicator is the primary instrument for bank. The supporting bank instruments are the turn coordinator and the attitude indicator.
Answer (B) is incorrect because the heading indicator is the primary, not supporting, bank instrument in a straight climb. Answer (C) is incorrect because the heading indicator is the primary, not supporting, bank instrument in a straight climb.

37.

4866. Which instruments are considered primary and supporting for bank, respectively, when establishing a level standard rate turn?

A— Turn coordinator and attitude indicator.
B— Attitude indicator and turn coordinator.
C— Turn coordinator and heading indicator.

Answer (B) is correct (4866). *(IFH Chap V)*
When you are establishing a level standard-rate turn, the attitude indicator is the primary bank instrument and is used to establish the approximate angle of bank. The turn coordinator is the supporting bank instrument as you check for the standard-rate turn indication.
Answer (A) is incorrect because the turn coordinator is the primary bank instrument and the attitude indicator is the supporting bank instrument only after the standard-rate turn is established, not while entering the turn. Answer (C) is incorrect because the turn coordinator is the supporting, not primary, bank instrument and the heading indicator is neither the primary nor the supporting bank instrument when establishing a standard-rate turn.

38.

4865. Which instrument provides the most pertinent information (primary) for bank control in straight-and-level flight?

A— Turn-and-slip indicator.
B— Attitude indicator.
C— Heading indicator.

Answer (C) is correct (4865). *(IFH Chap V)*
The primary instrument for bank control in straight-and-level flight is the heading indicator.
Answer (A) is incorrect because the turn-and-slip indicator is a supporting, not primary, bank instrument in straight-and-level flight. Answer (B) is incorrect because the attitude indicator is a supporting, not primary, bank and pitch instrument in straight-and-level flight.

39.

4869. Which instruments, in addition to the attitude indicator, are pitch instruments?

A— Altimeter and airspeed only.
B— Altimeter and VSI only.
C— Altimeter, airspeed indicator, and vertical speed indicator.

Answer (C) is correct (4869). *(IFH Chap V)*
The pitch control instruments are the attitude indicator, altimeter, vertical speed indicator, and airspeed indicator.
Answer (A) is incorrect because it omits the vertical speed indicator and the airspeed indicator. Answer (B) is incorrect because it omits the airspeed indicator.

40.

4871. Which instrument provides the most pertinent information (primary) for pitch control in straight-and-level flight?

A— Attitude indicator.
B— Airspeed indicator.
C— Altimeter.

Answer (C) is correct (4871). *(IFH Chap V)*
The primary pitch instrument for straight-and-level flight is the altimeter.
Answer (A) is incorrect because the attitude indicator is a supporting, not primary, pitch instrument in straight-and-level flight. Answer (B) is incorrect because the airspeed indicator is the primary power, not pitch, control instrument in straight-and-level flight.

41.
4920. For maintaining level flight at constant thrust, which instrument would be the least appropriate for determining the need for a pitch change?

A— Altimeter.
B— VSI.
C— Attitude indicator.

Answer (C) is correct (4920). *(IFH Chap V)*
To maintain level flight at constant thrust, the attitude indicator is the least appropriate for determining the need for pitch change. Until you have established and identified the level flight attitude for that airspeed, you have no way of knowing whether level flight as indicated on the attitude indicator is resulting in level flight as shown on the altimeter, vertical speed indicator, and airspeed indicator.
Answer (A) is incorrect because, since level flight means a constant altitude, the altimeter is the primary pitch instrument in level flight. Answer (B) is incorrect because the vertical speed indicator (as a trend instrument) shows immediately the initial vertical movement of the airplane, which, disregarding turbulence, can be a reflection of pitch change at a constant thrust.

42.
4832. The gyroscopic heading indicator is inoperative. What is the primary bank instrument in unaccelerated straight-and-level flight?

A— Magnetic compass.
B— Attitude indicator.
C— Miniature aircraft of turn coordinator.

Answer (A) is correct (4832). *(IFH Appendix)*
With the gyroscopic heading indicator inoperative, the primary bank instrument in unaccelerated straight-and-level flight is the magnetic compass. Since any banking results in a turn and change in heading, the magnetic compass is the only other instrument that indicates direction.
Answer (B) is incorrect because, although the attitude indicator shows any change in bank, it does not provide information (i.e., heading) needed to maintain straight flight. Answer (C) is incorrect because the miniature aircraft of the turn coordinator is the primary bank instrument in established standard-rate turns, not in straight flight.

43.
4837. What instruments are primary for pitch, bank, and power, respectively, when transitioning into a constant airspeed climb from straight-and-level flight?

A— Attitude indicator, heading indicator, and manifold pressure gauge or tachometer.
B— Attitude indicator for both pitch and bank; airspeed indicator for power.
C— Vertical speed, attitude indicator, and manifold pressure or tachometer.

Answer (A) is correct (4837). *(IFH Chap V)*
When you are entering a constant airspeed climb, the attitude indicator is the primary pitch instrument, the heading indicator is the primary bank instrument, and the tachometer or manifold pressure gauge is the primary power instrument.
Answer (B) is incorrect because the heading indicator, not attitude indicator, is primary for bank, and the manifold pressure gauge, not airspeed indicator, is primary for power. Answer (C) is incorrect because the attitude indicator, not vertical speed indicator, is the primary instrument for pitch, and the heading indicator, not attitude indicator, is primary for bank.

44.
4838. What is the primary bank instrument once a standard rate turn is established?

A— Attitude indicator.
B— Turn coordinator.
C— Heading indicator.

Answer (B) is correct (4838). *(IFH Chap V)*
After a standard-rate turn is established, the turn coordinator is the primary bank instrument.
Answer (A) is incorrect because the attitude indicator is the primary bank instrument in establishing a standard-rate turn but not for maintaining the turn once established. Answer (C) is incorrect because the heading indicator is the primary bank instrument for straight flight.

44a.
0601-892. During standard-rate turns, which instrument is considered "primary" for bank?

A— Heading indicator.
B— Turn and slip indicator or turn coordinator.
C— Attitude indicator.

Answer (B) is correct (0601-892). *(IFH Chap V)*
After a standard-rate turn is established, the turn coordinator or turn and slip indicator is the primary bank instrument.
Answer (A) is incorrect because the heading indicator is the primary bank instrument for straight flight.
Answer (C) is incorrect because the attitude indicator is the primary bank instrument in establishing a standard-rate turn but not for maintaining the turn once established.

45.
4850. What is the primary pitch instrument when establishing a constant altitude standard rate turn?

A— Altimeter.
B— VSI.
C— Airspeed indicator.

46.
4851. What is the initial primary bank instrument when establishing a level standard rate turn?

A— Turn coordinator.
B— Heading indicator.
C— Attitude indicator.

47.
4858. What is the primary bank instrument while transitioning from straight-and-level flight to a standard rate turn to the left?

A— Attitude indicator.
B— Heading indicator.
C— Turn coordinator (miniature aircraft).

48.
4853. What instrument(s) is(are) supporting bank instrument when entering a constant airspeed climb from straight-and-level flight?

A— Heading indicator.
B— Attitude indicator and turn coordinator.
C— Turn coordinator and heading indicator.

49.
4848. What is the primary pitch instrument during a stabilized climbing left turn at cruise climb airspeed?

A— Attitude indicator.
B— VSI.
C— Airspeed indicator.

Answer (A) is correct (4850). *(IFH Chap V)*
The primary pitch instrument in level flight, either straight or turns, is the altimeter.
Answer (B) is incorrect because the vertical speed indicator is a supporting, not primary, pitch instrument for establishing a level standard-rate turn. Answer (C) is incorrect because the airspeed indicator is the primary power, not pitch, instrument when establishing a constant altitude standard-rate turn.

Answer (C) is correct (4851). *(IFH Chap V)*
The initial primary bank instrument when establishing a level standard-rate turn is the attitude indicator.
Answer (A) is incorrect because only after the turn is established does the turn coordinator become the primary bank instrument. Answer (B) is incorrect because the heading indicator is the primary bank instrument for straight flight.

Answer (A) is correct (4858). *(IFH Chap V)*
The initial primary bank instrument when establishing a level standard-rate of turn is the attitude indicator.
Answer (B) is incorrect because the heading indicator is the primary bank instrument for straight flight. Answer (C) is incorrect because only after the turn is established does the turn coordinator become the primary bank instrument.

Answer (B) is correct (4853). *(IFH Chap V)*
When entering a constant-airspeed climb from straight-and-level flight, the primary bank instrument is the heading indicator. Supporting bank instruments are the turn coordinator and the attitude indicator.
Answer (A) is incorrect because the heading indicator is the primary, not supporting, bank instrument for straight flight. Answer (C) is incorrect because the heading indicator is the primary, not supporting, bank instrument for straight flight.

Answer (C) is correct (4848). *(IFH Chap V)*
In a climbing left turn at a constant airspeed, the airspeed indicator is the primary instrument for pitch once the climb is established.
Answer (A) is incorrect because the attitude indicator is a supporting, not primary, pitch instrument in a stabilized climb. Answer (B) is incorrect because the vertical speed indicator is a supporting, not primary, pitch instrument in a stabilized climb.

50.
4872. Which instruments are considered to be supporting instruments for pitch during change of airspeed in a level turn?

A— Airspeed indicator and VSI.
B— Altimeter and attitude indicator.
C— Attitude indicator and VSI.

51.
4874. Which instrument is considered primary for power as the airspeed reaches the desired value during change of airspeed in a level turn?

A— Airspeed indicator.
B— Attitude indicator.
C— Altimeter.

52.
4884. Which instrument indicates the quality of a turn?

A— Attitude indicator.
B— Heading indicator or magnetic compass.
C— Ball of the turn coordinator.

53.
4845. As power is increased to enter a 500 feet per minute rate of climb in straight flight, which instruments are primary for pitch, bank, and power respectively?

A— Attitude indicator, heading indicator, and manifold pressure gauge or tachometer.
B— VSI, attitude indicator, and airspeed indicator.
C— Airspeed indicator, attitude indicator, and manifold pressure gauge or tachometer.

Answer (C) is correct (4872). *(IFH Chap V)*
The supporting instruments for pitch during a change of airspeed in a level turn are the attitude indicator and the vertical speed indicator. The primary instrument is the altimeter.
Answer (A) is incorrect because the airspeed indicator is a supporting power, not pitch, instrument during a change of airspeed in a level turn. It becomes the primary power instrument as the desired airspeed is reached. Answer (B) is incorrect because the altimeter is the primary, not supporting, pitch instrument in level flight.

Answer (A) is correct (4874). *(IFH Chap V)*
The airspeed indicator is the primary power instrument as the airspeed reaches the desired value during a change of airspeed in a level turn.
Answer (B) is incorrect because the attitude indicator is a supporting pitch and bank instrument. Answer (C) is incorrect because the altimeter is the primary pitch instrument.

Answer (C) is correct (4884). *(IFH Chap V)*
The quality (coordination) of a turn relates to whether the horizontal component of lift balances the centrifugal force. It is indicated by the ball of the turn coordinator or the ball in a turn-and-slip indicator. The airplane is neither slipping nor skidding when the ball is centered, indicating the desired quality of a turn.
Answer (A) is incorrect because the attitude indicator provides both pitch and bank information. Answer (B) is incorrect because the heading indicator and/or magnetic compass show current direction and changes in direction, not quality of a turn.

Answer (A) is correct (4845). *(IFH Chap V)*
As the power is increased to enter a constant-rate climb in straight flight, the primary pitch instrument is the attitude indicator until the vertical speed indicator stabilizes at the desired rate of climb (then the vertical speed indicator becomes primary). The primary bank instrument is the heading indicator. The primary power instrument is the manifold pressure gauge or tachometer.
Answer (B) is incorrect because the vertical speed indicator is the primary pitch instrument once the constant-rate climb is established. Also, the manifold pressure gauge, not the airspeed indicator, is primary for power. Answer (C) is incorrect because the heading indicator, not the attitude indicator, is primary for bank in straight flight.

2.6 Unusual Attitudes

54.
4936. (Refer to figure 145 below.) What is the correct sequence for recovery from the unusual attitude indicated?

A— Reduce power, increase back elevator pressure, and level the wings.
B— Reduce power, level the wings, bring pitch attitude to level flight.
C— Level the wings, raise the nose of the aircraft to level flight attitude, and obtain desired airspeed.

Answer (B) is correct (4936). *(IFH Chap V)*
In Fig. 145, a nose-low attitude is indicated by a negative vertical speed indicator, high airspeed (i.e., near V_{NE}), and the airplane below the horizon on the attitude indicator. For nose-low unusual attitudes, the correct sequence for recovery is to reduce power to prevent excessive airspeed and loss of altitude; level the wings with coordinated aileron and rudder pressure to straight flight by referring to the turn coordinator; and raise the nose to level flight attitude by smooth back elevator pressure.
Answer (A) is incorrect because the wings should be level before you increase back pressure to decrease the load factor during leveling off. Answer (C) is incorrect because the power should be reduced first.

FIGURE 145.—Instrument Sequence (Unusual Attitude).

55.
4867. While recovering from an unusual flight attitude without the aid of the attitude indicator, approximate level pitch attitude is reached when the

A— airspeed and altimeter stop their movement and the VSI reverses its trend.
B— airspeed arrives at cruising speed, the altimeter reverses its trend, and the vertical speed stops its movement.
C— altimeter and vertical speed reverse their trend and the airspeed stops its movement.

56.
4938. (Refer to figure 147 below.) Which is the correct sequence for recovery from the unusual attitude indicated?

A— Level wings, add power, lower nose, descend to original attitude, and heading.
B— Add power, lower nose, level wings, return to original attitude and heading.
C— Stop turn by raising right wing and add power at the same time, lower the nose, and return to original attitude and heading.

Answer (A) is correct (4867). *(IFH Chap V)*
As the rate of movement of the altimeter and airspeed indicator needles decreases, the attitude is approaching level flight. When the needles stop and reverse direction, the aircraft is passing through level flight.
Answer (B) is incorrect because the vertical speed indicator will be lagging, i.e., showing a decrease in vertical movement when vertical movement has stopped. Answer (C) is incorrect because the rate is only slowing and has not stabilized when the altimeter reverses its trend; i.e., it must stop to indicate level flight.

Answer (B) is correct (4938). *(IFH Chap V)*
In Fig. 147, a nose-high attitude is indicated by the increasing altitude, the rate-of-climb indication on the vertical speed indicator, and the decreasing airspeed. The correct sequence for recovery is to add power, apply forward elevator pressure to lower the nose and prevent a stall, level the wings with coordinated aileron and rudder pressure to straight flight, and return to original altitude and heading.
Answer (A) is incorrect because you should both add power and lower the nose before you level the wings. Answer (C) is incorrect because you should both add power and lower the nose before you level the wings.

FIGURE 147.—Instrument Sequence (Unusual Attitude).

57.
4873. If an airplane is in an unusual flight attitude and the attitude indicator has exceeded its limits, which instruments should be relied on to determine pitch attitude before starting recovery?

A— Turn indicator and VSI.
B— Airspeed and altimeter.
C— VSI and airspeed to detect approaching VSI or VMO.

Answer (B) is correct (4873). *(IFH Chap V)*
If the attitude indicator is inoperative, a nose-low or nose-high attitude can be determined by the airspeed and altimeter. In a nose-high attitude, airspeed is decreasing and altimeter is increasing, and vice versa for nose-low attitudes.
Answer (A) is incorrect because the turn indicator indicates nothing about pitch attitude. Answer (C) is incorrect because the altimeter, not the VSI, is the primary pitch instrument. Note the FAA answer selection has VSI and VMO, which should be V_{S1} and V_{MO}, respectively.

58.
4875. Which is the correct sequence for recovery from a spiraling, nose-low, increasing airspeed, unusual flight attitude?

A— Increase pitch attitude, reduce power, and level wings.
B— Reduce power, correct the bank attitude, and raise the nose to a level attitude.
C— Reduce power, raise the nose to level attitude, and correct the bank attitude.

Answer (B) is correct (4875). *(IFH Chap V)*
For nose-low unusual attitudes, one should reduce the power, level the wings, and then increase the pitch to raise the nose to a level attitude.
Answer (A) is incorrect because the power should be decreased first, then the wings leveled. Answer (C) is incorrect because the wings should be leveled before the nose is raised to minimize the load factor.

59.
4927. During recoveries from unusual attitudes, level flight is attained the instant

A— the horizon bar on the attitude indicator is exactly overlapped with the miniature airplane.
B— a zero rate of climb is indicated on the VSI.
C— the altimeter and airspeed needles stop prior to reversing their direction of movement.

Answer (C) is correct (4927). *(IFH Chap V)*
In unusual attitudes, you can determine the attainment of level flight (not vertical movement) when the altimeter and airspeed needles stop prior to reversing their direction of movement.
Answer (A) is incorrect because the attitude indicator has a tendency to precess during an unusual attitude and may not be reliable. Answer (B) is incorrect because there is a lag or delay in the vertical speed indicator. It cannot be relied on for determining the instant level flight is attained.

2.7 Inoperative Instruments

60.
4937. (Refer to figure 146 below.) Identify the system that has failed and determine a corrective action to return the airplane to straight-and-level flight.

A— Static/pitot system is blocked; lower the nose and level the wings to level-fight attitude by use of attitude indicator.

B— Vacuum system has failed; reduce power, roll left to level wings, and pitchup to reduce airspeed.

C— Electrical system has failed; reduce power, roll left to level wings, and raise the nose to reduce airspeed.

Answer (A) is correct (4937). *(IFH Chap IV)*

In Fig. 146, the airplane is in a right turn as indicated by the attitude indicator, the heading indicator, and the turn coordinator; thus the vacuum and electrical instruments are consistent with each other. Since the attitude indicator indicates a climb, which is consistent with the altimeter and the VSI, the airspeed should not be increasing. Thus, the pitot tube ram air and drain holes are blocked, causing the airspeed indicator to react like an altimeter. To return the airplane to straight-and-level flight, you should lower the nose and level the wings to level-flight attitude by use of the attitude indicator.

Answer (B) is incorrect because the attitude indicator and heading indicator are consistent with the turn coordinator. Answer (C) is incorrect because the turn coordinator, which is normally electric, is consistent with the attitude indicator, which is normally a vacuum system instrument.

FIGURE 146.—Instrument Sequence (System Failed).

61.
4939. (Refer to figure 148 below.) What is the flight attitude? One system which transmits information to the instruments has malfunctioned.

A— Climbing turn to left.
B— Climbing turn to right.
C— Level turn to left.

Answer (B) is correct (4939). *(IFH Chap IV)*
Fig. 148 illustrates a climbing turn to the right. Note that the attitude indicator shows a climbing turn to the right, the heading indicator shows a turn to the right, and both the altimeter and vertical speed indicator indicate a climb. The turn coordinator shows no turn and is malfunctioning.
Answer (A) is incorrect because the turn is to the right, not the left. Answer (C) is incorrect because the attitude indicator, altimeter, and vertical speed indicator all indicate a climb, and the turn is to the right, not left.

FIGURE 148.—Instrument Interpretation (System Malfunction).

62.
4940. (Refer to figure 149 below.) What is the flight attitude? One system which transmits information to the instruments has malfunctioned.

A— Level turn to the right.
B— Level turn to the left.
C— Straight-and-level flight.

Answer (C) is correct (4940). *(IFH Chap IV)*
In Fig. 149, the vertical speed indicator, altimeter, and turn coordinator all indicate straight-and-level flight. The heading indicator indicates a turn to the south from west, which is a turn to the left. The attitude indicator indicates a turn to the right; i.e., the attitude indicator and heading indicator are in conflict. Thus, the vacuum system must be malfunctioning, and the airplane must be in straight-and-level flight.
Answer (A) is incorrect because the vacuum system (i.e., the attitude and heading indicators) is inoperative, and the airplane is in straight flight, not a right turn.
Answer (B) is incorrect because the vacuum system (i.e., the attitude and heading indicators) is inoperative, and the airplane is in straight flight, not a left turn.

Figure 149.—Instrument Interpretation (System Malfunction).

63.
4941. (Refer to figure 150 below.) What is the flight attitude? One instrument has malfunctioned.

A— Climbing turn to the right.
B— Climbing turn to the left.
C— Descending turn to the right.

Answer (A) is correct (4941). *(IFH Chap IV)*
In Fig. 150, the airplane is in a climb as evidenced by the vertical speed indicator, altimeter, and airspeed indicator. The heading indicator indicates a turn from west to north, which is a turn to the right. The turn coordinator also indicates a turn to the right. Thus, the airplane is in a climbing turn to the right. The attitude indicator is the instrument that is malfunctioning since it indicates a level turn to the left.

Answer (B) is incorrect because the attitude indicator is inoperative; thus, the airplane is turning to the right, not left. Answer (C) is incorrect because the airspeed indicator, altimeter, and vertical speed indicator all show that the airplane is climbing, not descending.

Figure 150.—Instrument Interpretation (Instrument Malfunction).

64.
4942. (Refer to figure 151 below.) What is the flight attitude? One instrument has malfunctioned.

A— Climbing turn to the right.
B— Level turn to the right.
C— Level turn to the left.

Answer (B) is correct (4942). *(IFH Chap IV)*
The vertical speed indicator, altimeter, and attitude indicator indicate level flight. The turn coordinator, attitude indicator, and heading indicator indicate a turn to the right. Accordingly, there is a level turn to the right, and the airspeed should not be near the stall speed. Thus, the ram air inlet and the drain hole of the pitot tube are clogged. The airspeed indicator will react the same way as an altimeter, if the static port is open, by showing a decrease in airspeed as altitude decreases and an increase in speed as altitude increases.
Answer (A) is incorrect because flight is level, not climbing, according to the vertical speed indicator, altimeter, and attitude indicator. Answer (C) is incorrect because the turn is to the right, not left.

FIGURE 151.—Instrument Interpretation (Instrument Malfunction).

2.8 Turbulence and Wind Shear

65.
4160. If you fly into severe turbulence, which flight condition should you attempt to maintain?

A— Constant airspeed (V_A).
B— Level flight attitude.
C— Constant altitude and constant airspeed.

Answer (B) is correct (4160). *(AvW Chap 11)*
In severe turbulence, you should attempt to maintain a level flight attitude. You will not be able to maintain a constant altitude and/or airspeed, but you should fly at or below design maneuvering speed (V_A) and attempt to maintain a level flight attitude.
Answer (A) is incorrect because you want to maintain an airspeed at or below V_A, but in severe turbulence, there will be large variations in airspeed, and you will not be able to keep it constant. Answer (C) is incorrect because, in severe turbulence, you will not be able to maintain a constant altitude and/or constant airspeed.

66.
4916. If severe turbulence is encountered during your IFR flight, the airplane should be slowed to the design maneuvering speed because the

A— maneuverability of the airplane will be increased.
B— amount of excess load that can be imposed on the wing will be decreased.
C— airplane will stall at a lower angle of attack, giving an increased margin of safety.

Answer (B) is correct (4916). *(AvW Chap 11)*
Flight at or below the design maneuvering speed (V_A) means that the airplane will stall before excess loads can be imposed on the wings.
Answer (A) is incorrect because you should slow the airspeed to reduce excessive loads, not because the airplane will be more maneuverable at a slow airspeed. Answer (C) is incorrect because an airplane will always stall when the critical angle of attack is exceeded.

67.
4917. When a climb or descent through an inversion or wind-shear zone is being performed, the pilot should be alert for which of the following change in airplane performance?

A— A fast rate of climb and a slow rate of descent.
B— A sudden change in airspeed.
C— A sudden surge of thrust.

Answer (B) is correct (4917). *(AvW Chap 10)*
When climbing through an inversion or wind-shear zone, the danger is a sudden change in airspeed. If the airplane were to move abruptly from a headwind to a tailwind, the airspeed would slow dramatically, and a stall or rapid descent could be induced.
Answer (A) is incorrect because a fast rate of climb and a slow rate of descent are usually not a safety problem, as the reverse could be. Answer (C) is incorrect because the amount of thrust does not change as a result of wind shears.

END OF CHAPTER

CHAPTER THREE
NAVIGATION SYSTEMS

This chapter contains outlines of major concepts tested, all FAA test questions and answers regarding navigation systems, and an explanation of each answer. Each module, or subtopic, within this chapter is listed above with the number of questions from the FAA knowledge test pertaining to that particular module. For each module, the first number following the parentheses is the page number on which the outline begins, and the next number is the page number on which the questions begin.

There are 88 questions in this chapter. We separate and organize the FAA questions into meaningful study units, i.e., chapters and modules. As an analogy, it is easier to deal with the "trees" if you understand the "forest." In this context, "trees" are individual FAA questions and the "forest" is the instrument rating knowledge test. The organizational units between the overall instrument rating knowledge test and the individual instrument rating test questions are chapters and modules in this book.

CAUTION: The **sole purpose** of this book is to expedite your passing the FAA instrument rating knowledge test. Accordingly, all extraneous material (i.e., topics or regulations not directly tested on the FAA knowledge test) is omitted, even though much more information and knowledge are necessary to fly safely. This additional material is presented in *Instrument Pilot Flight Maneuvers and Practical Test Prep*, *Pilot Handbook*, *Aviation Weather and Weather Services*, and *FAR/AIM*, available from Gleim Publications, Inc. See the order form on page 488.

3.1 DISTANCE MEASURING EQUIPMENT (DME) AND LORAN (Questions 1-6)

1.   DME displays slant range distance in nautical miles.

2.   Ignore slant range error if the airplane is 1 NM or more from the ground facility for each 1,000 ft. AGL.

   a.   The greatest slant range error comes at high altitudes very close to the VORTAC.

   b.   EXAMPLE: If you are 6,000 ft. AGL directly above a VORTAC, your DME will read 1.0 NM.

3.   A pilot can check the Airplane Flight Manual Supplement to determine if a LORAN C-equipped aircraft is approved for IFR operations.

3.2 AUTOMATIC DIRECTION FINDER (ADF) (Questions 7-21)

1.   The ADF indicator always has its needle pointing toward the NDB station (nondirectional beacon, also known as a radio beacon).

   a.   If the NDB is directly in front of the airplane, the needle will point straight up.

   b.   If the NDB is directly off the right wing, i.e., 3 o'clock, the needle will point directly to the right.

   c.   If the NDB is directly behind the aircraft, the needle will point straight down, etc.

   d.   The figure below illustrates the terms that are used with the ADF.

2.   Relative bearing (RB) to the station is the number of degrees you would have to turn to the right to fly directly to the NDB. When using a fixed card ADF, the

   a.   Relative bearing TO the station is shown by the head of the needle.

      1)   In the figure below, the RB to the station is 220°.

   b.   Relative bearing FROM the station is given by the tail of the needle.

      1)   In the figure below, the RB from the station is 40° (220 − 180).

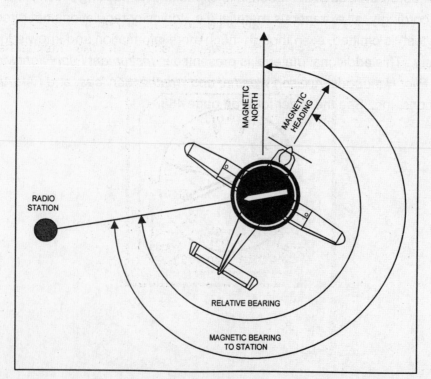

3. Magnetic bearing (MB) to the station is the actual heading you would have to fly to the station.

    a. If you turn right from your present heading to fly to the station, you are adding the number of degrees of turn to your heading.

    b. Thus, magnetic heading + relative bearing = magnetic bearing to the station, or MH + RB = MB (TO).

        1) For MB (FROM), subtract or add 180°.

        2) EXAMPLE: If the airplane shown above has an MH of 40° and an RB of 220°, the MB (TO) is 260° (40 + 220). The MB (FROM) is 80° (260 − 180).

    c. If MH and MB (TO) are known, use the formula: RB = MB (TO) − MH.

        1) Add or subtract 360° to obtain a figure between 0° and 360°, if needed.

4. A fixed card ADF always shows 0° at the top.

    a. Thus, RB may be read directly from the card, and MB must be calculated using the above formula.

    b. If the MB is given, the MH may be calculated as follows: MB − RB = MH.

5. A movable card ADF always shows magnetic heading (MH) at the top.

    a. Thus, MB (TO) may be read directly from the card under the head of the needle.
    b. MB (FROM) is indicated by the tail of the needle.
    c. RB may be calculated as follows: MB − MH = RB.

6. When working ADF problems, it is often helpful to draw the information given (as illustrated on page 72) to provide a picture of the airplane's position relative to the NDB station.

3.3 RADIO MAGNETIC INDICATOR (RMI) (Questions 22-31)

1. The **radio magnetic indicator (RMI)** consists of a rotating compass card and one or more navigation indicators which point to stations.

2. The knobs at the bottom of the RMI allow you to select ADF or VOR stations.

3. The magnetic heading of the airplane is always directly under the index at the top of the instrument.

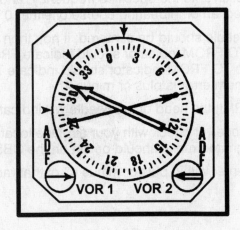

4.   The bearing pointer displays magnetic bearings to selected navigation stations.

    a.   The tail of the indicator tells you which radial you are on or the magnetic bearing FROM the station.

5.   DME arcs with the RMI. The RMI needle should point to the right wingtip on right-hand arcs and the left wingtip on left-hand arcs. This assumes a no-wind situation.

    a.   Crosswind from the inside of the arc (e.g., left crosswind on a left-hand arc) -- requires you to turn toward the NAVAID to compensate for the crosswind, putting the RMI needle in front of the wingtip reference

    b.   Crosswind from the outside of the arc -- requires you to turn to the outside of the arc, putting the RMI needle behind the wingtip reference

3.4 VOR RECEIVER CHECK (Questions 32-43)

1.   The *Airport/Facility Directory* provides a listing of available VOR receiver ground checkpoints and VOTs (VOR receiver test facilities).

    a.   VOT frequencies are also listed on En Route Low Altitude Charts.

2.   Over airborne checkpoints designated by the FAA, the maximum permissible bearing error for the VOR receiver is plus or minus 6° of the designated radial.

    a.   An alternative to a certified airborne checkpoint is a prominent ground reference point that is more than 20 NM from a VOR station that is along an established VOR airway.

        1)   Once over this point with the CDI needle centered, the OBS should indicate plus or minus 6° of the published radial.

3.   The maximum difference between two indicators of a dual VOR system is 4° between the two indicated bearings to the VOR.

    a.   The CDI needles should be centered and the indicated bearings checked rather than setting to identical radials and looking at the CDI needles.

4.   VOTs are available at a specified frequency at certain airports. The facility permits you to check the accuracy of your VOR receiver while you are on the ground.

    a.   The VOT transmits only the 360° radial in all directions.

    b.   Tune the VOR receiver to the specified frequency, and turn the OBS (omnibearing selector) to select an omnibearing course of either 0° or 180°.

        1)   The CDI needle should be centered; if not, then center the needle.
        2)   If 0°, the TO/FROM indicator should indicate FROM.
        3)   If 180°, the TO/FROM indicator should indicate TO.
        4)   The maximum error is plus or minus 4°.

    c.   When using an RMI, the head of the needle will indicate 180°.

5.   When making a VOR receiver check with your airplane located on the designated ground checkpoint, the designated radial should be set on the OBS.

    a.   The CDI must center within plus or minus 4° of that radial with a FROM indication.

3.5 VERY HIGH FREQUENCY OMNIDIRECTIONAL RANGE (VOR) STATION (Questions 44-59)

1. When VORs are undergoing maintenance, the coded and/or voice identification is not broadcast from the VOR.

2. DME/TACAN coded identification is transmitted one time for each three or four times the VOR identification is transmitted.

    a. If the VOR is out of service, the DME identification will be transmitted about once every 30 seconds at 1350 Hz.

3. A full-scale (from the center position to either side of the dial) deflection of a VOR CDI indicates a 10° deviation from the course centerline.

    a. About 10° to 12° of change of the OBS setting should deflect the CDI from the center to the last dot.

4. An (H) Class VORTAC facility has a range of 40 NM from 1,000 ft. AGL to 14,500 ft. AGL, and a range of 100 NM from 14,500 ft. AGL to 18,000 ft.

    a. To use (H) Class VORTAC facilities to define a direct route of flight at 17,000 ft. MSL, the facilities should be no farther apart than 200 NM.

    b. Generally, for IFR operation off of established airways below 18,000 ft., VOR navigational aids should be no more than 80 NM apart.

5. VOR station passage is indicated by a complete reversal of the TO/FROM indicator.

    a. If after station passage the CDI shows a ½-scale deflection and remains constant for a period of time, you are flying away from the selected radial.

6. Airplane displacement from a course is approximately 200 ft. per dot per NM on VORs.

    a. At 30 NM out, one dot is 1 NM displacement; two dots, 2 NM.
    b. At 60 NM out, one dot is 2 NM displacement; two dots, 4 NM.

7. Time/distance to station formula. When tracking inbound, make a 90° turn and measure time and degrees of bearing change.

    a. $Min.\ to\ station\ =\ \dfrac{60 \times Min.\ between\ bearings}{Degrees\ of\ bearing\ change}$

    b. $Distance\ to\ station\ =\ \dfrac{TAS \times Min.\ between\ bearings}{Degrees\ of\ bearing\ change}$

    1) You may also use your flight computer to calculate the distance.

3.6 HORIZONTAL SITUATION INDICATOR (HSI) (Questions 60-74)

1.   The **horizontal situation indicator (HSI)** is a combination of the heading indicator and the VOR/ILS indicator, as illustrated and explained below.

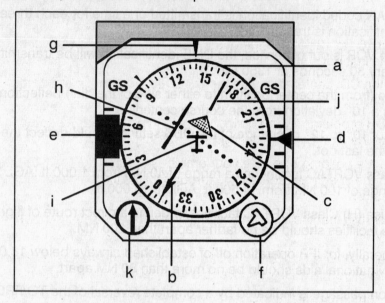

a.   The azimuth card -- rotates so that the heading is shown under the index at the top of the instrument

   1)   The azimuth card may be part of a remote indicating compass (RIC), or

   2)   The azimuth card must be checked against the magnetic compass and reset with a heading set knob.

b.   The course indicating arrow -- the VOR (OBS) indicator

c.   The TO/FROM indicator for the VOR

d.   Glide slope deviation pointer -- indicates above or below the glide slope, which is the longer center line

e.   Glide slope warning flag -- comes out when reliable signals are not received by the glide slope receiver

f.   Heading set knob -- used to coordinate the heading indicator (directional gyro, etc.) with the actual compass

   1)   If the azimuth card is part of an RIC, this knob is normally a heading bug (pointer) set knob that moves a bug around the periphery of the azimuth card.

g.   Lubber line -- shows the current heading

h.   Course deviation bar -- indicates the direction you would have to turn to intercept the desired radial if you were on the approximate heading of the OBS selection

i.   The airplane symbol -- a fixed symbol that shows the airplane relative to the selected course as though you were above the airplane looking down

j.   The tail of the course indicating arrow -- shows the reciprocal of the OBS heading

k.   The course setting knob -- used to adjust the OBS

2. Airplane displacement from a course is approximately 200 ft. per dot per NM on VORs.

    a. At 30 NM out, one dot is 1 NM displacement; two dots, 2 NM.

    b. At 60 NM out, one dot is 2 NM displacement; two dots, 4 NM.

3. A full-scale deflection of a VOR CDI indicates a 10° deviation from the course centerline.

    a. About 10° to 12° of change of the OBS setting should deflect the CDI from the center to the last dot.

    b. With the CDI centered, rotate the OBS 180° to change the ambiguity (TO/FROM) indication.

4. Solve all VOR problems by imagining yourself in an airplane heading in the general direction of the omnibearing setting.

    a. If you are heading opposite your omnibearing course, the CDI needle will point away from the imaginary course line through the VOR determined by your omnibearing selector.

    b. Remember that the VOR shows only your location (not your heading) with respect to the VOR.

5. A few of the questions on the FAA instrument rating knowledge test require you to identify the position of your airplane relative to a VOR given an HSI presentation.

    a. First, remember that the CDI needle does not point to the VOR. It indicates the position of the airplane relative to VOR radials.

        1) Irrespective of your direction of flight, the CDI needle always points toward the imaginary course line through the VOR determined by your omnibearing selector.

    b. The TO/FROM indicator operates independently of the direction (heading) of your airplane. It indicates which side of the VOR your airplane is on, based on the radial set on your omnibearing selector.

        1) Irrespective of your direction of flight, the TO/FROM indicator shows you whether you are before, on, or past a line 90° (perpendicular) to the course line determined by your omnibearing setting.

6. The following diagram explains the TO/FROM indicator and the CDI needle.

    a. Remember that you must rotate the diagram so the omnibearing direction is pointed in the general direction in which your omnibearing selector is set.

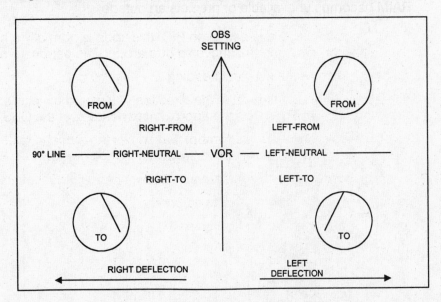

3.7 HSI/LOCALIZER (Questions 75-83)

1.   When VOR is tuned to a localizer frequency (108.10 to 111.95), the OBS (course selection) setting has no impact on the indications of the VOR.

2.   When an HSI is tuned to a localizer frequency (108.10 to 111.95), the setting of the front course heading with the head of the needle will eliminate reverse sensing on back courses.

    a.   Inbound on a back course, the tail of the needle will be at the top of the instrument, and you will have positive sensing.

    b.   If the HSI needle is set to the front course heading, you will have normal sensing on the HSI, whether you are flying a front course or a back course approach.

    c.   If the HSI needle is set to the back course heading, you will have reverse sensing on the HSI, whether you are flying a front course or a back course approach.

3.   The localizer information is reported on the face of the HSI instrument just as VOR signals are.

    a.   That is, it is based upon position rather than heading.

4.   Similar to VORs, if you are going in the direction specified for an approach to a runway, a left deflection means you are to the right of course if you are facing in the approximate direction of the localizer.

3.8 GLOBAL POSITIONING SYSTEM (GPS) (Questions 84-87)

1.   You should refer to the flight manual supplement to determine if an installed GPS is approved for IFR en route and IFR approaches.

    a.   Hand-held GPS systems and GPS systems certified for VFR operation may be used during IFR operations only as an aid to situational awareness.

2.   During IFR en route and terminal operations using an approved GPS system for navigation, the aircraft must be equipped with an approved and operational alternate navigation system that is appropriate to the route.

    a.   Any ground-based navigational facilities required for use with the alternate navigation system (e.g., VORs, NDBs, etc.) must be available and operational along the entire route of flight.

    b.   It is not necessary to actively monitor an alternate means of navigation unless the GPS is not equipped with Receiver Autonomous Integrity Monitoring (RAIM), or RAIM becomes unavailable or predicts an outage.

QUESTIONS AND ANSWER EXPLANATIONS

All the FAA questions from the instrument rating knowledge test relating to navigation systems and the material outlined previously are reproduced on the following pages in the same modules as the outlines. To the immediate right of each question are the correct answer and answer explanation. You should cover these answers and answer explanations with your hand or a piece of paper while responding to the questions. Refer to the general discussion in the Introduction on how to take the FAA knowledge test.

Remember that the questions from the FAA instrument rating knowledge test bank have been reordered by topic, and the topics have been organized into a meaningful sequence. Accordingly, the first line of the answer explanation gives the FAA question number and the citation of the authoritative source for the answer.

3.1 Distance Measuring Equipment (DME) and LORAN

1.
4397. Which distance is displayed by the DME indicator?

A— Slant range distance in NM.
B— Slant range distance in SM.
C— Line-of-sight direct distance from aircraft to VORTAC in SM.

Answer (A) is correct (4397). *(IFH Chap VII)*
DME (distance measuring equipment) displays line-of-sight direct distance, i.e., slant range, from the aircraft to the VORTAC in nautical miles.
Answer (B) is incorrect because the measurement is in nautical miles, not statute miles. Answer (C) is incorrect because the measurement is in nautical miles, not statute miles.

2.
4472. As a rule of thumb, to minimize DME slant range error, how far from the facility should you be to consider the reading as accurate?

A— Two miles or more for each 1,000 feet of altitude above the facility.
B— One or more miles for each 1,000 feet of altitude above the facility.
C— No specific distance is specified since the reception is line-of-sight.

Answer (B) is correct (4472). *(IFH Chap VII)*
You should consider the DME slant range error negligible if the airplane is 1 NM or more from the ground facility for each 1,000 ft. of altitude above the elevation of the facility.
Answer (A) is incorrect because the accuracy is 1 NM, not 2 NM, for each 1,000 ft. AGL. Answer (C) is incorrect because a specific distance is required because the reception is line-of-sight.

3.
4487. As a rule of thumb, to minimize DME slant range error, how far from the facility should you be to consider the reading as accurate?

A— Two miles or more for each 1,000 feet of altitude above the facility.
B— One or more miles for each 1,000 feet of altitude above the facility.
C— No specific distance is specified since the reception is line-of-sight.

Answer (B) is correct (4487). *(IFH Chap VII)*
You should consider the DME slant range error negligible if the airplane is 1 NM or more from the ground facility for each 1,000 ft. of altitude above the elevation of the facility.
Answer (A) is incorrect because the accuracy is 1 NM, not 2 NM, for each 1,000 ft. AGL. Answer (C) is incorrect because a specific distance is required because the reception is line-of-sight.

4.
4399. Where does the DME indicator have the greatest error between ground distance to the VORTAC and displayed distance?

A— High altitudes far from the VORTAC.
B— High altitudes close to the VORTAC.
C— Low altitudes far from the VORTAC.

Answer (B) is correct (4399). *(IFH Chap VII)*
Because the DME reads slant range distance, its greatest error occurs at high altitudes very close to the VORTAC. For example, if one were at 12,000 ft. directly over the VOR, the DME would show a distance from the VOR of approximately 2 NM.
Answer (A) is incorrect because, as you get farther away from the station, the slant range error of the DME becomes minimal. Answer (C) is incorrect because the DME has the greatest error at high, not low, altitudes close to, not far from, the VORTAC.

5.
4413. Which DME indication should you receive when you are directly over a VORTAC site at approximately 6,000 feet AGL?

A— 0.
B— 1.
C— 1.3.

Answer (B) is correct (4413). *(IFH Chap VII)*
Because the DME indicates slant range distance, it will indicate your altitude if you are directly above the VORTAC. One nautical mile equals approximately 6,000 ft., so the DME would read 1 NM.
Answer (A) is incorrect because the DME would only indicate zero if you were at ground level next to the VORTAC. Answer (C) is incorrect because it would mean that your altitude was about 8,000 ft. AGL (6,000 x 1.3).

6.
4665. By which means may a pilot determine if a Loran C equipped aircraft is approved for IFR operations?

A— Not necessary; Loran C is not approved for IFR.
B— Check aircraft logbook.
C— Check the Airplane Flight Manual Supplement.

Answer (C) is correct (4665). *(AIM Para 1-1-15)*
Pilots must be aware of the authorized operational approval level (e.g., VFR or IFR) of a LORAN receiver installed in their aircraft. Approval information is contained in the Aircraft Flight Manual Supplement, on FAA Form 337, in aircraft maintenance records, or possibly on a placard installed near or on the control panel.
Answer (A) is incorrect because some LORAN C receivers are approved for IFR operations by the FAA. Answer (B) is incorrect because the operational approval level may be found in the aircraft maintenance records, not necessarily the aircraft logbook.

3.2 Automatic Direction Finder (ADF)

7.
4578. (Refer to figure 101 below.) What is the magnetic bearing TO the station?

A— 060°.
B— 260°.
C— 270°.

Answer (B) is correct (4578). *(IFH Chap VII)*
Magnetic bearing TO the station is equal to the sum of magnetic heading plus relative bearing. Magnetic heading is given on the heading indicator as 350°, and the relative bearing is given as 270°. The sum is 620°. To obtain answers between 0° and 360°, you may have to add or subtract 360°. 620° − 360° = 260° magnetic bearing TO the station.

$$MH + RB = MB$$
$$620° = MB$$
$$620° - 360° = MB$$
$$260° = MB$$

Answer (A) is incorrect because 060° would be the MB FROM, not TO, the station if the MH were 330°. Answer (C) is incorrect because 270° is the relative bearing, not the magnetic bearing, TO the station.

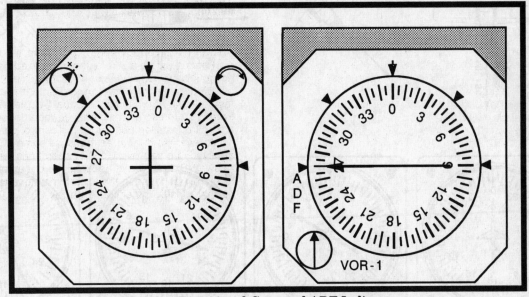

FIGURE 101.—Directional Gyro and ADF Indicator.

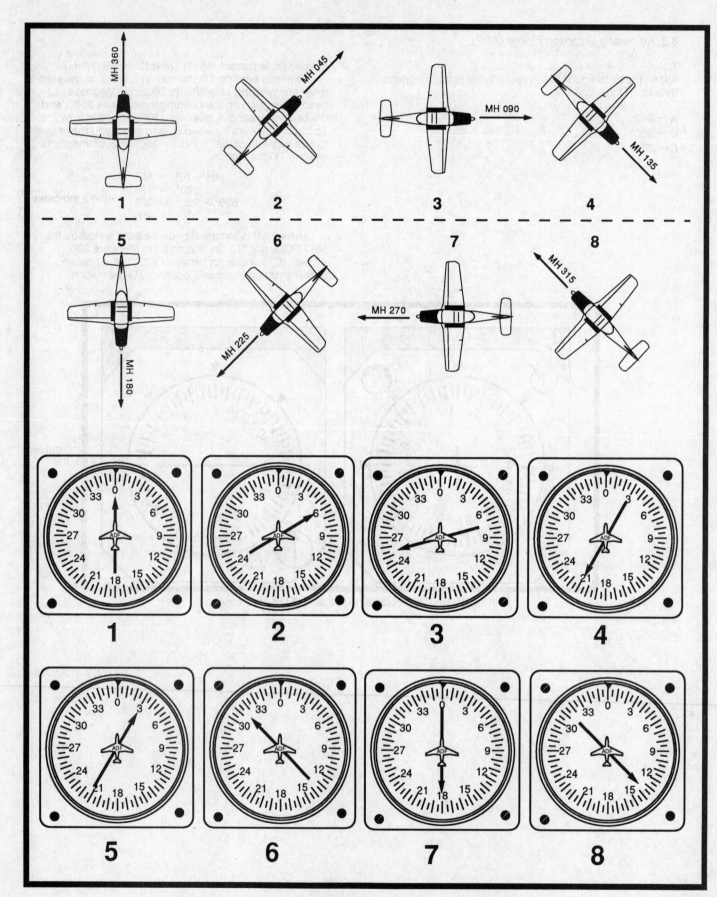

FIGURE 105.—Aircraft Magnetic Heading and ADF Illustration.

8.
4591. (Refer to figure 105 on page 82.) If the magnetic heading shown for aircraft 7 is maintained, which ADF illustration would indicate the aircraft is on the 120° magnetic bearing FROM the station?

A— 2.
B— 4.
C— 5.

Answer (C) is correct (4591). *(IFH Chap VII)*
On Fig. 105, airplane 7 has a magnetic heading of 270°. To use the standard magnetic bearing formula, you must first convert to magnetic bearing TO by adding 180° to MB FROM (120° + 180° = 300° MB TO). Also note that you may have to add or subtract 360° from the final answer to arrive at a figure between 0° and 360°.

$$MH + RB = MB$$
$$270° + RB = 300°$$
$$RB = 30°$$

Illustration 5 indicates a 30° relative bearing.
Answer (A) is incorrect because illustration 2 indicates you are on the 150°, not 120°, MB FROM the NDB. Answer (B) is incorrect because illustration 4 indicates you are on the 120° MB TO, not FROM, the NDB.

9.
4592. (Refer to figure 105 on page 82.) If the magnetic heading shown for aircraft 5 is maintained, which ADF illustration would indicate the aircraft is on the 210° magnetic bearing FROM the station?

A— 2.
B— 3.
C— 4.

Answer (C) is correct (4592). *(IFH Chap VII)*
On Fig. 105, airplane 5 has a magnetic heading of 180°. To determine the relative bearing given a 210° magnetic bearing FROM the station, convert to MB TO by adding or subtracting 180° (210° − 180° = 30° MB TO). Then use the standard formula.

$$MH + RB = MB$$
$$180° + RB = 30°$$
$$RB = -150°$$
$$RB = -150° + 360°$$
$$RB = 210°$$

Illustration 4 indicates a of 210° relative bearing.
Answer (A) is incorrect because illustration 2 indicates you are on the 240°, not 210°, MB TO, not FROM, the NDB. Answer (B) is incorrect because illustration 3 indicates you are on the 75°, not 210°, MB TO the NDB.

10.
4593. (Refer to figure 105 on page 82.) If the magnetic heading shown for aircraft 3 is maintained, which ADF illustration would indicate the aircraft is on the 120° magnetic bearing TO the station?

A— 4.
B— 5.
C— 8.

Answer (B) is correct (4593). *(IFH Chap VII)*
On Fig. 105, airplane 3 has a magnetic heading of 090°. To determine the relative bearing given a 120° magnetic bearing TO the station, use the standard magnetic bearing formula to get the bearing to the station.

$$MH + RB = MB$$
$$90° + RB = 120°$$
$$RB = 30°$$

Illustration 5 indicates a 30° relative bearing.
Answer (A) is incorrect because illustration 4 indicates you are on the 120° MB FROM, not TO, the NDB. Answer (C) is incorrect because illustration 8 indicates you are on the 225°, not 120°, MB TO the NDB.

11.
4594. (Refer to figure 105 on page 82.) If the magnetic heading shown for aircraft 1 is maintained, which ADF illustration would indicate the aircraft is on the 060° magnetic bearing TO the station?

A— 2.
B— 4.
C— 5.

12.
4595. (Refer to figure 105 on page 82.) If the magnetic heading shown for aircraft 2 is maintained, which ADF illustration would indicate the aircraft is on the 255° magnetic bearing TO the station?

A— 2.
B— 4.
C— 5.

13.
4596. (Refer to figure 105 on page 82.) If the magnetic heading shown for aircraft 4 is maintained, which ADF illustration would indicate the aircraft is on the 135° magnetic bearing TO the station?

A— 1.
B— 4.
C— 8.

14.
4597. (Refer to figure 105 on page 82.) If the magnetic heading shown for aircraft 6 is maintained, which ADF illustration would indicate the aircraft is on the 255° magnetic bearing FROM the station?

A— 2.
B— 4.
C— 5.

Answer (A) is correct (4594). *(IFH Chap VII)*
On Fig. 105, airplane 1 has a magnetic heading of 360° or 0°. To determine the relative bearing given a 060° magnetic bearing TO the station, use the standard magnetic bearing formula to get the bearing to the station.

$$MH + RB = MB$$
$$0° + RB = 60°$$
$$RB = 60°$$

Illustration 2 indicates a 60° relative bearing.
Answer (B) is incorrect because illustration 4 indicates you are on the 210°, not 060°, MB TO the NDB. Answer (C) is incorrect because illustration 5 indicates you are on the 030°, not 060°, MB TO the NDB.

Answer (B) is correct (4595). *(IFH Chap VII)*
On Fig. 105, airplane 2 has a magnetic heading of 045°. To determine the relative bearing given a 255° magnetic bearing TO the station, use the standard magnetic bearing formula to get the bearing to the station.

$$MH + RB = MB$$
$$45° + RB = 255°$$
$$RB = 210°$$

Illustration 4 indicates a 210° relative bearing.
Answer (A) is incorrect because illustration 2 indicates you are on the 105°, not 255°, MB TO the NDB. Answer (C) is incorrect because illustration 5 indicates you are on the 255° MB FROM, not TO, the NDB.

Answer (A) is correct (4596). *(IFH Chap VII)*
On Fig. 105, airplane 4 has a magnetic heading of 135°. To determine the relative bearing given a 135° magnetic bearing TO the station, use the standard magnetic bearing formula to get the magnetic bearing to the station.

$$MH + RB = MB$$
$$135° + RB = 135°$$
$$RB = 0°$$

Illustration 1 indicates a 0° relative bearing.
Answer (B) is incorrect because illustration 4 indicates you are on the 345°, not 135°, MB TO the NDB. Answer (C) is incorrect because illustration 8 indicates you are on the 270°, not 135°, MB TO the NDB.

Answer (B) is correct (4597). *(IFH Chap VII)*
On Fig. 105, airplane 6 has a magnetic heading of 225°. To determine the relative bearing given a 255° magnetic bearing FROM the station, convert to MB TO by subtracting 180° (255° – 180° = 75° MB TO). Then use the standard formula.

$$MH + RB = MB$$
$$225° + RB = 75°$$
$$RB = -150° + 360°$$
$$RB = 210°$$

Illustration 4 indicates a 210° relative bearing.
Answer (A) is incorrect because illustration 2 indicates you are on the 105°, not 255°, MB FROM the NDB. Answer (C) is incorrect because illustration 5 indicates you are on the 255° MB TO, not FROM, the NDB.

15.
4598. (Refer to figure 105 on page 82.) If the magnetic heading shown for aircraft 8 is maintained, which ADF illustration would indicate the aircraft is on the 090° magnetic bearing FROM the station?

A— 3.
B— 4.
C— 6.

Answer (C) is correct (4598). *(IFH Chap VII)*
    On Fig. 105, airplane 8 has a magnetic heading of 315°. To determine the relative bearing given a 090° magnetic bearing FROM the station, convert to MB TO by adding 180° (90° + 180° = 270° MB TO). Then use the standard formula.

$$
\begin{aligned}
MH + RB &= MB \\
315° + RB &= 270° \\
RB &= -45° + 360° \\
RB &= 315°
\end{aligned}
$$

Illustration 6 indicates a 315° relative bearing.
    Answer (A) is incorrect because illustration 3 indicates you are on the 030°, not 090°, MB FROM the NDB. Answer (B) is incorrect because illustration 4 indicates you are on the 345°, not 090°, MB FROM the NDB.

16.
4599. (Refer to figure 105 on page 82.) If the magnetic heading shown for aircraft 5 is maintained, which ADF illustration would indicate the aircraft is on the 240° magnetic bearing TO the station?

A— 2.
B— 3.
C— 4.

Answer (A) is correct (4599). *(IFH Chap VII)*
    On Fig. 105, airplane 5 has a magnetic heading of 180°. To determine the relative bearing given a 240° magnetic bearing TO the station, use the standard magnetic bearing formula to get the relative bearing to the station.

$$
\begin{aligned}
MH + RB &= MB \\
180° + RB &= 240° \\
RB &= 60°
\end{aligned}
$$

Illustration 2 indicates a 60° relative bearing.
    Answer (B) is incorrect because illustration 3 indicates you are on the 075°, not 240°, MB TO the NDB. Answer (C) is incorrect because illustration 4 indicates you are on the 030°, not 240°, MB TO the NDB.

17.
4600. (Refer to figure 105 on page 82.) If the magnetic heading shown for aircraft 8 is maintained, which ADF illustration would indicate the aircraft is on the 315° magnetic bearing TO the station?

A— 3.
B— 4.
C— 1.

Answer (C) is correct (4600). *(IFH Chap VII)*
    On Fig. 105, airplane 8 has a magnetic heading of 315°. To determine the relative bearing given a 315° magnetic bearing TO the station, use the standard magnetic bearing formula to get the bearing to the station.

$$
\begin{aligned}
MH + RB &= MB \\
315° + RB &= 315° \\
RB\ TO &= 0°
\end{aligned}
$$

Illustration 1 indicates a 0° relative bearing.
    Answer (A) is incorrect because illustration 3 indicates you are on the 210°, not 315°, MB TO the NDB. Answer (B) is incorrect because illustration 4 indicates you are on the 165°, not 315°, MB TO the NDB.

18.
4583. (Refer to instruments in figure 102 below.) On the basis of this information, the magnetic bearing TO the station would be

A— 175°.
B— 255°.
C— 355°.

Answer (C) is correct (4583). (IFH Chap VII)
On Fig. 102, the airplane has a magnetic heading of 215° and a relative bearing of 140°. To determine the magnetic bearing TO the station, use the standard magnetic bearing formula to get the bearing TO the station.

$$MH + RB = MB$$
$$215° + 140° = MB$$
$$MB = 355°$$

Answer (A) is incorrect because 175° is the MB FROM, not TO, the NDB. Answer (B) is incorrect because 255° is not a related direction in this problem.

FIGURE 102.—Directional Gyro and ADF Indicator.

19.
4584. (Refer to instruments in figure 102 above.) On the basis of this information, the magnetic bearing FROM the station would be

A— 175°.
B— 255°.
C— 355°.

Answer (A) is correct (4584). (IFH Chap VII)
On Fig. 102, the airplane has a magnetic heading of 215° and a relative bearing of 140°. To determine the magnetic bearing FROM the station, use the standard magnetic bearing formula to get the magnetic bearing TO the station, and then add or subtract 180° to convert MB TO to MB FROM.

$$MH + RB = MB$$
$$215° + 140° = 355° \text{ MB TO}$$
$$MB \text{ FROM} = 355° - 180° = 175°$$

Answer (B) is incorrect because 255° is not a related direction in this problem. Answer (C) is incorrect because 355° is the MB TO, not FROM, the NDB.

20.
4586. (Refer to instruments in figure 103 below.) On the basis of this information, the magnetic bearing TO the station would be

A— 060°.
B— 240°.
C— 270°.

Answer (B) is correct (4586). *(IFH Chap VII)*
On Fig. 103, the airplane has a magnetic heading of 330° and a relative bearing of 270°. To determine the magnetic bearing TO the station, use the standard magnetic bearing formula to get the magnetic bearing TO the station.

$$MH + RB = MB$$
$$330° + 270° = MB$$
$$MB = 600°$$
$$600° - 360° = 240°$$

Answer (A) is incorrect because 060° is the MB FROM, not TO, the NDB. Answer (C) is incorrect because 270° is the RB, not MB, TO the NDB.

FIGURE 103.—Directional Gyro and ADF Indicator.

21.
4585. (Refer to instruments in figure 103 above.) On the basis of this information, the magnetic bearing FROM the station would be

A— 030°.
B— 060°.
C— 240°.

Answer (B) is correct (4585). *(IFH Chap VII)*
On Fig. 103, the airplane has a magnetic heading of 330° and a relative bearing of 270°. To determine the magnetic bearing FROM the station, use the standard magnetic bearing formula to get the magnetic bearing TO the station. Then add or subtract 180° to convert MB TO to MB FROM.

$$MH + RB = MB$$
$$330° + 270° = MB$$
$$MB = 600°$$
$$600° - 360° = 240° \text{ MB TO}$$
$$MB \text{ FROM} = 240° - 180° = 60°$$

Answer (A) is incorrect because 030° is a heading unrelated to this problem. Answer (C) is incorrect because 240° is the MB TO, not FROM, the NDB.

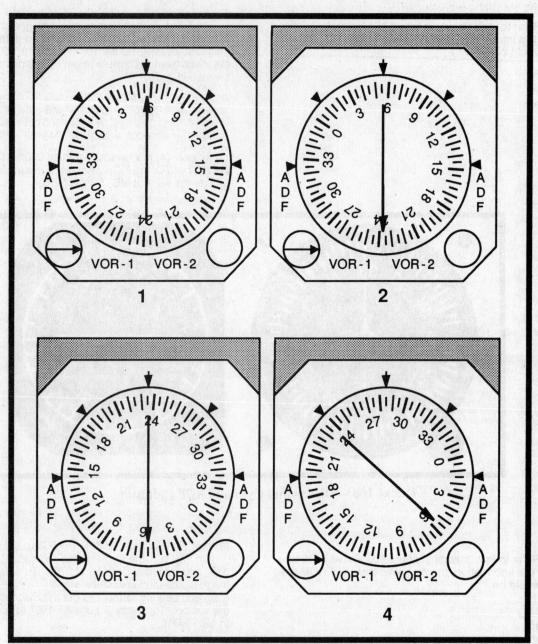

Figure 100.—RMI Illustrations.

3.3 Radio Magnetic Indicator (RMI)

22.
4579. (Refer to figure 100 on page 88.) Which RMI illustration indicates the aircraft to be flying outbound on the magnetic bearing of 235° FROM the station? (Wind 050° at 20 knots.)

A— 2.
B— 3.
C— 4.

Answer (B) is correct (4579). (IFH Chap VIII)
A radio magnetic indicator (RMI) consists of a compass card which rotates as the airplane turns. The magnetic heading of the airplane is always directly under the index at the top of the instrument. The bearing pointer displays magnetic bearings TO the selected station. The tail of the indicator tells you which radial you are on or the magnetic bearing FROM the station. Thus, a magnetic bearing of 235° FROM the station is indicated when the tail of the needle is on 235°, as in RMI 3. The airplane's heading is also 235°, which indicates that it is tracking outbound on the 235° MB FROM. The 20-kt. wind from 50° is almost a direct tailwind, which would not require a significant wind correction.
Answer (A) is incorrect because RMI 2 indicates outbound on the 235° MB TO, not FROM, the station. Answer (C) is incorrect because RMI 4 indicates a large wind correction to the right, e.g., to compensate for a strong crosswind, which does not exist in this question.

23.
4580. (Refer to figure 100 on page 88.) What is the magnetic bearing TO the station as indicated by illustration 4?

A— 285°.
B— 055°.
C— 235°.

Answer (B) is correct (4580). (IFH Chap VIII)
The magnetic heading of the airplane is always directly under the index at the top of the instrument. The bearing pointer displays the magnetic bearing TO the selected station. In RMI 4, the needle is pointing to 055°, which is the magnetic bearing TO the station.
Answer (A) is incorrect because 285° is the magnetic heading, not magnetic bearing. Answer (C) is incorrect because 235° is the magnetic bearing FROM, not TO, the station.

24.
4581. (Refer to figure 100 on page 88.) Which RMI illustration indicates the aircraft is southwest of the station and moving closer TO the station?

A— 1.
B— 2.
C— 3.

Answer (A) is correct (4581). (IFH Chap VIII)
If the airplane is to the southwest of the station and moving toward it, both the heading and the needle should be indicating northeast, which is shown in RMI 1. It indicates a magnetic bearing TO the station of 055°. The magnetic heading is also 055°, which means the airplane is flying to the station.
Answer (B) is incorrect because RMI 2 shows a heading of 055° and the VOR behind the airplane, i.e., the airplane is northeast, not southwest, of the station, and moving away FROM the station. Answer (C) is incorrect because RMI 3 shows a heading of 235° and the VOR behind the airplane, i.e., the airplane moving further FROM, not TO, the station.

25.
4582. (Refer to figure 100 on page 88.) Which RMI illustration indicates the aircraft is located on the 055° radial of the station and heading away from the station?

A— 1.
B— 2.
C— 3.

Answer (B) is correct (4582). (IFH Chap VIII)
A radial, or bearing FROM, is indicated by the tail of the needle. Thus, the 055° radial is indicated when the tail of the needle is on 055°, as in RMI 2. The heading is also 055°, which means you are flying toward the northeast away from the station and are on the 055° radial.
Answer (A) is incorrect because RMI 1 indicates flying toward the station on the 235° radial. Answer (C) is incorrect because RMI 3 indicates flying away from the station on the 235° radial.

26.

4602. (Refer to figure 107 below.) Where should the bearing pointer be located relative to the wing-tip reference to maintain the 16 DME range in a right-hand arc with a right crosswind component?

A— Behind the right wing-tip reference for VOR-2.
B— Ahead of the right wing-tip reference for VOR-2.
C— Behind the right wing-tip reference for VOR-1.

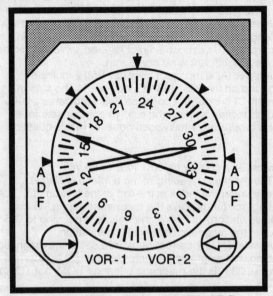

FIGURE 107.—RMI—DME—ARC

Illustration Wind Component.

Answer (B) is correct (4602). *(IFH Chap VIII)*

Normally when flying a DME arc with an RMI, the RMI needle will point directly to the VORTAC, and in a no-wind situation it will be on either a 90° or 3 o'clock (for right-hand arc) or 270° or 9 o'clock (for left-hand arc) indication. Since you are flying a right-hand arc, you should be using VOR 2, which points to the right. The right crosswind component will be blowing you away from the VORTAC. You should crab to the right so the VOR 2 bearing pointer is in front of the right wing-tip reference. This indicates you are correcting back into the wind and toward the VORTAC.

Answer (A) is incorrect because the bearing pointer would be behind the wing-tip reference if you were crabbed away from the VORTAC such as in a left-hand crosswind and a right-hand arc. Answer (C) is incorrect because VOR 1 is pointing toward the left, which would indicate a left-hand, not right-hand, DME arc.

27.
4603. (Refer to figure 108 below.) Where should the
bearing pointer be located relative to the wing-tip
reference to maintain the 16 DME range in a left-hand arc
with a left crosswind component?

A— Ahead of the left wing-tip reference for the VOR-2.
B— Ahead of the right wing-tip reference for the VOR-1.
C— Behind the left wing-tip reference for the VOR-2.

Answer (A) is correct (4603). *(IFH Chap VIII)*
    Since you are flying a left-hand arc, you should be
using VOR 2, which points to the left. The left crosswind
component will be blowing you away from the VORTAC.
You should crab to the left so the VOR 2 bearing pointer
is in front of the left wing-tip reference. This indicates you
are correcting back into the wind and toward the
VORTAC.
    Answer (B) is incorrect because you should use
VOR 2 as you are making a left-hand, not right-hand, turn.
Answer (C) is incorrect because the needle would be
behind the wing-tip if you were crabbed away from, not
toward, the VORTAC.

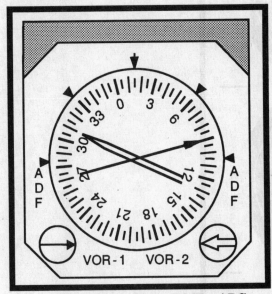

FIGURE 108.—RMI—DME—ARC
Illustration Wind Component.

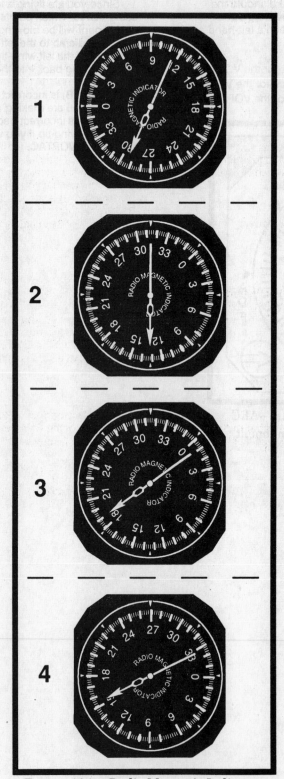

FIGURE 104.—Radio Magnetic Indicator.

28.
4590. (Refer to figure 104 on page 92.) If the radio magnetic indicator is tuned to a VOR, which illustration indicates the aircraft is on the 010° radial?

A— 1.
B— 2.
C— 3.

29.
4587. (Refer to figure 104 on page 92.) If the radio magnetic indicator is tuned to a VOR, which illustration indicates the aircraft is on the 115° radial?

A— 1.
B— 2.
C— 3.

30.
4588. (Refer to figure 104 on page 92.) If the radio magnetic indicator is tuned to a VOR, which illustration indicates the aircraft is on the 335° radial?

A— 2.
B— 3.
C— 4.

31.
4589. (Refer to figure 104 on page 92.) If the radio magnetic indicator is tuned to a VOR, which illustration indicates the aircraft is on the 315° radial?

A— 2.
B— 3.
C— 4.

Answer (C) is correct (4590). *(IFH Chap VIII)*
A radio magnetic indicator (RMI) consists of a rotating compass card and one or more indicators which point to stations. The tail of the indicator tells you what radial you are on. RMI 3 shows the tail of the indicator on 010°, which means that you are on the 010° radial.
Answer (A) is incorrect because RMI 1 indicates the 115° radial, not the 010° radial. Answer (B) is incorrect because RMI 2 indicates the 315° radial, not the 010° radial.

Answer (A) is correct (4587). *(IFH Chap VIII)*
The tail of the RMI indicator tells you what radial you are on. RMI 1 shows the tail of the indicator on 115°, which means that you are on the 115° radial.
Answer (B) is incorrect because RMI 2 indicates the 315° radial, not the 115° radial. Answer (C) is incorrect because RMI 3 indicates the 010° radial, not the 115° radial.

Answer (C) is correct (4588). *(IFH Chap VIII)*
The tail of the RMI indicator tells you what radial you are on. RMI 4 shows the tail of the indicator on 335°, which means that you are on the 335° radial.
Answer (A) is incorrect because RMI 2 indicates the 315° radial, not the 335° radial. Answer (B) is incorrect because RMI 3 indicates the 010° radial, not the 335° radial.

Answer (A) is correct (4589). *(IFH Chap VIII)*
The tail of the RMI indicator tells you what radial you are on. RMI 2 shows the tail of the indicator on 315°, which means that you are on the 315° radial.
Answer (B) is incorrect because RMI 3 indicates the 010° radial, not the 315° radial. Answer (C) is incorrect because RMI 4 indicates the 335° radial, not the 315° radial.

3.4 VOR Receiver Check

32.
4388. In which publication can the VOR receiver ground checkpoint(s) for a particular airport be found?

A— Airman's Information Manual.
B— En Route Low Altitude Chart.
C— Airport/Facility Directory.

Answer (C) is correct (4388). *(AIM Para 1-4-1)*
The *Airport/Facility Directory* provides a listing of available VOR receiver ground checkpoints.
Answer (A) is incorrect because the *Aeronautical Information Manual* contains general flight information, not data concerning specific airports. Answer (B) is incorrect because En Route Low Altitude Charts do not indicate VOR receiver ground checkpoints, only VOT frequencies.

33.
4389. Which is the maximum tolerance for the VOR indication when the CDI is centered and the aircraft is directly over the airborne checkpoint?

A— Plus or minus 6° of the designated radial.
B— Plus 6° or minus 4° of the designated radial.
C— Plus or minus 4° of the designated radial.

Answer (A) is correct (4389). *(AIM Para 1-4-1)*
Airborne checkpoints consist of certified radials that should be received over specific landmarks while airborne in the immediate vicinity of an airport. The maximum tolerance when the CDI is centered is ±6°.
Answer (B) is incorrect because the tolerance for an airborne checkpoint is ±6°, not +6° or –4°. Answer (C) is incorrect because the tolerance for an airborne checkpoint is ±6°, not ±4°, which is the tolerance for a ground checkpoint or a VOT.

34.
4378. When the CDI needle is centered during an airborne VOR check, the omni-bearing selector and the TO/FROM indicator should read

A— within 4° of the selected radial.
B— within 6° of the selected radial.
C— 0° TO, only if you are due south of the VOR.

Answer (B) is correct (4378). *(AIM Para 1-4-1)*
Airborne VOR checkpoints consist of certified radials that should be received over specific landmarks. If no checkpoint is available, a prominent ground point should be selected more than 20 NM from a VOR station that is along an established VOR airway. Once over this point with the CDI centered, the OBS should indicate within 6° of the published radial.
Answer (A) is incorrect because the maximum error for a ground, not airborne, VOR check is ±4°. Answer (C) is incorrect because you should use a certified airborne checkpoint or select a ground reference that is under an established VOR airway, not a randomly selected radial.

35.
4391. When making an airborne VOR check, what is the maximum allowable tolerance between the two indicators of a dual VOR system (units independent of each other except the antenna)?

A— 4° between the two indicated radials of a VOR.
B— Plus or minus 4° when set to identical radials of a VOR.
C— 6° between the two indicated radials of a VOR.

Answer (A) is correct (4391). *(AIM Para 1-4-1)*
If a dual system VOR (units independent of each other except for the antenna) is installed in the airplane, one system may be checked against the other in place of other VOR check procedures. The test consists of tuning both systems to the same VOR and centering the CDI needles, then noting the bearing variation between the two VOR units. It should be less than 4°.
Answer (B) is incorrect because the CDIs are to be centered, not set to the same radials. Answer (C) is incorrect because it is a maximum tolerance of 4°, not 6°.

36.
4383. While airborne, what is the maximum permissible variation between the two indicated bearings when checking one VOR system against the other?

A— Plus or minus 4° when set to identical radials of a VOR.
B— 4° between the two indicated bearings to a VOR.
C— Plus or minus 6° when set to identical radials of a VOR.

Answer (B) is correct (4383). *(AIM Para 1-4-1)*
If a dual system VOR (units independent of each other except for the antenna) is installed in the airplane, one system may be checked against the other in place of other check procedures. The test consists of tuning both systems to the same VOR with the CDI centered and noting the bearing variation between the two VOR units. It should be less than 4°.
Answer (A) is incorrect because the CDIs must be centered, not set to identical radials. Answer (C) is incorrect because it is a maximum permissible variation of 4°, not 6°, between the indicated bearings.

37.
4384. How should the pilot make a VOR receiver check when the aircraft is located on the designated checkpoint on the airport surface?

A— With the aircraft headed directly toward the VOR and the OBS set to 000°, the CDI should center within plus or minus 4° of that radial with a TO indication.
B— Set the OBS on the designated radial. The CDI must center within plus or minus 4° of that radial with a FROM indication.
C— Set the OBS on 180° plus or minus 4°; the CDI should center with a FROM indication.

Answer (B) is correct (4384). *(AIM Para 1-1-4)*
A VOR receiver check is a checkpoint on the airport surface near a VOR. When the aircraft is on the checkpoint, the designated radial should be set on the OBS. The CDI must then center within 4° of the radial. Also, there will be a FROM indication.
Answer (A) is incorrect because VOR indications are given the same no matter which heading the aircraft is on. The VOR indication is based upon position, not heading. Answer (C) is incorrect because the specified radial, not 180°, should be set on the OBS.

38.
4377. How should the pilot make a VOR receiver check when the aircraft is located on the designated checkpoint on the airport surface?

A— Set the OBS on 180° plus or minus 4°; the CDI should center with a FROM indication.
B— Set the OBS on the designated radial. The CDI must center within plus or minus 4° of that radial with a FROM indication.
C— With the aircraft headed directly toward the VOR and the OBS set to 000°, the CDI should center within plus or minus 4° of that radial with a TO indication.

Answer (B) is correct (4377). *(AIM Para 1-1-4)*
A VOR receiver check is a checkpoint on the airport surface near a VOR. When the airplane is on the checkpoint, the designated radial should be set on the OBS. The CDI must then center within 4° of the radial. Also, there will be a FROM indication.
Answer (A) is incorrect because the specified radial, not 180°, should be set on the OBS. Answer (C) is incorrect because VOR indications are given the same no matter which heading the aircraft is on. The VOR indication is based upon position, not heading.

39.
4386. Where can the VOT frequency for a particular airport be found?

A— On the IAP Chart and in the Airport/Facility Directory.
B— Only in the Airport/Facility Directory.
C— In the Airport/Facility Directory and on the A/G Voice Communication Panel of the En Route Low Altitude Chart.

Answer (C) is correct (4386). *(AIM Para 1-1-4)*
Both the *Airport/Facility Directory* and the A/G voice communication panel of the En Route Low Altitude Chart provide a listing of the VOT frequency for a particular airport.
Answer (A) is incorrect because VOT frequencies are not listed on approach charts. Answer (B) is incorrect because VOT frequencies are also published in En Route Low Altitude Charts.

40.
4376. When using VOT to make a VOR receiver check, the CDI should be centered and the OBS should indicate that the aircraft is on the

A— 090 radial.
B— 180 radial.
C— 360 radial.

Answer (C) is correct (4376). *(AIM Para 1-1-4)*
A VOT transmits only the 360° radial. Thus, with the CDI centered, the OBS should indicate 0° with a FROM indication and 180° with a TO indication.
Answer (A) is incorrect because the VOT transmits only the 360°, not 090°, radial in all directions. Answer (B) is incorrect because the VOT transmits only the 360°, not 180°, radial in all directions.

41.
4387. Which indications are acceptable tolerances when checking both VOR receivers by use of the VOT?

A— 360° TO and 003° TO, respectively.
B— 001° FROM and 005° FROM, respectively.
C— 176° TO and 003° FROM, respectively.

Answer (C) is correct (4387). *(AIM Para 1-1-4)*
A VOT transmits a 360° radial in all directions. Thus, with the course deviation indicator (CDI) centered, the omnibearing selector (OBS) should read 0° with the TO-FROM indicator showing FROM, or the OBS should read 180° with the TO-FROM indicator showing TO, with a maximum error of 4°.
Answer (A) is incorrect because at 000°, FROM, not TO, should be indicated. Answer (B) is incorrect because it exceeds the 4° maximum error limit.

42.
4382. (Refer to figure 81 below.) When checking a dual VOR system by use of a VOT, which illustration indicates the VOR's are satisfactory?

A— 1.
B— 2.
C— 4.

Answer (A) is correct (4382). *(AIM Para 1-1-4)*
   A VOT transmits a 360° radial in all directions. Thus, when using an RMI, the tail of each indicator should point to 360°, ±4°.
   Answer (B) is incorrect because illustration 2 shows the head, not the tail, of one indicator pointing to 360°.
   Answer (C) is incorrect because illustration 4 shows the heads, not the tails, of both indicators pointing to 360°.

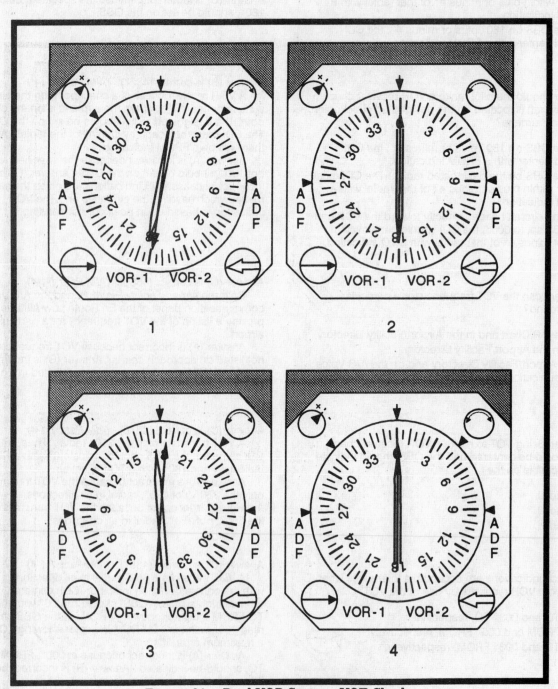

FIGURE 81.—Dual VOR System, VOT Check.

43.
4385. (Refer to figure 82 below.) Which is an acceptable range of accuracy when performing an operational check of dual VOR's using one system against the other?

A— 1.
B— 2.
C— 4.

Answer (C) is correct (4385). *(AIM Para 1-1-4)*
When performing an operational check of dual VORs using one system against the other, the difference between the two indicated bearings must be 4° or less. On an RMI, which has two VOR indicators, the VORs should point in the same direction, as in illustration 4 of Fig. 82.
Answer (A) is incorrect because, in illustration 1, the needles have a 180° difference. Answer (B) is incorrect because, in illustration 2, there is a 10° difference.

FIGURE 82.—Dual VOR System, Accuracy Check.

3.5 Very High Frequency Omnidirectional Range (VOR) Station

44.
4410. What indication should a pilot receive when a VOR station is undergoing maintenance and may be considered unreliable?

A— No coded identification, but possible navigation indications.
B— Coded identification, but no navigation indications.
C— A voice recording on the VOR frequency announcing that the VOR is out of service for maintenance.

Answer (A) is correct (4410). *(AIM Para 1-1-3)*
    The only positive method of identifying a VOR is by Morse Code identification and/or by the recorded voice identification, which is always indicated by use of the word "VOR" following the VOR name. During periods of maintenance, the facility identification is removed, although navigational signals may still be transmitted.
    Answer (B) is incorrect because the coded identification is removed when the station is undergoing maintenance. Answer (C) is incorrect because an out-of-service VOR is not announced by a voice recording.

45.
4411. A particular VOR station is undergoing routine maintenance. This is evidenced by

A— removal of the navigational feature.
B— broadcasting a maintenance alert signal on the voice channel.
C— removal of the identification feature.

Answer (C) is correct (4411). *(AIM Para 1-1-3)*
    The only positive method of identifying a VOR is by Morse Code identification or by the recorded voice identification, which is always indicated by use of the word "VOR" following the VOR name. During periods of maintenance, the coded and/or voice facility identification is removed, although navigational signals may still be transmitted.
    Answer (A) is incorrect because the navigational signals may continue even though they are not accurate. Answer (B) is incorrect because an out-of-service VOR is not announced by a voice recording.

46.
4663. When a VOR/DME is collocated under frequency pairings and the VOR portion is inoperative, the DME identifier will repeat at an interval of

A— 20 second intervals at 1020 Hz.
B— 30 second intervals at 1350 Hz.
C— 60 second intervals at 1350 Hz.

Answer (B) is correct (4663). *(AIM Para 1-1-7)*
    The DME/TACAN coded identification is transmitted at 1350 Hz once for each three or four times the VOR or localizer coded identification is transmitted. When either the VOR or the DME is operative, but not both, it is important to recognize which identifier is retained for the operative facility. A single-coded identification repeated at intervals of approximately 30 sec. indicates that the DME is operative and the VOR is not.
    Answer (A) is incorrect because the DME identifier repeats at 30-sec., not 20-sec., intervals at 1350 Hz, not 1020 Hz. Answer (C) is incorrect because the DME identifier repeats at 30-sec., not 60-sec., intervals.

47.
4412. What is the meaning of a single coded identification received only once approximately every 30 seconds from a VORTAC?

A— The VOR and DME components are operative.
B— VOR and DME components are both operative, but voice identification is out of service.
C— The DME component is operative and the VOR component is inoperative.

Answer (C) is correct (4412). *(AIM Para 1-1-7)*
    The DME/TACAN coded identification is transmitted at 1350 Hz once for each three or four times the VOR or localizer coded identification is transmitted. When either the VOR or the DME is operative, but not both, it is important to recognize which identifier is retained for the operative facility. A single-coded identification repeated at intervals of approximately 30 sec. indicates that the DME is operative and the VOR is not.
    Answer (A) is incorrect because a constant series of identity codes indicates that both the VOR and DME are operative. Answer (B) is incorrect because voice identification operates independently of the identity codes.

48.
4548. What angular deviation from a VOR course centerline is represented by a full-scale deflection of the CDI?

A— 4°.
B— 5°.
C— 10°.

Answer (C) is correct (4548). *(IFH Chap VII)*
On VORs, full needle deflection from the center position to either side of the dial indicates that the aircraft is 10° or more off course, assuming normal needle sensitivity.
Answer (A) is incorrect because 4° is indicated by a 2-dot deflection on a 5-dot VOR scale. Answer (B) is incorrect because 5° is indicated by a 2-dot deflection on a 4-dot VOR scale.

49.
4666. Full scale deflection of a CDI occurs when the course deviation bar or needle

A— deflects from left side of the scale to right side of the scale.
B— deflects from the center of the scale to either far side of the scale.
C— deflects from half scale left to half scale right.

Answer (B) is correct (4666). *(IFH Chap VII)*
Full-scale deflection of a CDI occurs when the needle deflects from the center of the scale to either far side of the scale. This indicates that the aircraft is 10° or more off course, assuming normal needle sensitivity.
Answer (A) is incorrect because it indicates moving from a left full deflection to a right full deflection, i.e., 10° left of course to 10° right of course. Answer (C) is incorrect because it indicates moving from a left half deflection to a right half deflection, i.e., 5° left of course to 5° right of course.

50.
4400. For operations off established airways at 17,000 feet MSL in the contiguous U.S., (H) Class VORTAC facilities used to define a direct route of flight should be no farther apart than

A— 75 NM.
B— 100 NM.
C— 200 NM.

Answer (C) is correct (4400). *(AIM Para 1-1-8)*
(H) Class VORTAC facilities have a range of 100 NM from 14,500 ft. AGL up to 18,000 ft. Thus, (H) Class VORTAC facilities should be no farther apart than 200 NM.
Answer (A) is incorrect because 75 NM is the range of an (HH) Class NDB facility, not an (H) Class VORTAC. Answer (B) is incorrect because 100 NM is the range of an (H) Class VORTAC at 17,000 ft. MSL; thus the distance between two (H) Class VORTAC facilities can be 200 NM.

50a.
4639. For IFR operations off of established airways below 18,000 feet, VOR navigational aids used to describe the "route of flight" should be no more than

A— 80 NM apart.
B— 40 NM apart.
C— 70 NM apart.

Answer (A) is correct (4639). *(AIM Para 1-1-8)*
(H) Class VOR facilities have a range of 40 NM from 1,000 ft. AGL up to 14,500 ft. AGL and a range of 100 NM from 14,500 ft. AGL up to 18,000 ft. Thus, in general, VOR navigational aids used to describe a route of flight off of established airways below 18,000 ft. (more specifically, below 14,500 ft. AGL) should be no more than 80 NM apart.
Answer (B) is incorrect because 40 NM is the range of an (H) Class VOR from 1,000 ft. AGL to 14,500 ft. AGL. VORs used to describe a route of flight off of established airways below 14,500 ft. AGL should be no more than 80 NM apart. Answer (C) is incorrect because VORs should be no more than 80 NM, not 70 NM, apart to define a route of flight off of established airways below 14,500 ft. AGL.

51.
4549. When using VOR for navigation, which of the following should be considered as station passage?

A— The first movement of the CDI as the airplane enters the zone of confusion.
B— The moment the TO-FROM indicator becomes blank.
C— The first positive, complete reversal of the TO-FROM indicator.

Answer (C) is correct (4549). *(IFH Chap VII)*
When approaching a VOR, the TO-FROM indicator and the CDI flicker as the airplane flies into the zone of confusion (no signal area). Station passage is shown by complete reversal of the TO-FROM indicator.
Answer (A) is incorrect because it indicates flight into the zone of confusion over the VOR, not station passage. Answer (B) is incorrect because it is an indication that you are in the zone of confusion over the VOR, not an indication of station passage.

52.
4550. Which of the following should be considered as station passage when using VOR?

A— The first flickering of the TO-FROM indicator and CDI as the station is approached.
B— The first full-scale deflection of the CDI.
C— The first complete reversal of the TO-FROM indicator.

Answer (C) is correct (4550). *(IFH Chap VII)*
When approaching a VOR, the TO-FROM indicator and the CDI flicker as the airplane flies into the zone of confusion (no signal area). Station passage is shown by complete reversal of the TO-FROM indicator.
Answer (A) is incorrect because it indicates flight into the zone of confusion over the VOR, not station passage. Answer (B) is incorrect because it is an indication that you are in the zone of confusion over the VOR, not an indication of station passage.

53.

4551. When checking the sensitivity of a VOR receiver, the number of degrees in course change as the OBS is rotated to move the CDI from center to the last dot on either side should be between

A— 5° and 6°.
B— 8° and 10°.
C— 10° and 12°.

Answer (C) is correct (4551). *(IFH Chap VIII)*
    In addition to VOR receiver checks, course sensitivity may be checked by noting the number of degrees of change in the course selected as you rotate the OBS to move the CDI from center to the last dot on either side. This range should be between 10° and 12°.
    Answer (A) is incorrect because 5° to 6° of course change should result in a ½-scale, not full-scale, needle deflection. Answer (B) is incorrect because 8° to 10° of course change should result in a ¾-scale, not full-scale, needle deflection.

54.

4552. A VOR receiver with normal five-dot course sensitivity shows a three-dot deflection at 30 NM from the station. The aircraft would be displaced approximately how far from the course centerline?

A— 2 NM.
B— 3 NM.
C— 5 NM.

Answer (B) is correct (4552). *(IFH Chap VIII)*
    Airplane displacement from a course is approximately 200 ft. per dot per nautical mile for VORs. For example, at 30 NM from the station, a one-dot deflection indicates approximately 1 NM displacement of the airplane from the course centerline. A full course deflection is 5 dots. With a 3-dot deflection, one would be about 3 NM from the course centerline.
    Answer (A) is incorrect because two dots, not three dots, indicate 2 NM off course. Answer (C) is incorrect because five dots, not three dots, indicate 5 NM off course.

55.

4553. An aircraft which is located 30 miles from a VOR station and shows a ½ scale deflection on the CDI would be how far from the selected course centerline?

A— 1½ miles.
B— 2½ miles.
C— 3½ miles.

Answer (B) is correct (4553). *(IFH Chap VIII)*
    Airplane displacement from a course is approximately 200 ft. per dot per nautical mile for VORs. For example, at 30 NM from the station, a 1-dot deflection indicates approximately 1 NM displacement of the airplane from the course centerline. A full course deflection is 5 dots. Since a ½-scale deflection on the CDI would be 2½ dots, the airplane would be about 2½ mi. from the course centerline.
    Answer (A) is incorrect because 1½ mi. would be indicated by a 1½-dot deflection. Answer (C) is incorrect because 3½ mi. would be indicated by a 3½-dot deflection.

56.

4554. What angular deviation from a VOR course centerline is represented by a ½ scale deflection of the CDI?

A— 2°.
B— 4°.
C— 5°.

Answer (C) is correct (4554). *(IFH Chap VIII)*
    A full course deflection is 5 dots, which is approximately 10°. Since rotation of the OBS to move the CDI from the center to the last dot is approximately 10°, a ½-scale deflection would be approximately 5°.
    Answer (A) is incorrect because a full-scale deflection is 10°, not 4°. Answer (B) is incorrect because a full-scale deflection is 10°, not 8°.

57.

4556. After passing a VORTAC, the CDI shows ½ scale deflection to the right. What is indicated if the deflection remains constant for a period of time?

A— The airplane is getting closer to the radial.
B— The OBS is erroneously set on the reciprocal heading.
C— The airplane is flying away from the radial.

Answer (C) is correct (4556). *(IFH Chap VIII)*
    If the CDI shows a ½-scale deflection to the right, the airplane is flying 5° to the left of course. If it is constant, it means the airplane is flying away from the radial because the 5° off course increases in actual distance as one gets farther away from the VORTAC.
    Answer (A) is incorrect because a steady deflection would indicate the airplane is getting closer to the radial if it were flying TO, not FROM, the station. Answer (B) is incorrect because, if you use the reciprocal heading, you get reverse indications from the CDI.

58.
4604. Determine the approximate time and distance to a station if a 5° wingtip bearing change occurs in 1.5 minutes with a true airspeed of 95 knots.

A— 16 minutes and 14.3 NM.
B— 18 minutes and 28.5 NM.
C— 18 minutes and 33.0 NM.

Answer (B) is correct (4604). *(IFH Chap VIII)*
Use the following formula to compute the time to station:

$$\text{Time to station} = \frac{60 \times \text{Min. between bearings}}{\text{Degrees of bearing change}}$$

$$= (60 \times 1.5) \div 5 = 18 \text{ min.}$$

Thus, it is 18 min. to the station, which is less than 1/3 of an hour. One-third of 95 is less than 33, and thus must be 28.5 rather than 33.0. On the computer side of your flight computer, put 95 kt. on the outer scale over 60 on the inner scale. Find 18 min. on the inner scale; 28.5 NM is on the outer scale.

Answer (A) is incorrect because the time is 18 min., not 16 min. Answer (C) is incorrect because 18 min. is less than 1/3 hr., and 1/3 of 95 kt. is less than 33 NM.

59.
4601. (Refer to figure 106 below.) The course selector of each aircraft is set on 360°. Which aircraft would have a FROM indication on the ambiguity meter and the CDI pointing left of center?

A— 1.
B— 2.
C— 3.

Answer (B) is correct (4601). *(IFH Chap VIII)*
If airplane 2 were heading 360°, the course would be to the left, and the airplane would fly away FROM the VOR. See discussion of VOR orientation presented at the end of the HSI outline.

Answer (A) is incorrect because, if airplane 1 were heading 360°, the course would be to the right, not left. Answer (C) is incorrect because, as airplane 3 is heading 360°, it is flying closer TO, not further FROM, the station, and the CDI would be pointing right, not left, of center.

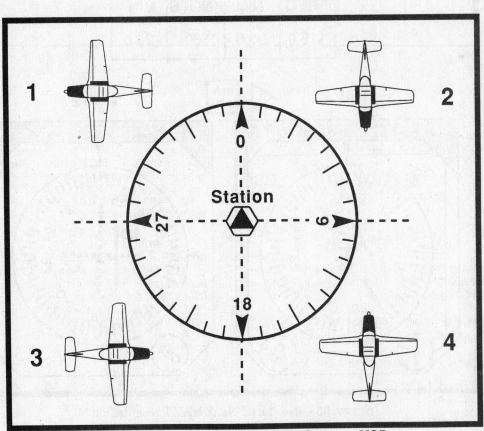

FIGURE 106.—Aircraft Location Relative to VOR.

3.6 Horizontal Situation Indicator (HSI)

60.
4557. (Refer to figure 95 below.) What is the lateral displacement of the aircraft in NM from the radial selected on the No. 1 NAV?

A— 5.0 NM.
B— 7.5 NM.
C— 10.0 NM.

61.
4558. (Refer to figure 95 below.) On which radial is the aircraft as indicated by the No. 1 NAV?

A— R-175.
B— R-165.
C— R-345.

Answer (A) is correct (4557). *(IFH Chap VIII)*
On VORs, the displacement from course is approximately 200 ft. per dot per nautical mile. At 30 NM from the station, one-dot deflection indicates approximately 1 NM displacement of the airplane from the course centerline. At 60 NM, it would be 2 NM for every dot of displacement. Since here displacement is 2½ dots, the airplane would be 5 NM from the centerline.
Answer (B) is incorrect because 7.5 NM would be indicated by a ¾ deflection. Answer (C) is incorrect because 10 NM would be indicated by a full deflection.

Answer (C) is correct (4558). *(IFH Chap VIII)*
The course selector in Fig. 95 is set on 350° with a FROM reading, indicating that, if the course deviation bar were centered, the airplane would be on R-350. Since a total deflection is approximately 10° to 12°, one-half deflection is 5° to 6°. Here, deflection is less than one-half, so it is about 5°. The course deviation bar indicates that this airplane is to the west of R-350, which would be R-345.
Answer (A) is incorrect because R-175 would require a TO indicator and a left deflection. Answer (B) is incorrect because R-165 would require a TO indicator.

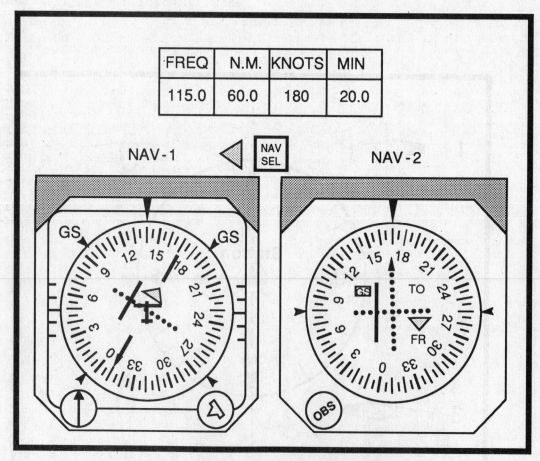

FIGURE 95.—No. 1 and No. 2 NAV Presentation.

62.
4559. (Refer to figure 95 on page 102.) Which OBS selection on the No. 1 NAV would center the CDI and change the ambiguity indication to a TO?

A— 175°.
B— 165°.
C— 345°.

63.
4560. (Refer to figure 95 on page 102.) What is the lateral displacement in degrees from the desired radial on the No. 2 NAV?

A— 1°.
B— 2°.
C— 4°.

64.
4561. (Refer to figure 95 on page 102.) Which OBS selection on the No. 2 NAV would center the CDI?

A— 174°.
B— 166°.
C— 335°.

65.
4562. (Refer to figure 95 on page 102.) Which OBS selection on the No. 2 NAV would center the CDI and change the ambiguity indication to a TO?

A— 166°.
B— 346°.
C— 354°.

Answer (B) is correct (4559). *(IFH Chap VIII)*
The course selector in Fig. 95 is set on 350°, resulting in a FROM reading and a ½-scale needle deflection. Thus, the airplane is 5° or 6° west of R-350, i.e., R-345. Setting the OBS to the reciprocal course of 165° would center the CDI with a TO indication.
Answer (A) is incorrect because the airplane is currently on R-345, not R-355. Answer (C) is incorrect because the airplane is currently on R-345 with a FROM, not TO, indication.

Answer (C) is correct (4560). *(IFH Chap VIII)*
Since on a standard 5-dot VOR indicator a full deflection of 5 dots is about 10°, 2 dots means a 4° deflection.
Answer (A) is incorrect because each dot is 2°, not ½°. Answer (B) is incorrect because each dot is 2°, not 1°.

Answer (A) is correct (4561). *(IFH Chap VIII)*
The course selector in Fig. 95 is set to 170° (it is not an HSI; it is a VOR), and the TO-FROM indicator indicates FROM, which means the airplane would be on R-170 if the course deviation bar were centered. Since the bar indicates a left 2-dot deflection, the airplane is 4° to the west of the radial, or on R-174.
Answer (B) is incorrect because a right, not left, deflection would indicate R-166. Answer (C) is incorrect because, on R-335 with an OBS setting of 170°, there would be a TO, not FROM, indication.

Answer (C) is correct (4562). *(IFH Chap VIII)*
The course selector in Fig. 95 is set to 170° (it is not an HSI; it is a VOR), and the TO-FROM indicator indicates FROM, which means the airplane would be on R-170 if the course deviation bar were centered. Since the bar indicates a 2-dot left deflection, the airplane is 4° to the west of the radial, or on R-174. To obtain a TO indication, one would have to change the OBS selection by 180° from 174° to 354°.
Answer (A) is incorrect because the airplane is on R-174, not R-346. Answer (B) is incorrect because the airplane is on R-174, not R-166.

66.
4606. (Refer to figure 109 below.) In which general direction from the VORTAC is the aircraft located?

A— Northeast.
B— Southeast.
C— Southwest.

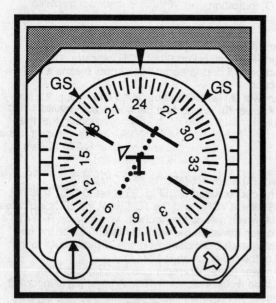

FIGURE 109.—CDI Direction from
VORTAC.

Answer (A) is correct (4606). *(IFH Chap VIII)*
    The course indicating arrow (OBS) is set to 180°, and the TO-FROM indicator indicates TO (triangle pointing TO arrowhead), which means the airplane is north of the VORTAC. Since the course deviation bar indicates that the airplane needs to be flown to the right, the airplane is to the east of the 360° radial of the VORTAC. Thus, the airplane is northeast of the VORTAC.
    Answer (B) is incorrect because, if the airplane were southeast of the VORTAC, there would be a FROM, not TO, indication. Answer (C) is incorrect because, if the airplane were southwest of the VORTAC, there would be a FROM, not TO, indication and a left, not right, bar deflection.

67.
4575. (Refer to figures 98 and 99 on pages 106 and 107.) To which aircraft position does HSI presentation "A" correspond?

A— 1.
B— 8.
C— 11.

Answer (A) is correct (4575). *(IFH Chap VIII)*
On Figs. 98 and 99, HSI "A" has a VOR course selection of 090°, with a TO indication, meaning the airplane is to the left of the 360/180 radials. It has a right deflection, which means it is north of the 270/90 radials. The airplane heading is 205°, which means airplane 1 is described.
Answer (B) is incorrect because airplane 8 is to the right of the 360/180 radials, which would require a FROM, not TO, indication. Answer (C) is incorrect because airplane 11 is to the right of the 360/180 radials and is south of the 270/090 radials, which would require a FROM, not TO, indication and a left, not right, bar deflection.

68.
4576. (Refer to figures 98 and 99 on pages 106 and 107.) To which aircraft position does HSI presentation "B" correspond?

A— 9.
B— 13.
C— 19.

Answer (C) is correct (4576). *(IFH Chap VIII)*
On Figs. 98 and 99, HSI "B" has a VOR course selection of 270° with a FROM indication, meaning that the airplane is to the left of the 360/180 radials. Since it has a right deflection, the airplane is south of R-270. Given a heading of 135°, airplane 19 is described.
Answer (A) is incorrect because airplane 9 would require a TO, not FROM, indication and a left, not right, bar deflection. Answer (B) is incorrect because airplane 13 is to the right of the 360/180 radials, which would require a TO, not FROM, indication.

69.
4577. (Refer to figures 98 and 99 on pages 106 and 107.) To which aircraft position does HSI presentation "C" correspond?

A— 6.
B— 7.
C— 12.

Answer (C) is correct (4577). *(IFH Chap VIII)*
On Figs. 98 and 99, HSI "C" has a VOR course selection of 360° with a TO indication, meaning the airplane is south of the 270/090 radials. Since the course deflection bar is to the left, the airplane is to the east of the 180° radial. Given a 310° heading, airplane 12 is described.
Answer (A) is incorrect because airplane 6 is north of the 270/090 radials, which would require a FROM, not TO, indication and has a north, not 310°, heading. Answer (B) is incorrect because airplane 7 is north of the 270/090 radials, which would require a FROM, not TO, indication.

70.
4572. (Refer to figures 98 and 99 on pages 106 and 107.) To which aircraft position does HSI presentation "D" correspond?

A— 4.
B— 15.
C— 17.

Answer (C) is correct (4572). *(IFH Chap VIII)*
On Figs. 98 and 99, HSI "D" has a VOR course selection (OBS) of 180°. Its FROM indication means the airplane is south of R-270/90. Since the course deflection bar is to the left, the airplane is west of R-180. Given the heading of 180°, the position describes airplane 17.
Answer (A) is incorrect because airplane 4 is north of the 270/090 radials, which would have a TO, not FROM, indication. Answer (B) is incorrect because airplane 15 would have a centered deflection bar and a north, not 180°, heading.

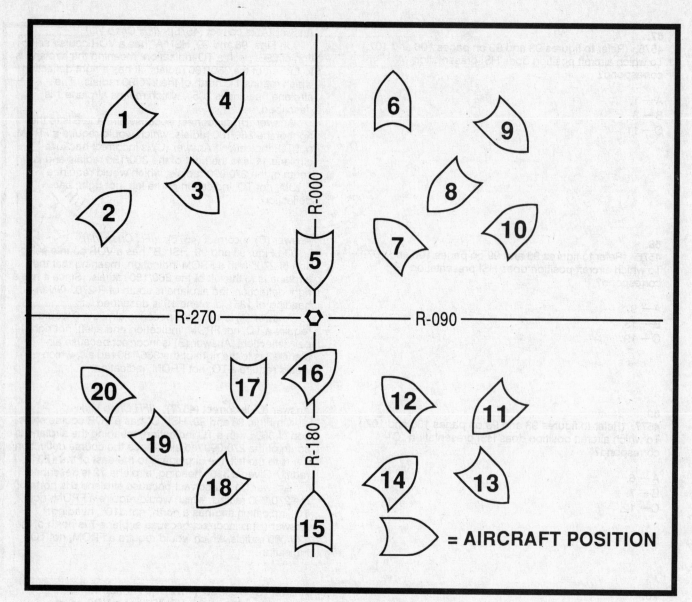

FIGURE 98.—Aircraft Position.

71.
4573. (Refer to figure 98 above and 99 on page 107.) To which aircraft position does HSI presentation "E" correspond?

A— 5.
B— 6.
C— 15.

Answer (B) is correct (4573). *(IFH Chap VIII)*
On Figs. 98 and 99, HSI "E" has a VOR course selection of 360°. Its FROM indication means the airplane is north of R-270/90. Given the course deflection bar to the left, the airplane is to the east of the 360° radial. Given the 360° heading, the position describes airplane 6.

Answer (A) is incorrect because airplane 5 would require a centered deflection bar, and has a south, not 360°, heading. Answer (C) is incorrect because airplane 15 is south of the 270/090 radials, which would require a centered deflection bar and a TO, not FROM, indication.

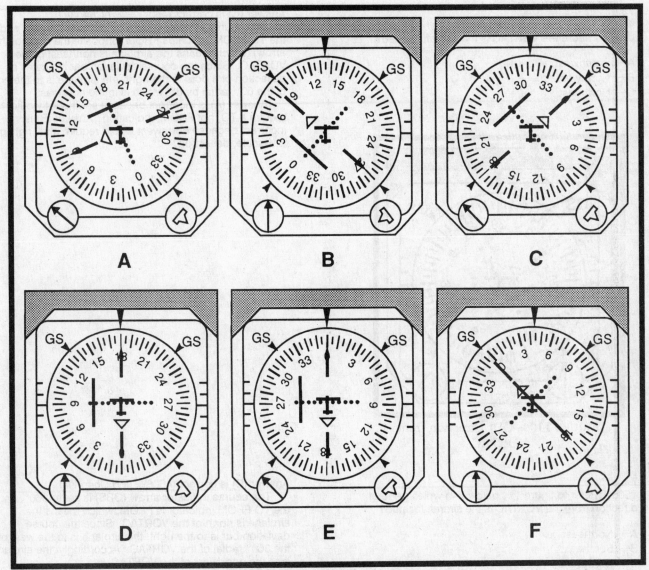

FIGURE 99.—HSI Presentation.

72.

4574. (Refer to figure 98 on page 106 and 99 above.) To which aircraft position does HSI presentation "F" correspond?

A— 10.
B— 14.
C— 16.

Answer (C) is correct (4574). *(IFH Chap VIII)*

On Figs. 98 and 99, HSI "F" has a VOR course selection of 180° with a FROM indication, meaning that the airplane is south of the 270/90 radials. Since the course deflection bar is centered, the airplane is on R-180. Given a heading of 045° (at the top of the HSI), airplane 16 is described.

Answer (A) is incorrect because airplane 10 is east of the 360/180 radials and north of the 270/090 radials, which would require a bar deflection, not a centered bar, and a TO, not FROM, indication. Answer (B) is incorrect because airplane 14 is east of the 360/180 radials, which would require a bar deflection, not a centered bar.

73.
4607. (Refer to figure 110 below.) In which general direction from the VORTAC is the aircraft located?

A— Southwest.
B— Northwest.
C— Northeast.

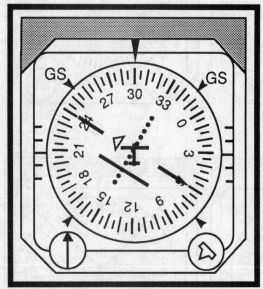

FIGURE 110.—CDI Direction from
VORTAC.

74.
4608. (Refer to figure 111 below.) In which general direction from the VORTAC is the aircraft located?

A— Northeast.
B— Southeast.
C— Northwest.

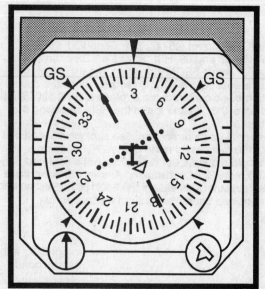

FIGURE 111.—CDI Direction from
VORTAC.

Answer (C) is correct (4607). *(IFH Chap VIII)*
The course indicator arrow (OBS) is set to 60°, and the TO-FROM indicates FROM (opposite the head of the arrow), which means the airplane is northeast of the VORTAC. Since the course deviation bar indicates a deflection of 3 dots to the right, the airplane is to the north of the 60° radial by 6°, which is in the northeast.
Answer (A) is incorrect because southwest would require a TO, not FROM, indication. Answer (B) is incorrect because northwest would require a full right, not a ½-scale, deflection.

Answer (C) is correct (4608). *(IFH Chap VIII)*
The course indicator arrow (OBS) is set to 360°, and the TO-FROM indicator is FROM, which means the airplane is north of the VORTAC. Since the course deviation bar is to the right, the airplane is to the west of the 360° radial of the VORTAC. Accordingly, the airplane is to the northwest of the VORTAC.
Answer (A) is incorrect because a left, not right, deflection would indicate the airplane is in the northeast. Answer (B) is incorrect because a TO, not FROM, indication would indicate the airplane is south of the VORTAC.

3.7 HSI/Localizer

Note: HSI presentations B, C, D, E, and I have backcourse settings of 090°, which means there is reverse sensing irrespective of the airplane's heading.

75.
4563. (Refer to figures 96 and 97 on pages 110 and 111.)
To which aircraft position(s) does HSI presentation "A" correspond?

A— 9 and 6.
B— 9 only.
C— 6 only.

Answer (A) is correct (4563). *(IFH Chap VII)*
On Figs. 96 and 97, HSI "A" has a heading of 360° with no localizer deviation, which means the airplane is on the localizer. Airplanes 6 and 9 are on the localizer with a 360° heading.
Answer (B) is incorrect because the indication will be the same on either localizer. Answer (C) is incorrect because the indication will be the same on either localizer.

76.
4564. (Refer to figures 96 and 97 on pages 110 and 111.)
To which aircraft position(s) does HSI presentation "B" correspond?

A— 11.
B— 5 and 13.
C— 7 and 11.

Answer (B) is correct (4564). *(IFH Chap VII)*
On Figs. 96 and 97, HSI "B" has a heading of 090°. It has localizer course setting of 090° with a right deflection, meaning the airplane is south of the localizer. Both airplanes 5 and 13 are described. Note the backcourse setting. If the front course 270° (instead of 90°) had been set, normal (rather than reverse) sensing would be indicated.
Answer (A) is incorrect because airplane 11 has a 270°, not 090°, heading. Answer (C) is incorrect because airplanes 7 and 11 have 270°, not 090°, headings.

77.
4565. (Refer to figures 96 and 97 on pages 110 and 111.)
To which aircraft position does HSI presentation "C" correspond?

A— 9.
B— 4.
C— 12.

Answer (C) is correct (4565). *(IFH Chap VII)*
On Figs. 96 and 97, HSI "C" has a heading of 090° with a centered course deviation bar; thus the airplane is on the localizer with a 090° heading, which describes airplane 12. The backcourse setting (090) has no effect because the deviation bar is centered.
Answer (A) is incorrect because airplane 9 has a 360°, not 090°, heading. Answer (B) is incorrect because airplane 4 has a 270°, not 090°, heading.

78.
4566. (Refer to figures 96 and 97 on pages 110 and 111.)
To which aircraft position does HSI presentation "D" correspond?

A— 1.
B— 10.
C— 2.

Answer (C) is correct (4566). *(IFH Chap VII)*
On Figs. 96 and 97, HSI "D" has a heading of 315°. Airplane 2 is the only one with a northwest heading.
Answer (A) is incorrect because airplane 1 has a heading of 215°, not 315°. Answer (B) is incorrect because airplane 10 has a heading of 135°, not 315°.

79.
4567. (Refer to figures 96 and 97 on pages 110 and 111.)
To which aircraft position(s) does HSI presentation "E" correspond?

A— 8 only.
B— 3 only.
C— 8 and 3.

Answer (C) is correct (4567). *(IFH Chap VII)*
On Figs. 96 and 97, HSI "E" has a heading of 045°. It has a right deflection with a backcourse HSI setting of 090. This results in reverse sensing, meaning the airplane is south of the localizer. Thus, airplanes 3 and 8 are described.
Answer (A) is incorrect because airplane 3 is also south of the localizer with a 045° heading. Answer (B) is incorrect because airplane 8 also has a 045° heading and is south of the localizer.

80.
4568. (Refer to figures 96 and 97 on pages 110 and 111.)
To which aircraft position does HSI presentation "F" correspond?

A— 4.
B— 11.
C— 5.

Answer (A) is correct (4568). *(IFH Chap VII)*
On Figs. 96 and 97, HSI "F" has a setting of 270° with a centered bar and a 270° heading, which corresponds to airplane 4.
Answer (B) is incorrect because airplane 11 would have a left, not centered, course deviation bar. Answer (C) is incorrect because airplane 5 has a heading of 090°, not 270°.

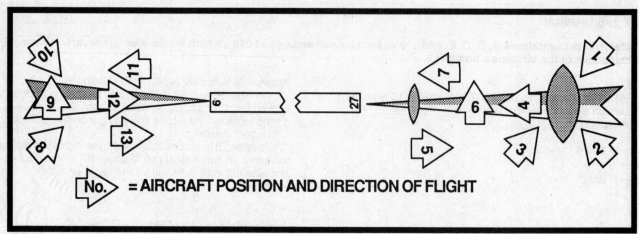

FIGURE 96.—Aircraft Position and Direction of Flight.

81.
4570. (Refer to figures 96 above and 97 on page 111.)
To which aircraft position does HSI presentation "H"
correspond?

A— 8.
B— 1.
C— 2.

Answer (B) is correct (4570). *(IFH Chap VII)*
    On Figs. 96 and 97, HSI "H" has a heading of 215°.
Airplane 1 is the only one with a southwest heading.
    Answer (A) is incorrect because airplane 8 has a
heading of 045°, not 215°. Answer (C) is incorrect
because airplane 2 has a heading of 315°, not 215°.

82.
4569. (Refer to figures 96 above and 97 on page 111.)
To which aircraft position(s) does HSI presentation "G"
correspond?

A— 7 only.
B— 7 and 11.
C— 5 and 13.

Answer (B) is correct (4569). *(IFH Chap VII)*
    On Figs. 96 and 97, HSI "G" has a localizer setting
at 270° with a left deviation, meaning the airplane is north
of the localizer. With a 270° heading, it corresponds to
airplanes 7 and 11.
    Answer (A) is incorrect because airplane 11 is also
north of the localizer with a 270° heading. Answer (C) is
incorrect because airplanes 5 and 13 have a heading of
090°, not 270°, and are also south, not north, of the
localizer.

83.
4571. (Refer to figures 96 above and 97 on page 111.)
To which aircraft position does HSI presentation "I"
correspond?

A— 4.
B— 12.
C— 11.

Answer (C) is correct (4571). *(IFH Chap VII)*
    On Figs. 96 and 97, HSI "I" has a left deviation with a
backcourse HSI setting of 090 resulting in reverse
sensing. Thus, the airplane is north of the localizer.
Airplane 11 has a 270° heading and is north of the
localizer.
    Answer (A) is incorrect because airplane 4 would have
a centered CDI, not a right deviation. Answer (B) is
incorrect because airplane 12 would have a centered CDI,
not a right deviation, and has a heading of 090°, not
270°.

3.8 Global Positioning System (GPS)

84.
4284. How can a pilot determine if a Global Positioning
System (GPS) installed in an aircraft is approved for IFR
en route and IFR approaches?

A— Flight manual supplement.
B— GPS operator's manual.
C— Aircraft owner's handbook.

Answer (A) is correct (4284). *(AC 20-138)*
    A supplement to the aircraft's *POH* (flight manual) is
required for newly installed equipment. A supplement
should state that the GPS is approved for IFR operations
(en route and approaches).
    Answer (B) is incorrect because the GPS operator's
manual will describe how to operate the GPS unit but will
not provide approval for its use in a particular aircraft.
Answer (C) is incorrect because the aircraft owner's
handbook (i.e., information manual or *POH*) may not have
any information on a GPS unit unless the unit was
installed as a standard feature.

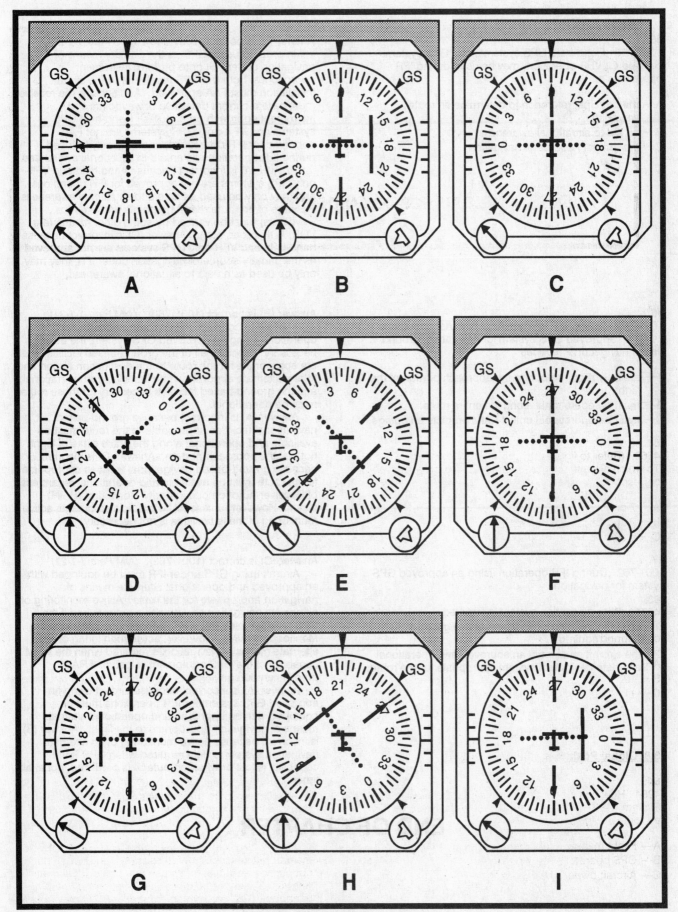

FIGURE 97.—HSI Presentation.

85.
1001-758. Hand-held GPS systems, and GPS systems certified for VFR operation, may be used during IFR operations as

A— the principal reference to determine en route waypoints.
B— an aid to situational awareness.
C— the primary source of navigation.

Answer (B) is correct (1001-758). *(AIM Para 1-1-21)*
In order to use a GPS as the primary means of navigation under IFR or to perform instrument approaches, both the GPS receiver and the aircraft installation must FAA-approved. Additionally, the receiver must have a current database of waypoints and instrument approach procedures. Hand-held GPS systems and VFR-only GPS systems are not FAA-approved for IFR operations, and may only be used during IFR operations as an aid to situational awareness.
Answer (A) is incorrect because hand-held and VFR-only GPS systems are not approved for IFR operations, and may only be used as an aid to situational awareness. Passage of en route reporting points and fixes (i.e., waypoints) must be verified by some other means (e.g., VOR, ADF, radar, etc.). Answer (C) is incorrect because hand-held and VFR-only GPS systems are not approved as the primary source of navigation under IFR; they may only be used as an aid to situational awareness.

86.
1001-760. During IFR en route and terminal operations using an approved GPS system for navigation, ground based navigational facilities

A— are only required during the approach portion of the flight.
B— must be operational along the entire route.
C— must be operational only if RAIM predicts an outage.

Answer (B) is correct (1001-760). *(AIM Para 1-1-21)*
In order to conduct IFR en route and terminal operations using an approved GPS system, the avionics necessary to receive all of the ground-based facilities that are appropriate for the route to the destination airport and to any alternate airport must be installed and operational, and the ground-based facilities necessary for these routes must be operational.
Answer (A) is incorrect because ground-based navigational facilities appropriate to the route must be available and operational along the entire route of flight, not just the approach portion. Answer (C) is incorrect because ground-based navigational facilities appropriate to the route must be available and operational regardless of Receiver Autonomous Integrity Monitoring (RAIM) status. However, unless RAIM predicts an outage, active monitoring of these facilities is not necessary.

87.
1001-762. During IFR operation using an approved GPS system for navigation,

A— no other navigation system is required.
B— active monitoring of an alternate navigation system is always required.
C— the aircraft must have an approved and operational alternate navigation system appropriate for the route.

Answer (C) is correct (1001-762). *(AIM Para 1-1-21)*
Aircraft using GPS under IFR must be equipped with an approved and operational alternate means of navigation appropriate for the route. Active monitoring of alternative navigation equipment is not required if the GPS receiver uses Receiver Autonomous Integrity Monitoring (RAIM). However, active monitoring of an alternate means of navigation is required when the RAIM capability of the GPS equipment is lost, or if RAIM predicts an outage.
Answer (A) is incorrect because aircraft using an approved GPS system for IFR operations must be equipped with an approved and operational alternate means of navigation appropriate to the flight. Answer (B) is incorrect because active monitoring of an alternate navigation system is only required when GPS RAIM capability is lost or when an outage is predicted, not at all times.

END OF CHAPTER

CHAPTER FOUR
FEDERAL AVIATION REGULATIONS

* Gleim module number
** FAR section number

This chapter contains outlines of major concepts tested, all FAA test questions and answers regarding Federal Aviation Regulations (FARs), and an explanation of each answer. Each module, or subtopic, within this chapter is listed above with the number of questions from the FAA knowledge test pertaining to that particular module. For each module, the first number following the parentheses is the page number on which the outline begins, and the next number is the page number on which the questions begin.

There are 84 questions in this chapter. We separate and organize the FAA questions into meaningful study units, i.e., chapters and modules. As an analogy, it is easier to deal with the "trees" if you understand the "forest." In this context, "trees" are individual FAA questions, and the "forest" is the instrument rating knowledge test. The organizational units between the overall instrument rating knowledge test and the individual instrument rating test questions are chapters and modules in this book.

CAUTION: The **sole purpose** of this book is to expedite your passing the FAA instrument rating knowledge test. Accordingly, all extraneous material (i.e., topics or regulations not directly tested on the FAA knowledge test) is omitted, even though much more information and knowledge are necessary to fly safely. This additional material is presented in *Instrument Pilot Flight Maneuvers and Practical Test Prep*, *Pilot Handbook*, *Aviation Weather and Weather Services*, and *FAR/AIM*, available from Gleim Publications, Inc. See the order form on page 488.

FARs ARE NOW REFERRED TO AS CFRs

The FAA is referring to the Federal Aviation Regulations as "14 CFR" rather than "FARs." The Office of Management and Budget uses FAR as an acronym for Federal Acquisition Regulations. CFR stands for Code of Federal Regulations, and the Federal Aviation Regulations are in Title 14. For example, FAR Part 1 and FAR 61.109 are now referred to as 14 CFR Part 1 and 14 CFR Sec. 61.109, respectively.

Due to CFIs' and pilots' widespread use of the acronym FAR, we continue to use FAR rather than CFR.

4.1 FAR PART 61
61.3 Requirements for Certificates, Ratings, and Authorizations (Questions 1-2)

1. The pilot in command must hold an instrument rating when operating under IFR or in weather conditions less than the minimums prescribed for VFR flight.

2. An IFR clearance is required when operating in Class A airspace.

61.51 Pilot Logbooks (Questions 3-5)

1. Instrument flight time may be logged when flight is solely by reference to instruments under actual or simulated flight conditions.

   a. The location and type of each instrument approach completed and the name of the safety pilot must be included in the logbook for each simulated instrument flight.

2. An instrument flight instructor (CFII) may log instrument time when acting as an instrument flight instructor in actual instrument weather conditions.

61.57 Recent Flight Experience: Pilot in Command (Questions 6-16)

1. In order to act as pilot in command under IFR, one must have logged instrument time (actual or simulated) within the preceding 6 months in either the same category of aircraft (airplane) to be used or in an airplane flight simulator or flight training device and must have performed the following procedures:

   a. At least six instrument approaches
   b. Holding procedures
   c. Intercepting and tracking courses through the use of navigation systems

2. An instrument pilot who does not meet the experience requirements during the prescribed time or 6 months thereafter must then pass an instrument proficiency check.

   a. This check may be conducted by an FAA inspector, an FAA-designated examiner, or a certificated instrument flight instructor.

61.133 Commercial Pilot Privileges and Limitations (Questions 17-21)

1. Commercial pilots without an instrument rating cannot carry passengers for hire on cross-country flights during the day beyond a radius of 50 NM.

   a. Carrying passengers at night is also prohibited without an instrument rating.

4.2 FAR PART 91
91.3 Responsibility and Authority of the Pilot in Command (Question 22)

1. The pilot in command of an aircraft is directly responsible for, and is the final authority as to, determining the airworthiness and operation of that aircraft prior to each flight.

91.21 Portable Electronic Devices (Question 23)

1. The use of certain portable electronic devices is prohibited on aircraft that are being operated under IFR.

91.103 Preflight Action (Questions 24-25)

1. Before beginning any IFR flight, the pilot must obtain and become familiar with information about weather reports and forecasts, fuel requirements, alternatives available if the planned flight cannot be completed, any known traffic delays, runway lengths at airports of intended use, and takeoff and landing distance information.

91.109 Flight Instruction; Simulated Instrument Flight and Certain Flight Tests (Question 26)

1. To operate an airplane in simulated instrument flight, you must have at least a private pilot who is appropriately rated in your aircraft occupying the other control seat as a safety pilot.

91.123 Compliance with ATC Clearances and Instructions (Questions 27-29)

1. If you deviate from an ATC clearance in an emergency, you must notify ATC as soon as possible.

2. If you are given priority by ATC in an emergency, ATC may request that you submit a detailed report within 48 hr. to the manager of that ATC facility.

    a. The report may be required even though no rule has been violated.

3. During an IFR flight in IMC, if a distress condition is encountered, the pilot should immediately declare an emergency and obtain an amended clearance.

    a. Distress is a condition of being threatened by serious and/or imminent danger and of requiring immediate assistance.

91.129 Operations in Class D Airspace (Question 30)

1. If an aircraft's transponder fails during flight within Class D airspace, no deviation is required because a transponder is not required in Class D airspace.

91.131 Operations in Class B Airspace (Questions 31-32)

1. Operations in Class B airspace require two-way radio communications with ATC and a Mode C transponder.

    a. If operating IFR, you must have a VOR receiver.

2. If it is necessary to conduct training operations within Class B airspace, procedures established by ATC for these flights within the Class B airspace will be followed.

91.135 Operations in Class A Airspace (Questions 33-36)

1. An IFR flight plan is required when flying in IFR conditions in controlled airspace and at all times in Class A airspace.

    a. Class A airspace includes the airspace from 18,000 ft. MSL up to and including FL 600.

91.155 Basic VFR Weather Minimums (Questions 37-43)

Cloud Clearance and Visibility Required for VFR

Airspace	Flight Visibility	Distance from Clouds		Airspace	Flight Visibility	Distance from Clouds
Class A	Not applicable	Not applicable		Class G: 1,200 ft. or less above the surface (regardless of MSL altitude)		
Class B	3 SM	Clear of clouds		Day	1 SM	Clear of clouds
				Night, except as provided in 1. below	3 SM	500 ft. below 1,000 ft. above 2,000 ft. horiz.
Class C	3 SM	500 ft. below 1,000 ft. above 2,000 ft. horiz.		More than 1,200 ft. above the surface but less than 10,000 ft. MSL		
Class D	3 SM	500 ft. below 1,000 ft. above 2,000 ft. horiz.		Day	1 SM	500 ft. below 1,000 ft. above 2,000 ft. horiz.
Class E:				Night	3 SM	500 ft. below 1,000 ft. above 2,000 ft. horiz.
Less than 10,000 ft. MSL	3 SM	500 ft. below 1,000 ft. above 2,000 ft. horiz.		More than 1,200 ft. above the surface and at or above 10,000 ft. MSL	5 SM	1,000 ft. below 1,000 ft. above 1 SM horiz.
At or above 10,000 ft. MSL	5 SM	1,000 ft. below 1,000 ft. above 1 SM horiz.				

1. An airplane may be operated clear of clouds in Class G airspace at night below 1,200 ft. AGL when the visibility is less than 3 SM but more than 1 SM in an airport traffic pattern and within ½ NM of the runway.

2. When flying under a "VFR-on-top" clearance on IFR flights, you must fly at VFR altitudes and comply with VFR visibility and distance-from-clouds criteria.

91.157 Special VFR Weather Minimums (Question 44)

1. With some exceptions, special VFR clearances can be requested in Class B, Class C, Class D, or Class E airspace areas.

    a. The flight requirements are to remain clear of clouds and have visibility of at least 1 SM.

2. Flight under special VFR clearance at night is permitted only if the pilot is instrument rated and the airplane is IFR equipped.

91.167 Fuel Requirements for Flight in IFR Conditions (Questions 45-46)

1. When flying IFR, you must carry sufficient fuel to fly to the first airport of intended landing, fly to the alternate airport (if required), and then fly for 45 min. at normal cruising speed.

2. An alternate airport is not required if the destination airport has

    a. At least one approved instrument approach procedure (IAP), and
    b. From 1 hr. before to 1 hr. after the ETA, a forecast of at least

        1) 2,000 ft. ceiling
        2) 3 SM visibility

91.169 IFR Flight Plan: Information Required (Questions 47-56a)

1. Intended airports of landing on an IFR flight must have a forecast ceiling of at least 2,000 ft. and visibility of at least 3 SM for 1 hr. before and 1 hr. after the ETA. Otherwise, an alternate must be listed on your IFR flight plan.

2. When a pilot elects to proceed to the selected alternate airport, the landing minimums used should be the minimums specified for the approach procedure selected.

    a. To list an airport with a nonprecision approach as an alternate, the forecast weather must be for at least an 800-ft. ceiling and 2 SM visibility at your ETA.

    b. To list an airport with a precision approach as an alternate, the forecast weather must indicate at least a 600-ft. ceiling and 2 SM visibility at your ETA.

3. If no instrument approaches are prescribed, the minimums for listing an airport as an alternate on an IFR flight are forecast weather allowing descent from the MEA, approach, and landing under basic VFR.

91.171 VOR Equipment Check for IFR Operations (Questions 57-62)

1. When making VOR operation checks, the date, place, bearing error, and pilot signature should be placed in the aircraft log or other record.

2. Operational checks of VORs must be made every 30 days.

3. The maximum allowable tolerance when performing an operational check of a dual VOR system is a 4° variation between the two indicated bearings.

    a. When performing an operational check using a VOT, the maximum tolerance is ±4°.

4. In addition to the VOR check that must be made at least every 30 days, the altimeter system and the transponder must have been inspected within 24 calendar months.

91.173 ATC Clearance and Flight Plan Required (Questions 63-67)

1. No person may operate an aircraft in controlled airspace under IFR unless that person has

    a. Filed an IFR flight plan, and
    b. Received an appropriate ATC clearance.

91.177 Minimum Altitudes for IFR Operations (Question 68)

1. Except when necessary for takeoff or landing, the minimum altitude for IFR flight (if none is prescribed in FAR Parts 95 or 97) is one of the following:

   a. 2,000 ft. above the highest obstacle within a horizontal distance of 4 NM over designated mountainous terrain

   b. 1,000 ft. above the highest obstacle within a horizontal distance of 4 NM over nonmountainous terrain

91.205 Powered Civil Aircraft with Standard Category U.S. Airworthiness Certificates: Instrument and Equipment Requirements (Questions 69-71b)

1. For IFR flight, navigation equipment must be appropriate to the ground facilities to be used.

2. Above 24,000 ft. MSL, DME is required if VOR navigational equipment is required.

3. A gyroscopic directional indicator, a gyroscopic attitude indicator, and a gyroscopic rate-of-turn indicator are required for IFR flight.

4. Aircraft being operated under IFR are required to have a slip-skid indicator and a clock with a sweep second pointer or digital presentation.

91.211 Supplemental Oxygen (Questions 72-75)

1. At cabin pressure altitudes above 15,000 ft. MSL, each passenger of the aircraft must be provided with supplemental oxygen.

2. At cabin pressure altitudes above 14,000 ft. MSL, the required minimum flight crew must be provided and use supplemental oxygen during the entire flight time at those altitudes.

3. Pilots can fly at cabin pressure altitudes above 12,500 ft. MSL up to and including 14,000 ft. MSL for up to 30 min. without supplemental oxygen.

   a. If a flight is conducted at these altitudes for more than 30 min., oxygen must be provided to and used by the required minimum flight crew for the time in excess of 30 min.

91.215 ATC Transponder and Altitude Reporting Equipment and Use (Questions 76-80)

1. All aircraft must have and use an altitude encoding transponder (Mode C) when operating

   a. Within Class B airspace
   b. Within 30 NM of the primary Class B airport
   c. Within and above Class C airspace
   d. Above 10,000 ft. MSL except at and below 2,500 ft. AGL
   e. In Class A airspace

2. Request for deviations must be made to the controlling ATC facility.

   a. If the transponder fails during flight, ATC may authorize the aircraft to continue to the airport of ultimate destination.

      1) An aircraft with an operating transponder but without Mode C can request a deviation at any time.

   b. For operation of an aircraft that is not equipped with a transponder, the request for a deviation must be made at least 1 hr. before the proposed operation.

91.411 Altimeter System and Altitude Reporting Equipment Tests and Inspections
(Questions 81-82)

1. Each static pressure system and altimeter instrument must be tested and inspected by the end of the 24th calendar month following the current inspection.

4.3 NTSB PART 830 NOTIFICATION AND REPORTING OF AIRCRAFT ACCIDENTS OR INCIDENTS AND OVERDUE AIRCRAFT, AND PRESERVATION OF AIRCRAFT WRECKAGE, MAIL, CARGO, AND RECORDS (Question 83)

1. NTSB Part 830 covers the procedures required for aircraft accident- and incident-reporting responsibilities for pilots.

QUESTIONS AND ANSWER EXPLANATIONS

All the FAA questions from the instrument rating knowledge test relating to FARs and the material outlined previously are reproduced on the following pages in the same modules as the outlines. To the immediate right of each question are the correct answer and answer explanation. You should cover these answers and answer explanations with your hand or a piece of paper while responding to the questions. Refer to the general discussion in the Introduction on how to take the FAA knowledge test.

Remember that the questions from the FAA instrument rating knowledge test bank have been reordered by topic, and the topics are organized into a meaningful sequence. Accordingly, the first line of the answer explanation gives the FAA question number and the citation of the authoritative source for the answer.

4.1 FAR PART 61
61.3 Requirements for Certificates, Ratings, and Authorizations

1.
4031. Under which condition must the pilot in command of a civil aircraft have at least an instrument rating?

A— When operating in Class E airspace.
B— For a flight in VFR conditions while on an IFR flight plan.
C— For any flight above an altitude of 1,200 feet AGL, when the visibility is less than 3 miles.

Answer (B) is correct (4031). *(FAR 61.3)*
No person may act as pilot in command of a civil aircraft under IFR or in weather conditions less than the minimums prescribed for VFR flight unless (s)he holds an instrument rating.
Answer (A) is incorrect because an instrument rating is required at all times when operating in Class A, not Class E, airspace. Answer (C) is incorrect because VFR is permitted in uncontrolled airspace during the day with visibilities of as little as 1 SM when more than 1,200 ft. AGL but below 10,000 ft. MSL.

2.
4025. The pilot in command of a civil aircraft must have an instrument rating only when operating

A— under IFR in positive control airspace.
B— under IFR, in weather conditions less than the minimum for VFR flight or in Class A airspace.
C— in weather conditions less than the minimum prescribed for VFR flight.

Answer (B) is correct (4025). *(FAR 61.3 and 91.135)*
No person may act as pilot in command of a civil aircraft under IFR, in weather conditions less than the minimums prescribed for VFR flight, or in Class A airspace unless (s)he holds an instrument rating.
Answer (A) is incorrect because you must have an instrument rating when operating under IFR, in weather conditions less than the minimum for VFR flight, or in Class A airspace, not only under IFR in positive control airspace. Positive control airspace means that ATC will provide separation to all aircraft within that airspace. Answer (C) is incorrect because it omits flying in VFR conditions with an IFR clearance.

61.51 Pilot Logbooks

3.
4010. Which flight time may be logged as instrument time when on an instrument flight plan?

A— All of the time the aircraft was not controlled by ground references.
B— Only the time you controlled the aircraft solely by reference to flight instruments.
C— Only the time you were flying in IFR weather conditions.

Answer (B) is correct (4010). *(FAR 61.51)*
A pilot may log as instrument flight time only that time during which (s)he operates the aircraft solely by reference to instruments, under actual or simulated instrument flight conditions.
Answer (A) is incorrect because VFR flight can be conducted above a cloud layer without visual ground references, i.e., VFR-on-top. Answer (C) is incorrect because time under the hood (i.e., simulated IFR) as well as actual IFR conditions counts as instrument time.

4.
4009. What portion of dual instruction time may a certificated instrument flight instructor log as instrument flight time?

A— All time during which the instructor acts as instrument instructor, regardless of weather conditions.
B— All time during which the instructor acts as instrument instructor in actual instrument weather conditions.
C— Only the time during which the instructor flies the aircraft by reference to instruments.

Answer (B) is correct (4009). *(FAR 61.51)*
An instrument flight instructor may log as instrument time that time during which (s)he acts as instrument flight instructor in actual instrument weather conditions.
Answer (A) is incorrect because the flight conditions must be IMC for the instructor to log flight instruction as instrument time. Answer (C) is incorrect because instructing in (as well as flying in) actual IFR weather conditions can be logged as instrument time by the instructor.

5.
4008. To meet instrument experience requirements of CFR Part 61, section 61.57(c), a pilot enters the condition of flight in the pilot logbook as simulated instrument conditions, what other qualifying information must also be entered?

A— Location and type of each instrument approach completed and name of safety pilot.
B— Number and type of instrument approaches completed and route of flight.
C— Name and pilot certificate number of safety pilot and type of approaches completed.

Answer (A) is correct (4008). *(FAR 61.51)*
A pilot may log as instrument flight time only that time during which (s)he operates the aircraft solely by reference to instruments, under actual or simulated instrument flight conditions. Each entry must include the location and type of each instrument approach completed and the name of the safety pilot for each simulated instrument flight.
Answer (B) is incorrect because the location and type of instrument approaches must be entered along with the safety pilot's name, not the route of flight. Answer (C) is incorrect because the location is required, but the safety pilot's certificate number is not.

61.57 Recent Flight Experience: Pilot in Command

6.
4021. How long does a pilot meet the recency of experience requirements for IFR flight after successfully completing an instrument proficiency check if no further IFR flights are made?

A— 90 days.
B— 6 calendar months.
C— 12 6 calendar months.

Answer (B) is correct (4021). *(FAR 61.57)*
No pilot may act as pilot in command when operating under IFR or in weather conditions less than the minimums prescribed for VFR unless (s)he has, within the past 6 months, logged instrument time under actual or simulated IFR conditions in the category of aircraft involved or in an appropriate flight simulator or flight training device and has performed at least six instrument approaches, holding procedures, and intercepting and tracking courses through the use of navigation systems. An alternative way to remain current is to pass an instrument proficiency check in the category of aircraft involved.
Answer (A) is incorrect because 90 days refers to takeoff and landing currency to carry passengers. Answer (C) is incorrect because 12 months is the time whereafter another instrument proficiency check is required.

7.

4001. No pilot may act as pilot-in-command of an aircraft, under IFR or in weather conditions less than the minimums prescribed for VFR unless that pilot has, within the preceding 6 calendar months, completed at least

A— six instrument approaches, holding procedures, intercepting and tracking courses using navigational systems, or passed an instrument proficiency check.

B— six instrument flights under actual IFR conditions.

C— three instrument approaches and logged 3 hours.

Answer (A) is correct (4001). *(FAR 61.57)*

No person may act as pilot in command under IFR or in weather conditions less than the minimums prescribed for VFR unless, within the preceding 6 calendar months, that person has performed and logged under actual or simulated instrument conditions, either in flight in the appropriate category of aircraft for the instrument privileges sought or in a flight simulator or flight training device that is representative of the aircraft category for the instrument privileges sought, at least six instrument approaches, holding procedures, and intercepting and tracking courses through the use of navigation systems. Alternatively, the pilot may pass an instrument proficiency check in the category of aircraft involved.

Answer (B) is incorrect because a pilot must complete, under actual or simulated instrument conditions, at least six instrument approaches, holding procedures, and intercepting and tracking courses through the use of navigation systems, not six instrument flights under actual IFR conditions. Answer (C) is incorrect because a pilot must complete at least six, not three, instrument approaches, holding procedures, and intercepting and tracking courses through the use of navigation systems. There is no required minimum number of hours to be logged.

8.

4027. To meet the minimum required instrument flight experience to act as pilot in command of an aircraft under IFR, you must have logged within the preceding 6 calendar months in the same category aircraft: six instrument approaches,

A— holding procedures, intercepting and tracking courses through the use of navigation systems.

B— three of which must be in the same category and class of aircraft to be flown, and 6 hours of instrument time in any aircraft.

C— and 6 hours of instrument time in any aircraft.

Answer (A) is correct (4027). *(FAR 61.57)*

No person may act as pilot in command under IFR or in weather conditions less than VFR minimums unless, within the preceding 6 calendar months, (s)he has performed and logged, under actual or simulated instrument conditions, at least six instrument approaches, holding procedures, and intercepting and tracking courses through the use of navigation systems, in the category of aircraft to be flown.

Answer (B) is incorrect because all six, not three, approaches must be in the same category and aircraft. Additionally, you must have accomplished holding procedures and intercepting and tracking courses through the use of navigation systems, not accumulated 6 hr. of instrument time. Answer (C) is incorrect because you must have also accomplished holding procedures and intercepting and tracking courses through the use of navigation systems in the same category and class of aircraft, not accumulated 6 hr. of instrument time in any aircraft.

9.
4012. To meet the minimum instrument experience requirements, within the last 6 calendar months you need

A—six instrument approaches, holding procedures, and intercepting and tracking courses in the appropriate category of aircraft.
B—six hours in the same category aircraft.
C—six hours in the same category aircraft, and at least 3 of the 6 hours in actual IFR conditions.

Answer (A) is correct (4012). *(FAR 61.57)*
No person may act as pilot in command under IFR or in weather conditions less than VFR minimums unless, within the preceding 6 calendar months, (s)he has performed and logged, under actual or simulated instrument conditions, at least six instrument approaches, holding procedures, and intercepting and tracking courses through the use of navigation systems, in the category of aircraft to be flown.
Answer (B) is incorrect because, to be current for IFR, you must have performed six instrument approaches, holding procedures, and intercepting and tracking courses in the same category of aircraft, not accumulated 6 hr. in the same category of aircraft. Answer (C) is incorrect because, to be current for IFR, you must have performed six instrument approaches, holding procedures, and intercepting and tracking courses in the same category of aircraft, not accumulated 6 hr. in the same category aircraft with at least 3 hr. in actual IFR conditions.

10.
4023. What recent instrument flight experience requirements must be met before you may act as pilot in command of an airplane under IFR?

A— A minimum of six instrument approaches in an airplane, or an approved simulator (airplane) or ground trainer, within the preceding 6 calendar months.
B— A minimum of six instrument approaches, at least three of which must be in an aircraft within the preceding 6 calendar months.
C— A minimum of six instrument approaches in an aircraft, at least three of which must be in the same category within the preceding 6 calendar months.

Answer (A) is correct (4023). *(FAR 61.57)*
No person may act as pilot in command under IFR or in weather conditions less than VFR minimums unless, within the preceding 6 calendar months, (s)he has performed and logged, under actual or simulated instrument conditions, at least six instrument approaches, holding procedures, and intercepting and tracking courses through the use of navigation systems, in the category of aircraft to be flown, in an approved simulator or flight training device, or in any combination of these.
Answer (B) is incorrect because all six approaches may be done in an approved flight simulator or flight training device; none are required to be done in an aircraft. Answer (C) is incorrect because all six approaches may be done in an approved flight simulator or flight training device; none are required to be done in an aircraft. In addition, all six approaches, not just three, must be done in the same category of aircraft or a simulator or flight training device representative of that aircraft category.

11.
4014. An instrument rated pilot, who has not logged any instrument experience in 1 year or more, cannot serve as pilot in command under IFR, unless the pilot

A— completes the required 6 hours and six approaches, followed by an instrument proficiency check given by an FAA-designated examiner.
B— passes an instrument proficiency check in the category of aircraft involved, given by an approved FAA examiner, instrument instructor, or FAA inspector.
C— passes an instrument proficiency check in the category of aircraft involved, followed by 6 hours and six instrument approaches, 3 of those hours in the category of aircraft involved.

Answer (B) is correct (4014). *(FAR 61.57)*
A pilot who does not meet the recent instrument experience requirements during the prescribed time or 6 months thereafter may not serve as pilot in command under IFR or in weather conditions less than the minimums prescribed for VFR until (s)he passes an instrument proficiency check in the category of aircraft involved, given by an FAA inspector, a member of an armed force of the U.S. authorized to conduct flight tests, an FAA-approved check pilot, or a certificated instrument flight instructor. The proficiency check may be completed in an appropriate flight simulator or flight training device.
Answer (A) is incorrect because an instrument proficiency check by itself provides currency. Additional time and approaches are not required. Answer (C) is incorrect because an instrument proficiency check by itself provides currency. Additional time and approaches are not required.

12.
4013. After your recent IFR experience lapses, how much time do you have before you must pass an instrument proficiency check to act as pilot in command under IFR?

A— 6 months.
B— 90 days.
C— 12 months.

Answer (A) is correct (4013). *(FAR 61.57)*
A pilot who does not meet the recent instrument experience requirements during the prescribed time or 6 months thereafter may not serve as pilot in command under IFR or in weather conditions less than the minimums prescribed for VFR until (s)he passes an instrument proficiency check.
Answer (B) is incorrect because 90 days refers to the takeoff and landing currency requirements to carry passengers. Answer (C) is incorrect because 12 months is the time from when you gain IFR currency to when you are required to pass another instrument proficiency check (assuming you have not maintained currency since you gained proficiency).

13.
4017. What minimum conditions are necessary for the instrument approaches required for IFR currency?

A— The approaches may be made in an aircraft, approved instrument ground trainer, or any combination of these.
B— At least three approaches must be made in the same category of aircraft to be flown.
C— The approaches must be made in the same category and class of aircraft to be flown.

Answer (A) is correct (4017). *(FAR 61.57)*
For IFR currency, the six instrument approaches must be made either in the same category of aircraft to be flown or in a flight simulator or training device representative of the aircraft category to be flown, or in any combination of these.
Answer (B) is incorrect because all six approaches may be done in an approved flight simulator or training device, not necessarily in an airplane. Answer (C) is incorrect because all six approaches may be done in an approved flight simulator or training device, not necessarily in an airplane.

14.
4015. A pilot's recent IFR experience expires on July 1 of this year. What is the latest date the pilot can meet the IFR experience requirement without having to take an instrument proficiency check?

A— December 31, this year.
B— June 30, next year.
C— July 31, this year.

Answer (A) is correct (4015). *(FAR 61.57)*
A pilot who does not meet the recent instrument experience requirements during the prescribed time or 6 months thereafter may not serve as pilot in command under IFR or in weather conditions less than the minimums prescribed for VFR until (s)he passes an instrument proficiency check. If the 6 months' recency experience period expires on July 1, the 6 months thereafter would expire on December 31 this year.
Answer (B) is incorrect because this date represents 12 months instead of 6 months. Answer (C) is incorrect because this date represents 1 month instead of 6 months.

15.
4020. How may a pilot satisfy the recent flight experience requirement necessary to act as pilot in command in IMC in powered aircraft? Within the previous 6 calendar months, logged

A— six instrument approaches, holding procedures, and intercepting and tracking courses using navigational systems.
B— six instrument approaches and 3 hours under actual or simulated IFR conditions within the last 6 months; three of the approaches must be in the category of aircraft involved.
C— 6 hours of instrument time under actual or simulated IFR conditions within the last 3 months, including at least six instrument approaches of any kind. Three of the 6 hours must be in flight in any category aircraft.

Answer (A) is correct (4020). *(FAR 61.57)*
No pilot may act as pilot in command of a powered aircraft under IFR or in weather conditions less than VFR minimums unless, within the preceding 6 calendar months, (s)he has performed and logged, under actual or simulated instrument conditions, at least six instrument approaches, holding procedures, and intercepting and tracking courses through the use of navigation systems, in the category of aircraft to be flown or in an airplane flight simulator or training device.
Answer (B) is incorrect because there is no instrument flight time requirement. In addition to the six instrument approaches, you must also log holding procedures and intercepting and tracking courses using navigational systems. Answer (C) is incorrect because there is no instrument flight time requirement. You must log six instrument approaches, holding procedures, and intercepting and tracking courses using navigational systems within the past 6 months, not 3 months.

16.
4026. What additional instrument experience is required for you to meet the recent flight experience requirements to act as pilot in command of an airplane under IFR?

Your present instrument experience within the preceding 6 calendar months is

1. three hours with holding, intercepting and tracking courses in an approved airplane flight simulator.
2. two instrument approaches in an airplane.

A— Three hours of simulated or actual instrument flight time in a helicopter, and two instrument approaches in an airplane or helicopter.
B— Four instrument approaches in an airplane, or an approved airplane flight simulator or training device.
C— Three instrument approaches in an airplane.

Answer (B) is correct (4026). *(FAR 61.57)*
No person may act as pilot in command under IFR or in weather conditions less than the minimums prescribed for VFR, unless within the preceding 6 calendar months that person has performed and logged under actual or simulated instrument conditions, either in flight in the appropriate category of aircraft for the instrument privileges being sought or in a flight simulator or flight training device that is representative of the aircraft category for the instrument privileges sought; at least six instrument approaches, holding procedures, and intercepting and tracking courses through the use of navigation systems. Having logged only two instrument approaches, the pilot must log four more.
Answer (A) is incorrect because no minimum time is required; four, not two, more approaches are required; and all approaches must be in an airplane or flight simulator or flight training device representative of an airplane, not a helicopter. Answer (C) is incorrect because four, not three, more approaches are required to have the required minimum of six.

61.133 Commercial Pilot Privileges and Limitations

17.
4035. To carry passengers for hire in an airplane on cross-country flights of more than 50 NM from the departure airport, the pilot in command is required to hold at least

A— a Category II pilot authorization.
B— a First-Class Medical certificate.
C— a Commercial Pilot Certificate with an instrument rating.

Answer (C) is correct (4035). *(FAR 61.133)*
To carry passengers for hire, the pilot in command is required to hold at least a commercial pilot certificate. Additionally, to carry those passengers for hire in an airplane on cross-country flights of more than 50 NM (or at night), (s)he must also hold an instrument rating on the commercial certificate.
Answer (A) is incorrect because Category II refers to an authorization for reduced ILS approach minimums. Answer (B) is incorrect because a first-class medical certificate is required for operations requiring an airline transport pilot certificate.

18.
4034. Which limitation is imposed on the holder of a Commercial Pilot Certificate if that person does not hold an instrument rating?

A— That person is limited to private pilot privileges at night.
B— The carrying of passengers or property for hire on cross-country flights at night is limited to a radius of 50 NM.
C— The carrying of passengers for hire on cross-country flights is limited to 50 NM and the carrying of passengers for hire at night is prohibited.

Answer (C) is correct (4034). *(FAR 61.133)*
The applicant for a commercial pilot certificate must hold an instrument rating (airplane), or the commercial pilot certificate must be endorsed with a limitation prohibiting the carriage of passengers for hire in airplanes on cross-country flights of more than 50 NM or at night.
Answer (A) is incorrect because that person may exercise commercial pilot privileges at night, but with limitations. Answer (B) is incorrect because no passengers may be carried at night without an instrument rating.

19.
4002. What limitation is imposed on a newly certificated commercial airplane pilot if that person does not hold an instrument pilot rating?

A— The carrying of passengers or property for hire on cross-country flights at night is limited to a radius of 50 nautical miles (NM).
B— The carrying of passengers for hire on cross-country flights is limited to 50 NM for night flights, but not limited for day flights.
C— The carrying of passengers for hire on cross-country flights is limited to 50 NM and the carrying of passengers for hire at night is prohibited.

Answer (C) is correct (4002). *(FAR 61.133)*
The applicant for a commercial pilot certificate must hold an instrument rating (airplane), or the commercial pilot certificate must be endorsed with a limitation prohibiting the carriage of passengers for hire in airplanes on cross-country flights of more than 50 NM or at night.
Answer (A) is incorrect because the carriage of property (freight) is not limited at night. Answer (B) is incorrect because no passengers may be carried at night and the flight is limited to 50 NM, not unlimited, for day flights without an instrument rating.

20.
4028. A certificated commercial pilot who carries passengers for hire at night or in excess of 50 NM is required to have at least

A— an associated type rating if the airplane is of the multiengine class.
B— a First-Class Medical Certificate.
C— an instrument rating in the same category and class of aircraft.

Answer (C) is correct (4028). *(FAR 61.133)*
A certificated commercial pilot who carries passengers for hire at night or in excess of 50 NM is required to have an instrument rating in the same category and class of aircraft.
Answer (A) is incorrect because, even if the airplane requires a type rating, the commercial pilot must have at least an instrument rating to carry passengers for hire at night or in excess of 50 NM. Answer (B) is incorrect because only a second-class medical certificate is required of commercial pilots. First-class medical certificates are required of airline transport pilots.

21.
4029. You intend to carry passengers for hire on a night VFR flight in a single-engine airplane within a 25-mile radius of the departure airport. You are required to possess at least which rating(s)?

A— A Commercial Pilot Certificate with a single-engine land rating.
B— A Commercial Pilot Certificate with a single-engine and instrument (airplane) rating.
C— A Private Pilot Certificate with a single-engine land and instrument airplane rating.

Answer (B) is correct (4029). *(FAR 61.133)*
A commercial pilot certificate with a single-engine airplane rating is required for a pilot to carry passengers for hire and to operate that class of aircraft. Also, an applicant for a commercial pilot certificate must hold an instrument rating (airplane), or the commercial pilot certificate will be endorsed with a limitation prohibiting carrying passengers for hire on cross-country flights of more than 50 NM or at night.
Answer (A) is incorrect because, to carry passengers for hire at night, one must have an instrument rating as well as a commercial pilot certificate. Answer (C) is incorrect because a commercial, not private, pilot certificate is required to carry passengers for hire.

4.2 FAR PART 91
91.3 Responsibility and Authority of the Pilot in Command

22.
4039. Who is responsible for determining that the altimeter system has been checked and found to meet 14 CFR Part 91 requirements for a particular instrument flight?

A— Owner.
B— Operator.
C— Pilot in command.

Answer (C) is correct (4039). *(FAR 91.3)*
The pilot in command of an aircraft is directly responsible for, and is the final authority as to, the airworthiness and operation of that aircraft.
Answer (A) is incorrect because the owner is primarily responsible for maintaining the aircraft, but the pilot in command is responsible for determining that the aircraft is airworthy. Answer (B) is incorrect because the operator is primarily responsible for maintaining the aircraft, but the pilot in command is responsible for determining that the aircraft is airworthy.

91.21 Portable Electronic Devices

23.
4004. The use of certain portable electronic devices is prohibited on aircraft that are being operated under

A— IFR.
B— VFR.
C— DVFR.

Answer (A) is correct (4004). *(FAR 91.21)*
The use of portable electronic devices in carrier aircraft and other aircraft operated under IFR is prohibited. This prohibition does not apply to portable voice recorders, hearing aids, heart pacemakers, electric shavers, and other devices which do not interfere with the aircraft's navigation and communication systems.
Answer (B) is incorrect because portable electronic devices are not prohibited in aircraft operated under VFR. Answer (C) is incorrect because portable electronic devices are not prohibited in aircraft operated under DVFR (defense VFR).

91.103 Preflight Action

24.
4033. Before beginning any flight under IFR, the pilot in command must become familiar with all available information concerning that flight. In addition, the pilot must

A— list an alternate airport on the flight plan and become familiar with the instrument approaches to that airport.
B— list an alternate airport on the flight plan and confirm adequate takeoff and landing performance at the destination airport.
C— be familiar with the runway lengths at airports of intended use, and the alternatives available if the flight cannot be completed.

25.
4003. Before beginning any flight under IFR, the pilot in command must become familiar with all available information concerning that flight including:

A— all instrument approaches at the destination airport.
B— an alternate airport and adequate takeoff and landing performance at the destination airport.
C— the runway lengths at airports of intended use, and the aircraft's takeoff and landing data.

91.109 Flight Instruction; Simulated Instrument Flight and Certain Flight Tests

26.
4011. What are the minimum qualifications for a person who occupies the other control seat as safety pilot during simulated instrument flight?

A— Private pilot certificate with appropriate category and class ratings for the aircraft.
B— Private pilot with instrument rating.
C— Private pilot with appropriate category, class, and instrument ratings.

Answer (C) is correct (4033). *(FAR 91.103)*
Each pilot in command shall, before beginning a flight, familiarize him/herself with all available information concerning that flight. For a flight under IFR or a flight not in the vicinity of an airport, this information should include weather reports and forecasts, fuel requirements, alternatives available if the planned flight cannot be completed, and any known traffic delays of which (s)he has been advised by ATC. For any flight, the preflight information should include runway lengths at airports of intended use and takeoff and landing distance data.
Answer (A) is incorrect because listing an alternate airport is not required for all IFR flights, i.e., when the destination is forecast to have ceilings above 2,000 ft. and visibility of at least 3 SM. Answer (B) is incorrect because listing an alternate airport is not required for all IFR flights, i.e., when the destination is forecast to have ceilings above 2,000 ft. and visibility of at least 3 SM.

Answer (C) is correct (4003). *(FAR 91.103)*
Each pilot in command shall, before beginning a flight, familiarize him/herself with all available information concerning that flight. For a flight under IFR or a flight not in the vicinity of an airport, this information should include weather reports and forecasts, fuel requirements, alternatives available if the planned flight cannot be completed, and any known traffic delays of which (s)he has been advised by ATC. For any flight, the preflight information should include runway lengths at airports of intended use and takeoff and landing distance information.
Answer (A) is incorrect because, while knowing what approaches are available is a good operating procedure, it is not a required preflight action. Answer (B) is incorrect because a pilot must be familiar with the airplane's takeoff and landing performance at all airports of intended use, not just the destination airport.

Answer (A) is correct (4011). *(FAR 91.109)*
No person may operate a civil aircraft in simulated instrument flight unless the other control seat is occupied by a safety pilot who possesses at least a private pilot certificate with category and class ratings appropriate to the aircraft being flown.
Answer (B) is incorrect because the safety pilot's certificate must carry an appropriate category and class (but not instrument) rating, e.g., a private pilot (helicopter) may not act as safety pilot in an airplane. Answer (C) is incorrect because the safety pilot does not need to be instrument rated.

91.123 Compliance with ATC Clearances and Instructions

27.
4407. When may ATC request a detailed report of an
emergency even though a rule has not been violated?

A— When priority has been given.
B— Any time an emergency occurs.
C— When the emergency occurs in controlled airspace.

Answer (A) is correct (4407). *(FAR 91.123)*
  Each pilot in command who is given priority by ATC in
an emergency (even though no FAR has been violated)
shall, if requested by ATC, submit a detailed report of that
emergency within 48 hr. to the manager of that ATC
facility.
  Answer (B) is incorrect because a written report may
be requested when priority is given in an emergency, not
any time an emergency occurs. Answer (C) is incorrect
because a written report may be requested when priority
is given in an emergency, regardless of where the
emergency occurs.

28.
4461. While on an IFR flight, a pilot has an emergency
which causes a deviation from an ATC clearance. What
action must be taken?

A— Notify ATC of the deviation as soon as possible.
B— Squawk 7700 for the duration of the emergency.
C— Submit a detailed report to the chief of the ATC
    facility within 48 hours.

Answer (A) is correct (4461). *(FAR 91.123)*
  Each pilot in command who, in an emergency,
deviates from an ATC clearance or instruction shall notify
ATC of that deviation as soon as possible.
  Answer (B) is incorrect because, in an emergency,
you must report a deviation from an ATC clearance as
soon as possible, not just squawk 7700 during the
emergency. Answer (C) is incorrect because a report in
48 hr. is required only if you are given priority during the
emergency and ATC requests such a report.

29.
4381. During an IFR flight in IMC, a distress condition is
encountered, (fire, mechanical, or structural failure). The
pilot should

A— not hesitate to declare an emergency and obtain an
    amended clearance.
B— wait until the situation is immediately perilous before
    declaring an emergency.
C— contact ATC and advise that an urgency condition
    exists and request priority consideration.

Answer (A) is correct (4381). *(FAR 91.123, P/C Glossary)*
  Distress is a condition of being threatened by serious
and/or imminent danger and of requiring immediate
assistance. Thus, during an IFR flight in IMC, if a distress
condition is encountered, you should immediately declare
an emergency and obtain an amended clearance.
  Answer (B) is incorrect because a distress condition is
perilous and you should not hesitate to declare an
emergency. Answer (C) is incorrect because you should
contact ATC and declare that an emergency, not urgency,
condition exists and obtain an amended clearance, not a
request for consideration.

91.129 Operations in Class D Airspace

30.
4375. The aircraft's transponder fails during flight within
Class D airspace.

A— The pilot should immediately request clearance to
    depart the Class D airspace.
B— No deviation is required because a transponder is
    not required in Class D airspace.
C— Pilot must immediately request priority handling to
    proceed to destination.

Answer (B) is correct (4375). *(FAR 91.129)*
  If an aircraft's transponder fails during flight within
Class D airspace, no deviation is required because a
transponder is not required in Class D airspace.
  Answer (A) is incorrect because, since a transponder
is not required in Class D airspace, the pilot does not
need to depart the Class D airspace. Answer (C) is
incorrect because, since a transponder is not required in
Class D airspace, a pilot does not need priority handling
to proceed to his/her destination.

91.131 Operations in Class B Airspace

31.
4426. In addition to a VOR receiver and two-way communications capability, which additional equipment is required for IFR operation in Class B airspace?

A— DME and an operable coded transponder. having Mode C capability.

B— Standby communications receiver, DME, and coded transponder.

C— An operable coded transponder having Mode C capability.

Answer (C) is correct (4426). *(FAR 91.131)*
Unless otherwise authorized by ATC, no person may operate an aircraft within Class B airspace unless that aircraft is equipped with

1. An operable two-way radio,
2. An operable 4096-code transponder having Mode C capability, and
3. For IFR operations, an operable VOR or TACAN receiver.

Answer (A) is incorrect because DME is not required. Answer (B) is incorrect because a standby radio receiver and DME are not required, and the transponder must have Mode C capability.

32.
4440. Which of the following is required equipment for operating an aircraft within Class B airspace?

A— A 4096 code transponder with automatic pressure altitude reporting equipment.

B— A VOR receiver with DME.

C— A 4096 code transponder.

Answer (A) is correct (4440). *(FAR 91.131)*
Unless otherwise authorized by ATC, no person may operate an aircraft within Class B airspace unless that aircraft is equipped with

1. An operable two-way radio,
2. An operable 4096-code transponder having Mode C capability, and
3. For IFR operations, an operable VOR or TACAN receiver.

Answer (B) is incorrect because DME is not required and a VOR receiver is only required when operating IFR. Answer (C) is incorrect because the 4096-code transponder must also have Mode C capability.

91.135 Operations in Class A Airspace

33.
4024. When are you required to have an instrument rating for flight in VMC?

A— Flight through an MOA.

B— Flight into an ADIZ.

C— Flight into Class A airspace.

Answer (C) is correct (4024). *(FAR 91.135)*
No person may operate an aircraft within Class A airspace at any time unless (s)he is rated for instrument flight and is on an instrument flight plan.
Answer (A) is incorrect because an instrument rating is not required for flight through an MOA in VMC. Answer (B) is incorrect because an instrument rating is not required for flight into an ADIZ (air defense identification zone) in VMC.

34.
4066. When is an IFR clearance required during VFR weather conditions?

A— When operating in the Class E airspace.

B— When operating in a Class A airspace.

C— When operating in airspace above 14,500 feet.

Answer (B) is correct (4066). *(FAR 91.135, 91.173)*
No person may operate an aircraft within Class A airspace unless the aircraft is operated under an IFR clearance, regardless of the weather conditions. Class A airspace includes the airspace from 18,000 ft. MSL up to and including FL 600.
Answer (A) is incorrect because an IFR clearance is not required in VMC in Class E airspace. Answer (C) is incorrect because an IFR clearance is not required in VMC in Class E airspace from 14,500 ft. MSL up to but not including 18,000 ft. MSL.

35.
4062. When is an IFR flight plan required?

A— When less than VFR conditions exist in either Class E or Class G airspace and in Class A airspace.

B— In all Class E airspace when conditions are below VFR, in Class A airspace, and in defense zone airspace.

C— In Class E airspace when IMC exists or in Class A airspace.

Answer (C) is correct (4062). *(FAR 91.135, 91.173)*
No person may operate an aircraft in Class E airspace in IMC unless (s)he has filed an IFR flight plan and received an appropriate ATC clearance. Furthermore, under FAR 91.135, no one may operate in Class A airspace unless the aircraft is operated under IFR at a specific flight level assigned by ATC. This implies having filed an IFR flight plan for Class A airspace also.
Answer (A) is incorrect because, while an instrument rating is required, an IFR flight plan is not required in Class G airspace. Answer (B) is incorrect because VFR flights are permitted when VFR weather conditions exist in air defense identification zones (ADIZ).

36.
4067. Operation in which airspace requires filing an IFR flight plan?

A— Any airspace when the visibility is less than 1 mile.

B— Class E airspace with IMC and Class A airspace.

C— Positive control area, Continental Control Area, and all other airspace, if the visibility is less than 1 mile.

Answer (B) is correct (4067). *(FAR 91.135, 91.173)*
No person may operate an aircraft in Class E airspace in IMC unless (s)he has filed an IFR flight plan and received an appropriate ATC clearance. Furthermore, under FAR 91.135, no one may operate in Class A airspace unless the aircraft is operated under IFR at a specific flight level assigned by ATC. This implies having filed an IFR flight plan for Class A airspace also.
Answer (A) is incorrect because an IFR flight plan is not required in Class G airspace. Answer (C) is incorrect because an IFR flight plan is not required in uncontrolled Class G airspace.

91.155 Basic VFR Weather Minimums

37.
4519. What is the required flight visibility and distance from clouds if you are operating in Class E airspace at 9,500 feet MSL with a VFR-on-Top clearance during daylight hours?

A— 3 SM, 1,000 feet above, 500 feet below, and 2,000 feet horizontal.

B— 5 SM, 500 feet above, 1,000 feet below, and 2,000 feet horizontal.

C— 3 SM, 500 feet above, 1,000 feet below, and 2,000 feet horizontal.

Answer (A) is correct (4519). *(FAR 91.155)*
In Class E airspace below 10,000 ft. MSL, the basic VFR weather minimums are flight visibility of 3 SM and a distance from clouds of 500 ft. below, 1,000 ft. above, and 2,000 ft. horizontal.
Answer (B) is incorrect because the visibility requirement is 3, not 5, SM and the distances from clouds above and below are reversed. It should be 1,000 ft. above and 500 ft. below. Answer (C) is incorrect because the distances from clouds above and below are reversed. It should be 1,000 ft. above and 500 ft. below.

38.
4518. What is the minimum flight visibility and distance from clouds for flight at 10,500 feet with a VFR-on-Top clearance during daylight hours? (Class E airspace.)

A— 3 SM, 1,000 feet above, 500 feet below, and 2,000 feet horizontal.

B— 5 SM, 1,000 feet above, 1,000 feet below, and 1 mile horizontal.

C— 5 SM, 1,000 feet above, 500 feet below, and 1 mile horizontal.

Answer (B) is correct (4518). *(FAR 91.155)*
In Class E airspace at or above 10,000 ft. MSL, the basic VFR weather minimums are flight visibility of 5 SM and a distance from clouds of 1,000 ft. above or below and 1 SM horizontal.
Answer (A) is incorrect because 3 SM, 1,000 ft. above, 500 ft. below, and 2,000 ft. horizontal are the minimum flight visibility and distance from clouds in Class E airspace below, not at or above, 10,000 ft. MSL. Answer (C) is incorrect because the vertical separation from clouds is 1,000 ft. both above and below.

39.
4524. (Refer to figure 92 on page 132.) What is the minimum in-flight visibility and distance from clouds required for an airplane operating less than 1,200 feet AGL during daylight hours in area 6?

A— 3 miles; (I) 1,000 feet; (K) 2,000 feet; (L) 500 feet.
B— 1 mile; (I) clear of clouds; (K) clear of clouds; (L) clear of clouds.
C— 1 mile; (I) 500 feet; (K) 1,000 feet; (L) 500 feet.

40.
4522. (Refer to figure 92 on page 132.) What is the minimum in-flight visibility and distance from clouds required in VFR conditions above clouds at 13,500 feet MSL (above 1,200 feet AGL) in Class G airspace during daylight hours for area 2?

A— 5 miles; (A) 1,000 feet; (C) 2,000 feet; (D) 500 feet.
B— 3 miles; (A) 1,000 feet; (C) 1 mile; (D) 1,000 feet.
C— 5 miles; (A) 1,000 feet; (C) 1 mile; (D) 1,000 feet.

41.
4523. (Refer to figure 92 on page 132.) What in-flight visibility and distance from clouds is required for a flight at 8,500 feet MSL (above 1,200 feet AGL) in Class G airspace in VFR conditions during daylight hours in area 4?

A— 1 mile; (E) 1,000 feet; (G) 2,000 feet; (H) 500 feet.
B— 3 miles; (E) 1,000 feet; (G) 2,000 feet; (H) 500 feet.
C— 5 miles; (E) 1,000 feet; (G) 1 mile; (H) 1,000 feet.

42.
4520. (Refer to figure 92 on page 132.) What is the minimum in-flight visibility and distance from clouds required for a VFR-on-Top flight at 9,500 feet MSL (above 1,200 feet AGL) during daylight hours for area 3?

A— 2,000 feet; (E) 1,000 feet; (F) 2,000 feet; (H) 500 feet.
B— 5 miles; (E) 1,000 feet; (F) 2,000 feet; (H) 500 feet.
C— 3 miles; (E) 1,000 feet; (F) 2,000 feet; (H) 500 feet.

43.
4521. (Refer to figure 92 on page 132.) A flight is to be conducted in VFR-on-Top conditions at 12,500 feet MSL (above 1,200 feet AGL). What is the in-flight visibility and distance from clouds required for operation in Class E airspace during daylight hours for area 1?

A— 5 miles; (A) 1,000 feet; (B) 2,000 feet; (D) 500 feet.
B— 5 miles; (A) 1,000 feet; (B) 1 mile; (D) 1,000 feet.
C— 3 miles; (A) 1,000 feet; (B) 2,000 feet; (D) 1,000 feet.

Answer (B) is correct (4524). *(FAR 91.155)*
In Class G airspace at or below 1,200 ft. AGL (Area 6 in Fig. 92), the basic VFR weather minimums during daylight hours are in-flight visibility of 1 SM and clear of clouds.
Answer (A) is incorrect because 3 SM visibility, 1,000 ft. above, 500 ft. below, and 2,000 ft. horizontal are the minimum visibility and distance from clouds in VFR flight in Area 6 at night, not in daylight. Answer (C) is incorrect because no such combination of requirements exists in any airspace.

Answer (C) is correct (4522). *(FAR 91.155)*
In Class G airspace at more than 1,200 ft. AGL and at or above 10,000 ft. MSL (Area 2 in Fig. 92), the basic VFR weather minimums are in-flight visibility of 5 SM and a distance from clouds of 1,000 ft. above or below and 1 SM horizontal.
Answer (A) is incorrect because 1,000 ft. above, 2,000 ft. horizontal, and 500 ft. below are the minimum cloud distances for VFR in Class G airspace above 1,200 ft. AGL and below, not at or above, 10,000 ft. MSL. Answer (B) is incorrect because visibility minimum is 5 SM, not 3 SM.

Answer (A) is correct (4523). *(FAR 91.155)*
In Class G airspace at more than 1,200 ft. AGL but less than 10,000 ft. MSL (Area 4 in Fig. 92), the basic VFR weather minimums during daylight hours are in-flight visibility of 1 SM and a distance from clouds of 500 ft. below, 1,000 ft. above, and 2,000 ft. horizontal.
Answer (B) is incorrect because the in-flight visibility of 3 SM is required for a night, not day, flight. Answer (C) is incorrect because in-flight visibility of 5 SM and a distance from clouds of 1,000 ft. above or below and 1 SM horizontal are the VFR weather minimums in Class G airspace above 1,200 ft. AGL and at or above, not below, 10,000 ft. MSL.

Answer (C) is correct (4520). *(FAR 91.155)*
In Class E airspace at less than 10,000 ft. MSL (Area 3 in Fig. 92), the basic VFR weather minimums are in-flight visibility of 3 SM and a distance from clouds of 500 ft. below, 1,000 ft. above, and 2,000 ft. horizontal.
Answer (A) is incorrect because the visibility required is 3 SM, not 2,000 ft. Answer (B) is incorrect because the visibility required is 3 SM, not 5 SM.

Answer (B) is correct (4521). *(FAR 91.155)*
In Class E airspace at or above 10,000 ft. MSL (Area 1 in Fig. 92), the basic VFR weather minimums are in-flight visibility of 5 SM and a distance from clouds of 1,000 ft. above or below and 1 SM horizontal.
Answer (A) is incorrect because the distance-from-clouds requirements listed are for below, not at or above, 10,000 ft. MSL. Answer (C) is incorrect because the visibility requirement is 5 SM, not 3 SM, and the horizontal separation requirement from clouds is 1 SM, not 2,000 ft.

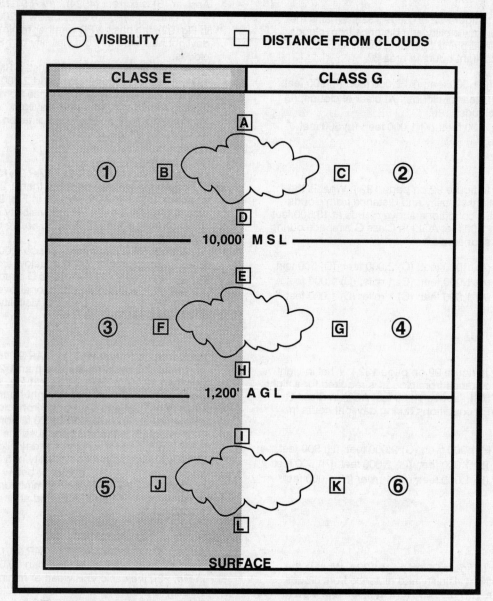

FIGURE 92.—Minimum In-Flight Visibility and Distance from Clouds.

91.157 Special VFR Weather Minimums

44.
4525. (Refer to figure 92 above.) What is the minimum in-flight visibility and distance from clouds required for an airplane operating less than 1,200 feet AGL under special VFR during daylight hours in area 5?

A— 1 mile; (I) 2,000 feet; (J) 2,000 feet; (L) 500 feet.
B— 3 miles; (I) clear of clouds; (J) clear of clouds; (L) 500 feet.
C— 1 mile; (I) clear of clouds; (J) clear of clouds; (L) clear of clouds.

Answer (C) is correct (4525). *(FAR 91.157)*
In Class E airspace when an airplane is operating under special VFR, the distance-from-clouds requirement is clear of clouds. No one may take off or land an airplane under special VFR unless ground visibility is at least 1 SM. If ground visibility is not reported, the in-flight visibility during takeoff or landing must be at least 1 SM.
Answer (A) is incorrect because special VFR permits operation just clear of clouds. Answer (B) is incorrect because special VFR permits operation just clear of clouds and with a minimum visibility of 1 SM, not 3 SM.

91.167 Fuel Requirements for Flight in IFR Conditions

45.
4032. What are the minimum fuel requirements in IFR conditions, if the first airport of intended landing is forecast to have a 1,500-foot ceiling and 3 miles visibility at flight-planned ETA? Fuel to fly to the first airport of intended landing,

A— and fly thereafter for 45 minutes at normal cruising speed.

B— fly to the alternate, and fly thereafter for 45 minutes at normal cruising speed.

C— fly to the alternate, and fly thereafter for 30 minutes at normal cruising speed.

Answer (B) is correct (4032). *(FAR 91.167)*
In general, no person may operate a civil aircraft in IFR conditions unless it carries enough fuel (considering weather reports, forecasts, and conditions) to complete the flight to the first airport of intended landing, fly from that airport to the alternate airport, and fly after that for 45 min. at normal cruising speed.

Answer (A) is incorrect because an alternate airport is required because the destination airport, from 1 hr. before to 1 hr. after ETA, has a forecast ceiling of less than 2,000 ft. AGL. Answer (C) is incorrect because the fuel requirement after the alternate is 45 min., not 30 min.

46.
4005. During your preflight planning for an IFR flight, you determine that the first airport of intended landing has no instrument approach prescribed in 14 CFR part 97. The weather forecast for one hour before through one hour after your estimated time of arrival is 3,000 ft. scattered with 5 miles visibility. To meet the fuel requirements for this flight, you must be able to fly to the first airport of intended landing,

A— and then fly for 45 minutes at normal cruising speed.

B— then to the alternate airport, and then for 45 minutes at normal cruising speed.

C— then to the alternate airport, and then for 30 minutes at normal cruising speed.

Answer (B) is correct (4005). *(FAR 91.167)*
You may not operate an aircraft (other than a helicopter) under IFR unless it carries sufficient fuel to fly to the first airport of intended landing, fly from that airport to the alternate airport, and fly thereafter for 45 minutes at normal cruising speed. An alternate airport is not required if the forecast weather conditions from one hour before to one hour after your estimated time of arrival call for a 2,000-ft. ceiling and 3 SM visibility, and your destination airport has at least one approved instrument approach procedure (IAP). Because your destination airport (first airport of intended landing) has no IAP, you must file an alternate airport and meet the applicable fuel requirements.

Answer (A) is incorrect because you are required to file an alternate airport and meet the applicable fuel requirements because your destination airport has no IAP. Answer (C) is incorrect because you would be required to carry fuel sufficient for only 30 minutes at normal cruising speed after flying to the alternate airport if you were flying a helicopter, not an airplane. Airplanes must be able to fly for 45 minutes at normal cruising speed.

91.169 IFR Flight Plan: Information Required

47.
4082. For aircraft other than helicopters, is an alternate airport required for an IFR flight to ATL (Atlanta Hartsfield) if the proposed ETA is 1930Z?

TAF KATL 121720Z 121818 20012KT 5SM HZ BKN030
  FM2000 3SM TSRA OVC025CB
  FM2200 33015G20KT P6SM BKN015 OVC040 BECMG
  0608 02008KT BKN040 BECMG 1012 00000KT P6SM
  CLR=

A— Yes, because the ceiling could fall below 2,000 feet within 2 hours before to 2 hours after the ETA.

B— No, because the ceiling and visibility are forecast to remain at or above 1,000 feet and 3 miles, respectively.

C— No, because the ceiling and visibility are forecast to be at or above 2,000 feet and 3 miles within 1 hour before to 1 hour after the ETA.

Answer (C) is correct (4082). *(FAR 91.169)*
Since the ETA is 1930Z, you must check the forecast from 1830Z to 2030Z. In the TAF given, you will use the first forecast period (which is valid from 1800 to 2000Z) and the second forecast period (which is valid from 2000 to 2200Z). The lowest visibility and ceiling are forecast from 2000 to 2200Z. The visibility is 3 SM, and the ceiling is 2,500 ft. Thus, no alternate airport is required because the ceiling and visibility are forecast to be at or above 2,000 ft. and 3 SM within 1 hr. before to 1 hr. after the ETA.

Answer (A) is incorrect because the time frame of concern is 1 hr., not 2 hr., before and after the ETA. Answer (B) is incorrect because the ceiling must remain at least 2,000 ft., not 1,000 ft., for an alternate not to be required.

48.
4719. When a pilot elects to proceed to the selected alternate airport, which minimums apply for landing at the alternate?

A— 600-1 if the airport has an ILS.

B— Ceiling 200 feet above the published minimum; visibility 2 miles.

C— The landing minimums for the approach to be used.

Answer (C) is correct (4719). *(FAR 91.169)*
When one goes to an alternate airport to land, the landing minimums for the particular approach, not the minimums for listing the airport as an alternate, are the minimums to be used for the approach.

Answer (A) is incorrect because, to be listed on the flight plan as an alternate airport, the weather conditions at the estimated time of arrival at the alternate must be a 600-ft. ceiling and 2 SM, not 1 SM, visibility. Answer (B) is incorrect because the published approach minimums, not some adjustment thereof, should be used.

49.
4630. If a pilot elects to proceed to the selected alternate, the landing minimums used at that airport should be the

A— minimums specified for the approach procedure selected.
B— alternate minimums shown on the approach chart.
C— minimums shown for that airport in a separate listing of "IFR Alternate Minimums."

Answer (A) is correct (4630). *(FAR 91.169)*
When one goes to an alternate airport to land, the landing minimums for the particular approach, not the minimums for listing the airport as an alternate, are the approach minimums to be used for the approach.
Answer (B) is incorrect because alternate minimums shown on the approach chart refer to the weather conditions required to list that airport as an alternate on your IFR flight plan, not to land there. Answer (C) is incorrect because alternate minimums shown on the approach chart refer to the weather conditions required to list that airport as an alternate on your IFR flight plan, not to land there.

50.
4081. What minimum weather conditions must be forecast for your ETA at an alternate airport, that has only a VOR approach with standard alternate minimums, for the airport to be listed as an alternate on the IFR flight plan?

A— 800-foot ceiling and 1 statute mile visibility.
B— 800-foot ceiling and 2 statute miles visibility.
C— 1,000-foot ceiling and visibility to allow descent from minimum en route altitude (MEA), approach, and landing under basic VFR.

Answer (B) is correct (4081). *(FAR 91.169)*
Unless otherwise authorized, no one may include an alternate airport with only a nonprecision approach in an IFR flight plan unless current weather forecasts indicate that, at the ETA at the alternate airport, the ceiling will be at least 800 ft. and 2 SM visibility.
Answer (A) is incorrect because the visibility requirement is 2 SM, not 1 SM. Answer (C) is incorrect because, if no instrument approach procedure is available at an airport, the ceiling and visibility minimums are those allowing descent from the MEA, approach, and landing under basic VFR.

51.
4083. For aircraft other than helicopters, what minimum conditions must exist at the destination airport to avoid listing an alternate airport on an IFR flight plan when a standard IAP is available?

A— From 2 hours before to 2 hours after ETA, forecast ceiling 2,000, and visibility 2 and ½ miles.
B— From 2 hours before to 2 hours after ETA, forecast ceiling 3,000, and visibility 3 miles.
C— From 1 hour before to 1 hour after ETA, forecast ceiling 2,000, and visibility 3 miles.

Answer (C) is correct (4083). *(FAR 91.169)*
An alternate airport is not required to be listed on an IFR flight plan if the destination airport has a standard instrument approach procedure available and, for at least 1 hr. before and 1 hr. after the estimated time of arrival, the weather reports or forecasts, or any combination of them, indicate

1. The ceiling will be at least 2,000 ft. above the airport elevation; and
2. The visibility will be at least 3 SM.

Answer (A) is incorrect because the destination weather condition forecast is from 1 hr., not 2 hr., before and after ETA, and the visibility must be at least 3 SM, not 2½ SM. Answer (B) is incorrect because the destination weather condition forecast is from 1 hr., not 2 hr., before and after ETA, and the ceiling must be at least 2,000 ft. AGL, not 3,000 ft. AGL.

52.
4086. What are the minimum weather conditions that must be forecast to list an airport as an alternate when the airport has no approved IAP?

A— The ceiling and visibility at ETA, 2,000 feet and 3 miles, respectively.
B— The ceiling and visibility from 2 hours before until 2 hours after ETA, 2,000 feet and 3 miles, respectively.
C— The ceiling and visibility at ETA must allow descent from MEA, approach, and landing, under basic VFR.

Answer (C) is correct (4086). *(FAR 91.169)*
Unless otherwise authorized, no one may include an alternate airport that has no instrument approach in an IFR flight plan unless current weather forecasts indicate that, at the ETA at the alternate airport, the ceiling and visibility will allow descent from the MEA, approach, and landing under basic VFR.
Answer (A) is incorrect because an alternate must be listed on your IFR flight plan unless the weather at your destination is forecast, from 1 hr. before to 1 hr. after ETA, to have a ceiling of 2,000 ft. and visibility of 3 SM. Answer (B) is incorrect because an alternate must be listed on your IFR flight plan, unless the weather at your destination is forecast, from 1 hr., not 2 hr., before to 1 hr. after ETA, to have at least a 2,000-ft. ceiling and visibility of 3 SM.

53.
4085. What standard minimums are required to list an airport as an alternate on an IFR flight plan if the airport has VOR approach only?

A— Ceiling and visibility at ETA, 800 feet and 2 miles, respectively.

B— Ceiling and visibility from 2 hours before until 2 hours after ETA, 800 feet and 2 miles, respectively.

C— Ceiling and visibility at ETA, 600 feet and 2 miles, respectively.

54.
4087. For aircraft other than helicopters, what minimum weather conditions must be forecast for your ETA at an alternate airport that has a precision approach procedure, with standard alternate minimums, in order to list it as an alternate for the IFR flight?

A— 600-foot ceiling and 2 SM visibility at your ETA.

B— 600-foot ceiling and 2 SM visibility from 2 hours before to 2 hours after your ETA.

C— 800-foot ceiling and 2 SM visibility at your ETA.

55.
4760. What are the alternate minimums that must be forecast at the ETA for an airport that has a precision approach procedure?

A— 400-foot ceiling and 2 miles visibility.

B— 600-foot ceiling and 2 miles visibility.

C— 800-foot ceiling and 2 miles visibility.

56.
4769. An airport without an authorized IAP may be included on an IFR flight plan as an alternate, if the current weather forecast indicates that the ceiling and visibility at the ETA will

A— allow for descent from the IAF to landing under basic VFR conditions.

B— be at least 1,000 feet and 1 mile.

C— allow for a descent from the MEA, approach, and a landing under basic VFR conditions.

56a.
0601-772. When an alternate airport is required, what are the weather minimums that must be forecast at the ETA for an alternate airport that has a precision approach procedure?

A— Ceiling 200 feet above the approach minimums and at least 1 statute mile visibility, but not less than the minimum visibility for the approach.

B— 600 foot ceiling and 2 statute miles visibility.

C— Ceiling 200 feet above field elevation and visibility 1 statute mile, but not less than the minimum visibility for the approach.

Answer (A) is correct (4085). *(FAR 91.169)*
Unless otherwise authorized, no person may include an alternate airport that has only a VOR (i.e., nonprecision) approach in an IFR flight plan unless current weather forecasts indicate that at the ETA at the alternate airport the ceiling is at least 800 ft. and visibility is 2 SM.
Answer (B) is incorrect because the alternate airport weather minimums apply to the ETA, not 2 hr. plus or minus. Answer (C) is incorrect because 600 ft. and 2 SM are the alternate airport weather minimums for a precision approach, i.e., ILS.

Answer (A) is correct (4087). *(FAR 91.169)*
Unless otherwise authorized, no person may include an alternate airport that has a precision (ILS) approach in an IFR flight plan unless current weather forecasts indicate that at the ETA at the alternate airport the ceiling is at least 600 ft. and visibility is 2 SM.
Answer (B) is incorrect because the alternate airport weather minimums apply to the ETA, not 2 hr. plus or minus. Answer (C) is incorrect because 800 ft. and 2 SM are the alternate airport minimums for a nonprecision approach.

Answer (B) is correct (4760). *(FAR 91.169)*
Unless otherwise authorized, no person may include an alternate airport that has a precision (ILS) approach in an IFR flight plan unless current weather forecasts indicate that at the ETA at the alternate airport the ceiling is at least 600 ft. and visibility is 2 SM.
Answer (A) is incorrect because 400 ft. is not a standard minimum ceiling used as an alternative airport minimum. Answer (C) is incorrect because 800 ft. and 2 SM are the alternate airport minimums for nonprecision approaches.

Answer (C) is correct (4769). *(FAR 91.169)*
Unless otherwise authorized, no person may include an alternate airport that does not have a standard instrument approach on an IFR flight plan unless current weather forecasts indicate that at the ETA at the alternate airport the ceiling and visibility will allow for a descent from the MEA, approach, and landing under basic VFR conditions.
Answer (A) is incorrect because descent must be possible from the MEA, not the IAF (initial approach fix), under basic VFR conditions. Answer (B) is incorrect because 800 ft., not 1,000 ft., and 2 SM, not 1 SM, are the standard alternate airport weather minimums at ETA for a nonprecision approach procedure.

Answer (B) is correct (0601-772). *(FAR 91.169)*
Unless otherwise authorized, no person may include an alternate airport that has a precision (ILS) approach in an IFR flight plan unless current weather forecasts indicate that at the ETA at the alternate airport the ceiling is at least 600 ft. and visibility is 2 SM.
Answer (A) is incorrect because 600 ft., not 200 ft. above minimums, is the minimum ceiling; and 2 SM, not 1 SM, is the minimum visibility required to list an airport with a precision approach as an alternate. Answer (C) is incorrect because 600 ft., not 200 ft., and 2 SM, not 1 SM, are the alternate minimums for airports with precision approaches.

91.171 VOR Equipment Check for IFR Operations

57.
4046. What record shall be made in the aircraft log or other permanent record by the pilot making the VOR operational check?

A— The date, place, bearing error, and signature.
B— The date, frequency of VOR or VOT, number of flight hours since last check, and signature.
C— The date, place, bearing error, aircraft total time, and signature.

Answer (A) is correct (4046). *(FAR 91.171)*
Each person making the VOR operational check shall enter the date, place, and bearing error and sign the aircraft log or other record.
Answer (B) is incorrect because VOR frequency and number of flight hr. since last check are not required. Answer (C) is incorrect because the aircraft's total time is not required.

58.
4036. When must an operational check on the aircraft VOR equipment be accomplished when used to operate under IFR?

A— Within the preceding 10 days or 10 hours of flight time.
B— Within the preceding 30 days or 30 hours of flight time.
C— Within the preceding 30 days.

Answer (C) is correct (4036). *(FAR 91.171)*
No person may operate a civil aircraft under IFR using the VOR system of radio navigation unless the VOR equipment of that aircraft is maintained, checked, and inspected under an approved procedure, or has been operationally checked within the preceding 30 days and was found to be within the limits of the permissible indicated bearing error.
Answer (A) is incorrect because it must be checked every 30 days, not 10 days or 10 hr. Answer (B) is incorrect because there is no time requirement regarding hours of flight time.

59.
4044. Which data must be recorded in the aircraft log or other appropriate log by a pilot making a VOR operational check for IFR operations?

A— VOR name or identification, date of check, amount of bearing error, and signature.
B— Place of operational check, amount of bearing error, date of check, and signature.
C— Date of check, VOR name or identification, place of operational check, and amount of bearing error.

Answer (B) is correct (4044). *(FAR 91.171)*
Each person making the VOR operational check shall enter the date, place, and bearing error and sign the aircraft log or other record.
Answer (A) is incorrect because the place of operational check rather than the VOR name or identification is required. Answer (C) is incorrect because a signature is required, but the VOR name is not required.

60.
4054. When making an airborne VOR check, what is the maximum allowable tolerance between the two indicators of a dual VOR system (units independent of each other except the antenna)?

A— 4° between the two indicated bearings of a VOR.
B— Plus or minus 4° when set to identical radials of a VOR.
C— 6° between the two indicated radials of a VOR.

Answer (A) is correct (4054). *(FAR 91.171)*
If a dual VOR system (units independent of each other except the antenna) is installed in the aircraft, you may check one system against the other. You tune both systems to the same VOR station and note the indicated bearings to that station. The maximum permissible variation between the two indicated bearings is 4°.
Answer (B) is incorrect because you center the CDI and note the bearing, not set both VORs to the same radial. Answer (C) is incorrect because the maximum allowable difference between the two VORs is 4°, not 6°, of the indicated radial.

61.
4048. Which checks and inspections of flight instruments or instrument systems must be accomplished before an aircraft can be flown under IFR?

A— VOR within 30 days, altimeter systems within 24 calendar months, and transponder within 24 calendar months.
B— ELT test within 30 days, altimeter systems within 12 calendar months, and transponder within 24 calendar months.
C— VOR within 24 calendar months, transponder within 24 calendar months, and altimeter system within 12 calendar months.

Answer (A) is correct (4048). *(FARs 91.171, 91.411, and 91.413)*
No person may operate a civil aircraft under IFR using the VOR system of radio navigation unless the VOR equipment of that aircraft is maintained, checked, and inspected under an approved procedure, or has been operationally checked within the preceding 30 days and was found to be within the limits of the permissible indicated bearing error. Also, within the preceding 24 calendar months, each altimeter system and transponder must be tested, inspected, and found to comply with the regulations.
Answer (B) is incorrect because check and inspection of the altimeter system is required every 24 months, not 12 months, and ELTs must be inspected every 12 months, not tested within 30 days. Answer (C) is incorrect because VORs must be checked within 30 days, not 24 months, and altimeter systems must be inspected within 24 months, not 12 months.

62.
4372. What is the maximum tolerance allowed for an operational VOR equipment check when using a VOT?

A— Plus or minus 4°.
B— Plus or minus 6°.
C— Plus or minus 8°.

Answer (A) is correct (4372). *(FAR 91.171)*
When using a VOT for an operational VOR equipment check, the maximum permissible indicated bearing error is plus or minus 4°.
Answer (B) is incorrect because plus or minus 6° is the maximum error allowed when using an airborne checkpoint. Answer (C) is incorrect because plus or minus 8° is not an acceptable error for any type of VOR equipment check.

91.173 ATC Clearance and Flight Plan Required

63.
4068. When departing from an airport located outside controlled airspace during IMC, you must file an IFR flight plan and receive a clearance before

A— takeoff.
B— entering IFR conditions.
C— entering Class E airspace.

Answer (C) is correct (4068). *(FAR 91.173)*
No person may operate an aircraft in controlled airspace under IFR unless (s)he has filed an IFR flight plan and received an appropriate ATC clearance.
Answer (A) is incorrect because an IFR flight plan and clearance are not required until you enter controlled airspace. Answer (B) is incorrect because an IFR flight plan and clearance are not required until you enter controlled airspace.

64.
4065. To operate an aircraft under IFR, a flight plan must have been filed and an ATC clearance received prior to

A— controlling the aircraft solely by use of instruments.
B— entering weather conditions in any airspace.
C— entering controlled airspace.

Answer (C) is correct (4065). *(FAR 91.173)*
No person may operate an aircraft in controlled airspace under IFR unless (s)he has filed an IFR flight plan and received an appropriate ATC clearance.
Answer (A) is incorrect because an IFR flight plan and clearance are not required until you enter controlled airspace. Answer (B) is incorrect because an IFR flight plan and clearance are not required until you enter controlled airspace.

65.
4064. To operate under IFR below 18,000 feet, a pilot must file an IFR flight plan and receive an appropriate ATC clearance prior to

A— entering controlled airspace.
B— entering weather conditions below VFR minimums.
C— takeoff.

Answer (A) is correct (4064). *(FAR 91.173)*
No person may operate an aircraft in controlled airspace under IFR unless (s)he has filed an IFR flight plan and received an appropriate ATC clearance.
Answer (B) is incorrect because an IFR flight plan and clearance are not required until you enter controlled airspace. Answer (C) is incorrect because an IFR flight plan and clearance are not required until you enter controlled airspace.

66.
4063. Prior to which operation must an IFR flight plan be filed and an appropriate ATC clearance received?

A— Flying by reference to instruments in controlled airspace.
B— Entering controlled airspace when IMC exists.
C— Takeoff when IFR weather conditions exist.

Answer (B) is correct (4063). *(FAR 91.173)*
No person may operate an aircraft in controlled airspace under IFR unless (s)he has filed an IFR flight plan and received an appropriate ATC clearance.
Answer (A) is incorrect because you may fly by reference to instruments with a safety pilot in VFR weather conditions without an IFR flight plan or an IFR clearance. Answer (C) is incorrect because an IFR flight plan is not required until you enter controlled airspace.

67.
4427. No person may operate an aircraft in controlled airspace under IFR unless he/she files a flight plan

A— and receives a clearance by telephone prior to takeoff.
B— prior to takeoff and requests the clearance upon arrival on an airway.
C— and receives a clearance prior to entering controlled airspace.

Answer (C) is correct (4427). *(FAR 91.173)*
No person may operate an aircraft in controlled airspace under IFR unless (s)he has filed an IFR flight plan and received an appropriate ATC clearance.
Answer (A) is incorrect because it does not matter how the clearance is obtained. Answer (B) is incorrect because a person must file an IFR flight plan and receive clearance before operating in controlled airspace, e.g., a federal airway.

91.177 Minimum Altitudes for IFR Operations

68.
4006. Except when necessary for takeoff or landing or unless otherwise authorized by the Administrator, the minimum altitude for IFR flight is

A— 3,000 feet over all terrain.
B— 3,000 feet over designated mountainous terrain; 2,000 feet over terrain elsewhere.
C— 2,000 feet above the highest obstacle over designated mountainous terrain; 1,000 feet above the highest obstacle over terrain elsewhere.

Answer (C) is correct (4006). *(FAR 91.177)*
Except when necessary for takeoff or landing, no person may operate an aircraft under IFR below 2,000 ft. above the highest obstacle within a horizontal distance of 4 NM from the course to be flown over designated mountainous terrain, or 1,000 ft. above the highest obstacle within a horizontal distance of 4 NM from the course to be flown over terrain elsewhere.
Answer (A) is incorrect because the minimum IFR altitude is 2,000 ft. above the highest obstacle over mountainous terrain or 1,000 ft. over the highest obstacle over terrain elsewhere, not 3,000 ft. over all terrain. Answer (B) is incorrect because the minimum IFR altitude is 2,000 ft., not 3,000 ft., above the highest obstacle over mountainous terrain, or 1,000 ft., not 2,000 ft., above the highest obstacle over terrain elsewhere.

91.205 Powered Civil Aircraft with Standard Category U.S. Airworthiness Certificates: Instrument and Equipment Requirements

69.
4055. What minimum navigation equipment is required for IFR flight?

A— VOR/LOC receiver, transponder, and DME.
B— VOR receiver and, if in ARTS III environment, a coded transponder equipped for altitude reporting.
C— Navigation equipment appropriate to the ground facilities to be used.

Answer (C) is correct (4055). *(FAR 91.205)*
The minimum navigation equipment requirement for IFR flight is navigation equipment that is appropriate to the ground facilities to be used.
Answer (A) is incorrect because a VOR/LOC receiver and DME are required only if VORTAC stations will be used for navigation and DME fixes need to be identified. If you are using alternative means of navigation (e.g., LORAN), this equipment is not needed. A transponder is not a navigation system. Answer (B) is incorrect because a VOR is required only if using VOR stations for navigation. If using NDB stations, a VOR is not required. A transponder is not a navigation system.

70.
4050. Where is DME required under IFR?

A— At or above 24,000 feet MSL if VOR navigational equipment is required.
B— In positive control airspace.
C— Above 18,000 feet MSL.

Answer (A) is correct (4050). *(FAR 91.205)*
If VOR navigational equipment is required, no person may operate a U.S.-registered civil aircraft within the 50 states and the District of Columbia, at or above 24,000 ft. MSL (FL 240), unless that aircraft is equipped with approved distance measuring equipment (DME).
Answer (B) is incorrect because, if VOR navigational equipment is required, DME is required at or above FL 240, not only in positive control airspace. Positive control airspace is that airspace in which ATC separates all aircraft, e.g., Class A, Class B, Class C. Answer (C) is incorrect because Class A airspace begins at 18,000 ft. MSL and DME is required at or above FL 240, if VOR navigational equipment is required.

71.
4051. An aircraft operated during IFR under 14 CFR Part 91 is required to have which of the following?

A— Radar altimeter.
B— Dual VOR system.
C— Gyroscopic direction indicator.

Answer (C) is correct (4051). *(FAR 91.205)*
An aircraft operated during IFR under FAR Part 91 is required to have a gyroscopic direction indicator (directional gyro or equivalent).
Answer (A) is incorrect because only a sensitive altimeter, not a radar altimeter, is required. Answer (B) is incorrect because, if VOR navigation is to be used, only one, not two, VOR is required under FAR Part 91.

71a.
4043. Aircraft being operated under IFR are required to have, in addition to the equipment required for VFR and night, at least

A— a slip skid indicator.
B— dual VOR receivers.
C— distance measuring equipment.

Answer (A) is correct (4043). *(FAR 91.205)*
An aircraft operated under FAR Part 91 under IFR is required to have a slip-skid indicator (e.g., the ball of the turn coordinator).
Answer (B) is incorrect because the requirement is for navigational equipment appropriate to the ground facilities to be used, not necessarily dual VOR receivers. Answer (C) is incorrect because DME is required only above 24,000 ft. MSL when VOR navigational equipment is required.

71b.
4057. To meet the requirements for flight under IFR, an aircraft must be equipped with certain operable instruments and equipment. One of those required is

A— a radar altimeter.
B— a transponder with altitude reporting capability.
C— a clock with sweep second pointer or digital presentation.

Answer (C) is correct (4057). *(FAR 91.205)*
An aircraft operated under FAR Part 91 under IFR is required to have a clock displaying hours, minutes, and seconds with a sweep-second pointer or digital presentation.
Answer (A) is incorrect because a radio (radar) altimeter is required under some circumstances for Category II operations with decision heights below 150 ft. AGL, not for all flights under IFR. Answer (B) is incorrect because a transponder with altitude encoding capability is required in certain airspace areas, not for all flights under IFR.

91.211 Supplemental Oxygen

72.
4053. What is the oxygen requirement for an unpressurized aircraft at 15,000 feet?

A— All occupants must use oxygen for the entire time at this altitude.
B— Crew must start using oxygen at 12,000 feet and passengers at 15,000 feet.
C— Crew must use oxygen for the entire time above 14,000 feet and passengers must be provided supplemental oxygen only above 15,000 feet.

Answer (C) is correct (4053). *(FAR 91.211)*
No one may operate a U.S. civil aircraft at cabin pressure altitudes above 14,000 ft. MSL unless the required minimum flight crew is provided with and uses supplemental oxygen during the entire flight time at those altitudes. At cabin pressure altitudes above 15,000 ft. MSL, each passenger must be provided with supplemental oxygen.
Answer (A) is incorrect because the required minimum flight crew must use oxygen above 14,000 ft. MSL and others must be provided with oxygen above 15,000 ft. MSL. Answer (B) is incorrect because the crew must start using oxygen at 14,000 ft. MSL or after 30 min. above 12,500 ft. MSL.

73.
4052. What is the maximum IFR altitude you may fly in an unpressurized aircraft without providing passengers with supplemental oxygen?

A— 12,500 feet.
B— 14,000 feet.
C— 15,000 feet.

Answer (C) is correct (4052). *(FAR 91.211)*
At cabin pressure altitudes above 15,000 ft. MSL, each occupant must be provided with supplemental oxygen.
Answer (A) is incorrect because, at cabin pressure altitudes above 12,500 ft. MSL up to and including 14,000 ft. MSL, only the minimum flight crew must use supplemental oxygen for that part of the flight at those altitudes that is more than 30 min. duration. Answer (B) is incorrect because, at cabin pressure altitudes above 14,000 ft. MSL, only the required minimum flight crew must use supplemental oxygen.

74.
4045. What is the maximum cabin pressure altitude at which a pilot can fly for longer than 30 minutes without using supplemental oxygen?

A— 10,500 feet.
B— 12,000 feet.
C— 12,500 feet.

Answer (C) is correct (4045). *(FAR 91.211)*
No one may operate a U.S. civil aircraft at cabin pressure altitudes above 12,500 ft. MSL up to and including 14,000 ft. MSL unless the required minimum flight crew uses supplemental oxygen for that part of the flight at those altitudes that is of more than 30 min. duration.
Answer (A) is incorrect because supplemental oxygen is not required at any time at 10,500 ft. Answer (B) is incorrect because supplemental oxygen is not required at any time at 12,000 ft.

75.
4042. If an unpressurized aircraft is operated above 12,500 feet MSL, but not more than 14,000 feet MSL, for a period of 2 hours 20 minutes, how long during that time is the minimum flightcrew required to use supplemental oxygen?

A— 2 hours 20 minutes.
B— 1 hour 20 minutes.
C— 1 hour 50 minutes.

Answer (C) is correct (4042). *(FAR 91.211)*
No one may operate a U.S. civil aircraft at cabin pressure altitudes above 12,500 ft. MSL up to and including 14,000 ft. MSL unless the required minimum flight crew uses supplemental oxygen for that part of the flight at those altitudes that is of more than 30 min. duration. If the flight lasts 2 hr. and 20 min., the crew must use supplemental oxygen for all but 30 min., or 1 hr. and 50 min.
Answer (A) is incorrect because one may fly for 30 min. without supplemental oxygen between 12,500 ft. MSL and 14,000 ft. MSL. Answer (B) is incorrect because 30 min. of flight, not 1 hr., is permitted without supplemental oxygen between 12,500 ft. MSL up to and including 14,000 ft. MSL.

91.215 ATC Transponder and Altitude Reporting Equipment and Use

76.
4037. In the 48 contiguous states, excluding the airspace at or below 2,500 feet AGL, an operable coded transponder equipped with Mode C capability is required in all controlled airspace at and above

A— 12,500 feet MSL.
B— 10,000 feet MSL.
C— Flight level (FL) 180.

Answer (B) is correct (4037). *(FAR 91.215)*
Unless otherwise authorized or directed by ATC, no person may operate an aircraft in the 48 contiguous states at and above 10,000 ft. MSL, excluding the airspace at or below 2,500 ft. AGL, unless the aircraft is equipped with an operable Mode C transponder.
Answer (A) is incorrect because 12,500 ft. MSL pertains to supplemental oxygen, not Mode C, requirements. Answer (C) is incorrect because FL 180 is the floor of Class A airspace.

77.
4038. A coded transponder equipped with altitude reporting capability is required in all controlled airspace

A— at and above 10,000 feet MSL, excluding at and below 2,500 feet AGL.
B— at and above 2,500 feet above the surface.
C— below 10,000 feet MSL, excluding at and below 2,500 feet AGL.

Answer (A) is correct (4038). *(FAR 91.215)*
Unless otherwise authorized or directed by ATC, no person may operate an aircraft in the 48 contiguous states at and above 10,000 ft. MSL, excluding the airspace at or below 2,500 ft. AGL, unless the aircraft is equipped with an operable Mode C transponder.
Answer (B) is incorrect because the airspace above 2,500 ft. AGL must also be at or above 10,000 ft. MSL. Answer (C) is incorrect because the limit is at and above, not below, 10,000 ft. MSL.

78.
4439. Prior to operating an aircraft not equipped with a transponder in Class B airspace, a request for a deviation must be submitted to the

A— FAA Administrator at least 24 hours before the proposed operation.
B— nearest FAA General Aviation District Office 24 hours before the proposed operation.
C— controlling ATC facility at least 1 hour before the proposed flight.

Answer (C) is correct (4439). *(FAR 91.215)*
ATC may authorize deviations on a continuing basis, or for individual flights, for operations of aircraft without a transponder. The request for a deviation must be submitted to the ATC facility having jurisdiction over the airspace concerned at least 1 hr. before the proposed operation.
Answer (A) is incorrect because a request for a deviation to operate in Class B airspace in an airplane not equipped with a transponder must be submitted to the controlling ATC facility at least 1 hr. before the proposed flight, not to the FAA Administrator at least 24 hr. before the operation. Answer (B) is incorrect because a request for a deviation to operate in Class B airspace in an airplane not equipped with a transponder must be submitted to the controlling ATC facility at least 1 hr. before the proposed flight, not to the nearest FSDO (formerly called GADO) 24 hr. before the proposed operation.

79.
4438. When an aircraft is not equipped with a transponder, what requirement must be met before ATC will authorize a flight within Class B airspace?

A— A request for the proposed flight must be made to ATC at least 1 hour before the flight.
B— The proposed flight must be conducted when operating under instrument flight rules.
C— The proposed flight must be conducted in visual meteorological conditions (VMC).

Answer (A) is correct (4438). *(FAR 91.215)*
Requests for ATC authorized deviations must be made to the ATC facility having jurisdiction over the concerned airspace. A request for a deviation from the transponder equipment requirement in Class B airspace must be made to the controlling ATC facility at least 1 hr. before the flight.
Answer (B) is incorrect because you must request a deviation from the transponder equipment requirement from ATC. The requirement is not that the proposed flight be conducted under IFR. Answer (C) is incorrect because you must request a deviation from the transponder equipment requirement from ATC. The requirement is not that the proposed flight be conducted in VMC.

80.
4007. If the aircraft's transponder fails during flight within Class B airspace,

A— the pilot should immediately request clearance to depart the Class B airspace.
B— ATC may authorize deviation from the transponder requirement to allow aircraft to continue to the airport of ultimate destination.
C— aircraft must immediately descend below 1,200 feet AGL and proceed to destination.

Answer (B) is correct (4007). *(FAR 91.215)*
If an aircraft's transponder fails during flight within Class B airspace, ATC may authorize deviation from the transponder requirement to allow the aircraft to continue to the airport of ultimate destination, including any intermediate stops, or to proceed to a place where suitable repairs can be made, or both.
Answer (A) is incorrect because ATC can immediately authorize a deviation from the transponder requirement without requiring the pilot to request clearance to depart the Class B airspace area. Answer (C) is incorrect because a pilot may descend only if clearance from ATC is obtained.

91.411 Altimeter System and Altitude Reporting Equipment Tests and Inspections

81.
4047. Your aircraft had the static pressure system and altimeter tested and inspected on January 5, of this year, and was found to comply with FAA standards. These systems must be reinspected and approved for use in controlled airspace under IFR by

A— January 5, next year.
B— January 5, 2 years hence.
C— January 31, 2 years hence.

Answer (C) is correct (4047). *(FAR 91.411)*
Within the preceding 24 calendar months, each static pressure system, each altimeter instrument, and each automatic pressure altitude reporting system must be tested, inspected, and found to comply with the regulations. The 24-calendar-month period following January of this year begins February 1, this year, and ends on January 31, 2 years hence.
Answer (A) is incorrect because these tests must be completed every 24 calendar months, not 1 year from the date of the last inspection. Answer (B) is incorrect because these tests must be completed within the preceding 24 calendar months, not 2 years from the date of the last inspection.

82.
4049. An aircraft altimeter system test and inspection must be accomplished within

A— 12 calendar months.
B— 18 calendar months.
C— 24 calendar months.

Answer (C) is correct (4049). *(FAR 91.411)*
Within the preceding 24 calendar months, each static pressure system, each altimeter instrument, and each automatic pressure altitude reporting system must be tested, inspected, and found to comply with the regulations.
Answer (A) is incorrect because an annual inspection, not the altimeter system, must be accomplished within the preceding 12 calendar months. Answer (B) is incorrect because the aircraft's altimeter system must be tested and inspected within 24, not 18, calendar months.

4.3 NTSB PART 830 NOTIFICATION AND REPORTING OF AIRCRAFT ACCIDENTS OR INCIDENTS AND OVERDUE AIRCRAFT, AND PRESERVATION OF AIRCRAFT WRECKAGE, MAIL, CARGO, AND RECORDS

83.
4088. Which publication covers the procedures required for aircraft accident and incident reporting responsibilities for pilots?

A— FAR Part 61.
B— FAR Part 91.
C— NTSB Part 830.

Answer (C) is correct (4088). *(NTSB 830.1)*
NTSB Part 830 contains rules pertaining to the following:

1. Notification and reporting aircraft accidents and incidents and certain other occurrences in the operation of aircraft when they involve civil aircraft of the U.S. wherever they occur, or foreign civil aircraft when such events occur in the U.S., its territories, or possessions.
2. Reporting aircraft accidents and listed incidents in the operation of aircraft when they involve certain public aircraft.
3. Preservation of aircraft wreckage, mail, cargo, and records involving all civil aircraft in the U.S., its territories, or possessions.

Answer (A) is incorrect because FAR Part 61 concerns certification of pilots, flight instructors, and ground instructors. Answer (B) is incorrect because FAR Part 91 concerns general operating and flight rules.

END OF CHAPTER

CHAPTER FIVE
AIRPORTS, AIR TRAFFIC CONTROL, AND AIRSPACE

This chapter contains outlines of major concepts tested; all FAA test questions and answers regarding airports, air traffic control, and airspace; and an explanation of each answer. Each module, or subtopic, within this chapter is listed above with the number of questions from the FAA knowledge test pertaining to that particular module. For each module, the first number following the parentheses is the page number on which the outline begins, and the next number is the page number on which the questions begin.

There are 114 questions in this chapter. We separate and organize the FAA questions into meaningful study units, i.e., chapters and modules. As an analogy, it is easier to deal with the "trees" if you understand the "forest." In this context, "trees" are individual FAA questions, and the "forest" is the instrument rating knowledge test. The organizational units between the overall instrument rating knowledge test and the individual instrument rating test questions are chapters and modules in this book.

CAUTION: The **sole purpose** of this book is to expedite your passing the FAA instrument rating knowledge test. Accordingly, all extraneous material (i.e., topics or regulations not directly tested on the FAA knowledge test) is omitted, even though much more information and knowledge are necessary to fly safely. This additional material is presented in *Instrument Pilot Flight Maneuvers and Practical Test Prep*, *Pilot Handbook*, *Aviation Weather and Weather Services*, and *FAR/AIM*, available from Gleim Publications, Inc. See the order form on page 488.

5.1 PRECISION INSTRUMENT RUNWAY MARKINGS (Questions 1-8)

1. The figure below depicts a precision instrument runway.

    a. The distance from the runway threshold to the fixed distance marker is 1,000 ft. (distance A).

    b. The distance from the runway threshold to the touchdown zone marker is 500 ft. (distance B).

    c. The distance from the beginning of the touchdown zone marker to the beginning of the fixed distance marker is 500 ft. (distance C).

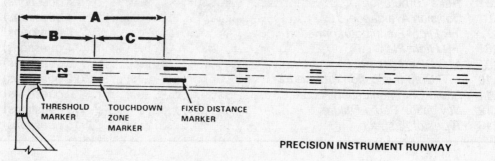

PRECISION INSTRUMENT RUNWAY

2. A displaced threshold is a threshold that is not at the beginning of a runway. It is indicated by arrows in the middle of the runway pointing to a broad, solid line across the runway. The remainder of the runway, following the displaced threshold, is the landing portion of the runway.

    a. The paved area before the displaced threshold is available for taxiing, the landing rollout, and the takeoff of aircraft, but not for landing.

    b. In Fig. 138 on page 154, the approach end of the runway is on the right. Thus, taxiing and takeoff are permitted toward the green threshold lights (marked by the arrow).

3. Runway end identifier lights (REIL) consist of a pair of synchronized flashing lights, one on each side of the runway threshold facing the approach area.

    a. REIL permit the rapid and positive identification of a runway surrounded by other lighting, lacking contrast with surrounding terrain, and/or experiencing reduced visibility.

4. Hydroplaning occurs when an aircraft's tires are separated from the runway by water.

    a. It usually occurs at high speeds when water is standing on a smooth runway.

5.2 AIRPORT SIGNS AND MARKINGS (Questions 9-12d)

1. Mandatory airport instruction signs have a red background with white lettering. Mandatory instruction signs include

    a. Runway approach area holding position signs and runway holding position signs

        1) These signs denote an entrance to a runway from a taxiway or from an intersecting runway.

2. Runway holding position markings (hold lines) at the intersection of taxiways and runways consist of four yellow lines, two solid and two dashed, that extend across the width of the taxiway with the dashed lines nearest the runway.

    a. These markings identify where an aircraft is to hold short of the runway.

3. Direction signs consist of black lettering on a yellow background.

    a. These signs indicate the designation (name) and direction (orientation) of taxiways leading out of an intersection.

5.3 VISUAL APPROACH SLOPE INDICATOR (VASI) (Questions 13-24)

1. Visual approach slope indicators (VASIs) are a system of lights that provide visual descent information during the approach to a runway.

2. The standard VASI consists of a two-barred tier of lights.

   a. If both light bars appear red, you are below the glide path. Remember this with "red means dead."

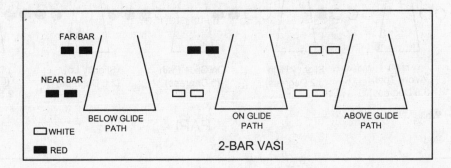

   b. If the far lights (on top visually) appear red and the near lights (on bottom visually) appear white, you are on the glide path.

      1) This glide path is normally set at 3°.

   c. If both light bars appear white, you are above the glide path.

3. Actually, each light bar marks a separate glide path. The far light bar marks a higher glide path than the glide path extended from the nearer light bar. You are between them when you are below the higher glide path and above the lower glide path.

   a. Remember that red over white (i.e., R before W alphabetically) is the desired sequence.

      1) White over red is impossible.

4. VASIs also may have three light bars, which provide a lower glide path and a higher glide path. The higher glide path marked by the middle and far light bars is intended for use by high cockpit aircraft.

   a. If the nearest light bar is white and the two farther light bars are red, you are on the lower glide path, usually 3°.

   b. If the farthest light bar is red and the two nearer light bars are white, you are on the upper glide path, usually 3.25°.

   c. Above both glide paths, all lights will be white. Below both glide paths, all lights will be red.

5. If all VASI lights appear red as you reach the MDA, you should level off momentarily to intercept the proper glide path.

6. A tricolor VASI is a single light unit projecting three colors visible for ½ to 1 mi. in daylight and about 5 mi. at night.

   a. The below glide path indicator is red.
   b. The above glide path indicator is amber.
   c. The on glide path indicator is green.

7. VASI provides only glide path guidance and safe obstruction clearance within ±10° of the extended runway centerline from as far as 4 NM from the runway threshold.

   a. It does not provide information on alignment with the runway.

5.4 PRECISION APPROACH PATH INDICATOR (PAPI) (Questions 25-29)

1.   PAPI lights are similar to VASIs, but they are installed in a single row of either two or four lights.

2.   The glide path indications are depicted below.

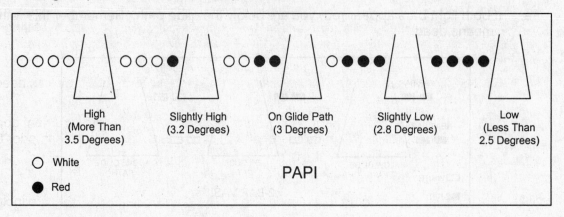

5.5 WAKE TURBULENCE (Questions 30-33)

1.   The greatest vortex strength occurs behind heavy, clean, and slow aircraft (e.g., during the takeoff of a jet transport because it has a high gross weight and a high angle of attack).

2.   Light quartering tailwinds prolong the hazards of wake turbulence the longest because they move the vortices of preceding aircraft forward to the touchdown zone and hold the upwind vortex on the runway.

    a.   A light crosswind of 3 to 7 kt. would result in an upwind vortex tending to remain over the runway.

3.   When landing behind a large aircraft on the same runway, stay at or above the other aircraft's final approach flight path, and land beyond that airplane's touchdown point.

5.6 COLLISION AVOIDANCE (Questions 34-37)

1.   When climbing to an assigned altitude on an airway, use the centerline except to avoid other aircraft when in VFR conditions.

2.   During climbs and descents in VFR conditions, execute gentle banks left and right to permit continual scanning of surrounding airspace.

3.   When weather conditions permit, i.e., VFR, you must assume the responsibility to see and avoid other aircraft, regardless of whether operating under IFR or VFR.

5.7 IFR FLIGHT PLANNING INFORMATION (Questions 38-44)

1.   Every pilot should receive a preflight briefing from a Flight Service Station (FSS), whether by telephone, radio, or personal visit.

    a.   The briefing should contain weather advisories and notices about en route airports and other navigational aids.

2.   The **Notice to Airmen (NOTAM) System** disseminates time-critical aeronautical information that is temporary in nature or not known in time to publish on charts or in procedural publications.

    a.   NOTAMs include airport or primary runway closures, changes in the status of navigational aids, instrument landing systems, radar service availability, and other information that could affect a pilot's decision to make a flight.

3. There are three categories of NOTAMs:

    a. NOTAM (D), or distant NOTAM, contains information for all navigational facilities that are part of the National Airspace System (NAS) and all public-use airports that are listed in the *Airport/Facility Directory* (A/FD).

    b. NOTAM (L), or local NOTAM, contains information that includes such data as runway closures, personnel and equipment near or crossing runways, airport rotating beacon outages, and airport lighting aids that do not affect instrument approach criteria, such as VASI.

    c. FDC NOTAM is a temporary or permanent regulatory change published as needed by the National Flight Data Center (FDC).

        1) FDC NOTAMs advise of changes in flight data which affect instrument approach procedures, and amend aeronautical charts and flight restrictions prior to normal publication.

4. NOTAMs are disseminated by two means:

    a. The most current data are disseminated via telecommunications. They are included as part of a routine pilot weather briefing given by an FSS specialist.

    b. The *Notices to Airmen Publication* (formerly Class II NOTAMs) is published every 28 days. Once published, these NOTAMs are not provided during pilot weather briefing unless specifically requested.

5. The best source of airport conditions would be to combine data available from

    a. The *Airport/Facility Directory*
    b. NOTAMs (L)
    c. NOTAMs (D)

6. **Automatic Terminal Information Service (ATIS)** broadcasts are updated whenever any official weather data are received, regardless of content change or reported values, or when there is a change in other pertinent data such as active runway, instrument approach in use, etc.

    a. Absence of the sky condition and visibility from the ATIS broadcast specifically implies that the ceiling is more than 5,000 ft. and visibility is more than 5 SM.

7. In Class B, C, D, and E surface areas, operation of an airport beacon during daylight hours usually indicates IFR weather conditions (ground visibility less than 3 SM and/or ceiling less than 1,000 ft.).

5.8 IFR FLIGHT PLAN (Questions 45-55)

1. To operate under instrument flight rules in controlled airspace, you are required to file an IFR flight plan.

    a. The FAA's standard flight plan form appears in Fig. 1 on page 164.

2. When you file a composite (part VFR, part IFR) flight plan, you should check both VFR and IFR in block 1.

3. In block 3, you are to indicate the aircraft type and special equipment.

    a. After the aircraft type, a slash is followed by a letter indicating the combination of

        1) Usable transponder
        2) DME
        3) Area navigation (RNAV) equipment

    b. Not reported are ADF or airborne radar capability.

4. When an IFR flight plan has different altitudes for different legs, you should enter the altitude only for the first leg in block 7.

5. Time en route (block 10) should be based on arrival at the point of first intended landing.

6. The fuel-on-board time (block 12) should be based upon the total usable fuel on board.

7. On composite flight plans for which the first portion of the flight is IFR, the flight plan should be a standard IFR flight plan, including

   a. Points of transition from one airway to another

   b. Fixes defining direct route segments

   c. The clearance limit fix, i.e., the point at which you will begin the VFR portion of the flight

8. When transitioning from VFR to IFR on a composite flight plan, you should contact the nearest FSS to close the VFR portion and request an ATC IFR clearance.

   a. You must obtain an IFR clearance before entering IFR conditions.

9. IFR flight plans can be canceled only if you are flying in VFR conditions outside Class A airspace.

10. When landing at an airport without a control tower or FSS on the field, the pilot must initiate IFR flight plan cancellation. The pilot may cancel

    a. By radio while airborne if conditions are VFR
    b. By radio or telephone as soon as (s)he is on the ground

11. A waypoint on an IFR flight is a predetermined geographical position used for an RNAV route or RNAV instrument approach identification or progress reporting. It is defined relative to a VORTAC position **or** by longitude and latitude; i.e., it does not have to be relative to a VORTAC.

5.9 ATC CLEARANCES (Questions 56-64)

1. Pilots of airborne aircraft should read back ATC clearances concerning altitude assignments and/or vectors and any part requiring verification.

2. An abbreviated IFR clearance includes

   a. Destination airport
   b. The route of flight, given fix-by-fix, or "as filed."
   c. Initial altitude
   d. DP (instrument departure procedure) name, number, and/or transition, if appropriate

3. When a departure clearance from an airport without an operating control tower contains a void time, the pilot must advise ATC as soon as possible (but no later than 30 min. after the void time) if a decision is made NOT to take off.

4. A cruise clearance assigns a pilot a block of airspace from the minimum IFR altitude up to and including the altitude specified in the cruise clearance.

   a. Climb and descent within the block are at the discretion of the pilot.

5.10 ATC COMMUNICATION PROCEDURES (Questions 65-86)

1. You should state your position on the airport when calling the tower for takeoff from a runway intersection (i.e., an intersection other than at the end of the runway).

2. When flying IFR, the pilot must maintain continuous contact with assigned ATC frequencies.

   a. All radio frequency changes are made at the direction of ATC.

3. When climbing or descending per ATC clearance, the pilot should use the optimum rate consistent with the aircraft to 1,000 ft. above or below the assigned altitude and then climb or descend at the rate of between 500 and 1,500 fpm until attaining the assigned altitude.

    a. It is sufficient to use a cruise climb rather than a maximum angle of climb.
    b. If you cannot climb or descend at least 500 fpm, you should notify ATC.
    c. You should lead your turns so that you remain in the center of the airway.

4. The reports that a pilot must make to ATC without a specific ATC request include

    a. At all times:

        1) Inability to climb or descend at a rate of at least 500 fpm
        2) Change in the average true airspeed at cruising altitude when it varies by more than 5% or 10 kt. from that filed in your flight plan
        3) Change from assigned altitude
        4) Missed approach
        5) Departure from any assigned holding fix or point
        6) The time and altitude when reaching holding fix or clearance limit
        7) Loss of communication or navigation capability or anything else affecting the safety of flight

    b. When not in radar contact:

        1) Departure from final approach fix inbound on final approach
        2) Correction of an estimate which appears to be more than 3 min. in error
        3) Passage over certain reporting points:

            a) Compulsory reporting points as marked by solid black triangles on en route charts
            b) Each fix used in the flight plan to define the route of flight on a direct flight not flown on radials or courses of established airways or routes

5. Your Mode C transponder should always be set to Mode C and turned ON unless otherwise requested by ATC.

6. When receiving traffic advisories from ATC, remember that the controller sees only the airplane's direction of travel, not the airplane heading.

    a. You must adjust traffic reports for any wind correction you are holding.

7. **Radar contact** means your airplane has been identified on the radar screen and radar flight following will be provided until radar identification is terminated by the controller.

8. **Resume own navigation** means that you continue to be under ATC radar surveillance but are responsible for your own navigation. No more vectors will be given.

    a. You are still in radar contact with ATC. Thus, you do not need to make position reports.

9. **Radar service terminated** means that you are no longer under ATC radar surveillance and must resume position reports at compulsory reporting points.

10. IFR flights receive separation from all IFR aircraft and participating VFR aircraft operating within the outer area of Class C airspace.

11. When flying VFR on practice instrument approaches, you must avoid IFR conditions. You do not have an IFR clearance.

12. While you should comply with all headings and altitudes assigned by ATC, you should feel free to question any assigned altitude or heading believed to be incorrect. The pilot has ultimate responsibility for safe flight.

13. When ATC requests a specified airspeed, you are expected to maintain the speed plus or minus 10 kt. based upon indicated airspeed.

14. If you cancel your IFR flight plan 10 mi. from your destination airport (located in Class D airspace), you must establish communications with the tower prior to entering the Class D airspace.

15. At airports which have a part-time control tower and an FSS located on the same airport, the FSS will provide Local Airport Advisory (LAA) service when the control tower is not in operation.

    a. The FSS provides advisory data on runways, weather, traffic patterns, etc. Advisory data do **not** constitute ATC clearance or other authoritative ATC actions.

    b. Remember, if ATC is not operating, you must cancel your own flight plan by notifying the FSS.

16. **Minimum fuel** is just an advisory to ATC that indicates an emergency situation is possible should any undue delay occur.

5.11 RADIO COMMUNICATION FAILURE (Questions 87-91a)

1. In the event of two-way communications failure, ATC will assume the pilot is operating in accordance with FAR 91.185.

    a. As always, pilot judgment is the final determinant of safest flying.

2. According to FAR 91.185, if you lose two-way communications

    a. When you are holding and you receive an expected further clearance (EFC) time, you should leave the holding pattern at the EFC time.

    b. When you are on an IFR flight in VFR weather conditions, you should continue your flight under VFR and land as soon as practicable.

    c. When you are in IFR conditions, you should continue on the route specified in your clearance (for each leg of your flight) at the highest of

        1)   The last assigned altitude
        2)   Expected altitude per ATC
        3)   MEA (minimum en route altitude)

3. When losing radio communications, you should alert ATC by setting your transponder code to 7600.

    a. If you are in an emergency situation, you should set and leave the transponder at 7700.

5.12 NAVIGATION RADIO FAILURE (Questions 92-94)

1. If your DME fails above FL 240, you should notify ATC of the failure and continue to the next airport of intended landing at which repairs or replacement of the equipment can be made.

2. When operating under IFR, you must immediately report to ATC the loss of VOR, TACAN, ADF, or LF navigation receiver capability; complete or partial loss of ILS receiver; and/or any impairment of radio communications capability.

5.13 TYPES OF AIRSPACE (Questions 95-109)

1. En Route Low-Altitude Charts show Class B, Class C, Class D, Class E, and special-use airspace.

    a. However, they do not show Class A airspace.

2. Class G (uncontrolled) airspace is airspace where ATC does not control air traffic.

3. Transition areas are Class E airspace and are used to transition between the terminal area and en route flight.

    a. When designated in conjunction with an airport which has a prescribed instrument approach, Class E airspace extends upward from 700 ft. AGL.

    b. When designated in conjunction with airway route structures, etc., Class E airspace extends upward from 1,200 ft. AGL.

    c. Both types of transition areas terminate at the base of overlying controlled airspace, i.e., Class A airspace.

4. Class A airspace is from 18,000 ft. MSL to FL 600.

5. Military operations areas (MOA) consist of airspace established for the purpose of separating certain military training activities from IFR traffic.

6. The maximum altitude at which Class G airspace will exist is 14,500 ft. MSL (excluding the airspace less than 1,500 ft. AGL).

7. Generally, the maximum altitude for Class B airspace is 10,000 ft. MSL.

8. The normal lateral limit for Class D airspace is 4 NM.

9. The normal upper limit of Class D airspace is 2,500 ft. AGL.

10. Class C airspace consists of controlled airspace within which all aircraft are subject to the operating rules and equipment requirements specified in FAR Part 91.

    a. Aircraft must be equipped with two-way radio communications and a Mode C transponder.

QUESTIONS AND ANSWER EXPLANATIONS

All the FAA questions from the instrument rating knowledge test relating to airports, Air Traffic Control, and airspace and the material outlined previously are reproduced on the following pages in the same modules as the outlines. To the immediate right of each question are the correct answer and answer explanation. You should cover these answers and answer explanations with your hand or a piece of paper while responding to the questions. Refer to the general discussion in the Introduction on how to take the FAA knowledge test.

Remember that the questions from the FAA instrument rating knowledge test bank have been reordered by topic, and the topics have been organized into a meaningful sequence. Accordingly, the first line of the answer explanation gives the FAA question number and the citation of the authoritative source for the answer.

5.1 Precision Instrument Runway Markings

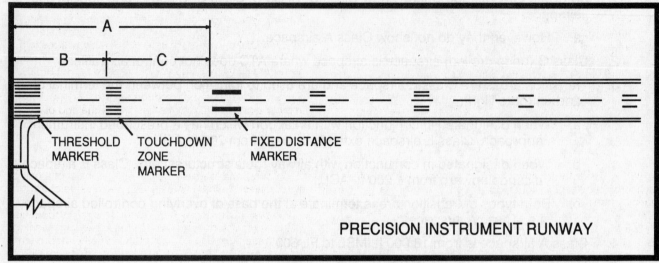

FIGURE 137.—Precision Instrument Runway.

1.
4791. (Refer to figure 137 above.) What is the distance (A) from the beginning of the runway to the fixed distance marker?

A— 500 feet.
B— 1,000 feet.
C— 1,500 feet.

Answer (B) is correct (4791). (AIM Para 2-3-3)
The fixed distance marker on precision instrument runways consists of two heavy lines parallel to the direction of the runway, 1,000 ft. from the runway threshold.
Answer (A) is incorrect because the six parallel lines (somewhat lighter and narrower than the fixed distance marker) 500 ft. from the threshold of the runway are the touchdown zone marker. Answer (C) is incorrect because the marker at roughly 1,500 ft. from the threshold is the next marker beyond the fixed distance marker, not the fixed distance marker.

2.
4792. (Refer to figure 137 above.) What is the distance (B) from the beginning of the runway to the touchdown zone marker?

A— 250 feet.
B— 500 feet.
C— 750 feet.

Answer (B) is correct (4792). (AIM Para 2-3-3)
The distance from the runway threshold to the touchdown zone marker is 500 ft. The touchdown zone marker consists of six lines parallel to the runway.
Answer (A) is incorrect because there is no standardized marking 250 ft. from the beginning of the runway. Answer (C) is incorrect because there is no standardized marking 750 ft. from the beginning of the runway.

3.
4793. (Refer to figure 137 above.) What is the distance (C) from the beginning of the touchdown zone marker to the beginning of the fixed distance marker?

A— 1,000 feet.
B— 500 feet.
C— 250 feet.

Answer (B) is correct (4793). (AIM Para 2-3-3)
Since the touchdown zone marker is 500 ft. from the runway threshold and the fixed distance marker is 1,000 ft. from the runway threshold, the distance from the beginning of the touchdown zone marker to the beginning of the fixed distance marker is 500 ft. (1,000 – 500).
Answer (A) is incorrect because 1,000 ft. is the distance from the beginning of the runway to the fixed distance marker. Answer (C) is incorrect because 250 ft. is not a standard distance between runway markings.

4.
4796. The primary purpose of runway end identifier lights, installed at many airfields, is to provide

A— rapid identification of the approach end of the runway during reduced visibility.
B— a warning of the final 3,000 feet of runway remaining as viewed from the takeoff or approach position.
C— rapid identification of the primary runway during reduced visibility.

Answer (A) is correct (4796). *(AIM Para 2-1-3)*
    Runway end identifier lights (REIL) are effective for rapid and positive identification of the approach end of a runway which is surrounded by a preponderance of other lighting, which lacks contrast with surrounding terrain, and/or which has reduced visibility. They are white strobe lights, one on each side of the runway threshold.
    Answer (B) is incorrect because it describes runway remaining lights in the center of the runway, not REIL. Answer (C) is incorrect because REIL of other than the primary runway may be used to help identify the airport. In other words, REIL may be flashing at the end of a runway which is not the primary runway.

5.
4795. Which type of runway lighting consists of a pair of synchronized flashing lights, one on each side of the runway threshold?

A— RAIL.
B— HIRL.
C— REIL.

Answer (C) is correct (4795). *(AIM Para 2-1-3)*
    Runway end identifier lights (REIL) consist of a pair of synchronized flashing lights, one on each side of the runway threshold.
    Answer (A) is incorrect because RAIL refers to runway alignment indicator lights, which are sequenced flashing lights that are used in combination with other approach lighting systems. Answer (B) is incorrect because HIRL refers to high-intensity runway lights, which are a runway edge light system.

6.
4794. Which runway marking indicates a displaced threshold on an instrument runway?

A— Arrows leading to the threshold mark.
B— Centerline dashes starting at the threshold.
C— Red chevron marks in the nonlanding portion of the runway.

Answer (A) is correct (4794). *(AIM Para 2-3-3)*
    On any runway, a displaced threshold is marked with a series of arrows in the middle of the runway pointing to the threshold mark, which is a solid line across the runway. A displaced threshold is available for taxiing, landing rollout, and takeoff, but not landing.
    Answer (B) is incorrect because it describes the centerline marking of a runway. Answer (C) is incorrect because chevron marks are usually yellow. They indicate a nonusable portion of the runway that is only available for emergency use (overrun and stopway areas).

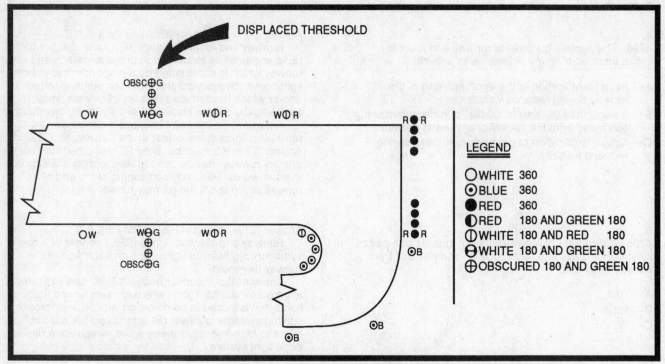

FIGURE 138.—Runway Legend.

7.
4797. (Refer to figure 138 above.) What night operations, if any, are authorized between the approach end of the runway and the threshold lights?

A— No aircraft operations are permitted short of the threshold lights.
B— Only taxi operations are permitted in the area short of the threshold lights.
C— Taxi and takeoff operations are permitted, providing the takeoff operations are toward the visible green threshold lights.

Answer (C) is correct (4797). *(AIM Para 2-3-3)*
On displaced thresholds, runway edge lights appear red when taxiing toward the green threshold lights and white when taxiing away from the threshold to the departure end of the runway. The area behind the displaced runway threshold is available for taxiing, landing rollout, and takeoff of aircraft.
Answer (A) is incorrect because overrun areas are areas where only emergency operations are permitted. Overrun areas do not have any runway edge lights. Answer (B) is incorrect because landing rollout and takeoff operations are also permitted behind displaced thresholds.

8.
4738. Under which conditions is hydroplaning most likely to occur?

A— When rudder is used for directional control instead of allowing the nosewheel to contact the surface early in the landing roll on a wet runway.
B— During conditions of standing water, slush, high speed, and smooth runway texture.
C— During a landing on any wet runway when brake application is delayed until a wedge of water begins to build ahead of the tires.

Answer (B) is correct (4738). *(FAA-P-8740-50)*
In hydroplaning, the aircraft tire is separated from the runway by water. It is more apt to happen at higher speeds, with standing water or slush on the runway, and on a runway with a smooth texture.
Answer (A) is incorrect because the nosewheel cannot hydroplane if it is not put down to the runway surface. Answer (C) is incorrect because hydroplaning occurs regardless of brake timing.

5.2 Airport Signs and Markings

9.
4534. (Refer to figure 94 on page 427.) Mandatory airport instruction signs are designated by having

A— yellow lettering with a black background.
B— white lettering with a red background.
C— black lettering with a yellow background.

Answer (B) is correct (4534). *(AIM Para 2-3-8)*
Mandatory airport instruction signs have a red background with white lettering and are used to denote an entrance to a runway or critical area, and areas where an aircraft is prohibited from entering.
Answer (A) is incorrect because yellow lettering on a black background denotes taxiway or runway location signs (where the aircraft is located). Answer (C) is incorrect because black lettering on a yellow background denotes direction, destination, and information signs.

10.
4535. (Refer to figure 94 on page 427.) What sign is designated by illustration 7?

A— Location sign.
B— Mandatory instruction sign.
C— Direction sign.

Answer (B) is correct (4535). *(AIM Para 2-3-8)*
Mandatory instruction signs have a red background with white lettering. The sign designated by illustration 7 (15-APCH) protects the approach to RWY 15 and/or the departure for RWY 33.
Answer (A) is incorrect because location signs use yellow lettering on a black background. Answer (C) is incorrect because direction signs use black lettering on a yellow background.

11.
4536. (Refer to figure 94 on page 427.) What colors are runway holding position signs?

A— White with a red background.
B— Red with a white background.
C— Yellow with a black background.

Answer (A) is correct (4536). *(AIM Para 2-3-8)*
Runway holding position signs, like other mandatory instruction signs, have white lettering on a red background. Runway holding position signs are located at the holding position on taxiways that intersect a runway or on runways that intersect other runways.
Answer (B) is incorrect because red lettering on a white background is used on the landing area of a hospital heliport but is not used on any airport signs. Answer (C) is incorrect because taxiway and runway location signs, not runway holding position signs, have yellow lettering on a black background.

12.
4537. (Refer to figure 94 on page 427.) Hold line markings at the intersection of taxiways and runways consist of four lines that extend across the width of the taxiway. These lines are

A— white, and the dashed lines are nearest the runway.
B— yellow, and the dashed lines are nearest the runway.
C— yellow, and the solid lines are nearest the runway.

Answer (B) is correct (4537). *(AIM Para 2-3-5)*
Runway holding position markings on taxiways identify the location where you are supposed to stop when you do not have a clearance to proceed onto the runway. These markings consist of four yellow lines, two solid and two dashed, spaced 6 inches apart and extending across the width of the taxiway, with the dashed lines nearest the runway. The solid lines are always on the side where the aircraft is to hold.
Answer (A) is incorrect because the lines are yellow, not white. Answer (C) is incorrect because solid lines are always on the holding side, not the runway side.

12a.
1001-1. The "runway hold position" sign denotes

A— intersecting runways.
B— an entrance to runway from a taxiway
C— an area protected for an aircraft approaching a runway.

Answer (B) is correct (1001-1). *(AIM Para 2-3-8)*
Runway holding position signs, consisting of white numbering on a red background, are found adjacent to runway holding position markings that are painted on a taxiway or a runway. These signs and markings indicate the point at which aircraft are expected to hold short of a runway if an ATC clearance to proceed onto that runway has not been received at an airport with an operating control tower or without making sure of adequate separation at an airport without an operating control tower. Runway holding position signs therefore denote the entrance to a runway from a taxiway or from an intersecting runway.
Answer (A) is incorrect because a runway hold position sign is used only to denote an intersecting runway when that runway is used for "Land, Hold Short" operations or as a taxiway. Answer (C) is incorrect because a runway approach area holding position sign, not a runway holding position sign, denotes an area protected for aircraft approaching or departing a runway.

12b.
1001-2. "Runway hold position" markings on the taxiway

A— identifies where aircraft hold short of the runway.
B— identifies area where aircraft are prohibited.
C— allows an aircraft permission onto the runway.

Answer (A) is correct (1001-2). *(AIM Para 2-3-5)*
Runway holding position markings on taxiways identify the location where you are supposed to stop when you do not have an ATC clearance to proceed at an airport with an operating control tower or without making sure of adequate separation at an airport without an operating control tower. These markings consist of four yellow lines, two solid and two dashed, spaced 6 inches apart and extending across the width of the taxiway, with the dashed lines nearest the runway. The solid lines are always on the side where the aircraft is to hold.
Answer (B) is incorrect because a no entry sign, not a runway hold position marking, identifies an area where aircraft are prohibited. Answer (C) is incorrect because runway holding position markings indicate that aircraft should hold short of the runway, not taxi onto it, until a clearance to proceed onto the runway is received.

12c.

1001-3. The "No Entry" sign identifies

A— the exit boundary for the runway protected area.
B— an area that does not continue beyond intersection.
C— paved area where aircraft entry is prohibited.

Answer (C) is correct (1001-3). *(AIM 2-3-8)*
No entry signs consist of a white horizontal line surrounded by a white circle on a red background. These signs are posted at points where aircraft entry is prohibited. These signs are typically found on taxiways that are intended to be used in only one direction and at the intersection of vehicle roadways with runways, taxiways, or ramp areas where the roadway may be mistaken for a taxiway or other aircraft movement area.
Answer (A) is incorrect because a runway boundary sign, not a no entry sign, identifies the boundary of the runway protected area for aircraft leaving the runway. Runway boundary signs consist of a black depiction of a runway holding position marking on a yellow background. Answer (B) is incorrect because a taxiway ending marker sign, not a no entry sign, indicates that a taxiway does not continue beyond the next intersection. Taxiway ending marker signs consist of alternating yellow and black diagonal stripes.

12d.

1001-4. When turning onto a taxiway from another taxiway, the "taxiway directional sign" indicates

A— direction to the take-off runway.
B— designation and direction of taxiway leading out of an intersection.
C— designation and direction of exit taxiway from runway.

Answer (B) is correct (1001-4). *(AIM Para 2-3-10)*
Direction signs consist of black lettering on a yellow background. These signs identify the designations of taxiways leading out of an intersection. An arrow next to each taxiway designation indicates the direction that an aircraft must turn in order to taxi onto that taxiway.
Answer (A) is incorrect because outbound destination signs, not direction signs, indicate the direction that must be taken out of an intersection in order to follow the preferred taxi route to a runway. Answer (C) is incorrect because the question specifies that you are turning onto a taxiway from another taxiway, not from a runway.

5.3 Visual Approach Slope Indicator (VASI)

13.

4781. Which approach and landing objective is assured when the pilot remains on the proper glidepath of the VASI?

A— Continuation of course guidance after transition to VFR.
B— Safe obstruction clearance in the approach area.
C— Course guidance from the visual descent point to touchdown.

Answer (B) is correct (4781). *(AIM Para 2-1-2)*
The VASI system provides visual descent guidance and provides safe obstruction clearance within plus or minus 10° of the extended runway centerline from as far as 4 NM from the runway threshold.
Answer (A) is incorrect because VASI does not provide course guidance. Answer (C) is incorrect because VASI does not provide course guidance.

14.

4774. (Refer to figure 134 below.) Unless a higher angle is necessary for obstacle clearance, what is the normal glidepath angle for a 2-bar VASI?

A— 2.75°.
B— 3.00°.
C— 3.25°.

Answer (B) is correct (4774). *(AIM Para 2-1-2)*
Two-bar VASI installations provide one visual glide path, which is normally set at 3°. Angles at some locations may be as high as 4.5°, however, to give proper obstacle clearance. This greater angle may necessitate increased runway for landing and rollout of some high-performance airplanes.
Answer (A) is incorrect because the normal glide path angle for a 2-bar VASI is 3°, not 2.75°. Answer (C) is incorrect because 3.25° is the normal upper glide path provided by a 3-bar VASI.

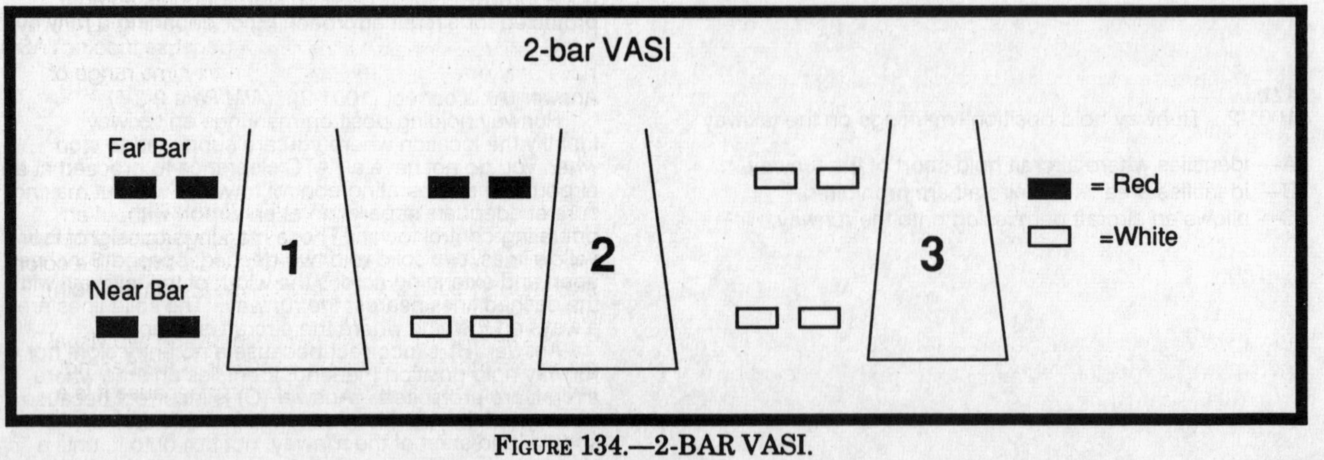

FIGURE 134.—2-BAR VASI.

15.
4775. Which of the following indications would a pilot see while approaching to land on a runway served by a 2-bar VASI?

A— If on the glidepath, the near bars will appear red, and the far bars will appear white.
B— If departing to the high side of the glidepath, the far bars will change from red to white.
C— If on the glidepath, both near bars and far bars will appear white.

16.
4778. When on the proper glidepath of a 2-bar VASI, the pilot will see the near bar as

A— white and the far bar as red.
B— red and the far bar as white.
C— white and the far bar as white.

17.
4779. If an approach is being made to a runway that has an operating 3-bar VASI and all the VASI lights appear red as the airplane reaches the MDA, the pilot should

A— start a climb to reach the proper glidepath.
B— continue at the same rate of descent if the runway is in sight.
C— level off momentarily to intercept the proper approach path.

18.
4776. The middle and far bars of a 3-bar VASI will

A— both appear white to the pilot when on the upper glidepath.
B— constitute a 2-bar VASI for using the lower glidepath.
C— constitute a 2-bar VASI for using the upper glidepath.

19.
4777. Tricolor Visual Approach Indicators normally consist of

A— a single unit, projecting a three-color visual approach path.
B— three separate light units, each projecting a different color approach path.
C— three separate light projecting units of very high candle power with a daytime range of approximately 5 miles.

20.
4780. Which is a feature of the tricolor VASI?

A— One light projector with three colors: red, green, and amber.
B— Two visual glidepaths for the runway.
C— Three glidepaths, with the center path indicated by a white light.

Answer (B) is correct (4775). *(AIM Para 2-1-2)*
As you move to the high side of a VASI glide slope, the far bar will change from red to white. When you are on the glide slope, the far bar is red. When you are above the glide slope, the far bar is white.
Answer (A) is incorrect because, if you are on the glide slope, the near bars are white, not red, and the far bars are red, not white (the opposite is impossible). Answer (C) is incorrect because, if both near and far bars are white, you are above, not on, the glide slope.

Answer (A) is correct (4778). *(AIM Para 2-1-2)*
When you are on the proper glide path of a 2-bar VASI, the near lights will be white and the far lights red.
Answer (B) is incorrect because white over red is impossible. Answer (C) is incorrect because white over white means you are above, not on, the glide path.

Answer (C) is correct (4779). *(AIM Para 2-1-2)*
If all three VASI bars are red, you are beneath both glide paths and should level off momentarily to intercept the proper approach path.
Answer (A) is incorrect because a climb is not necessary. If you level off you will soon be back on the glide path. Answer (B) is incorrect because you should briefly stop, not continue, your rate of descent to get back on the desired glide path.

Answer (C) is correct (4776). *(AIM Para 2-1-2)*
On 3-bar VASIs, the lower glide path is provided by the near and middle bars at a 3° glide slope. The middle and far bars normally have a 1/4° greater glide slope and are used for the upper glide path.
Answer (A) is incorrect because, when both the middle and far bars are white, the airplane is above both glide paths. Answer (B) is incorrect because the near and middle bars are used for the lower glide path.

Answer (A) is correct (4777). *(AIM Para 2-1-2)*
Tricolor visual approach indicators consist of a single light unit projecting a three-color visual approach path. The unit has a useful range of ½ to 1 mi. in daylight and as much as 5 mi. at night.
Answer (B) is incorrect because tricolor visual approach indicators have only one light unit and only one glide path. Answer (C) is incorrect because tricolor VASIs have only one projecting unit with a daytime range of about 1, not 5, mi.

Answer (A) is correct (4780). *(AIM Para 2-1-2)*
Tricolor VASIs normally consist of a single light unit projecting a three-color visual approach path. The colors are amber (above the glide path), green (on the path), and red (below the path).
Answer (B) is incorrect because having two visual glide paths for the runway is a feature of a 3-bar, not tricolor, VASI. Answer (C) is incorrect because it is a nonsense concept; i.e., there is not a three-glide path VASI.

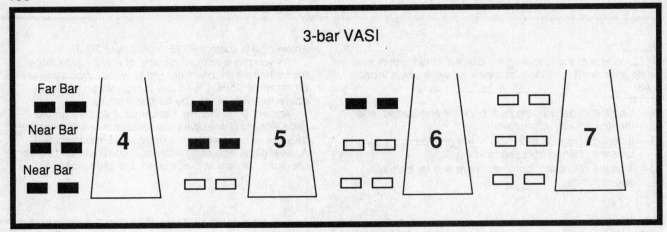

FIGURE 135.—3-BAR VASI.

21.
4782. (Refer to figure 135 above.) Unless a higher angle is required for obstacle clearance, what is the normal glidepath for a 3-bar VASI?

A— 2.3°.
B— 2.75°.
C— 3.0°.

Answer (C) is correct (4782). *(AIM Para 2-1-2)*
    The normal glide path for a 3-bar VASI (the lower glide path) is 3°. The upper glide path is usually a 3.25° slope. Higher-angle glide slopes, up to 4.5°, are used in some places for adequate obstruction clearance.
    Answer (A) is incorrect because 2.3° is not a VASI glide path angle. Answer (B) is incorrect because 2.75° is not a VASI glide path angle.

22.
4783. (Refer to figure 135 above.) Which illustration would a pilot observe when on the lower glidepath?

A— 4.
B— 5.
C— 6.

Answer (B) is correct (4783). *(AIM Para 2-1-2)*
    On the lower glide path of a 3-bar VASI, the near lights should be white and the middle and far bars should be red, which is illustration 5.
    Answer (A) is incorrect because illustration 4 indicates that you are below both glide paths. Answer (C) is incorrect because illustration 6 indicates that you are on the upper glide path.

23.
4784. (Refer to figure 135 above.) Which illustration would a pilot observe if the aircraft is above both glidepaths?

A— 5.
B— 6.
C— 7.

Answer (C) is correct (4784). *(AIM Para 2-1-2)*
    If you are above both glide paths on a 3-bar VASI, you will observe that all three rows of lights appear white, which is illustration 7.
    Answer (A) is incorrect because illustration 5 indicates that you are on the lower glide path. Answer (B) is incorrect because illustration 6 indicates that you are on the upper glide path.

24.
4785. (Refer to figure 135 above.) Which illustration would a pilot observe if the aircraft is below both glidepaths?

A— 4.
B— 5.
C— 6.

Answer (A) is correct (4785). *(AIM Para 2-1-2)*
    If you are below both glide paths on a 3-bar VASI, you will observe that all three rows of lights appear red, which is illustration 4.
    Answer (B) is incorrect because illustration 5 indicates that you are on the lower glide path. Answer (C) is incorrect because illustration 6 indicates that you are on the upper glide path.

5.4 Precision Approach Path Indicator (PAPI)

25.
4786. (Refer to figure 136 on page 159.) Which illustration depicts an "on glidepath" indication?

A— 8.
B— 10.
C— 11.

Answer (B) is correct (4786). *(AIM Para 2-1-2)*
    The precision approach path indicator (PAPI) uses light units similar to the VASI, but they are installed in a single row of either two or four units, rather than bars. If all the light units indicate white, you are above the glide slope. If all indicate red, you are below the glide slope. If two lights indicate red and two lights indicate white, you are on the glide slope, as shown in illustration 10.
    Answer (A) is incorrect because illustration 8 indicates that you are above the glide slope. Answer (C) is incorrect because illustration 11 indicates that you are slightly below (2.8°) the glide slope.

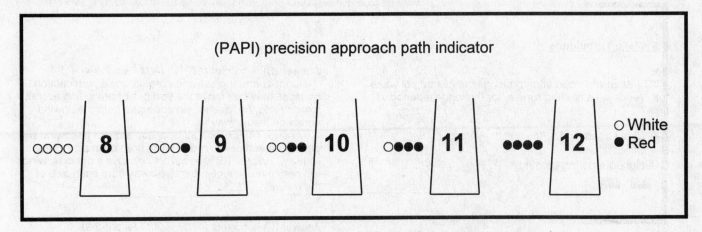

Figure 136. -- Precision Approach Path Indicator (PAPI)

26.
4787. (Refer to figure 136 above.) Which illustration depicts a "slightly low" (2.8°) indication?

A— 9.
B— 10.
C— 11.

Answer (C) is correct (4787). *(AIM Para 2-1-2)*
On PAPI, you are slightly below (2.8°) the glide path when three of the four lights indicate red as in illustration 11.
Answer (A) is incorrect because illustration 9 indicates that you are slightly above (3.2°) the glide path. Answer (B) is incorrect because illustration 10 indicates that you are on (3.0°) the glide path.

27.
4788. (Refer to figure 136 above.) Which illustration would a pilot observe if the aircraft is on a glidepath higher than 3.5°?

A— 8.
B— 9.
C— 11.

Answer (A) is correct (4788). *(AIM Para 2-1-2)*
Higher than the glide path on PAPIs means 3.5° or more, which is indicated by all white lights as in illustration 8.
Answer (B) is incorrect because illustration 9 indicates that you are slightly high (3.2°). Answer (C) is incorrect because illustration 11 indicates that you are slightly low (2.8°).

28.
4789. (Refer to figure 136 above.) Which illustration would a pilot observe if the aircraft is "slightly high" (3.2°) on the glidepath?

A— 8.
B— 9.
C— 11.

Answer (B) is correct (4789). *(AIM Para 2-1-2)*
Slightly high on a PAPI is about 3.2°, which is indicated by three white lights out of four. The remaining light is red as in illustration 9.
Answer (A) is incorrect because illustration 8 indicates a glide slope that is high or more than 3.5°. Answer (C) is incorrect because illustration 11 indicates a glide slope that is slightly low or about 2.8°.

29.
4790. (Refer to figure 136 above.) Which illustration would a pilot observe if the aircraft is less than 2.5°?

A— 10.
B— 11.
C— 12.

Answer (C) is correct (4790). *(AIM Para 2-1-2)*
On PAPI systems, low is indicated by all red lights as in illustration 12. Low means the aircraft is on a glide slope of less than 2.5°.
Answer (A) is incorrect because illustration 10 indicates that you are on the glide path (3.0°). Answer (B) is incorrect because illustration 11 indicates that you are slightly low (2.8°).

5.5 Wake Turbulence

30.
4707. What wind condition prolongs the hazards of wake turbulence on a landing runway for the longest period of time?

A— Direct headwind.
B— Direct tailwind.
C— Light quartering tailwind.

Answer (C) is correct (4707). *(AIM Para 7-3-4)*
Light quartering tailwinds require maximum caution because they can move the vortices of preceding aircraft forward into the touchdown zone and hold the upwind vortex on the runway.
Answer (A) is incorrect because a direct headwind will permit the vortices to move away from each side of the runway. Answer (B) is incorrect because a direct tailwind will permit the vortices to move away from each side of the runway.

31.
4708. Wake turbulence is near maximum behind a jet transport just after takeoff because

A— the engines are at maximum thrust output at slow airspeed.
B— the gear and flap configuration increases the turbulence to maximum.
C— of the high angle of attack and high gross weight.

Answer (C) is correct (4708). *(AIM Para 7-3-3)*
The greatest vortex strength occurs when the generating aircraft is heavy, clean, and slow, such as in takeoff climbout. At this time there is a high gross weight and also a high angle of attack.
Answer (A) is incorrect because vortices have to do with airflows about the wingtips, not the engines. Answer (B) is incorrect because the gear and flap configuration will change the characteristics of the vortex.

32.
4709. What effect would a light crosswind of approximately 7 knots have on vortex behavior?

A— The light crosswind would rapidly dissipate vortex strength.
B— The upwind vortex would tend to remain over the runway.
C— The downwind vortex would tend to remain over the runway.

Answer (B) is correct (4709). *(AIM Para 7-3-4)*
A light crosswind of 1 to 7 kt. could result in the upwind vortex of a preceding aircraft remaining in the touchdown zone for a period of time. Also, it could hasten the drift of the downwind vortex toward another runway.
Answer (A) is incorrect because strong, not light, winds would help rapidly dissipate vortex strength. Answer (C) is incorrect because the upwind, not downwind, vortex would tend to remain over the runway in a light crosswind.

33.
4710. When landing behind a large jet aircraft, at which point on the runway should you plan to land?

A— If any crosswind, land on the windward side of the runway and prior to the jet's touchdown point.
B— At least 1,000 feet beyond the jet's touchdown point.
C— Beyond the jet's touchdown point.

Answer (C) is correct (4710). *(AIM Para 7-3-6)*
When landing behind a large aircraft on the same runway, stay at or above the large aircraft's final approach flight path, and land beyond its touchdown point.
Answer (A) is incorrect because you must land beyond, not prior to, the touchdown point. Answer (B) is incorrect because there is no minimum distance (i.e., 1,000 ft.) that you should land beyond the jet's touchdown point.

5.6 Collision Avoidance

34.
4441. Which procedure is recommended while climbing to an assigned altitude on the airway?

A— Climb on the centerline of the airway except when maneuvering to avoid other air traffic in VFR conditions.
B— Climb slightly on the right side of the airway when in VFR conditions.
C— Climb far enough to the right side of the airway to avoid climbing or descending traffic coming from the opposite direction if in VFR conditions.

Answer (A) is correct (4441). *(FAR 91.181)*
When climbing to an assigned altitude on an airway, one should use the centerline except to avoid other aircraft when in VFR conditions. This procedure is specified in FAR 91.181, which requires aircraft to operate along the centerline of federal airways.
Answer (B) is incorrect because you are required to maintain the centerline, not remain on the right side, while operating on a federal airway. Answer (C) is incorrect because you are required to maintain the centerline, not remain on the right side, while operating on a federal airway.

35.
4634. What is expected of you as pilot on an IFR flight plan if you are descending or climbing in VFR conditions?

A— If on an airway, climb or descend to the right of the centerline.
B— Advise ATC you are in visual conditions and will remain a short distance to the right of the centerline while climbing.
C— Execute gentle banks, left and right, at a frequency which permits continuous visual scanning of the airspace about you.

Answer (C) is correct (4634). *(AIM Para 4-4-14)*
During climbs and descents in VFR conditions, pilots should execute gentle banks left and right to permit continual scanning of surrounding airspace.
Answer (A) is incorrect because you are required to maintain, not remain to the right of, the centerline while operating on a federal airway, except when maneuvering to avoid other traffic in VFR conditions. Answer (B) is incorrect because you are not required to advise ATC that you are in visual conditions, but you are required to maintain, not remain to the right of, the centerline while operating on a federal airway, except when maneuvering to avoid other traffic in VFR conditions.

36.
4373. When is a pilot on an IFR flight plan responsible for avoiding other aircraft?

A— At all times when not in radar contact with ATC.
B— When weather conditions permit, regardless of whether operating under IFR or VFR.
C— Only when advised by ATC.

Answer (B) is correct (4373). *(FAR 91.113)*
When weather conditions permit, regardless of whether an operation is conducted under IFR or VFR, each pilot shall maintain vigilance in order to see and avoid other aircraft.
Answer (A) is incorrect because, if weather conditions permit, each pilot is responsible for avoiding other aircraft, whether in radar contact or not. Answer (C) is incorrect because, if weather conditions permit, each pilot, not ATC, is responsible for avoiding other aircraft.

37.
4471. What responsibility does the pilot in command of an IFR flight assume upon entering VFR conditions?

A— Report VFR conditions to ARTCC so that an amended clearance may be issued.
B— Use VFR operating procedures.
C— To see and avoid other traffic.

Answer (C) is correct (4471). *(FAR 91.113)*
When weather conditions permit, regardless of whether an operation is conducted under IFR or VFR, each pilot shall maintain vigilance in order to see and avoid other aircraft.
Answer (A) is incorrect because VFR conditions are not reported unless so requested by ATC. Answer (B) is incorrect because IFR operating procedures are to be followed on an IFR flight.

5.7 IFR Flight Planning Information

38.
4405. The most current en route and destination flight information for planning an instrument flight should be obtained from

A— the ATIS broadcast.
B— the FSS.
C— Notices to Airmen (Class II).

Answer (B) is correct (4405). *(AIM Para 5-1-1)*
The FAA urges every pilot to receive a preflight briefing, which may be obtained from a Flight Service Station (FSS) by telephone, radio, or personal visit. The preflight briefing should cover weather, airport, and en route navigation data.
Answer (A) is incorrect because the ATIS (Automatic Terminal Information Service) broadcasts only information pertaining to landing and departing operations at one airport. ATIS does not provide any en route information. Answer (C) is incorrect because *Notices to Airmen Publication* (formerly Class II) is published every 28 days and contains NOTAMs still in effect but not transmitted with weather information. It is only one aspect of a complete flight briefing.

39.
4080. What is the purpose of FDC NOTAMs?

A— To provide the latest information on the status of navigation facilities to all FSS facilities for scheduled broadcasts.
B— To issue notices for all airports and navigation facilities in the shortest possible time.
C— To advise of changes in flight data which affect instrument approach procedures (IAP), aeronautical charts, and flight restrictions prior to normal publication.

Answer (C) is correct (4080). *(AIM Para 5-1-3)*
FDC (Flight Data Center) NOTAMs are regulatory in nature and issued to establish restrictions to flight or amend charts or published instrument approach procedures. FDC NOTAMs are published as needed and indexed in the *Notices to Airmen Publication*.
Answer (A) is incorrect because NOTAMs (D), not FDC NOTAMs, provide information for the status of navigational facilities. These NOTAMs are appended to the hourly weather reports. Answer (B) is incorrect because the purpose of NOTAMs (D) or (L) is to issue notices for all public-use airports and navigation facilities in the shortest possible time.

40.
4406. From what source can you obtain the latest FDC NOTAM's?

A— Notices to Airmen Publication.
B— FAA AFSS/FSS.
C— Airport/Facility Directory.

Answer (B) is correct (4406). *(AIM Para 5-1-3)*
The National Flight Data Center occasionally publishes regulatory changes (either permanent or temporary) in FDC (Flight Data Center) NOTAMs. They are also used to advertise temporary flight restrictions caused by such things as natural disasters, large public events, and other events that may generate congested air traffic. FSSs are required to keep a file of current FDC NOTAMs.
Answer (A) is incorrect because the *Notices to Airmen Publication* is published every 28 days. The FSSs may have more current data. Answer (C) is incorrect because the *Airport/Facility Directory* is only published every 56 days. The *A/FD* includes only permanent changes that were known at the time of publication.

41.
4079. Which sources of aeronautical information, when used collectively, provide the latest status of airport conditions (e.g., runway closures, runway lighting, snow conditions)?

A— Aeronautical Information Manual, aeronautical charts, and Distant (D) Notice to Airmen (NOTAM's).
B— Airport Facility Directory, FDC NOTAM's, and Local (L) NOTAM's.
C— Airport Facility Directory, Distant (D) NOTAM's, and Local (L) NOTAM's.

Answer (C) is correct (4079). *(AIM Para 5-1-3)*
The latest status of airport conditions can be determined by using the *Airport/Facility Directory* for items that have been known for some time, and distant (D) NOTAMs and local (L) NOTAMs, which contain the most up-to-date data.
Answer (A) is incorrect because the *Aeronautical Information Manual (AIM)* is a source of basic flight information and ATC procedures, not specific airport information, and aeronautical charts do not indicate the latest status of runway conditions. Answer (B) is incorrect because FDC NOTAMs deal with regulatory changes or unusual air traffic congestion, not local airport conditions.

42.
4403. When are ATIS broadcasts updated?

A— Every 30 minutes if weather conditions are below basic VFR; otherwise, hourly.
B— Upon receipt of any official weather, regardless of content change or reported values.
C— Only when the ceiling and/or visibility changes by a reportable value.

Answer (B) is correct (4403). *(AIM Para 4-1-13)*
    ATIS broadcasts are updated upon the receipt of any official weather regardless of content change or reported values. A new recording will also be made when there is a change in other pertinent data such as runway change, instrument approach in use, etc.
    Answer (A) is incorrect because the frequency of ATIS updates does not differ under VFR or IFR conditions. Answer (C) is incorrect because the recording will be updated whenever official weather is received, even if there is no change.

43.
4404. Absence of the sky condition and visibility on an ATIS broadcast specifically implies that

A— the ceiling is more than 5,000 feet and visibility is 5 miles or more.
B— the sky condition is clear and visibility is unrestricted.
C— the ceiling is at least 3,000 feet and visibility is 5 miles or more.

Answer (A) is correct (4404). *(AIM Para 4-1-13)*
    The ATIS broadcast generally includes the latest weather sequence, sky conditions, temperature, dew point, wind direction and velocity, altimeter, runways in use, etc. Absence of the sky condition and visibility on an ATIS broadcast specifically implies that the ceiling is more than 5,000 ft. and visibility is more than 5 SM.
    Answer (B) is incorrect because the absence of the sky condition and visibility on an ATIS broadcast implies that ceilings are more than 5,000 ft., not clear, and visibility is 5 SM or more, not unrestricted. Answer (C) is incorrect because the absence of the sky condition on an ATIS broadcast implies a ceiling of more than 5,000 ft., not at least 3,000 ft.

44.
4408. The operation of an airport rotating beacon during daylight hours may indicate that

A— the in-flight visibility is less than 3 miles and the ceiling is less than 1,500 feet within Class E airspace.
B— the ground visibility is less than 3 miles and/or the ceiling is less than 1,000 feet in Class B, C, or D airspace.
C— an IFR clearance is required to operate within the airport traffic area.

Answer (B) is correct (4408). *(AIM Para 2-1-8)*
    In Class B, C, D, and E surface areas, operation of an airport beacon during daylight hours often indicates that the ground visibility is less than 3 SM and/or the ceiling is less than 1,000 ft. Pilots should not rely solely on the beacon to indicate weather conditions because there is no regulatory requirement for daylight operation of the airport's rotating beacon.
    Answer (A) is incorrect because the operation of an airport rotating beacon during daylight hours at an airport located in Class E airspace may indicate that in-flight visibility (if ground is not reported) is less than 3 SM and/or the ceiling is less than 1,000 ft., not 1,500 ft. Answer (C) is incorrect because an IFR clearance is required only in controlled airspace when IMC exists, not at an airport that is operating a rotating beacon during the day.

5.8 IFR Flight Plan

45.
4072. (Refer to figure 1 below.) Which item(s) should be checked in block 1 for a composite flight plan?

A— VFR with an explanation in block 11.
B— IFR with an explanation in block 11.
C— VFR and IFR.

Answer (C) is correct (4072). *(AIM Para 5-1-7)*
If you are filing a composite VFR/IFR flight plan, you should check both VFR and IFR in Block 1 of the flight plan. A DVFR flight plan is required for flights through air defense identification zones (ADIZ) for national security reasons.
Answer (A) is incorrect because both VFR and IFR should be checked. Answer (B) is incorrect because both VFR and IFR should be checked.

46.
4075. (Refer to figure 1 below.) Which equipment determines the code to be entered in block 3 as a suffix to aircraft type on the flight plan form?

A— DME, ADF, and airborne radar.
B— DME, transponder, and ADF.
C— DME, transponder, and RNAV.

Answer (C) is correct (4075). *(AIM Para 5-1-7)*
Block 3 asks for the aircraft type and special equipment. After the aircraft type, a slash is followed by a letter indicating the combination of transponder, DME, and area navigation (RNAV) equipment that you have in the airplane.
Answer (A) is incorrect because you need not report ADF (automatic direction finder) or airborne radar. Answer (B) is incorrect because an ADF is not considered a special type of navigation equipment.

47.
4074. (Refer to figure 1 below.) What information should be entered in block 7 of an IFR flight plan if the flight has three legs, each at a different altitude?

A— Altitude for first leg.
B— Altitude for first leg and highest altitude.
C— Highest altitude.

Answer (A) is correct (4074). *(AIM Para 5-1-7)*
Block 7 of IFR flight plans is for altitude. You should enter only the initial request for altitude. When more than one altitude or flight level is desired along the route of flight, it is best to make subsequent requests direct to the controller.
Answer (B) is incorrect because initial, not highest, altitude is to be submitted on your flight plan. Answer (C) is incorrect because initial, not highest, altitude is to be entered on your flight plan.

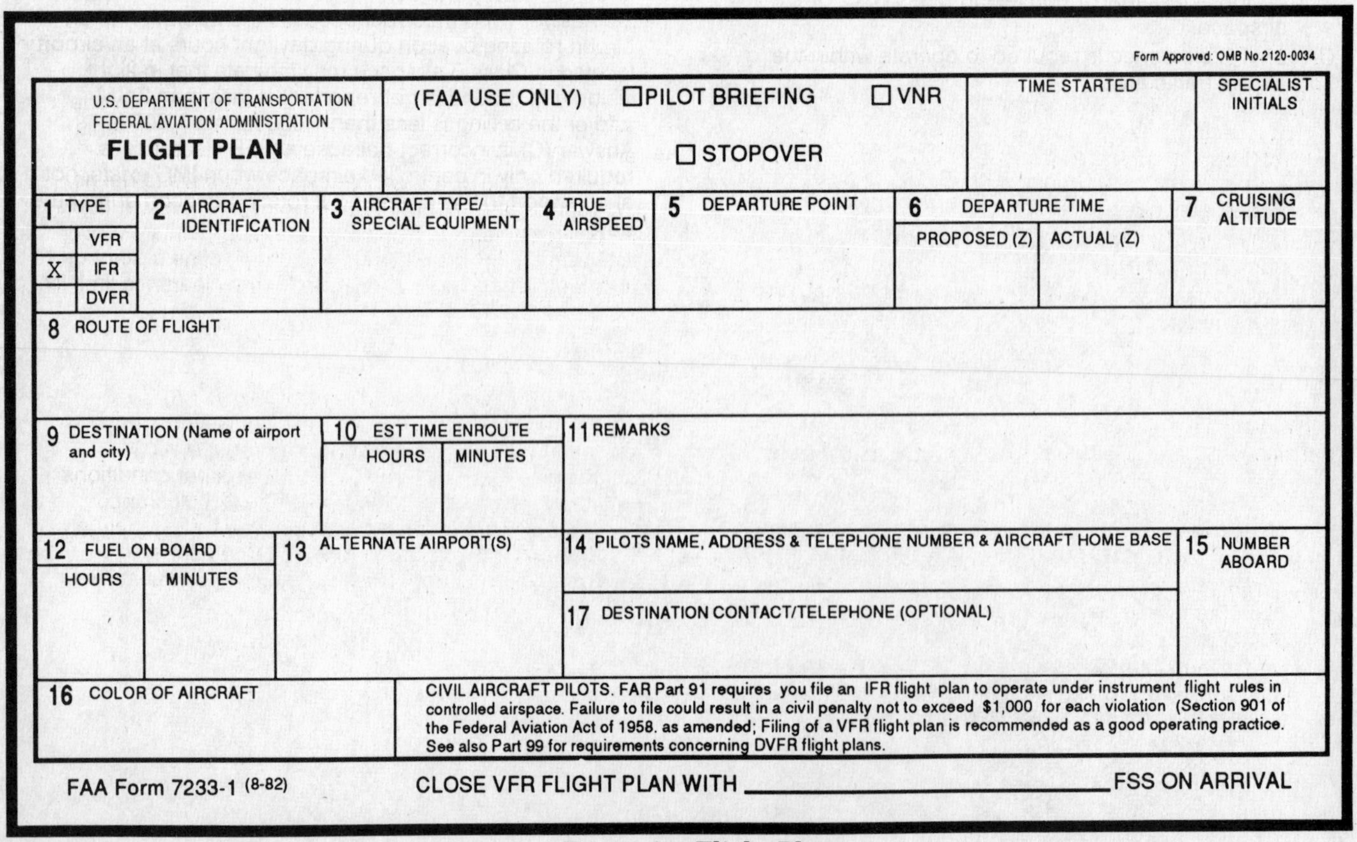
Form Approved: OMB No.2120-0034
U.S. DEPARTMENT OF TRANSPORTATION
FEDERAL AVIATION ADMINISTRATION
FLIGHT PLAN
(FAA USE ONLY) ☐ PILOT BRIEFING ☐ VNR ☐ STOPOVER
TIME STARTED
SPECIALIST INITIALS
1 TYPE: VFR; X IFR; DVFR
2 AIRCRAFT IDENTIFICATION
3 AIRCRAFT TYPE/ SPECIAL EQUIPMENT
4 TRUE AIRSPEED
5 DEPARTURE POINT
6 DEPARTURE TIME: PROPOSED (Z); ACTUAL (Z)
7 CRUISING ALTITUDE
8 ROUTE OF FLIGHT
9 DESTINATION (Name of airport and city)
10 EST TIME ENROUTE: HOURS; MINUTES
11 REMARKS
12 FUEL ON BOARD: HOURS; MINUTES
13 ALTERNATE AIRPORT(S)
14 PILOTS NAME, ADDRESS & TELEPHONE NUMBER & AIRCRAFT HOME BASE
15 NUMBER ABOARD
17 DESTINATION CONTACT/TELEPHONE (OPTIONAL)
16 COLOR OF AIRCRAFT
CIVIL AIRCRAFT PILOTS. FAR Part 91 requires you file an IFR flight plan to operate under instrument flight rules in controlled airspace. Failure to file could result in a civil penalty not to exceed $1,000 for each violation (Section 901 of the Federal Aviation Act of 1958. as amended; Filing of a VFR flight plan is recommended as a good operating practice. See also Part 99 for requirements concerning DVFR flight plans.
FAA Form 7233-1 (8-82) CLOSE VFR FLIGHT PLAN WITH ____________ FSS ON ARRIVAL

FIGURE 1.—Flight Plan.

48.
4073. (Refer to figure 1 on page 164.) The time entered in block 12 for an IFR flight should be based on which fuel quantity?

A— Total fuel required for the flight.
B— Total useable fuel on board.
C— The amount of fuel required to fly to the destination airport, then to the alternate, plus a 45-minute reserve.

49.
4761. What point at the destination should be used to compute estimated time en route on an IFR flight plan?

A— The final approach fix on the expected instrument approach.
B— The initial approach fix on the expected instrument approach.
C— The point of first intended landing.

50.
4059. When may a pilot file a composite flight plan?

A— When requested or advised by ATC.
B— Any time a portion of the flight will be VFR.
C— Any time a landing is planned at an intermediate airport.

51.
4060. When filing a composite flight plan where the first portion of the flight is IFR, which fix(es) should be indicated on the flight plan form?

A— All points of transition from one airway to another, fixes defining direct route segments, and the clearance limit fix.
B— Only the fix where you plan to terminate the IFR portion of the flight.
C— Only those compulsory reporting points on the IFR route segment.

52.
4061. What is the recommended procedure for transitioning from VFR to IFR on a composite flight plan?

A— Prior to transitioning to IFR, contact the nearest FSS, close the VFR portion, and request ATC clearance.
B— Upon reaching the proposed point for change to IFR, contact the nearest FSS and cancel your VFR flight plan, then contact ARTCC and request an IFR clearance.
C— Prior to reaching the proposed point for change to IFR, contact ARTCC, request your IFR clearance, and instruct them to cancel the VFR flight plan.

Answer (B) is correct (4073). *(AIM Para 5-1-7)*
Block 12 should be filled in with the time at normal cruising speed using total usable fuel on board. It should be computed from the departure point.
Answer (A) is incorrect because total fuel required for the flight is determined in your flight planning but is not an item that is listed on an IFR flight plan. Answer (C) is incorrect because it describes the IFR fuel requirement.

Answer (C) is correct (4761). *(FAR 91.153)*
Estimated time en route on an IFR flight plan should be the time from takeoff at the departure airport to touchdown at the point of first intended landing.
Answer (A) is incorrect because, due to varying weather conditions, runways in use, traffic, etc., there is no way of accurately telling which approach will be used. Answer (B) is incorrect because, due to varying weather conditions, runways in use, traffic, etc., there is no way of accurately telling which approach will be used.

Answer (B) is correct (4059). *(AIM Para 5-1-6)*
A composite flight plan should be filed whenever VFR operation is specified for one portion of the flight and IFR for another portion.
Answer (A) is incorrect because ATC does not request or advise on the type of flight plan to file other than IFR flight plans required in certain weather conditions and in the positive control area. Answer (C) is incorrect because you are not required to convert a flight plan from or to IFR or VFR when landing is planned at an intermediate airport.

Answer (A) is correct (4060). *(AIM Para 5-1-6)*
On composite flight plans for which the first portion of the flight is IFR, the flight plan should be a standard IFR flight plan, which includes points of transition from one airway to another, fixes defining direct route segments, and the clearance limit fix.
Answer (B) is incorrect because you have to define the route to get to your clearance limit fix. Answer (C) is incorrect because compulsory reporting points are not listed on an IFR flight plan unless they define a point of transition, direct route segments, or the clearance limit fix.

Answer (A) is correct (4061). *(AIM Para 5-1-6)*
Prior to transitioning from VFR to IFR, you should close the VFR portion with FSS and request ATC clearance. You must remain in VFR weather conditions until operating in accordance with the IFR clearance.
Answer (B) is incorrect because you must obtain an IFR clearance before beginning IFR operations. Answer (C) is incorrect because you should cancel your VFR flight plan with FSS, not ATC.

53.
4076. When may a pilot cancel the IFR flight plan prior to completing the flight?

A— Any time.
B— Only if an emergency occurs.
C— Only in VFR conditions when not in Class A airspace.

Answer (C) is correct (4076). *(AIM Para 5-1-13)*
An IFR flight plan may be canceled at any time you are operating in VFR conditions when not in Class A airspace by stating, "Cancel my IFR flight plan" to ATC. Once accepted by ATC, you should change to the appropriate communications frequency, transponder code, and altitude.
Answer (A) is incorrect because you cannot proceed under VFR when IFR conditions exist or when you are flying above FL 180 (i.e., in Class A airspace). Answer (B) is incorrect because ATC will provide needed assistance in emergencies while you are operating under an IFR flight plan.

54.
4058. How is your flight plan closed when your destination airport has IFR conditions and there is no control tower or flight service station (FSS) on the field?

A— The ARTCC controller will close your flight plan when you report the runway in sight.
B— You may close your flight plan any time after starting the approach by contacting any FSS or ATC facility.
C— Upon landing, you must close your flight plan by radio or by telephone to any FSS or ATC facility.

Answer (C) is correct (4058). *(AIM Para 5-1-13)*
IFR flight plans are automatically closed by ATC if you land at an airport with an operating control tower. However, if operating under an IFR flight plan to an airport with no functioning control tower, you must cancel the IFR flight plan. You may cancel your IFR flight plan while airborne only if weather permits. If your destination airport has IFR conditions and there is no tower or FSS on the field, you should close your IFR flight plan upon landing by radio or telephone to any FSS or ATC facility.
Answer (A) is incorrect because you, not ATC, must close your IFR flight plan at airports without an operating control tower or FSS on the field. Answer (B) is incorrect because, when an airport has IFR conditions, you must have IFR clearances until you have safely landed.

55.
4069. What is a way point when used for an IFR flight?

A— A predetermined geographical position used for an RNAV route or an RNAV instrument approach.
B— A reporting point defined by the intersection of two VOR radials.
C— A location on a victor airway which can only be identified by VOR and DME signals.

Answer (A) is correct (4069). *(IFH Chap VII)*
A waypoint on an IFR flight is a predetermined geographical position used for an RNAV route or an RNAV instrument approach definition or progress-reporting purposes. It is defined relative to a VORTAC position or in terms of latitude/longitude coordinates.
Answer (B) is incorrect because a point defined by the intersection of two VOR radials is called an intersection, not a way point. Answer (C) is incorrect because a location on a victor airway which can be identified only by VOR and DME signals is called a DME fix, not a way point.

5.9 ATC Clearances

56.
4395. What response is expected when ATC issues an IFR clearance to pilots of airborne aircraft?

A— Read back the entire clearance as required by regulation.
B— Read back those parts containing altitude assignments or vectors and any part requiring verification.
C— Read-back should be unsolicited and spontaneous to confirm that the pilot understands all instructions.

Answer (B) is correct (4395). *(AIM Para 4-4-6)*
Pilots of airborne aircraft should read back those parts of ATC clearances and instructions containing altitude assignments or vectors and any part requiring verification. The read-back serves as a double-check between pilots and ATC and reduces the kinds of communications errors that occur when a number is either misheard or incorrect.
Answer (A) is incorrect because the read-back is an expected procedure, but there is no regulatory requirement to read back an ATC clearance. Only those parts containing altitude assignments or vectors and any part requiring verification, not the entire clearance, should be read back. Answer (C) is incorrect because only those parts containing altitude assignments or vectors and any part requiring verification, not all instructions, should be read back.

57.
4396. Which clearance items are always given in an abbreviated IFR departure clearance? (Assume radar environment.)

A— Altitude, destination airport, and one or more fixes which identify the initial route of flight.
B— Destination airport, altitude, DP Name, Number, and/or Transition, if appropriate.
C— Clearance limit, DP Name, Number, and/or Transition, if appropriate.

Answer (B) is correct (4396). *(AIM Para 5-2-3)*
An abbreviated IFR departure clearance will include the destination airport. En route altitude will be stated in the clearance, and the pilot will be advised to expect an assigned or filed altitude within a given time or at a certain point after departure. Any DP (instrument departure procedure) will also be specified by ATC stating the DP name, the current number, and the DP transition name.
Answer (A) is incorrect because the fixes are already included in the flight plan and do not need to be repeated in an abbreviated IFR departure clearance. Answer (C) is incorrect because an en route altitude is always given in an abbreviated IFR departure clearance.

58.
4414. Which information is always given in an abbreviated departure clearance?

A— DP or transition name and altitude to maintain.
B— Name of destination airport or specific fix and altitude.
C— Altitude to maintain and code to squawk.

Answer (B) is correct (4414). *(AIM Para 5-2-3)*
An abbreviated IFR departure clearance always contains the name of your destination airport or clearance limit; altitude; and, if a DP is to be flown, the DP name, the current number, and the DP transition name.
Answer (A) is incorrect because the destination airport or clearance limit is always given in an abbreviated clearance. Answer (C) is incorrect because the destination airport or clearance limit is always given in an abbreviated clearance.

59.
4486. An abbreviated departure clearance "...CLEARED AS FILED..." will always contain the name

A— and number of the STAR to be flown when filed in the flight plan.
B— of the destination airport filed in the flight plan.
C— of the first compulsory reporting point if not in a radar environment.

Answer (B) is correct (4486). *(AIM Para 5-2-3)*
An abbreviated IFR departure clearance will include the destination airport. En route altitude will be stated, and the pilot will be advised to expect an assigned or filed altitude by a certain time or at a certain point after departure either separately or as part of a DP. The abbreviated clearance also includes the DP name-number-transition, if appropriate.
Answer (A) is incorrect because a STAR, when filed in a flight plan, is considered a part of the filed route of flight and will not normally be stated in an initial departure clearance. Answer (C) is incorrect because compulsory reporting points are not given in an abbreviated clearance.

60.
4398. On the runup pad, you receive the following clearance from ground control:

CLEARED TO THE DALLAS-LOVE AIRPORT AS FILED — MAINTAIN SIX THOUSAND — SQUAWK ZERO SEVEN ZERO FOUR JUST BEFORE DEPARTURE — DEPARTURE CONTROL WILL BE ONE TWO FOUR POINT NINER.

An abbreviated clearance, such as this, will always contain the

A— departure control frequency.
B— requested en route altitude.
C— destination airport and route.

Answer (C) is correct (4398). *(AIM Para 5-2-3)*
An IFR departure clearance will always contain the destination airport and the route of flight. The route of flight will either be given fix-by-fix by the controller, or it will be given "as filed," in which case the route on the IFR flight plan is the assigned route. The statement, "Cleared to the Dallas-Love airport as filed," contains the destination airport and the specific route to be taken (the filed route).
Answer (A) is incorrect because if the abbreviated clearance contains a DP, the departure control frequency may not be given if the frequency is published in the DP. Answer (B) is incorrect because "Cleared to (destination) airport as filed" does NOT include the en route altitude filed (requested) in the flight plan. An en route altitude will be stated in the clearance or the pilot will be advised to expect an assigned or filed altitude.

61.
4394. When departing from an airport not served by a control tower, the issuance of a clearance containing a void time indicates that

A— ATC will assume the pilot has not departed if no transmission is received before the void time.
B— the pilot must advise ATC as soon as possible, but no later than 30 minutes, of their intentions if not off by the void time.
C— ATC will protect the airspace only to the void time.

Answer (B) is correct (4394). *(AIM Para 5-2-4)*
    If operating from an airport not served by a control tower, the pilot may receive a clearance containing a provision that, if the flight has not departed by a specific time (void time), the clearance is void. In this situation, the pilot who does not depart prior to the void time must advise ATC of his/her intentions as soon as possible, but no later than 30 min. after the void time.
    Answer (A) is incorrect because ATC will assume a departure unless it hears from the pilot. Answer (C) is incorrect because the airspace is protected until ATC hears from the pilot.

62.
4443. What is the significance of an ATC clearance which reads "...CRUISE SIX THOUSAND..."?

A— The pilot must maintain 6,000 until reaching the IAF serving the destination airport, then execute the published approach procedure.
B— It authorizes a pilot to conduct flight at any altitude from minimum IFR altitude up to and including 6,000.
C— The pilot is authorized to conduct flight at any altitude from minimum IFR altitude up to and including 6,000, but each change in altitude must be reported to ATC.

Answer (B) is correct (4443). *(AIM Para 4-4-3)*
    The term "cruise" in a clearance assigns a pilot a block of airspace from the minimum IFR altitude up to and including the specified altitude (e.g., 6,000 ft. MSL). The pilot may level off at any intermediate altitude within this block of airspace. Climb and descent within the block are to be made at the discretion of the pilot. However, once the pilot starts descent and verbally reports leaving an altitude in the block, (s)he may not return to that altitude without additional ATC clearance.
    Answer (A) is incorrect because the pilot need not maintain 6,000 ft. Answer (C) is incorrect because the pilot may change altitude without reporting to ATC.

63.
4392. What is the significance of an ATC clearance which reads "...CRUISE SIX THOUSAND..."?

A— The pilot must maintain 6,000 feet until reaching the IAF serving the destination airport, then execute the published approach procedure.
B— Climbs may be made to, or descents made from, 6,000 feet at the pilot's discretion.
C— The pilot may utilize any altitude from the MEA/MOCA to 6,000 feet, but each change in altitude must be reported to ATC.

Answer (B) is correct (4392). *(AIM Para 4-4-3)*
    The term "cruise" in a clearance assigns a pilot a block of airspace from the minimum IFR altitude up to and including the specified altitude (e.g., 6,000 ft. MSL). The pilot may climb to, level off at, or descend from any intermediate altitude within this block of airspace. Once the pilot starts descent and verbally reports leaving an altitude in the block, however, (s)he may not return to that altitude without additional ATC clearance.
    Answer (A) is incorrect because the pilot need not maintain 6,000 ft. Answer (C) is incorrect because the pilot is assigned all the airspace from the minimum IFR altitude to 6,000 ft. MSL and may change altitudes without reporting to ATC.

64.
4458. A "CRUISE FOUR THOUSAND FEET" clearance would mean that the pilot is authorized to

A— vacate 4,000 feet without notifying ATC.
B— climb to, but not descend from 4,000 feet, without further ATC clearance.
C— use any altitude from minimum IFR to 4,000 feet, but must report leaving each altitude.

Answer (A) is correct (4458). *(AIM Para 4-4-3)*
    The term "cruise" in a clearance assigns a pilot a block of airspace from the minimum IFR altitude up to and including the specified altitude (e.g., 4,000 ft. MSL). The pilot may level off at any intermediate altitude within this block of airspace. Climb and descent within the block are to be made at the discretion of the pilot. However, once the pilot starts descent and verbally reports leaving an altitude in the block, (s)he may not return to that altitude without additional ATC clearance.
    Answer (B) is incorrect because any airspace between the minimum IFR altitude and 4,000 ft. MSL may be used without further ATC clearance. Answer (C) is incorrect because cruise clearances do not require reporting a change in altitude to ATC.

5.10 ATC Communication Procedures

65.
4538. When should pilots state their position on the airport when calling the tower for takeoff?

A— When visibility is less than 1 mile.
B— When parallel runways are in use.
C— When departing from a runway intersection.

Answer (C) is correct (4538). *(AIM Para 4-3-10)*
You should state your position on the airport when calling the tower for takeoff from a runway intersection. Additionally, you are expected to request from ground control approval for the intersection departure (i.e., a departure from any runway intersection except the end of the runway) prior to taxi.
Answer (A) is incorrect because a pilot is not expected to state his/her position on the airport when calling the tower for takeoff when visibility is less than 1 mile.
Answer (B) is incorrect because a pilot is not expected to state his/her position on the airport when calling the tower for takeoff when parallel runways are in use.

66.
4420. During a takeoff into IFR conditions with low ceilings, when should the pilot contact departure control?

A— Before penetrating the clouds.
B— When advised by the tower.
C— Upon completing the first turn after takeoff or upon establishing cruise climb on a straight-out departure.

Answer (B) is correct (4420). *(AIM Para 5-2-5)*
A pilot should not change to the departure control frequency until advised by ATC. Because the pilot maintains continuous contact with assigned ATC frequencies, all frequency changes are at the direction of ATC.
Answer (A) is incorrect because the tower will advise the pilot when to contact departure control, and such contact is not based on whether the aircraft has penetrated the clouds. Answer (C) is incorrect because the tower will advise the pilot when to contact departure control, which may or may not be upon completion of the first turn after takeoff or establishment of a cruise climb on departure.

67.
4393. What is the recommended climb procedure when a nonradar departure control instructs a pilot to climb to the assigned altitude?

A— Maintain a continuous optimum climb until reaching assigned altitude and report passing each 1,000 foot level.
B— Climb at a maximum angle of climb to within 1,000 feet of the assigned altitude, then 500 feet per minute the last 1,000 feet.
C— Maintain an optimum climb on the centerline of the airway without intermediate level-offs until 1,000 feet below assigned altitude, then 500 to 1,500 feet per minute.

Answer (C) is correct (4393). *(AIM Para 4-4-9)*
When ATC clearances are given to descend or climb to a certain altitude, the pilot should use the optimum rate consistent with the operating characteristics of the aircraft to 1,000 ft. above or below the assigned altitude and then attempt to descend or climb at a rate of between 500 and 1,500 fpm until reaching the assigned altitude. Also, on airways, one should climb and descend on the centerline of the airway with no intermediate level-offs.
Answer (A) is incorrect because the pilot is not required to report passing each 1,000 ft. of altitude. Answer (B) is incorrect because one should normally use a cruise climb rather than a maximum angle of climb.

68.
4555. To comply with ATC instructions for altitude changes of more than 1,000 feet, what rate of climb or descent should be used?

A— As rapidly as practicable to 500 feet above/below the assigned altitude, and then at 500 feet per minute until the assigned altitude is reached.

B— 1,000 feet per minute during climb and 500 feet per minute during descents until reaching the assigned altitude.

C— As rapidly as practicable to 1,000 feet above/below the assigned altitude, and then between 500 and 1,500 feet per minute until reaching the assigned altitude.

69.
4380. When ATC has not imposed any climb or descent restrictions and aircraft are within 1,000 feet of assigned altitude, pilots should attempt to both climb and descend at a rate of between

A— 500 feet per minute and 1,000 feet per minute.

B— 500 feet per minute and 1,500 feet per minute.

C— 1,000 feet per minute and 2,000 feet per minute.

70.
4456. Which report should be made to ATC without a specific request when not in radar contact?

A— Entering instrument meteorological conditions.

B— When leaving final approach fix in bound on final approach.

C— Correcting an E.T.A. any time a previous E.T.A. is in error in excess of 2 minutes.

Answer (C) is correct (4555). *(AIM Para 4-4-9)*
When ATC clearances are given to descend or climb to a certain altitude, the pilot should use the optimum rate consistent with the operating characteristics of the aircraft to 1,000 ft. above or below the assigned altitude and then attempt to descend or climb at a rate of between 500 and 1,500 fpm until reaching the assigned altitude. Also, one should climb and descend on the centerline of the airway with no intermediate level-offs.

Answer (A) is incorrect because the rate should be between 500 and 1,500 fpm after you are within 1,000 ft., not 500 ft., of the target altitude. Answer (B) is incorrect because the rate of climb and descent should be based upon aircraft capability. Also, when 1,000 ft. above or below the assigned altitude, the pilot should attempt to descend or climb at a rate of between 500 and 1,500 fpm until the assigned altitude is reached.

Answer (B) is correct (4380). *(AIM Para 4-4-9)*
When ATC clearances are given to descend or climb to a certain altitude, the pilot should use the optimum rate consistent with the operating characteristics of the aircraft to 1,000 ft. above or below the assigned altitude and then attempt to descend or climb at a rate of between 500 and 1,500 fpm until reaching the assigned altitude. Also, on airways, one should climb and descend on the centerline of the airway with no intermediate level-offs.

Answer (A) is incorrect because, within 1,000 ft. of the assigned altitude, pilots should attempt to climb/descend at a rate of between 500 and 1,500 fpm, not 1,000 fpm. Answer (C) is incorrect because, within 1,000 ft. of the assigned altitude, pilots should attempt to climb/descend at a rate of between 500 and 1,500 fpm, not 1,000 and 2,000 fpm.

Answer (B) is correct (4456). *(AIM Para 5-3-3)*
The following reports (in addition to those that are made at all times) should be made to ATC without a specific request when not in radar contact:

1. A report when leaving final approach fix in bound on final approach (nonprecision approach) or when leaving the outer marker or fix used in lieu of the outer marker in bound on final approach (precision approach).
2. Position reports over compulsory reporting points.
3. A corrected ETA to a reporting point at any time it becomes apparent that an estimate as previously submitted is in error in excess of 3 min.

Answer (A) is incorrect because a report should be made to ATC whether or not in radar contact anytime you encounter any type of weather conditions that have not been forecast. If IMC were forecast, no report is necessary. Answer (C) is incorrect because a report should be made to ATC when correcting an ETA anytime a previous ETA is in error in excess of 3 min., not 2 min.

71.
4078. For IFR planning purposes, what are the compulsory reporting points when using VOR/DME or VORTAC fixes to define a direct route not on established airways?

A— Fixes selected to define the route.
B— There are no compulsory reporting points unless advised by ATC.
C— At the changeover points.

72.
4390. When should your transponder be on Mode C while on an IFR flight?

A— Only when ATC requests Mode C.
B— At all times if the equipment has been calibrated, unless requested otherwise by ATC.
C— When passing 12,500 feet MSL.

73.
4421. During a flight, the controller advises "traffic 2 o'clock 5 miles southbound." The pilot is holding 20° correction for a crosswind from the right. Where should the pilot look for the traffic?

A— 40° to the right of the aircraft's nose.
B— 20° to the right of the aircraft's nose.
C— Straight ahead.

74.
4605. During the en route phase of an IFR flight, the pilot is advised "Radar service terminated." What action is appropriate?

A— Set transponder to code 1200.
B— Resume normal position reporting.
C— Activate the IDENT feature of the transponder to re-establish radar contact.

Answer (A) is correct (4078). *(AIM Para 5-3-2)*
When using VOR/DME or VORTAC fixes to define a direct route not on an established airway, those fixes selected to define the route automatically become compulsory reporting points (when not in radar contact) for the flight.
Answer (B) is incorrect because, on a direct flight, the compulsory reporting points are those fixes used to define the route. Answer (C) is incorrect because some navigation systems used on direct flights do not require COPs to prevent the loss of navigation guidance, e.g., GPS.

Answer (B) is correct (4390). *(AIM Para 4-1-19)*
If your airplane's transponder is equipped to reply on Mode C, it should be on at all times unless deactivation is directed by ATC.
Answer (A) is incorrect because Mode C should be turned off, not on, only when directed by ATC.
Answer (C) is incorrect because Mode C is a requirement anytime you are flying above 10,000 ft. MSL, not 12,500 ft. MSL.

Answer (A) is correct (4421). *(AIM Para 4-1-14)*
ATC issues traffic advisories in terms of the aircraft's course (i.e., ground track), not its heading. Allowance must be made for drift correction or course change made simultaneously with the radar traffic information. 2 o'clock is approximately 60° to the right of the aircraft's course. Since the pilot is already holding a 20° right-wind correction, (s)he should look only 40° to the right of the aircraft's nose for the traffic.
Answer (B) is incorrect because 20° to the right of the aircraft's nose is 40° to the right of the aircraft's track, which is between 1 and 2 o'clock. Answer (C) is incorrect because straight ahead is 20° (wind correction) to the right of the aircraft's track, which is between 12 and 1 o'clock.

Answer (B) is correct (4605). *(AIM Para 5-3-2)*
During the en route phase of an IFR flight, if you are advised of "radar service terminated" or "radar contact lost," you should resume normal position reporting as required when not in radar contact.
Answer (A) is incorrect because you should set the transponder to code 1200 (VFR) only when you cancel your IFR flight plan with ATC and you are instructed to squawk VFR. Answer (C) is incorrect because you should activate the IDENT feature of the transponder only upon the request of ATC.

75.
4423. What does the ATC term "Radar Contact" signify?

A— Your aircraft has been identified and you will receive separation from all aircraft while in contact with this radar facility.

B— Your aircraft has been identified on the radar display and radar flight-following will be provided until radar identification is terminated.

C— You will be given traffic advisories until advised the service has been terminated or that radar contact has been lost.

Answer (B) is correct (4423). *(P/C Glossary)*
The term "radar contact" is used by ATC to inform an aircraft that it is identified on the radar display and that radar flight following will be provided until radar service is terminated. Reporting over compulsory reporting points is not required when an aircraft is in radar contact.
Answer (A) is incorrect because separation from all aircraft occurs only in Class A, B, and C airspace. Answer (C) is incorrect because traffic advisory service is provided only to the extent possible. Higher-priority duties take precedence, such as controlling or other limitations, volume of traffic, frequency congestion, or controller workload.

76.
4422. What is meant when departure control instructs you to "resume own navigation" after you have been vectored to a Victor airway?

A— You should maintain the airway by use of your navigation equipment.

B— Radar service is terminated.

C— You are still in radar contact, but must make position reports.

Answer (A) is correct (4422). *(P/C Glossary)*
Assuming you have been vectored to an airway on your intended route of flight, you should maintain your course along the airway by use of your navigation equipment when ATC advises you to resume your own navigation.
Answer (B) is incorrect because "resume navigation" means that the radar controller will stop vectoring you, not stop observing you. Answer (C) is incorrect because position reporting is not required when you are in radar contact with ATC.

77.
4424. Upon intercepting the assigned radial, the controller advises you that you are on the airway and to "RESUME OWN NAVIGATION." This phrase means that

A— you are still in radar contact, but must make position reports.

B— radar services are terminated and you will be responsible for position reports.

C— you are to assume responsibility for your own navigation.

Answer (C) is correct (4424). *(P/C Glossary)*
Assuming you have been vectored to an airway on your intended route of flight, you should maintain your course along the airway by use of your navigation equipment when ATC advises you to resume your own navigation.
Answer (A) is incorrect because position reporting is not required when in radar contact. Answer (B) is incorrect because "resume navigation" means only that the radar controller is going to stop vectoring you, not stop observing you.

78.
4409. What service is provided by departure control to an IFR flight when operating from an airport within the outer area of Class C airspace?

A— Separation from all aircraft.

B— Position and altitude of all traffic within 2 miles of the IFR pilot's line of flight and altitude.

C— Separation from all IFR aircraft and participating VFR aircraft.

Answer (C) is correct (4409). *(FAR 91.130)*
In the outer area of Class C airspace, ATC provides an IFR flight with separation from all IFR aircraft and participating VFR aircraft. VFR aircraft participation in the outer area is voluntary.
Answer (A) is incorrect because an IFR flight is provided traffic advisories and conflict resolution with other IFR aircraft and with only participating VFR aircraft within the outer area of Class C airspace. Answer (B) is incorrect because ATC provides position and altitude of aircraft that may conflict, not position and altitude of all traffic within 2 NM of your line of flight.

79.
4758. If during a VFR practice instrument approach, Radar Approach Control assigns an altitude or heading that will cause you to enter the clouds, what action should be taken?

A— Enter the clouds, since ATC authorization for practice approaches is considered an IFR clearance.

B— Avoid the clouds and inform ATC that altitude/heading will not permit VFR.

C— Abandon the approach.

Answer (B) is correct (4758). *(AIM Para 4-3-21)*
During a VFR practice instrument approach, you are responsible to comply with basic visual flight rules. Thus, if radar approach assigns an altitude or heading that will cause you to enter the clouds, you must avoid the clouds and inform ATC that that altitude/heading will not permit VFR.
Answer (A) is incorrect because pilots may not enter clouds without an IFR clearance. Answer (C) is incorrect because the pilot need only modify, not abandon the approach, to maintain VFR.

80.
4726. You are being vectored to the ILS approach course, but have not been cleared for the approach. It becomes evident that you will pass through the localizer course. What action should be taken?

A— Turn outbound and make a procedure turn.

B— Continue on the assigned heading and query ATC.

C— Start a turn to the inbound heading and inquire if you are cleared for the approach.

Answer (B) is correct (4726). *(AIM Para 5-4-3)*

Normally, you will be informed by ATC when it is necessary to vector across the final approach course for spacing or other reasons. If you have not been cleared for the approach and it becomes evident that you will cross the approach course, you must continue on your assigned heading and question ATC.

Answer (A) is incorrect because, while you are being radar vectored, you are not authorized to make a procedure turn unless cleared by ATC. Answer (C) is incorrect because you must maintain your assigned heading, not turn inbound on the final approach course.

81.
4725. What is the pilot in command's responsibility when flying a propeller aircraft within 20 miles of the airport of intended landing and ATC requests the pilot to reduce speed to 160? (Pilot complies with speed adjustment.)

A— Reduce TAS to 160 knots and maintain until advised by ATC.

B— Reduce IAS to 160 MPH and maintain until advised by ATC.

C— Reduce IAS to 160 knots and maintain that speed within 10 knots.

Answer (C) is correct (4725). *(AIM Para 4-4-11)*

ATC will express all speed adjustments in terms of knots based on indicated airspeed (IAS) in 10-kt. increments below FL 240. When complying with an ATC speed adjustment to reduce to 160, you should reduce IAS to 160 kt. and maintain that speed within 10 kt.

Answer (A) is incorrect because ATC speed restrictions are based on indicated airspeed (IAS), not true airspeed (TAS). Answer (B) is incorrect because airspeeds are given in knots, not MPH.

82.
4071. For which speed variation should you notify ATC?

A— When the ground speed changes more than 5 knots.

B— When the average true airspeed changes 5 percent or 10 knots, whichever is greater.

C— Any time the ground speed changes 10 MPH.

Answer (B) is correct (4071). *(AIM Para 5-3-3)*

There are a number of things a pilot needs to report to ATC without being requested. One is a change in the average TAS at cruising altitude when it varies by 5% or 10 kt. (whichever is greater) from that filed in the flight plan.

Answer (A) is incorrect because ATC should be notified if TAS, not ground speed, varies more than 10 kt., not 5 kt., or 5%, whichever is greater. Answer (C) is incorrect because ATC should be notified if TAS, not ground speed, varies more than 10 kt., not 10 MPH, or 5%, whichever is greater.

83.
4469. When are you required to establish communications with the tower (Class D airspace), if you cancel your IFR flight plan 10 miles from the destination?

A— Immediately after canceling the flight plan.

B— When advised by ARTCC.

C— Before entering Class D airspace.

Answer (C) is correct (4469). *(FAR 91.129)*

You must establish two-way radio communication with the tower before entering Class D airspace. Thus, if you cancel your IFR flight plan, you must notify the tower of your position and intentions prior to entering Class D airspace.

Answer (A) is incorrect because, while it is a good operating practice to make an initial call to the tower up to 15 mi. from a Class D airport, it is required only before entering Class D airspace. Answer (B) is incorrect because, while ARTCC may advise you to contact the tower when the controller accepts your IFR flight plan cancellation, you are required to contact the tower only prior to entering Class D airspace.

84.

4415. If a control tower and an FSS are located on the same airport, which function is provided by the FSS during those periods when the tower is closed?

A— Automatic closing of the IFR flight plan.

B— Approach control services.

C— Airport Advisory Service.

Answer (C) is correct (4415). *(AIM Para 4-1-9)*

An FSS located on an airport will provide Local Airport Advisory (LAA) service at that airport when there is no operating control tower. This service provides arriving and departing aircraft with wind direction and speed, favored runway, altimeter setting, pertinent known traffic, pertinent known field condition, and airport taxi routes and traffic patterns. The information is advisory in nature.

Answer (A) is incorrect because the pilot must initiate cancellation of the IFR plan if operating IFR to an airport with no functioning control tower. Answer (B) is incorrect because FSS personnel can only issue advisories, not provide ATC services, to pilots.

85.

4416. Which service is provided for IFR arrivals by a FSS located on an airport without a control tower?

A— Automatic closing of the IFR flight plan.

B— Airport advisories.

C— All functions of approach control.

Answer (B) is correct (4416). *(AIM Para 4-1-9)*

An FSS located on an airport will provide Local Airport Advisory (LAA) service at that airport if there is no operating control tower. This service provides arriving and departing aircraft with wind direction and speed, favored runway, altimeter setting, pertinent known traffic, pertinent known field condition, and airport taxi routes and traffic patterns. The information is advisory in nature.

Answer (A) is incorrect because the pilot must initiate cancellation of the IFR plan if operating IFR to an airport with no operating control tower. Answer (C) is incorrect because FSS personnel can issue only advisories, not ATC clearances and instructions, to pilots.

86.

4379. What does declaring "minimum fuel" to ATC imply?

A— Traffic priority is needed to the destination airport.

B— Emergency handling is required to the nearest useable airport.

C— Merely an advisory that indicates an emergency situation is possible should any undue delay occur.

Answer (C) is correct (4379). *(AIM Para 5-5-15)*

You should advise ATC of your minimum fuel status when your fuel supply has reached a state in which, upon reaching your destination, you cannot accept any undue delay. Be aware that this is not an emergency situation, but merely an advisory that indicates an emergency situation is possible should any undue delay occur.

Answer (A) is incorrect because priority may be issued when declaring an emergency, not when declaring minimum fuel. Answer (B) is incorrect because minimum fuel advisory is not an emergency situation.

5.11 Radio Communication Failure

87.

4462. You enter a holding pattern (at a fix that is not the same as the approach fix) with an EFC time of 1530. At 1520 you experience complete two-way communications failure. Which procedure should you follow to execute the approach to a landing?

A— Depart the holding fix to arrive at the approach fix as close as possible to the EFC time and complete the approach.

B— Depart the holding fix at the EFC time, and complete the approach.

C— Depart the holding fix at the earliest of the flight planned ETA or the EFC time, and complete the approach.

Answer (B) is correct (4462). *(FAR 91.185)*

If you experience two-way radio communication failure at a holding fix that is not the same as the approach fix, leave the holding fix at the EFC time, and complete the approach.

Answer (A) is incorrect because you leave for, not arrive at, the approach fix at the EFC time. Answer (C) is incorrect because the EFC time takes precedence over the flight plan ETA.

88.
4463. Which procedure should you follow if you experience two-way communications failure while holding at a holding fix with an EFC time? (The holding fix is not the same as the approach fix.)

A— Depart the holding fix to arrive at the approach fix as close as possible to the EFC time.
B— Depart the holding fix at the EFC time.
C— Proceed immediately to the approach fix and hold until EFC.

89.
4464. You are in IMC and have two-way radio communications failure. If you do not exercise emergency authority, what procedure are you expected to follow?

A— Set transponder to code 7600, continue flight on assigned route and fly at the last assigned altitude or the MEA, whichever is higher.
B— Set transponder to code 7700 for 1 minute, then to 7600, and fly to an area with VFR weather conditions.
C— Set transponder to 7700 and fly to an area where you can let down in VFR conditions.

90.
4466. What altitude and route should be used if you are flying in IMC and have two-way radio communications failure?

A— Continue on the route specified in your clearance, fly at an altitude that is the highest of last assigned altitude, altitude ATC has informed you to expect, or the MEA.
B— Fly direct to an area that has been forecast to have VFR conditions, fly at an altitude that is at least 1,000 feet above the highest obstacles along the route.
C— Descend to MEA and, if clear of clouds, proceed to the nearest appropriate airport. If not clear of clouds, maintain the highest of the MEA's along the clearance route.

91.
4465. Which procedure should you follow if, during an IFR flight in VFR conditions, you have two-way radio communications failure?

A— Continue the flight under VFR and land as soon as practicable.
B— Continue the flight at assigned altitude and route, start approach at your ETA, or, if late, start approach upon arrival.
C— Land at the nearest airport that has VFR conditions.

Answer (B) is correct (4463). *(FAR 91.185)*
If you experience two-way radio communication failure at a holding fix that is not the same as the approach fix, leave the holding fix at the EFC time, and complete the approach.
Answer (A) is incorrect because you would leave for, not arrive at, the approach fix at the EFC time.
Answer (C) is incorrect because you should not leave the holding fix to go to the approach fix until the EFC time.

Answer (A) is correct (4464). *(FAR 91.185, AIM Para 6-4-2)*
When you lose two-way radio capability, you should alert ATC by changing your transponder to code 7600. If you experience two-way radio communication failure while in IMC, continue your flight on the assigned route and maintain the last assigned altitude or the MEA, whichever is higher.
Answer (B) is incorrect because the transponder should be set on 7600 at all times, not 7700 for 1 min., and you must maintain your assigned route and altitude (or MEA). If VMC are encountered, continue the flight under VFR and land as soon as practicable. Answer (C) is incorrect because you should set the transponder to 7600. While in IMC, you must maintain your assigned route and altitude (or MEA).

Answer (A) is correct (4466). *(FAR 91.185)*
When you lose two-way radio communication in IMC, continue the flight by the route assigned by the last ATC clearance, by the route that ATC has advised may be expected to be assigned, or by the flight plan. Use the highest of the altitude assigned in the last ATC clearance, the MEA, or the flight level ATC may be expected to assign.
Answer (B) is incorrect because you should continue the assigned route. Answer (C) is incorrect because you should use the highest of the altitude assigned, the altitude expected to be assigned, or MEA.

Answer (A) is correct (4465). *(FAR 91.185)*
If a radio failure occurs during an IFR flight in VFR conditions or if VFR conditions are encountered after the failure, the pilot should continue the flight under VFR and land as soon as practicable.
Answer (B) is incorrect because this procedure applies only if you are in instrument meteorological conditions, not VFR. Answer (C) is incorrect because the pilot retains the prerogative of exercising good judgment and is not required to land at an unauthorized airport or an airport unsuitable for the type of aircraft flown, nor is the pilot required to land only minutes short of the destination.

91a.
4374. While flying on an IFR flight plan, you experience two-way communications radio failure while in VFR conditions. In this situation, you should continue your flight under

A— VFR and land as soon as practicable.
B— IFR and maintain the last assigned route and altitude to your flight plan destination.
C— VFR and proceed to your flight plan destination.

Answer (A) is correct (4374). *(FAR 91.185)*
If a radio failure occurs during an IFR flight in VFR conditions or if VFR conditions are encountered after the failure, the pilot should continue the flight under VFR and land as soon as practicable.
Answer (B) is incorrect because this procedure applies only if you are in instrument meteorological conditions, not VFR. Answer (C) is incorrect because you should land as soon as practicable rather than proceeding to your flight plan destination.

5.12 Navigation Radio Failure

92.
4448. What action should you take if your DME fails at FL 240?

A— Advise ATC of the failure and land at the nearest available airport where repairs can be made.
B— Notify ATC that it will be necessary for you to go to a lower altitude, since your DME has failed.
C— Notify ATC of the failure and continue to the next airport of intended landing where repairs can be made.

Answer (C) is correct (4448). *(FAR 91.205)*
When required DME fails at or above FL 240, the pilot should notify ATC immediately and may continue operations at and above FL 240 to the next airport of intended landing at which repairs or replacement of the equipment can be made.
Answer (A) is incorrect because you can continue to your destination, not the nearest airport, and have repairs made there. Answer (B) is incorrect because you need not descend to a lower altitude after you notify ATC. You may continue to operate at or above FL 240.

93.
4459. What is the procedure when the DME malfunctions at or above 24,000 feet MSL?

A— Notify ATC immediately and request an altitude below 24,000 feet.
B— Continue to your destination in VFR conditions and report the malfunction.
C— After immediately notifying ATC, you may continue to the next airport of intended landing where repairs can be made.

Answer (C) is correct (4459). *(FAR 91.205)*
When required DME fails at or above FL 240, the pilot should notify ATC immediately and may continue operations at and above FL 240 to the next airport of intended landing at which repairs or replacement of the equipment can be made.
Answer (A) is incorrect because there is no need to descend to a lower altitude. You may continue to your destination and have repairs made there. Answer (B) is incorrect because you may continue your flight as normal, even under IFR, and make repairs at your destination.

94.
4460. What action should you take if your No. 1 VOR receiver malfunctions while operating in controlled airspace under IFR? Your aircraft is equipped with two VOR receivers. The No. 1 receiver has Omni/Localizer/Glide Slope capability, and the No. 2 receiver has only VOR/Localizer capability.

A— Report the malfunction immediately to ATC.
B— Continue the flight as cleared; no report is required.
C— Continue the approach and request a VOR or NDB approach.

Answer (A) is correct (4460). *(FAR 91.187)*
When operating under IFR in controlled airspace, you must immediately report to ATC as soon as practical any malfunctions of navigational, approach, or communication equipment occurring in flight. Each report should include the following:

1. Aircraft identification,
2. Equipment affected,
3. Degree to which the capability of the pilot to operate under IFR in the ATC system is impaired, and
4. Nature and extent of assistance desired from ATC.

Answer (B) is incorrect because a report to ATC is required. Answer (C) is incorrect because ATC will know that you need a VOR or NDB approach if you report the ILS receiver inoperative.

5.13 Types of Airspace

95.
4077. Which types of airspace are depicted on the En Route Low Altitude Chart?

A— Class D, Class C, Class B, Class E, and special use airspace.
B— Class A, special use airspace, Class D, and Class E.
C— Special use airspace, Class E, Class D, Class A, Class B, and Class C.

Answer (A) is correct (4077). *(ACL)*
En Route Low Altitude Charts depict Class B, Class C, Class D, Class E, and special-use airspace up to but not including 18,000 ft. MSL.
Answer (B) is incorrect because Class A airspace is airspace above FL 180. It is not depicted on En Route Low-Altitude Charts. Answer (C) is incorrect because Class A airspace is not depicted on En Route Low-Altitude Charts.

96.
4475. Class G airspace is that airspace where

A— ATC does not control air traffic.
B— ATC controls only IFR flights.
C— the minimum visibility for VFR flight is 3 miles.

Answer (A) is correct (4475). *(AIM Para 3-3-1)*
Class G airspace is that portion of the airspace that has not been designated as Class A, Class B, Class C, Class D, or Class E. In Class G airspace, ATC has neither the authority nor the responsibility for exercising control over air traffic in any weather condition.
Answer (B) is incorrect because ATC does not control IFR flight in Class G airspace. Answer (C) is incorrect because the minimum visibility for VFR flight is 1 SM, not 3 SM, in Class G airspace during the day when below 10,000 ft. MSL.

97.
4473. Which airspace is defined as a transition area when designated in conjunction with an airport which has a prescribed IAP?

A— The Class E airspace extending upward from 700 feet or more above the surface and terminating at the base of the overlying controlled airspace.
B— That Class D airspace extending from the surface and terminating at the base of the continental control area.
C— The Class C airspace extending from the surface to 700 or 1,200 feet AGL, where designated.

Answer (A) is correct (4473). *(AIM Para 3-2-6)*
Transition areas are Class E airspace that extends upward from 700 ft. or more above the surface when designated in conjunction with an airport for which an instrument approach procedure (IAP) has been pre-scribed. Class E airspace extends up to but does not include 18,000 ft. MSL, i.e., the base of Class A airspace.
Answer (B) is incorrect because a transition area is classified as Class E, not Class D, airspace. Answer (C) is incorrect because transition areas are Class E, not Class C, airspace and extend upward from, not to, 700 ft.

98.
4476. What are the vertical limits of a transition area that is designated in conjunction with an airport having a prescribed IAP?

A— Surface to 700 feet AGL.
B— 1,200 feet AGL to the base of the overlying controlled airspace.
C— 700 feet AGL or more to the base of the overlying controlled airspace.

Answer (C) is correct (4476). *(AIM Para 3-2-6)*
Transition areas are controlled airspace extending upward from 700 ft. or more above the surface when designated in conjunction with an airport for which an instrument approach procedure has been prescribed. Transition areas terminate at the base of overlying controlled airspace (i.e., Class A airspace).
Answer (A) is incorrect because a transition area begins at 700 ft. AGL, not the surface, when it is designated in conjunction with an IAP. Answer (B) is incorrect because transition areas begin at 1,200 ft. AGL when designated in conjunction with an airway route structure or segment, not with an airport with an instrument approach.

99.
4474. The vertical extent of the Class A airspace throughout the conterminous U.S. extends from

A— 18,000 feet to and including FL 450.
B— 18,000 feet to and including FL 600.
C— 12,500 feet to and including FL 600.

Answer (B) is correct (4474). *(AIM Para 3-2-2)*
Class A airspace extends from 18,000 ft. MSL to and including FL 600.
Answer (A) is incorrect because FL 450 is the top of the jet routes. Answer (C) is incorrect because the base of Class A airspace is 18,000 ft. MSL, not 12,500 ft. MSL.

100.
4434. MOAs are established to

A— prohibit all civil aircraft because of hazardous or secret activities.
B— separate certain military activities from IFR traffic.
C— restrict civil aircraft during periods of high-density training activities.

Answer (B) is correct (4434). *(AIM Para 3-4-5)*
MOAs consist of airspace of defined vertical and lateral limits established for the purpose of separating certain military training activities from IFR traffic. When an MOA is in use, nonparticipating IFR traffic may be cleared to fly through if ATC can provide IFR separation. Otherwise, ATC will reroute or restrict nonparticipating IFR traffic.
Answer (A) is incorrect because a prohibited area, not an MOA, prohibits all aircraft for reasons of national security. Answer (C) is incorrect because a restricted area, not an MOA, is used to restrict aircraft during certain periods.

101.
4526. (Refer to figure 93 below.) What is the floor of Class E airspace when designated in conjunction with an airway?

A— 700 feet AGL.
B— 1,200 feet AGL.
C— 1,500 feet AGL.

Answer (B) is correct (4526). *(AIM Para 3-2-6)*
The floor of Class E airspace when designated in conjunction with an airway is 1,200 ft. AGL.
Answer (A) is incorrect because 700 ft. AGL is the floor of Class E airspace when designated in conjunction with an airport which has an approved IAP, not with an airway. Answer (C) is incorrect because the floor of Class E airspace when designated in conjunction with an airway is 1,200 ft. AGL, not 1,500 ft. AGL.

102.
4527. (Refer to figure 93 below.) Which altitude is the normal upper limit for Class D airspace?

A— 1,000 feet AGL.
B— 2,500 feet AGL.
C— 4,000 feet AGL.

Answer (B) is correct (4527). *(AIM Para 3-2-5)*
Class D airspace extends from the surface up to and including 2,500 ft. AGL.
Answer (A) is incorrect because 1,000 ft. AGL is the normal traffic pattern altitude for piston aircraft, not the ceiling of Class D airspace. Answer (C) is incorrect because 4,000 ft. AGL is the upper limit for Class C, not Class D, airspace.

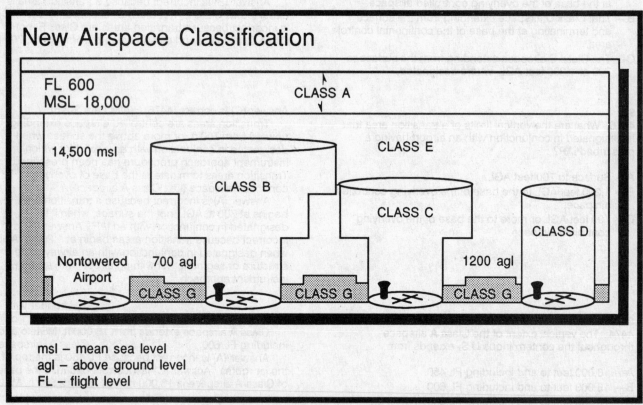

FIGURE 93.—New Airspace Classification.

103.
4528. (Refer to figure 93 above.) What is the floor of Class E airspace when designated in conjunction with an airport which has an approved IAP?

A— 500 feet AGL.
B— 700 feet AGL.
C— 1,200 feet AGL.

Answer (B) is correct (4528). *(AIM Para 3-2-6)*
The floor of Class E airspace when designated in conjunction with an airport which has an approved IAP is 700 ft. AGL.
Answer (A) is incorrect because 500 ft. AGL is not an altitude which defines airspace. Answer (C) is incorrect because 1,200 ft. AGL is the floor of Class E airspace when designated in conjunction with an airway, not an approved IAP.

104.
4529. (Refer to figure 93 on page 178.) Which altitude is the upper limit for Class A airspace?

A— 14,500 feet MSL.
B— 18,000 feet MSL.
C— 60,000 feet MSL.

Answer (C) is correct (4529). *(AIM Para 3-2-2)*
Class A airspace extends from 18,000 ft. MSL to and including 60,000 ft. MSL (i.e., FL 600).
Answer (A) is incorrect because 14,500 ft. MSL is the upper limit for Class G, not Class A, airspace. Answer (B) is incorrect because 18,000 ft. MSL is the floor, not the upper limit, of Class A airspace.

105.
4530. (Refer to figure 93 on page 178.) What is the maximum altitude that Class G airspace will exist? (Does not include airspace less than 1,500 feet AGL.)

A— 18,000 feet MSL.
B— 14,500 feet MSL.
C— 14,000 feet MSL.

Answer (B) is correct (4530). *(AIM Para 3-2-6)*
The maximum altitude at which Class G airspace will exist (not including airspace less than 1,500 ft. AGL) is 14,500 ft. MSL.
Answer (A) is incorrect because 18,000 ft. MSL is the floor of Class A airspace, not the maximum altitude at which Class G airspace will exist. Answer (C) is incorrect because 14,000 ft. MSL is not an altitude which defines airspace.

106.
4531. (Refer to figure 93 on page 178.) What is generally the maximum altitude for Class B airspace?

A— 4,000 feet MSL.
B— 10,000 feet MSL.
C— 14,500 feet MSL.

Answer (B) is correct (4531). *(AIM Para 3-2-3)*
The maximum altitude for Class B airspace will generally be 10,000 ft. MSL.
Answer (A) is incorrect because 4,000 ft. MSL is not an altitude which defines airspace. Answer (C) is incorrect because 14,500 ft. MSL is the maximum altitude at which Class G, not Class B, airspace will exist.

107.
4532. (Refer to figure 93 on page 178.) What are the normal lateral limits for Class D airspace?

A— 8 NM.
B— 5 NM.
C— 4 NM.

Answer (C) is correct (4532). *(AIM Para 3-2-5)*
The normal lateral limit for Class D airspace is approximately 4 NM.
Answer (A) is incorrect because 8 NM is not a defined lateral limit of any class of airspace surface area. Answer (B) is incorrect because 5 NM defines the lateral limit of a Class C, not Class D, surface area.

108.
4533. (Refer to figure 93 on page 178.) What is the floor of Class A airspace?

A— 10,000 feet MSL.
B— 14,500 feet MSL.
C— 18,000 feet MSL.

Answer (C) is correct (4533). *(AIM Para 3-2-2)*
Class A airspace extends from 18,000 ft. MSL up to, and including, FL 600.
Answer (A) is incorrect because 10,000 ft. MSL is the floor of controlled airspace in which a transponder with altitude encoding capability is required, not the floor of Class A airspace. Answer (B) is incorrect because 14,500 ft. MSL is a floor of Class E, not Class A, airspace.

109.
4539. What minimum aircraft equipment is required for operation within Class C airspace?

A— Two-way communications and Mode C transponder.
B— Two-way communications.
C— Transponder and DME.

Answer (A) is correct (4539). *(AIM Para 3-2-4)*
In Class C airspace, the equipment requirement is an operating two-way communications radio and a Mode C transponder.
Answer (B) is incorrect because a Mode C transponder is also required. Answer (C) is incorrect because two-way communications and Mode C capability are also required and DME is not required.

END OF CHAPTER

CHAPTER SIX
HOLDING AND INSTRUMENT APPROACHES

This chapter contains outlines of major concepts tested, all FAA test questions and answers regarding holding and instrument approaches, and an explanation of each answer. Each module, or subtopic, within this chapter is listed above with the number of questions from the FAA pilot knowledge test pertaining to that particular module. For each module, the first number following the parentheses is the page number on which the outline begins, and the next number is the page number on which the questions begin.

There are 155 questions in this chapter. We separate and organize the FAA questions into meaningful study units, i.e., chapters and modules. As an analogy, it is easier to deal with the "trees" if you understand the "forest." In this context, "trees" are individual FAA questions, and the "forest" is the instrument rating knowledge test. The organizational units between the overall instrument rating knowledge test and the individual instrument rating test questions are chapters and modules in this book.

CAUTION: The **sole purpose** of this book is to expedite your passing the FAA instrument rating knowledge test. Accordingly, all extraneous material (i.e., topics or regulations not directly tested on the FAA knowledge test) is omitted, even though much more information and knowledge are necessary to fly safely. This additional material is presented in *Instrument Pilot Flight Maneuvers and Practical Test Prep*, *Pilot Handbook*, *Aviation Weather and Weather Services*, and *FAR/AIM*, available from Gleim Publications, Inc. See the order form on page 488.

6.1 CONTACT AND VISUAL APPROACHES (Questions 1-6)

1.   You may request a contact approach if there is 1 SM flight visibility and you can operate clear of clouds to the destination airport.

   a.   A contact approach is an alternative to a standard instrument approach procedure (SIAP).

   b.   It cannot be assigned by ATC.

2.   ATC may assign a visual approach to an airport or authorize you to follow other airplanes for a landing if the approach can be accomplished in VFR.

   a.   You must have the airport or the preceding aircraft in sight.

   b.   Visual approaches can be assigned by ATC; contact approaches cannot.

   c.   On visual approaches, radar service is automatically terminated when the aircraft is instructed to contact the tower.

6.2 SDF AND LDA APPROACHES (Questions 7-10)

1.   LDA (localizer-type directional aid) is as useful and accurate as a localizer (3° to 6° course width).

   a.   The LDA is very similar to an instrument landing system (ILS), but it usually does not have a glide slope (i.e., it has only a localizer) and is **not** aligned with the runway.

2.   SDF (simplified directional facility) has a course width of either 6° or 12°.

   a.   SDF approaches may or may not be aligned with a runway (and their courses are wider). SDF does not have a glide slope.

6.3 RUNWAY VISUAL RANGE (RVR) (Questions 11-15)

1.   RVR is an instrumentally derived value that represents the horizontal distance the pilot can see down the runway from the approach end.

   a.   It is based on the measurement of a transmissometer near the touchdown point of the instrument runway and is reported in hundreds of feet.

2.   If RVR is inoperative and cannot be reported, convert the RVR minimum to ground visibility, and use that as the visibility minimum for takeoffs and landings.

   a.   See Legend 11 on page 193 for a chart of RVR/visibility comparable values.

3.   The normal ILS visibility minimum is ½ SM, which is 2400 RVR.

6.4 MISSED APPROACHES (Questions 16-17)

1.   When executing a missed approach prior to the missed approach point (MAP), continue the approach to the MAP at or above the minimum descent altitude (MDA) or decision height (DH) before executing any turns.

2.   If you lose visual reference in a circle to land from an instrument approach, you should make a climbing turn toward your landing runway to become established on the missed approach course.

6.5 ILS SPECIFICATIONS (Questions 18-28)

1.   The ILS missed approach should be executed upon arrival at the DH on the glide slope if the visual reference requirements are not met.

2.   The normal decision height for a Category I ILS is 200 ft. AGL.

   a.   This is the height of the glide slope centerline at the middle marker.

3.   The amount of deflection and distance from the localizer and the glide slope for an ILS is presented as Fig. 139 on page 211.

   a.   A series of questions asks how far you are from the localizer or glide slope centerlines given certain types of deflection on your glide slope indicator. These questions require interpreting Fig. 139.

4.   Compass locators, when used for the outer marker (OM) and middle marker (MM) of an ILS, transmit two-letter identification groups.

   a.   The outer compass locator (LOM) transmits the first two letters of the localizer identification group.

   b.   The middle compass locator (LMM) transmits the last two letters of the localizer identification group.

   c.   If the OM and/or MM are not compass locators, there is no two-letter identification transmission.

5.   An inner marker (IM) is identified by continuous dots at the rate of 6 per second and a flashing white marker beacon.

6.   If DME is available on an ILS or localizer approach, the DME/TACAN channel will be indicated in the localizer frequency box on the instrument approach chart.

7.   Parallel ILS approaches provide aircraft a minimum of 2 mi. radar separation between successive aircraft on the adjacent localizer course.

8.   Legend 28 on page 184 contains the ILS standard characteristics and terminology.

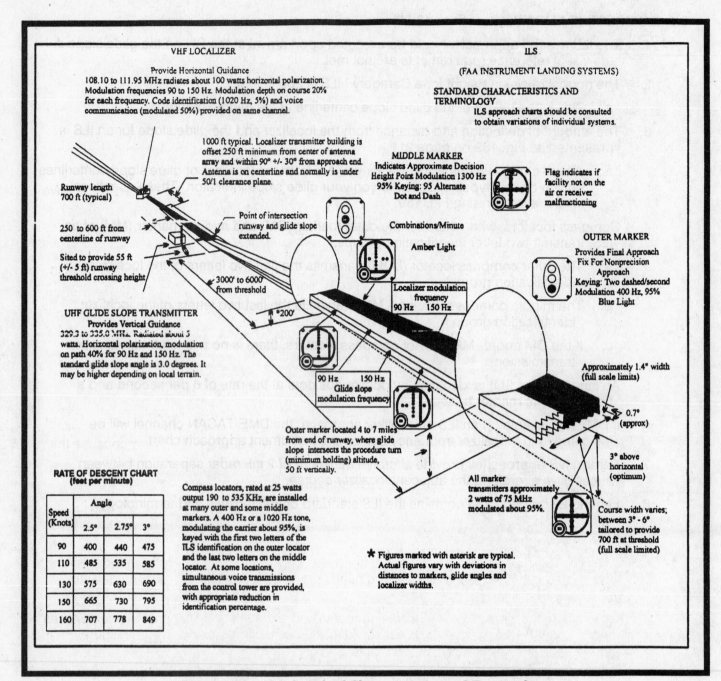

LEGEND 28.—ILS Standard Characteristics and Terminology.

6.6 UNUSABLE ILS COMPONENTS (Questions 29-36)

1. ILS components include

   a. Localizer
   b. Glide slope
   c. Outer marker
   d. Middle marker
   e. Approach lights

2. If more than one component is unusable, each minimum is raised to the highest minimum required by any single component that is inoperative.

3. A compass locator or precision approach radar (PAR) may be substituted for an inoperative OM or MM.

   a. An inoperative MM does not change the landing minimums; thus no substitution is necessary.

4. When installed with the ILS and specified in the approach procedure, DME may be used in lieu of the OM.

5. When the glide slope fails, the ILS reverts to a nonprecision localizer (LOC) approach.

   a. The LOC MDA and visibility minimums will be used.

6. If you are on the glide slope when the ILS fails and a VASI is in sight, you should continue the approach using the VASI, and report the malfunction to ATC.

6.7 FLYING THE APPROACH (Questions 37-48)

1. Rate of descent on the glide slope is dependent on the airplane groundspeed because the descent must be constant relative to the distance traveled over the ground.

   a. As groundspeed increases, the descent rate must increase.
   b. As groundspeed decreases, the descent rate must decrease.

2. If the airspeed is too fast and the glide slope and localizer are centered, you should initially reduce power.

3. When you are being vectored for an ILS approach and are about to fly through the localizer, you should maintain your last assigned heading and question ATC rather than deviate from a clearance.

4. If a wind shear changes from a headwind to a tailwind, the airspeed drops, the nose pitches down, and the vertical speed increases. You must initially increase power to resume normal approach speed.

   a. Then power must be reduced as airspeed stabilizes so you can maintain the glide slope due to the increased groundspeed.

   b. The tendency is to go below the glide slope.

5. If a wind shear changes from a tailwind to a headwind (or even to calm), you must decrease your power initially and then increase it once you are through the shear to maintain the glide slope.

   a. The tendency is to go above the glide slope.

6. In tracking the localizer, you should have your drift correction established to maintain the localizer centerline before reaching the outer marker.

   a. Then completion of the approach should be accomplished with heading corrections no greater than 2°.

6.8 ASR APPROACHES (Questions 49-53)

1. During airport surveillance radar (ASR) approaches, ATC provides headings, tells when to commence descent to MDA, gives the airplane's position each mile on final from the runway, and indicates arrival at the MAP.

2. Surveillance approaches may be used at airports for which civil radar instrument approach minimums have been published.

3. ATC radar, when approved for approach control service, may be used for course guidance to the final approach, ASR and PAR approaches, and monitoring of nonradar approaches.

4. During a no-gyro approach (i.e., when your gyroscopic instruments have failed), all turns prior to final approach should be made at the standard rate.

    a. After being handed off to the final approach controller, all turns should be at one-half the standard rate.

6.9 SIDE-STEP APPROACHES (Questions 54-55)

1. A side-step approach is an instrument approach to one runway until you can see a parallel runway and "side step" to land on the parallel runway.

2. A side-step approach is used when a pilot executes an approach procedure serving one of parallel runways that are separated by 1,200 ft. or less and then diverts to a parallel runway using a straight-in approach.

3. Execute a side-step procedure as soon as possible after the runway environment is in sight.

6.10 TIMED APPROACHES FROM HOLDING FIXES (Questions 56-59)

1. A timed approach is one in which you are cleared to leave the final approach fix or outer marker at a specified future time.

2. Timed approaches from a holding fix may be executed only under the following conditions:

    a. A control tower is in operation at the airport where the approach is conducted.

    b. Direct communication is maintained between pilot and approach control or center until the pilot is instructed to contact tower.

    c. If more than one missed approach procedure is available, none may require a course reversal; i.e., the missed approach procedure must not take you back to the final approach fix.

    d. If only one missed approach procedure is available, course reversal is not required, and the reported ceiling and visibility must be greater than the highest circling minimum for the IAP.

    e. When cleared for the approach, the pilot shall not execute a procedure turn.

3. When making a timed approach from a holding fix at the outer marker, you should adjust the holding pattern to leave the final approach fix inbound at the assigned time.

NOTE: Timed approaches are primarily used in nonradar environments.

6.11 HOLDING (Questions 60-80)

1. A holding procedure is a predetermined maneuver which keeps aircraft within a specified airspace while awaiting further clearance from ATC.

2. Holding patterns are race track-shaped patterns based on a fix which is a radio navigation facility (VOR, ADF, or other NAVAID); an intersection of NAVAID bearings, radials, or a DME fix; or a waypoint (GPS or other RNAV equipment).

3. Holding patterns consist of the following components (note that the fix is always at the end of the inbound leg):

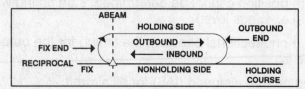

a. A **standard pattern** means the turns in the holding pattern are to the right.
b. A **nonstandard pattern** means the turns in the holding pattern are to the left.

    1) ATC will specify in the holding clearance if left turns are to be made.

4. You enter a holding pattern using one of three procedures as illustrated in the figure below. This illustrates a standard pattern; the same concept is used in a nonstandard pattern.

a. Parallel procedure. Fly a parallel holding course as in (a). Turn left and return to the holding fix or intercept the holding course.

b. Teardrop procedure. Proceed on an outbound track of 30° or less to the holding course; turn right to intercept the holding course, as in (b).

c. Direct entry procedure. Turn right and fly the pattern, as in (c).

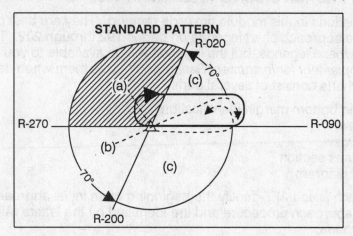

5. The best way to determine the entry method on the FAA knowledge test is to draw a holding pattern complete with the fix and inbound leg.

a. Through the fix, draw the 70° angle such that it intersects the outbound leg at about 1/3 of the outbound leg length.

b. Then slightly shade the (a) area, which is the 110° angle between the extension of the inbound leg and the 70° line.

c. The (b) area is the 70° angle between the 70° line and the extension of the inbound leg.

d. EXAMPLE: In the above illustration, the inbound leg to the fix is 270°, and the outbound leg is 090°. If the fix is a VOR station, the following radials define which entry procedure to use:

    R-200 to R-270 -- teardrop procedure
    R-270 to R-020 -- parallel procedure
    R-020 to R-200 -- direct procedure

6. The timing of the outbound leg begins over or abeam the fix, whichever occurs later.

    a. If the abeam position cannot be determined, start timing when the turn to outbound is complete (i.e., wings level).

    b. At an NDB (nondirectional beacon), the timing for the outbound leg should be when abeam the fix.

7. Maximum holding pattern airspeed (IAS) for all aircraft

    a. From the minimum holding altitude (MHA) through 6,000 ft. -- 200 kt.
    b. From 6,001 ft. through 14,000 ft. -- 230 kt.
    c. From 14,001 ft. and above -- 265 kt.

8. When a holding pattern is used in lieu of a procedure turn, the holding maneuver must still be executed within the time or leg length specified in the profile view on the instrument approach procedure (IAP) chart.

9. When more than one circuit of the holding pattern is needed to lose altitude or become better established on course, additional circuits can be made at the pilot's discretion only if the pilot advises ATC and ATC approves.

6.12 INSTRUMENT APPROACH CHARTS (Questions 81-138)

1. The FAA questions in this module are wide ranging. They are best prepared for by studying the approach chart legends on pages 192 through 202. The questions will not refer you to these legends, but the legends will be available to you in the FAA's *Computer Testing Supplement for Instrument Rating* book. Use them when needed. Remember that approach charts consist of several parts:

    a. Top and bottom margin identification
    b. Planview
    c. Profile view
    d. Minimums section
    e. Airport diagram

2. Initial approach fixes (IAF) identify the beginning of an initial approach segment of an instrument approach procedure and are identified by the letters IAF on the planview of approach charts.

3. Aircraft approach categories are listed as A, B, C, D, and E based upon 1.3 times the stall speed of the aircraft in the landing configuration at maximum certified gross landing weight ($1.3 \, V_{so}$).

4. The symbol "T" in a point-down black triangle indicates that takeoff minimums are not standard and/or departure minimums are published and you should consult alternative takeoff procedures.

    a. The symbol "A" in a point-up black triangle indicates that nonstandard minimums exist to list the airport as an IFR alternate.

        1) Standard alternate minimums are 800-2 for a nonprecision approach and 600-2 for a precision approach.

5. The absence of the procedure turn barb on the planview on an approach chart indicates that a procedure turn is not authorized for that approach.

    a. The term NoPT means that there is no procedure turn.

6. A course reversal (procedure turn) is not required (or authorized) when radar vectors are being provided.

7. Minimum safe sector altitudes are depicted on approach charts. These provide at least 1,000 ft. of obstacle clearance within a 25-NM radius of the navigation facility upon which the procedure is predicated but do not necessarily assure acceptable navigational signal coverage.

8. Published landing minimums apply when you are making an instrument approach to an airport.

9. If you adhere to the minimum altitudes depicted on the IAP, you can be assured of terrain and obstacle clearance.

10. When being radar vectored to an instrument approach, you should comply with the last assigned altitude until the airplane is established on a segment of a published route or IAP and you have been cleared for the approach, after which you should continue descents to the listed minimum altitudes.

11. When simultaneous approaches are in progress, each pilot will be advised to monitor the tower frequency to receive advisories and instructions.

12. When straight-in minimums are not published, you can make a straight-in landing if the active runway is in sight, there is sufficient time to make a normal landing, and you have been cleared to land.

13. If you are doing an approach in a category B airplane but maintaining a speed faster than the maximum specified for that category, you should use category C minimums.

14. When an instrument approach procedure involves a procedure turn, the maximum allowable indicated airspeed is 200 kt.

15. When a DME is inoperative, there will be no code tone (identifier) broadcast.

16. On instrument approach segments, the minimum altitudes are indicated on the planview and profile view, which YOU are expected to be able to interpret and specify on the FAA instrument rating knowledge test.

17. When holding patterns exist in lieu of outbound procedure turns, the length of the outbound leg may be indicated as a distance rather than time. This information is given in both the planview and the profile view of the approach chart.

18. On RNAV approaches, the MAP is identified when the TO/FROM indicator changes, which indicates station passage at the MAP waypoint.

    a. On some RNAV approach charts, the distance from the MAP to another, more prominent way point located along the extended final approach course may be shown in the profile and plan views.

19. RNAV waypoints, when used for an instrument approach, contain boxes in which the latitude and longitude are listed on the first line and the VOR direction and distance on the second line.

20. RNAV approaches require an approved RNAV receiver; no other navigation equipment is specifically required.

21. LDA is as useful and accurate as an ILS localizer but is not part of a complete ILS.

    a. The LDA is not aligned with the runway.

22. On procedure turns, there may be a distance limitation from a NAVAID, and procedural turns should be made entirely on the side of the inbound radial or bearing to which the procedural turn arrow points.

    a. If a teardrop turn is depicted, only a teardrop course reversal can be executed.

23. If you are not able to identify a NAVAID marking a descent to a lower altitude on a nonprecision approach, you cannot descend to the next lower altitude.

24. The MAP of a precision approach is arrival at the DH on the glide slope.

25. The appropriate approach and tower frequencies are indicated at the top of the planview.

26. When a marker beacon receiver becomes inoperative and you cannot identify the MM during an ILS approach, you should use the published minimums.

27. A second VOR receiver may be needed when doing a localizer approach with a final step-down fix to be identified by a VOR radial.

28. Some nonprecision approaches will allow descents to lower altitudes at specified DME distances.

    a.   The advantage of DME can be determined by comparing the two MDA values.

29. Use the recommended entry into holding patterns as discussed in the previous module.

30. The minimum navigation equipment required for a VOR/DME approach is one VOR receiver and DME.

31. Restrictions to circle to land procedures are found below the minimums section of the IAP chart.

32. The height above touchdown (HAT) is the height of the MDA or DH above the touchdown zone. It is the smaller numbers that appear after the MDA or DH.

    a.   The numbers in parentheses are military minimums.

33. The minimums section of the approach chart provides the MDA or DH and the visibility (expressed as RVR or SM).

34. When making an LOC approach to the primary airport of the Class B airspace, the aircraft must be equipped with

    a.   Two-way radio communication
    b.   Mode C transponder
    c.   VOR

35. When the glide slope becomes inoperative during an ILS approach, the approach becomes a nonprecision LOC approach.

    a.   The LOC minimums then apply.

36. The final approach fix (FAF) for a precision approach is identified on the approach chart by a lightning bolt (⤳).

    a.   The intercept altitude is indicated next to the symbol.

37. On a nonprecision approach, the distance from the FAF to the MAP is indicated below the airport diagram.

38. If a runway has a displaced threshold, the distance available for landing will be shown by a notation in the airport diagram. For example, "Rwy 21 ldg 5957'" signifies that 5,957 ft. of the total length of runway 21 are available for landing.

39. A category C aircraft must use category C minimums, even if using category B approach speed.

40. Legends 10 through 22 (except 16 and 17) concern instrument approaches and are presented on pages 192 through 202.

6.13 DPs AND STARs (Questions 139-151)

1. DPs (instrument departure procedures), STARs (standard terminal arrival routes), and visual approaches are all routinely assigned by ATC as appropriate.

2. DPs and STARs are issued to simplify clearance delivery procedures when ATC deems it appropriate unless you have requested "no DP" or "no STAR" in the remarks section of your flight plan.

   a. Less desirably, pilots may refuse DPs and STARs when they are part of a clearance.

3. When a DP requires a minimum climb rate of a specified number of ft. per NM, you may be requested to convert the climb rate into feet per minute.

   a. Use the Rate of Climb Table in Legend 16 on page 204.

   b. Another method is first to divide the groundspeed by 60 to get the NM per min. Then multiply NM per min. times the required climb rate per NM to determine climb rate in feet per minute (fpm).

      1) EXAMPLE: If 200 ft. per NM is required to a specified altitude and your groundspeed is 120 kt., you will be traveling 2 NM/min. (120 NM/60 min.), which will require a minimum climb rate of 400 fpm (200 required ft./NM x 2 NM/min.).

4. To accept a DP, you must have at least a textual description of it.

5. Preferred IFR routes are correlated with DPs and STARs and may be defined by airways, jet routes, and direct routes between NAVAIDs.

6. The departure route description of a DP explains the departure procedures. It also explains the route to be used if communication is lost.

7. You will be asked to interpret VOR indication to determine your position relative to a fix.

8. A STAR's purpose is to simplify clearance delivery procedures.

9. Legend 17 concerns DPs (formerly known as SIDs) and STARs and is presented on page 203.

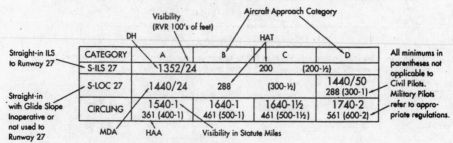

TERMS   NDING MINI.   DATA

IFR LANDING MINIMA

The United States Standard for Terminal Instrument Procedures (TERPS) is the approved criteria for formulating instrument approach procedures. Landing minima are established for six aircraft approach categories (ABCDE and COPTER).
In the absence of COPTER MINIMA, helicopters may use the CAT A minimums of other procedures.
The standard format for RNAV minima and landing minima portrayal follows:

RNAV MINIMA

CATEGORY	A	B	C	D
GLS PA DA		1382/24 200 (200-½)		
LNAV/ DA. VNAV	1500/24 318 (400-½)			1500/40 318 (400-¾)
LNAV MDA	1700/24 518 (600-½)		1700/50 518 (600-1)	1700/60 518 (600-1¼)
CIRCLING	1760-1 578 (600-1)		1760-1½ 578 (600-1½)	1760-2 578 (600-2)

RNAV minimums are dependent on navigation equipment capability, as stated in the applicable AFM or AFMS and as outlined below.

GLS (GLobal Navigation System (GNSS) Landing System)
Must have WAAS (Wide Area Augmentation System) equipment approved for precise approach.
Note: "PA" indicates that the runway environment, i.e., runway markings, runway lights, parallel taxiway, etc., meets precision approach requirements. If the GLS minimums line does not contain "PA", then the runway environment does not support precision requirements.

LNAV/VNAV (Lateral Navigation/Vertical Navigation)
Must have WAAS equipment approved for precision approach, or RNP-0.3 system based on GPS or DME/DME, with an IFR approach approved Baro-VNAV system. Other RNAV approach systems require special approval.
Use of Baro-VNAV systems is limited by temperature, i.e., "Baro-VNAV NA below -20 C(-4 F)".
(Not applicable if chart is annotated "Baro-VNAV NA".)
NOTE: DME/DME based RNP-0.3 systems may be used only when a chart note indicates DME/DME availability, for example, "DME/DME RNP-0.3 Authorized." Specific DME facilities may be required, for example: "DME/DME RNP-0.3 Authorized. ABC, XYZ required."

LNAV (Lateral Navigation)
Must have IFR approach approved WAAS, GPS, GPS based FMS systems, or RNP-0.3 systems based on GPS or DME/DME. Other RNAV approach systems require special approval.
NOTE: DME/DME based RNP-0.3 systems may be used only when a chart note indicates DME/DME availability, for example, "DME/DME RNP-0.3 Authorized." Specific DME facilities may be required, for example: "DME/DME RNP-0.3 Authorized. ABC, XYZ required."

LANDING MINIMA FORMAT

In this example airport elevation is 1179, and runway touchdown zone elevation is 1152.

CATEGORY	A	B	C	D
S-ILS 27	1352/24	200 (200-½)		
S-LOC 27	1440/24	288 (300-½)		1440/50 288 (300-1)
CIRCLING	1540-1 361 (400-1)	1640-1 461 (500-1)	1640-1½ 461 (500-1½)	1740-2 561 (600-2)

Straight-in ILS to Runway 27

Straight-in with Glide Slope Inoperative or not used to Runway 27

All minimums in parentheses not applicable to Civil Pilots. Military Pilots refer to appropriate regulations.

Visibility (RVR 100's of feet)

Aircraft Approach Category

DH   HAT

MDA   HAA   Visibility in Statute Miles

TERMS/LANDING MINIMA DATA

A1

LEGEND 10.—Instrument Approach Procedures Explanation of Terms.

SC-1, 24 FEB 2000   A2

00055

TERMS/LANDING MINIMA DATA

COPTER MINIMA ONLY

CATEGORY	COPTER		
H-176°	680-½	363	(400-½)

Copter Approach Direction   Height of MDA/DH
Above Landing Area (HAL)

No circling minimums are provided

RADAR MINIMA

								Visibility (RVR 100's of feet)		
PAR (c)	10	2.5°/42/1000	ABCDE	**195/16**	100	(100-¼)				
(d)	28	2.5°/48/1068	ABCDE	**187/16**	100	(100-¼)				
ASR	10		ABC	**560/40**	463	(500-¾)	D	**560/50**	463	(500-1)
			E	**580/60**	463	(500-1¼)				
	28		AB	**600/50**	513	(600-1)	C	**600/60**	513	(600-1¼)
			DE	**600-1½**	513	(600-1½)				
CIR (b)	10		AB	**560-1¼**	463	(500-1¼)	C	**560-1½**	463	(500-1½)
	28		AB	**600-1¼**	503	(600-1¼)	C	**600-1½**	503	(600-1½)
	10, 28		DE	**660-2**	563	(600-2)				

All minimums in parentheses not applicable to Civil Pilots. Military Pilots refer to appropriate regulations.

Visibility in Statute Miles

Radar Minima:
1. Minima shown are the lowest permitted by established criteria. Pilots should consult applicable directives for their category of aircraft.
2. The circling MDA and weather minima to be used are those for the runway to which the final approach is flown - not the landing runway. In the above RADAR MINIMA example, a category C aircraft flying a radar approach to runway 10, circling to land on runway 28, must use an MDA of 560 feet with weather minima of 500-1½ .

⚠ Alternate Minimums not standard. Civil users refer to tabulation. USA/USN/USAF pilots refer to appropriate regulations.

⚠ NA   Alternate minimums are Not Authorized due to unmonitored facility or absence of weather reporting service.

▼ Take-off Minimums not standard and/or Departure Procedures are published. Refer to tabulation.

AIRCRAFT APPROACH CATEGORIES

Speeds are based on 1.3 times the stall speed in the landing configuration of maximum gross landing weight. An aircraft shall fit in only one category. If it is necessary to maneuver at speeds in excess of the upper limit of a speed range for a category, the minimums for the next higher category should be used. For example, an aircraft which falls in Category A, but is circling to land at a speed in excess of 91 knots, should use the approach Category B minimums when circling to land. See following category limits:

MANEUVERING TABLE

Approach Category	A	B	C	D	E
Speed (Knots)	0-90	91-120	121-140	141-165	Abv 165

RVR/ Meteorological Visibility Comparable Values

The following table shall be used for converting RVR to meteorological visibility when RVR is not reported for the runway of intended operation. Adjustments of landing minima may be required - see Inoperative Components Table.

RVR (feet)	Visibility (statute miles)	RVR (feet)	Visibility (statute miles)
1600	¼	4000	¾
2000	⅜	4500	⅞
2400	½	5000	1
3200	⅝	6000	1¼

TERMS/ NDING MINIM DATA

LEGEND 11.—Instrument Approach Procedures Explanation of Terms.

F1

99252
GENERAL INFO

GENERAL INFORMATION

This publication includes Instrument Approach Procedures (IAPs), Departure Procedures (DPs), and Standard Terminal Arrivals (STARs) for use by both civil and military aviation and is issued every 56 days.

STANDARD TERMINAL ARRIVALS AND DEPARTURE PROCEDURES

The use of the associated codified STAR/DP and transition identifiers are requested of users when filing flight plans via teletype and are required for users filing flight plans via computer interface. It must be noted that when filing a STAR/DP with a transition, the first three coded characters of the STAR and the last three coded characters of the DP are replaced by the transition code. Examples: ACTON SIX ARRIVAL, file (AQN.AQN6); ACTON SIX ARRIVAL, EDNAS TRANSITION, file (EDNAS.AQN6). FREEHOLD THREE DEPARTURE, file (FREH3.RBV), FREEHOLD THREE DEPARTURE, ELWOOD CITY TRANSITION, file (FREH3.EWC).

PILOT CONTROLLED AIRPORT LIGHTING SYSTEMS

Available pilot controlled lighting (PCL) systems are indicated as follows:
1. Approach lighting systems that bear a system identification are symbolized using negative symbology, e.g., ●, ●, ☺
2. Approach lighting systems that do not bear a system identification are indicated with a negative "●" besides the name.
A star (✱) indicates non-standard PCL, consult Directory/Supplement, e.g., ●✱
To activate lights use frequency indicated in the communication section of the chart with a ● or the appropriate lighting system identification e.g., UNICOM 122.8 ●, ●, ●

KEY MIKE	FUNCTION
7 times within 5 seconds	Highest intensity available
5 times within 5 seconds	Medium or lower intensity (Lower REIL or REIL-off)
3 times within 5 seconds	Lowest intensity available (Lower REIL or REIL-off)

CHART CURRENCY INFORMATION

FAA procedure amendment number ——— Amdt 11A 99365 ——— Date of latest change
                                     Orig 00365

The Chart Date indentifies the Julian date the chart was added to the volume or last revised for any reason. The first two digits indicate the year, the last three digits indicate the day of the year (001 to 365/6) in which the latest addition or change was first published.
The Procedure Amendment Number precedes the Chart Date, and changes any time instrument information (e.g., DH, MDA, approach routing, etc.) changes. Procedure changes also cause the Chart Date to change.

MISCELLANEOUS

★ Indicates a non-continuously operating facility, see A/FD or flight supplement.
# Indicates control tower temporarily closed UFN.
"Radar required" on the chart indicates that radar vectoring is required for the approach.
Distances in nautical miles (except visibility in statute miles and Runway Visual Range in hundreds of feet). Runway Dimensions in feet. Elevations in feet. Mean Sea Level (MSL). Ceilings in feet above airport elevation. Radials/bearings/headings/courses are magnetic. Horizontal Datum: Unless otherwise noted on the chart, all coordinates are referenced to North American Datum 1983 (NAD 83), which for charting purposes is considered equivalent to World Geodetic System 1984 (WGS 84).

LEGEND 12.—General Information.

99140

GENERAL INFO

ABBREVIATIONS

ADF	Automatic Direction Finder
ALS	Approach Light System
ALSF	Approach Light System with Sequenced Flashing Lights
APP CON	Approach Control
ARR	Arrival
ASOS	Automated Surface Observing System
ASR/PAR	Published Radar Minimums at this Airport
ATIS	Automatic Terminal Information Service
AWOS	Automated Weather Observing System
AZ	Azimuth
BC	Back Course
C	Circling
CAT	Category
CCW	Counter Clockwise
Chan	Channel
CLNC DEL	Clearance Delivery
CNF	Computer Navigation Fix
CTAF	Common Traffic Advisory Frequency
CW	Clockwise
DH	Decision Height
DME	Distance Measuring Equipment
DR	Dead Reckoning
ELEV	Elevation
FAF	Final Approach Fix
FM	Fan Marker
FMS	Flight Management System
GCO	Ground Communications Outlet
GPI	Ground Point of Interception
GPS	Global Positioning System
GS	Glide Slope
HAA	Height above Airport
HAL	Height above Landing
HAT	Height above Touchdown
HIRL	High Intensity Runway Lights
IAF	Initial Approach Fix
ICAO	International Civil Aviation Organization
IM	Inner Marker
Intcp	Intercept
INT	Intersection
LDA	Localizer Type Directional Aid
Ldg	Landing
LDIN	Lead in Light System
LIRL	Low Intensity Runway Lights
LOC	Localizer
LR	Lead Radial. Provides at least 2 NM (Copter 1 NM) of lead to assist in turning onto the intermediate/final course.
MALS	Medium Intensity Approach Light System

MALSR	Medium Intensity Approach Light System with RAIL
MAP	Missed Approach Point
MDA	Minimum Descent Altitude
MIRL	Medium Intensity Runway Lights
MLS	Microwave Landing System
MM	Middle Marker
NA	Not Authorized
NDB	Non-directional Radio Beacon
NM	Nautical Mile
NoPT	No Procedure Turn Required (Procedure Turn shall not be executed without ATC clearance)
ODALS	Omnidirectional Approach Light System
OM	Outer Marker
R	Radial
RA	Radio Altimeter setting height
RAIL	Runway Alignment Indicator Lights
RBn	Radio Beacon
RCLS	Runway Centerline Light System
REIL	Runway End Identifier Lights
RNAV	Area Navigation
RNP	Required Navigation Performance
RPI	Runway Point of Intercept(ion)
RRL	Runway Remaining Lights
Rwy	Runway
RVR	Runway Visual Range
S	Straight-in
SALS	Short Approach Light System
SSALR	Simplified Short Approach Light System with RAIL
SDF	Simplified Directional Facility
TA	Transition Altitude
TAC	TACAN
TCH	Threshold Crossing Height (height in feet Above Ground level)
TDZ	Touchdown Zone
TDZE	Touchdown Zone Elevation
TDZ/CL	Touchdown Zone and Runway Centerline Lighting
TDZL	Touchdown Zone Lights
TLv	Transition Level
VASI	Visual Approach Slope Indicator
VDP	Visual Descent Point
VGSI	Visual Glide Slope Indicator
WP/WPT	Waypoint (RNAV)
X	Radar Only Frequency

GENERAL INFO
99140

LEGEND 13.—Abbreviations.

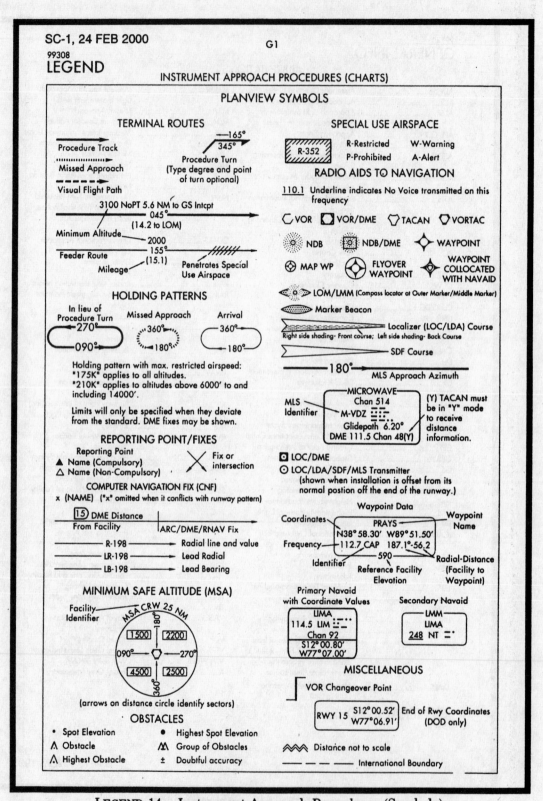

LEGEND 14.—Instrument Approach Procedures (Symbols).

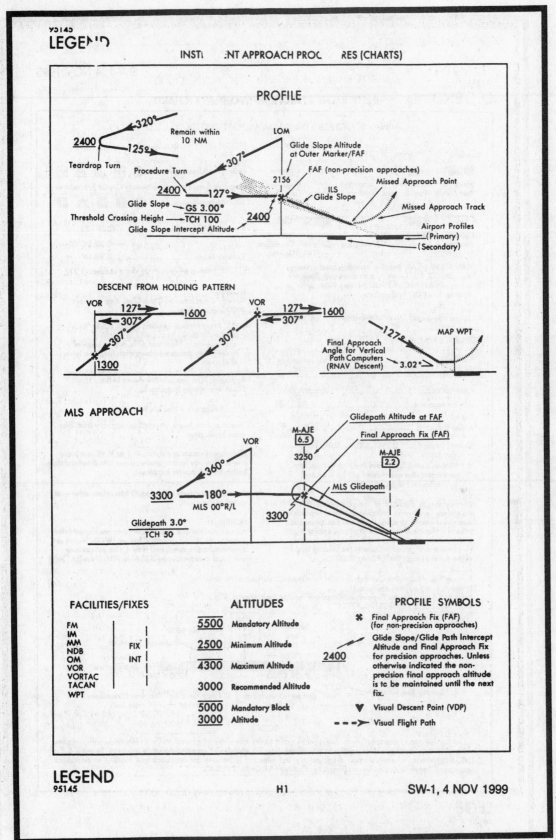

LEGEND 15.—Instrument Approach Procedures (Profile).

95201

K1   SW-1, 4 NOV 1999

LEGEND   INSTRUMENT APPROACH PROCEDURES (CHARTS)

AIRPORT DIAGRAM/AIRPORT SKETCH

Runways

| Hard Surface | Other Than Hard Surface | Stopways, Taxiways, Parking Areas | Displaced Threshold |

| Closed Runway | Closed Taxiway | Under Construction | Metal Surface | Runway Centerline Lighting |

ARRESTING GEAR: Specific arresting gear systems; e.g., BAK-12, MA-1A etc., shown on airport diagrams, not applicable to Civil Pilots. Military Pilots Refer to Appropriate DOD Publications.

uni-directional   bi-directional   Jet Barrier

REFERENCE FEATURES

Buildings...■

Tanks...●

Obstruction...△

Airport Beacon #....................................☆

Runway
Radar Reflectors....................................⧗

Control Tower #......................................▪

\# When Control Tower and Rotating Beacon are co-located, Beacon symbol will be used and further identified as TWR.

Runway length depicted is the physical length of the runway (end-to-end, including displaced thresholds if any) but excluding areas designated as stopways. Where a displaced threshold is shown and/or part of the runway is otherwise not available for landing, an annotation is added to indicate the landing length of the runway; e.g., RWY 13 ldg 5000'.

Runway Weight Bearing Capacity/or PCN Pavement Classification Number is shown as a codified expression.
Refer to the appropriate Supplement/Directory for applicable codes; e.g.,
RWY 14-32 S75, T185, ST175, TT325
PCN 80 F/D/X/U

Helicopter Alighting Areas Ⓗ ⊞ Ⓗ ⚠ ⊞

Negative Symbols used to identify Copter Procedures

landing point.................... Ⓗ ⊞ Ⓗ ⚠ ⊞

Runway TDZ elevation..................TDZE 123

→0.3% DOWN

Runway Slope...............................0.8% UP→

(shown when runway slope exceeds 0.3%)

NOTE:
Runway Slope measured to midpoint on runways 8000 feet or longer.

◧ U.S. Navy Optical Landing System (OLS) "OLS" location is shown because of its height of approximately 7 feet and proximity to edge of runway may create an obstruction for some types of aircraft.

Approach light symbols are shown in the Flight Information Handbook.

Airport diagram scales are variable.

True/magnetic North orientation may vary from diagram to diagram.

Coordinate values are shown in 1 or ½ minute increments. They are further broken down into 6 second ticks, within each 1 minute increment.

Positional accuracy within ±600 feet unless otherwise noted on the chart.

NOTE:
All new and revised airport diagrams are shown referenced to the World Geodetic System (WGS) (noted on appropriate diagram), and may not be compatible with local coordinates published in FLIP. (Foreign Only)

BAK-12   Runway Slope   FIELD ELEV 174   Rwy 2 ldg 8000'
Displaced Threshold
0.7% UP →   Runway Identification
20   9000 X 200   ←023.2°   1000 X 200
Runway End Elevation ← ELEV 164   Runway Dimensions (in feet)   Runway Heading (Magnetic)   Stopway Dimensions (in feet)

SCOPE

Airport diagrams are specifically designed to assist in the movement of ground traffic at locations with complex runway/taxiway configurations and provide information for updating Computer Based Navigation Systems (I.E., INS, GPS) aboard aircraft. Airport diagrams are not intended to be used for approach and landing or departure operations. For revisions to Airport Diagrams: Consult FAA Order 7910.4B.

LEGE
95201

LEGEND 18.—Airport Diagram.

RATE OF DESCENT TABLE

A rate of descent table is provided for use in planning and executing precision descents under known or approximate ground speed conditions. It will be especially useful for approaches when the localizer only is used for course guidance. A best speed, power, altitude combination can be programmed which will result in a stable glide rate and altitude favorable for executing a landing if minimums exist upon breakout. Care should always be exercised so that minimum descent altitude and missed approach point are not exceeded.

ANGLE OF DESCENT (degrees and tenths)		FEET /NM	GROUND SPEED (knots)										
			30	45	60	75	90	105	120	135	150	165	180
2.0		210	105	160	210	265	320	370	425	475	530	585	635
2.5		265	130	200	265	330	395	465	530	595	665	730	795
V E R T I C A L P A T H A N G L E	2.7	287	143	215	287	358	430	501	573	645	716	788	860
	2.8	297	149	223	297	371	446	520	594	669	743	817	891
	2.9	308	154	231	308	385	462	539	616	693	769	846	923
	3.0	318	159	239	318	398	478	557	637	716	796	876	955
	3.1	329	165	247	329	411	494	576	658	740	823	905	987
	3.2	340	170	255	340	425	510	594	679	764	849	934	1019
	3.3	350	175	263	350	438	526	613	701	788	876	963	1051
	3.4	361	180	271	361	451	541	632	722	812	902	993	1083
3.5		370	185	280	370	465	555	650	740	835	925	1020	1110
4.0		425	210	315	425	530	635	740	845	955	1060	1165	1270
4.5		475	240	355	475	595	715	835	955	1075	1190	1310	1430
5.0		530	265	395	530	660	795	925	1060	1190	1325	1455	1590
5.5		580	290	435	580	730	875	1020	1165	1310	1455	1600	1745
6.0		635	315	475	635	795	955	1110	1270	1430	1590	1745	1950
6.5		690	345	515	690	860	1030	1205	1375	1550	1720	1890	2065
7.0		740	370	555	740	925	1110	1295	1480	1665	1850	2035	2220
7.5		795	395	595	795	990	1190	1390	1585	1785	1985	2180	2380
8.0		845	425	635	845	1055	1270	1480	1690	1905	2115	2325	2540
8.5		900	450	675	900	1120	1345	1570	1795	2020	2245	2470	2695
9.0		950	475	715	950	1190	1425	1665	1900	2140	2375	2615	2855
9.5		1005	500	750	1005	1255	1505	1755	2005	2255	2510	2760	3010
10.0		1055	530	790	1055	1320	1585	1845	2110	2375	2640	2900	3165
10.5		1105	555	830	1105	1385	1660	1940	2215	2490	2770	3045	3320
11.0		1160	580	870	1160	1450	1740	2030	2320	2610	2900	3190	3480
11.5		1210	605	910	1210	1515	1820	2120	2425	2725	3030	3335	3635
12.0		1260	630	945	1260	1575	1890	2205	2520	2835	3150	3465	3780

DESCENT TABLE 99028

LEGEND 21.—Instrument Approach Procedure Charts, Rate-of-Descent Table.

INOP COMPONENTS
99084

INOPERATIVE COMPONENTS OR VISUAL AIDS TABLE

Landing minimums published on instrument approach procedure charts are based upon full operation of all components and visual aids associated with the particular instrument approach chart being used. Higher minimums are required with inoperative components or visual aids as indicated below. If more than one component is inoperative, each minimum is raised to the highest minimum required by any single component that is inoperative. ILS glide slope inoperative minimums are published on the instrument approach charts as localizer minimums. This table may be amended by notes on the approach chart. Such notes apply only to the particular approach catergory(ies) as stated. See legend page for description of components indicated below.

(1) ILS, MLS, and PAR

Inoperative Component or Aid	Approach Category	Increase Visibility
ALSF 1 & 2, MALSR, & SSALR	ABCD	1/4 mile

(2) ILS with visibility minimum 0f 1,800 RVR

Inoperative	Approach Category	Increase Visibility
ALSF 1 & 2, MALSR, & SSALR	ABCD	To 4000 RVR
TDZL RCLS	ABCD	To 2400 RVR
RVR	ABCD	To 1/2 mile

(3) VOR,VOR/DME, VORTAC, VOR (TAC), VOR/DME (TAC), LOC, LOC/DME, LDA, LDA/DME, SDF, SDF/DME, GPS, RNAV,and ASR

Inoperative Visual Aid	Approach Category	Increase Visibility
ALSF 1 & 2, MALSR, & SSALR	ABCD	1/2 mile
SSALS,MALS, & ODALS	ABC	1/4 mile

(4) NDB

Inoperative	Approach Category	Increase Visibility
ALSF 1 & 2, MALSR, & SSALR	C	1/2 mile
	ABD	1/4 mile
MALS, SSALS, ODALS	ABC	1/4 mile

CORRECTIONS, COMMENTS AND/OR PROCUREMENT

FOR CHARTING ERRORS CONTACT:
National Ocean Service/NOAA
N/ACC1, SSMC-4, Sta. #2335
1305 East-West Highway
Silver Spring, MD 20910-3281
Telephone Toll-Free (800) 626-3677
Internet/E-Mail: Aerochart@NOAA.GOV

FOR CHANGES, ADDITIONS, OR RECOMMENDATIONS ON PROCEDURAL ASPECTS:
Contact Federal Aviation Administration, ATA 110
800 Independence Avenue, SW
Washington, DC 20591
Telephone Toll Free (800) 457-6656

TO PURCHASE CHARTS CONTACT:
National Ocean Service
NOAA, N/ACC3
Distribution Division
Riverdale, MD 20737
Telephone Toll Free (800) 638-8972

Requests for the creation or revisions to Airport Diagrams should be in accordance with FAA Order 7910.4B.

LEGEND 22.—Inoperative Components or Visual Aids Table.

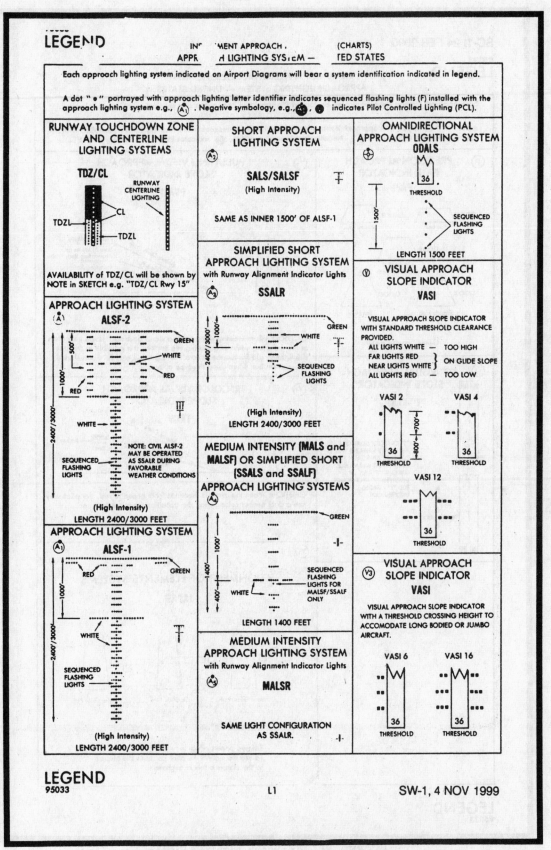

LEGEND 19.—Approach Lighting Systems.

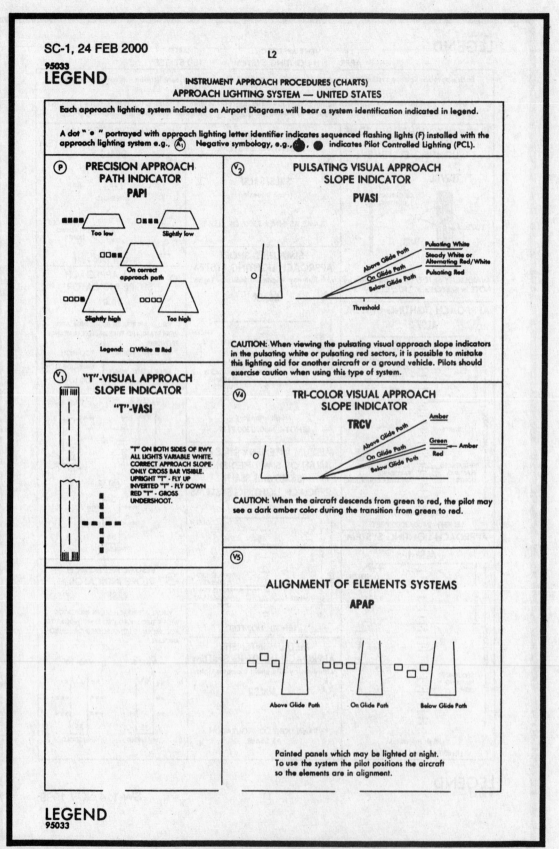

SC-1, 24 FEB 2000

95033

LEGEND

L2

INSTRUMENT APPROACH PROCEDURES (CHARTS)

APPROACH LIGHTING SYSTEM — UNITED STATES

Each approach lighting system indicated on Airport Diagrams will bear a system identification indicated in legend.

A dot " • " portrayed with approach lighting letter identifier indicates sequenced flashing lights (F) installed with the approach lighting system e.g., (A₁) Negative symbology, e.g., ●, ● indicates Pilot Controlled Lighting (PCL).

(P) PRECISION APPROACH PATH INDICATOR

PAPI

Too low

Slightly low

On correct approach path

Slightly high

Too high

Legend: □ White ■ Red

(V₁) "T"-VISUAL APPROACH SLOPE INDICATOR

"T"-VASI

"T" ON BOTH SIDES OF RWY ALL LIGHTS VARIABLE WHITE. CORRECT APPROACH SLOPE- ONLY CROSS BAR VISIBLE. UPRIGHT "T" - FLY UP INVERTED "T" - FLY DOWN RED "T" - GROSS UNDERSHOOT.

(V₂) PULSATING VISUAL APPROACH SLOPE INDICATOR

PVASI

Above Glide Path — Pulsating White
Steady White or Alternating Red/White
On Glide Path — Pulsating Red
Below Glide Path

Threshold

CAUTION: When viewing the pulsating visual approach slope indicators in the pulsating white or pulsating red sectors, it is possible to mistake this lighting aid for another aircraft or a ground vehicle. Pilots should exercise caution when using this type of system.

(V₄) TRI-COLOR VISUAL APPROACH SLOPE INDICATOR

TRCV

Above Glide Path — Amber
On Glide Path — Green — Amber
Below Glide Path — Red

CAUTION: When the aircraft descends from green to red, the pilot may see a dark amber color during the transition from green to red.

(V₅)

ALIGNMENT OF ELEMENTS SYSTEMS

APAP

Above Glide Path

On Glide Path

Below Glide Path

Painted panels which may be lighted at night. To use the system the pilot positions the aircraft so the elements are in alignment.

LEGEND
95033

LEGEND 20.—Approach Lighting System.

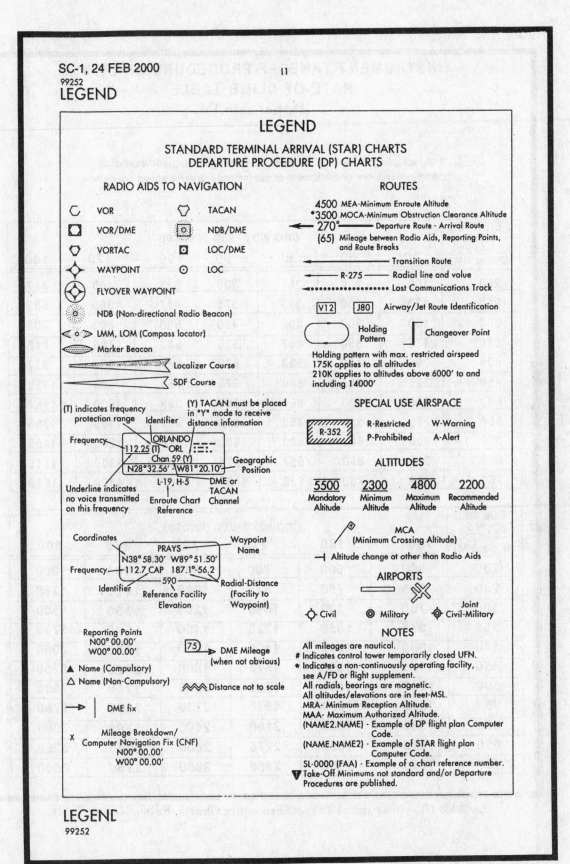

LEGEND 17.—Standard Arrival/Departure Charts.

INSTRUMENT TAKEOFF PROCEDURE CHARTS
RATE-OF-CLIMB TABLE
(ft. per min.)

A rate-of-climb table is provided for use in planning and executing
takeoff procedures under known or approximate ground speed conditions.

REQUIRED CLIMB RATE (ft. per NM)	GROUND SPEED (KNOTS)						
	30	60	80	90	100	120	140
200	100	200	267	300	333	400	467
250	125	250	333	375	417	500	583
300	150	300	400	450	500	600	700
350	175	350	467	525	583	700	816
400	200	400	533	600	667	800	933
450	225	450	600	675	750	900	1050
500	250	500	667	750	833	1000	1167
550	275	550	733	825	917	1100	1283
600	300	600	800	900	1000	1200	1400
650	325	650	867	975	1083	1300	1516
700	350	700	933	1050	1167	1400	1633

REQUIRED CLIMB RATE (ft. per NM)	GROUND SPEED (KNOTS)					
	150	180	210	240	270	300
200	500	600	700	800	900	1000
250	625	750	875	1000	1125	1250
300	750	900	1050	1200	1350	1500
350	875	1050	1225	1400	1575	1750
400	1000	1200	1400	1600	1700	2000
450	1125	1350	1575	1800	2025	2250
500	1250	1500	1750	2000	2250	2500
550	1375	1650	1925	2200	2475	2750
600	1500	1800	2100	2400	2700	3000
650	1625	1950	2275	2600	2925	3250
700	1750	2100	2450	2800	3150	3500

LEGEND 16.—Instrument Takeoff Procedure Charts, Rate-of-Climb Table.

6.14 MICROWAVE LANDING SYSTEM AND GPS APPROACHES (Questions 152-154)

1. Microwave landing system (MLS) identification is a four-character alphabetical designation starting with the letter M transmitted in Morse Code at least six times per minute.

2. If receiver autonomous integrity monitoring (RAIM) is not available when setting up a GPS approach, you must select another type of navigation and approach system.

3. When you are using GPS for navigation and instrument approaches, any required alternate airport must have an approved instrument approach procedure, other than GPS, which is anticipated to be operational and available at the estimated time of arrival (ETA) and which the airplane is equipped to fly.

QUESTIONS AND ANSWER EXPLANATIONS

All the FAA questions from the instrument rating knowledge test relating to holding and instrument approaches and the material outlined previously are reproduced on the following pages in the same modules as the outlines. To the immediate right of each question are the correct answer and answer explanation. You should cover these answers and answer explanations with your hand or a piece of paper while responding to the questions. Refer to the general discussion in the Introduction on how to take the FAA knowledge test.

Remember that the questions from the FAA instrument rating knowledge test bank have been reordered by topic, and the topics have been organized into a meaningful sequence. Accordingly, the first line of the answer explanation gives the FAA question number and the citation of the authoritative source for the answer.

6.1 Contact and Visual Approaches

1.
4743. What conditions are necessary before ATC can authorize a visual approach?

A— You must have the preceding aircraft in sight, and be able to remain in VFR weather conditions.
B— You must have the airport in sight or the preceding aircraft in sight, and be able to proceed to, and land in IFR conditions.
C— You must have the airport in sight or a preceding aircraft to be followed, and be able to proceed to the airport in VFR conditions.

Answer (C) is correct (4743). *(AIM Para 5-4-20)*
ATC may authorize airplanes to conduct visual approaches to an airport or to follow another airplane when flight to and landing at the airport can be accomplished in VFR weather. You must have the airport or preceding aircraft in sight before the clearance is issued.
Answer (A) is incorrect because you can have the airport in sight instead of having the preceding aircraft in sight. Answer (B) is incorrect because you must be able to land in VFR, not IFR, conditions.

2.
4718. What are the main differences between a visual approach and a contact approach?

A— The pilot must request a contact approach; the pilot may be assigned a visual approach and higher weather minimums must exist.
B— The pilot must request a visual approach and report having the field in sight; ATC may assign a contact approach if VFR conditions exist.
C— Anytime the pilot reports the field in sight, ATC may clear the pilot for a contact approach; for a visual approach, the pilot must advise that the approach can be made under VFR conditions.

Answer (A) is correct (4718). *(AIM Para 5-4-22)*
Contact approaches can be issued only upon pilot request, but visual approaches may be assigned by ATC. Visual approaches require VFR conditions. Contact approaches require 1 SM flight visibility and the ability to remain clear of clouds.
Answer (B) is incorrect because ATC may assign visual approaches without pilot request, and ATC cannot issue a contact approach clearance without the pilot's request. Answer (C) is incorrect because ATC cannot issue a contact approach clearance without the pilot's request.

3.
4750. A contact approach is an approach procedure that may be used

A— in lieu of conducting a SIAP.
B— if assigned by ATC and will facilitate the approach.
C— in lieu of a visual approach.

Answer (A) is correct (4750). *(AIM Para 5-4-22)*
A contact approach may be requested by the pilot if there is 1 SM flight visibility and the pilot can operate clear of clouds. It is an alternative to a standard instrument approach procedure (SIAP).
Answer (B) is incorrect because ATC cannot assign a contact approach; pilots must request them. Answer (C) is incorrect because using a contact approach is not necessary if a visual approach is possible.

3a.
4712. You arrive at your destination airport on an IFR flight plan. Which is a prerequisite condition for the performance of a contact approach?

A— A ground visibility of at least 2 SM.
B— A flight visibility of at least 1/2 NM.
C— Clear of clouds and at least 1 SM flight visibility.

Answer (C) is correct (4712). *(AIM Para 5-4-22)*
A contact approach may be requested by the pilot if there is 1 SM flight visibility and the pilot can operate clear of clouds.
Answer (A) is incorrect because the flight, not ground, visibility must be at least 1 SM, not 2 SM. Answer (B) is incorrect because the flight visibility must be at least 1 SM, not 1/2 NM.

4.

4735. What are the requirements for a contact approach to an airport that has an approved IAP, if the pilot is on an instrument flight plan and clear of clouds?

A— The controller must determine that the pilot can see the airport at the altitude flown and can remain clear of clouds.

B— The pilot must agree to the approach when given by ATC and the controller must have determined that the visibility was at least 1 mile and be reasonably sure the pilot can remain clear of clouds.

C— The pilot must request the approach, have at least 1-mile visibility, and be reasonably sure of remaining clear of clouds.

Answer (C) is correct (4735). *(AIM Para 5-4-22)*
Pilots operating in accordance with an IFR flight plan, provided they are clear of clouds, have at least 1 SM flight visibility, and can reasonably expect to continue to the destination airport in those conditions, may request ATC authorization for a contact approach.
Answer (A) is incorrect because the pilot must determine whether (s)he can reasonably expect to continue to the airport in at least 1 SM flight visibility and clear of clouds, not the controller. Answer (B) is incorrect because the pilot must request a contact approach; ATC does not solicit or assign contact approaches.

5.

4736. When is radar service terminated during a visual approach?

A— Automatically when ATC instructs the pilot to contact the tower.

B— Immediately upon acceptance of the approach by the pilot.

C— When ATC advises, "Radar service terminated; resume own navigation."

Answer (A) is correct (4736). *(AIM Para 5-4-20)*
During a visual approach, radar service is automatically terminated without advising the pilot once the pilot has been instructed to contact the tower or change to advisory frequency.
Answer (B) is incorrect because approach clearance is given well before radar service is terminated.
Answer (C) is incorrect because "resume own navigation" is generally an en route instruction and is not applicable to approaches.

6.

4737. When may you obtain a contact approach?

A— ATC may assign a contact approach if VFR conditions exist or you report the runway in sight and are clear of clouds.

B— ATC may assign a contact approach if you are below the clouds and the visibility is at least 1 mile.

C— ATC will assign a contact approach only upon request if the reported visibility is at least 1 mile.

Answer (C) is correct (4737). *(AIM Para 5-4-22)*
ATC will assign a contact approach only upon pilot request if the pilot is operating clear of clouds, has at least 1 SM flight visibility, and expects to reach the airport and land in those conditions.
Answer (A) is incorrect because ATC may assign a visual, not a contact, approach if VFR weather conditions exist. ATC may not assign a contact approach.
Answer (B) is incorrect because ATC may not assign a contact approach. The pilot must request one.

6.2 SDF and LDA Approaches

7.

4705. What are the main differences between the SDF and the localizer of an ILS?

A— The useable off-course indications are limited to 35° for the localizer and up to 90° for the SDF.

B— The SDF course may not be aligned with the runway and the course may be wider.

C— The course width for the localizer will always be 5° while the SDF course will be between 6° and 12°.

Answer (B) is correct (4705). *(AIM Para 1-1-10)*
The approach techniques and procedures used in performance of an SDF instrument approach are essentially identical to those employed to execute a standard localizer approach, except that the SDF course may not be aligned with the runway and the course may be wider, resulting in less precision.
Answer (A) is incorrect because the off-course indications are limited to 35° for both types of approach.
Answer (C) is incorrect because the course width for the localizer is usually between 3° and 6°, and SDF is either 6° or 12° (not between).

8.

4703. What is the difference between a Localizer-Type Directional Aid (LDA) and the ILS localizer?

A— The LDA is not aligned with the runway.

B— The LDA uses a course width of 6° or 12°, while an ILS uses only 5°.

C— The LDA signal is generated from a VOR-type facility and has no glide slope.

Answer (A) is correct (4703). *(AIM Para 1-1-9)*
The localizer-type directional aid (LDA) is similar to a localizer but is not part of a complete ILS, and it is not aligned with the runway.
Answer (B) is incorrect because the LDA uses the same course width as the ILS, i.e., 3° to 6°. The SDF uses 6° or 12°. Answer (C) is incorrect because the LDA is a localizer-type, not VOR-type, signal.

9.
4704. How wide is an SDF course?

A— Either 3° or 6°.
B— Either 6° or 12°.
C— Varies from 5° to 10°.

Answer (B) is correct (4704). *(AIM Para 1-1-10)*
    The simplified directional facility (SDF) signal is fixed at either 6° or 12° as necessary to provide maximum flyability and optimum course quality.
    Answer (A) is incorrect because either 3° or 6° is half the course width of an SDF. Answer (C) is incorrect because a course 5° to 10° wide does not relate to ILS, LDA, or SDF.

10.
4702. What is a difference between an SDF and an LDA facility?

A— The SDF course width is either 6° or 12° while the LDA course width is approximately 5°.
B— The SDF course has no glide slope guidance while the LDA does.
C— The SDF has no marker beacons while the LDA has at least an OM.

Answer (A) is correct (4702). *(AIM Para 1-1-9)*
    The localizer-type directional aid (LDA) is of comparable utility and accuracy as a localizer but is not part of a complete ILS. The LDA usually provides a more precise approach course than the simplified directional facility (SDF) installation, which has a course width of 6° or 12°. The LDA course widths are from 3° to 6°.
    Answer (B) is incorrect because only some LDA approaches provide glide slope guidance, but this is not a requirement of the system. Answer (C) is incorrect because both SDF and LDA may have marker beacons.

6.3 Runway Visual Range (RVR)

11.
4401. What does the Runway Visual Range (RVR) value, depicted on certain straight-in IAP Charts, represent?

A— The slant range distance the pilot can see down the runway while crossing the threshold on glide slope.
B— The horizontal distance a pilot should see when looking down the runway from a moving aircraft.
C— The slant visual range a pilot should see down the final approach and during landing.

Answer (B) is correct (4401). *(AWS Sect 2)*
    RVR is an instrumentally derived value that represents the horizontal distance the pilot will see down the runway from the approach end. It is based on the measurement of a transmissometer near the touchdown point of the instrument runway and is reported in hundreds of feet.
    Answer (A) is incorrect because RVR is the horizontal, not slant range, distance the pilot will see down the runway. Answer (C) is incorrect because RVR is the horizontal, not slant range, distance the pilot will see down the runway, not the final approach.

12.
4759. The RVR minimums for takeoff or landing are published in an IAP, but RVR is inoperative and cannot be reported for the runway at the time. Which of the following would apply?

A— RVR minimums which are specified in the procedure should be converted and applied as ground visibility.
B— RVR minimums may be disregarded, providing the runway has an operative HIRL system.
C— RVR minimums may be disregarded, providing all other components of the ILS system are operative.

Answer (A) is correct (4759). *(FAR 91.175)*
    If RVR minimums for takeoff or landing are prescribed in an instrument approach procedure, but RVR is inoperative and cannot be reported for the runway of intended operation, the RVR minimum shall be converted to ground visibility and shall be the visibility minimum for takeoff or landing on that runway.
    Answer (B) is incorrect because RVR minimums must be converted to ground visibility, not disregarded. Answer (C) is incorrect because RVR minimums must be converted to ground visibility, not disregarded.

13.
4716. RVR minimums for landing are prescribed in an IAP, but RVR is inoperative and cannot be reported for the intended runway at the time. Which of the following would be an operational consideration?

A— RVR minimums which are specified in the procedures should be converted and applied as ground visibility.
B— RVR minimums may be disregarded, providing the runway has an operative HIRL system.
C— RVR minimums may be disregarded, providing all other components of the ILS system are operative.

Answer (A) is correct (4716). *(FAR 91.175)*
    If RVR minimums for takeoff or landing are prescribed in an instrument approach procedure, but RVR is inoperative and cannot be reported for the runway of intended operation, the RVR minimum shall be converted to ground visibility and shall be the visibility minimum for takeoff or landing on that runway.
    Answer (B) is incorrect because RVR minimums must be converted to ground visibility, not disregarded. Answer (C) is incorrect because RVR minimums must be converted to ground visibility, not disregarded.

14.
4762. If the RVR equipment is inoperative for an IAP that requires a visibility of 2400 RVR, how should the pilot expect the visibility requirement to be reported in lieu of the published RVR?

A— As a slant range visibility of 2,400 feet.
B— As an RVR of 2,400 feet.
C— As a ground visibility of ½ SM.

Answer (C) is correct (4762). *(FAR 91.175)*
Refer to Legend 11 on page 193 for a chart of RVR/visibility comparable values. An RVR of 2,400 ft. may be converted to ½ SM visibility when the RVR is not reported.
Answer (A) is incorrect because RVR is a horizontal, not slant range, visibility. Answer (B) is incorrect because RVR cannot be reported if the RVR equipment is inoperative. It must be converted to ground visibility.

15.
4754. If the RVR is not reported, what meteorological value should you substitute for 2400 RVR?

A— A ground visibility of ½ NM.
B— A slant range visibility of 2,400 feet for the final approach segment of the published approach procedure.
C— A ground visibility of ½ SM.

Answer (C) is correct (4754). *(FAR 91.175)*
Refer to Legend 11 on page 193 for a chart of RVR/visibility comparable values. An RVR of 2,400 ft. may be converted to ½ SM visibility when the RVR is not reported.
Answer (A) is incorrect because RVR is converted into statute, not nautical, miles. Answer (B) is incorrect because when RVR is not reported, ground visibility, not slant range visibility on approach, is substituted.

6.4 Missed Approaches

16.
4667. If an early missed approach is initiated before reaching the MAP, the following procedure should be used unless otherwise cleared by ATC.

A— Proceed to the missed approach point at or above the MDA or DH before executing a turning maneuver.
B— Begin a climbing turn immediately and follow missed approach procedures.
C— Maintain altitude and continue past MAP for 1 minute or 1 mile whichever occurs first.

Answer (A) is correct (4667). *(AIM Para 5-4-19)*
When an early missed approach is executed, the pilot should, unless otherwise directed by ATC, fly the IAP as specified on the approach plate to the missed approach point at or above the MDA or DH before executing a turning maneuver.
Answer (B) is incorrect because one should continue to the MAP before executing any turns. Answer (C) is incorrect because one need only continue to, not past, the MAP.

17.
4631. If the pilot loses visual reference while circling to land from an instrument approach and ATC radar service is not available, the missed approach action should be to

A— execute a climbing turn to parallel the published final approach course and climb to the initial approach altitude.
B— climb to the published circling minimums then proceed direct to the final approach fix.
C— make a climbing turn toward the landing runway and continue the turn until established on the missed approach course.

Answer (C) is correct (4631). *(AIM Para 5-4-19)*
If visual reference is lost while circling to land, the missed approach specified for that particular procedure must be followed. To become established on the prescribed missed approach course, the pilot should make an initial climbing turn toward the landing runway and continue the turn until established on the missed approach course.
Answer (A) is incorrect because the climbing turn should be toward the landing runway; then the pilot should execute the published missed approach procedures. Answer (B) is incorrect because there should be a climbing turn toward the landing runway.

6.5 ILS Specifications

18.
4744. If all ILS components are operating and the required visual references are not established, the missed approach should be initiated upon

A— arrival at the DH on the glide slope.
B— arrival at the middle marker.
C— expiration of the time listed on the approach chart for missed approach.

Answer (A) is correct (4744). *(FAR 91.175)*
The missed approach procedure should be executed upon arrival at the decision height (DH) on the glide slope if the visual reference requirements are not met. Thus, DH on an ILS is the MAP.
Answer (B) is incorrect because the DH rather than the middle marker is the MAP. Answer (C) is incorrect because the time listed on the approach chart for missed approaches is used in conjunction with the localizer for a timed approach if the glide slope fails during the ILS approach; i.e., it is not the primary indicator.

19.
4763. If during an ILS approach in IFR conditions, the approach lights are not visible upon arrival at the DH, the pilot is

A— required to immediately execute the missed approach procedure.
B— permitted to continue the approach and descend to the localizer MDA.
C— permitted to continue the approach to the approach threshold of the ILS runway.

Answer (A) is correct (4763). *(FAR 91.175)*
The missed approach procedure should be executed upon arrival at the decision height (DH) on the glide slope if the visual reference requirements are not met. Thus, the DH on an ILS is the MAP.
Answer (B) is incorrect because the DH is the MAP on an ILS, which is lower than the localizer MDA. Answer (C) is incorrect because the pilot may continue the approach below the DH only if the required visual references (e.g., approach lights) are established.

20.
4669. How does a pilot determine if DME is available on an ILS/LOC?

A— IAP indicate DME\TACAN channel in LOC frequency box.
B— LOC\DME are indicated on en route low altitude frequency box.
C— LOC\DME frequencies available in the Airman's Information Manual.

Answer (A) is correct (4669). *(IFH Chap X)*
If DME is available on an ILS or localizer approach, the DME/TACAN channel will be indicated in the localizer frequency box on the approach plate.
Answer (B) is incorrect because LOC/DME frequencies are available on approach plates, not en route charts. Answer (C) is incorrect because the *AIM* gives general information on navigation systems, not specific frequencies.

21.
4753. Approximately what height is the glide slope centerline at the MM of a typical ILS?

A— 100 feet.
B— 200 feet.
C— 300 feet.

Answer (B) is correct (4753). *(AIM Para 1-1-9)*
The ILS glide path projection angle is normally 3° above horizontal so it intersects the middle marker (MM) at 200 ft. and the outer marker (OM) at about 1,400 ft. above the touchdown zone elevation (TDZE).
Answer (A) is incorrect because the glide slope centerline at the inner, not middle, marker on a Category II ILS is at 100 ft. above the TDZE. Answer (C) is incorrect because the glide slope centerline at the MM is usually 200 ft. AGL, not 300 ft.

22.
4824. (Refer to figures 139 and 140 on page 211.) Which displacement from the localizer and glide slope at the 1.9 NM point is indicated?

A— 710 feet to the left of the localizer centerline and 140 feet below the glide slope.
B— 710 feet to the right of the localizer centerline and 140 feet above the glide slope.
C— 430 feet to the right of the localizer centerline and 28 feet above the glide slope.

Answer (B) is correct (4824). *(AIM Para 1-1-9)*
The airplane is to the right of the localizer and above the glide slope each by 2 dots at 1.9 NM out. Per Fig. 139, 2 dots at 1.9 NM are 140 ft. above the glide slope and 710 ft. to the right of the localizer.
Answer (A) is incorrect because the airplane is to the right, not left, of the localizer and above, not below, the glide slope. Answer (C) is incorrect because the 430-ft. and 28-ft. deviations are at 1,300 ft., not 1.9 NM.

23.
4825. (Refer to figures 139 and 141 on page 211.) Which displacement from the localizer centerline and glide slope at the 1,300-foot point from the runway is indicated?

A— 21 feet below the glide slope and approximately 320 feet to the right of the runway centerline.
B— 28 feet above the glide slope and approximately 250 feet to the left of the runway centerline.
C— 21 feet above the glide slope and approximately 320 feet to the left of the runway centerline.

Answer (C) is correct (4825). *(AIM Para 1-1-9)*
The airplane is above the glide slope and to the left of the localizer by 1½ dots each at 1,300 ft. out. Per extrapolation and Fig. 139, this displacement is 21 ft. above the glide slope and about 320 ft. to the left of the localizer.
Answer (A) is incorrect because the airplane is above, not below, the glide slope, and to the left, not right, of the localizer. Answer (B) is incorrect because 28 ft. is 2 dots, and 250 ft. is less than 1¼ dots.

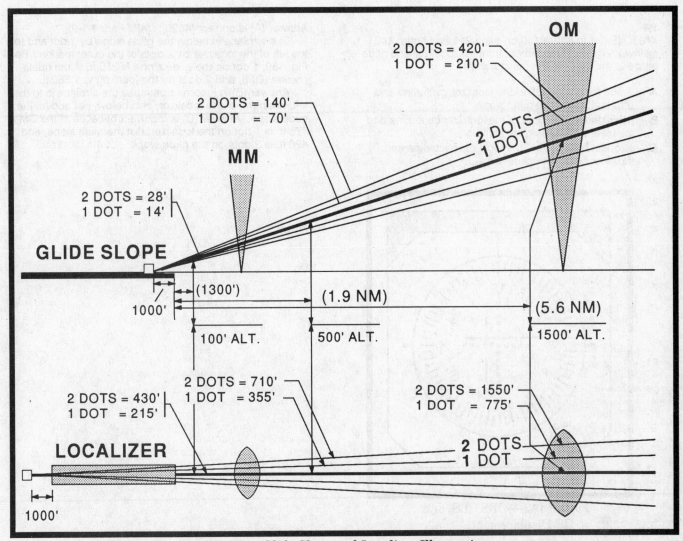

FIGURE 139.—Glide Slope and Localizer Illustration.

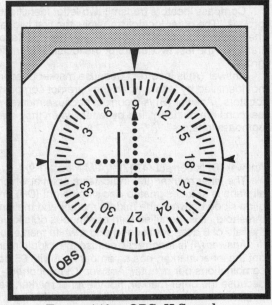

FIGURE 140.—OBS, ILS, and
GS Displacement.

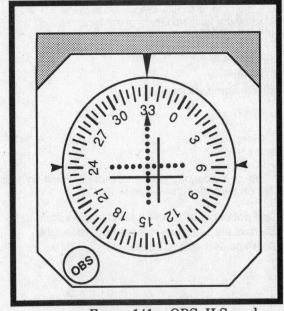

FIGURE 141.—OBS, ILS, and
GS Displacement.

24.
4826. (Refer to figure 139 on page 211 and figure 142 below.) Which displacement from the localizer and glide slope at the outer marker is indicated?

A— 1,550 feet to the left of the localizer centerline and 210 feet below the glide slope.

B— 1,550 feet to the right of the localizer centerline and 210 feet above the glide slope.

C— 775 feet to the left of the localizer centerline and 420 feet below the glide slope.

Answer (A) is correct (4826). *(AIM Para 1-1-9)*
The airplane is below the glide slope by 1 dot and to the left of the localizer by 2 dots at the outer marker. Per Fig. 139, 1 dot on the glide slope is 210 ft. at the outer marker (OM), and 2 dots on the localizer is 1,550 ft.
Answer (B) is incorrect because the airplane is to the left, not right, of the localizer, and below, not above, the glide slope. Answer (C) is incorrect because at the OM 775 ft. is 1 dot on the localizer, not the glide slope, and 420 ft. is 2 dots on the glide slope, not the localizer.

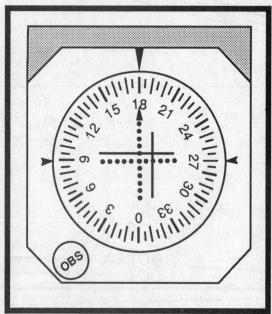

FIGURE 142.—OBS, ILS, and
GS Displacement.

25.
4729. Which range facility associated with the ILS is identified by the last two letters of the localizer identification group?

A— Inner marker.
B— Outer marker.
C— Middle compass locator.

Answer (C) is correct (4729). *(AIM Para 1-1-9)*
Compass locators transmit two-letter identification groups. The outer locator transmits the first two letters of the localizer identification group, and the middle locator transmits the last two letters of the localizer identification group.
Answer (A) is incorrect because marker beacons are not identified by letters when they are not compass locators. Answer (B) is incorrect because marker beacons are not identified by letters when they are not compass locators.

26.
4747. Which indications will a pilot receive where an IM is installed on a front course ILS approach?

A— One dot per second and a steady amber light.
B— Six dots per second and a flashing white light.
C— Alternate dashes and a blue light.

Answer (B) is correct (4747). *(AIM Para 1-1-9)*
The inner marker (IM) indicates a point at which an airplane is at a designated decision height (DH) on the glide slope between the middle marker and the landing threshold. It is identified with continuous dots keyed at the rate of 6 dots per second and a white marker beacon.
Answer (A) is incorrect because the middle marker, not the inner marker, has an amber light with 95 dot-dash combinations per minute. Answer (C) is incorrect because the outer marker, not the inner marker, has continuous, not alternate, dashes and a blue light.

27.
4730. Which range facility associated with the ILS can be identified by a two-letter coded signal?

A— Middle marker.
B— Outer marker.
C— Compass locator.

28.
4692. Which of the following statements is true regarding Parallel ILS approaches?

A— Parallel ILS approach runway centerlines are separated by at least 4,300 feet and standard IFR separation is provided on the adjacent runway.
B— Parallel ILS approaches provide aircraft a minimum of 1½ miles radar separation between successive aircraft on the adjacent localizer course.
C— Landing minimums to the adjacent runway will be higher than the minimums to the primary runway, but will normally be lower than the published circling minimums.

6.6 Unusable ILS Components

29.
4731. Which pilot action is appropriate if more than one component of an ILS is unusable?

A— Use the highest minimum required by any single component that is unusable.
B— Request another approach appropriate to the equipment that is useable.
C— Raise the minimums a total of that required by each component that is unusable.

30.
4732. Which substitution is permitted when an ILS component is inoperative?

A— A compass locator or precision radar may be substituted for the ILS outer or middle marker.
B— ADF or VOR bearings which cross either the outer or middle marker sites may be substituted for these markers.
C— DME, when located at the localizer antenna site, should be substituted for the outer or middle marker.

Answer (C) is correct (4730). *(AIM Para 1-1-9)*
Each compass locator (middle and outer) is identified by a two-letter coded signal.
Answer (A) is incorrect because marker beacons are not identified by letters when they are not a compass locator. Answer (B) is incorrect because marker beacons are not identified by letters when they are not a compass locator.

Answer (B) is correct (4692). *(AIM Para 5-4-12)*
Aircraft are afforded a minimum of 1½ mi. radar separation diagonally between successive aircraft on the adjacent localizer course and a minimum 2½ mi. radar separation from aircraft on the same final approach during parallel ILS operations.
Answer (A) is incorrect because, when parallel ILS runways are separated by at least 4,300 ft., a minimum of 2 mi. diagonal radar separation is between successive aircraft, not standard IFR separation. Answer (C) is incorrect because a side-step maneuver, not a parallel ILS approach, will have landing minimums to the adjacent runway which are higher than the minimums to the primary runway, but these minimums will normally be lower than the published circling minimums.

Answer (A) is correct (4731). *(AIM Para 1-1-9)*
Landing minimums published on instrument approach procedure charts are based upon full operation of all components and the use of visual aids associated with the particular instrument approach chart. Higher visibility minimums are required with inoperative components or visual aids as specified in FAA tables. If more than one component is inoperative, each minimum is raised to the highest minimum required by any single component that is inoperative.
Answer (B) is incorrect because an ILS can be used with some components inoperative. Those inoperative components would increase the approach minimums, but you would not need to request another approach appropriate to the equipment that is usable. Answer (C) is incorrect because it is not cumulative; you need only use the highest minimum required as a result of any one component's being unusable.

Answer (A) is correct (4732). *(FAR 91.175)*
A compass locator or precision radar may be substituted for an inoperative outer or middle marker. Compass locators, precision radar, DME, VOR, or nondirectional fixes authorized in the standard instrument approach or surveillance radar may be substituted for an inoperative outer marker.
Answer (B) is incorrect because ADF and VOR bearings can be substituted for the outer marker but not the middle marker. Answer (C) is incorrect because DME can be substituted for the outer marker but not the middle marker.

31.
4733. What facilities, if any, may be substituted for an inoperative middle marker during an ILS approach without affecting the straight-in minimums?

A— ASR.
B— Substitution not necessary, minimums do not change.
C— Compass locator, PAR, and ASR.

Answer (B) is correct (4733). *(FAR 91.175)*
Refer to Legend 22, Inoperative Components or Visual Aids Table, on page 200. Note that an inoperative middle marker (MM) is not listed as an inoperative ILS component that would require an increase in the visibility minimum. While a compass locator or PAR may be substituted for an inoperative MM, no substitution is necessary since the landing minimums are not changed.
Answer (A) is incorrect because no substitution is necessary for an inoperative MM since the landing minimums do not change. Answer (C) is incorrect because no substitution is necessary for an inoperative MM since the landing minimums do not change.

32.
4742. Which of these facilities may be substituted for an MM during a complete ILS IAP?

A— Surveillance and precision radar.
B— Compass locator and precision radar.
C— A VOR/DME fix.

Answer (B) is correct (4742). *(FAR 91.175)*
Compass locators or precision radar may be substituted for the outer or middle marker.
Answer (A) is incorrect because airport surveillance radar may be substituted for the outer marker but not the middle marker. Answer (C) is incorrect because a VOR/DME fix authorized in the standard instrument approach may only be substituted for the outer marker.

33.
4664. When installed with the ILS and specified in the approach procedures, DME may be used

A— in lieu of the OM.
B— in lieu of visibility requirements.
C— to determine distance from TDZ.

Answer (A) is correct (4664). *(AIM Para 1-1-9)*
When installed with the ILS and specified in the approach procedure, DME may be used in lieu of the outer marker (OM).
Answer (B) is incorrect because DME has no effect on visibility requirements. Answer (C) is incorrect because touchdown zone (TDZ) is the first 3,000 ft. of the runway, not a specific point.

34.
4770. Which substitution is appropriate during an ILS approach?

A— A VOR radial crossing the outer marker site may be substituted for the outer marker.
B— LOC minimums should be substituted for ILS minimums whenever the glide slope becomes inoperative.
C— DME, when located at the localizer antenna site, should be substituted for either the outer or middle marker.

Answer (B) is correct (4770). *(AIM Para 1-1-9)*
When the glide slope becomes inoperative during an ILS approach, the approach can be conducted as a localizer approach and the LOC minimums apply.
Answer (A) is incorrect because a VOR radial must be authorized in the standard approach procedure to be used as a substitute. Answer (C) is incorrect because DME can be substituted for the outer marker, but not the middle marker.

35.
4764. Immediately after passing the final approach fix in bound during an ILS approach in IFR conditions, the glide slope warning flag appears. The pilot is

A— permitted to continue the approach and descend to the DH.
B— permitted to continue the approach and descend to the localizer MDA.
C— required to immediately begin the prescribed missed approach procedure.

Answer (B) is correct (4764). *(AIM Para 1-1-9)*
When the glide slope fails, the approach can continue as a nonprecision localizer approach. Accordingly, if the glide slope fails on an ILS approach, the pilot may switch to the localizer approach and descend to the localizer MDA (minimum descent altitude).
Answer (A) is incorrect because, once the glide slope is inoperative, the localizer may be used only for a nonprecision approach, which uses MDA, not DH. Answer (C) is incorrect because one should execute the missed approach procedure only after reaching the missed approach point.

36.
4706. A pilot is making an ILS approach and is past the OM to a runway which has a VASI. What action should the pilot take if an electronic glide slope malfunction occurs and the pilot has the VASI in sight?

A— The pilot should inform ATC of the malfunction and then descend immediately to the localizer DH and make a localizer approach.
B— The pilot may continue the approach and use the VASI glide slope in place of the electronic glide slope.
C— The pilot must request an LOC approach, and may descend below the VASI at the pilot's discretion.

Answer (B) is correct (4706). *(FAR 91.175)*
Once the necessary specified visual requirements, e.g., the VASI, are attained for the intended runway, the pilot may continue the approach and use the VASI in place of the electronic glide slope.
Answer (A) is incorrect because, once the pilot has the necessary visual references, the approach may be continued visually. Answer (C) is incorrect because, once the pilot has the necessary visual references, the approach may be continued visually. Descent below the VASI glide path shall occur only when necessary for a safe landing.

6.7 Flying the Approach

37.
4752. The rate of descent on the glide slope is dependent upon

A— true airspeed.
B— calibrated airspeed.
C— ground speed.

Answer (C) is correct (4752). *(IFH Chap VIII)*
The rate of descent required to stay on the ILS glide slope depends on the ground speed because the descent must be constant relative to the distance traveled over the ground. Thus, the descent must be decreased if ground speed is decreased.
Answer (A) is incorrect because the rate of descent is based on ground speed, not true airspeed. Answer (B) is incorrect because the rate of descent is based on ground speed, not calibrated airspeed.

38.
4745. The rate of descent required to stay on the ILS glide slope

A— must be increased if the ground speed is decreased.
B— will remain constant if the indicated airspeed remains constant.
C— must be decreased if the ground speed is decreased.

Answer (C) is correct (4745). *(IFH Chap VIII)*
The rate of descent required to stay on the ILS glide slope is dependent on the ground speed because the descent must be constant relative to the distance traveled over the ground. Thus, the descent must be decreased if ground speed is decreased.
Answer (A) is incorrect because, if ground speed decreases and descent increases, the airplane will go below the glide slope. Answer (B) is incorrect because ground speed rather than airspeed determines the rate of descent.

39.
4748. To remain on the ILS glidepath, the rate of descent must be

A— decreased if the airspeed is increased.
B— decreased if the ground speed is increased.
C— increased if the ground speed is increased.

Answer (C) is correct (4748). *(IFH Chap VIII)*
The rate of descent required to stay on the ILS glide slope depends on the ground speed because the descent must be constant relative to the distance traveled over the ground. Thus, the descent must be increased if ground speed is increased.
Answer (A) is incorrect because the rate of descent must be based upon ground speed, not airspeed, while on the glide slope. Answer (B) is incorrect because, if one decreases the rate of descent with ground speed increasing, the airplane will rise above the glide slope.

40.
4720. When passing through an abrupt wind shear which involves a shift from a tailwind to a headwind, what power management would normally be required to maintain a constant indicated airspeed and ILS glide slope?

A— Higher than normal power initially, followed by a further increase as the wind shear is encountered, then a decrease.

B— Lower than normal power initially, followed by a further decrease as the wind shear is encountered, then an increase.

C— Higher than normal power initially, followed by a decrease as the shear is encountered, then an increase.

Answer (B) is correct (4720). *(AC 00-54)*
When an airplane is on the ILS glide slope and there is a change from a tailwind to a headwind, the groundspeed will decrease. During the tailwind, lower-than-normal power will be required. When the wind shear is encountered, even lower power will be required to decrease the spurt in airspeed. Once the wind shifts to a headwind, the airplane will require an increase in power to maintain the necessary groundspeed to stay on the ILS glide slope.
Answer (A) is incorrect because initially there is lower-than-normal, not higher-than-normal, power with a tailwind, and when the headwind is encountered, a decrease, not an increase, in power is required. Answer (C) is incorrect because initially there is lower-than-normal, not higher-than-normal, power with a tailwind.

41.
4721. What effect will a change in wind direction have upon maintaining a 3° glide slope at a constant true airspeed?

A— When ground speed decreases, rate of descent must increase.

B— When ground speed increases, rate of descent must increase.

C— Rate of descent must be constant to remain on the glide slope.

Answer (B) is correct (4721). *(IFH Chap VIII)*
The rate of descent required to stay on the ILS glide slope is dependent on the ground speed because the descent must be constant relative to the distance traveled over the ground. Thus, the descent must be increased if ground speed is increased.
Answer (A) is incorrect because, if you increase the rate of descent when the ground speed decreases, you will fly below the glide slope. Answer (C) is incorrect because the rate of descent must change with changes in ground speed.

42.
4756. The glide slope and localizer are centered, but the airspeed is too fast. Which should be adjusted initially?

A— Pitch and power.
B— Power only.
C— Pitch only.

Answer (B) is correct (4756). *(IFH Chap VIII)*
If the glide slope and localizer are centered but the airspeed is too fast, you should reduce power initially. Almost immediately, you will then have to make pitch adjustments to compensate for the power adjustment to maintain the glidepath.
Answer (A) is incorrect because, although the pitch and power adjustments must be closely coordinated, the power is actually adjusted first. Answer (C) is incorrect because adjusting pitch initially would cause you to fly above the glide path.

43.
4757. While being vectored, if crossing the ILS final approach course becomes imminent and an approach clearance has not been issued, what action should be taken by the pilot?

A— Turn outbound on the final approach course, execute a procedure turn, and inform ATC.

B— Turn inbound and execute the missed approach procedure at the outer marker if approach clearance has not been received.

C— Maintain the last assigned heading and query ATC.

Answer (C) is correct (4757). *(AIM Para 5-4-3)*
While being vectored, if you determine that crossing the final approach course is imminent and you have not been informed that you will be vectored across it, you should question the controller. You should not turn inbound on the final approach course unless you have received an approach clearance.
Answer (A) is incorrect because you should maintain the last assigned heading until you receive an amended clearance. When in doubt, query ATC. Answer (B) is incorrect because you should maintain the last assigned heading until you receive an amended clearance. When in doubt, query ATC.

44.
4739. Thrust is managed to maintain IAS, and glide slope is being flown. What characteristics should be observed when a headwind shears to be a constant tailwind?

A— PITCH ATTITUDE: Increases; REQUIRED THRUST: Increased, then reduced; VERTICAL SPEED: Increases; IAS: Increases, then decreases to approach speed.
B— PITCH ATTITUDE: Decreases; REQUIRED THRUST: Increased, then reduced; VERTICAL SPEED: Increases; IAS: Decreases, then increases to approach speed.
C— PITCH ATTITUDE: Increases; REQUIRED THRUST: Reduced, then increased; VERTICAL SPEED: Decreases; IAS: Decreases, then increases to approach speed.

Answer (B) is correct (4739). *(AC 00-54)*
When a headwind shears to a tailwind, the airplane's airspeed drops, its nose pitches down, and its vertical speed increases. The power must be increased initially to resume normal approach speed, then reduced as airspeed stabilizes to maintain the glide slope due to the increased groundspeed.
Answer (A) is incorrect because the airspeed decreases, not increases, initially as the headwind shears to a tailwind, causing the pitch to decrease, not increase. Answer (C) is incorrect because the pitch attitude decreases, not increases, due to the decreased airspeed, causing the vertical speed to increase, not decrease. Initially, the thrust must be increased, not decreased, to maintain approach airspeed.

45.
4727. While flying a 3° glide slope, a constant tailwind shears to a calm wind. Which conditions should the pilot expect?

A— Airspeed and pitch attitude decrease and there is a tendency to go below glide slope.
B— Airspeed and pitch attitude increase and there is a tendency to go below glide slope.
C— Airspeed and pitch attitude increase and there is a tendency to go above glide slope.

Answer (C) is correct (4727). *(AC 00-54)*
When a constant tailwind shears to a calm wind, the airplane's airspeed increases, its nose pitches up, and it has a tendency to go above the glide slope. The nose pitches up due to the increased lift from the increased airspeed.
Answer (A) is incorrect because the airspeed and pitch increase, not decrease, and there is a tendency to go above, not below, the glide slope. Answer (B) is incorrect because the tendency is to go above, not below, the glide slope.

46.
4755. While flying a 3° glide slope, a headwind shears to a tailwind. Which conditions should the pilot expect on the glide slope?

A— Airspeed and pitch attitude decrease and there is a tendency to go below glide slope.
B— Airspeed and pitch attitude increase and there is a tendency to go above glide slope.
C— Airspeed and pitch attitude decrease and there is a tendency to remain on the glide slope.

Answer (A) is correct (4755). *(AC 00-54)*
When a headwind shears to a tailwind, the airplane's airspeed drops, its nose pitches down, and it begins to drop below the glide slope. The airplane will be both slow and power deficient.
Answer (B) is incorrect because airspeed and pitch decrease, not increase, and there is a tendency to go below, not above, the glide slope. Answer (C) is incorrect because there is a tendency to go below, not remain on, the glide slope.

47.
4772. During a precision radar or ILS approach, the rate of descent required to remain on the glide slope will

A— remain the same regardless of groundspeed.
B— increase as the groundspeed increases.
C— decrease as the groundspeed increases.

Answer (B) is correct (4772). *(IFH Chap VIII)*
The rate of descent required to stay on the ILS glide slope is dependent on the groundspeed because the descent must be constant relative to the distance traveled over the ground. Thus, the descent must be increased if groundspeed is increased.
Answer (A) is incorrect because the descent rate varies with the groundspeed. Answer (C) is incorrect because the descent rate must increase, not decrease, as groundspeed increases.

48.
4773. When tracking in bound on the localizer, which of the following is the proper procedure regarding drift corrections?

A— Drift corrections should be accurately established before reaching the outer marker and completion of the approach should be accomplished with heading corrections no greater than 2°.
B— Drift corrections should be made in 5° increments after passing the outer marker.
C— Drift corrections should be made in 10° increments after passing the outer marker.

Answer (A) is correct (4773). *(IFH Chap VIII)*
When you are tracking in bound on the localizer, your drift correction should be small and reduced proportionally as the course narrows. By the time you reach the outer marker, your drift correction should be established accurately enough to permit completion of the approach with heading corrections no greater than 2°.
Answer (B) is incorrect because, after you pass the outer marker, your drift corrections should be no greater than 2°, not 5°. Answer (C) is incorrect because, after you pass the outer marker, your drift corrections should be no greater than 2°, not 10°.

6.8 ASR Approaches

49.
4741. Which information, in addition to headings, does the radar controller provide without request during an ASR approach?

A— The recommended altitude for each mile from the runway.
B— When reaching the MDA.
C— When to commence descent to MDA, the aircraft's position each mile on final from the runway, and arrival at the MAP.

Answer (C) is correct (4741). *(AIM Para 5-4-10)*
A surveillance approach (ASR) provides navigation guidance in azimuths (direction) only. The pilot is furnished headings to align the airplane with the extended centerline of the landing runway and will be advised when to commence descent to the MDA and the MAP. In addition, the pilot will be advised of the airplane's position each mile on the final approach from the runway or MAP as appropriate.
Answer (A) is incorrect because the recommended altitude for each mile from the runway is provided only upon request. Answer (B) is incorrect because the controller does not have precise altitude capability.

50.
4711. Where may you use a surveillance approach?

A— At any airport that has an approach control.
B— At any airport which has radar service.
C— At airports for which civil radar instrument approach minimums have been published.

Answer (C) is correct (4711). *(AIM Para 5-4-10)*
ASR (surveillance) approaches are available at airports for which radar instrument approach minimums have been published and a separate approach chart is available. That is, a surveillance approach must have previously been authorized and established by the FAA for a particular runway at a particular airport prior to its availability.
Answer (A) is incorrect because specific procedures, minimums, missed approach points, etc., must be established before a surveillance approach can be conducted by ATC. Answer (B) is incorrect because specific procedures, minimums, missed approach points, etc., must be established before a surveillance approach can be conducted by ATC.

51.
4728. How is ATC radar used for instrument approaches when the facility is approved for approach control service?

A— Precision approaches, weather surveillance, and as a substitute for any inoperative component of a navigation aid used for approaches.
B— ASR approaches, weather surveillance, and course guidance by approach control.
C— Course guidance to the final approach course, ASR and PAR approaches, and the monitoring of nonradar approaches.

Answer (C) is correct (4728). *(AIM Para 5-4-3)*
Where radar is approved for approach control service, it is used not only to provide course guidance for radar approaches but also to provide vectors in conjunction with published nonradar approaches based on radio NAVAIDs.
Answer (A) is incorrect because approach control radar is not designed for weather surveillance.
Answer (B) is incorrect because approach control radar is not designed for weather surveillance.

52.
4822. During a "no-gyro" approach and prior to being handed off to the final approach controller, the pilot should make all turns

A— one-half standard rate unless otherwise advised.
B— any rate not exceeding a 30° bank.
C— standard rate unless otherwise advised.

53.
4823. After being handed off to the final approach controller during a "no-gyro" surveillance or precision approach, the pilot should make all turns

A— one-half standard rate.
B— based upon the groundspeed of the aircraft.
C— standard rate.

6.9 Side-Step Approaches

54.
4740. When cleared to execute a published sidestep maneuver for a specific approach and landing on the parallel runway, at what point is the pilot expected to commence this maneuver?

A— At the published minimum altitude for a circling approach.
B— As soon as possible after the runway or runway environment is in sight.
C— At the localizer MDA minimum and when the runway is in sight.

55.
4771. Assume this clearance is received:

"CLEARED FOR ILS RUNWAY 07 LEFT APPROACH, SIDE-STEP TO RUNWAY 07 RIGHT."

When would the pilot be expected to commence the side-step maneuver?

A— As soon as possible after the runway environment is in sight.
B— Any time after becoming aligned with the final approach course of Runway 07 left, and after passing the final approach fix.
C— After reaching the circling minimums for Runway 07 right.

Answer (C) is correct (4822). *(AIM Para 5-4-10)*
During "no-gyro" approaches prior to the final approach, all turns should be made at the standard rate unless otherwise advised by ATC.
Answer (A) is incorrect because one-half the standard-rate turn should be used in conjunction with the final approach controller. Answer (B) is incorrect because the turn should be at the standard rate unless otherwise advised.

Answer (A) is correct (4823). *(AIM Para 5-4-10)*
After being handed off to the final approach controller on a "no-gyro" surveillance or precision approach, all turns should be at one-half the standard rate.
Answer (B) is incorrect because the established procedure is to turn at one-half the standard rate regardless of groundspeed. Answer (C) is incorrect because a standard-rate turn should be used on "no-gyro" approaches prior to working with the final approach controller.

Answer (B) is correct (4740). *(AIM Para 5-4-17)*
Pilots are expected to commence the side-step maneuver as soon as possible after the runway or runway environment is in sight.
Answer (A) is incorrect because the side-step maneuver should be performed only when the runway environment is in sight. Answer (C) is incorrect because the side-step maneuver should be performed as soon as the runway environment is in sight, which may be before reaching the MDA.

Answer (A) is correct (4771). *(AIM Para 5-4-17)*
Pilots are expected to commence the side-step maneuver as soon as possible after the runway or runway environment is in sight.
Answer (B) is incorrect because the side-step maneuver should be performed as soon as possible but only after the runway or runway environment is in sight. Answer (C) is incorrect because the side-step maneuver should be performed as soon as possible but only after the runway or runway environment is in sight.

6.10 Timed Approaches from Holding Fixes

56.
4768. Which of the following conditions is required before "timed approaches from a holding fix" may be conducted?

A— If more than one missed approach procedure is available, only one may require a course reversal.

B— If more than one missed approach procedure is available, none may require a course reversal.

C— Direct communication between the pilot and the tower must be established prior to beginning the approach.

Answer (B) is correct (4768). *(AIM Para 5-4-9)*
Timed approaches from a holding fix may be conducted when a control tower is in operation at the airport of intended landing and direct communications are maintained between the pilot and center approach until switching to the tower. Course reversals are not permitted when more than one missed approach procedure exists.
Answer (A) is incorrect because no course reversals are permitted on a missed approach procedure if more than one missed approach procedure is available.
Answer (C) is incorrect because, prior to beginning the approach, the pilot must be in contact with approach, not the tower.

57.
4627. If only one missed approach procedure is available, which of the following conditions is required when conducting "timed approaches from a holding fix"?

A— The pilot must contact the airport control tower prior to departing the holding fix in bound.

B— The reported ceiling and visibility minimums must be equal to or greater than the highest prescribed circling minimums for the IAP.

C— The reported ceiling and visibility minimums must be equal to or greater than the highest prescribed straight in MDA minimums for the IAP.

Answer (B) is correct (4627). *(AIM Para 5-4-9)*
If only one missed approach procedure is available, the reported ceiling and visibility must be equal to or greater than the highest prescribed circling minimums for the IAP.
Answer (A) is incorrect because the pilot contacts the tower when so directed by approach or center.
Answer (C) is incorrect because the ceiling and visibility minimums must exceed the highest circling, not straight in, minimums.

58.
4628. Prior to conducting "timed approaches from a holding fix," which one of the following is required?

A— The time required to fly from the primary facility to the field boundary must be determined by a reliable means.

B— The airport where the approach is to be conducted must have a control tower in operation.

C— The pilot must have established two-way communications with the tower before departing the holding fix.

Answer (B) is correct (4628). *(AIM Para 5-4-9)*
One requirement for timed approaches is that the airport where the approach is to be conducted must have a control tower in operation.
Answer (A) is incorrect because the times to fly from the holding fix to the runway at various groundspeeds are provided on approach plates. Answer (C) is incorrect because the pilot must be in communication with approach or center until told to switch to the tower.

59.
4629. When making a "timed approach" from a holding fix at the outer marker, the pilot should adjust the

A— holding pattern to start the procedure turn at the assigned time.

B— airspeed at the final approach fix in order to arrive at the missed approach point at the assigned time.

C— holding pattern to leave the final approach fix inbound at the assigned time.

Answer (C) is correct (4629). *(AIM Para 5-4-9)*
The pilot should adjust the holding pattern to leave the final approach fix inbound at the assigned time.
Answer (A) is incorrect because, in timed approaches, the pilot will not execute a procedure turn unless cleared to do so by ATC. Answer (B) is incorrect because the assigned time is the departure time from the final approach fix, not the arrival time at the MAP.

6.11 Holding

60.
4620. At what point should the timing begin for the first leg outbound in a nonstandard holding pattern?

A— Abeam the holding fix, or wings level, whichever occurs last.
B— When the wings are level at the completion of the 180° turn outbound.
C— When over or abeam the holding fix, whichever occurs later.

61.
4618. (Refer to figure 115 below.) You receive this ATC clearance:

"...HOLD WEST OF THE ONE FIVE DME FIX ON THE ZERO NINE ZERO RADIAL OF ABC VORTAC, FIVE MILE LEGS, LEFT TURNS..."

You arrive at the 15 DME fix on a heading of 350°. Which holding pattern correctly complies with these instructions, and what is the recommended entry procedure?

A— 1; teardrop.
B— 2; direct.
C— 1; direct.

Answer (C) is correct (4620). *(IFH Chap XII)*
Outbound leg timing begins when over or abeam the holding fix, whichever occurs later. If the abeam position cannot be determined, start timing when the turn to outbound is completed (i.e., wings return to level).
Answer (A) is incorrect because timing begins on the outbound leg when the wings are level only if the abeam position cannot be determined. Answer (B) is incorrect because the wings may be level before you are abeam the fix.

Answer (C) is correct (4618). *(AIM Para 5-3-7)*
Holding pattern 1 is correct because the holding fix is always at the end of the inbound leg. Draw the 70° line through the fix such that it intersects the outbound leg 1/3 of the leg length from abeam the fix.

Airplane Heading to Fix	Entry
340° to 160°	Direct
160° to 270°	Parallel
270° to 340°	Teardrop

A 350° heading to the fix requires a direct entry, which requires a standard-rate left turn to 270° beginning over the holding fix.
Answer (A) is incorrect because approaching the fix on a heading of 350° requires a direct, not teardrop, entry. Answer (B) is incorrect because holding pattern 2 does not show the holding fix at the end of the inbound leg.

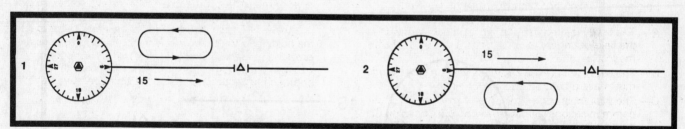

FIGURE 115.—DME Fix with Holding Pattern.

62.
4609. (Refer to figure 112 below.) You arrive at the
15 DME fix on a heading of 350°. Which holding pattern
correctly complies with the ATC clearance below, and
what is the recommended entry procedure?

"...HOLD WEST OF THE ONE FIVE DME FIX ON THE
ZERO NINE ZERO RADIAL OF THE ABC VORTAC, FIVE
MILE LEGS, LEFT TURNS..."

A— 1; teardrop entry.
B— 1; direct entry.
C— 2; direct entry.

Answer (B) is correct (4609). (AIM Para 5-3-7)
  Holding pattern 1 is correct because the holding fix is
always at the end of the inbound leg. Draw the 70° line
through the fix such that it intersects the outbound leg
1/3 of the leg length from abeam the fix.

Airplane Heading to Fix	Entry
340° to 160°	Direct
160° to 270°	Parallel
270° to 340°	Teardrop

A 350° heading to the fix requires a direct entry, which
requires a standard-rate left turn to 270° beginning over
the holding fix.
  Answer (A) is incorrect because approaching the fix
on a heading of 350° requires a direct, not teardrop,
entry. Answer (C) is incorrect because holding pattern 2
does not show the holding fix at the end of the inbound
leg.

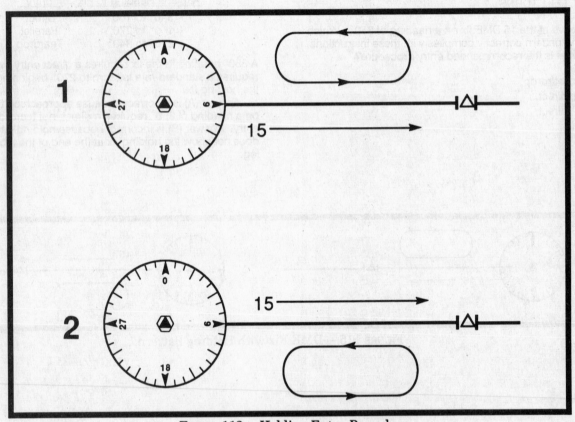

FIGURE 112.—Holding Entry Procedure.

63.
4617. To ensure proper airspace protection while in a
holding pattern, what is the maximum airspeed above
14,000 feet for civil turbojet aircraft?

A— 230 knots.
B— 265 knots.
C— 200 knots.

Answer (B) is correct (4617). (AIM Para 5-3-7)
  For civil turbojets, the maximum indicated airspeed
above 14,000 ft. MSL for holding patterns is 265 kt.
  Answer (A) is incorrect because 230 kt. is the
maximum holding airspeed for a civil turbojet from above
6,000 ft. through 14,000 ft., not above 14,000 ft.
Answer (C) is incorrect because 200 kt. is the maximum
holding airspeed for a turbojet aircraft from the MHA
through 6,000 ft., not above 14,000 ft.

64.
4766. To ensure proper airspace protection while in a holding pattern above 14,000 feet in a propeller-driven airplane, what is the maximum indicated airspeed a pilot should use?

A— 265 knots.
B— 175 knots.
C— 200 knots.

Answer (A) is correct (4766). *(AIM Para 5-3-7)*
The maximum indicated airspeed while in a holding pattern above 14,000 ft. in any airplane is 265 kt.
Answer (B) is incorrect because 175 kt. is a nonstandard maximum airspeed, which is depicted by an icon on the appropriate chart. Answer (C) is incorrect because 200 kt. is the maximum holding airspeed for an airplane from the MHA through 6,000 ft., not above 14,000 ft.

65.
4614. (Refer to figure 114 below.) A pilot receives this ATC clearance:

"...CLEARED TO THE ABC VORTAC. HOLD WEST ON THE TWO SEVEN ZERO RADIAL..."

What is the recommended procedure to enter the holding pattern?

A— Parallel or teardrop.
B— Parallel only.
C— Direct only.

Answer (C) is correct (4614). *(AIM Para 5-3-7)*
When holding west on the 270° radial, use right turns because left turns were not stated in the clearance. The holding pattern will be to the south of the 270° radial, so the VORTAC (the fix) is at the end of the inbound leg. To determine entry procedures, draw a 70° line through the holding fix such that it crosses through the outbound leg 1/3 of the leg length from abeam the fix.

R-020 to R-090	Teardrop
R-090 to R-200	Parallel
R-200 to R-020	Direct

Since you are approaching the holding fix from the northwest on R-330 of ABC VORTAC (Fig. 114), you will make a direct entry.
Answer (A) is incorrect because the parallel or teardrop entries are alternatives only when approaching on R-090. Answer (B) is incorrect because the parallel entry is appropriate only when approaching on R-090 to R-200.

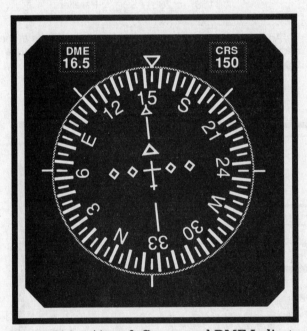

Figure 114.—Aircraft Course and DME Indicator.

66.
4615. (Refer to figure 114 above.) A pilot receives this ATC clearance:

"...CLEARED TO THE XYZ VORTAC. HOLD NORTH ON THE THREE SIX ZERO RADIAL, LEFT TURNS..."

What is the recommended procedure to enter the holding pattern?

A— Teardrop only.
B— Parallel only.
C— Direct only.

Answer (C) is correct (4615). *(AIM Para 5-3-7)*
Visualize a 360° radial with left turns. The pattern will be to the east of the radial with the holding fix being the VORTAC. Since you are approaching from the northwest on R-330 of XYZ VORTAC (see Fig. 114.), you will be able to make a direct entry.

R-180 to R-250	Teardrop
R-250 to R-070	Direct
R-070 to R-180	Parallel

Answer (A) is incorrect because, if you were approaching on R-180 to R-250, you would make a teardrop entry. Answer (B) is incorrect because, if you were approaching on R-070 to R-180, you would fly through the VOR, parallel the holding course, turn right to the holding course, and make an entry.

67.
4616. (Refer to figure 114 on page 223.) A pilot receives this ATC clearance:

"...CLEARED TO THE ABC VORTAC. HOLD SOUTH ON THE ONE EIGHT ZERO RADIAL..."

What is the recommended procedure to enter the holding pattern?

A— Teardrop only.
B— Parallel only.
C— Direct only.

68.
4619. (Refer to figure 116 below.) You arrive over the 15 DME fix on a heading of 350°. Which holding pattern correctly complies with the ATC clearance below, and what is the recommended entry procedure?

"...HOLD WEST OF THE ONE FIVE DME FIX ON THE TWO SIX EIGHT RADIAL OF THE ABC VORTAC, FIVE MILE LEGS, LEFT TURNS..."

A— 1; teardrop entry.
B— 2; direct entry.
C— 1; direct entry.

Answer (A) is correct (4616). *(AIM Para 5-3-7)*
    If you are holding south on the 180° radial, you will have right turns because left turns are not specified, and you will be on the east side of the radial (to cross the VORTAC at the end of your inbound leg). Draw the 70° line through the VORTAC on R-110/R-290. Since you are inbound on R-330 (Fig. 114), you will make a teardrop entry.

R-290 to R-360	Teardrop
R-360 to R-110	Parallel
R-110 to R-290	Direct

    Answer (B) is incorrect because a parallel entry is appropriate from R-360 to R-110. Answer (C) is incorrect because a direct entry is appropriate from R-110 to R-290.

Answer (B) is correct (4619). *(AIM Para 5-3-7)*
    Alternative 2 is acceptable and 1 is not because the holding fix is always at the end of the inbound leg. Draw in the 70° line through the fix such that it intersects the outbound leg 1/3 of the length from abeam the fix. Direct entry is used with a heading of 338° to 158°.

Airplane Heading to Fix	Entry
338° to 158°	Direct
158° to 268°	Parallel
268° to 338°	Teardrop

    Answer (A) is incorrect because the fix is always at the end of the inbound leg. Answer (C) is incorrect because the fix is always at the end of the inbound leg.

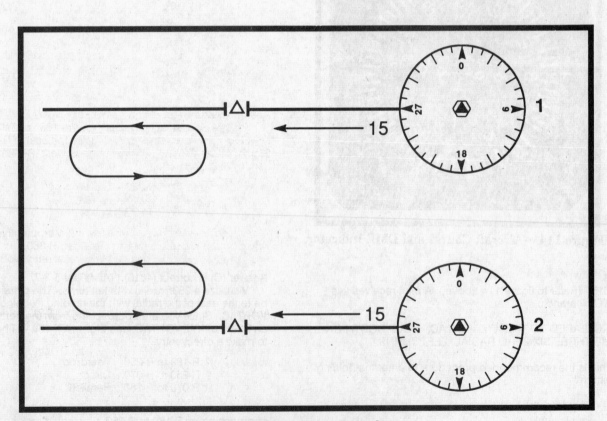

FIGURE 116.—Holding Entry Procedure.

69.
4610. (Refer to figure 113 below.) You receive this ATC clearance:

"...HOLD EAST OF THE ABC VORTAC ON THE ZERO NINER ZERO RADIAL, LEFT TURNS..."

What is the recommended procedure to enter the holding pattern?

A— Parallel only.
B— Direct only.
C— Teardrop only.

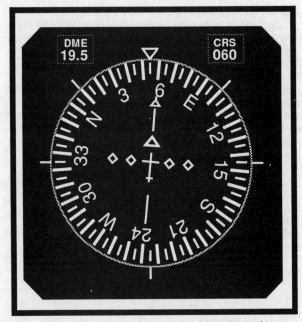

FIGURE 113.—Aircraft Course and DME Indicator.

70.
4611. (Refer to figure 113 above.) You receive this ATC clearance:

"...CLEARED TO THE ABC VORTAC. HOLD SOUTH ON THE ONE EIGHT ZERO RADIAL..."

What is the recommended procedure to enter the holding pattern?

A— Teardrop only.
B— Direct only.
C— Parallel only.

71.
4612. (Refer to figure 113 above.) You receive this ATC clearance:

"...CLEARED TO THE XYZ VORTAC. HOLD NORTH ON THE THREE SIX ZERO RADIAL, LEFT TURNS..."

What is the recommended procedure to enter the holding pattern.

A— Parallel only.
B— Direct only.
C— Teardrop only.

Answer (A) is correct (4610). (AIM Para 5-3-7)
    You are cleared to hold east of the ABC VORTAC with left turns on R-090. The holding side will be south of R-090, with the holding fix being the VORTAC. Draw the 70° line through the VORTAC on R-340/R-160.

R-270 to R-340	Teardrop
R-340 to R-160	Direct
R-160 to R-270	Parallel

Since you are approaching the VORTAC from the southwest on R-240 (see Fig. 113), you will make a parallel entry.
    Answer (B) is incorrect because a direct entry would be appropriate if you were coming in on R-340 to R-160.
Answer (C) is incorrect because a teardrop entry would be appropriate if you were coming in from R-270 to R-340.

Answer (B) is correct (4611). (AIM Para 5-3-7)
    You are cleared to hold south on the 180° radial with right turns, which means you will be to the east of R-180. Since you are coming in from the southwest (R-240), you can make a direct entry.

R-290 to R-360	Teardrop
R-360 to R-110	Parallel
R-110 to R-290	Direct

    Answer (A) is incorrect because a teardrop entry would be appropriate only from R-290 to R-360.
Answer (C) is incorrect because a parallel entry would be appropriate only from R-360 to R-110.

Answer (C) is correct (4612). (AIM Para 5-3-7)
    Holding north of the XYZ VORTAC with left turns on R-360 means you are on the east side of the radial. Since you are coming in from the southwest (R-240), you will be making a teardrop entry.

R-180 to R-250	Teardrop
R-250 to R-070	Direct
R-070 to R-180	Parallel

    Answer (A) is incorrect because a parallel approach would be appropriate only if you were coming in between R-070 and R-180. Answer (B) is incorrect because a direct entry is appropriate only between R-250 and R-070.

72.
4613. (Refer to figure 113 on page 225.) You receive this ATC clearance:

"...CLEARED TO THE ABC VORTAC. HOLD WEST ON THE TWO SEVEN ZERO RADIAL..."

What is the recommended procedure to enter the holding pattern?

A— Parallel only.
B— Direct only.
C— Teardrop only.

73.
4624. What timing procedure should be used when performing a holding pattern at a VOR?

A— Timing for the outbound leg begins over or abeam the VOR, whichever occurs later.
B— Timing for the inbound leg begins when initiating the turn inbound.
C— Adjustments in timing of each pattern should be made on the inbound leg.

74.
4621. (Refer to figure 117 below.) You receive this ATC clearance:

"...CLEARED TO THE ABC NDB. HOLD SOUTHEAST ON THE ONE FOUR ZERO DEGREE BEARING FROM THE NDB. LEFT TURNS..."

At station passage you note the indications in figure 117. What is the recommended procedure to enter the holding pattern?

A— Direct only.
B— Teardrop only.
C— Parallel only.

Answer (B) is correct (4613). *(AIM Para 5-3-7)*
You are cleared to hold west on R-270 with right turns, so you will be south of R-270. Since you are coming in on R-240, you need to make a direct entry.

R-020 to R-090	Teardrop
R-090 to R-200	Parallel
R-200 to R-020	Direct

Answer (A) is incorrect because a parallel entry is appropriate only on R-090 to R-200. Answer (C) is incorrect because a teardrop entry is appropriate only when coming in on R-020 to R-090.

Answer (A) is correct (4624). *(AIM Para 5-3-7)*
Outbound leg timing begins over or abeam the fix, whichever occurs later. If abeam the position cannot be determined, start timing when the turn to outbound is completed.
Answer (B) is incorrect because the timing for the inbound leg begins when the inbound turn is completed, not when it is initiated. Answer (C) is incorrect because the timing of the pattern is adjusted by varying the length of the outbound leg. Once inbound, you must fly to the holding fix and cannot adjust the length of the leg.

Answer (C) is correct (4621). *(AIM Para 5-3-7)*
Holding southeast on the 140° bearing means that you are south and to the west of the 140° and 320° bearings from the NDB with left turns. Since you are entering from the southwest on a 055° heading, you must make a parallel entry.

Airplane Heading to Fix	Entry
210° to 030°	Direct
030° to 140°	Parallel
140° to 210°	Teardrop

Answer (A) is incorrect because a direct entry would be appropriate if you were approaching from a heading of 210° to 030°. Answer (B) is incorrect because a teardrop entry would be appropriate if you were approaching from a heading of 140° to 210°.

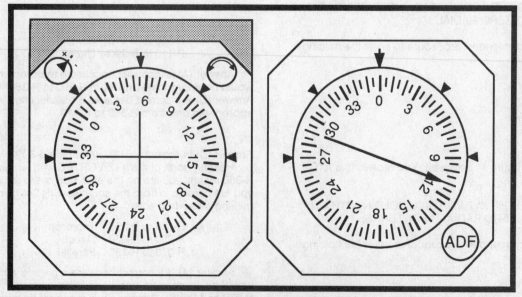

FIGURE 117.—Heading and ADF Indicators.

75.
4622. (Refer to figure 117 on page 226.) You receive this ATC clearance:

"...CLEARED TO THE XYZ NDB. HOLD NORTHEAST ON THE ZERO FOUR ZERO DEGREE BEARING FROM THE NDB. LEFT TURNS..."

At station passage you note the indications in figure 117. What is the recommended procedure to enter the holding pattern?

A— Direct only.
B— Teardrop only.
C— Parallel only.

76.
4623. (Refer to figure 117 on page 226.) You receive this ATC clearance:

"...CLEARED TO THE ABC NDB. HOLD SOUTHWEST ON THE TWO THREE ZERO DEGREE BEARING FROM THE NDB..."

At station passage you note the indications in figure 117. What is the recommended procedure to enter the holding pattern?

A— Direct only.
B— Teardrop only.
C— Parallel only.

77.
4625. When holding at an NDB, at what point should the timing begin for the second leg outbound?

A— When the wings are level and the wind drift correction angle is established after completing the turn to the outbound heading.
B— When the wings are level after completing the turn to the outbound heading, or abeam the fix, whichever occurs first.
C— When abeam the holding fix.

78.
4626. To ensure proper airspace protection while holding at 5,000 feet in a civil aircraft, what is the maximum indicated airspeed a pilot should use?

A— 230 knots.
B— 200 knots.
C— 210 knots.

79.
4767. Where a holding pattern is specified in lieu of a procedure turn, the holding maneuver must be executed within

A— the 1-minute time limitation or DME distance as specified in the profile view.
B— a radius of 5 miles from the holding fix.
C— 10 knots of the specified holding speed.

Answer (B) is correct (4622). *(AIM Para 5-3-7)*
You are holding northeast on the 040° bearing with left turns. This means you are to the east and south of 040° bearing from the NDB. Since you are entering from a 055° heading, you will make a teardrop entry.

Airplane Heading to Fix	Entry
110° to 290°	Direct
290° to 040°	Parallel
040° to 110°	Teardrop

Answer (A) is incorrect because a direct entry would be appropriate when approaching from a heading of 110° to 290°. Answer (C) is incorrect because you would use a parallel entry only if approaching on a heading from 290° to 040°.

Answer (A) is correct (4623). *(AIM Para 5-3-7)*
You are holding southwest on the 230° bearing from the NDB, but you will be on the southeast side of the inbound leg. Since you are approaching from the southwest on a 055° heading, you will make a direct entry.

Airplane Heading to Fix	Entry
340° to 160°	Direct
160° to 230°	Teardrop
230° to 340°	Parallel

Answer (B) is incorrect because a teardrop entry would be appropriate only if you were approaching the NDB on a heading from 160° to 230°. Answer (C) is incorrect because a parallel entry would be appropriate only if you were approaching the NDB on a heading from 230° to 340°.

Answer (C) is correct (4625). *(AIM Para 5-3-7)*
Outbound timing begins over or abeam the fix, whichever occurs later. If the abeam position cannot be determined, start timing when the turn to outbound is completed.
Answer (A) is incorrect because only when you cannot determine position abeam the fix should you start the timing when the turn is complete. Answer (B) is incorrect because timing of the outbound leg begins when abeam the fix, not when the wings are level.

Answer (B) is correct (4626). *(AIM Para 5-3-7)*
The maximum airspeed in holding patterns for a civil aircraft is 200 kt. from the minimum holding altitude (MHA) through 6,000 ft.
Answer (A) is incorrect because 230 kt. is the maximum holding speed from 6,001 ft. through 14,000 ft. Answer (C) is incorrect because 210 kt. is the maximum holding airspeed from 6,001 ft. through 14,000 ft. where published.

Answer (A) is correct (4767). *(AIM Para 5-3-7)*
Holding patterns should always be executed within the time or leg length published in the profile view of the IAP.
Answer (B) is incorrect because a radius of 5 mi. for a procedure turn can be specified only for category A or helicopter aircraft. Answer (C) is incorrect because ATC does not specify a holding speed. You need only remain below the maximum allowable holding speed.

80.
4668. When more than one circuit of the holding pattern is needed to lose altitude or become better established on course, the additional circuits can be made

A— at pilot's discretion.
B— only in an emergency.
C— only if pilot advises ATC and ATC approves.

Answer (C) is the best answer (4668). *(AIM Para 5-4-8)*
If you are cleared for the approach while in a holding pattern, ATC will not expect you to make any additional circuits in the hold. If you do elect to make additional circuits to lose altitude or become better established on course, it is your responsibility to so advise ATC when you receive your approach clearance.
Answer (A) is incorrect because, while you may elect to make additional circuits in the holding pattern, you are required to advise ATC of your intentions. Answer (B) is incorrect because additional circuits may be made at your discretion; declaring an emergency is not necessary.

6.12 Instrument Approach Charts

81.
4715. How can an IAF be identified on a Standard Instrument Approach Procedure (SIAP) Chart?

A— All fixes that are labeled IAF.
B— Any fix illustrated within the 10 mile ring other than the FAF or stepdown fix.
C— The procedure turn and the fixes on the feeder facility ring.

Answer (A) is correct (4715). *(AIM P/C Glossary)*
The fixes depicted on Instrument Approach Procedure Charts that identify the beginning of an initial approach segment are the initial approach fixes (IAF). Initial approach fixes are identified by the letters IAF on instrument approach charts. There may be more than one for any given approach.
Answer (B) is incorrect because IAFs are specifically identified with "IAF." Answer (C) is incorrect because IAFs are specifically identified with "IAF."

82.
4746. Which fixes on the IAP Charts are initial approach fixes?

A— Any fix on the en route facilities ring, the feeder facilities ring, and those at the start of arc approaches.
B— Only the fixes at the start of arc approaches and those on either the feeder facilities ring or en route facilities ring that have a transition course shown to the approach procedure.
C— Any fix that is identified by the letters IAF.

Answer (C) is correct (4746). *(AIM P/C Glossary)*
The fixes depicted on Instrument Approach Procedure Charts that identify the beginning of an initial approach segment are the initial approach fixes (IAF). Initial approach fixes are identified by the letters IAF on instrument approach charts. There may be more than one for any given approach.
Answer (A) is incorrect because IAFs are specifically identified with "IAF." Answer (B) is incorrect because IAFs are specifically identified with "IAF."

83.
4717. Aircraft approach categories are based on

A— certificated approach speed at maximum gross weight.
B— 1.3 times the stall speed in landing configuration at maximum gross landing weight.
C— 1.3 times the stall speed at maximum gross weight.

Answer (B) is correct (4717). *(IFH Chap X)*
IFR approach minimums are specified for various aircraft speed/weight combinations. Speeds are based upon the value of 1.3 times the stall speed of the aircraft in the landing configuration at maximum certified gross landing weight.
Answer (A) is incorrect because aircraft do not have certificated approach speeds. Answer (C) is incorrect because speeds are based on 1.3 times the stall speed in landing configuration at maximum gross landing weight, not just maximum gross weight.

84.
4470. What does the symbol T within a black triangle in the minimums section of the IAP for a particular airport indicate?

A— Takeoff minimums are 1 mile for aircraft having two engines or less and ½ mile for those with more than two engines.
B— Instrument takeoffs are not authorized.
C— Takeoff minimums are not standard and/or departure procedures are published.

Answer (C) is correct (4470). *(ACL)*
The symbol in the question indicates that takeoff minimums are not standard and/or departure procedures are published, and one should consult the alternate takeoff procedures. Takeoff minimums apply to operations under Parts 121, 125, 127, 129, and 135, i.e., operations other than Part 91.
Answer (A) is incorrect because it gives the standard minimums for takeoff when there is a published instrument approach. Answer (B) is incorrect because the alternate takeoff procedures will indicate if instrument takeoffs are not authorized.

85.
4636. What does the absence of the procedure turn barb on the plan view on an approach chart indicate?

A— A procedure turn is not authorized.
B— Teardrop-type procedure turn is authorized.
C— Racetrack-type procedure turn is authorized.

86.
4671. During an instrument approach, under what conditions, if any, is the holding pattern course reversal not required?

A— When radar vectors are provided.
B— When cleared for the approach.
C— None, since it is always mandatory.

87.
4637. When making an instrument approach at the selected alternate airport, what landing minimums apply?

A— Standard alternate minimums (600-2 or 800-2).
B— The IFR alternate minimums listed for that airport.
C— The landing minimums published for the type of procedure selected.

88.
4632. When the approach procedure involves a procedure turn, the maximum speed should not be greater than

A— 180 knots IAS.
B— 200 knots IAS.
C— 250 knots IAS.

89.
4540. What obstacle clearance and navigation signal coverage is a pilot assured with the Minimum Sector Altitudes depicted on the IAP charts?

A— 1,000 feet and acceptable navigation signal coverage within a 25 NM radius of the navigation facility.
B— 1,000 feet within a 25 NM radius of the navigation facility but not acceptable navigation signal coverage.
C— 500 feet and acceptable navigation signal coverage within a 10 NM radius of the navigation facility.

90.
4672. During an instrument precision approach, terrain and obstacle clearance depends on adherence to

A— minimum altitude shown on the IAP.
B— terrain contour information.
C— natural and man-made reference point information.

Answer (A) is correct (4636). *(AIM Para 5-4-8)*
The absence of the procedure turn barb in the plan view indicates that a procedure turn is not authorized for that approach.
Answer (B) is incorrect because the absence of a procedure turn barb indicates that all, not just teardrop-type, procedure turns are not authorized. Answer (C) is incorrect because the absence of a procedure turn barb indicates that all, not just racetrack-type, procedure turns are not authorized.

Answer (A) is correct (4671). *(AIM Para 5-4-8)*
A course reversal (procedure turn) is not required when radar vectors are being provided.
Answer (B) is incorrect because a course reversal may be required when cleared for a full approach. Answer (C) is incorrect because a course reversal is not mandatory when radar vectors are provided.

Answer (C) is correct (4637). *(FAR 91.175)*
Published landing minimums always apply when making an instrument approach to an airport.
Answer (A) is incorrect because alternate minimums refer to the minimum forecast weather allowable to list an airport as an alternate on the flight plan. Answer (B) is incorrect because alternate minimums refer to the minimum forecast weather allowable to list an airport as an alternate on the flight plan.

Answer (B) is correct (4632). *(AIM Para 5-4-8)*
When the approach procedure involves a procedure turn, a maximum speed of not greater than 200 kt. IAS should be observed, and the turn should be executed within the distance specified in the profile view.
Answer (A) is incorrect because the maximum speed that should be used is 200 kt., not 180 kt. Answer (C) is incorrect because the maximum speed that should be used is 200 kt., not 250 kt.

Answer (B) is correct (4540). *(AIM Para 5-4-5)*
Minimum sector altitudes are depicted on approach charts and provide at least 1,000 ft. of obstacle clearance within a 25-NM radius of the navigation facility upon which the procedure is predicated. These altitudes are for emergency use only and do not necessarily assure acceptable navigational signal coverage.
Answer (A) is incorrect because minimum sector altitudes do not guarantee acceptable signal coverage. Answer (C) is incorrect because minimum sector altitudes do not guarantee acceptable signal coverage, and they provide 1,000 ft., not 500 ft., of obstacle clearance.

Answer (A) is correct (4672). *(AIM Para 5-4-5)*
A pilot adhering to the altitudes, flight paths, and weather minimums depicted on the IAP chart is assured of terrain and obstruction clearance.
Answer (B) is incorrect because the design of IAPs takes terrain and obstacle clearance into account. Answer (C) is incorrect because, during instrument approaches, instrument, not visual, reference points are used to assure terrain and obstacle clearance.

91.
4734. When being radar vectored for an ILS approach, at what point may you start a descent from your last assigned altitude to a lower minimum altitude if cleared for the approach?

A— When established on a segment of a published route or IAP.
B— You may descend immediately to published glide slope interception altitude.
C— Only after you are established on the final approach unless informed otherwise by ATC.

92.
4641. While being radar vectored, an approach clearance is received. The last assigned altitude should be maintained until

A— reaching the FAF.
B— advised to begin descent.
C— established on a segment of a published route or IAP.

93.
4670. When simultaneous approaches are in progress, how does each pilot receive radar advisories?

A— On tower frequency.
B— On approach control frequency.
C— One pilot on tower frequency and the other on approach control frequency.

94.
4749. When may a pilot make a straight-in landing, if using an IAP having only circling minimums?

A— A straight-in landing may not be made, but the pilot may continue to the runway at MDA and then circle to land on the runway.
B— The pilot may land straight-in if the runway is the active runway and (s)he has been cleared to land.
C— A straight-in landing may be made if the pilot has the runway in sight in sufficient time to make a normal approach for landing, and has been cleared to land.

95.
4714. Which procedure should be followed by a pilot who is circling to land in a Category B airplane, but is maintaining a speed 5 knots faster than the maximum specified for that category?

A— Use the approach minimums appropriate for Category C.
B— Use Category B minimums.
C— Use Category D minimums since they apply to all circling approaches.

Answer (A) is correct (4734). *(AIM Para 5-4-7)*
When you are cleared for the approach while being radar vectored, you must maintain your last assigned altitude until the airplane is established on a segment of a published route or IAP. Then use the published altitude to descend within each succeeding route or approach segment.
Answer (B) is incorrect because you must wait to descend until you are on part of the published procedure. Answer (C) is incorrect because you should follow prescribed altitudes whenever you are on a segment of a published route or IAP.

Answer (C) is correct (4641). *(AIM Para 5-4-7)*
When an approach clearance is received, the last assigned altitude should be maintained until the aircraft is established on a segment of a published route or IAP. Then published altitudes apply.
Answer (A) is incorrect because published altitudes may be used as soon as the aircraft is on a published route, which should be before the FAF. Answer (B) is incorrect because, when ATC issues an approach clearance, descent to published altitudes is left to the discretion of the pilot.

Answer (A) is correct (4670). *(AIM Para 5-4-12)*
When simultaneous approaches are in progress, each pilot will be advised to monitor the tower frequency to receive advisories and instructions.
Answer (B) is incorrect because pilots will receive radar advisories on tower, not approach control, frequency. Answer (C) is incorrect because both pilots will receive radar advisories on tower frequency.

Answer (C) is correct (4749). *(IFH Chap X)*
When the normal rate of descent or the runway alignment factor of 30° is exceeded, a straight-in minimum is not published, and a circling minimum applies. Even without published straight-in minimums, the pilot may land straight-in if (s)he has the active runway in sight in sufficient time to make a normal landing and has been cleared to land.
Answer (A) is incorrect because a straight-in landing may be made if it is the appropriate runway. Answer (B) is incorrect because the pilot must also have sufficient time to make a normal approach for a landing.

Answer (A) is correct (4714). *(IFH Chap X)*
If it is necessary to maneuver at speeds in excess of the upper limit of the speed range for any category, the minimums for the next higher category should be used.
Answer (B) is incorrect because a pilot should use minimums for the category appropriate to the approach speed being used. Answer (C) is incorrect because Category D minimums do not necessarily apply to all circling approaches.

96.
4662. (Refer to figure 127 below.) If cleared for NDB RWY 28 approach (Lancaster/Fairfield) over ZZV VOR, the flight would be expected to

Category A Aircraft
Last assigned altitude 3,000 feet

A— proceed straight in from CRISY, descending to MDA after CASER.
B— proceed to CRISY, then execute the teardrop procedure as depicted on the approach chart.
C— proceed direct to CASER, then straight in to S-28 minimums of 1620-1.

Answer (A) is correct (4662). *(IFH Chap X)*
From ZZV VOR (which is an IAF), there is a NoPT transition published through CRISY INT. Thus, the flight would proceed straight in from CRISY, descending to the MDA after CASER. The straight-in minimums for a Category A aircraft are an MDA of 1,620 ft. MSL and visibility of 1 SM.
Answer (B) is incorrect because the NoPT symbol just under ZZV VOR indicates that the procedure turn is not authorized when approaching from ZZV. Answer (C) is incorrect because the arrow southwest of ZZV VOR indicates the route to CRISY, not CASER, and then straight in.

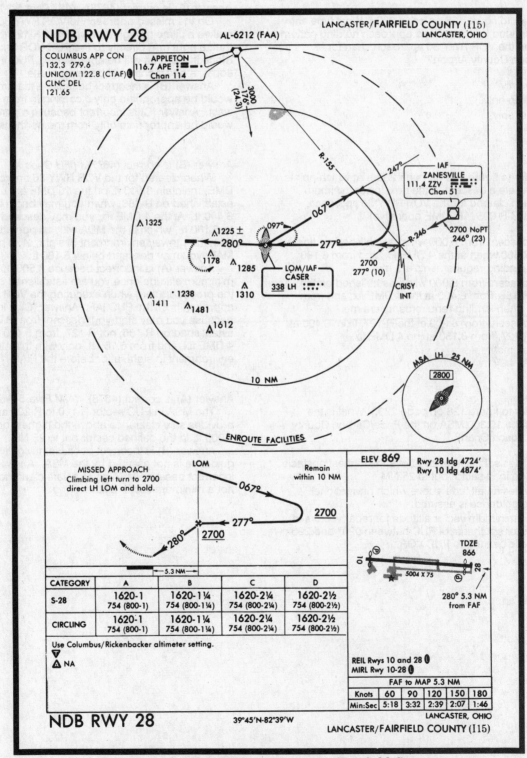

FIGURE 127.—NDB RWY 28, Lancaster/Fairfield County.

97.
4674. (Refer to figure 128 on page 233.) How should a pilot determine when the DME at Price/Carbon County Airport is inoperative?

A— The airborne DME will always indicate "0" mileage.
B— The airborne DME will "search," but will not "lock on."
C— The airborne DME may appear normal, but there will be no code tone.

Answer (C) is correct (4674). *(AIM Para 1-1-7)*
When a DME is inoperative, the code tone (identifier) will not be broadcast, although a signal may still be received.
Answer (A) is incorrect because the airborne DME will give no indication if the DME is inoperative. Answer (B) is incorrect because the airborne DME may be inoperative.

98.
4675. (Refer to figure 128 on page 233.) What type entry is recommended for the missed approach holding pattern depicted on the VOR RWY 36 approach chart for Price/Carbon County Airport?

A— Direct only.
B— Teardrop only.
C— Parallel only.

Answer (A) is correct (4675). *(AIM Para 5-3-7)*
On the missed approach to VOR RWY 36, the pilot makes a climbing right turn via PUC R-127 to 8,100 ft. and then a right turn directly to the PUC VOR and to 9,000 ft. Since the aircraft will be approaching PUC VOR from the south, a direct entry will be appropriate.
Answer (B) is incorrect because a teardrop entry would be appropriate only if coming in from the northwest. Answer (C) is incorrect because a parallel entry would be appropriate only from the northeast.

99.
4677. (Refer to figure 128 on page 233.) At which points may you initiate a descent to the next lower minimum altitude when cleared for the VOR RWY 36 approach, from the PUC R-095 IAF (DME operative)?

A— Start descent from 8,000 when established on final, from 7,500 when at the 4 DME fix, and from 6,180 when landing requirements are met.
B— Start descent from 8,000 when established on the PUC R-186, from 6,400 at the 4 DME fix, and from 6,180 when landing requirements are met.
C— Start descent from 8,000 at the R-127, from 6,400 at the LR-127, from 6,180 at the 4 DME fix.

Answer (B) is correct (4677). *(IFH Chap X)*
When cleared for the VOR RWY 36 approach with DME, maintain 8,000 ft. on the 10 DME arc until established on R-186, when you may begin descent to 6,400 ft. At the 4 DME fix, you may descend from 6,400 to 6,180 ft., which is the MDA with an operative DME. With the runway environment in sight, at or before the MAP, you may descend below 6,180 ft.
Answer (A) is incorrect because 7,500 ft. is the minimum altitude once you are established outbound on the procedure turn when executing the VOR RWY 36 approach from the PUC IAF. Answer (C) is incorrect because you may start your descent from 8,000 ft. when established on R-186, not R-127, from 6,400 ft. at the 4 DME fix, and from 6,180 ft. only with the runway environment in sight, at or before the MAP.

100.
4678. (Refer to figure 128 on page 233.) What is the purpose of the 10,300 MSA on the Price/Carbon County Airport Approach Chart?

A— It provides safe clearance above the highest obstacle in the defined sector out to 25 NM.
B— It provides an altitude above which navigational course guidance is assured.
C— It is the minimum vector altitude for radar vectors in the sector southeast of PUC between 020° and 290° magnetic bearing to PUC VOR.

Answer (A) is correct (4678). *(AIM Para 5-4-5)*
The MSA in PUC sector R-110 to R-200 at 10,300 ft. provides safe clearance above the highest obstacle plus 1,000 ft. in the defined sector out to 25 NM.
Answer (B) is incorrect because navigational course guidance is not assured by the MSA. Answer (C) is incorrect because MSA gives a safe clearance altitude, not a minimum vector altitude.

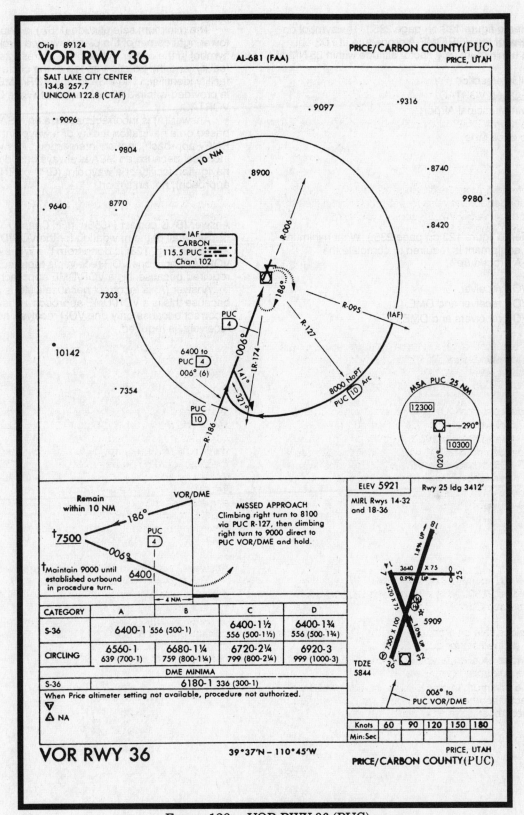

FIGURE 128.—VOR RWY 36 (PUC).

101.
4654. (Refer to figure 123 on page 235.) The symbol on the plan view of the VOR/DME-A procedure at 7D3 represents a minimum safe sector altitude within 25 NM of

A— DEANI intersection.
B— White Cloud VORTAC.
C— Baldwin Municipal Airport.

Answer (B) is correct (4654). *(ACL)*
    The minimum safe altitude (MSA) is depicted on the lower right corner of the plan view by a circle. The symbol in the center of the circle represents the type of facility, and the notation on top of the circle provides the facility identifier. The MSA for the VOR/DME-A IAP at 7D3 is provided within a 25-NM radius of White Cloud (HIC) VORTAC.
    Answer (A) is incorrect because an MSA is always based on a navigation facility or a waypoint (GPS or RNAV approach), not an intersection. Answer (C) is incorrect because an MSA is always based on a navigation facility or a waypoint (GPS or RNAV approach), not an airport.

102.
4653. (Refer to figure 123 on page 235.) What minimum navigation equipment is required to complete the VOR/DME-A procedure?

A— One VOR receiver.
B— One VOR receiver and DME.
C— Two VOR receivers and DME.

Answer (B) is correct (4653). *(IFH Chap X)*
    Since all of the navigation for the VOR/DME-A approach (Fig. 123) is done from the White Cloud VORTAC, only one VOR receiver is required. DME is also required because it is a VOR/DME approach.
    Answer (A) is incorrect because DME is also required because this is a VOR/DME approach. Answer (C) is incorrect because only one VOR receiver, not two receivers, is required.

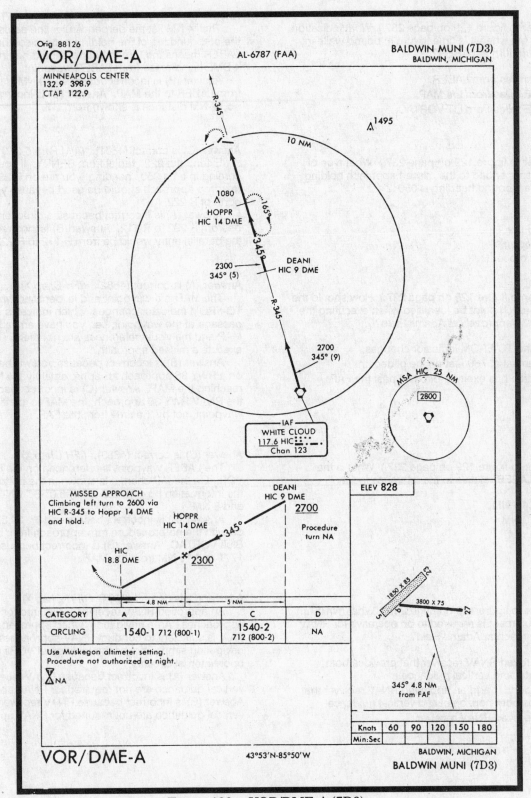

FIGURE 123.—VOR/DME-A (7D3).

103.
4680. (Refer to figure 129 on page 237.) What indication should you get when it is time to turn in bound while in the procedure turn at LABER?

A— 4 DME miles from LABER.
B— 10 DME miles from the MAP.
C— 12 DME miles from LIT VORTAC.

Answer (A) is correct (4680). *(AIM Para 5-3-7)*
    The "4 NM" at the perpendicular line across the end of the outbound leg of the holding pattern southeast of LABER means the turn in bound should begin when 4 DME is indicated from LABER waypoint.
    Answer (B) is incorrect because 10 NM is the distance from LABER to the MAP. Answer (C) is incorrect because no 12-NM distance is shown from LIT.

104.
4681. (Refer to figure 129 on page 237.) What type of entry is recommended to the missed approach holding pattern if the inbound heading is 050°?

A— Direct.
B— Parallel.
C— Teardrop.

Answer (C) is correct (4681). *(AIM Para 5-3-7)*
    Extend the 222° radial from BENDY. If you are coming in on a 050° heading, you are on R-230. The teardrop approach should be used because you are north of R-222.
    Answer (A) is incorrect because a direct entry would be from R-292 to R-112. Answer (B) is incorrect because the parallel entry would be from R-112 to R-222.

105.
4682. (Refer to figure 129 on page 237.) How should the missed approach point be identified when executing the RNAV RWY 36 approach at Adams Field?

A— When the TO-FROM indicator changes.
B— Upon arrival at 760 feet on the glidepath.
C— When time has expired for 5 NM past the FAF.

Answer (A) is correct (4682). *(IFH Chap X)*
    The MAP is a waypoint and is identified when the TO-FROM indicator changes, which indicates station passage at the waypoint; i.e., you have arrived at the MAP and the visual references are not there, so you must execute a missed approach.
    Answer (B) is incorrect because you will be at 760 ft. on a RWY 36 approach for approximately 1½ NM before reaching the MAP. Answer (C) is incorrect because, on the RNAV RWY 36 approach, the MAP is identified by a waypoint, not by the time from the FAF.

106.
4683. (Refer to figure 129 on page 237.) What is the position of LABER relative to the reference facility?

A— 316°, 24.3 NM.
B— 177°, 10 NM.
C— 198°, 8 NM.

Answer (C) is correct (4683). *(IFH Chap X)*
    The LABER waypoint is referenced on the Little Rock VOR. On the IAP chart, it is shown in the bottom line of the information box, "113.9 LIT 198.0°-8," which is 198° and 8 NM.
    Answer (A) is incorrect because 316°, 24.3 NM has to do with the no procedure turn approach from the Pine Bluff VORTAC. Answer (B) is incorrect because LABER is 177° and 10 NM from the MAP.

107.
4684. (Refer to figure 129 on page 237.) What minimum airborne equipment is required to be operative for RNAV RWY 36 approach at Adams Field?

A— An approved RNAV receiver that provides both horizontal and vertical guidance.
B— A transponder and an approved RNAV receiver that provides both horizontal and vertical guidance.
C— Any approved RNAV receiver.

Answer (C) is correct (4684). *(IFH Chap X)*
    An approved RNAV receiver is required for RNAV approaches. Area navigation, when approved by the FAA, is sufficient to conduct RNAV approaches. Area navigation simply moves the location of VORs based upon internal circuitry.
    Answer (A) is incorrect because RNAV receivers with vertical guidance are not required for RNAV approaches. Answer (B) is incorrect because RNAV receivers with vertical guidance are not required for RNAV approaches.

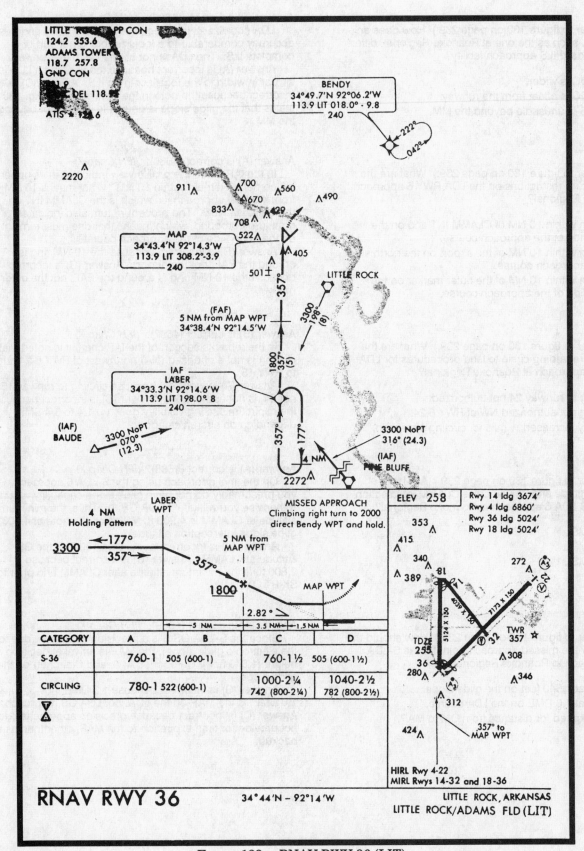

FIGURE 129.—RNAV RWY 36 (LIT).

108.
4685. (Refer to figure 130 on page 239.) How does an LDA facility, such as the one at Roanoke Regional, differ from a standard ILS approach facility?

A— The LOC is wider.
B— The LOC is offset from the runway.
C— The GS is unusable beyond the MM.

109.
4686. (Refer to figure 130 on page 239.) What are the procedure turn restrictions on the LDA RWY 6 approach at Roanoke Regional?

A— Remain within 10 NM of CLAMM INT and on the north side of the approach course.
B— Remain within 10 NM of the airport on the north side of the approach course.
C— Remain within 10 NM of the outer marker on the north side of the approach course.

110.
4687. (Refer to figure 130 on page 239.) What are the restrictions regarding circle to land procedures for LDA RWY/GS 6 approach at Roanoke Regional?

A— Circling to runway 24 not authorized.
B— Circling not authorized NW of RWY 6-24.
C— Visibility increased ½ mile for circling approach.

111.
4688. (Refer to figure 130 on page 239.) At what minimum altitude should you cross CLAMM intersection during the S-LDA 6 approach at Roanoke Regional?

A— 4,200 MSL.
B— 4,182 MSL.
C— 2,800 MSL.

112.
4689. (Refer to figure 130 on page 239.) How should the pilot identify the missed approach point for the S-LDA GS 6 approach to Roanoke Regional?

A— Arrival at 1,540 feet on the glide slope.
B— Arrival at 1.0 DME on the LDA course.
C— Time expired for distance from OM to MAP.

Answer (B) is correct (4685). *(AIM Para 1-1-9)*
LDA (localizer-type directional aid) has utility and accuracy comparable to a localizer but is not part of a complete ILS. The LDA is not aligned with the runway.
Answer (A) is incorrect because the LOC in an LDA is similar in width to the localizer in an ILS. Answer (C) is incorrect because the note in the profile view of Fig. 130 states that the glide slope is unusable inside, not beyond, the MM.

Answer (A) is correct (4686). *(IFH Chap X)*
In the IAP chart, the profile view indicates in its upper left corner: "Remain within 10 NM." That means 10 NM from the final approach fix, which is the CLAMM INT on the Callahan NDB. The procedure turn also indicates right turn outbound, which means that one must remain on the north side of the approach course.
Answer (B) is incorrect because the 10-NM ring is around the FAF, not the airport. Answer (C) is incorrect because the 10-NM ring is around the FAF, not the outer marker.

Answer (B) is correct (4687). *(IFH Chap X)*
In the remarks section of the IAP chart, it is noted that circling is not authorized (NA) northwest of RWY 6-24 and to RWY 15.
Answer (A) is incorrect because circling to runway 15, not 24, is not authorized. Answer (C) is incorrect because the minimum circling visibility goes up 1/4 to 3/4 SM, depending on aircraft category.

Answer (A) is correct (4688). *(IFH Chap X)*
On the final approach using the S-LDA 6 approach, you presumably do not have glide slope capability (otherwise you will use S-LDA/GS 6). Thus, the minimum altitude at CLAMM is 4,200 ft. MSL (see the note at 4,500 glide slope interception altitude).
Answer (B) is incorrect because 4,182 ft. is the GS altitude at CLAMM. Answer (C) is incorrect because 2,800 ft. is the minimum altitude after CLAMM and prior to SKIRT OM.

Answer (A) is correct (4689). *(IFH Chap X)*
Since the S-LDA/GS 6 is a precision approach (due to the electronic glide slope), the MAP is arrival at decision height (1,540 ft. for Categories A, B, and C aircraft) on the glide slope.
Answer (B) is incorrect because 1.3 DME, not 1.0 DME, is the MAP on the LDA, not LDA GS, approach. Answer (C) is incorrect because precision approaches do not provide for time expiration to the MAP, other than as a backup.

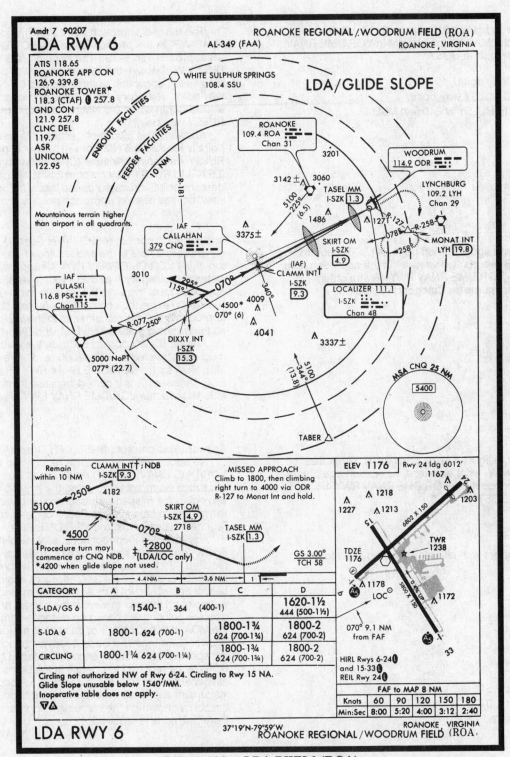

FIGURE 130.—LDA RWY 6 (ROA).

113.
4691. (Refer to figure 131 on page 241.) What determines the MAP for the straight-in VOR/DME RNAV RWY 4R approach at BOS?

A— RULSY way point.
B— .5 NM to RULSY way point.
C— 2.5 NM to RULSY at 840 feet MSL.

Answer (B) is correct (4691). *(ACL)*
The missed approach point (MAP) is identified by "MAP WP" in the profile view of the VOR/DME RNAV RWY 4R approach into BOS. The notation "0.5 NM from RULSY WP" above the missed approach point means that the missed approach point is located 0.5 NM from RULSY way point. Therefore, the missed approach procedure should begin when 0.5 NM remains before reaching RULSY way point.
Answer (A) is incorrect because the missed approach point is located 0.5 NM from RULSY way point, not at RULSY way point. Answer (C) is incorrect because 2.5 NM to RULSY way point at 840 ft. MSL is the visual descent point, indicated by the heavy "V" in the profile view, not the missed approach point.

114.
4690. (Refer to figure 131 on page 241.) The control tower at BOS reports "tall vessels" in the approach area. What are the VOR/DME RNAV RWY 4R straight-in approach minimums for Category A aircraft?

A— 840/40
B— 890/24
C— 890/40

Answer (A) is correct (4690). *(IFH Chap X)*
There is a note in the second line of information at the top of the VOR/DME RNAV RWY 4R approach chart which states that category A aircraft making the straight-in approach must increase the visibility minimums to RVR 4,000 when the control tower reports tall vessels in the approach area. No adjustments to the MDA are required, so the minimums are 840 ft. MSL and RVR 4,000.
Answer (B) is incorrect because the visibility minimums must be increased to RVR 4,000, and there is no 890 ft. MSL MDA for the VOR/DME RNAV RWY 4R approach at BOS. Answer (C) is incorrect because there is no 890 ft. MSL MDA for the VOR/DME RNAV RWY 4R approach at BOS.

115.
4695. (Refer to figure 131 on page 241.) Other than VOR/DME RNAV, what additional navigation equipment is required to conduct the VOR/DME RNAV RWY 4R approach at BOS?

A— None.
B— VNAV.
C— Transponder with altitude encoding and Marker Beacon.

Answer (A) is correct (4695). *(IFH Chap XI)*
No additional equipment is required to conduct the VOR/DME RNAV RWY 4R approach at Boston. All approach waypoints, including the missed approach waypoint, the missed approach holding waypoint, and the minimum safe altitude (MSA) circle center waypoint, require the use of just the VOR/DME RNAV equipment.
Answer (B) is incorrect because vertical navigation (VNAV) equipment may be used if available, but it is not required. If it is available and is used, the profile view of the approach chart shows a 3.00° descent angle. The visual descent point shown 2 miles from the missed approach waypoint on the profile view of the chart is not a mandatory descent point and is based on distance from the runway at the MDA of 840 ft. MSL, not on vertical navigation. Answer (C) is incorrect because, even though a transponder with altitude encoding (Mode C) would normally be required to operate in the Boston Class B airspace, it is not required equipment to conduct any instrument approach procedure. In addition, no marker beacon is shown on the instrument approach chart, therefore, none is required.

116.
4693. (Refer to figure 131 on page 241.) What is the landing distance available for the VOR/DME RNAV RWY 4R approach at BOS?

A— 7,000 ft.
B— 8,850 ft.
C— 10,005 ft.

Answer (B) is correct (4693). *(ACL)*
In the upper right corner of the airport diagram, there is a notation that says "Rwy 4R ldg 8850'." This notation signifies that the runway length available for landing is 8,850 ft.; the remainder of the 10,005 ft. runway length is a displaced threshold.
Answer (A) is incorrect because 7,000 ft. is the length of runway 9-27, not the available landing distance on runway 4R. Answer (C) is incorrect because 10,005 ft. is the total length of runway 4R, not the runway length available for landing.

117.
4694. (Refer to figure 131 below.) During a missed approach from the VOR/DME RNAV RWY 4R approach at BOS, what course should be flown to the missed approach holding way point?

A— 036°.
B— Runway heading.
C— 033°.

Answer (C) is correct (4694). *(IFH Chap XI)*
In the upper right corner of Fig. 131, just under "Boston, Massachusetts," there is a missed approach procedure information box. It reads, "MISSED APPROACH: Climb to 3000 via 033° track to WAXEN WP and hold." Also, on the profile view just above the MAP WP, the data box shows a climb to 3,000 feet on a track of 033° to WAXEN.

Answer (A) is incorrect because the missed approach procedure is fly to WAXEN via the 033° track (course), not 036°, which is the final approach course. Answer (B) is incorrect because the missed approach procedure is fly to WAXEN via the 033° track (course), not via runway heading.

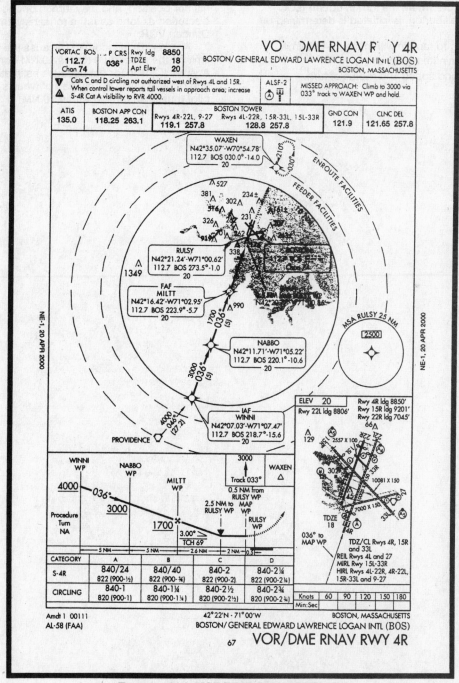

FIGURE 131.—VOR/DME RNAV RWY 4R.

118.
4655. (Refer to figure 124 on page 243.) What options are available concerning the teardrop course reversal for LOC RWY 35 approach to Duncan/Halliburton Field?

A— If a course reversal is required, only the teardrop can be executed.
B— The point where the turn is begun and the type and rate of turn are optional.
C— A normal procedure turn may be made if the 10 DME limit is not exceeded.

119.
4656. (Refer to figure 124 on page 243.) The point on the teardrop procedure where the turn in bound (LOC RWY 35) Duncan/Halliburton, is initiated is determined by

A— DME and timing to remain within the 10-NM limit.
B— Timing for a 2 minute maximum.
C— Estimating ground speed and radius of turn.

Answer (A) is correct (4655). *(AIM Para 5-4-8)*
When a procedure turn track is specified for the LOC RWY 35 approach, the turn must be flown exactly as depicted. Thus, only the teardrop can be executed.
Answer (B) is incorrect because the turn must be begun at a point such that the aircraft remains within 10 NM of the VOR, and the procedure turn must be a teardrop. Answer (C) is incorrect because the procedure turn must be a teardrop.

Answer (A) is correct (4656). *(AIM Para 5-4-8)*
The pilot may use DME and/or timing to determine his/her position, and may turn in bound at his/her discretion as long as (s)he remains within 10 NM of Duncan VOR.
Answer (B) is incorrect because the only maximum limit on the procedure turn is 10 NM from the VOR. Answer (C) is incorrect because estimating ground speed and radius of turn is only part of what is required. The pilot must also remain within 10 NM.

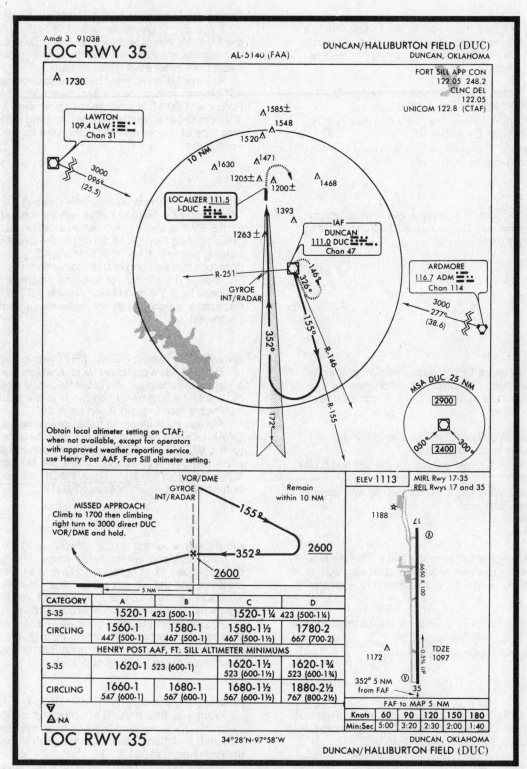

FIGURE 124.—LOC RWY 35, Duncan, Oklahoma.

120.
4696. (Refer to figure 133 on page 245.) How should a pilot reverse course to get established on the in bound course of the ILS RWY 9, if radar vectoring or the three IAF's are not utilized?

A— Execute a standard 45° procedure turn toward Seal Beach VORTAC or Pomona VORTAC.
B— Make an appropriate entry to the depicted holding pattern at Swan Lake OM/INT.
C— Use any type of procedure turn, but remain within 10 NM of Riverside VOR.

Answer (B) is correct (4696). *(AIM Para 5-4-8)*
If you do not use radar vectoring or the three IAFs for the ILS RWY 9 approach, you should make an appropriate entry into the depicted holding pattern at the Swan Lake outer marker/intersection.
Answer (A) is incorrect because to execute a standard 45° procedure turn toward Seal Beach VORTAC or Pomona VORTAC is a nonsense statement. Answer (C) is incorrect because the depicted holding pattern is the only type of course reversal authorized for the ILS RWY 9 approach.

121.
4698. (Refer to figure 133 on page 245.) What type of entry is recommended for the missed approach holding pattern at Riverside Municipal?

A— Direct.
B— Parallel.
C— Teardrop.

Answer (A) is correct (4698). *(IFH Chap X)*
To enter the holding pattern on the missed approach for ILS RWY 9, use a direct entry because you will arrive at the holding fix (PDZ VORTAC) in the direction of the holding pattern. Thus, at PDZ VORTAC, you will make a right turn to a heading of 078° (direct entry).
Answer (B) is incorrect because a parallel entry would be made from the northwest. Answer (C) is incorrect because a teardrop entry would be made from the southwest.

122.
4699. (Refer to figure 133 on page 245.) What action should the pilot take if the marker beacon receiver becomes inoperative during the S-ILS 9 approach at Riverside Municipal?

A— Substitute SWAN LAKE INT for the OM and surveillance radar for the MM.
B— Raise the DH 100 feet (50 feet for the OM and 50 feet for the MM).
C— Substitute SWAN LAKE INT for the OM and use published minimums.

Answer (C) is correct (4699). *(IFH Chap X)*
The OM has a compass locator, which is an acceptable substitute. An inoperative MM does not require any adjustment to be made to the published minimums (see Legend 22 on page 200).
Answer (A) is incorrect because you can substitute SWAN LAKE INT for the OM, but no substitute is required for the MM. Answer (B) is incorrect because you can substitute SWAN LAKE INT for the OM, but no substitute is necessary for the MM. Thus, the DH will be as published on the IAP, not raised 100 ft.

123.
4700. (Refer to figure 133 on page 245.) Why are two VOR/LOC receivers recommended to obtain an MDA of 1,160 when making an S-LOC 9 approach to Riverside Municipal?

A— To obtain R-327 of PDZ when on the localizer course.
B— In order to identify Riverside VOR.
C— To utilize the published stepdown fix.

Answer (C) is correct (4700). *(IFH Chap X)*
Two VOR/localizer receivers are necessary to identify the step-down fix at Agnes INT. One VOR is set on the localizer, and the other is set to Paradise VOR (R-032). The MDA for the S-LOC 9 approach is 1,260 ft. until Agnes INT, after which a descent to 1,160 ft. is permitted.
Answer (A) is incorrect because R-327 of PDZ can be determined when on the localizer through the Swan Lake NDB. Answer (B) is incorrect because the Riverside VOR is not used in the S-LOC 9 approach.

124.
4701. (Refer to figure 133 on page 245.) What is the minimum altitude descent procedure if cleared for the S-ILS 9 approach from Seal Beach VORTAC?

A— Descend and maintain 3,000 to JASER INT, descend to and maintain 2,500 until crossing SWAN LAKE, descend and maintain 1,260 until crossing AGNES, and to 991 (DH) after passing AGNES.
B— Descend and maintain 3,000 to JASER INT, descend to 2,800 when established on the LOC course, intercept and maintain the GS to 991 (DH).
C— Descend and maintain 3,000 to JASER INT, descend to 2,500 while established on the LOC course inbound, intercept and maintain the GS to 991 (DH).

Answer (C) is correct (4701). *(IFH Chap X)*
From Seal Beach VORTAC, descend to 3,000 ft. to Jaser INT, then descend to 2,500 ft. on the localizer inbound, and then descend on the glide slope to the decision height of 991 ft.
Answer (A) is incorrect because 2,500 ft. is maintained until the glide slope, and the ILS glide slope is flown down to 991 ft. Answer (B) is incorrect because, when on the localizer, you should descend to 2,500 ft., not 2,800 ft., until intercepting the glide slope.

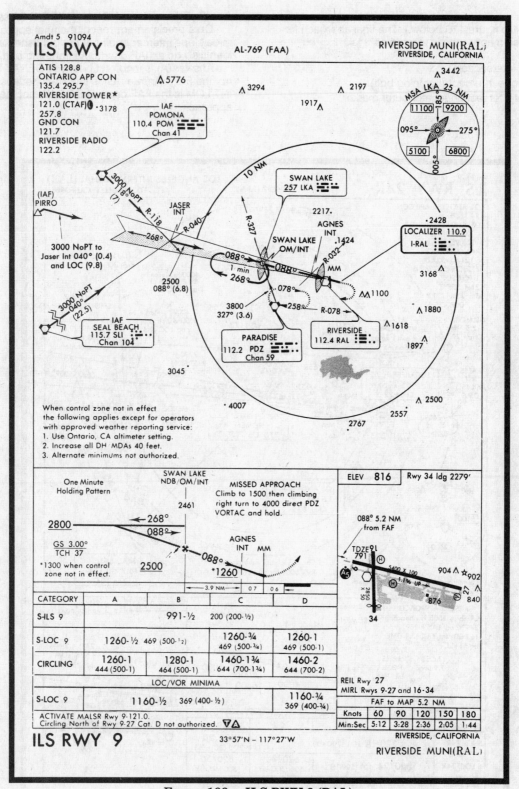

FIGURE 133.—ILS RWY 9 (RAL).

125.
4642. (Refer to figure 119 below.) The final approach fix for the precision approach is located at

A— DENAY intersection.
B— Glide slope intercept (lightning bolt).
C— ROMEN intersection/locator outer marker.

Answer (B) is correct (4642). *(AIM P/C Glossary)*
On a precision approach, the final approach fix is the glide slope intercept point at the published altitude. It is identified on an IAP chart by a lightning bolt.
Answer (A) is incorrect because DENAY INT is an IAF, not the FAF. Answer (C) is incorrect because ROMEN INT/LOM is the FAF on the LOC 24R, not the ILS 24R, approach.

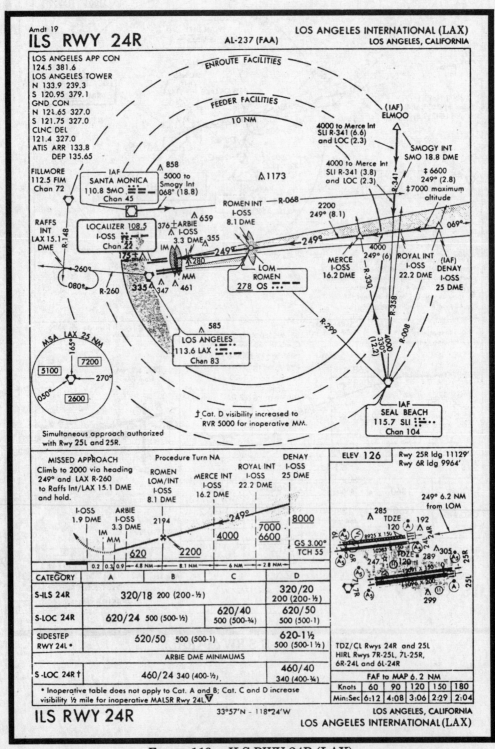

FIGURE 119.—ILS RWY 24R (LAX).

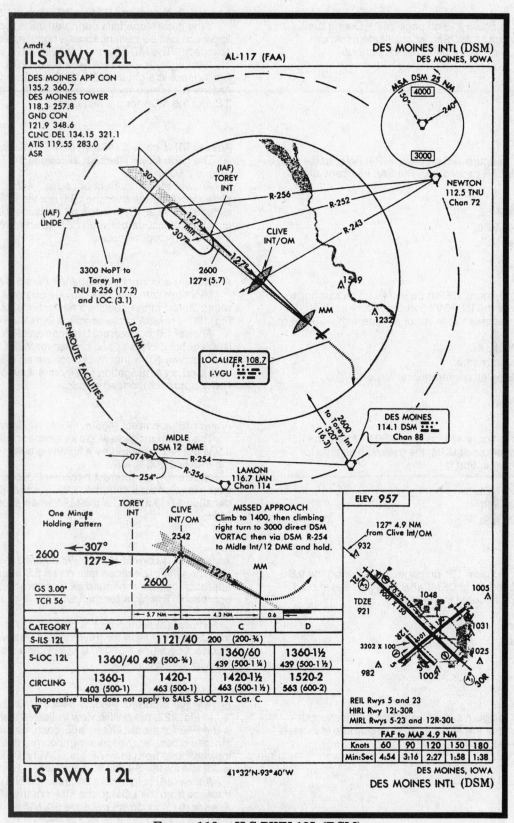

FIGURE 118.—ILS RWY 12L (DSM).

126.
4635. (Refer to figure 118 on page 247.) During the ILS RWY 12L procedure at DSM, what altitude minimum applies if the glide slope becomes inoperative?

A— 1,420 feet.
B— 1,360 feet.
C— 1,121 feet.

Answer (B) is correct (4635). *(AIM Para 1-1-9)*
If the glide slope fails during an ILS approach, the approach can be continued as a nonprecision localizer approach. The MDA for the LOC RWY 12L is 1,360 ft.
Answer (A) is incorrect because 1,420 ft. is the circling, not straight-in, MDA for Categories B and C. Answer (C) is incorrect because 1,121 ft. is the DH for the ILS, not the MDA for the localizer.

127.
4648. (Refer to figure 120 on page 249.) Refer to the DEN ILS RWY 35R procedure. The FAF intercept altitude is

A— 7,488 feet MSL.
B— 7,500 feet MSL.
C— 9,000 feet MSL.

Answer (B) is correct (4648). *(AIM P/C Glossary)*
The glide slope intercept altitude at the FAF (lightning bolt) is 7,500 ft. MSL.
Answer (A) is incorrect because 7,488 ft. MSL is the glide slope altitude over the OM, not the FAF intercept altitude. Answer (C) is incorrect because 9,000 ft. MSL is a minimum altitude between SEDAL and ENGLE INTs, not the FAF intercept altitude.

128.
4649. (Refer to figure 120 on page 249.) The symbol on the plan view of the ILS RWY 35R procedure at DEN represents a minimum safe sector altitude within 25 NM of

A— Denver VORTAC.
B— Gandi outer marker.
C— Denver/Stapleton International Airport.

Answer (A) is correct (4649). *(AIM Para 5-4-5)*
Minimum safe altitudes provide obstacle clearance within 25 NM of the specified navigational facility. In Fig. 120, the MSA circle specifies DEN VORTAC.
Answer (B) is incorrect because an MSA for the ILS RWY 35R at DEN is based on Denver VORTAC, not the OM. Answer (C) is incorrect because an MSA will always be based on a navigation facility or a waypoint (GPS or RNAV approach), not an airport.

129.
4650. (Refer to figure 121 on page 250.) During the ILS RWY 30R procedure at DSM, the minimum altitude for glide slope interception is

A— 2,365 feet MSL.
B— 2,500 feet MSL.
C— 3,000 feet MSL.

Answer (B) is correct (4650). *(AIM P/C Glossary)*
The minimum glide slope interception altitude for an ILS is the FAF (marked by a lightning bolt). In Fig. 121, the FAF is 2,500 ft. MSL.
Answer (A) is incorrect because 2,365 ft. MSL is the glide slope altitude over the LOM. Answer (C) is incorrect because 3,000 ft. MSL is the MSA when south of the LOM.

130.
4651. (Refer to figure 121 on page 250.) During the ILS RWY 30R procedure at DSM, what MDA applies should the glide slope become inoperative?

A— 1,157 feet.
B— 1,320 feet.
C— 1,360 feet.

Answer (B) is correct (4651). *(AIM Para 1-1-9)*
When the glide slope fails on an ILS approach, the approach can be continued as a nonprecision localizer approach. The MDA for the LOC 30R (Fig. 121) is 1,320 ft.
Answer (A) is incorrect because 1,157 ft. is the DH for the ILS, not the MDA for the localizer. Answer (C) is incorrect because 1,360 ft. is the circling, not straight-in, MDA for Category A.

131.
4652. (Refer to figure 122 on page 251.) The missed approach point of the ATL S-LOC 8L procedure is located how far from the LOM?

A— 4.8 NM.
B— 5.1 NM.
C— 5.2 NM.

Answer (C) is correct (4652). *(AIM P/C Glossary)*
In Fig. 122, the profile view indicates that CATTA LOM is the FAF for the S-LOC 8L approach, as indicated by the Maltese cross. At the lower right corner of the IAP chart, it indicates that from the FAF (i.e., CATTA LOM) to the MAP is 5.2 NM for the S-LOC 8L approach.
Answer (A) is incorrect because 4.8 NM is the distance from the LOM to the MM, not the MAP. Answer (B) is incorrect because 5.1 NM is the distance from the LOM to the IM, not the MAP.

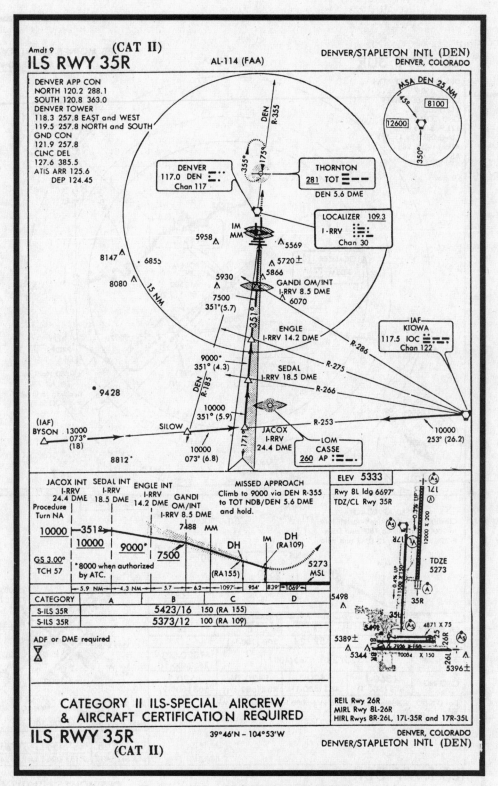

FIGURE 120.—ILS RWY 35R (DEN).

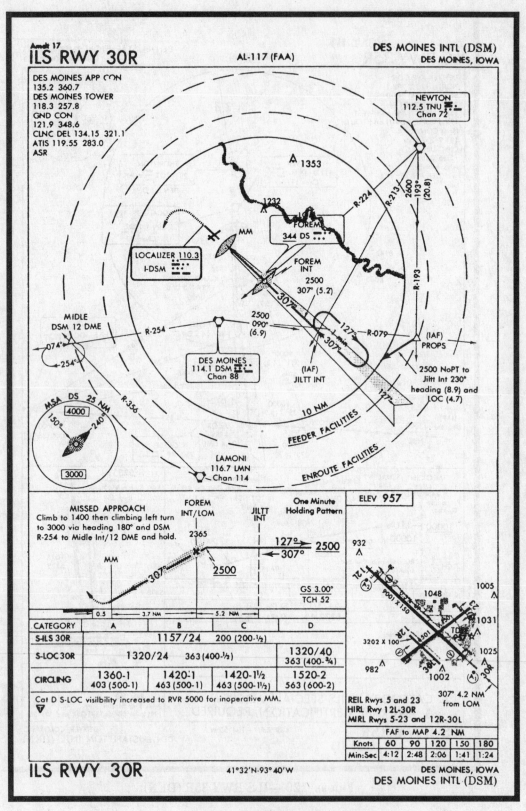

FIGURE 121.—ILS RWY 30R (DSM).

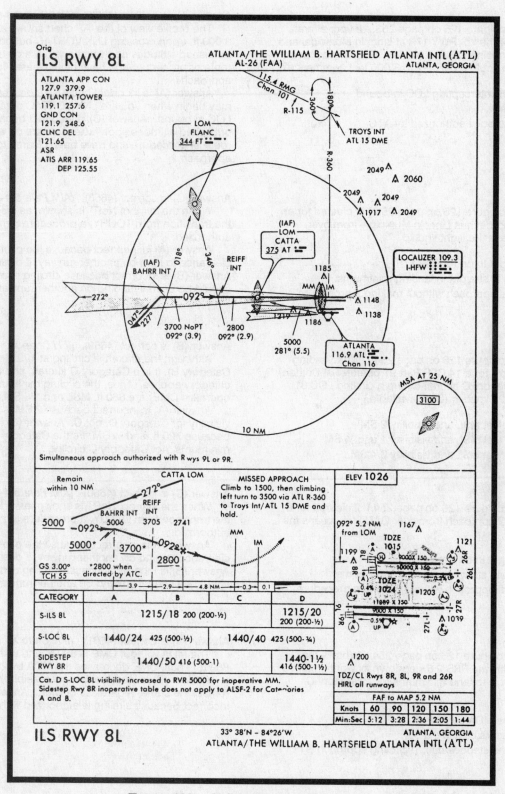

FIGURE 122.—ILS RWY 8L (ATL).

132.
4657. (Refer to figure 125 on page 253.) If your aircraft was cleared for the ILS RWY 17R at Lincoln Municipal and crossed the Lincoln VOR at 5,000 feet MSL, at what point in the teardrop could a descent to 3,000 feet commence?

A— As soon as intercepting LOC in bound.
B— Immediately.
C— Only at the point authorized by ATC.

133.
4658. (Refer to figure 125 on page 253.) If cleared for an S-LOC 17R approach at Lincoln Municipal from over TOUHY, it means the flight should

A— land straight in on runway 17R.
B— comply with straight-in landing minimums.
C— begin final approach without making a procedure turn.

134.
4659. (Refer to figure 126 on page 254.) What landing minimums apply for a 14 CFR Part 91 operator at Dothan, AL using a category C aircraft during a circling LOC 31 approach at 120 knots? (DME available.)

A— MDA 860 feet MSL and visibility 2 SM.
B— MDA 860 feet MSL and visibility 1 and ½ SM.
C— MDA 720 feet MSL and visibility 3/4 SM.

135.
4660. (Refer to figure 126 on page 254.) If cleared for a straight-in LOC approach from over OALDY, it means the flight should

A— land straight in on runway 31.
B— comply with straight-in landing minimums.
C— begin final approach without making a procedure turn.

136.
4661. (Refer to figure 126 on page 254.) What is the ability to identify the RRS 2.5 stepdown fix worth in terms of localizer circle-to-land minimums for a category C aircraft?

A— Decreases MDA by 20 feet.
B— Decreases visibility by ½ SM.
C— Without the stepdown fix, a circling approach is not available.

Answer (B) is correct (4657). *(AIM Para 5-4-8)*
The profile view of the IAP chart shows a descent to 3,000 ft. upon crossing LNK VORTAC out bound. Published altitudes apply when you are on a published route or procedure and have been cleared for the approach.
Answer (A) is incorrect because a descent to 3,000 ft. may begin when you are LNK VORTAC out bound, not LOC in bound. Answer (C) is incorrect because published altitudes apply when you are on a published route or procedure and have been cleared for the approach.

Answer (C) is correct (4658). *(AIM Para 5-4-8)*
When the symbol NoPT is shown, as in Fig. 125 on the transition from TOUHY, a procedure turn is not authorized.
Answer (A) is incorrect because the pilot may request clearance to land on another runway, if desired. Answer (B) is incorrect because circling minimums should be used if landing on another runway is desired.

Answer (B) is correct (4659). *(IFH Chap X)*
Although the aircraft is circling at 120 kt. (which is Category B), it is a Category C aircraft, and the higher category applies. Thus, the circling minimums (with an operative DME) are 860 ft. MSL and 1½ SM.
Answer (A) is incorrect because 2 SM is the minimum visibility for Category D, not C. Answer (C) is incorrect because 720 ft. and ¾ SM are the Category D straight-in minimums, not Category C circling.

Answer (C) is correct (4660). *(AIM Para 5-4-8)*
When the symbol NoPT is shown, as in Fig. 126 on the transition from OALDY, a procedure turn is not authorized.
Answer (A) is incorrect because the pilot may request clearance to land on another runway, if desired. Answer (B) is incorrect because circling minimums should be used if landing on another runway is desired.

Answer (A) is correct (4661). *(IFH Chap X)*
The MDA without DME is 880 ft. and with DME is 860 ft. Thus, DME decreases the MDA by 20 ft.
Answer (B) is incorrect because visibility minimums remain the same, regardless of DME. Answer (C) is incorrect because circling is authorized without DME.

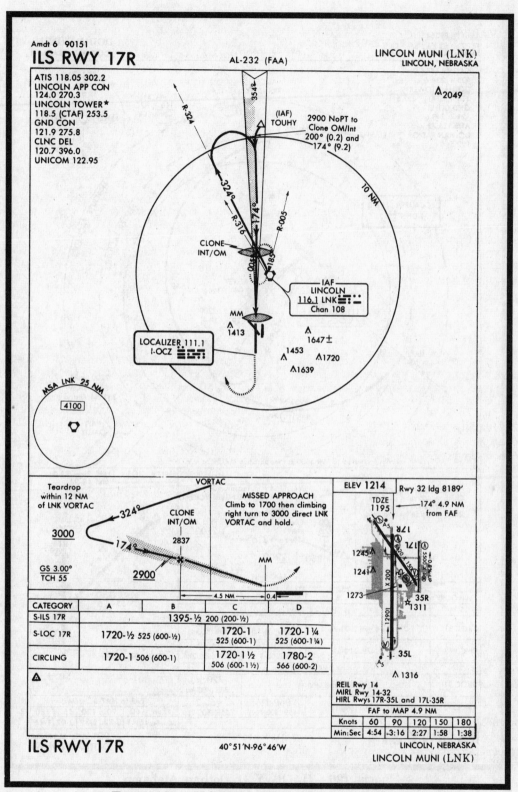

FIGURE 125.—ILS RWY 17R, Lincoln, Nebraska.

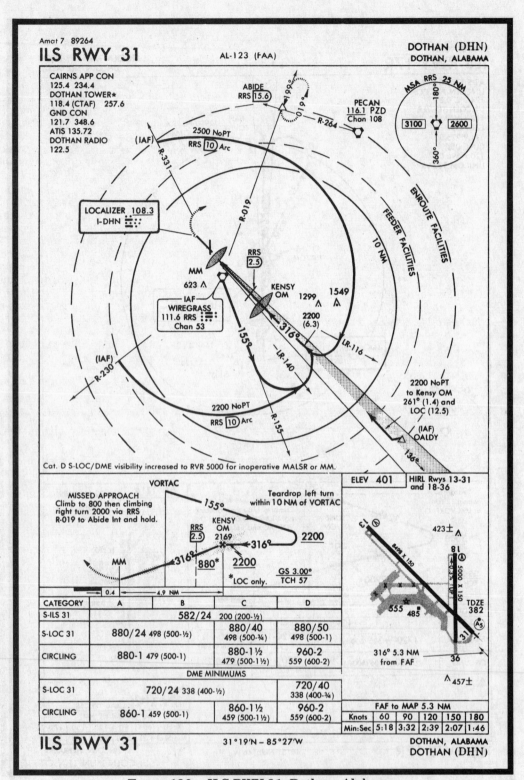

FIGURE 126.—ILS RWY 31, Dothan, Alabama.

137.
4332. (Refer to figure 60A on page 256.) What is the elevation of the TDZE for RWY 4?

A— 70 feet MSL.
B— 54 feet MSL.
C— 46 feet MSL.

Answer (C) is correct (4332). *(IFH Chap X)*
The TDZE (touchdown zone elevation) is the highest elevation in the first 3,000 ft. of the runway on a straight-in landing approach. On an NOS chart, it is marked in the airport diagram near the approach end of the runway. Thus, the TDZE for RWY 4 is 46 ft. MSL.
Answer (A) is incorrect because 70 ft. MSL is the elevation of a tower near the approach end of RWY 4. Answer (B) is incorrect because 54 ft. MSL is the TCH (threshold crossing height) on the ILS RWY 4 approach, i.e., the height at which the airplane's glide slope antenna should cross the runway's threshold on the glide slope.

138.
4331. (Refer to figure 60A on page 256 and figure 61 below.) What is your position relative to the PLATS intersection, glide slope, and the localizer course?

A— Past PLATS, below the glide slope, and right of the localizer course.
B— Approaching PLATS, above the glide slope, and left of the localizer course.
C— Past PLATS, above the glide slope, and right of the localizer course.

Answer (C) is correct (4331). *(IFH Chap VIII)*
The VOR in Fig. 61 is tuned to the localizer. The CDI and glide slope needles show your position as above glide slope and right of the localizer course. The RMI #2 indicator is tuned to the Scholes VORTAC and shows your position as R-300 (tail of the double needle). Since PLATS Intersection is on R-291, you are northeast of PLATS, or past it on the inbound course.
Answer (A) is incorrect because the glide slope needle is below center, indicating above, not below, glide slope. Answer (B) is incorrect because R-300 of Scholes VORTAC is northeast, not southwest, of PLATS, and the CDI is left of center, indicating right, not left, of course.

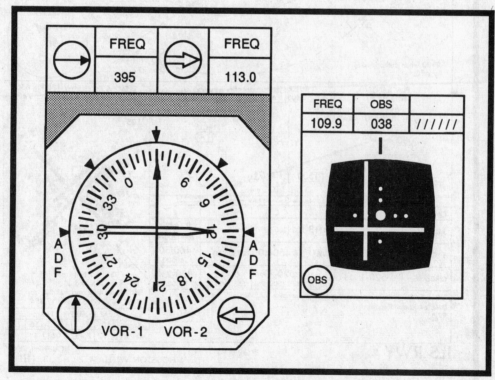

FIGURE 61.—RMI and CDI Indicators.

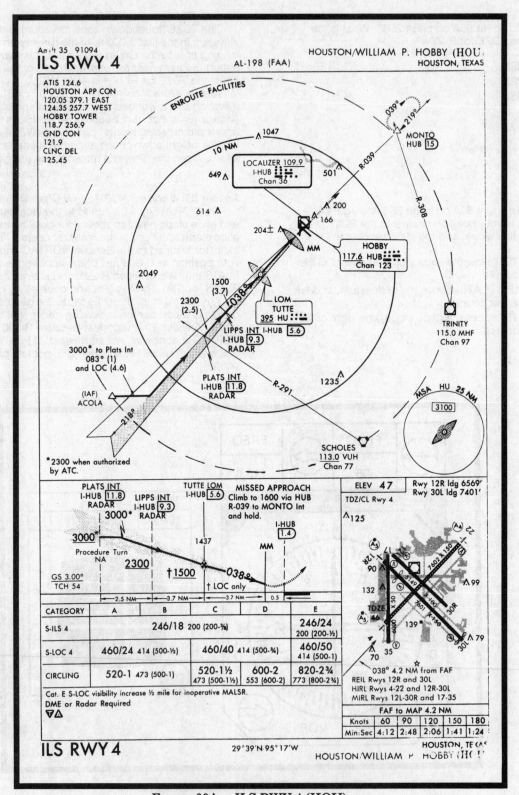

FIGURE 60A.—ILS RWY 4 (HOU).

6.13 DPs and STARs

139.
4488. (Refer to figure 85 on page 259 and 86 below.) Which combination of indications confirm that you are approaching WAGGE intersection slightly to the right of the LOC centerline on departure?

A— 1 and 3.
B— 1 and 4.
C— 2 and 3.

Answer (C) is correct (4488). *(IFH Chap VIII)*
    If you are flying out on the back course, you have front course indications. Therefore, if you are to the right of the localizer centerline, you will get a left needle deflection, such as in 2 (see Figs. 85 and 86). To determine whether you are at WAGGE INT, visualize yourself flying out on Squaw Valley R-062 (113.2). If you were north of the radial, you would get a right needle deflection, such as in 3.
    Answer (A) is incorrect because illustration 1 would mean you are left, not right, of the localizer centerline. Answer (B) is incorrect because illustration 1 would mean you are left, not right, of the localizer centerline. Also, a left needle deflection on 113.2 (as in 4) would mean that you were south of R-062 and would thus be beyond WAGGE INT.

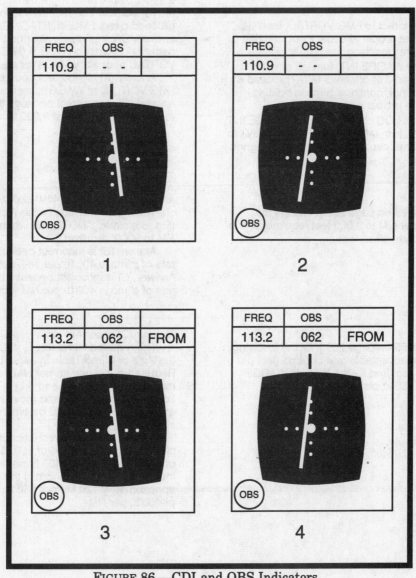

FIGURE 86.—CDI and OBS Indicators.

140.
4489. (Refer to figure 85 on page 259.) What route should you take if cleared for the Washoe Two Departure and your assigned route is V6?

A— Climb on the LOC south course to WAGGE where you will be vectored to V6.
B— Climb on the LOC south course to cross WAGGE at 9,000, turn left and fly direct to FMG VORTAC and cross at or above 10,000, and proceed on FMG R-241.
C— Climb on the LOC south course to WAGGE, turn left and fly direct to FMG VORTAC. If at 10,000 turn left and proceed on FMG R-241; if not at 10,000 enter depicted holding pattern and climb to 10,000 before proceeding on FMG R-241.

141.
4490. (Refer to figure 85 on page 259.) What procedure should be followed if communications are lost before reaching 9,000 feet?

A— At 9,000, turn left direct to FMG VORTAC, then via assigned route if at proper altitude; if not, climb in holding pattern until reaching the proper altitude.
B— Continue climb to WAGGE INT, turn left direct to FMG VORTAC, then if at or above MCA, proceed on assigned route; if not, continue climb in holding pattern until at the proper altitude.
C— Continue climb on LOC course to cross WAGGE INT at or above 9,000, turn left direct to FMG VORTAC to cross at 10,000 or above, and continue on assigned course.

142.
4491. (Refer to figure 85 on page 259.) What is the minimum rate climb per NM to 9,000 feet required for the WASH2 WAGGE Departure?

A— 400 feet.
B— 750 feet.
C— 875 feet.

143.
4492. (Refer to figure 85 on page 259.) Of the following, which is the minimum acceptable rate of climb (feet per minute) to 9,000 feet required for the WASH2 WAGGE departure at a GS of 150 knots?

A— 750 feet per minute.
B— 825 feet per minute.
C— 1,000 feet per minute.

Answer (A) is correct (4489). *(AIM Para 5-2-6)*
The instructions on Fig. 85 for the Washoe Two Departure are to "climb via Reno localizer south course to WAGGE INT for radar vector to assigned route."
Answer (B) is incorrect because it describes the lost communication procedure. Answer (C) is incorrect because it describes the lost communication procedure.

Answer (B) is correct (4490). *(AIM Para 5-2-6)*
The Lost Communications section under the departure route description states, "...if communications are lost before reaching 9,000 ft., continue climb via I-RNO localizer south course to WAGGE INT, turn left proceed direct FMG VORTAC. Cross FMG VORTAC at or above MCA, thence via assigned route or climb in holding pattern northeast on FMG R-041, left turns to cross FMG VORTAC at or above MCA for assigned route."
Answer (A) is incorrect because you are to turn left to FMG VORTAC at WAGGE, irrespective of altitude. Answer (C) is incorrect because there is no requirement to cross WAGGE INT at 9,000 ft.

Answer (A) is correct (4491). *(AIM Para 5-2-6)*
The right-hand side of the Washoe Two Departure (Fig. 85) states, "NOTE: Minimum climb rate of 400' per NM to 9000' required."
Answer (B) is incorrect because the required minimum rate of climb is 400 ft. per NM, not 750 ft. per NM. Answer (C) is incorrect because the required minimum rate of climb is 400 ft. per NM, not 875 ft. per NM.

Answer (C) is correct (4492). *(ACL)*
The required climb rate is 400 ft./NM (Fig. 85). Use the Rate of Climb Table in Legend 16 on page 204. Required climb rate (ft. per NM) is found on the left margin, and groundspeed (kt.) is found on the top. Locate 400 ft. per NM and move right to the 150-kt. groundspeed column to determine a 1,000-fpm rate of climb.
Answer (A) is incorrect because 750 fpm is the rate of climb at a groundspeed of 150 kt. that results in a climb of 300 ft. per NM, not 400 ft. per NM. Answer (B) is incorrect because 825 fpm is the rate of climb at approximately 125 kt., not 150 kt., that results in a climb of 400 ft. per NM.

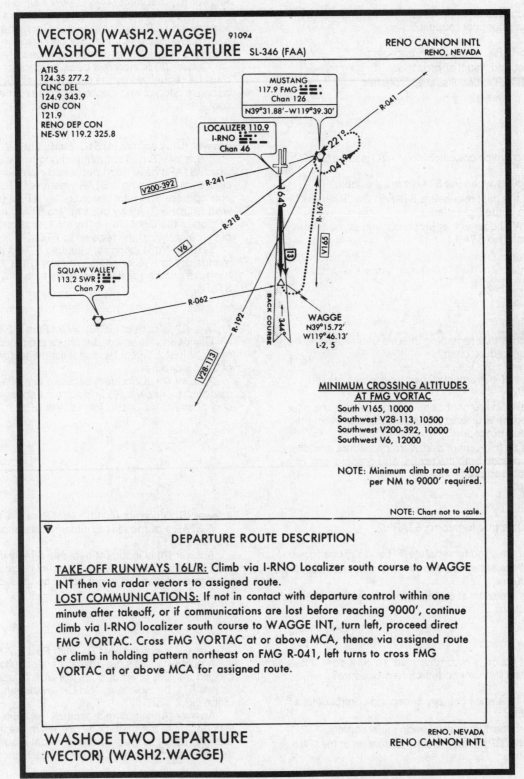

(VECTOR) (WASH2.WAGGE) 91094
WASHOE TWO DEPARTURE SL-346 (FAA)

RENO CANNON INTL
RENO, NEVADA

ATIS
124.35 277.2
CLNC DEL
124.9 343.9
GND CON
121.9
RENO DEP CON
NE-SW 119.2 325.8

MUSTANG
117.9 FMG
Chan 126
N39°31.88'–W119°39.30'

R-041

LOCALIZER 110.9
I-RNO
Chan 46

221°

041°

R-241

V200-392

R-167

R-218

V165

V6

13

SQUAW VALLEY
113.2 SWR
Chan 79

R-062

BACK COURSE

344°

WAGGE
N39°15.72'
W119°46.13'
L-2, 5

R-192

V28-113

MINIMUM CROSSING ALTITUDES
AT FMG VORTAC
South V165, 10000
Southwest V28-113, 10500
Southwest V200-392, 10000
Southwest V6, 12000

NOTE: Minimum climb rate at 400'
per NM to 9000' required.

NOTE: Chart not to scale.

DEPARTURE ROUTE DESCRIPTION

TAKE-OFF RUNWAYS 16L/R: Climb via I-RNO Localizer south course to WAGGE
INT then via radar vectors to assigned route.
LOST COMMUNICATIONS: If not in contact with departure control within one
minute after takeoff, or if communications are lost before reaching 9000', continue
climb via I-RNO localizer south course to WAGGE INT, turn left, proceed direct
FMG VORTAC. Cross FMG VORTAC at or above MCA, thence via assigned route
or climb in holding pattern northeast on FMG R-041, left turns to cross FMG
VORTAC at or above MCA for assigned route.

WASHOE TWO DEPARTURE
(VECTOR) (WASH2.WAGGE)

RENO, NEVADA
RENO CANNON INTL

FIGURE 85.—WASHOE TWO DEPARTURE.

144.
4442. Which clearance procedures may be issued by ATC without prior pilot request?

A— DP's, STAR's, and contact approaches.
B— Contact and visual approaches.
C— DP's, STAR's, and visual approaches.

Answer (C) is correct (4442). *(AIM Para 5-5-14)*
DPs, STARs, and visual approaches are all routinely assigned by ATC as appropriate. Contact approaches must be requested by the pilot and made in lieu of a standard or special instrument approach.
Answer (A) is incorrect because contact approaches must be requested by the pilot. Answer (B) is incorrect because contact approaches must be requested by the pilot.

145.
4751. Under which condition does ATC issue a STAR?

A— To all pilots wherever STAR's are available.
B— Only if the pilot requests a STAR in the "Remarks" section of the flight plan.
C— When ATC deems it appropriate, unless the pilot requests "No STAR."

Answer (C) is correct (4751). *(AIM Para 5-4-1)*
Pilots of IFR civil aircraft destined to locations for which STARs have been published may be issued a clearance containing a STAR whenever ATC deems it appropriate. The pilot should notify ATC if (s)he does not wish to use a STAR by placing "No STAR" in the remarks section of the flight plan or by the less desirable method of verbally stating the request to ATC.
Answer (A) is incorrect because STARs are not mandatory to ATC or pilots. Answer (B) is incorrect because pilot request is necessary to avoid, not obtain, STARs.

146.
4638. Which is true regarding the use of an instrument departure procedure chart?

A— The use of instrument departure procedures is mandatory.
B— To use an instrument departure procedure, the pilot must possess at least the textual description of the approved procedure.
C— To use an instrument departure procedure, the pilot must possess both the textual and graphic form of the approved procedure.

Answer (B) is correct (4638). *(AIM Para 5-2-6)*
Use of an instrument departure procedure (DP) requires that the pilot have at least the textual description of the procedure.
Answer (A) is incorrect because use of a DP is never mandatory. Answer (C) is incorrect because a pilot need only possess the textual form of the DP.

147.
4640. Which is true regarding STAR's?

A— STAR's are used to separate IFR and VFR traffic.
B— STAR's are established to simplify clearance delivery procedures.
C— STAR's are used at certain airports to decrease traffic congestion.

Answer (B) is correct (4640). *(AIM Para 5-4-1)*
A STAR's purpose is to simplify clearance delivery procedures.
Answer (A) is incorrect because STARs do not pertain to VFR traffic. Answer (C) is incorrect because STARs are used to decrease radio, not traffic, congestion.

148.
4417. What action is recommended if a pilot does not wish to use an instrument departure procedure?

A— Advise clearance delivery or ground control before departure.
B— Advise departure control upon initial contact.
C— Enter "No DP" in the REMARKS section of the IFR flight plan.

Answer (C) is correct (4417). *(AIM Para 5-2-6)*
A pilot who does not possess an instrument departure procedure (DP) chart or does not wish to use a DP should advise ATC by indicating "No DP" in the remarks section of the flight plan.
Answer (A) is incorrect because verbal requests are less desirable than entering "No DP" in the flight plan. Answer (B) is incorrect because verbal requests are less desirable than entering "No DP" in the flight plan.

149.
4418. A particular instrument departure procedure requires a minimum climb rate of 210 feet per NM to 8,000 feet. If you climb with a ground speed of 140 knots, what is the rate of climb required in feet per minute?

A— 210.
B— 450.
C— 490.

150.
4419. Which procedure applies to instrument departure procedures?

A— Instrument departure clearances will not be issued unless requested by the pilot.
B— The pilot in command must accept an instrument departure procedure when issued by ATC.
C— If an instrument departure procedure is accepted, the pilot must possess at least a textual description.

151.
4070. Preferred IFR routes beginning with a fix, indicate that departing aircraft will normally be routed to the fix by

A— the established airway(s) between the departure airport and the fix.
B— an instrument departure procedure (DP), or radar vectors.
C— direct route only.

6.14 Microwave Landing System and GPS Approaches

152.
4798. What international Morse Code identifier is used to identify a specific interim standard microwave landing system?

A— A two letter Morse Code identifier preceded by the Morse Code for the letters "IM".
B— A three letter Morse Code identifier preceded by the Morse Code for the letter "M".
C— A three letter Morse Code identifier preceded by the Morse Code for the letters "ML".

Answer (C) is correct (4418). *(ACL)*
Use the Rate of Climb Table in Legend 16 on page 204. Required climb rate (ft. per NM) is found on the left margin and ground speed (kt.) is found on the top. Since 210 ft. per NM is not on the chart, you must interpolate between 200 and 250 ft. per NM at 140 kt. At 200 ft. per NM the climb rate is 467 fpm, and at 250 ft. per NM it is 583 fpm. Interpolate for 210 ft. per NM to determine a rate of climb of 490 fpm.
Answer (A) is incorrect because 210 is the required ft. per NM, not fpm. Answer (B) is incorrect because the required climb rate is 490 fpm, not 450 fpm.

Answer (C) is correct (4419). *(AIM Para 5-2-6)*
Once an instrument departure procedure (DP) is accepted, the presumption by ATC is that the pilot possesses a textual description of the DP.
Answer (A) is incorrect because pilots operating from locations with DPs may expect ATC clearances containing a DP. Answer (B) is incorrect because you must reject a DP clearance if you do not have a text of the DP or if it is otherwise unacceptable.

Answer (B) is correct (4070). *(P/C Glossary)*
Preferred IFR routes are correlated with DPs and STARs and may be defined by airways, jet routes, and direct routes between NAVAIDs. Thus, preferred routes beginning with a fix indicate that the departing traffic will normally be routed to the fix via a DP or radar vectors.
Answer (A) is incorrect because established airways may not exist between the airport and the fix, and other methods may be more efficient and effective. Answer (C) is incorrect because a direct route may not be appropriate due to obstructions or traffic flows.

Answer (B) is correct (4798). *(AIM Para 1-1-11)*
MLS identification is a four-character alphabetic designation starting with the letter "M," transmitted in international Morse Code at least 6 times per minute.
Answer (A) is incorrect because the identifier letter is the single character "M," which is followed by three other letters. Answer (C) is incorrect because the identifier letter is the single character "M," which is followed by three other letters.

153.
4799. If Receiver Autonomous Integrity Monitoring (RAIM) is not available when setting up a GPS approach, the pilot should

A— select another type of navigation and approach system.
B— continue to the MAP and hold until the satellites are recaptured.
C— continue the approach, expecting to recapture the satellites before reaching the FAF.

Answer (A) is correct (4799). *(AIM Para 1-1-21)*
RAIM outages may occur due to an insufficient number of satellites or due to unsuitable satellite geometry, which causes the error in the position solution to become too large. If RAIM is not available when setting up a GPS approach, you must select another type of navigation and approach system.
Answer (B) is incorrect because, if RAIM is not available when setting up a GPS approach, you should select another type of navigation and approach system. You should not fly to the MAP and hold. Additionally, there is no holding pattern at the MAP. Answer (C) is incorrect because, if RAIM is not available when setting up a GPS approach, you should select another type of navigation and approach system. If RAIM failure occurs while you are setting up the GPS approach or conducting a GPS approach, you must not continue the approach hoping that RAIM will become available before the FAF.

154.
4801. When using GPS for navigation and instrument approaches, any required alternate airport must have

A— an approved operational instrument approach procedure other than GPS.
B— authorization to fly approaches under IFR using GPS avionics systems.
C— a GPS approach that is anticipated to be operational and available at the ETA.

Answer (A) is correct (4801). *(AIM Para 1-1-21)*
When you are using GPS for navigation and instrument approaches, any required alternate airport must have an approved instrument approach procedure, other than GPS, which is anticipated to be operational and available at the estimated time of arrival (ETA) and which the airplane is equipped to fly.
Answer (B) is incorrect because authorization to fly approaches under IFR using GPS avionics systems requires that the GPS unit and installation meet FAA standards and receive FAA approval. Answer (C) is incorrect because any required alternate airport must have an approved instrument approach procedure other than GPS, not a GPS approach, that is anticipated to be operational and available at the ETA.

END OF CHAPTER

CHAPTER SEVEN
AEROMEDICAL FACTORS

This chapter contains outlines of major concepts tested, all FAA test questions and answers regarding aeromedical factors, and an explanation of each answer. Each module, or subtopic, within this chapter is listed above with the number of questions from the FAA knowledge test pertaining to that particular module. For each module, the first number following the parentheses is the page number on which the outline begins, and the next number is the page number on which the questions begin.

There are 18 questions in this chapter. We separate and organize the FAA questions into meaningful study units, i.e., chapters and modules. As an analogy, it is easier to deal with the "trees" if you understand the "forest." In this context, "trees" are individual FAA questions, and the "forest" is the instrument rating knowledge test. The organizational units between the overall instrument rating knowledge test and the individual instrument rating test questions are chapters and modules in this book.

CAUTION: The **sole purpose** of this book is to expedite passing the FAA instrument rating knowledge test. Accordingly, extraneous material (i.e., topics or regulations not directly tested on the FAA knowledge test) is omitted, even though much more information and knowledge are necessary to fly safely. This additional material is presented in *Instrument Pilot Flight Maneuvers and Practical Test Prep*, *Pilot Handbook*, *Aviation Weather and Weather Services*, and *FAR/AIM*, available from Gleim Publications, Inc. See the order form on page 488.

7.1 HYPOXIA AND HYPERVENTILATION (Questions 1-2)

1. Hypoxia results from a lack of oxygen in the bloodstream and causes a lack of clear thinking, fatigue, euphoria, and, shortly thereafter, unconsciousness.

    a. Symptoms of hypoxia are difficult to detect before the pilot's reactions are affected.

2. Hyperventilation occurs when an excessive amount of air is breathed into the lungs at an excessive rate, e.g., when one becomes excited as a result of stress, fear, or anxiety.

    a. Overcome hyperventilation symptoms by slowing the breathing rate, by placing a paper bag over your nose and mouth and breathing into it, or by talking aloud.

7.2 SPATIAL DISORIENTATION (Questions 3-12)

1. Spatial disorientation (sometimes called vertigo) is a state of temporary confusion resulting from misleading information sent to the brain by various sensory organs.

2. The best way to overcome the effects of spatial disorientation is to rely on the airplane instruments and ignore body (kinesthetic) signals.

3. The nervous system often interprets centrifugal force as vertical movement, i.e., rising or falling.

4. Coriolis illusion is caused by an abrupt head movement in a prolonged constant-rate turn.

    a. This can cause spatial disorientation.

5. An abrupt change from a climb to straight-and-level flight can create the illusion of tumbling backwards.

6. A rapid acceleration during takeoff can create the illusion of being in a nose-up attitude.

7. False horizon is an illusion that is caused by a sloping cloud formation, an obscured horizon, or a dark scene spread with ground lights and stars.

7.3 VISION AND VISUAL ILLUSION (Questions 13-18)

1. Pilots should adapt their eyes for night flying by avoiding bright white lights for 30 min. prior to flight.

    a. Thereafter, white light must be avoided because it will cause temporary night blindness and impair night vision adaptation.

2. The most effective way to scan for other aircraft in daylight is to use a series of short, regularly spaced eye movements that bring successive areas of the sky into your central vision field.

    a. Each movement should not exceed 10°, and each area should be observed for at least 1 second to enable detection.

    b. Only a very small center area of the eye has the ability to send clear, sharply focused messages to the brain. All other areas provide less detail.

    c. At night, however, the eyes are most effective at seeing objects off center. Accordingly, pilots should scan slowly back and forth to facilitate off-center viewing.

3. Haze can also create the illusion of being a greater distance from the runway, resulting in the pilot's flying a lower-than-normal approach.

4. A narrower-than-usual runway may create the illusion that the airplane is higher than it actually is.

    a. This illusion results in a lower-than-normal approach.
    b. A wider-than-usual runway creates the opposite illusion and problem.

5. An upward-sloping runway may create the illusion that the airplane is at a higher-than-actual altitude.

    a. This illusion results in a lower-than-normal approach.
    b. A downward-sloping runway creates the opposite illusion and problem.

7.1 Hypoxia and Hyperventilation

1.
4809. Why is hypoxia particularly dangerous during flights with one pilot?

A— Night vision may be so impaired that the pilot cannot see other aircraft.
B— Symptoms of hypoxia may be difficult to recognize before the pilot's reactions are affected.
C— The pilot may not be able to control the aircraft even if using oxygen.

Answer (B) is correct (4809). *(AIM Para 8-1-2)*
Hypoxia symptoms are gradual, and a pilot may not recognize the symptoms before his/her reactions are affected. Because the symptoms of hypoxia vary with the individual, having two pilots increases the chance of detection before pilot reactions are affected.
Answer (A) is incorrect because hypoxia, which is a lack of sufficient oxygen, affects all mental and physical activity, not just night vision. Answer (C) is incorrect because hypoxia will not occur if supplemental oxygen is used properly.

2.
4816. What action should be taken if hyperventilation is suspected?

A— Breathe at a slower rate by taking very deep breaths.
B— Consciously breathe at a slower rate than normal.
C— Consciously force yourself to take deep breaths and breathe at a faster rate than normal.

Answer (B) is correct (4816). *(AIM Para 8-1-3)*
Hyperventilation occurs when abnormally large amounts of air are breathed in and out of the lungs. Early symptoms of hyperventilation and hypoxia are similar and include dizziness, drowsiness, tingling of the fingers and toes, and sensation of body heat. If hyperventilation is suspected, you should consciously breathe at a slower rate than normal.
Answer (A) is incorrect because taking deep breaths will only aggravate hyperventilation. Answer (C) is incorrect because taking deep breaths and breathing at a faster rate than normal is the cause, not cure, of hyperventilation.

7.2 Spatial Disorientation

3.
4814. A pilot is more subject to spatial disorientation if

A— kinesthetic senses are ignored.
B— eyes are moved often in the process of cross-checking the flight instruments.
C— body signals are used to interpret flight attitude.

Answer (C) is correct (4814). *(MHP Chap 14)*
Spatial disorientation is a state of temporary confusion resulting from misleading information being sent to the brain by various sensory organs. Thus, the pilot should ignore sensations of muscles and inner ear and kinesthetic senses (those which sense motion).
Answer (A) is incorrect because spatial disorientation is prevented/overcome by ignoring the kinesthetic senses. Answer (B) is incorrect because spatial disorientation is prevented/overcome by using and trusting the flight instruments.

4.
4815. Which procedure is recommended to prevent or overcome spatial disorientation?

A— Reduce head and eye movements to the extent possible.
B— Rely on the kinesthetic sense.
C— Rely on the indications of the flight instruments.

Answer (C) is correct (4815). *(MHP Chap 14)*
To overcome the effect of spatial disorientation, pilots should rely entirely on the indications of the flight instruments.
Answer (A) is incorrect because, although rapid head movements should be avoided, eye movement is necessary for proper scanning of the flight instruments. Answer (B) is incorrect because the kinesthetic sense is creating the problem; i.e., it should be ignored.

5.
4810. The sensations which lead to spatial disorientation during instrument flight conditions

A— are frequently encountered by beginning instrument pilots, but never by pilots with moderate instrument experience.
B— occur, in most instances, during the initial period of transition from visual to instrument flight.
C— must be suppressed and complete reliance placed on the indications of the flight instruments.

Answer (C) is correct (4810). *(AIM Para 8-1-5)*
In instrument flight conditions, the only way to prevent spatial disorientation is by visual reference to and reliance on the flight instruments.
Answer (A) is incorrect because pilots with moderate and even heavy instrument experience can experience spatial disorientation. Answer (B) is incorrect because spatial disorientation can occur at any time outside visual references are lost. This can happen on a clear day flying in VMC or in IMC.

6.
4811. How can an instrument pilot best overcome spatial disorientation?

A— Rely on kinesthetic sense.
B— Use a very rapid cross-check.
C— Read and interpret the flight instruments, and act accordingly.

Answer (C) is correct (4811). *(IFH Chap II)*
To overcome spatial disorientation, the IFR pilot should read and interpret the flight instruments and ignore all the body senses.
Answer (A) is incorrect because the kinesthetic sense is what causes the problem; i.e., it should be ignored. Answer (B) is incorrect because the flight instruments should be read and understood in a deliberate manner, not in haste or panic.

7.
4813. How can an instrument pilot best overcome spatial disorientation?

A— Use a very rapid cross-check.
B— Properly interpret the flight instruments and act accordingly.
C— Avoid banking in excess of 30°.

Answer (B) is correct (4813). *(IFH Chap II)*
To overcome spatial disorientation, the IFR pilot should read and interpret the flight instruments and ignore all the body senses.
Answer (A) is incorrect because the flight instruments should be read and understood in a deliberate manner, not in haste or panic. Answer (C) is incorrect because spatial disorientation can also occur in bank angles less than 30°.

8.
4802. Without visual aid, a pilot often interprets centrifugal force as a sensation of

A— rising or falling.
B— turning.
C— motion reversal.

Answer (A) is correct (4802). *(IFH Chap II)*
Nerves in tendons and muscles, including shifting of abdominal muscles, often incorrectly interpret centrifugal force as vertical movement, i.e., rising or falling.
Answer (B) is incorrect because centrifugal force is caused by turning but is often misinterpreted as rising or falling. Answer (C) is incorrect because centrifugal force is caused by turning, not motion reversal.

9.
4805. Abrupt head movement during a prolonged constant rate turn in IMC or simulated instrument conditions can cause

A— pilot disorientation.
B— false horizon.
C— elevator illusion.

Answer (A) is correct (4805). *(AIM Para 8-1-5)*
An abrupt head movement in a prolonged constant-rate turn that has ceased stimulating the motion sensing system can create the illusion of rotation or movement in an entirely different axis. This illusion is called the Coriolis illusion and can lead to spatial disorientation.
Answer (B) is incorrect because a false horizon is an illusion caused by sloping cloud formations, an obscured horizon, a dark scene spread with ground lights and stars, or certain geometric patterns of ground light. This illusion creates the impression of not being aligned correctly with the actual horizon and can also lead to spatial disorientation. Answer (C) is incorrect because an elevator illusion is caused by an abrupt upward vertical acceleration, usually by an updraft. This illusion can also lead to spatial disorientation.

10.

4807. An abrupt change from climb to straight-and-level flight can create the illusion of

A— tumbling backwards.
B— a noseup attitude.
C— a descent with the wings level.

11.

4808. A rapid acceleration during takeoff can create the illusion of

A— spinning in the opposite direction.
B— being in a noseup attitude.
C— diving into the ground.

12.

4806. A sloping cloud formation, an obscured horizon, and a dark scene spread with ground lights and stars can create an illusion known as

A— elevator illusions.
B— autokinesis.
C— false horizons.

7.3 Vision and Visual Illusion

13.

4817. Which use of cockpit lighting is correct for night flight?

A— Reducing the interior lighting intensity to a minimum level.
B— The use of regular white light, such as a flashlight, will not impair night adaptation.
C— Coloration shown on maps is least affected by the use of direct red lighting.

Answer (A) is correct (4807). *(AIM Para 8-1-5)*
An abrupt change from climb to straight-and-level flight can create the illusion of tumbling backwards. The disoriented pilot will push the airplane abruptly into a nose-low attitude, possibly intensifying this illusion, which is called an inversion illusion.
Answer (B) is incorrect because a rapid acceleration during takeoff can create an illusion of being in a nose-up attitude. This is called a somatogravic illusion. Answer (C) is incorrect because an observed loss of altitude during a coordinated constant-rate turn that has ceased stimulating the motion sensing system (i.e., inner ear) can create the illusion of being in a descent with the wings level. This illusion is called a graveyard spiral.

Answer (B) is correct (4808). *(AIM Para 8-1-5)*
A rapid acceleration during takeoff can create the illusion of being in a nose-up attitude. The disoriented pilot will push the airplane into a nose-low, or dive, attitude. This is called a somatogravic illusion.
Answer (A) is incorrect because a proper recovery from a spin that has ceased stimulating the motion sensing system (i.e., inner ear) can create the illusion of spinning in the opposite direction. This is known as a graveyard spin. Answer (C) is incorrect because a rapid deceleration or an abrupt downward vertical acceleration (usually caused by a downdraft) can cause the illusion of a nose-down, or dive, attitude.

Answer (C) is correct (4806). *(AIM Para 8-1-5)*
A sloping cloud formation, an obscured horizon, a dark scene spread with ground lights and stars, and certain geometric patterns of ground light can create an illusion known as false horizons. The disoriented pilot will place the airplane in a dangerous attitude.
Answer (A) is incorrect because elevator illusions are caused by abrupt upward or downward vertical accelerations, usually by updrafts and downdrafts. These lead to illusions of being in a climb or descent. Answer (B) is incorrect because, at night, a static light will appear to move about when stared at for many seconds, creating an illusion known as autokinesis.

Answer (A) is correct (4817). *(AIM Para 8-1-6)*
In darkness, vision becomes more sensitive to light, making it possible for the pilot to see distant objects. A pilot can achieve a moderate degree of this dark adaptation within 20 min. under dim red cockpit lighting. White cockpit lighting is required for map and instrument reading, especially when operating under IFR. To maintain some night vision, the interior lighting intensity is to be kept at a minimum level.
Answer (B) is incorrect because, after a pilot's eyes have become adapted to darkness, the pilot must avoid exposing them to any bright white light, which would cause temporary night blindness and impair night adaptation. Answer (C) is incorrect because the colors on maps can be severely distorted when using a red light.

14.
4812. Which statement is correct regarding the use of cockpit lighting for night flight?

A— Reducing the lighting intensity to a minimum level will eliminate blind spots.
B— The use of regular white light, such as a flashlight, will impair night adaptation.
C— Coloration shown on maps is least affected by the use of direct red lighting.

15.
4818. Which technique should a pilot use to scan for traffic to the right and left during straight-and-level flight?

A— Systematically focus on different segments of the sky for short intervals.
B— Concentrate on relative movement detected in the peripheral vision area.
C— Continuous sweeping of the windshield from right to left.

16.
4819. What effect does haze have on the ability to see traffic or terrain features during flight?

A— Haze causes the eyes to focus at infinity, making terrain features harder to see.
B— The eyes tend to overwork in haze and do not detect relative movement easily.
C— Haze creates the illusion of being a greater distance than actual from the runway, and causes pilots to fly a lower approach.

17.
4803. Due to visual illusion, when landing on a narrower-than-usual runway, the aircraft will appear to be

A— higher than actual, leading to a lower-than-normal approach.
B— lower than actual, leading to a higher-than-normal approach.
C— higher than actual, leading to a higher-than-normal approach.

18.
4804. What visual illusion creates the same effect as a narrower-than-usual runway?

A— An upsloping runway.
B— A wider-than-usual runway.
C— A downsloping runway.

Answer (B) is correct (4812). *(AIM Para 8-1-6)*
After a pilot's eyes have become adapted to darkness, the pilot must avoid exposing them to any bright white light, which would cause temporary night blindness and impair night adaptation.
Answer (A) is incorrect because the minimum level of cockpit lighting may be insufficient to read maps, gauges, etc. Answer (C) is incorrect because the colors on maps can be severely distorted when using a red light.

Answer (A) is correct (4818). *(AIM Para 8-1-6)*
The most effective way to scan for other aircraft during daylight is to use a series of short, regularly spaced eye movements that bring successive areas of the sky into your central vision field. Only a very small center area of the eye has the ability to send clear, sharply focused messages to the brain. All other areas provide less detail.
Answer (B) is incorrect because the peripheral areas do not send sharply focused messages to the brain. Peripheral vision is more effective at night. Answer (C) is incorrect because concentration for at least 1 second is needed for each 10° sector.

Answer (C) is correct (4819). *(AIM Para 8-1-5)*
Haze can create the illusion of being at a greater distance from the runway and often causes pilots to fly a lower approach.
Answer (A) is incorrect because haze may cause the condition known as empty-field myopia. This condition results when the pilot has nothing specific to focus on outside the airplane and the eyes relax and focus at a range of about 10 to 30 ft., not infinity. Answer (B) is incorrect because in haze the eyes tend to relax, not overwork, thus causing empty-field myopia, or looking without seeing.

Answer (A) is correct (4803). *(AIM Para 8-1-5)*
A narrower-than-usual runway may create the illusion that the aircraft is higher than actual, resulting in a lower-than-normal approach.
Answer (B) is incorrect because wider, not narrower, runways give a lower-than-actual altitude illusion. Answer (C) is incorrect because a higher-than-actual altitude illusion results in a lower-than-usual, not higher-than-usual, approach.

Answer (A) is correct (4804). *(AIM Para 8-1-5)*
Both narrower-than-usual runway and an upsloping runway may create the illusion that the airplane is at a higher altitude than it actually is. The pilot will fly a lower approach and risk striking obstructions or landing short.
Answer (B) is incorrect because a wider-than-usual runway may create the illusion that the aircraft is at a lower altitude than it actually is, and the unknowing pilot may land hard or overshoot the runway. Answer (C) is incorrect because a downsloping runway may create the illusion that the aircraft is at a lower altitude than it actually is, and the unknowing pilot may land hard or overshoot the runway.

END OF CHAPTER

CHAPTER EIGHT
AVIATION WEATHER

This chapter contains outlines of major concepts tested, all FAA test questions and answers regarding aviation weather, and an explanation of each answer. Each module, or subtopic, within this chapter is listed above with the number of questions from the FAA knowledge test pertaining to that particular module. For each module, the first number following the parentheses is the page number on which the outline begins, and the next number is the page number on which the questions begin.

There are 85 questions in this chapter. We separate and organize the FAA questions into meaningful study units, i.e., chapters and modules. As an analogy, it is easier to deal with the "trees" if you understand the "forest." In this context, "trees" are individual FAA questions, and the "forest" is the instrument rating knowledge test. The organizational units between the overall instrument rating knowledge test and the individual instrument rating test questions are chapters and modules in this book.

CAUTION: The **sole purpose** of this book is to expedite your passing the FAA instrument rating knowledge test. Accordingly, all extraneous material (i.e., topics or regulations not directly tested on the FAA knowledge test) is omitted, even though much more information and knowledge are necessary to fly safely. This additional material is presented in *Instrument Pilot Flight Maneuvers and Practical Test Prep*, *Pilot Handbook*, *Aviation Weather and Weather Services*, and *FAR/AIM*, available from Gleim Publications, Inc. See the order form on page 488.

8.1 CAUSES OF WEATHER (Questions 1-15)

1. Every physical process of weather is accompanied by, or is the result of, heat exchanges.

2. Unequal heating of the Earth's surface causes differences in pressure and, thus, altimeter settings.

    a. On weather maps, the lines drawn to connect points of equal pressure show pressure contours called **isobars**.

3. Three of the forces at work on winds are discussed below.

    a. The pressure gradient force causes wind to flow from an area of high pressure to one of low pressure.

        1) This flow is thus perpendicular to the isobars.

    b. Coriolis force deflects winds to the right in the Northern Hemisphere. Coriolis force is a result of the Earth's rotation.

        1) The Coriolis force is at a right angle to wind direction and directly proportional to wind speed. Its effect is more forceful at greater altitudes (above approximately 2,000 ft. AGL) because surface winds are slowed by friction.

        2) It deflects winds so strongly that they flow parallel to isobars.

    c. Friction with the Earth's surface weakens the wind.

        1) Since these winds are slower, they are less affected by Coriolis force. The pressure gradient becomes stronger than Coriolis force, and the wind flows across, rather than parallel to, the isobars.

4. An **air mass** is an extensive body of air having uniform moisture and temperature properties.

5. The average height of the layer of the Earth's atmosphere called the **troposphere** is about 37,000 ft. in mid-latitudes. It varies between approximately 25,000 ft. at the poles to 65,000 ft. at the equator.

6. The boundary between the troposphere and the stratosphere is the thin layer called the **tropopause**.

    a. Temperature and wind vary greatly in the vicinity of the tropopause.
    b. It is associated with an abrupt change in the temperature lapse rate.

7. The **stratosphere** is the layer of atmosphere above the tropopause.

    a. It is characterized by low moisture content and absence of clouds.
    b. It has relatively small changes in temperature with an increase in altitude.

8. The **jet stream** is a narrow, disjointed, wandering "river" of maximum winds.

    a. It moves with pressure ridges and troughs in the upper atmosphere near the tropopause.

    b. It blows from a generally westerly direction and by definition has a speed of 50 kt. or more.

    c. The jet stream is normally weaker and farther north in the summer.

    d. The jet stream is normally stronger and farther south in the winter.

9. A **front** is the zone of transition between two air masses of different temperature, humidity, and wind.

    a. There is always a change in wind when you fly across a front.

    b. The threat of low-level wind shear occurs just before the warm front passes the airport.

    c. With a cold front, the most critical period for wind shear occurs just as or just after the cold front passes the airport.

10. Frontal waves and cyclones (and areas of low pressure) usually form in slow-moving cold fronts or in stationary fronts.

11. Squall lines usually develop ahead of a cold front.

8.2 STABILITY OF AIR MASSES (Questions 16-28)

1. The **lapse rate** is a measure of how much temperature decreases (or possibly increases) with an increase in altitude. This is the actual temperature change associated with increases in altitude and sometimes is referred to as the **ambient lapse rate**.

    a. In contrast to the ambient or actual lapse rate is the **adiabatic lapse rate**. The adiabatic, or "expansional cooling" lapse rate, is the temperature decrease due only to expansion of air as it rises. The adiabatic lapse rate means no heat gain or loss -- just a decrease in temperature because of expansion.

        1) The dry adiabatic lapse rate is 3°C per 1,000 ft.

        2) The adiabatic lapse rate varies from about 1.1°C to 2.8°C based on moisture content of the air.

        3) The average adiabatic lapse rate is 2°C per 1,000 ft.

2. The ambient lapse rate can thus be used by pilots to determine the stability of air masses.

    a. The greater the ambient lapse rate (more than 2°C per 1,000 ft.) and the higher the humidity, the more unstable the air -- and the more thunderstorms can be expected.

    b. Moist air is less stable than dry air because it cools adiabatically at a slower rate, which means that moist air must rise higher before its temperature cools to that of the air around it (i.e., cumulus build-up).

3. Cloud formation after lifting is determined by the stability of the air before lifting.

    a. Turbulence and clouds with vertical development (cumuliform) result when unstable air rises (due to convective currents).

    b. Moist, stable air moving up a mountain slope produces stratiform clouds as it cools.

        1) Unstable air moving up a mountain slope produces clouds with extensive vertical development.

4. When a cold air mass moves over a warm surface, heating from below provides unstable lifting action, giving rise to cumuliform clouds, turbulence, and good visibility.

5. The growth rate of precipitation is enhanced by upward air currents carrying water droplets upward where condensation increases droplet size.

6. Stable air characteristics

   a. Stratiform clouds and fog
   b. Smooth air
   c. Continuous (steady) precipitation
   d. Fair-to-poor visibility in haze and smoke

7. Unstable air characteristics

   a. Cumuliform clouds
   b. Turbulent air
   c. Showery precipitation
   d. Good visibility

8.3 TEMPERATURE INVERSIONS (Questions 29-32)

1. Normally, temperature decreases as altitude increases. A temperature inversion occurs when temperature increases as altitude increases.

2. Temperature inversions usually result in a stable layer of warm air below the inversion.

3. A temperature inversion often develops near the ground on clear, cool nights when the wind is light.

   a. It is caused by terrestrial radiation.

4. Smooth air with restricted visibility (due to fog, haze, or low clouds) is usually found beneath a low-level temperature inversion.

8.4 TEMPERATURE, DEW POINT, AND FOG (Questions 33-45)

1. When the temperature-dew point spread is 3°C (5°F) or less and decreasing, you should expect fog and/or low clouds.

2. Air temperature largely determines how much water vapor can be held by the air.

   a. **Dew point** is the temperature at which the air will be saturated with moisture, i.e., 100% humidity.

3. Frost forms when the temperature of the collecting surface (e.g., the airplane) is below the dew point of the surrounding air and the dew point is below freezing (0°C or 32°F).

4. Water vapor becomes visible as it condenses into clouds, fog, or dew.

   a. **Evaporation** is the conversion of liquid water to water vapor.
   b. **Sublimation** is the conversion of ice to water vapor or water vapor to ice.

5. **Radiation fog** is most likely to occur when there is a clear sky, little or no wind, and a small temperature-dew point spread over a land surface (especially low, flatland areas).

   a. As the ground cools rapidly due to radiation, the air close to the surface cools more quickly than slightly higher air.

      1) This is the most frequent type of surface-based temperature inversion.

   b. As the air reaches its dew point, radiation fog forms.

6. **Advection fog** forms as a result of moist air condensing as it moves over a colder surface (i.e., water or ground).

   a. It requires wind to force the movement.

   b. Advection fog is most likely to occur in coastal areas, when air moves inland from the coast in winter.

7. **Upslope fog** results from warm, moist air being cooled as it is forced up sloping terrain.

8. **Precipitation-induced fog** results from warm fronts (warmer air over cooler air), i.e., when warm rain or drizzle falls through the cooler air.

   a. Evaporation from the precipitation saturates the cooler air, causing fog.

9. Fog can also form easily in industrial areas where combustion pollution provides a high concentration of condensation nuclei (tiny particles on which moisture can condense as the air cools).

8.5 CLOUDS (Questions 46-53)

1. Clouds are divided into four families based on their height:

   a. High clouds (consist of ice crystals and do not pose an icing threat)
   b. Middle clouds
   c. Low clouds
   d. Clouds with extensive vertical development

2. Lifting action, unstable air, and moisture are the ingredients for the formation of cumulonimbus clouds.

   a. Fair weather cumulus clouds form in convective currents and often indicate turbulence at and below the cloud level.

   b. Nimbus means rain cloud.

   c. Towering cumulus is an early stage of cumulonimbus.

   d. The greatest turbulence is in cumulonimbus clouds (thunderstorms).

3. Standing lenticular altocumulus clouds (ACSL) are almond or lens-shaped and form on the crests of waves created by barriers in the wind flow (e.g., on the leeward side of a mountain).

   a. The presence of these clouds indicate very strong turbulence.

8.6 THUNDERSTORMS (Questions 54-63)

1. Thunderstorms have three phases in their life cycle:

   a. **Cumulus** -- the building stage of a thunderstorm when there are continuous updrafts

   b. **Mature** -- the time of greatest intensity when there are both updrafts and downdrafts (causing severe wind shear and turbulence)

      1) The commencing of rain on the Earth's surface indicates the beginning of the mature stage of a thunderstorm.

   c. **Dissipating** -- characterized predominantly by downdrafts; i.e., the phase of the storm raining itself out

2. A thunderstorm, by definition, always has lightning because lightning causes thunder.

3. Thunderstorms are produced by cumulonimbus clouds. They form when there is

   a. Sufficient water vapor
   b. An unstable lapse rate
   c. An initial upward boost (i.e., a lifting action) to start the process

4. Thunderstorms produce wind shear turbulence, a hazardous and invisible phenomenon, particularly for airplanes landing and taking off.

   a. If a thunderstorm is penetrated, a pilot should fly straight ahead, set power for recommended turbulence penetration airspeed, and attempt to maintain a level attitude.

5. The most severe thunderstorm conditions (heavy hail, destructive winds, tornadoes, etc.) are generally associated with squall line thunderstorms.

   a. A **squall line** is a nonfrontal, narrow band of thunderstorms usually ahead of a cold front.

6. A **squall** (not squall line) is defined as a sudden increase in wind speed of at least 16 kt., the speed rising to 22 kt. or more and lasting at least 1 min.

7. Embedded thunderstorms are obscured because they occur in very cloudy conditions or thick haze layers.

8. Airborne weather-avoidance radar detects only precipitation drops. It does not detect minute cloud droplets (i.e., clouds and fog).

   a. Thus, airborne weather-avoidance radar provides no assurance of avoiding instrument weather conditions.

8.7 ICING (Questions 64-71)

1. Structural icing requires two conditions:

   a. Flight through visible moisture
   b. The temperature at freezing or below

2. Freezing rain usually causes the greatest accumulation of structural ice.

   a. Freezing rain indicates that temperatures are above freezing at some higher altitude.

3. Ice pellets are caused when rain droplets freeze at a higher altitude; i.e., freezing rain exists above.

4. Heavy, wet snow indicates the temperature is above freezing at your altitude.

   a. Snow that is heavy and wet formed above you but is on the verge of melting.

5. Frost on wings disrupts the airflow over the wings causing early airflow separation and resulting in a loss of lift. It should be removed before flight is attempted.

6. Test data indicate that ice, snow, or frost having a thickness and roughness similar to medium or coarse sandpaper on the leading edge and upper surface of a wing can reduce wing lift by as much as 30% and increase drag by 40%.

7. With a standard (average) temperature lapse rate of 2°C per 1,000 ft., the freezing level can be determined by knowing the current temperature and elevation.

   a. EXAMPLE: At a field elevation of 1,350 ft. MSL, the temperature is +8°C. To reach the freezing level, the temperature must drop 8°C. Thus the freezing level is 4,000 ft. (8°C ÷ 2°C/1,000 ft.) above field elevation, or 5,350 ft. MSL (1,350 + 4,000).

8.8 WIND SHEAR (Questions 72-77)

1. **Wind shear** is any change in wind velocity (speed and/or direction).

    a. If the change is abrupt and of more than slight magnitude, it can be an extreme hazard to flight.

2. Wind shear can occur at any level in the atmosphere and be horizontal and/or vertical; i.e., it occurs wherever adjacent air flows in different directions and/or at different speeds.

3. Wind shear is an atmospheric condition that may be associated with a low-level temperature inversion, a jet stream, or a frontal zone.

4. **Light turbulence** momentarily causes slight, erratic changes in altitude and/or attitude.

5. **Severe turbulence** and wind shear may be found on all sides of a thunderstorm, including directly beneath it and as much as 20 mi. laterally.

6. Hazardous wind shear is commonly encountered near the ground during periods of strong temperature inversion and near thunderstorms.

    a. Expect wind shear in a temperature inversion whenever wind speed at 2,000 to 4,000 ft. AGL is 25 kt. or more.

8.9 MICROBURSTS (Questions 78-85)

1. Microbursts are small-scale intense downdrafts which, on reaching the surface, spread outward in all directions from the downdraft center. This causes the presence of both vertical and horizontal wind shears that can be extremely hazardous to all types and categories of aircraft, especially at low altitudes.

2. Parent clouds producing microburst activity can be any of the low or middle layer convective cloud types.

    a. Microbursts commonly occur within the heavy rain portion of thunderstorms but also occur in much weaker, benign-appearing convective cells that have little or no precipitation reaching the ground.

3. The life cycle of a microburst as it descends in a convective rain shaft is illustrated below.

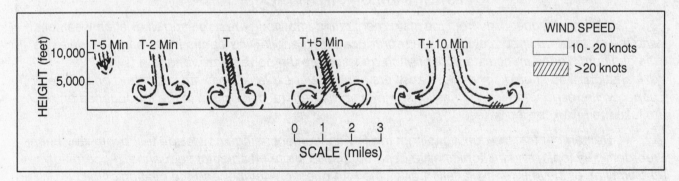

    a. "T" is the time the microburst strikes the ground.

4. Characteristics of microbursts include

    a. Size. The microburst downdraft is typically less than 1 mi. in diameter as it descends from the cloud base to about 1,000-3,000 ft. above the ground.

        1) In the transition zone near the ground, the downdraft changes to a horizontal outflow that can extend to approximately 2½ mi. in diameter.

b. Intensity. The downdrafts can be as strong as 6,000 fpm.

1) Horizontal winds near the surface can be as strong as 45 kt., resulting in a 90-kt. shear (headwind to tailwind change for a traversing aircraft) across the microburst.

2) These strong horizontal winds occur within a few hundred feet of the ground.

c. Visual signs. Microbursts can be found almost anywhere there is convective activity.

1) They may be embedded in heavy rain associated with a thunderstorm or in light rain in benign-appearing virga.

2) When there is little or no precipitation at the surface accompanying the microburst, a ring of blowing dust may be the only visual clue of its existence.

d. Duration. An individual microburst will seldom last longer than 15 min. from the time it strikes the ground until dissipation.

1) An important consideration for pilots is that the microburst intensifies for about 5 min. after it strikes the ground, with the maximum-intensity winds lasting approximately 2 to 4 min.

2) Once microburst activity starts, multiple microbursts in the same general area are not uncommon and should be expected.

3) Sometimes microbursts are concentrated into a line structure, and under these conditions, activity may continue for as long as an hour.

5. Microburst wind shear may create a severe hazard for aircraft within 1,000 ft. of the ground, particularly during the approach to landing and landing and takeoff phases.

a. The aircraft may encounter a headwind (performance increasing) followed by a downdraft and tailwind (both performance decreasing), possibly resulting in terrain impact.

b. See Fig. 13 on page 292.

QUESTIONS AND ANSWER EXPLANATIONS

All the FAA questions from the instrument rating knowledge test relating to aviation weather and the material outlined previously are reproduced on the following pages in the same modules as the outlines. To the immediate right of each question are the correct answer and answer explanation. You should cover these answers and answer explanations with your hand or a piece of paper while responding to the questions. Refer to the general discussion in the Introduction on how to take the FAA knowledge test.

Remember that the questions from the FAA instrument rating knowledge test bank have been reordered by topic, and the topics have been organized into a meaningful sequence. Accordingly, the first line of the answer explanation gives the FAA question number and the citation of the authoritative source for the answer.

8.1 Causes of Weather

1.
4096.   The primary cause of all changes in the Earth's weather is

A— variation of solar energy received by the Earth's regions.
B— changes in air pressure over the Earth's surface.
C— movement of the air masses.

Answer (A) is correct (4096). *(AvW Chap 2)*
   Every physical process of weather is accompanied by, or is the result of, a heat exchange. Unequal solar heating of the Earth's surface causes differences in air pressure, which result in all changes in the Earth's weather.
   Answer (B) is incorrect because changes in air pressure are a result of varying temperatures. Answer (C) is incorrect because movement of air masses (wind) is a result of varying temperatures and pressures.

2.
4108.   Which force, in the Northern Hemisphere, acts at a right angle to the wind and deflects it to the right until parallel to the isobars?

A— Centrifugal.
B— Pressure gradient.
C— Coriolis.

Answer (C) is correct (4108). *(AvW Chap 4)*
   Coriolis force is a result of the Earth's rotation. As the wind moves perpendicular to the isobars (from high to low pressure), it is apparently deflected to the right in the Northern Hemisphere, until it is moving parallel to the isobars. This effect is most pronounced above 2,000 ft. AGL.
   Answer (A) is incorrect because centrifugal force is a force that acts outwardly on any object moving in a curved path. Answer (B) is incorrect because pressure gradient causes the wind to move perpendicular to the isobars. The wind is then deflected by Coriolis force.

3.
4107.   What relationship exists between the winds at 2,000 feet above the surface and the surface winds?

A— The winds at 2,000 feet and the surface winds flow in the same direction, but the surface winds are weaker due to friction.
B— The winds at 2,000 feet tend to parallel the isobars while the surface winds cross the isobars at an angle toward lower pressure and are weaker.
C— The surface winds tend to veer to the right of the winds at 2,000 feet and are usually weaker.

Answer (B) is correct (4107). *(AvW Chap 4)*
   Generally, winds near the surface are weaker than those aloft due to the friction between the Earth's surface and the wind. Also, because they are slower, winds near the surface are less affected by the Coriolis force. The pressure gradient forces are thus stronger near the surface, and the winds cross the isobars at an angle instead of flowing parallel to them.
   Answer (A) is incorrect because the Coriolis force is less at the surface, so surface winds flow in a direction different from those aloft. Answer (C) is incorrect because the winds aloft veer to the right of surface winds, not the opposite.

4.
4106.   Winds at 5,000 feet AGL on a particular flight are southwesterly while most of the surface winds are southerly. This difference in direction is primarily due to

A— a stronger pressure gradient at higher altitudes.
B— friction between the wind and the surface.
C— stronger Coriolis force at the surface.

Answer (B) is correct (4106). *(AvW Chap 4)*
   Southerly winds at the surface will become southwesterly winds at 5,000 ft. because the Coriolis force deflects winds aloft to the right. This force has less effect on surface winds which have been slowed by friction with the Earth's surface.
   Answer (A) is incorrect because the pressure differentials are approximately uniform through the altitudes. Answer (C) is incorrect because the Coriolis force at the surface is weaker with slower wind speed.

5.
4105.   What causes surface winds to flow across the isobars at an angle rather than parallel to the isobars?

A— Coriolis force.
B— Surface friction.
C— The greater density of the air at the surface.

Answer (B) is correct (4105). *(AvW Chap 4)*
   Generally, winds near the surface are weaker than those aloft due to the friction between the Earth's surface and the wind. Also, because they are slower, winds near the surface are less affected by the Coriolis force. The pressure gradient forces are thus stronger near the surface, and the winds cross the isobars at an angle instead of flowing parallel to them.
   Answer (A) is incorrect because the Coriolis force is directly proportional to wind speed. At higher altitudes (above 2,000 to 3,000 ft. AGL), winds not slowed by surface friction are so deflected by the Coriolis force that they flow parallel to the isobars, not across them. Answer (C) is incorrect because the greater air density at the surface has little effect on the relationship of winds to the isobars.

6.
4158. An air mass is a body of air that

A— has similar cloud formations associated with it.
B— creates a wind shift as it moves across the Earth's surface.
C— covers an extensive area and has fairly uniform properties of temperature and moisture.

Answer (C) is correct (4158). *(AvW Chap 8)*
    An air mass is an extensive body of air within which the conditions of temperature and moisture in a horizontal plane are essentially uniformly distributed. Generally, an air mass takes on the properties of the large area it overlies.
    Answer (A) is incorrect because an air mass may have cloud formations or it may be clear and dry. Answer (B) is incorrect because changes in wind, temperature, etc., indicate a frontal zone between two air masses.

7.
4097. A characteristic of the stratosphere is

A— an overall decrease of temperature with an increase in altitude.
B— a relatively even base altitude of approximately 35,000 feet.
C— relatively small changes in temperature with an increase in altitude.

Answer (C) is correct (4097). *(AvW Chap 1)*
    The stratosphere is the atmospheric layer above the tropopause. It is the band of altitude from about 7 to 22 mi. It is characterized by a slight average increase in temperature from base to top and thus is very stable. It also has a low moisture content and an absence of clouds.
    Answer (A) is incorrect because there is a slight increase, not decrease, in temperature with increase in altitude. Answer (B) is incorrect because the base of the stratosphere is considerably higher at the equator than at the poles.

8.
4155. A jet stream is defined as wind of

A— 30 knots or greater.
B— 40 knots or greater.
C— 50 knots or greater.

Answer (C) is correct (4155). *(AvW Chap 13)*
    The jet stream is a roughly horizontal stream of wind of 50 kt. or more (by definition) concentrated within a narrow band embedded in the westerly winds in the high troposphere. It occurs in an area of intensified pressure gradients. A second or even third jet stream may form at one time, and these may not be continuous.
    Answer (A) is incorrect because a jet stream, by definition, is a wind of 50 kt., not 30 kt., or greater. Answer (B) is incorrect because a jet stream, by definition, is a wind of 50 kt., not 40 kt., or greater.

9.
4154. The average height of the troposphere in the middle latitudes is

A— 20,000 feet.
B— 25,000 feet.
C— 37,000 feet.

Answer (C) is correct (4154). *(AvW Chap 1)*
    In the mid-latitudes, the average height of the troposphere is about 37,000 ft. It is 25,000 to 30,000 ft. at the poles and 55,000 to 65,000 ft. at the equator. It is generally higher in summer than in winter.
    Answer (A) is incorrect because the average height of the troposphere is 25,000 to 30,000 ft. at the poles, not the mid-latitudes. Answer (B) is incorrect because the average height of the troposphere is 25,000 to 30,000 ft. at the poles, not the mid-latitudes.

10.
4168. The strength and location of the jet stream is normally

A— stronger and farther north in the winter.
B— weaker and farther north in the summer.
C— stronger and farther north in the summer.

Answer (B) is correct (4168). *(AvW Chap 13)*
    In the mid-latitudes, the wind speed in the jet stream averages considerably less in the summer than in the winter. Also, the jet stream shifts farther north in summer than in winter.
    Answer (A) is incorrect because the jet stream is usually farther south, not north, in winter. Answer (C) is incorrect because the jet stream is usually weaker, not stronger, in summer.

11.
4227. Which feature is associated with the tropopause?

A— Absence of wind and turbulent conditions.
B— Absolute upper limit of cloud formation.
C— Abrupt change in temperature lapse rate.

Answer (C) is correct (4227). *(AvW Chap 13)*
The tropopause is the transition layer of atmosphere between the troposphere (surface to about 7 to 22 mi.) and the stratosphere. A characteristic of the tropopause is that there is an abrupt change in the temperature lapse rate, i.e., the rate at which temperature decreases with height.
Answer (A) is incorrect because there are usually very strong winds in the tropopause. These create narrow zones of wind shear, which may generate hazardous turbulence. Answer (B) is incorrect because clouds may form above the tropopause even though there is little moisture in the stratosphere.

12.
4136. Which weather phenomenon is always associated with the passage of a frontal system?

A— A wind change.
B— An abrupt decrease in pressure.
C— Clouds, either ahead or behind the front.

Answer (A) is correct (4136). *(AvW Chap 8)*
Whenever a front passes, a wind shift will always occur. This discontinuity may be in direction, speed, or both.
Answer (B) is incorrect because the pressure and/or temperature may not change significantly as a weak front passes. Answer (C) is incorrect because some fronts do not contain enough moisture to produce clouds. Therefore, clouds are not always associated with a frontal system.

13.
4140. Which is a characteristic of low-level wind shear as it relates to frontal activity?

A— With a warm front, the most critical period is before the front passes the airport.
B— With a cold front, the most critical period is just before the front passes the airport.
C— Turbulence will always exist in wind-shear conditions.

Answer (A) is correct (4140). *(PHAK Chap 5)*
Wind shear associated with a warm front occurs above an airport before the front passes the airport. A warm front is warmer air overtaking colder air.
Answer (B) is incorrect because cold front wind shear occurs just as or just after the front passes rather than before it passes. Answer (C) is incorrect because wind shear can sometimes occur with no forewarning from turbulence.

14.
4127. Frontal waves normally form on

A— slow moving cold fronts or stationary fronts.
B— slow moving warm fronts and strong occluded fronts.
C— rapidly moving cold fronts or warm fronts.

Answer (A) is correct (4127). *(AvW Chap 8)*
Frontal waves and cyclones (areas of low pressure) usually form in slow-moving cold fronts or in stationary fronts.
Answer (B) is incorrect because frontal waves are usually not associated with warm fronts or occluded fronts. Answer (C) is incorrect because frontal waves usually form on slow-moving, not rapidly moving, cold fronts and not on warm fronts.

15.
4137. Where do squall lines most often develop?

A— In an occluded front.
B— In a cold air mass.
C— Ahead of a cold front.

Answer (C) is correct (4137). *(AvW Chap 11)*
A squall line is a nonfrontal band of active thunderstorms that sometimes develops ahead of a cold front.
Answer (A) is incorrect because squall lines are usually associated with a fast-moving cold front. Answer (B) is incorrect because they occur ahead of the cold front, not behind the front in the cold air.

8.2 Stability of Air Masses

16.
4128. Which are characteristics of an unstable cold air mass moving over a warm surface?

A— Cumuliform clouds, turbulence, and poor visibility.
B— Cumuliform clouds, turbulence, and good visibility.
C— Stratiform clouds, smooth air, and poor visibility.

Answer (B) is correct (4128). *(AvW Chap 8)*
When a cold air mass moves over a warm surface, the warm air near the surface rises and creates an unstable situation. These convective currents give rise to cumuliform clouds, turbulence, and good visibility.
Answer (A) is incorrect because unstable air lifts and blows haze away, resulting in good, not poor, visibility. Answer (C) is incorrect because unstable conditions produce cumuliform rather than stratiform clouds. Also, the air is turbulent, and visibility is good.

17.
4119. What are the characteristics of stable air?

A— Good visibility, steady precipitation, and stratus-type clouds.
B— Poor visibility, intermittent precipitation, and cumulus-type clouds.
C— Poor visibility, steady precipitation, and stratus-type clouds.

Answer (C) is correct (4119). *(AvW Chap 8)*
Stable air is air which is still or moving horizontally but not vertically. As a result, the pollutants hang in the air and visibility is poor. Also, stable air forms stratus-type clouds since the air is moving in layers. Relatedly, precipitation spreads out over a wide area and is relatively steady.
Answer (A) is incorrect because the visibility is poor rather than good in stable air. Answer (B) is incorrect because the precipitation is steady and the clouds are stratiform.

18.
4118. What type clouds can be expected when an unstable air mass is forced to ascend a mountain slope?

A— Layered clouds with little vertical development.
B— Stratified clouds with considerable associated turbulence.
C— Clouds with extensive vertical development.

Answer (C) is correct (4118). *(AvW Chap 6)*
Unstable air has a greater lapse rate. Because the air above is much colder than the air below, the lower (warmer) air tends to rise very easily. When an unstable air mass is forced to ascend up a mountain slope, it will probably continue to ascend beyond the mountain slope. Once the air expands and cools to the dew point, cumulus clouds will form with considerable vertical development. Any unstable air mass movement will usually result in turbulence as well.
Answer (A) is incorrect because layered clouds are associated with stable air. Answer (B) is incorrect because stratified clouds are associated with stable air and no turbulence.

19.
4117. Which is a characteristic of stable air?

A— Fair weather cumulus clouds.
B— Stratiform clouds.
C— Unlimited visibility.

Answer (B) is correct (4117). *(AvW Chap 8)*
Stratiform clouds, i.e., layer-type clouds, characteristically form in stable air. A stable atmosphere resists any upward or downward displacement, so clouds tend to lie horizontally instead of developing vertically.
Answer (A) is incorrect because cumulus clouds indicate unstable conditions. Answer (C) is incorrect because restricted, not unlimited, visibility near the ground is an indication of stable air.

20.
4116. The general characteristics of unstable air are

A— good visibility, showery precipitation, and cumuliform-type clouds.
B— good visibility, steady precipitation, and stratiform-type clouds.
C— poor visibility, intermittent precipitation, and cumuliform-type clouds.

Answer (A) is correct (4116). *(AvW Chap 8)*
Unstable air is moving vertically and usually produces cumulus clouds. The precipitation from cumulus clouds is showery. The lifting associated with unstable air generally clears smoke and other pollution away; thus visibility is relatively good.
Answer (B) is incorrect because unstable air generally has showery, not steady, precipitation and cumulus, not stratiform, clouds. Answer (C) is incorrect because unstable air generally has good, not poor, visibility.

21.
4115. What type of clouds will be formed if very stable moist air is forced up slope?

A— First stratified clouds and then vertical clouds.
B— Vertical clouds with increasing height.
C— Stratified clouds with little vertical development.

Answer (C) is correct (4115). *(AvW Chap 6)*
Even when being forced up slope, stable air forms stratus-type clouds. This is because the air resists any further upward movement.
Answer (A) is incorrect because there would be vertical clouds if the air were unstable rather than stable. Answer (B) is incorrect because there would be vertical clouds if the air were unstable rather than stable.

22.
4098. Steady precipitation, in contrast to showers, preceding a front is an indication of

A— stratiform clouds with moderate turbulence.
B— cumuliform clouds with little or no turbulence.
C— stratiform clouds with little or no turbulence.

Answer (C) is correct (4098). *(AvW Chap 8)*
Steady precipitation is a characteristic of stable air because of its lack of lifting action. Also characteristic are stratiform clouds with relatively little turbulence.
Answer (A) is incorrect because stable air has little or no turbulence. Answer (B) is incorrect because stratiform rather than cumuliform clouds form in stable air.

23.
4159. What enhances the growth rate of precipitation?

A— Advective action.
B— Upward currents.
C— Cyclonic movement.

24.
4123. Which of the following combinations of weather producing variables would likely result in cumuliform-type clouds, good visibility, rain showers, and possible clear-type icing in clouds?

A— Unstable, moist air, and no lifting mechanism.
B— Stable, dry air, and orographic lifting.
C— Unstable, moist air, and orographic lifting.

25.
4122. What determines the structure or type of clouds which form as a result of air being forced to ascend?

A— The method by which the air is lifted.
B— The stability of the air before lifting occurs.
C— The amount of condensation nuclei present after lifting occurs.

26.
4121. Stability can be determined from which measurement of the atmosphere?

A— Low-level winds.
B— Ambient lapse rate.
C— Atmospheric pressure.

27.
4120. What are some characteristics of unstable air?

A— Nimbostratus clouds and good surface visibility.
B— Turbulence and poor surface visibility.
C— Turbulence and good surface visibility.

Answer (B) is correct (4159). (AvW Chap 5)
The growth rate of precipitation is enhanced by upward currents, which carry moisture particles to cooler levels. The particles grow in size and weight (due to condensation) until the atmosphere can no longer hold them (saturation point) and they fall as precipitation.
Answer (A) is incorrect because advective action usually refers to the horizontal transport of atmospheric properties by wind, such as warm advection (warm land air moving out over colder water). Answer (C) is incorrect because cyclonic movement refers to the counterclockwise movement around a low-pressure area.

Answer (C) is correct (4123). (AvW Chap 6)
Cumuliform clouds, good visibility, and showery rain are produced as unstable, moist air is lifted into higher, cooler regions. When the lifting is the result of movement over terrain (e.g., up a mountain slope), it is called orographic lifting. Clear icing is formed from large drops such as those found in cumuliform clouds.
Answer (A) is incorrect because, without a lifting mechanism, there would be no vertical development of clouds to result in showery rain and icing in clouds. Answer (B) is incorrect because stable conditions result in stratiform rather than cumuliform clouds, and dry air does not result in showery rain or icing even when lifted.

Answer (B) is correct (4122). (AvW Chap 6)
The structure of clouds is determined by the stability of the air before it is lifted. If unstable, the clouds will have vertical development. If stable, the clouds will be horizontal, i.e., stratiform.
Answer (A) is incorrect because the stability of the air, not the lifting mechanism, determines the type of cloud formations. Answer (C) is incorrect because condensation nuclei encourage the formation of rain droplets or ice but have no effect on the type of cloud formations.

Answer (B) is correct (4121). (AvW Chap 6)
The ambient lapse rate is the actual rate of decrease in temperature with height. A great decrease in temperature as altitude increases encourages warm air from below to rise and creates an unstable air mass. Lifting is inhibited by lesser or very small temperature decreases with altitude (i.e., a low lapse rate).
Answer (A) is incorrect because stability refers to vertical air movement, not horizontal air movement. Answer (C) is incorrect because atmospheric pressure is a measure of the weight or downward force of air and does not affect air stability.

Answer (C) is correct (4120). (AvW Chap 8)
The lifting tendency of unstable air creates turbulence and clears the surface air of clouds, dust, and other pollution.
Answer (A) is incorrect because stratus clouds are characteristic of stable, not unstable, air. Answer (B) is incorrect because poor surface visibility is a characteristic of stable, not unstable, air.

28.
4124. Unsaturated air flowing up slope will cool at the rate of approximately (dry adiabatic lapse rate)

A— 3 °C per 1,000 feet.
B— 2 °C per 1,000 feet.
C— 2.5 °C per 1,000 feet.

Answer (A) is correct (4124). *(AvW Chap 6)*
    The dry adiabatic lapse rate signifies a prescribed rate of expansional cooling or compressional heating. The dry adiabatic rate is 3°C for each 1,000 ft. Note that this rate differs from the average normal lapse rate of 2°C for each 1,000 ft. of altitude. The average lapse rate does NOT occur in dry air, but rather in air with "average" humidity.
    Answer (B) is incorrect because 2°C per 1,000 ft. is the standard lapse rate in stable air. Answer (C) is incorrect because 2.5°C per 1,000 ft. is the rate at which the temperature and dew point converge in a convective current of unsaturated air.

8.3 Temperature Inversions

29.
4114. What feature is associated with a temperature inversion?

A— A stable layer of air.
B— An unstable layer of air.
C— Air mass thunderstorms.

Answer (A) is correct (4114). *(AvW Chaps 2 and 6)*
    A temperature inversion is defined as an increase in temperature with height; i.e., the lapse rate is less than standard. The cooler air stays near the surface, and there is little or no vertical movement.
    Answer (B) is incorrect because instability occurs when the temperature decreases, not increases as in a temperature inversion, with an increase in height, and the warmer air continues to rise. Answer (C) is incorrect because air mass thunderstorms result from instability. They do not occur when there is a temperature inversion.

30.
4200. Which weather conditions should be expected beneath a low-level temperature inversion layer when the relative humidity is high?

A— Smooth air and poor visibility due to fog, haze, or low clouds.
B— Light wind shear and poor visibility due to haze and light rain.
C— Turbulent air and poor visibility due to fog, low stratus-type clouds, and showery precipitation.

Answer (A) is correct (4200). *(AvW Chap 2)*
    A temperature inversion is an increase in temperature as altitude increases; normally temperature decreases with increases in altitude. In an inversion, warm air rises to its own temperature and forms a stable layer of air. A low-level inversion results in poor visibility by trapping fog, smoke, dust, etc., in low levels of the atmosphere.
    Answer (B) is incorrect because wind shear may be expected within, not beneath, a low-level temperature inversion. Answer (C) is incorrect because an inversion forms a stable layer of air, thus making it smooth, not turbulent, and causing steady, not showery, precipitation.

31.
4125. A temperature inversion will normally form only

A— in stable air.
B— in unstable air.
C— when a stratiform layer merges with a cumuliform mass.

Answer (A) is correct (4125). *(AvW Chap 2)*
    In a temperature inversion, warm air overlies colder air; i.e., the lapse rate is inverted. By definition, this is a stable condition since there is no lifting action.
    Answer (B) is incorrect because unstable air has colder air above warm air. Answer (C) is incorrect because a merger of stratus and cumulus clouds is associated with an occluded front, not necessarily a temperature inversion.

32.
4094. A common type of ground or surface based temperature inversion is that which is produced by

A— warm air being lifted rapidly aloft in the vicinity of mountainous terrain.
B— the movement of colder air over warm air, or the movement of warm air under cold air.
C— ground radiation on clear, cool nights when the wind is light.

Answer (C) is correct (4094). *(AvW Chap 2)*
    A temperature inversion means the temperature becomes warmer rather than cooler with increases in altitude. A ground- or surface-based temperature inversion is produced when the air near the surface is cooled faster than the overlying air as a result of radiation of heat on a clear, still night. The air very close to the surface is thus cooler than the air a few hundred feet above.
    Answer (A) is incorrect because, when warm air is lifted, unstable, not stable, air is the result. Answer (B) is incorrect because a temperature inversion consists of warm air over colder air, not colder over warm.

8.4 Temperature, Dew Point, and Fog

33.
4169. Which conditions are favorable for the formation of radiation fog?

A— Moist air moving over colder ground or water.
B— Cloudy sky and a light wind moving saturated warm air over a cool surface.
C— Clear sky, little or no wind, small temperature/dew point spread, and over a land surface.

Answer (C) is correct (4169). (AvW Chap 12)
Conditions favorable for radiation fog are a clear sky, little or no wind, and a small temperature-dew point spread. The fog forms as terrestrial radiation cools the ground. The air near the ground is cooled to dew point, and fog forms.
Answer (A) is incorrect because advection fog, not radiation fog, forms when moist air moves over colder ground or water. The sky may be cloudy over advection fog. Answer (B) is incorrect because advection fog, not radiation fog, forms when moist air moves over colder ground or water. The sky may be cloudy over advection fog.

34.
4167. What situation is most conducive to the formation of radiation fog?

A— Warm, moist air over low, flatland areas on clear, calm nights.
B— Moist, tropical air moving over cold, offshore water.
C— The movement of cold air over much warmer water.

Answer (A) is correct (4167). (AvW Chap 12)
Conditions favorable for radiation fog are a clear sky, little or no wind, and a small temperature-dew point spread. The fog forms as terrestrial radiation cools the ground. The air close to the surface cools more quickly than the slightly higher air. The air near the ground is cooled to dew point, and fog forms.
Answer (B) is incorrect because advection fog forms as a result of warm air moving over a colder surface. Answer (C) is incorrect because steam fog forms when cold air moves over a warmer surface.

35.
4112. The most frequent type of ground- or surface-based temperature inversion is that produced by

A— radiation on a clear, relatively still night.
B— warm air being lifted rapidly aloft in the vicinity of mountainous terrain.
C— the movement of colder air under warm air, or the movement of warm air over cold air.

Answer (A) is correct (4112). (AvW Chap 2)
An inversion often develops near the ground on clear, cool nights when the wind is light. The ground radiates heat and cools much faster than the overlying air. Air in contact with the ground becomes cold, while the temperature a few hundred feet above changes very little. Thus temperature increases with height.
Answer (B) is incorrect because it describes orographic lifting. Answer (C) is incorrect because it describes a cold front and a warm front, respectively.

36.
4166. What types of fog depend upon a wind in order to exist?

A— Steam fog and down slope fog.
B— Precipitation-induced fog and ground fog.
C— Advection fog and up slope fog.

Answer (C) is correct (4166). (AvW Chap 12)
Up slope fog forms as a result of moist, stable air being cooled as it moves up a sloping terrain. Advection fog forms when moist air is blown over a cold surface, decreasing the moist air's temperature to its dew point. Thus, both up slope fog and advection fog depend on air moving from one area to another; i.e., they depend on wind.
Answer (A) is incorrect because down slope fog is a nonsense term. Answer (B) is incorrect because precipitation fog forms when warm rain or drizzle falls through cool air, and ground fog requires little or no wind.

37.
4165. In what localities is advection fog most likely to occur?

A— Coastal areas.
B— Mountain slopes.
C— Level inland areas.

Answer (A) is correct (4165). (AvW Chap 12)
Advection fog forms when moist air moves over colder ground or water. This type of fog is thus most common along coastal areas. During the winter, advection fog over the central and eastern United States results when moist air from the Gulf of Mexico spreads northward over cold ground.
Answer (B) is incorrect because mountain slopes are required for upslope, not advection, fog. Answer (C) is incorrect because level inland areas will most likely produce radiation, not advection, fog.

38.
4164. In which situation is advection fog most likely to form?

A— An air mass moving inland from the coast in winter.
B— A light breeze blowing colder air out to sea.
C— Warm, moist air settling over a warmer surface under no-wind conditions.

39.
4163. Fog is usually prevalent in industrial areas because of

A— atmospheric stabilization around cities.
B— an abundance of condensation nuclei from combustion products.
C— increased temperatures due to industrial heating.

40.
4162. Which weather condition can be expected when moist air flows from a relatively warm surface to a colder surface?

A— Increased visibility.
B— Convective turbulence due to surface heating.
C— Fog.

41.
4156. Under which condition does advection fog usually form?

A— Moist air moving over colder ground or water.
B— Warm, moist air settling over a cool surface under no-wind conditions.
C— A land breeze blowing a cold air mass over a warm water current.

42.
4103. The amount of water vapor which air can hold largely depends on

A— relative humidity.
B— air temperature.
C— stability of air.

43.
4104. Clouds, fog, or dew will always form when

A— water vapor condenses.
B— water vapor is present.
C— the temperature and dew point are equal.

Answer (A) is correct (4164). *(AvW Chap 12)*
Advection fog forms when moist air moves over colder ground or water. This type of fog is most likely to form when an air mass moves from the warmer water inland from the coast in winter. As the air moves over the cooler land, it cools to the dew point and forms advection fog.
Answer (B) is incorrect because colder air blowing out to sea results in steam, not advection, fog. Answer (C) is incorrect because warm, moist air settling over a warmer surface would not cool, so fog would not form.

Answer (B) is correct (4163). *(AvW Chap 12)*
Fog often forms in industrial areas because the combustion products leave dust in the air on which water can condense. These particles are called condensation nuclei.
Answer (A) is incorrect because cities, *per se*, have no effect on air stability. Answer (C) is incorrect because the amount of heat that factories release into the air is not significant in the formation of fog.

Answer (C) is correct (4162). *(AvW Chap 12)*
When moist air flows from a relatively warm surface to a colder surface, the warm, moist air is cooled to its dew point, and advection fog is produced.
Answer (A) is incorrect because fog forms, which decreases, not increases, visibility. Answer (B) is incorrect because the surface cools the air, resulting in stable air with little or no convective turbulence.

Answer (A) is correct (4156). *(AvW Chap 12)*
Advection fog forms when moist air moves over colder ground or water. The moist air is cooled to the dew point, and fog forms.
Answer (B) is incorrect because radiation fog, not advection fog, forms when warm, moist air settles over a cool surface under no-wind conditions. Answer (C) is incorrect because steam fog, not advection fog, forms when a land breeze blows a cold air mass over a warm water current.

Answer (B) is correct (4103). *(AvW Chap 5)*
Air temperature largely determines how much water vapor can be held by the air. Warm air, which is less dense, can hold more water vapor than cold air.
Answer (A) is incorrect because relative humidity is the ratio of the existing amount of water vapor in the air at a given temperature to the maximum amount that could be held at that temperature. Answer (C) is incorrect because air stability is related to the temperature lapse rate, not moisture.

Answer (A) is correct (4104). *(AvW Chap 5)*
As water vapor condenses, it becomes visible as clouds, fog, or dew.
Answer (B) is incorrect because some water vapor is usually present, but it does not necessarily form clouds, fog, or dew. Answer (C) is incorrect because, even at 100% humidity (when the dew point equals actual temperature), water vapor may not condense if sufficient condensation nuclei are not present.

44.
4101. To which meteorological condition does the term "dew point" refer?

A— The temperature to which air must be cooled to become saturated.
B— The temperature at which condensation and evaporation are equal.
C— The temperature at which dew will always form.

Answer (A) is correct (4101). *(AvW Chap 5)*
Dew point refers to the temperature to which air must be cooled to become saturated by the water vapor in the air. Dew point, when related to air temperature in aviation weather reports, reveals how close the air is to saturation and possible cloud, fog, or precipitation formation.
Answer (B) is incorrect because condensation (vapor to water) occurs at low temperatures, and evaporation (water to vapor) occurs at high temperatures. Answer (C) is incorrect because the formation of dew depends on relative humidity and the temperature of the collecting surface.

45.
4100. Which conditions result in the formation of frost?

A— The temperature of the collecting surface is at or below freezing and small droplets of moisture are falling.
B— When dew forms and the temperature is below freezing.
C— Temperature of the collecting surface is below the dewpoint of surrounding air and the dewpoint is colder than freezing.

Answer (C) is correct (4100). *(AvW Chap 5)*
If the air temperature drops below the dew point, the air becomes more dense and can no longer hold the water vapor. The water vapor will condense to form visible moisture. Frost will form only if the temperature of the collecting surfaces is below the dew point of the surrounding air AND the dew point is below freezing.
Answer (A) is incorrect because the dew point must also be below freezing and droplets of moisture are not necessary. Answer (B) is incorrect because the formation of dew is not required. The dew point of surrounding air must be below freezing, and the temperature of the collecting surface must be less than the dew point.

8.5 Clouds

46.
4134. What are the four families of clouds?

A— Stratus, cumulus, nimbus, and cirrus.
B— Clouds formed by updrafts, fronts, cooling layers of air, and precipitation into warm air.
C— High, middle, low, and those with extensive vertical development.

Answer (C) is correct (4134). *(AvW Chap 7)*
For identification purposes, clouds are divided into four "families" based on their height range. The families are high clouds, middle clouds, low clouds, and clouds with extensive vertical development.
Answer (A) is incorrect because it describes cloud formation and characteristic. Answer (B) is incorrect because it describes the way various clouds are formed.

47.
4133. Which family of clouds is least likely to contribute to structural icing on an aircraft?

A— Low clouds.
B— High clouds.
C— Clouds with extensive vertical development.

Answer (B) is correct (4133). *(AvW Chaps 7, 10)*
High clouds are least likely to contribute to structural icing since they usually consist entirely of ice crystals. Since ice is already frozen, it will not freeze onto the structural surface of the airplane.
Answer (A) is incorrect because low clouds can contain supercooled water, which freezes on contact with the airplane. Answer (C) is incorrect because clouds with extensive vertical development can contain supercooled water, which freezes on contact with the airplane.

48.
4132. The presence of standing lenticular altocumulus clouds is a good indication of

A— a jetstream.
B— very strong turbulence.
C— heavy icing conditions.

Answer (B) is correct (4132). *(AvW Chaps 7, 9)*
When stable air crosses a mountain barrier, it tends to flow in layers. The barrier may set up waves in these layers, which remain stationary while the wind blows rapidly through them. Wave crests extend well above the highest mountain tops. Under each wave crest is a rotary circulation, which can create very violent turbulence. Crests of the standing waves may be marked by stationary lens-shaped clouds known as standing lenticular clouds.
Answer (A) is incorrect because the jet stream flows around the world at high altitudes and at varying latitudes. Answer (C) is incorrect because standing lenticular clouds occur at varying temperatures, not only below freezing.

49.
4131. The suffix "nimbus", used in naming clouds, means a

A— cloud with extensive vertical development.
B— rain cloud.
C— dark massive, towering cloud.

Answer (B) is correct (4131). *(AvW Chap 7)*
The prefix "nimbo" or the suffix "nimbus" means rain-cloud. For example, stratified clouds from which rain is falling are called nimbostratus clouds. A heavy, swelling, cumulus-type cloud which produces precipitation is called a cumulonimbus cloud.
Answer (A) is incorrect because "cumulo," not "nimbus," denotes a cloud with extensive vertical development. Answer (C) is incorrect because it specifies a cumulonimbus cloud, not any nimbus cloud.

50.
4130. Standing lenticular clouds, in mountainous areas, indicate

A— an inversion.
B— unstable air.
C— turbulence.

Answer (C) is correct (4130). *(AvW Chaps 7, 9)*
The "waves" generated as wind flows across a mountain barrier may form standing lenticular clouds at the crest of each wave. Their presence indicates very strong turbulence, and they should be avoided.
Answer (A) is incorrect because stratus, not standing lenticular, clouds indicate stable air which may be the result of a temperature inversion. Answer (B) is incorrect because cumulus, not standing lenticular, clouds indicate unstable air.

51.
4129. Which clouds have the greatest turbulence?

A— Towering cumulus.
B— Cumulonimbus.
C— Altocumulus castellanus.

Answer (B) is correct (4129). *(AvW Chap 7)*
Cumulonimbus clouds are thunderstorms and the ultimate manifestation of instability. They are huge vertically developed clouds with dense, billowy tops often crowned with thick veils of dense cirrus, called the "anvil." Nearly the entire spectrum of flying hazards is contained in these clouds, including violent turbulence.
Answer (A) is incorrect because towering cumulus clouds are only a preliminary stage of the cumulonimbus cloud. Answer (C) is incorrect because altocumulus castellanus is a middle-level convective cloud which indicates rough turbulence with some icing, but thunderstorms are far more turbulent.

52.
4157. A high cloud is composed mostly of

A— ozone.
B— condensation nuclei.
C— ice crystals.

Answer (C) is correct (4157). *(AvW Chap 7)*
The high cloud family is cirriform. It includes cirrus, cirrocumulus, and cirrostratus clouds. They are composed almost entirely of ice crystals. Their bases range from 16,500 ft. to 45,000 ft.
Answer (A) is incorrect because ozone is an unstable form of oxygen. The heaviest concentrations are in the stratosphere, not in clouds. Answer (B) is incorrect because condensation nuclei are the small particles in the air onto which water vapor condenses or sublimates.

53.
4149. Fair weather cumulus clouds often indicate

A— turbulence at and below the cloud level.
B— poor visibility.
C— smooth flying conditions.

Answer (A) is correct (4149). *(AvW Chap 7)*
Fair weather cumulus clouds form in convective currents and are characterized by relatively flat bases and dome-shaped tops. They indicate a shallow layer of instability, some turbulence, and no significant icing.
Answer (B) is incorrect because the instability producing the cumulus clouds provides good, not poor, visibility. Answer (C) is incorrect because the instability producing the cumulus clouds creates some turbulence, not smooth conditions.

8.6 Thunderstorms

54.
4148. What are the requirements for the formation of a thunderstorm?

A— A cumulus cloud with sufficient moisture.
B— A cumulus cloud with sufficient moisture and an inverted lapse rate.
C— Sufficient moisture, an unstable lapse rate, and a lifting action.

Answer (C) is correct (4148). *(AvW Chap 11)*
For a thunderstorm to form, the air must have sufficient water vapor, an unstable lapse rate, and an initial upward lifting action to start the storm process in motion. Surface heating, converging winds, sloping terrain, a frontal surface, or any combination of these can provide the lift.
Answer (A) is incorrect because a lifting action is also required for formation of a thunderstorm. Answer (B) is incorrect because a lifting action and an unstable, not inverted, lapse rate are required for the formation of a thunderstorm.

55.
4147. What is an indication that downdrafts have developed and the thunderstorm cell has entered the mature stage?

A— The anvil top has completed its development.
B— Precipitation begins to fall from the cloud base.
C— A gust front forms.

Answer (B) is correct (4147). *(AvW Chap 11)*
The mature stage of a thunderstorm is signaled when rain begins falling at the surface. This means that the downdrafts have developed sufficiently to carry water all the way through the thunderstorm.
Answer (A) is incorrect because an anvil top does not necessarily develop over every thunderstorm. Answer (C) is incorrect because gust front is a nonsense term.

56.
4146. Which procedure is recommended if a pilot should unintentionally penetrate embedded thunderstorm activity?

A— Reverse aircraft heading or proceed toward an area of known VFR conditions.
B— Reduce airspeed to maneuvering speed and maintain a constant altitude.
C— Set power for recommended turbulence penetration airspeed and attempt to maintain a level flight attitude.

Answer (C) is correct (4146). *(AvW Chap 11)*
If a thunderstorm is penetrated, you should always attempt to maintain a constant attitude at or below the maneuvering or turbulence penetration speed recommended for the airplane. Note that the airspeed cannot always be kept constant, but the power can be set so that you will be operating generally at or below the maneuvering speed.
Answer (A) is incorrect because a straight course will probably take you out of the storm most quickly. Also, turning maneuvers increase stresses on the aircraft. Answer (B) is incorrect because maintaining a constant airspeed (V_A) in updrafts and downdrafts may be impossible. It is best to set power so you will operate at or below V_A. Also, attempting to maintain constant altitude, not attitude, increases the stress on the airplane.

57.
4145. Which thunderstorms generally produce the most severe conditions, such as heavy hail and destructive winds?

A— Warm front.
B— Squall line.
C— Air mass.

Answer (B) is correct (4145). *(AvW Chap 11)*
A squall line is a nonfrontal narrow band of active thunderstorms. It often contains severe, steady-state thunderstorms and presents the single most intense weather hazard to airplanes.
Answer (A) is incorrect because warm fronts indicate stable air, which does not usually produce thunderstorms. Answer (C) is incorrect because an air mass thunderstorm is the least severe type of thunderstorm.

58.
4144. Which weather phenomenon is always associated with a thunderstorm?

A— Lightning.
B— Heavy rain showers.
C— Supercooled raindrops.

Answer (A) is correct (4144). *(AvW Chap 11)*
A thunderstorm, by definition, has lightning, because lightning causes the thunder. Lightning is the discharge of electricity generated by thunderstorms.
Answer (B) is incorrect because hail may occur instead of heavy rain showers. Answer (C) is incorrect because supercooled raindrops may not occur if the lifting process does not extend above the freezing level.

59.
4143. During the life cycle of a thunderstorm, which stage is characterized predominately by downdrafts?

A— Cumulus.
B— Dissipating.
C— Mature.

60.
4142. If squalls are reported at your destination, what wind conditions should you anticipate?

A— Sudden increases in wind speed of at least 16 knots rising to 22 knots or more, lasting for at least 1 minute.
B— Peak gusts of at least 35 knots for a sustained period of 1 minute or longer.
C— Rapid variation in wind direction of at least 20° and changes in speed of at least 10 knots between peaks and lulls.

61.
4141. What is indicated by the term "embedded thunderstorms"?

A— Severe thunderstorms are embedded within a squall line.
B— Thunderstorms are predicted to develop in a stable air mass.
C— Thunderstorms are obscured by massive cloud layers and cannot be seen.

62.
4126. Which weather phenomenon signals the beginning of the mature stage of a thunderstorm?

A— The start of rain at the surface.
B— Growth rate of cloud is maximum.
C— Strong turbulence in the cloud.

63.
4092. Which is true regarding the use of airborne weather-avoidance radar for the recognition of certain weather conditions?

A— The radarscope provides no assurance of avoiding instrument weather conditions.
B— The avoidance of hail is assured when flying between and just clear of the most intense echoes.
C— The clear area between intense echoes indicates that visual sighting of storms can be maintained when flying between the echoes.

Answer (B) is correct (4143). *(AvW Chap 11)*
Thunderstorms have three stages in their life cycle: cumulus, mature, and dissipating. In the dissipating stage, the storm is characterized by downdrafts as the storm rains itself out.
Answer (A) is incorrect because the cumulus stage is the building stage characterized by updrafts. Answer (C) is incorrect because the mature stage has both updrafts and downdrafts, which create strong wind shears.

Answer (A) is correct (4142). *(AvW Glossary)*
A squall is a sudden increase in wind speed by at least 16 kt. rising to 22 kt. or more and lasting for at least 1 min. In contrast, a wind gust is a brief increase in wind with a variation between peaks and lulls of at least 10 kt. Note that these definitions involve variations in wind speed, not wind direction.
Answer (B) is incorrect because a squall is a sudden increase in wind speed of at least 16 kt., rising to a peak of 22 kt. or more, not a peak gust of at least 35 kt. lasting for at least 1 min. Answer (C) is incorrect because squalls refer to changes in wind speed, not direction. Additionally, the wind is reported as gusty when there are changes in speed of at least 10 kt. between peaks and lulls.

Answer (C) is correct (4141). *(AvW Chap 11)*
The term "embedded thunderstorms" means that the storms are embedded in clouds or thick haze layers and cannot be seen.
Answer (A) is incorrect because a squall line consists of severe thunderstorms which can usually be seen. Answer (B) is incorrect because thunderstorms do not usually occur in stable air masses.

Answer (A) is correct (4126). *(AvW Chap 11)*
The mature stage of a thunderstorm is indicated when rain begins falling at the surface. This means that downdrafts have developed sufficiently to carry water all the way through the thunderstorm.
Answer (B) is incorrect because maximum growth rate occurs in the first or cumulus stage. Answer (C) is incorrect because strong turbulence can occur in all stages.

Answer (A) is correct (4092). *(AvW Chap 11)*
Weather-avoidance radar provides information on precipitation based on echo returns. Avoiding the heaviest areas of precipitation will often (not always) keep you out of the greatest turbulence. Radar does not show water vapor. Thus, clouds and fog, i.e., instrument weather conditions, are not indicated.
Answer (B) is incorrect because intense thunderstorms can often hurl hail for miles. Answer (C) is incorrect because visual sighting of storms is not assured, because clouds and fog are not shown by radar.

8.7 Icing

64.
4152. In which meteorological environment is aircraft structural icing most likely to have the highest rate of accumulation?

A— Cumulonimbus clouds.
B— High humidity and freezing temperature.
C— Freezing rain.

65.
4171. Test data indicate that ice, snow, or frost having a thickness and roughness similar to medium or coarse sandpaper on the leading edge and upper surface of an airfoil can

A— reduce lift by as much as 50 percent and increase drag by as much as 50 percent.
B— increase drag and reduce lift by as much as 25 percent.
C— reduce lift by as much as 30 percent and increase drag by 40 percent.

66.
4161. Which precipitation type normally indicates freezing rain at higher altitudes?

A— Snow.
B— Hail.
C— Ice pellets.

67.
4153. What is an operational consideration if you fly into rain which freezes on impact?

A— You have flown into an area of thunderstorms.
B— Temperatures are above freezing at some higher altitude.
C— You have flown through a cold front.

68.
4102. What temperature condition is indicated if wet snow is encountered at your flight altitude?

A— The temperature is above freezing at your altitude.
B— The temperature is below freezing at your altitude.
C— You are flying from a warm air mass into a cold air mass.

Answer (C) is correct (4152). *(AvW Chap 10)*
The condition most favorable for very hazardous icing is the presence of many large, supercooled water drops (i.e., freezing rain). The heaviest icing will usually be found at altitudes at or slightly above the freezing level where the temperature is never more than a few degrees below freezing.
Answer (A) is incorrect because icing does not necessarily occur in thunderstorms due to the large variation in temperature in thunderstorms. Answer (B) is incorrect because visible moisture, not just high humidity, must be present for icing.

Answer (C) is correct (4171). *(AC 120-58)*
Test data indicate that ice, snow, or frost formations having a thickness and surface roughness similar to medium or coarse sandpaper on the leading edge and upper surface of an airfoil can reduce lift by as much as 30% and increase drag by 40%. These changes in lift and drag significantly increase stall speed, reduce controllability, and alter aircraft flight characteristics.
Answer (A) is incorrect because ice, snow, or frost having a thickness or roughness similar to medium or coarse sandpaper on the leading edge and upper surface of an airfoil can reduce lift by as much as 30%, not 50%, and increase drag by 40%, not 50%. Answer (B) is incorrect because ice, snow, or frost having a thickness or roughness similar to medium or coarse sandpaper on the leading edge and upper surface of an airfoil can reduce lift by as much as 30%, not 25%, and increase drag by 40%, not 25%.

Answer (C) is correct (4161). *(AvW Chap 5)*
Ice pellets normally indicate that rain droplets are freezing at a higher altitude. Warmer air above exists from which rain is falling and freezing on the way down, as it enters cooler air (i.e., freezing rain exists above).
Answer (A) is incorrect because snow indicates that the temperature of the air above you is well below freezing. Answer (B) is incorrect because hail indicates instability of the air aloft where supercooled droplets above the freezing level begin to freeze. Once a drop has frozen, other drops latch onto it, and the hailstone grows.

Answer (B) is correct (4153). *(AvW Chap 10)*
Rain which freezes on impact is called freezing rain. If rain falls through freezing air, it will usually form supercooled water droplets, i.e., freezing rain. It indicates that temperatures somewhere above the airplane are above freezing.
Answer (A) is incorrect because freezing rain does not necessarily indicate the presence of thunderstorms. Answer (C) is incorrect because freezing rain does not necessarily indicate the presence of cold fronts.

Answer (A) is correct (4102). *(AvW Chap 5)*
If snow is wet at your altitude, you are in above-freezing temperatures because the snow has started to melt.
Answer (B) is incorrect because the wet snow indicates the temperature is above freezing, not below freezing, at your altitude. Answer (C) is incorrect because the temperature is lower above you, but not necessarily in front of you.

69.
4099. The presence of ice pellets at the surface is evidence that

A— there are thunderstorms in the area.
B— a cold front has passed.
C— there is freezing rain at a higher altitude.

Answer (C) is correct (4099). *(AvW Chap 5)*
Ice pellets form as a result of rain freezing at a higher altitude. Rain droplets cool as they fall from a warmer layer through air with a temperature below freezing.
Answer (A) is incorrect because thunderstorms do not necessarily cause ice pellets. Answer (B) is incorrect because cold fronts do not necessarily cause ice pellets.

70.
4151. Why is frost considered hazardous to flight operation?

A— Frost changes the basic aerodynamic shape of the airfoil.
B— Frost decreases control effectiveness.
C— Frost causes early airflow separation resulting in a loss of lift.

Answer (C) is correct (4151). *(AvW Chap 10)*
Frost spoils the smooth flow of air, thus causing a slowing of the airflow. This causes early airflow separation over the affected airfoil, resulting in a loss of lift. A heavy coat of hard frost will cause a 5 to 10% increase in stall speed. Even a small amount of frost on airfoils may prevent an aircraft from becoming airborne at normal takeoff speed.
Answer (A) is incorrect because frost is very thin. It does not change the airfoil shape as structural icing does. Answer (B) is incorrect because frost has no bearing on control effectiveness, only airfoil lift.

71.
4113. If the air temperature is +8 °C at an elevation of 1,350 feet and a standard (average) temperature lapse rate exists, what will be the approximate freezing level?

A— 3,350 feet MSL.
B— 5,350 feet MSL.
C— 9,350 feet MSL.

Answer (B) is correct (4113). *(AvW Chap 2)*
The decrease of temperature with altitude is defined as the lapse rate. The standard lapse rate is 2°C per 1,000 ft. To reach the freezing level, you must have a drop of 8°C. Thus the freezing level is 4,000 ft. (8/2 x 1,000 ft.) up, or 5,350 ft. MSL (1,350 + 4,000).
Answer (A) is incorrect because it represents a standard lapse rate of 4° per 1,000 ft. Answer (C) is incorrect because it represents a standard lapse rate of 1° per 1,000 ft.

8.8 Wind Shear

72.
4150. What is an important characteristic of wind shear?

A— It is an atmospheric condition that is associated exclusively with zones of convergence.
B— The Coriolis phenomenon in both high- and low-level air masses is the principal generating force.
C— It is an atmospheric condition that may be associated with a low-level temperature inversion, a jet stream, or a frontal zone.

Answer (C) is correct (4150). *(AvW Chap 9)*
Wind shear can occur at any level where winds are blowing in different directions or at different speeds. It is an atmospheric condition associated with low-level temperature inversions, the jet stream, or a frontal zone.
Answer (A) is incorrect because zones of convergence are low-pressure areas. Wind shear can occur in highs as well as lows. Answer (B) is incorrect because the Coriolis force is the deflective force of the Earth's rotation which affects all wind flows, not just wind shear.

73.
4210. A pilot reporting turbulence that momentarily causes slight, erratic changes in altitude and/or attitude should report it as

A— light turbulence.
B— moderate turbulence.
C— light chop.

Answer (A) is correct (4210). *(AWS Sect 14)*
Light turbulence is defined as a disturbed air flow that momentarily causes slight erratic changes in altitude and/or attitude.
Answer (B) is incorrect because moderate turbulence is more intense. It is sufficient to cause changes in altitude, but the pilot maintains control throughout. Answer (C) is incorrect because light chop means slight or moderate, rapid, and somewhat rhythmic bumpiness without appreciable changes in altitude or attitude.

74.
4139. What is an important characteristic of wind shear?

A— It is primarily associated with the lateral vortices generated by thunderstorms.
B— It usually exists only in the vicinity of thunderstorms, but may be found near a strong temperature inversion.
C— It may be associated with either a wind shift or a wind speed gradient at any level in the atmosphere.

75.
4135. Where can wind shear associated with a thunderstorm be found? Choose the most complete answer.

A— In front of the thunderstorm cell (anvil side) and on the right side of the cell.
B— In front of the thunderstorm cell and directly under the cell.
C— On all sides of the thunderstorm cell and directly under the cell.

76.
4138. Where does wind shear occur?

A— Exclusively in thunderstorms.
B— Wherever there is an abrupt decrease in pressure and/or temperature.
C— With either a wind shift or a wind speed gradient at any level in the atmosphere.

77.
4238. Hazardous wind shear is commonly encountered near the ground

A— during periods when the wind velocity is stronger than 35 knots.
B— during periods when the wind velocity is stronger than 35 knots and near mountain valleys.
C— during periods of strong temperature inversion and near thunderstorms.

8.9 Microbursts

78.
4253. An aircraft that encounters a headwind of 45 knots, within a microburst, may expect a total shear across the microburst of

A— 40 knots.
B— 80 knots.
C— 90 knots.

Answer (C) is correct (4139). *(AvW Chap 9)*
Wind shear can occur at any level where winds are blowing in different directions or at different speeds.
Answer (A) is incorrect because wind shear is found in conditions other than thunderstorm turbulence, e.g., mountain waves, fronts, etc. Answer (B) is incorrect because wind shear is found in conditions other than thunderstorm turbulence, e.g., mountain waves, fronts, etc.

Answer (C) is correct (4135). *(AvW Chap 11)*
Wind shear associated with thunderstorms may be found on all sides of the thunderstorm cell, including directly beneath it and as much as 20 mi. laterally.
Answer (A) is incorrect because wind shear may be found on all sides and beneath the thunderstorm cell. Answer (B) is incorrect because wind shear may be found on all sides and beneath the thunderstorm cell.

Answer (C) is correct (4138). *(AvW Chap 9)*
Wind shear can occur at any level where winds are blowing in different directions (wind shift) or at different speeds (a wind speed gradient).
Answer (A) is incorrect because wind shear is also caused by barriers to wind flow, occurs behind and below airplanes generating lift, etc. Answer (B) is incorrect because wind shear is the result of wind change, not a change in temperature or pressure, *per se*.

Answer (C) is correct (4238). *(AvW Chap 9)*
Thunderstorms produce hazardous wind shear near the ground. Wind shear during temperature inversions is also hazardous when at low levels as it affects aircraft approaching and departing airports.
Answer (A) is incorrect because any wind, not only wind shear, is hazardous when in excess of 35 kt. Answer (B) is incorrect because wind shear usually occurs on the leeward side of mountains, not in valleys.

Answer (C) is correct (4253). *(AIM Para 7-1-23)*
If a headwind in a microburst is 45 kt., the wind will be going in the opposite direction on the other side of the microburst at presumably the same 45 kt., resulting in a wind shear between the headwind and tailwind of 90 kt.
Answer (A) is incorrect because the total wind shear expected across a microburst is twice the initial headwind, e.g., 45 kt. x 2 = 90 kt., not 40 kt. Answer (B) is incorrect because the total wind shear expected across a microburst is twice the initial headwind, e.g., 45 kt. x 2 = 90 kt., not 80 kt.

79.
4252. Maximum downdrafts in a microburst encounter may be as strong as

A— 8,000 feet per minute.
B— 7,000 feet per minute.
C— 6,000 feet per minute.

Answer (C) is correct (4252). *(AIM Para 7-1-23)*
Downdrafts in a microburst can be as strong as 6,000 FPM. Horizontal winds near the surface can be as strong as 45 kt., resulting in a 90-kt. wind shear. The strong horizontal winds occur within a few hundred feet of the ground.
Answer (A) is incorrect because maximum downdrafts are usually 6,000 FPM, not 8,000 FPM. Answer (B) is incorrect because maximum downdrafts are usually 6,000 FPM, not 7,000 FPM.

80.
4251. What is the expected duration of an individual microburst?

A— Two minutes with maximum winds lasting approximately 1 minute.
B— One microburst may continue for as long as 2 to 4 hours.
C— Seldom longer than 15 minutes from the time the burst strikes the ground until dissipation.

Answer (C) is correct (4251). *(AIM Para 7-1-23)*
An individual microburst will seldom last longer than 15 min. from the time it strikes ground until dissipation. The horizontal winds continue to increase during the first 5 min. with maximum-intensity winds lasting approximately 2 to 4 min.
Answer (A) is incorrect because microbursts last 15, not 2 min., and maximum winds last 2 to 4 min., not 1 min. Answer (B) is incorrect because the maximum winds last 2 to 4 min., not 2 to 4 hr., and the microburst is usually limited to about 15 min.

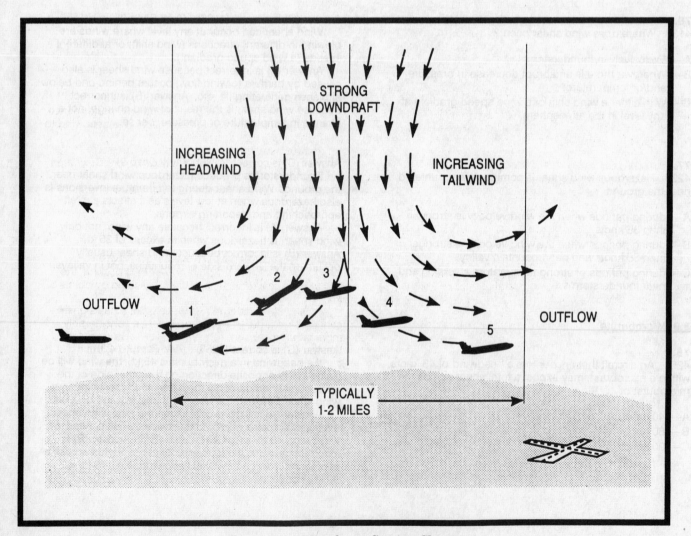

FIGURE 13.—Microburst Section Chart.

81.
4255. (Refer to figure 13 on page 292.) When penetrating a microburst, which aircraft will experience an increase in performance without a change in pitch or power?

A— 3.
B— 2.
C— 1.

82.
4256. (Refer to figure 13 on page 292.) The aircraft in position 3 will experience which effect in a microburst encounter?

A— Decreasing headwind.
B— Increasing tailwind.
C— Strong downdraft.

83.
4257. (Refer to figure 13 on page 292.) What effect will a microburst encounter have upon the aircraft in position 4?

A— Strong tailwind.
B— Strong updraft.
C— Significant performance increase.

84.
4258. (Refer to figure 13 on page 292.) How will the aircraft in position 4 be affected by a microburst encounter?

A— Performance increasing with a tailwind and updraft.
B— Performance decreasing with a tailwind and downdraft.
C— Performance decreasing with a headwind and downdraft.

85.
4254. (Refer to figure 13 on page 292.) If involved in a microburst encounter, in which aircraft positions will the most severe downdraft occur?

A— 4 and 5.
B— 2 and 3.
C— 3 and 4.

Answer (C) is correct (4255). *(AIM Para 7-1-23)*
Refer to Fig. 13 and note that, as the airplane at point 1 approaches the microburst, it will experience an increasing headwind and increasing performance.
Answer (A) is incorrect because at point 3 the airplane is experiencing a strong downdraft. Answer (B) is incorrect because at point 2 the airplane is experiencing a decreasing headwind component.

Answer (C) is correct (4256). *(AIM Para 7-1-23)*
At point 3 in Fig. 13, the airplane is experiencing a strong downdraft as it is approaching the center of the microburst.
Answer (A) is incorrect because at point 2, not 3, the airplane encounters decreasing headwind. Answer (B) is incorrect because at point 5 the airplane encounters an increasing tailwind that may result in an extreme situation as pictured, i.e., just before impact.

Answer (A) is correct (4257). *(AIM Para 7-1-23)*
At point 4 in Fig. 13, the airplane is encountering a strong tailwind in addition to a strong downdraft.
Answer (B) is incorrect because there are no updrafts in microbursts, only downdrafts. Answer (C) is incorrect because the significance in performance increase occurs at point 1, not 4, where there is an increase in headwind.

Answer (B) is correct (4258). *(AIM Para 7-1-23)*
In Fig. 13, point 4 represents decreased performance as a result of both the windshear shift from a headwind to a tailwind and a strong downdraft.
Answer (A) is incorrect because performance decreases at point 4 due to the tailwind and a downdraft, not an updraft. Answer (C) is incorrect because the performance decreases as a result of the tailwind, not headwind.

Answer (C) is correct (4254). *(AIM Para 7-1-23)*
In Fig. 13, the most severe downdrafts occur at the center of the microburst, which are indicated by points 3 and 4.
Answer (A) is incorrect because point 5 has significantly less downdraft even though it has considerably more tailwind. Answer (B) is incorrect because point 2 has not so significant a downdraft as 3 and 4, but it contains significant headwind even though it is decreasing.

END OF CHAPTER

CHAPTER NINE
AVIATION WEATHER SERVICES

This chapter contains outlines of major concepts tested, all FAA test questions and answers regarding aviation weather services, and an explanation of each answer. Each module, or subtopic, within this chapter is listed above with the number of questions from the FAA knowledge test pertaining to that particular module. For each module, the first number following the parentheses is the page number on which the outline begins, and the next number is the page number on which the questions begin.

There are 79 questions in this chapter. We separate and organize the FAA questions into meaningful study units, i.e., chapters and modules. As an analogy, it is easier to deal with the "trees" if you understand the "forest." In this context, "trees" are individual FAA questions, and the "forest" is the instrument rating knowledge test. The organizational units between the overall instrument rating knowledge test and the individual instrument rating test questions are chapters and modules in this book.

CAUTION: The **sole purpose** of this book is to expedite your passing the FAA instrument rating knowledge test. Accordingly, all extraneous material (i.e., topics or regulations not directly tested on the FAA knowledge test) is omitted, even though much more information and knowledge are necessary to fly safely. This additional material is presented in *Instrument Pilot Flight Maneuvers and Practical Test Prep*, *Pilot Handbook*, *Aviation Weather and Weather Services*, and *FAR/AIM*, available from Gleim Publications, Inc. See the order form on page 488.

Author's note: The NWS continually evaluates and updates the products that it produces for aviation. In this fluid environment, it is difficult for the FAA to maintain current figures and questions. Since the sole purpose of this book is to expedite your passing the FAA knowledge test, the outline covers only what is on the test. For up-to-date information, see Gleim's *Aviation Weather and Weather Services*, Part III, Aviation Weather Services, beginning on page 211.

9.1 IN-FLIGHT WEATHER ADVISORIES (Questions 1-6)

1. The Hazardous Inflight Weather Advisory Service (HIWAS) is a continuous broadcast over selected VORs of in-flight weather advisories, i.e., SIGMETs, convective SIGMETs, AIRMETs, severe weather forecast alerts (AWW), and center weather advisories.

2. AIRMETs are issued on a scheduled basis every 6 hr., with unscheduled amendments issued as required.

   a. An AIRMET is valid for 6 hr.

3. A SIGMET advises of nonconvective activity that is potentially hazardous to all aircraft.

4. SIGMETs are issued when the following phenomena occur or are expected to occur:

   a. Severe icing not associated with thunderstorms

   b. Severe or extreme turbulence or clear air turbulence (CAT) not associated with thunderstorms

   c. Duststorms, sandstorms, or volcanic ash lowering surface or in-flight visibilities to below 3 SM

   d. Volcanic eruption

5. Pilots of IFR flights seeking ATC in-flight weather avoidance assistance should keep in mind that ATC radar limitations and frequency congestion may limit the controller's capability to provide this service.

9.2 AVIATION ROUTINE WEATHER REPORT (METAR) (Questions 7-11)

1. Aviation routine weather reports (METARs) are actual weather observations at the time indicated on the report. There are two types of reports.

   a. METAR is an hourly routine observation (scheduled).
   b. SPECI is a special METAR observation (unscheduled).

2. Following the type of report are the elements listed beginning below:

   a. The four-letter ICAO station identifier

   b. Date and time of report. It is appended with a "Z" to denote Coordinated Universal Time (UTC).

   c. Modifier (as required)

   d. Wind

   e. Visibility

   f. Runway visual range (as required)

   g. Weather phenomena

    h.   Sky conditions

        1)   The ceiling is the lowest broken or overcast layer, or vertical visibility into an obscuration.

        2)   Cloud bases are reported with three digits in hundreds of feet AGL.

           a)   EXAMPLE: OVC007 means overcast cloud layer at 700 ft. AGL.

        3)   Total obscurations are reported in the format "VVhhh" with "VV" meaning vertical visibility and "hhh" being the vertical visibility in hundreds of feet.

           a)   EXAMPLE: VV008 means vertical visibility of 800 ft.

    i.   Temperature-dew point

    j.   Altimeter

    k.   Remarks (RMK)

        1)   RAE42SNB42 means rain ended at 42 min. past the hour and snow began at 42 min. past the hour.

3.   EXAMPLE: METAR KAUS 301651Z 12008KT 4SM −RA HZ BKN010 BKN023 OVC160 21/17 A3005 RMK RAB25

    a.   METAR is a routine weather observation.

    b.   KAUS is Austin, TX.

    c.   301651Z means the observation was taken on the 30th day at 1651 UTC (or Zulu).

    d.   12008KT means the wind is from 120° true at 8 kt.

    e.   4SM means the visibility is 4 statute miles.

    f.   −RA HZ means light rain and haze.

    g.   BKN010 BKN023 OVC160 means broken cloud layers at 1,000 ft. and 2,300 ft. and an overcast cloud layer at 16,000 ft.

    h.   21/17 means the temperature is 21°C and the dew point is 17°C.

    i.   A3005 means the altimeter setting is 30.05 in. of Hg.

    j.   RMK RAB25 means remarks, rain began at 25 min. past the hour.

9.3 PILOT WEATHER REPORTS (PIREPs) (Questions 12-13)

1. PIREPs are transmitted in the format illustrated below.

UUA/UA	Type of report: URGENT (UUA) - Any PIREP that contains any of the following weather phenomena: tornadoes, funnel clouds, or waterspouts; severe or extreme turbulence, including clear air turbulence (CAT); severe icing; hail; low-level wind shear (LLWS) (pilot reports air speed fluctuations of 10 knots or more within 2,000 feet of the surface); any other weather phenomena reported which are considered by the controller to be hazardous, or potentially hazardous, to flight operations. ROUTINE (UA) - Any PIREP that contains weather phenomena not listed above, including low-level wind shear reports with air speed fluctuations of less than 10 knots.
/OV	Location: Use VHF NAVAID(s) or an airport using the three- or four-letter location identifier. Position can be over a site, at some location relative to a site, or along a route. Ex: /OV KABC; /OV KABC090025; /OV KABC045020-DEF; /OV KABC-KDEF
/TM	Time: Four digits in UTC. Ex: /TM 0915
/FL	Altitude/Flight level: Three digits for hundreds of feet with no space between FL and altitude. If not known, use UNKN. Ex: /FL095; /FL310; /FLUNKN
/TP	Aircraft type: Four digits maximum; if not known, use UNKN. Ex: /TP L329; /TP B737; /TP UNKN
/SK	Sky cover: Describes cloud amount, height of cloud bases, and height of cloud tops. If unknown, use UNKN. Ex: /SK SCT040-TOP080; /SK BKNUNKN-TOP075; /SK BKN-OVC050-TOPUNKN; /SK OVCUNKN-TOP085
/WX	Flight visibility and weather: Flight visibility (FV) is reported first. Use standard METAR weather symbols. Intensity (– for light, no qualifier for moderate, and + for heavy) shall be coded for all precipitation types except ice crystals and hail. Ex: /WX FV05SM – RA; /WX FV01 SN BR; /WX RA
/TA	Temperature (Celsius): If below zero, prefix with an "M." Temperature should also be reported if icing is reported. Ex: /TA 15; /TA M06
/WV	Wind: Direction from which the wind is blowing coded in tens of degrees using three digits. Directions of less than 100 degrees shall be preceded by a zero. The wind speed shall be entered as a two- or three-digit group immediately following the direction, coded in whole knots using the hundreds, tens, and units digits. Ex: /WV 27045KT; /WV 280110KT
/TB	Turbulence: Use standard contractions for intensity and type (CAT or CHOP when appropriate). Include altitude only if different from FL. Ex: /TB EXTRM; /TB OCNL LGT-MDT BLO 090; /TB MOD-SEV CHOP 080-110
/IC	Icing: Describe using standard intensity and type contractions. Include altitude only if different from FL. Ex: /IC LGT-MDT RIME; /IC SEV CLR 028-045
/RM	Remarks: Use free form to clarify the report putting hazardous elements first Ex: /RM LLWS –15 KT SFC-030 DURGC RY 22 JFK

2. EXAMPLE: UA /OV OKC 063064/TM 1522/FL080/TP C172/TA –04/WV 245040/TB LGT/RM IN CLR.

DECODED: Pilot report, 64 NM on the 063° radial from Oklahoma City VOR at 1522 UTC (or Z), flight level 8,000 ft., type of aircraft is a Cessna 172, outside air temperature is –4°C, wind 245° at 40 kt., light turbulence, remarks are that the pilot is in clear skies.

9.4 WEATHER DEPICTION CHART (Questions 14-16)

1. The weather depiction chart is computer-prepared from both manual and automated METARs.

   a. A reporting station is depicted on the chart by a circle called a station circle.
   b. Automated stations are identified by a bracket ( ]) to the right of the station circle.

2. Station circle data

   a. Total sky cover is shown by the amount of shading of the station circle.

   b. Cloud height above ground level (AGL) is entered under the station circle in hundreds of feet.

      1) If the total sky cover is broken, overcast, or obscured, the cloud height is the ceiling.

   c. Weather and obstruction-to-vision symbols are entered to the left of the station circle.

      1) Some may be entered above the station circle for readability.

   d. When visibility is 6 SM or less, it is entered to the left of the weather or obstructions to visibility.

   e. EXAMPLES:

      means overcast sky, ceiling 500 ft., continuous rain (slight at time of observation), and visibility greater than 6 SM.

      means overcast sky, ceiling 1,500 ft., continuous rain (heavy at time of observation), and visibility 1/2 SM.

3. The chart shows observed ceiling and visibility by categories as follows:

   a. IFR -- Ceilings less than 1,000 ft. and/or visibility less than 3 SM is shown by a hatched area outlined by a smooth line.

   b. MVFR (marginal VFR) -- Ceilings 1,000 to 3,000 ft. inclusive and/or visibility 3 to 5 SM inclusive is shown by a nonhatched area outlined by a smooth line.

   c. VFR -- Ceilings greater than 3,000 ft. and visibility greater than 5 SM are not outlined.

9.5 RADAR SUMMARY CHART (Questions 17-25)

1. Radar summary charts graphically display a collection of radar reports concerning the intensity and movement of precipitation, e.g., squall lines, specific thunderstorm cells, and other areas of hazardous precipitation.

2. During preflight planning, the pilot should combine the radar summary chart information with indications of other charts, reports, and forecasts to gain a three-dimensional understanding of the weather.

3. Information presented on the radar summary chart includes

    a.   Echo pattern and coverage
    b.   Weather associated with echoes

         1)   EXAMPLE: TRW+ means increasing thunderstorms and rainshowers.

    c.   Intensity (contours)
    d.   Trend (+ or −) of precipitation
    e.   Height of echo bases and tops
    f.   Movement of echoes

4. The following symbols are used on radar summary charts:

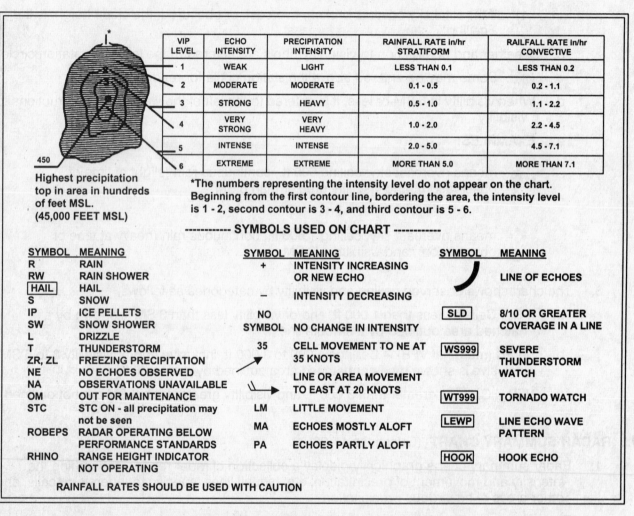

VIP LEVEL	ECHO INTENSITY	PRECIPITATION INTENSITY	RAINFALL RATE in/hr STRATIFORM	RAILFALL RATE in/hr CONVECTIVE
1	WEAK	LIGHT	LESS THAN 0.1	LESS THAN 0.2
2	MODERATE	MODERATE	0.1 - 0.5	0.2 - 1.1
3	STRONG	HEAVY	0.5 - 1.0	1.1 - 2.2
4	VERY STRONG	VERY HEAVY	1.0 - 2.0	2.2 - 4.5
5	INTENSE	INTENSE	2.0 - 5.0	4.5 - 7.1
6	EXTREME	EXTREME	MORE THAN 5.0	MORE THAN 7.1

Highest precipitation top in area in hundreds of feet MSL. (45,000 FEET MSL)

*The numbers representing the intensity level do not appear on the chart. Beginning from the first contour line, bordering the area, the intensity level is 1 - 2, second contour is 3 - 4, and third contour is 5 - 6.

------------ SYMBOLS USED ON CHART ------------

SYMBOL	MEANING
R	RAIN
RW	RAIN SHOWER
HAIL	HAIL
S	SNOW
IP	ICE PELLETS
SW	SNOW SHOWER
L	DRIZZLE
T	THUNDERSTORM
ZR, ZL	FREEZING PRECIPITATION
NE	NO ECHOES OBSERVED
NA	OBSERVATIONS UNAVAILABLE
OM	OUT FOR MAINTENANCE
STC	STC ON - all precipitation may not be seen
ROBEPS	RADAR OPERATING BELOW PERFORMANCE STANDARDS
RHINO	RANGE HEIGHT INDICATOR NOT OPERATING

SYMBOL	MEANING
+	INTENSITY INCREASING OR NEW ECHO
−	INTENSITY DECREASING
NO SYMBOL	NO CHANGE IN INTENSITY
35	CELL MOVEMENT TO NE AT 35 KNOTS
	LINE OR AREA MOVEMENT TO EAST AT 20 KNOTS
LM	LITTLE MOVEMENT
MA	ECHOES MOSTLY ALOFT
PA	ECHOES PARTLY ALOFT

SYMBOL	MEANING
	LINE OF ECHOES
SLD	8/10 OR GREATER COVERAGE IN A LINE
WS999	SEVERE THUNDERSTORM WATCH
WT999	TORNADO WATCH
LEWP	LINE ECHO WAVE PATTERN
HOOK	HOOK ECHO

RAINFALL RATES SHOULD BE USED WITH CAUTION

5. The height of the precipitation tops and bases of echoes are shown on the chart in hundreds of feet above mean sea level.

    a.   Tops are entered above a short line, while any available bases are entered below.

         1)   Top heights displayed are the highest in the indicated area.

    b.   EXAMPLES:

         450   Maximum top 45,000 ft.

         220/080   Bases 8,000 ft.; maximum top 22,000 ft.

9.6 TERMINAL AERODROME FORECAST (TAF) (Questions 26-32)

1.   Terminal aerodrome forecasts (TAFs) are weather forecasts for selected airports throughout the country. They are a source of weather to expect at your destination airport at your ETA.

   a.   The forecast is for a geographical area within a 5-SM radius of the airport's center.

      1)   **VC** (vicinity) is used to refer to weather expected to occur between a 5- to 10-SM radius of the airport.

2.   The elements of a TAF are listed below:

   a.   Type of report

      1)   TAF is a routine forecast.
      2)   TAF AMD is an amended forecast.

   b.   ICAO station identifier

   c.   Date and time the forecast is actually prepared

   d.   Valid period of the forecast

   e.   Forecast meteorological conditions. This is the body of the forecast and includes the following:

      1)   Wind

         a)   **VRB** means that the wind direction is forecast to fluctuate due to convective activity or low wind speeds (3 kt. or less).

      2)   Visibility

         a)   **P6SM** means the forecast visibility is greater than 6 SM.

      3)   Weather
      4)   Sky condition
      5)   Optional data (wind shear)

         a)   Wind shear in a TAF is a forecast of nonconvective low-level wind shear (up to 2,000 ft. AGL) and is forecast only when wind shear is expected.

         b)   EXAMPLE: **WS005/27050KT** means low-level wind shear at 500 ft. AGL, wind 270° true at 50 kt.

9.7 AVIATION AREA FORECAST (FA) (Questions 33-34)

1.   The VFR Clouds and Weather (VFR CLDS/WX) section of the aviation area forecast (FA) contains a 12-hr. specific forecast followed by a 6-hr. categorical outlook giving a total forecast period of 18 hr.

   a.   The VFR CLDS/WX section is usually several paragraphs long and is broken down by states or well-known geographical areas.

   b.   The specific forecast section covers an area the size of several states (an area greater than 3,000 sq. mi.) and gives a general description of clouds and weather that are significant to VFR flight operations.

2.   In the categorical outlook of an FA, the contraction **WND** is included if the winds, sustained or gusty, are expected to be 20 kt. or greater.

9.8 WINDS AND TEMPERATURES ALOFT FORECAST (FD) (Questions 35-44)

1. Forecast winds and temperatures, provided at specified altitudes for specific locations in the United States, are presented in table form.

2. A four-digit group (used when temperatures are not forecast) shows wind direction with reference to **true** north and the wind speed in **knots**.

   a. The first two digits indicate wind direction after a zero is added.
   b. The next two digits indicate the wind speed.

3. A six-digit group includes the forecast temperature aloft.

   a. The last two digits indicate the temperature in degrees Celsius.

   b. Plus or minus is indicated before the temperature, except at higher altitudes (above 24,000 ft. MSL) where it is always below freezing.

   c. The ISA (International Standard Atmosphere) temperature is 15°C at the surface with a standard lapse rate of 2°C per 1,000 ft.

4. When the wind speed is less than 5 kt., the forecast is coded **9900**, which means that the wind is light and variable.

5. Note that at some of the lower levels the wind and temperature information is omitted.

   a. Winds aloft are not forecast for levels within 1,500 ft. of the station elevation.

   b. No temperatures are forecast for the 3,000-ft. level or for a level within 2,500 ft. of the station elevation.

6. If the wind speed is forecast to be 100 to 199 kt., the forecaster adds 50 to the direction and subtracts 100 from the speed. To decode, you must do the reverse: subtract 50 from the direction and add 100 to the speed.

   a. EXAMPLE: If the forecast for the 39,000-ft. level appears as **731960**, subtract 50 from 73 and add 100 to 19. The wind would be 230° at 119 kt. with a temperature of −60°C (above 24,000 ft.).

   b. It is easy to know when the coded direction has been increased by 50. Coded direction (in tens of degrees) normally ranges from 01 (010°) to 36 (360°). Any coded direction with a numerical value greater than 36 indicates a wind of 100 kt. or greater. The coded direction for winds of 100 to 199 kt. thus ranges from 51 through 86.

7. If the wind speed is forecast to be 199 kt. or more, the wind group is coded as 199 kt.; e.g., **7799** is decoded 270° at 199 kt. or more.

8. EXAMPLES: Decode these FD winds and temperatures:

Coded	Decoded
9900+00	Winds light and variable, temperature 0°C
2707	270° at 7 kt.
850552	85 − 50 = 35; 05 + 100 = 105
	350° at 105 kt., temperature −52°C

9.9 LOW-LEVEL SIGNIFICANT WEATHER PROG (Questions 45-52)

1. Low-level prognostic charts contain four charts (panels) of conditions forecast to exist at a valid time shown on the chart.

    a. The two upper panels forecast significant weather from the surface up to 24,000 ft.: one for 12 hr. and the other for 24 hr. from the time of issuance.

    b. The two lower panels forecast surface conditions: one for 12 hr. and the other for 24 hr. from the time of issuance.

    c. See Fig. 18 on page 323.

2. The top panels show

    a. Ceilings less than 1,000 ft. and/or visibility less than 3 SM (IFR) indicated by a solid line around the area

    b. Ceilings 1,000 to 3,000 ft. and/or visibility 3 to 5 SM (MVFR) indicated by a scalloped line around the area

    c. Moderate or greater turbulence indicated by a broken line around the area

        1) Altitudes "up to" are above a line; e.g., 120 is up to 12,000 ft.

        2) Altitudes "down to" are below a line; e.g., 90 is down to 9,000 ft.

    d. Freezing levels indicated by a dashed line corresponding to the height of the freezing level

3. The bottom panels show location of

    a. Highs, lows, fronts
    b. Other areas of significant weather

4. The following symbols are used on "prog" charts:

    a. Standard weather symbols

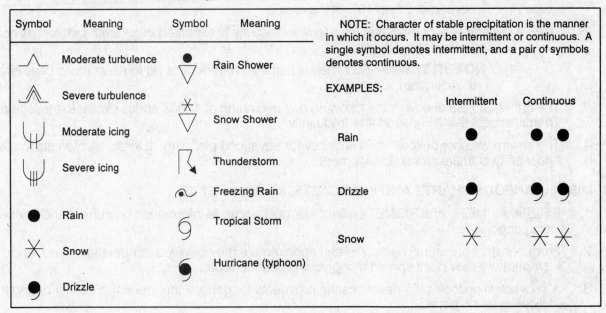

b.   Significant weather symbols

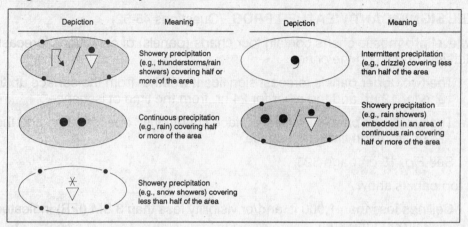

9.10 SEVERE WEATHER OUTLOOK CHART (Questions 53-56)

1.   The severe weather outlook chart is a 48-hr. outlook for thunderstorm activity presented in two panels.

2.   The left-hand panel covers the first 24-hr. period beginning at 1200Z (12Z) and depicts areas of possible general and severe thunderstorm activity in the continental U.S.

    a.   A line with an arrowhead delineates an area of probable thunderstorm activity located to the right of the line when facing in the direction of the arrow.

    b.   If severe thunderstorm activity is expected in an area, that area is labeled with a risk category.

        1)   **SLGT** means that there is a slight risk of severe thunderstorms; they are expected to cover 2% to 5% of the area.

        2)   **MDT** means that there is a moderate risk of severe thunderstorms; they are expected to cover 6% to 10% of the area.

        3)   **HIGH** means that there is a high risk of severe thunderstorms; they are expected to cover more than 10% of the area.

    c.   If general (i.e., non-severe) thunderstorm activity is expected in an area, that area is not labeled with a risk category.

        1)   **NO SVR TSTMS FCST** means that the chart depicts no forecast areas of severe thunderstorms.

3.   The right-hand panel covers the following day beginning at 1200Z and is similar to the left-hand panel, except that it is issued less frequently.

4.   The severe weather outlook chart is strictly for advanced planning. It alerts all interests to the possibility of future storm development.

9.11 MISCELLANEOUS CHARTS AND FORECASTS (Questions 57-65)

1.   PIREPs, AIRMETs, and SIGMETs reflect the most accurate information on current and forecast icing conditions.

2.   From constant pressure charts, you can approximate the observed temperature, wind, and temperature-dew point spread along your proposed route.

3.   A convective outlook (AC) describes the prospects for general thunderstorm activity during the following 24-hr. period.

    a.   Areas in which there is a high, moderate, or slight risk of severe thunderstorms are included as well as areas where thunderstorms may approach severe limits.

4.   The surface analysis chart depicts actual frontal positions, pressure patterns, temperature, dew point, wind, weather, and obstructions to vision at the valid time of the chart.

5.   A severe weather watch bulletin (WW) is unscheduled and is issued as required.

6.   A TWEB route forecast provides specific information concerning expected sky cover, cloud tops, visibility, weather, and obstructions to vision in a route format.

9.12 HIGH-LEVEL SIGNIFICANT WEATHER PROG (Questions 66-73)

1. The U.S. High-Level Significant Weather Prognostic Chart encompasses airspace from 25,000 ft. to 60,000 ft. pressure altitude (FL 250 to FL 600).

2. Tropopause heights are depicted in hundreds of feet MSL, which may be presented by a five-sided polygon or a small rectangular block.

    a. The five-sided polygon indicates areas of high and low tropopause heights.

    b. The rectangular block indicates the tropopause height in areas that have a very flat tropopause slope.

    c. Note that, in figure 20, which is out-of-date, all heights are given as flight levels, not hundreds of feet MSL.

3. The height and maximum wind speed of jet streams having a core speed of 80 kt. or greater are shown as a solid line with arrowheads indicating the flow direction.

    a. The height is given as a flight level (FL).

    b. The maximum core wind velocity is depicted by a shaft with a pennant equal to 50 kt. and a feather, or barb, equal to 10 kt.

        1) EXAMPLE: ▲▲ ||| ⎯⎯⎯ means a maximum core speed of 130 kt.

4. Areas of forecast moderate or greater clear air turbulence (CAT) are bounded by heavy, dashed lines.

    a. CAT includes all turbulence not caused by convective activity.

    b. Areas are labeled with the appropriate turbulence symbol(s) and the vertical extent in hundreds of feet MSL.

5. Small scalloped lines enclose areas of expected cumulonimbus development. "CB" denotes cumulonimbus.

    a. CB refers to the occurrence or expected occurrence of an area of widespread cumulonimbus clouds or cumulonimbus clouds along a line with little or no space between the individual clouds, or cumulonimbus clouds embedded in cloud layers or concealed by haze or dust.

    b. CB bases below 24,000 ft. (FL 240) are shown as XXX.

        1) CB tops are expressed in hundreds of feet MSL.

        2) The term "below 24,000 ft." (FL 240) is used because phenomena that extend beyond the lower limit of the High-Level Significant Weather Prognostic Chart are found on the Low-Level Significant Weather Prognostic Chart, the upper limit of which is 24,000 ft. pressure altitude (FL 240).

6. EXAMPLES:

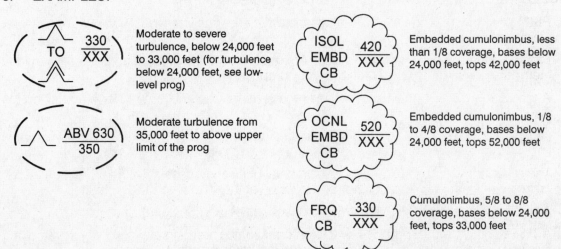

9.13 OBSERVED WINDS ALOFT CHART (Questions 76-79)

1.   Arrows with pennants and barbs show wind direction and speed.

  a.   Wind direction is drawn to the nearest 10°, with the second digit of the coded direction entered at the outer end of the arrow.

  1)   To determine wind direction, obtain the general direction from the arrow and then use the digit to determine the direction to the nearest 10°.

  2)   For example, wind from the northwest with a digit of "3" at the end of the arrow indicates 330°.

  b.   Wind speed is indicated by the sum of three symbols: A half barb is 5 kt., a full barb is 10 kt., and a pennant is 50 kt.

2.   Temperature is in whole degrees Celsius for each forecast point and is entered above and to the right of the station circle.

3.   EXAMPLES:

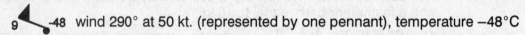

 wind 290° at 50 kt. (represented by one pennant), temperature −48°C

wind 230° at 35 kt. (represented by three and one-half barbs), temperature −47°C

QUESTIONS AND ANSWER EXPLANATIONS

All the FAA questions from the instrument rating knowledge test relating to aviation weather services and the material outlined previously are reproduced on the following pages in the same modules as the outlines. To the immediate right of each question are the correct answer and answer explanation. You should cover these answers and answer explanations with your hand or a piece of paper while responding to the questions. Refer to the general discussion in the Introduction on how to take the FAA knowledge test.

Remember that the questions from the FAA instrument rating knowledge test bank have been reordered by topic, and the topics have been organized into a meaningful sequence. Accordingly, the first line of the answer explanation gives the FAA question number and the citation of the authoritative source for the answer.

9.1 In-Flight Weather Advisories

1.
4467. AIRMETs are issued on a scheduled basis every

A— 15 minutes after the hour only.
B— 15 minutes until the AIRMET is canceled.
C— six hours.

Answer (C) is correct (4467). *(AWS Sect 4)*
AIRMETs are issued on a scheduled basis every 6 hr., with unscheduled amendments issued as required.
Answer (A) is incorrect because AIRMETs are issued on a scheduled basis every 6 hr., not every 15 min. past the hour. Answer (B) is incorrect because AIRMETs are issued on a scheduled basis every 6 hr., not every 15 min. until the AIRMET is canceled.

2.
4187. What is the maximum forecast period for AIRMET's?

A— Two hours.
B— Four hours.
C— Six hours.

Answer (C) is correct (4187). *(AWS Sect 4)*
The maximum forecast period for AIRMETs is 6 hr. If conditions persist beyond 6 hr., the AIRMET must be updated and reissued.
Answer (A) is incorrect because convective SIGMETs, not AIRMETs, are valid for up to 2 hr. Answer (B) is incorrect because SIGMETs, not AIRMETs, are valid for up to 4 hr.

3.
4181. SIGMET's are issued as a warning of weather conditions potentially hazardous

A— particularly to light aircraft.
B— to all aircraft.
C— only to light aircraft operations.

Answer (B) is correct (4181). *(AWS Sect 4)*
SIGMETs warn of weather considered potentially hazardous to all categories of aircraft. SIGMETs are forecasts of tornadoes, lines of thunderstorms, embedded thunderstorms, large hail, severe and extreme turbulence, severe icing, and widespread sandstorms and snowstorms.
Answer (A) is incorrect because SIGMETs apply to all aircraft. Answer (C) is incorrect because AIRMETs, not SIGMETs, apply to light aircraft.

4.
4183. Which meteorological condition is issued in the form of a SIGMET (WS)?

A— Widespread sand or dust storms lowering visibility to less than 3 miles.
B— Moderate icing.
C— Sustained winds of 30 knots or greater at the surface.

Answer (A) is correct (4183). *(AWS Sect 4)*
SIGMETs are issued for severe and extreme turbulence; severe icing; and widespread dust storms, sandstorms, or volcanic ash lowering visibility below 3 mi.
Answer (B) is incorrect because moderate icing is issued in the form of an AIRMET, not a SIGMET. Answer (C) is incorrect because sustained winds of 30 kt. or greater at the surface are issued in the form of an AIRMET, not a SIGMET.

5.

4468. Pilots of IFR flights seeking ATC in-flight weather avoidance assistance should keep in mind that

A— ATC radar limitations and, frequency congestion may limit the controllers capability to provide this service.

B— circumnavigating severe weather can only be accommodated in the en route areas away from terminals because of congestion.

C— ATC Narrow Band Radar does not provide the controller with weather intensity capability.

Answer (A) is correct (4468). *(AIM Para 7-1-12)*
The controllers' primary function is to provide safe separation between aircraft. Any additional service, such as weather avoidance, can be provided only to the extent it does not interfere with the primary function. Unfortunately, the separation workload is usually greater when weather disrupts the normal flow of traffic.
Answer (B) is incorrect because controllers can provide weather circumnavigation in terminal areas when workload permits. Answer (C) is incorrect because ATC narrowband radar is replacing digitized radar weather displays in ARTCC facilities to provide even better measurement of precipitation density.

6.

4241. The Hazardous Inflight Weather Advisory Service (HIWAS) is a continuous broadcast over selected VORs of

A— SIGMETs, CONVECTIVE SIGMETs, AIRMETs, Severe Weather Forecast Alerts (AWW), and Center Weather Advisories.

B— SIGMETs, CONVECTIVE SIGMETs, AIRMETs, Wind Shear Advisories, and Severe Weather Forecast Alerts (AWW).

C— Wind Shear Advisories, Radar Weather Reports, SIGMETs, CONVECTIVE SIGMETs, AIRMETs, and Center Weather Advisories (CWA).

Answer (A) is correct (4241). *(AWS Sect 1)*
The Hazardous Inflight Weather Advisory Service (HIWAS) is a continuous broadcast service over selected VORs of in-flight weather advisories, i.e., SIGMETs, convective SIGMETs, AIRMETs, severe weather forecast alerts (AWW), and center weather advisories (CWA).
Answer (B) is incorrect because a runway wind shear advisory would be given to arriving and departing aircraft by a tower controller, not the HIWAS. Answer (C) is incorrect because radar weather reports would be available from the En Route Flight Advisory Service (EFAS), not the HIWAS.

9.2 Aviation Routine Weather Report (METAR)

7.

4205. What is meant by the entry in the remarks section of METAR surface report for KBNA?

METAR KBNA 211250Z 33018KT 290V260 1/2SM
  R31/2700FT +SN BLSNFG VV008 00/M03 A2991
  RMK RAE42SNB42

A— The wind is variable from 290° to 360°.

B— Heavy blowing snow and fog on runway 31.

C— Rain ended 42 past the hour, snow began 42 past the hour.

Answer (C) is correct (4205). *(AWS Sect 2)*
The contraction RMK follows the altimeter in the body and precedes remarks. RMK RAE42SNB42 means remarks follow, rain ended 42 min. past the hour (RAE42), and snow began 42 min. past the hour (SNB42).
Answer (A) is incorrect because the remarks section indicates that rain ended 42 min. past the hour and snow began 42 min. past the hour, not that the wind is variable from 290° to 360°. Answer (B) is incorrect because the remarks section indicates that rain ended 42 min. past the hour and snow began 42 min. past the hour, not that there is heavy blowing snow and fog on Rwy 31.

8.

4202. A ceiling is defined as the height of the

A— highest layer of clouds or obscuring phenomena aloft that covers over 6/10 of the sky.

B— lowest layer of clouds that contributed to the overall overcast.

C— lowest layer of clouds or obscuring phenomena aloft that is reported as broken or overcast.

Answer (C) is correct (4202). *(AWS Sect 2)*
For aviation purposes, the ceiling is the lowest broken or overcast layer, or vertical visibility into an obscuration.
Answer (A) is incorrect because the ceiling is the base of the lowest, not highest, broken or overcast layer. Answer (B) is incorrect because the lowest layer of clouds must be broken or overcast, not simply a contributor to the overall overcast.

9.

4203. The reporting station originating this Aviation Routine Weather Report has a field elevation of 620 feet. If the reported sky cover is one continuous layer, what is its thickness (tops of OVC are reported at 6,500 feet)?

METAR KMDW 121856Z AUTO 32005KT 1 1/2SM +RA
  BR OVC007 17/16 A2980

A— 5,180 feet.

B— 5,800 feet.

C— 5,880 feet.

Answer (A) is correct (4203). *(AWS Sect 2)*
The sky cover for KMDW is reported as a ceiling of 700 ft. AGL, overcast (OVC007). The field elevation is 620 ft. MSL; thus, the base of the overcast layer is 1,320 ft. MSL (700+620). The tops of the overcast are reported at 6,500 ft.; thus, the thickness of the overcast layer is 5,180 ft. (6,500–1,320).
Answer (B) is incorrect because 5,800 ft. would be the thickness of the sky cover if the field elevation were 0 ft., not 620 ft. Answer (C) is incorrect because 5,880 ft. is the height above ground of the tops of the overcast layer, not the thickness of the overcast layer.

10.
4196. The station originating the following weather report has a field elevation of 1,300 feet MSL. From the bottom of the overcast cloud layer, what is its thickness (tops of OVC are reported at 3,800 feet)?

SPECI KOKC 2228Z 28024G36KT 3/4SM BKN008
  OVC020 28/23 A3000

A— 500 feet.
B— 1,700 feet.
C— 2,500 feet.

11.
4182. What significant sky condition is reported in this METAR observation?

METAR KBNA 1250Z 33018KT 290V360 1/2SM
  R31/2700FT +SN BLSNFG VV008 00/M03 A2991
  RMK RERAE42SNB42

A— Runway 31 ceiling is 2,700 feet.
B— Sky is obscured with vertical visibility of 800 feet.
C— Measured ceiling is 300 feet overcast.

9.3 Pilot Weather Reports (PIREPs)

12.
4220. Interpret this PIREP.

MRB UA/OV MRB/TM 1430/FL 060/TP C182/SK BKN BL
  /WX RA/TB MDT.

A— Ceiling 6,000 feet intermittently below moderate thundershowers; turbulence increasing westward.
B— FL 60,000, intermittently below clouds; moderate rain, turbulence increasing with the wind.
C— At 6,000 feet; between layers; moderate turbulence; moderate rain.

13.
4198. Which response most closely interprets the following PIREP?

UA/OV OKC 063064/TM 1522/FL080/TP C172/TA –04
  /WV245040/TB LGT/RM IN CLR.

A— 64 nautical miles on the 63 degree radial from Oklahoma City VOR at 1522 UTC, flight level 8,000 ft. Type of aircraft is a Cessna 172.
B— Reported by a Cessna 172, turbulence and light rime icing in climb to 8,000 ft.
C— 63 nautical miles on the 64 degree radial from Oklahoma City, thunderstorm and light rain at 1522 UTC.

Answer (A) is correct (4196). *(AWS Sect 2)*
The question is to determine the thickness of the overcast layer at KOKC. The SPECI reported the base of the overcast cloud layer at 2,000 ft. AGL (OVC020). The field elevation is 1,300 ft. MSL; thus, the base of the overcast layer is 3,300 ft. MSL (2,000+1,300). The tops of the overcast layer are reported at 3,800 ft. MSL; thus, the thickness of the overcast cloud layer is 500 ft. (3,800–3,300).
Answer (B) is incorrect because 1,700 ft. is the distance from the base of the broken (BKN), not overcast (OVC), cloud layer to the top of the overcast. Answer (C) is incorrect because 2,500 ft. is the height above the ground of the tops of the overcast, not the thickness of the overcast layer.

Answer (B) is correct (4182). *(AWS Sect 2)*
The sky condition follows the weather element. At KBNA, the sky cover is reported as VV008, which means the sky is obscured (indefinite ceiling) with a vertical visibility of 800 feet.
Answer (A) is incorrect because runway 31 RVR, not ceiling, is 2,700 ft. Answer (C) is incorrect because 00/M03 means the temperature is 0°C and the dew point is –3°C, not that there is a measured ceiling of 300 ft. overcast.

Answer (C) is correct (4220). *(AWS Sect 3)*
The PIREP decodes as follows: pilot report, over Martinsburg, WV at 1430 UTC, flight level is 6,000 ft., type of aircraft is a Cessna 182, and sky condition is broken with the pilot reporting between layers in moderate rain and moderate turbulence.
Answer (A) is incorrect because the flight level, not the ceiling, is 6,000 ft., and TB MDT means moderate turbulence, not thundershowers. Answer (B) is incorrect because the flight level is 6,000 ft., not 60,000 ft., and BL means between layers, not below clouds.

Answer (A) is correct (4198). *(AWS Sect 3)*
The PIREP decodes as follows: pilot report, 64 NM on the 063° radial from Oklahoma City VOR at 1522 UTC, flight level is 8,000 ft., type of aircraft is a Cessna 172, outside air temperature is –4°C, wind is from 245° at 40 kt. with light turbulence, remarks are that the pilot is in clear skies.
Answer (B) is incorrect because TB LGT RM IN CLR means light turbulence (remark) in clear, not turbulence and rime icing in climb. Answer (C) is incorrect because OKC 063064 means the aircraft was located 64 NM, not 63 NM, on the 063° radial, not the 064° radial. Additionally, there is no report of thunderstorm and rain.

9.4 Weather Depiction Chart

14.
4208. (Refer to figure 4 on page 311.) The Weather Depiction Chart in the area of northwestern Wyoming indicates

A— overcast with scattered rain showers.
B— 1,000-foot ceilings and visibility 3 miles or more.
C— 500-foot ceilings and continuous rain, less than 3 miles visibility.

Answer (C) is correct (4208). *(AWS Sect 6)*
The station circle in northwestern Wyoming indicates an overcast sky (darkened circle), 500-ft. ceiling ("5" under the circle), and continuous rain (two dots over circle). The station circle is in a shaded area, which indicates IFR with ceiling less than 1,000 ft. and/or visibility less than 3 SM.
Answer (A) is incorrect because the chart provides data only from observation stations. Rain showers would be reported as intermittent, not scattered. Intermittent showers (moderate intensity at time of observation) would be shown as two vertical, not horizontal, dots.
Answer (B) is incorrect because the station in Wyoming is reporting a ceiling of 500 ft., not 1,000 ft., and since visibility is not shown, it is interpreted to mean greater than 6 SM, not 3 SM or more.

15.
4207. (Refer to figure 4 on page 311.) The Weather Depiction Chart indicates the heaviest precipitation is occurring in

A— north central Florida.
B— north central Minnesota.
C— central South Dakota.

Answer (B) is correct (4207). *(AWS Sect 6)*
The heaviest precipitation is occurring in north central Minnesota. The station near the southern edge of the shaded area has four dots in a diamond shape above the circle, which means continuous rain (not freezing), heavy at the time of observation.
Answer (A) is incorrect because no precipitation is reported for north central Florida. Answer (C) is incorrect because no precipitation is reported for central South Dakota.

16.
4206. (Refer to figure 4 on page 311.) What is the meaning of a bracket ( ]) plotted to the right of the station circle on a weather depiction chart?

A— The station represents the en route conditions within a 50 mile radius.
B— The station is an automated observation location.
C— The station gives local overview of flying conditions for a six-hour period.

Answer (B) is correct (4206). *(AWS Sect 6)*
Data for the weather depiction chart come from the observations reported by both manual and automated observation locations. The automated stations are denoted by a bracket ( ]) plotted to the right of the station circle.
Answer (A) is incorrect because a bracket to the right of the station circle means the station is an automated site. The chart does not provide en route conditions between stations. Answer (C) is incorrect because a bracket to the right of the station circle means that the station is an automated site, not that the station gives a local overview of flying conditions for a 6-hr. period.

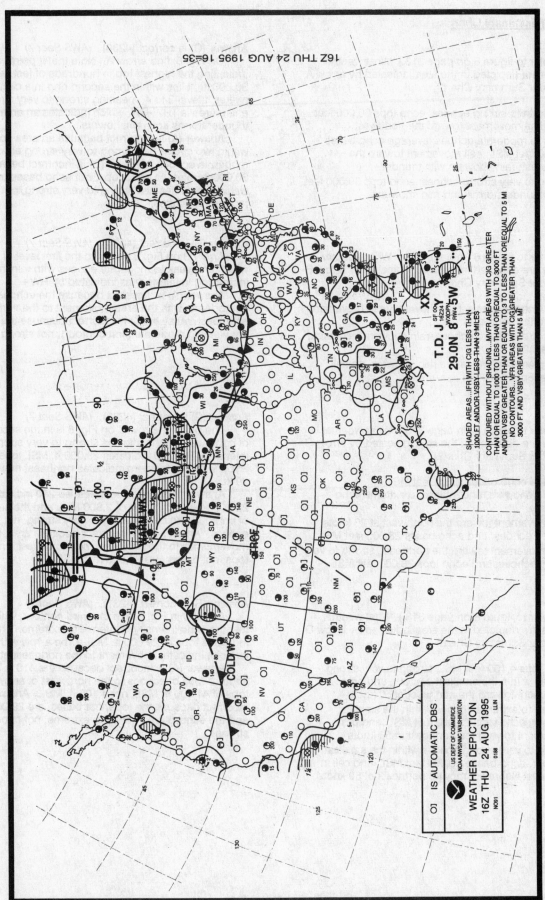

FIGURE 4.—Weather Depiction Chart.

9.5 Radar Summary Chart

17.
4230. (Refer to figure 8 on page 313.) What weather conditions are depicted in the area indicated by arrow A on the Radar Summary Chart?

A— Moderate to strong echoes; echo tops 30,000 feet MSL; line movement toward the northwest.
B— Weak to moderate echoes; average echo bases 30,000 feet MSL; cell movement toward the southeast; rain showers with thunder.
C— Strong to very strong echoes; echo tops 30,000 feet MSL; thunderstorms and rain showers.

Answer (C) is correct (4230). *(AWS Sect 7)*
On Fig. 8, find arrow A. Note that it points to a dot indicating the highest top in hundreds of feet, which is 30,000 ft. It lies within the second ring in a circuit, which makes it level 3 to 4, meaning strong to very strong. The entire area is TRW-RW, which indicates an area of thunderstorms and rainshowers.
Answer (A) is incorrect because an area contained within two circles has strong to very strong echoes, not moderate echoes. Answer (B) is incorrect because 30,000 ft. refers to echo tops, not echo bases and an area within two circles has strong to very strong, not weak to moderate, echoes.

18.
4233. (Refer to figure 8 on page 313.) What weather conditions are depicted in the area indicated by arrow B on the Radar Summary Chart?

A— Weak echoes, heavy rain showers, area movement toward the southeast.
B— Weak to moderate echoes, rain showers increasing in intensity.
C— Strong echoes, moderate rain showers, no cell movement.

Answer (B) is correct (4233). *(AWS Sect 7)*
Arrow B on Fig. 8 points to the first level of contours, which are weak to moderate echoes with rainshowers increasing in intensity as indicated by RW+.
Answer (A) is incorrect because the echoes are weak to moderate with the area movement to the northeast, not southeast. Answer (C) is incorrect because the echoes are weak to moderate (first contour), not strong.

19.
4232. (Refer to figure 8 on page 313.) What weather conditions are depicted in the area indicated by arrow C on the Radar Summary Chart?

A— Average echo bases 2,800 feet MSL, thundershowers, and intense to extreme echo intensity.
B— Cell movement toward the northwest at 20 knots, intense echoes, and echo bases 28,000 feet MSL.
C— Area movement toward the northeast, strong to very strong echoes, and echo tops 28,000 feet MSL.

Answer (C) is correct (4232). *(AWS Sect 7)*
The point of arrow C on Fig. 8 is in the second level of contours, which indicates strong to very strong echo intensity. The 280 indicates 28,000 ft. MSL tops. The arrow with two feathers indicates northeast movement at 20 kt.
Answer (A) is incorrect because 280 indicates tops of 28,000 MSL, not bases of 2,800 MSL and the second level of contours indicates strong to very strong, not intense, echoes. Answer (B) is incorrect because area, not cell, movement is to the northeast, not northwest, and echo tops, not bases, are 28,000 feet MSL.

20.
4231. (Refer to figure 8 on page 313.) What weather conditions are depicted in the area indicated by arrow D on the Radar Summary Chart?

A— Echo tops 4,100 feet MSL, strong to very strong echoes within the smallest contour, and area movement toward the northeast at 50 knots.
B— Intense to extreme echoes within the smallest contour, echo tops 29,000 feet MSL, and cell movement toward the northeast at 50 knots.
C— Strong to very strong echoes within the smallest contour, echo bases 29,000 feet MSL, and cell in northeast Nebraska moving northeast at 50 knots.

Answer (B) is correct (4231). *(AWS Sect 7)*
Arrow D in Fig. 8 is in the third contour, which means that the echo intensity is intense to extreme. The 290 indicates tops of 29,000 ft. MSL. The arrow with the 50 at its point indicates movement to the northeast at 50 kt.
Answer (A) is incorrect because the 410 is for another area of echoes to the northeast of arrow D, with tops of 41,000 ft. MSL, not 4,100 ft. MSL. Answer (C) is incorrect because the tops, not bases, are 29,000 ft. MSL and the echoes are intense to extreme, not strong to very strong.

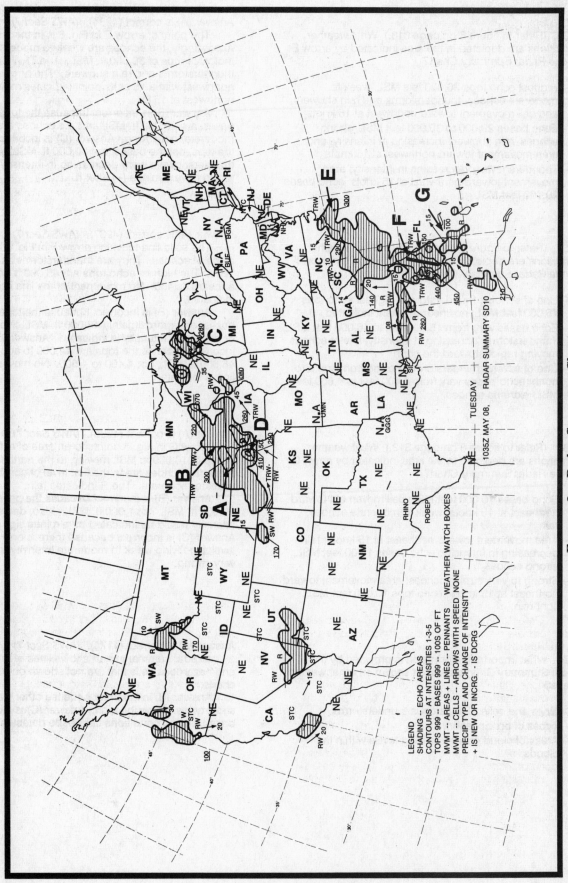

FIGURE 8.—Radar Summary Chart.

21.
4234. (Refer to figure 8 on page 313.) What weather conditions are depicted in the area indicated by arrow E on the Radar Summary Chart?

A— Highest echo tops 30,000 feet MSL, weak to moderate echoes, thunderstorms and rain showers, and cell movement toward northwest at 15 knots.

B— Echo bases 29,000 to 30,000 feet MSL, strong echoes, rain showers increasing in intensity, and area movement toward northwest at 15 knots.

C— Thundershowers decreasing in intensity; area movement toward northwest at 15 knots; echo bases 30,000 feet MSL.

Answer (A) is correct (4234). *(AWS Sect 7)*
The point of arrow E in Fig. 8 is in the first contour. Accordingly, the echoes are weak to moderate. The 300 indicates tops of 30,000 ft. MSL. The TRW indicates thunderstorms and rain showers. The arrow to the northwest with a 15 at its point indicates movement to the northwest at 15 kt.
Answer (B) is incorrect because the tops, not the bases, are 29,000 ft. MSL and the echoes are weak to moderate, not strong. Answer (C) is incorrect because the tops, not the bases, are 30,000 ft. MSL. Also, if thundershowers were decreasing in intensity, the TRW would have a minus (–) after it.

22.
4237. (Refer to figure 8 on page 313.) What weather conditions are depicted in the area indicated by arrow F on the Radar Summary Chart?

A— Line of echoes; thunderstorms; highest echo tops 45,000 feet MSL; no line movement indicated.

B— Echo bases vary from 15,000 feet to 46,000 feet MSL; thunderstorms increasing in intensity; line of echoes moving rapidly toward the north.

C— Line of severe thunderstorms moving from south to north; echo bases vary from 4,400 feet to 4,600 feet MSL; extreme echoes.

Answer (A) is correct (4237). *(AWS Sect 7)*
The solid line to which arrow F in Fig. 8 is pointing is a line of echoes. They are thunderstorms as indicated by TRW. The highest echo tops are 45,000 ft. MSL, which appears as 450. No movement of the line itself is indicated.
Answer (B) is incorrect because the tops, not the bases, are approximately 46,000 ft. MSL. No movement or change in intensity is indicated. Answer (C) is incorrect because the tops are 44,000 to approximately 46,000 ft. MSL, not 4,400 to 4,600. No movement of the line is indicated.

23.
4236. (Refer to figure 8 on page 313.) What weather conditions are depicted in the area indicated by arrow G on the Radar Summary Chart?

A— Echo bases 10,000 feet MSL; cell movement toward northeast at 15 knots; weak to moderate echoes; rain.

B— Area movement toward northeast at 15 knots; rain decreasing in intensity; echo bases 1,000 feet MSL; strong echoes.

C— Strong to very strong echoes; area movement toward northeast at 15 knots; echo tops 10,000 feet MSL; light rain.

Answer (A) is correct (4236). *(AWS Sect 7)*
Arrow G in Fig. 8 points to an area of echoes with bases of 10,000 ft. MSL moving to the northeast at 15 kt. Since the echoes are in the first level of contours, they are weak to moderate. The R indicates rain.
Answer (B) is incorrect because the bases are 10,000 ft. MSL, not 1,000 ft. MSL. Also, decreasing intensity would be indicated by a minus sign after the R. Answer (C) is incorrect because there is only one contour level, signifying weak to moderate intensity, not strong to very strong.

24.
4174. What important information is provided by the Radar Summary Chart that is not shown on other weather charts?

A— Lines and cells of hazardous thunderstorms.

B— Types of precipitation.

C— Areas of cloud cover and icing levels within the clouds.

Answer (A) is correct (4174). *(AWS Sect 7)*
A radar summary chart shows lines of thunderstorms and hazardous cells that are not shown on other weather charts.
Answer (B) is incorrect because other weather charts show types of precipitation. Answer (C) is incorrect because icing conditions cannot be detected by radar.

25.

4235. For the most effective use of the Radar Summary Chart during preflight planning, a pilot should

A— consult the chart to determine more accurate measurements of freezing levels, cloud cover, and wind conditions between reporting stations.

B— compare it with the charts, reports, and forecasts of a three-dimensional picture of clouds and precipitation.

C— utilize the chart as the only source of information regarding storms and hazardous conditions existing between reporting stations.

Answer (B) is correct (4235). *(AWS Sect 7)*
A radar summary chart graphically indicates a collection of radar reports, i.e., reports of echoes from thunderstorms and heavy precipitation. In conjunction with the weather depiction chart, which is a composite of METAR reports, a radar summary chart provides a more three-dimensional picture of clouds and precipitation.

Answer (A) is incorrect because a radar summary chart does not show freezing levels, cloud cover, or wind conditions. Answer (C) is incorrect because a radar summary chart must be used in conjunction with other reports and forecasts for an accurate picture of weather conditions.

9.6 Terminal Aerodrome Forecast (TAF)

26.

4228. From which primary source should you obtain information regarding the weather expected to exist at your destination at your estimated time of arrival?

A— Weather Depiction Chart.
B— Radar Summary and Weather Depiction Chart.
C— Terminal Aerodrome Forecast.

Answer (C) is correct (4228). *(AWS Sect 4)*
A terminal aerodrome forecast (TAF) is a concise statement of the expected meteorological conditions at an airport during a specified period (usually 24 hr.). Thus, a TAF contains information regarding the expected weather at the destination airport at the ETA.

Answer (A) is incorrect because a weather depiction chart is a national weather map of observed, not forecast, weather at the time specified on the chart. It is useful for flight planning to get a broad overview of the observed conditions. Answer (B) is incorrect because radar summary and weather depiction charts are national weather maps of observed, not forecast, weather at a specific time. They are useful for flight planning but do not provide specific information about a particular destination.

27.

4204. What is the wind shear forecast in the following TAF?

TAF
KCVG 231051Z 231212 12012KT 4SM –RA BR OVC008
  WS005/27050KT TEMPO 1719 1/2SM –RA FG
FM1930 09012KT 1SM –DZ BR VV003 BECMG 2021
  5SM HZ=

A— 5 feet AGL from 270° at 50 KT.
B— 50 feet AGL from 270° at 50 KT.
C— 500 feet AGL from 270° at 50 KT.

Answer (C) is correct (4204). *(AIM Para 7-1-28)*
Wind shear in a TAF is a forecast of nonconvective low-level wind shear (up to 2,000 ft. AGL) and is entered after the sky condition when wind shear is expected. The wind shear forecast for KCVG is coded as **WS005/27050KT**, which means low-level wind shear at 500 ft. AGL, wind from 270° true at 50 kt.

Answer (A) is incorrect because the height of the wind shear (WS005) is 500 ft. AGL, not 5 ft. AGL. Answer (B) is incorrect because the height of the wind shear (WS005) is 500 ft. AGL, not 50 ft. AGL.

28.
4180. What is the forecast wind at 1800Z in the following TAF?

KMEM 091740Z 1818 00000KT 1/2SM RAFG OVC005=

A— Calm.
B— Unknown.
C— Not recorded.

29.
4178. When the visibility is greater than 6 SM on a TAF it is expressed as

A— 6PSM.
B— P6SM.
C— 6SMP.

30.
4177. A "VRB" wind entry in a Terminal Aerodrome Forecast (TAF) will be indicated when the wind is

A— 3 knots or less.
B— 6 knots or less.
C— 9 knots or less.

31.
4176. Which primary source should be used to obtain forecast weather information at your destination for the planned ETA?

A— Area Forecast.
B— Radar Summary and Weather Depiction Charts.
C— Terminal Aerodrome Forecast (TAF).

32.
4170. The body of a Terminal Aerodrome Forecast (TAF) covers a geographical proximity within a

A— 5 nautical mile radius of the center of an airport.
B— 5 statute mile radius from the center of an airport runway complex.
C— 5 to 10 statute mile radius from the center of an airport runway complex.

Answer (A) is correct (4180). *(AWS Sect 4)*
In the TAF for KMEM, the forecast wind at 1800Z is coded as 00000KT, which means a calm wind.
Answer (B) is incorrect because the forecast wind at 1800Z is 00000KT, which means a calm, not unknown, wind. Answer (C) is incorrect because the forecast wind at 1800Z is 00000KT, which means a calm wind, not an unrecorded wind.

Answer (B) is correct (4178). *(AWS Sect 4)*
When the forecast visibility is greater than 6 SM, it will be coded as P6SM.
Answer (A) is incorrect because forecast visibility greater than 6 SM will be coded as P6SM, not 6PSM. Answer (C) is incorrect because forecast visibility greater than 6 SM will be coded as P6SM, not 6SMP.

Answer (A) is correct (4177). *(AWS Sect 4)*
A "VRB" wind entry in a TAF indicates that the wind direction is forecast to fluctuate due to convective activity or low wind speeds (3 kt. or less).
Answer (B) is incorrect because a "VRB" wind entry in a TAF indicates that the wind direction is forecast to fluctuate due to convective activity or low wind speeds of 3 kt., not 6 kt., or less. Answer (C) is incorrect because a "VRB" wind entry in a TAF indicates that the wind direction is forecast to fluctuate due to convective activity or low wind speeds of 3 kt., not 9 kt., or less.

Answer (C) is correct (4176). *(AWS Sect 4)*
A terminal aerodrome forecast (TAF) is a concise statement of the expected meteorological conditions at an airport during a specified period (usually 24 hr.). Thus, a TAF contains information regarding the expected weather at the destination airport at the ETA.
Answer (A) is incorrect because an area forecast (FA) is a forecast of general weather conditions over an area the size of several states, not for a specific airport. The FA is used if the destination airport does not have a TAF. Answer (B) is incorrect because radar summary and weather depiction charts are national weather maps of observed weather at a specific time. They are useful for flight planning but do not provide specific information about a particular destination airport.

Answer (B) is correct (4170). *(AWS Sect 4)*
The Terminal Aerodrome Forecast (TAF) is a concise statement of the expected meteorological conditions at an airport during a specified period (usually 24 hr.). The TAF covers a geographic area within a 5 SM radius of the airport's center.
Answer (A) is incorrect because the TAF covers a geographic area within a 5-SM radius of the airport's center, not a 5-NM radius. Answer (C) is incorrect because the TAF covers a geographic area within a 5 SM radius of the airport's center, not 5 to 10 statute miles. The letters VC in the TAF describe conditions that will occur within the vicinity of the airport (5 to 10 SM), not at the airport, and will be used only with FG (fog), SH (showers), or TS (thunderstorms).

9.7 Aviation Area Forecast (FA)

33.
4201. Area forecasts generally include a forecast period of 18 hours and cover a geographical

A— terminal area.
B— area less than 3,000 square miles.
C— area the size of several states.

Answer (C) is correct (4201). *(AWS Sect 4)*
Area forecasts (FA) generally include a total forecast period of 18 hr. and cover a geographical area the size of several states.
Answer (A) is incorrect because a TAF, not an FA, will forecast conditions at a terminal area. Answer (B) is incorrect because an FA forecast covers an area greater than, not less than, 3,000 sq. mi. and gives a general description of clouds and weather which are significant to VFR operations.

34.
4179. "WND" in the categorical outlook in the Aviation Area Forecast means that the wind during that period is forecast to be

A— At least 6 knots or stronger.
B— At least 15 knots or stronger.
C— At least 20 knots or stronger.

Answer (C) is correct (4179). *(AWS Sect 4)*
WND in the categorical outlook in the aviation area forecast (FA) means that the winds, sustained or gusty, are expected to be 20 kt. or greater during that period.
Answer (A) is incorrect because WND means the winds are expected to be at least 20 kt., not 6 kt., or stronger. Answer (B) is incorrect because WND means the winds are expected to be at least 20 kt., not 15 kt., or stronger.

9.8 Winds and Temperatures Aloft Forecast (FD)

35.
4193. (Refer to figure 2 on page 318.) What approximate wind direction, speed, and temperature (relative to ISA) should a pilot expect when planning for a flight over ALB at FL 270?

A— 270° magnetic at 97 knots; ISA –4 °C.
B— 260° true at 110 knots; ISA +5 °C.
C— 275° true at 97 knots; ISA +4 °C.

Answer (C) is correct (4193). *(AWS Sect 4)*
For conditions at FL 270 over ALB in Fig. 2, you must interpolate between values at FL 240 and FL 300. First, decode the two given flight levels:

$$FL\ 240 = 270° \text{ at } 77 \text{ kt. and } -28°C$$
$$FL\ 300 = 280° \text{ at } 118 \text{ kt. and } -42°C$$
$$\text{Difference} = 10° \quad 41 \text{ kt.} \quad -14°C$$

Interpolation for each value gives

$$FL\ 270 = 275° \text{ at } 97 \text{ kt. and } -35°C$$

Finally, note that the answer asks for ISA (standard temperature). At 2° per 1,000 ft., ISA would be 54°C (27 x 2) less than surface standard of 15°C. Thus, at FL 270, the standard temperature is 15° – 54° = –39°C. Thus the –35°C forecast temperature is ISA + 4°C.
Answer (A) is incorrect because winds aloft are always given in true, not magnetic, direction. Answer (B) is incorrect because interpolating between 270° and 280° results in 275°, not 260°.

FT	3000	6000	9000	12000	18000	24000	30000	34000	39000
EMI	2807	2715-07	2728-10	2842-13	2867-21	2891-30	751041	771150	780855
ALB	0210	9900-07	2714-09	2728-12	2656-19	2777-28	781842	760150	269658
PSB		1509+04	2119+01	2233-04	2262-14	2368-26	781939	760850	780456
STL	2308	2613+02	2422-03	2431-08	2446-19	2461-30	760142	782650	760559

VALID 141200Z FOR USE 0900-1500Z. TEMPS NEG ABV 24000

FIGURE 2.—Winds and Temperatures Aloft Forecast.

36.
4192. (Refer to figure 2 above.) What approximate wind direction, speed, and temperature (relative to ISA) should a pilot expect when planning for a flight over PSB at FL 270?

A— 260° magnetic at 93 knots; ISA +7 °C.
B— 280° true at 113 knots; ISA +3 °C.
C— 255° true at 93 knots; ISA +6 °C.

Answer (C) is correct (4192). (AWS Sect 4)
For conditions at FL 270 over PSB in Fig. 2, you must interpolate between values at FL 240 and FL 300. First, decode the two given flight levels:

FL 240 =	230° at	68 kt. and	−26.0°C
FL 300 =	280° at	119 kt. and	−39.0°C
Difference =	50°	51 kt.	−13.0°C

Interpolation for each value gives

FL 270 = 255° at 93 kt. and −33°C

Finally, to compare the temperature to standard, subtract the lapse rate at FL 270 [(27,000/1,000) x 2° = 54°] from surface standard of 15°C to get FL 270 standard of −39°C. The forecast temperature of about −33°C at FL 270 is thus 6°C warmer than standard.
Answer (A) is incorrect because winds aloft are always given in true, not magnetic, direction. Answer (B) is incorrect because interpolating between 230° and 280° results in 255°, not 280°.

37.
4194. (Refer to figure 2 above.) What approximate wind direction, speed, and temperature (relative to ISA) should a pilot expect when planning for a flight over EMI at FL 270?

A— 265° true; 100 knots; ISA +3 °C.
B— 270° true; 110 knots; ISA +5 °C.
C— 260° magnetic; 100 knots; ISA −5 °C.

Answer (A) is correct (4194). (AWS Sect 4)
For conditions at FL 270 over EMI in Fig. 2, you must interpolate between values at FL 240 and FL 300. First, decode the two given flight levels:

FL 240 =	280° at	91 kt. and	−30°C
FL 300 =	250° at	110 kt. and	−41°C
Difference =	30°	19 kt.	−11°C

Interpolation for each value gives approximately

FL 270 = 265° at 100 kt. and −36°C

Finally, to compare the temperature to standard, subtract the lapse rate at FL 270 [(27,000/1,000) x 2° = 54°] from surface standard of 15°C to get FL 270 standard of −39°C. The forecast temperature of about −36°C at FL 270 is thus 3°C warmer than standard.
Answer (B) is incorrect because interpolating between 250° and 280° results in 265°, not 270°. Answer (C) is incorrect because winds aloft are given in true, not magnetic, direction.

38.
4199. A station is forecasting wind and temperature aloft at FL 390 to be 300° at 200 knots; temperature –54°C. How would this data be encoded in the FD?

A— 300054.
B— 809954.
C— 309954.

39.
4095. How much colder than standard temperature is the forecast temperature at 9,000 feet, as indicated in the following excerpt from the Winds and Temperature Aloft Forecast?

FT	6000	9000
	0737-04	1043-10

A— 3°C.
B— 10°C.
C— 7°C.

40.
4172. What wind direction and speed is represented by the entry 9900+00 for 9,000 feet, on a Winds and Temperatures Aloft Forecast (FD)?

A— Light and variable; less than 5 knots.
B— Vortex winds exceeding 200 knots.
C— Light and variable; less than 10 knots.

41.
4189. When is the wind-group at one of the forecast altitudes omitted at a specific location or station in the Winds and Temperatures Aloft Forecast (FD)? When the wind

A— is less than 5 knots.
B— is less than 10 knots.
C— at the altitude is within 1,500 feet of the station elevation.

Answer (B) is correct (4199). *(AWS Sect 4)*
At FL 390, a 300° wind at 200 kt. is encoded as 809954. Note that the first two digits are the direction. The second two digits are velocity. 200 kt. or greater wind speeds are coded as 99 for the speed, and 50 is added to the two-digit direction code. Here, the direction is 80 for 300°. The temperature is the last two digits, and minus signs are omitted above 24,000 ft. MSL.
Answer (A) is incorrect because it indicates winds from 300° at 0 kt. However, when forecast speed is less than 5 kt., the code is 9900 for wind direction and speed. Answer (C) is incorrect because it indicates a 99-kt. wind speed from 300°.

Answer (C) is correct (4095). *(AWS Sect 4)*
At 9,000 ft., the forecast temperature is –10°C. Standard temperature is 15°C at sea level with a lapse rate of 2°C per 1,000 ft., which would bring the standard temperature to –3°C at 9,000 ft. (15° – 18°). Therefore, the forecast temperature of –10°C is 7° colder than the standard temperature of –3°C.
Answer (A) is incorrect because standard temperature at 9,000 ft. is –3°C, not –7°C. Answer (B) is incorrect because standard temperature at 9,000 ft. is –3°C, not 0°C.

Answer (A) is correct (4172). *(AWS Sect 4)*
The entry 9900 in a winds and temperatures aloft forecast indicates light and variable winds. +00 is the air temperature on the Celsius scale.
Answer (B) is incorrect because an example of the code for winds over 200 kt. would be 7099, for 200° at 199 kt. or greater. Answer (C) is incorrect because light and variable means less than 5 kt., not 10 kt.

Answer (C) is correct (4189). *(AWS Sect 4)*
No winds are forecast within 1,500 ft. of the station elevation. No temperatures are forecast for the 3,000-ft. MSL or for a level within 2,500 ft. of station elevation.
Answer (A) is incorrect because, when forecast wind speed is less than 5 kt., the code 9900 is used for direction and velocity. Answer (B) is incorrect because, when forecast wind speed is less than 5 kt., not 10 kt., the code 9900 is used for direction and velocity.

42.
4188. When is the temperature at one of the forecast altitudes omitted at a specific location or station in the Winds and Temperatures Aloft Forecast (FD)?

A— When the temperature is standard for that altitude.
B— For the 3,000-foot altitude (level) or when the level is within 2,500 feet of station elevation.
C— Only when the winds are omitted for that altitude (level).

Answer (B) is correct (4188). *(AWS Sect 4)*
No temperatures are forecast for the 3,000-ft. level or for a level within 2,500 ft. of station elevation. No winds are forecast within 1,500 ft. of the station elevation.
Answer (A) is incorrect because temperatures are reported whether standard or not. Answer (C) is incorrect because the winds are omitted within 1,500 ft. of the ground and temperatures are omitted within 2,500 ft. of the ground.

43.
4190. Decode the excerpt from the Winds and Temperature Aloft Forecast (FD) for OKC at 39,000 feet.

```
FT          3000   6000   39000
OKC                       830558
```

A— Wind 130° at 50 knots, temperature –58 °C.
B— Wind 330° at 105 knots, temperature –58 °C.
C— Wind 330° at 205 knots, temperature –58 °C.

Answer (B) is correct (4190). *(AWS Sect 4)*
At OKC at 39,000 ft., the 83 for wind direction means that 100 kt. have been deducted from the wind speed and 50 added to the wind direction. Thus, the wind speed is 105 kt. Also, subtract 50 from the first two-digit code for direction to get 330°. Above 24,000 ft., the temperatures are always negative.
Answer (A) is incorrect because 130° at 50 kt. and –58°C would be 135058. Answer (C) is incorrect because 330° at 205 kt. and –58°C would be 839958.

44.
4191. Which values are used for winds aloft forecasts?

A— Magnetic direction and knots.
B— Magnetic direction and MPH.
C— True direction and knots.

Answer (C) is correct (4191). *(AWS Sect 4)*
Winds aloft are forecast in true direction and knots.
Answer (A) is incorrect because true, not magnetic, direction is used. Answer (B) is incorrect because true, not magnetic, direction and knots, not MPH, are used.

9.9 Low-Level Significant Weather Prog

45.
4214. A prognostic chart depicts the conditions

A— existing at the surface during the past 6 hours.
B— which presently exist from the 1,000-millibar through the 700-millibar level.
C— forecast to exist at a specific time in the future.

Answer (C) is correct (4214). *(AWS Sect 11)*
Prognostic charts show conditions as they are forecast to be at the valid time (UTC or Zulu) for the chart. The charts are issued four times daily.
Answer (A) is incorrect because prognostic charts relate to the future, not the past. Answer (B) is incorrect because prognostic charts relate to the future, not the present.

46.
4213. (Refer to figure 5 below.) What is the meaning of the symbol depicted as used on the U.S. Low-Level Significant Weather Prognostic Chart?

A— Showery precipitation (e.g. rain showers) embedded in an area of continuous rain covering half or more of the area.
B— Continuous precipitation (e.g. rain) covering half or more of the area.
C— Showery precipitation (e.g. thunderstorms/rain showers) covering half or more of the area.

Answer (A) is correct (4213). *(AWS Sect 11)*
The dot over the triangle in Fig. 5 indicates showery precipitation. The two heavy, solid dots indicate continuous rain. The shaded area indicates that more than one-half of the area is obscured.
Answer (B) is incorrect because the dot over the triangle indicates showery precipitation within the area of continuous precipitation. Answer (C) is incorrect because thunderstorms are indicated by an R with an arrow on the leg.

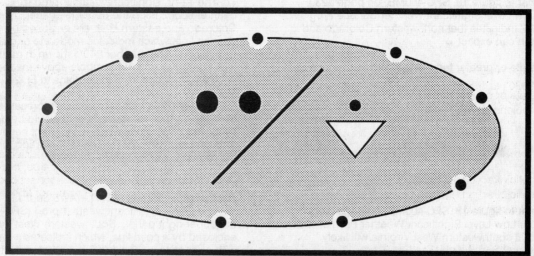

FIGURE 5.—Symbol Used on Low-Level Significant Weather Prognostic Chart.

47.
4212. Which meteorological conditions are depicted by a prognostic chart?

A— Conditions existing at the time of the observation.
B— Interpretation of weather conditions for geographical areas between reporting stations.
C— Conditions forecast to exist at a specific time shown on the chart.

Answer (C) is correct (4212). *(AWS Sect 11)*
Prognostic charts show conditions as they are forecast to be at the valid time for the chart. The charts are issued four times daily.
Answer (A) is incorrect because prognostic charts relate to the future, not the present. Answer (B) is incorrect because prognostic charts relate to the future, not the present.

48.
4211. The Low-Level Significant Weather Prognostic Chart depicts weather conditions

A— that are forecast to exist at a valid time shown on the chart.
B— as they existed at the time the chart was prepared.
C— that existed at the time shown on the chart which is about 3 hours before the chart is received.

Answer (A) is correct (4211). *(AWS Sect 11)*
Prognostic charts show conditions as they are forecast to be at the valid time for the chart. The charts are issued four times daily.
Answer (B) is incorrect because the low-level prog chart consists of 12- and 24-hr. forecasts. Answer (C) is incorrect because prognostic charts look to the future; they do not report the past.

49.
4219. (Refer to figure 18, SFC-PROG, on page 323.) The chart symbols shown in the Gulf of Mexico at 12Z and extending into AL, GA, SC, and northern FL indicate a

A— tropical storm.
B— hurricane.
C— tornado originating in the Gulf of Mexico.

Answer (A) is correct (4219). *(AWS Sect 11)*
    The SFC PROG chart at 1200Z is on the lower right panel. The symbol shown in the Gulf of Mexico and extending into AL, GA, SC, and northern FL indicates a tropical storm and associated precipitation.
    Answer (B) is incorrect because the symbol in the Gulf of Mexico indicates a tropical storm. A hurricane symbol would have the center circle darkened, not open. Answer (C) is incorrect because the symbol in the Gulf of Mexico indicates a tropical storm, not a tornado. Additionally, tornadoes are not forecast on a prog chart.

50.
4218. (Refer to figure 18, SFC-400MB, on page 323.) The U.S. Low Level Significant Weather Surface Prog Chart at 00Z indicates that northwestern Colorado and eastern Utah can expect

A— moderate or greater turbulence from the surface to FL 240.
B— moderate or greater turbulence above FL 240.
C— no turbulence is indicated.

Answer (A) is correct (4218). *(AWS Sect 11)*
    The 12-hr. significant weather prog (SFC-400MB) chart at 0000Z is on the upper left panel. Northwestern Colorado and eastern Utah are enclosed by a long, dashed line, which indicates moderate or greater turbulence. The number 240/ (shown in northwestern WY with an arrow) and the symbols above mean moderate-to-severe turbulence from the surface to FL 240 (24,000 ft. MSL).
    Answer (B) is incorrect because forecast turbulence from the surface to above FL 240 would be depicted as /SFC, not 240/. Answer (C) is incorrect because no turbulence is forecast for central Colorado, but it is indicated for northwestern Colorado.

51.
4217. (Refer to figure 18, SFC-400MB, on page 323.) The 24-Hour Low Level Significant Weather Prog at 12Z indicates that southwestern West Virginia will likely experience

A— ceilings less than 1,000 feet, visibility less than 3 miles.
B— clear sky and visibility greater than 6 miles.
C— ceilings 1,000 to 3,000 feet and visibility 3 to 5 miles.

Answer (A) is correct (4217). *(AWS Sect 11)*
    The 24-hr. significant weather prog (SFC-400MB) is on the upper right panel. Southwestern West Virginia is enclosed by a solid line, which indicates a forecast of IFR with ceilings less than 1,000 ft. and/or visibility less than 3 SM.
    Answer (B) is incorrect because the low-level significant weather prog does not show areas of clear skies, only areas of ceilings above 3,000 ft., by not being enclosed by solid or scalloped lines. Answer (C) is incorrect because forecast ceilings of 1,000 to 3,000 ft. inclusive and/or visibility 3 to 5 SM inclusive are indicated by an area enclosed by a scalloped, not solid, line.

52.
4216. (Refer to figure 18, SFC PROG, on page 323.) A planned low altitude flight from northern Florida to southern Florida at 00Z is likely to encounter

A— intermittent rain or rain showers, moderate turbulence, and freezing temperatures above 8,000 feet.
B— showery precipitation, thunderstorms/rain showers covering half or more of the area.
C— showery precipitation covering less than half the area, no turbulence below 18,000 feet, and freezing temperatures above 12,000 feet.

Answer (B) is correct (4216). *(AWS Sect 11)*
    The SFC PROG at 0000Z is on the lower left panel. The Florida peninsula is in a shaded area surrounded by a dash-dot line. The dash-dot line means showery precipitation, and the shading means the precipitation covers half or more of the area. The type of precipitation is depicted in north Florida. The triangle with the dot over it means rain showers, and the symbol resembling an "R" with an arrow means thunderstorms.
    Answer (A) is incorrect because intermittent precipitation would be indicated by a solid line, not a dash-dot line. Answer (C) is incorrect because showery precipitation covering less than half the area is depicted by a dash-dot line with no shading. The Florida peninsula has shading, which means precipitation covering half or more, not less, of the area.

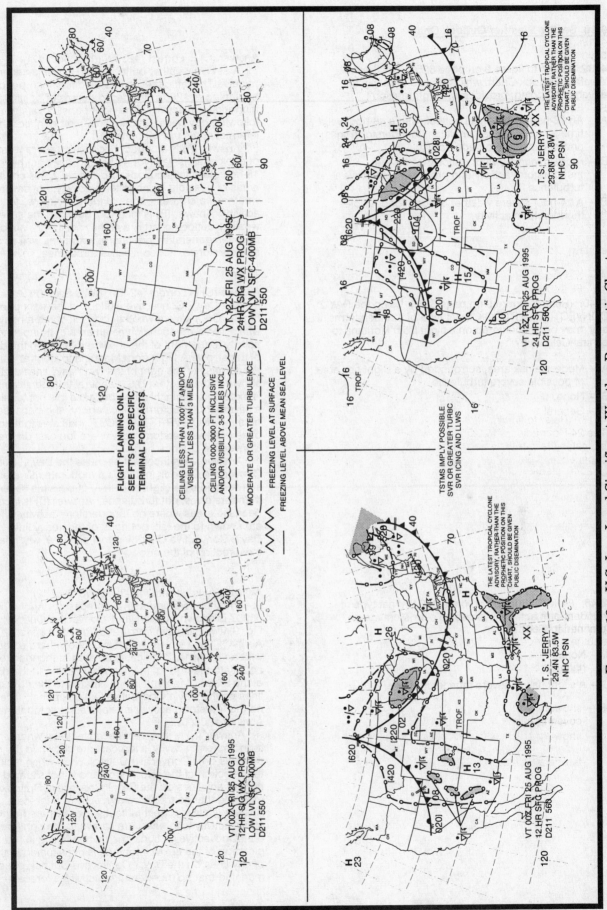

FIGURE 18.—U.S. Low-Level Significant Weather Prognostic Charts.

9.10 Severe Weather Outlook Chart

53.
4239. (Refer to figure 9 on page 325.) The Severe
Weather Outlook Chart, which is used primarily for
advance planning, provides what information?

A— An 18-hour categorical outlook with a 48-hour valid
time for severe weather watch, thunderstorm lines,
and of expected tornado activity.
B— A preliminary 12-hour outlook for severe
thunderstorm activity and probable convective
turbulence.
C— A 24-hour severe weather outlook for possible
thunderstorm activity.

Answer (C) is correct (4239). *(AWS Sect 12)*
    A severe weather outlook chart is presented in two
panels. The left panel covers the first 24-hr. period
beginning at 1200Z and depicts areas of possible
thunderstorm activity. The right panel covers the
following day beginning at 1200Z and contains the same
information as the left panel.
    Answer (A) is incorrect because a severe weather
outlook chart is valid for 48 hr. and does not have an
18-hr. categorical outlook. Additionally, this chart depicts
areas of possible thunderstorm activity, not severe
weather watch areas, lines of thunderstorms, or tornado
activity. Answer (B) is incorrect because the severe
weather outlook chart is a 48-hr., not 12-hr., outlook for
possible general thunderstorm activity as well as severe
thunderstorms, not convective turbulence.

54.
4240. (Refer to figure 9 on page 325.) Using the DAY 2
CONVECTIVE OUTLOOK, what type of thunderstorms, if
any, may be encountered on a flight from Montana to
central California?

A— Moderate risk area, surrounded by a slight risk area,
of possible severe turbulence.
B— None.
C— General.

Answer (C) is correct (4240). *(AWS Sect 12)*
    The Day 2 Convective Outlook is the right panel of
Fig. 9. On a severe weather outlook chart, a heavy line
with an arrowhead indicates an area of thunderstorm
activity to the right of the line when facing in the direction
of the arrow. A flight from Montana to Central California
would pass to the right of the two heavy lines that are
shown in the western U.S. General thunderstorm activity
is expected within this area because it is not labeled with
a severe thunderstorm risk category, and because the
notation "NO SVR TSTMS FCST" indicates that no areas
of severe thunderstorm activity are forecast on the Day 2
Convective Outlook panel.
    Answer (A) is incorrect because the Day 1, not Day 2,
Convective Outlook indicates a moderate risk area,
surrounded by a slight risk area, of possible severe
thunderstorms, not turbulence. Answer (B) is incorrect
because areas where no thunderstorm activity is forecast
are shown to the left, not right, of the heavy lines on the
Day 2 Convective Outlook panel of Fig. 9, when facing in
the direction of the arrow.

55.
4248. (Refer to figure 9 on page 325.) What type of
thunderstorm activity is expected over Montana on
April 4th at 0800Z?

A— None.
B— General.
C— A slight risk of severe thunderstorms.

Answer (A) is correct (4248). *(AWS Sect 12)*
    The thunderstorm activity forecast for April 4th at
0800Z is shown on the Day 1 Convective Outlook panel of
Fig. 9, which is valid from 1200Z on April 3rd to 1200Z on
April 4th. On a severe weather outlook chart, a heavy line
with an arrowhead indicates an area of thunderstorm
activity to the right of the line when facing in the direction
of the arrow. Montana is not situated to the right of any
lines on the Day 1 Convective Outlook panel. Therefore,
no thunderstorm activity is expected over Montana on
April 4th at 0800Z.
    Answer (B) is incorrect because areas where
thunderstorm activity is forecast are shown to the right of
the lines on a Convective Outlook chart when facing in
the direction of the arrow. Montana is not situated to the
right of any lines on the Day 1 Convective Outlook panel,
meaning that no thunderstorm activity is forecast.
Answer (C) is incorrect because areas where thunderstorm activity is forecast are shown to the right of the lines
on a Convective Outlook chart when facing in the
direction of the arrow. Montana is not situated to the right
of any lines on the Day 1 Convective Outlook panel,
meaning that no thunderstorm activity is forecast.

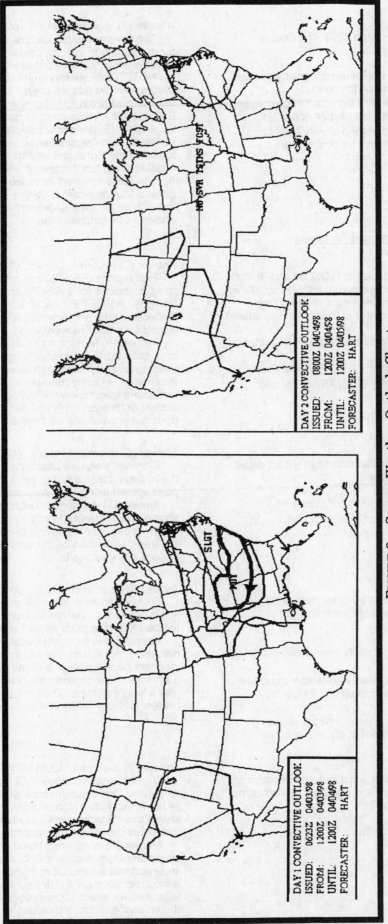

FIGURE 9.—Severe Weather Outlook Charts.

56.
4197. (Refer to figure 9 on page 325.) The Severe Weather Outlook Chart depicts

A— areas of probable severe thunderstorms by the use of single hatched areas on the chart.
B— areas of forecast, severe or extreme turbulence, and areas of severe icing for the next 24 hours.
C— areas of general thunderstorm activity (excluding severe) by the use of hatching on the chart.

Answer (A) is correct (4197). *(AWS Sect 12)*
    The severe weather outlook chart is a 48-hr. outlook for thunderstorm activity, presented in two panels. The hatched area indicates possible severe thunderstorms.
    NOTE: This question refers to an old version of the severe weather outlook chart. The current chart does not use hatched areas to indicate severe thunderstorms. Expect the FAA to revise this question in the future.
    Answer (B) is incorrect because areas of forecast severe or extreme turbulence for the next 24 hr. can be found on the significant weather panel of the significant weather prog, not the severe weather outlook chart. Answer (C) is incorrect because an area of possible general thunderstorm activity is shown to the right of a line with an arrowhead (when facing in the direction of the arrow), not a hatched area.

9.11 Miscellaneous Charts and Forecasts

57.
4184. A pilot planning to depart at 1100Z on an IFR flight is particularly concerned about the hazard of icing. What sources reflect the most accurate information on icing conditions (current and forecast) at the time of departure?

A— Low-Level Significant Weather Prognostic Chart, and the Area Forecast.
B— The Area Forecast, and the Freezing Level Chart.
C— Pilot weather reports (PIREP's), AIRMET's, and SIGMET's.

Answer (C) is correct (4184). *(AWS Sect 4)*
    Pilot reports (PIREPs) can reflect the most current icing conditions for a specific area, including type and intensity. AIRMET Zulu is for icing and freezing levels for a specified time and normally an outlook. A SIGMET is issued for areas of severe icing.
    Answer (A) is incorrect because low-level sig weather prog charts do not forecast icing conditions but do forecast freezing levels, and an area forecast does not provide any information on icing conditions. Answer (B) is incorrect because a freezing-level chart cannot be used to determine current or forecast icing conditions, and an area forecast does not provide any information on icing conditions.

58.
4195. What flight planning information can a pilot derive from constant pressure charts?

A— Clear air turbulence and icing conditions.
B— Levels of widespread cloud coverage.
C— Winds and temperatures aloft.

Answer (C) is correct (4195). *(AWS Sect 8)*
    Constant pressure charts provide information about the observed temperature, wind, and temperature-dew point spread along your proposed route.
    Answer (A) is incorrect because clear air turbulence is shown on the low-level prog chart. Answer (B) is incorrect because areas and levels of widespread cloud coverage are shown on the weather depiction and surface analysis charts.

59.
4173. What conclusion(s) can be drawn from a 500-millibar Constant Pressure Chart for a planned flight at FL 180?

A— Winds aloft at FL 180 generally flow across the height contours.
B— Observed temperature, wind, and temperature/dew point spread along the proposed route can be approximated.
C— Upper highs, lows, troughs, and ridges will be depicted by the use of lines of equal pressure.

Answer (B) is correct (4173). *(AWS Sect 8)*
    From a constant pressure analysis chart, you can approximate the observed temperature, wind, and temperature-dew point spread along a proposed route.
    Answer (A) is incorrect because the winds usually flow parallel to, not across, the height contours. Answer (C) is incorrect because heights of the specified pressure for each station are depicted via solid lines called contours to give a height pattern. The contours depict high height centers and low height centers, not highs and lows.

60.
4226. Which weather forecast describes prospects for an area coverage of both severe and general thunderstorms during the following 24 hours?

A— Terminal Aerodrome Forecast.
B— Convective outlook.
C— Radar Summary Chart.

Answer (B) is correct (4226). *(AWS Sect 4)*
    The convective outlook (AC) describes the prospects for general thunderstorm activity during the following 24 hr. Areas with a high, moderate, or slight risk of severe thunderstorms are included, as well as areas where thunderstorms may approach severe limits.
    Answer (A) is incorrect because a terminal aerodrome forecast (TAF) is a statement of expected conditions around an airport, not a forecast of thunderstorms only. Answer (C) is incorrect because a radar summary chart depicts observed radar returns, which show precipitation intensity, at the time shown on the chart. It provides an indication of observed, not forecast, severe and general thunderstorms.

61.
4209. The Surface Analysis Chart depicts

A— actual pressure systems, frontal locations, cloud tops, and precipitation at the time shown on the chart.

B— frontal locations and expected movement, pressure centers, cloud coverage, and obstructions to vision at the time of chart transmission.

C— actual frontal positions, pressure patterns, temperature, dew point, wind, weather, and obstructions to vision at the valid time of the chart.

Answer (C) is correct (4209). *(AWS Sect 5)*
The surface analysis chart provides the locations of pressure systems, dew points, wind, and obstructions to vision at the valid time of the chart.
Answer (A) is incorrect because the surface analysis chart does not depict cloud tops. Answer (B) is incorrect because expected movement of weather systems is not depicted. This chart depicts current conditions at the time of issuance.

62.
4215. What information is provided by a Convective Outlook (AC)?

A— It describes areas of probable severe icing and severe or extreme turbulence during the next 24 hours.

B— It provides prospects of both general and severe thunderstorm activity during the following 24 hours.

C— It indicates areas of probable convective turbulence and the extent of instability in the upper atmosphere (above 500 MB).

Answer (B) is correct (4215). *(AWS Sect 4)*
The convective outlook describes the prospects for general thunderstorm activity during the following 24 hr. Areas with a high, moderate, or slight risk of severe thunderstorms are included, as well as areas where thunderstorms may approach severe limits.
Answer (A) is incorrect because areas of severe or extreme turbulence are forecast in the significant weather prog charts, not in an AC. Additionally, icing is not specifically forecast but is implied in clouds and precipitation above the freezing level. Answer (C) is incorrect because areas of probable convective turbulence and with the extent of instability above 500 mb/hPa (18,000 ft. MSL) are depicted by the contraction "CB" in a high-level significant weather prog, not an AC.

63.
4175. What does a Convective Outlook (AC) describe for a following 24-hr. period?

A— General thunderstorm activity.

B— A severe weather watch bulletin.

C— When forecast conditions are expected to continue beyond the valid period.

Answer (A) is correct (4175). *(AWS Sect 4)*
A convective outlook (AC) describes the prospects for general thunderstorm activity during the following 24 hr.
Answer (B) is incorrect because a severe weather watch bulletin is a separate product. An AC forecasts general thunderstorm activity for the following 24 hr., while a severe weather watch bulletin is issued as necessary to define areas of possible severe thunderstorms or tornado activity. Answer (C) is incorrect because an AC is a forecast of thunderstorm activity for the following 24-hr. period, not a statement of forecast conditions that are expected to continue beyond the valid period.

64.
4186. When are severe weather watch bulletins (WW) issued?

A— Every 12 hours as required.

B— Every 24 hours as required.

C— Unscheduled and issued as required.

Answer (C) is correct (4186). *(AWS Sect 4)*
A severe weather watch bulletin (WW) defines areas of possible severe thunderstorms or tornado activity. WWs are unscheduled and are issued as required by the National Severe Storm Forecast Center.
Answer (A) is incorrect because severe weather watch bulletins are unscheduled and are issued as required, not every 12 hr. as required. Answer (B) is incorrect because severe weather watch bulletins are unscheduled and are issued as required, not every 24 hr. as required.

65.
4185. Which forecast provides specific information concerning expected sky cover, cloud tops, visibility, weather, and obstructions to vision in a route format?

A— DFW FA 131240.

B— MEM TAF 132222.

C— 249 TWEB 252317.

Answer (C) is correct (4185). *(AWS Sect 4)*
The TWEB route forecast provides expected sky cover, cloud tops, visibility, weather, and obstructions to vision in a route format. The forecast is for a corridor 25 mi. on either side of the route.
Answer (A) is incorrect because an FA covers an area of several states, not a specific route. Answer (B) is incorrect because a TAF is a forecast of weather within 5 SM of a specific airport, not a route.

9.12 High-Level Significant Weather Prog

66.
4225. (Refer to figure 7 on page 329.) What information is indicated by arrow A?

A— The height of the tropopause in meters above sea level.
B— The height of the existing layer of CAT.
C— The height of the tropopause in hundreds of feet above MSL.

Answer (C) is correct (4225). (AWS Sect 11)
On the U.S. High-Level Significant Weather Prognostic Chart, Fig. 7, tropopause heights are depicted in rectangular boxes in hundreds of feet MSL, i.e., 260, 300, 340, 390, 450, and 530. As you look at the map, you can see how the tropopause height varies around the center.
Answer (A) is incorrect because the height is in hundreds of feet, not meters. Answer (B) is incorrect because areas of clear air turbulence (CAT) are bounded by heavy dashed lines.

67.
4223. (Refer to figure 7 on page 329.) What weather conditions are predicted within the area indicated by arrow C?

A— Light turbulence at FL 370 within the area outlined by dashes.
B— Moderate turbulence at 32,000 feet MSL.
C— Moderate to severe CAT has been reported at FL 320.

Answer (B) is correct (4223). (AWS Sect 11)
The letter C points to a banana-shaped oval area outlined by a heavy dashed line. About an inch west-northwest of the letter C, there is a symbol composed of a single "mountain peak," or upside-down V, over the number 350, which is separated from 3 Xs by a horizontal line. This symbol indicates that moderate turbulence is forecast in the outlined area from 35,000 ft. MSL to below the lower limit of the chart (24,000 ft. MSL).
Answer (A) is incorrect because moderate, not light, turbulence is forecast within the area outlined by dashes. Answer (C) is incorrect because no clear air turbulence (CAT) has been reported by this chart, which is a forecast product, not an observation of existing weather; and the relevant area has moderate, not moderate to severe, CAT forecast from 35,000 ft. MSL to below the lower limit of the chart (24,000 ft. MSL).

68.
4224. (Refer to figure 7 on page 329.) What weather conditions are depicted within the area indicated by arrow B?

A— Light to moderate turbulence at and above 37,000 feet MSL.
B— Moderate turbulence from below 24,000 feet MSL to 37,000 feet MSL.
C— Moderate to severe CAT is forecast to exist at FL 370.

Answer (B) is correct (4224). (AWS Sect 11)
On the U.S. High-Level Significant Weather Prognostic Chart, arrow B on Fig. 7 refers to an area bounded by heavy dashed lines, which indicate moderate turbulence. The XXX beneath the line means the base is below FL 240 (the lower limit of all high-level progs), and the 370 means the top of the forecast CAT, FL 370.
Answer (A) is incorrect because the turbulence is moderate, not light to moderate. Answer (C) is incorrect because the turbulence is moderate, not moderate to severe.

69.
4222. (Refer to figure 7 on page 329.) What weather conditions are depicted within the area indicated by arrow D?

A— Forecast isolated thunderstorms, tops at FL 440, more than 1/8 coverage.
B— Existing isolated cumulonimbus clouds, tops above 43,000 feet with less than 1/8 coverage.
C— Forecast isolated embedded cumulonimbus clouds with tops at 43,000 feet MSL, and less than 1/8 coverage.

Answer (C) is correct (4222). (AWS Sect 11)
Arrow D on the High-Level Significant Weather Prognostic (forecast) Chart points to an area of forecast isolated embedded cumulonimbus clouds with tops at 43,000 feet MSL. The term isolated means less than 1/8 coverage. Approximately 1 inch southwest of the letter D, just off the southern Cuban coast, is the notation "ISOL EMBD CB," and just to the right of this is the notation "430" over a line with 3 Xs under it, meaning that the cumulonimbus clouds extend from 43,000 to below the lower limit of the chart (24,000 feet MSL). There is a thin, heavy line going from these notations due north along the 80°W meridian of longitude to the arrow coming from the letter D.
Answer (A) is incorrect because the chart notations indicate tops at 43,000 feet, not 44,000 feet, and isolated means less than 1/8 coverage, not more than 1/8 coverage. Answer (B) is incorrect because the High-Level Significant Weather Prognostic Chart depicts forecast, not existing, conditions, and the notations indicate CB tops at 43,000 feet MSL, not above 43,000 feet MSL.

70.
4221. (Refer to figure 7 on page 329.) What weather conditions are depicted within the area indicated by arrow E?

A— Frequent embedded thunderstorms, less than 1/8 coverage, and tops at FL 370.
B— Frequent lightning in thunderstorms at FL 370.
C— Occasional cumulonimbus, 1/8 to 4/8 coverage, bases below 24,000 feet MSL and tops at 40,000 feet MSL.

Answer (C) is correct (4221). (AWS Sect 11)
Arrow E on Fig. 7 points to an area indicating occasional (OCNL), i.e., 1/8 to 4/8 coverage of cumulonimbus clouds and thunderstorms. They are from below FL 240 to FL 400.
Answer (A) is incorrect because the thunderstorms are not embedded. Also, there is 5/8 to 8/8 area coverage (FRQ). Answer (B) is incorrect because the high-level prog does not indicate lightning.

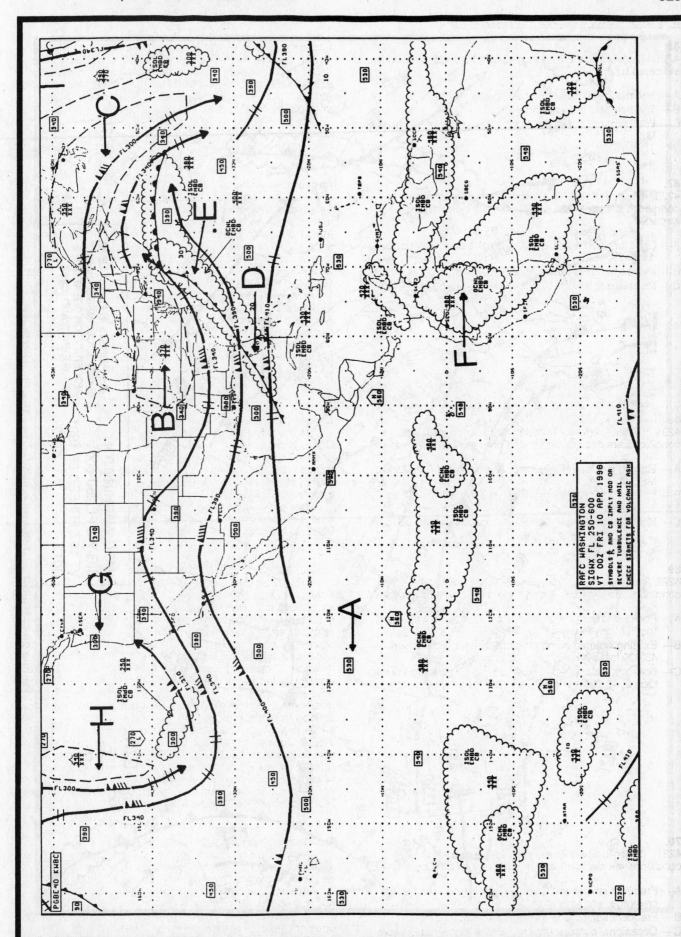

FIGURE 7.—High-Level Significant Weather Prognostic Chart.

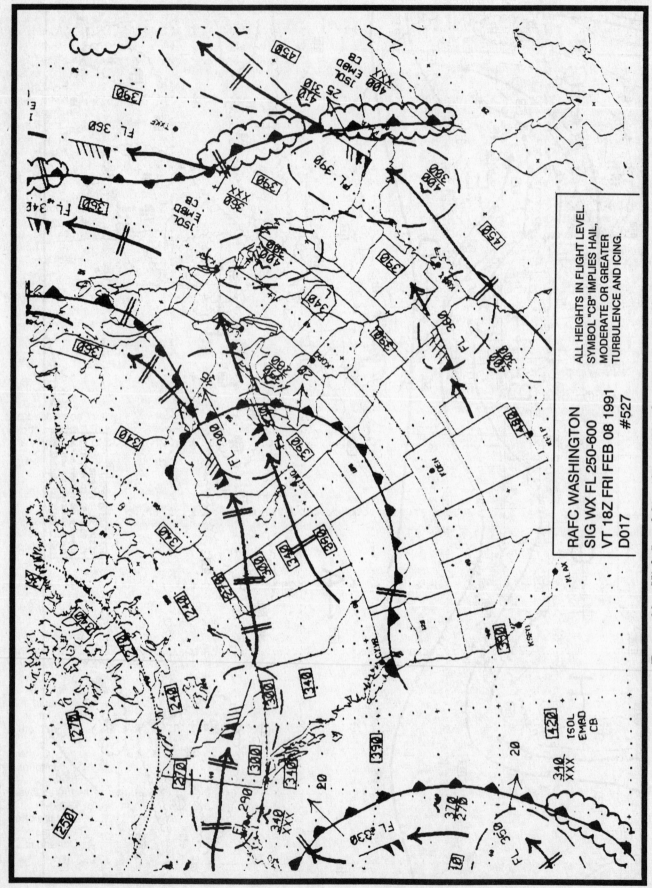

FIGURE 20.—High-Level Significant Weather Prognostic Chart.

71.
4229. (Refer to figure 7 on page 329.) What weather conditions are depicted within the area indicated by arrow F?

A— 2/8 to 6/8 coverage, occasional embedded thunderstorms, tops at FL 540.
B— 1/8 to 4/8 coverage, occasional embedded thunderstorms, maximum tops at 51,000 feet MSL.
C— Occasionally embedded cumulonimbus, bases below 24,000 feet with tops to 48,000 feet.

71a.
4242. (Refer to figure 7 on page 329.) The symbol on the U.S. HIGH-LEVEL SIGNIFICANT WEATHER PROG, indicated by arrow G, represents the

A— wind direction at the tropopause (300°).
B— height of the tropopause.
C— height of maximum wind shear (30,000 feet).

71b.
4245. (Refer to figure 7 on page 329.) The area indicated by arrow H indicates

A— light turbulence below 34,000 feet.
B— isolated embedded cumulonimbus clouds with bases below FL180 and tops at FL340.
C— moderate turbulence at and below 34,000 feet.

72.
4243. (Refer to figure 20 on page 330.) What is the maximum wind velocity forecast in the jet stream shown on the High Level Significant Weather Prognostic Chart over Canada?

A— 80 knots.
B— 103 knots.
C— 130 knots.

Answer (C) is correct (4229). *(AWS Sect 11)*
The scalloped area (on Fig. 7) to which arrow F points shows occasional embedded cumulonimbus clouds from below 24,000 ft. (XXX) to 48,000 ft. (480).
Answer (A) is incorrect because the coverage codes include ISOL (to 1/8), OCNL (1/8 to 4/8), and FRQ (5/8 to 8/8), not 2/8 to 6/8, and the tops are forecast to be at 48,000 ft. (480), not FL 540. Answer (B) is incorrect because the tops are forecast to be at 48,000 ft. (480), not 51,000 ft. MSL.

Answer (B) is correct (4242). *(AWS Sect 11)*
Arrow G points to a rectangular box with a number inside it. On the U.S. High-Level Significant Weather Prognostic Chart, the number inside this symbol indicates the height of the tropopause in hundreds of feet. The box at arrow G has "300," which means the height of the tropopause is 30,000 ft., or FL 300.
Answer (A) is incorrect because "300" is the height of the tropopause in hundreds of ft. (30,000 ft.), not the wind direction at the tropopause. Answer (C) is incorrect because "300" is the height of the tropopause, not the height of maximum wind shear, in hundreds of ft. (30,000 ft.).

Answer (C) is correct (4245). *(AWS Sect 11)*
Arrow H points to an area surrounded by heavy dashed lines. Inside that area is a symbol composed of a single "mountain peak," or upside-down V, shown above the number 340, which is separated from three Xs by a horizontal line. This symbol indicates that moderate turbulence is forecast in the outlined area from 34,000 ft. to below the lower limit of the chart (24,000 ft.).
Answer (A) is incorrect because an area outlined by heavy dashed lines indicates forecast moderate or greater, not light, clear air turbulence. Answer (B) is incorrect because isolated embedded cumulonimbus clouds with bases below 24,000 ft., not FL 180, and tops at 25,000 ft., not FL 340, are forecast in the area (enclosed by scalloped lines) which appears approximately 1 inch below the letter H.

Answer (C) is correct (4243). *(AWS Sect 11)*
The forecast jet streams having a core speed of 80 kt. or greater are shown on the high-level significant weather prog as a solid line with arrowheads indicating the flow direction. The forecast maximum core wind velocity is depicted by a shaft with each pennant (solid triangle) equal to 50 kt. and each feather (single line) equal to 10 kt. The maximum core speed forecast for the jet stream over Canada is 130 kt. (2 pennants + 3 feathers = 130 kt.)
Answer (A) is incorrect because the presence of the line depicting the jet stream indicates that the minimum core speed is 80 kt., but the maximum core speed is depicted by a shaft with pennants and/or feathers. Over Canada, the maximum speed is forecast at 130 kt. Answer (B) is incorrect because each feather on the shaft indicates 10 kt., not 1 kt., of wind speed. Thus, the maximum core speed of the jet stream over Canada is 130 kt., not 103 kt.

73.
4244. (Refer to figure 20 on page 330.) What is the height of the tropopause over Kentucky?

A— FL 300 sloping to FL 400 feet MSL.
B— FL 340.
C— FL 390.

Answer (B) is correct (4244). *(AWS Sect 11)*
Over the state of Kentucky is a five-sided polygon which has 340 over a letter "L." This indicates a low tropopause height of 34,000 ft. The chart legend states "All heights in flight level."
Answer (A) is incorrect because the area enclosed by a dashed line centered over Virginia, not Kentucky, is forecasting an area of moderate clear air turbulence (CAT) from FL 300 to FL 400, not a sloping tropopause. Answer (C) is incorrect because FL 390 is the height of the tropopause surrounding Kentucky (indicated by numerous occurrences of "FL 390" inside rectangles), not over Kentucky, where a low tropopause height of FL 340 is indicated by "FL 340 L" inside a five-sided polygon.

> The FAA has eliminated all questions that referred to Figure 10 - Tropopause Height/Vertical Wind Shear Prognostic Chart.

74.

The FAA has revised question 4245 to refer to Fig. 7, High-Level Significant Weather Prognostic Chart. Question 4245 is now question 71b on page 331.

75.

The FAA has revised question 4242 to refer to Fig. 7, High-Level Significant Weather Prognostic Chart. Question 4242 is now question 71a on page 331.

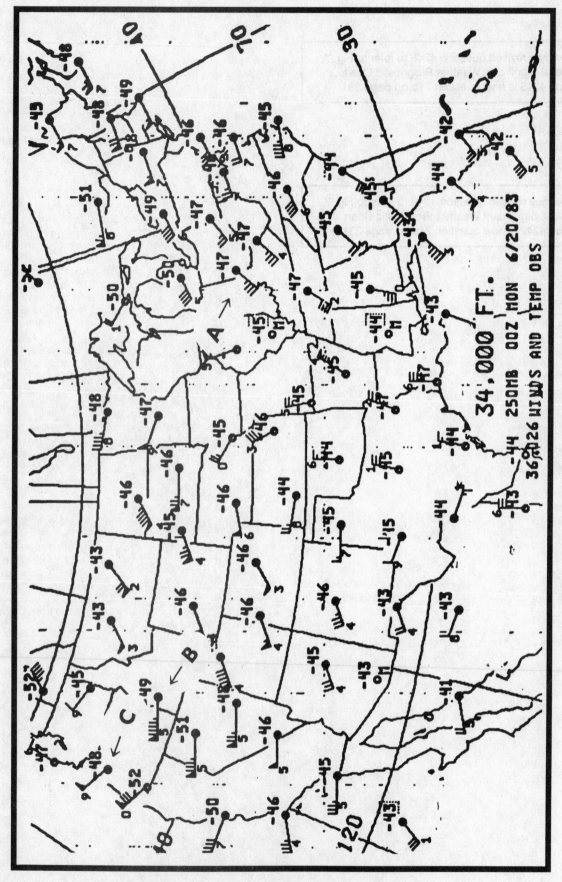

FIGURE 12.—Observed Winds Aloft for 34,000 Feet.

9.13 Observed Winds Aloft Chart

76.
4246. (Refer to figure 12 on page 334.) What is the approximate wind direction and velocity at 34,000 feet (see arrow C)?

A— 290°/50 knots.
B— 330°/50 knots.
C— 090°/48 knots.

Answer (A) is correct (4246). *(AWS Sect 10)*
Refer to arrow C in Fig. 12 (in Oregon) for Portland. The line is from the northwest with a 9 next to it, which means 290°. On the line is a solid triangle, or pennant, which means 50 kt. So the wind is from 290° at 50 kt.
Answer (B) is incorrect because the 9 next to a northwest line means 290°, not 330°. Answer (C) is incorrect because the 9 next to a northwest line means 290°, not 090°.

77.
4247. (Refer to figure 12 on page 334.) The wind direction and velocity on the Observed Winds Aloft Chart (see arrow A) is indicated from the

A— northeast at 35 knots.
B— northwest at 47 knots.
C— southwest at 35 knots.

Answer (C) is correct (4247). *(AWS Sect 10)*
Refer to arrow A in Fig. 12 (in southern Ohio). A line from the southwest with a 3 next to it = 230°. On the line are three 10-kt. symbols and one 5-kt. symbol indicating wind velocity of 35 kt. Thus, the wind is from 230° at 35 kt.
Answer (A) is incorrect because the line, and thus the wind, is from the southwest, not the northeast.
Answer (B) is incorrect because the line, and thus the wind, is from the southwest, not the northwest.

78.
4249. (Refer to figure 12 on page 334.) What is the approximate wind direction and velocity at CVG at 34,000 feet (see arrow A)?

A— 040°/35 knots.
B— 097°/40 knots.
C— 230°/35 knots.

Answer (C) is correct (4249). *(AWS Sect 10)*
Refer to arrow A in Fig. 12 (in southern Ohio). A line from the southwest with a 3 next to it = 230°. On the line are three 10-kt. symbols and one 5-kt. symbol indicating wind velocity of 35 kt. Thus, the wind is from 230° at 35 kt.
Answer (A) is incorrect because the line, and thus the wind, is from the southwest, not the northeast.
Answer (B) is incorrect because the line, and thus the wind, is from the southwest, not the east.

79.
4250. (Refer to figure 12, arrow B, on page 334.) What is the approximate wind direction and velocity at BOI (see arrow B)?

A— 270°/55 knots.
B— 250°/95 knots.
C— 080°/95 knots.

Answer (B) is correct (4250). *(AWS Sect 10)*
Refer to arrow B in Fig. 12 (in Idaho). The line plotted is from the west-southwest with a 5 by it; thus it is 250°. Adding the 50-kt. symbol with four 10-kt. symbols and one 5-kt. symbol, the wind velocity is 95 kt. Thus, the wind is from 250° at 95 kt.
Answer (A) is incorrect because the line has a 5 next to it, indicating 250°, not 270°. Answer (C) is incorrect because the line, and thus the wind, is from the west-southwest, not the east.

END OF CHAPTER

CHAPTER TEN
IFR EN ROUTE

This chapter contains outlines of major concepts tested, all FAA test questions and answers regarding IFR en route, and an explanation of each answer. Each module, or subtopic, within this chapter is listed above with the number of questions from the FAA knowledge test pertaining to that particular module. For each module, the first number following the parentheses is the page number on which the outline begins, and the next number is the page number on which the questions begin.

There are 60 questions in this chapter. We separate and organize the FAA questions into meaningful study units, i.e., chapters and modules. As an analogy, it is easier to deal with the "trees" if you understand the "forest." In this context, "trees" are individual FAA questions, and the "forest" is the instrument rating knowledge test. The organizational units between the overall instrument rating knowledge test and the individual instrument rating test questions are chapters and modules in this book.

CAUTION: The **sole purpose** of this book is to expedite your passing the FAA instrument rating knowledge test. Accordingly, all extraneous material (i.e., topics or regulations not directly tested on the FAA knowledge test) is omitted, even though much more information and knowledge are necessary to fly safely. This additional material is presented in *Instrument Pilot Flight Maneuvers and Practical Test Prep*, *Pilot Handbook*, *Aviation Weather and Weather Services*, and *FAR/AIM*, available from Gleim Publications, Inc. See the order form on page 488.

10.1 MINIMUM IFR ALTITUDES (Questions 1-13)

1. **Minimum reception altitude (MRA)** is the lowest altitude at which an intersection can be determined.

2. **Minimum obstruction clearance altitude (MOCA)** assures acceptable navigational signal coverage only within 22 NM (25 SM) of a VOR.

   a. ATC may assign the MOCA as an assigned altitude when certain special conditions exist and when the airplane is within 22 NM of a VOR.

3. **Minimum en route altitude (MEA)** is the lowest published altitude between radio fixes which assures acceptable navigational signal coverage and meets obstacle clearance requirements between those fixes.

   a. It is the minimum altitude to cross a fix beyond which a higher minimum applies.

4. MOCA and all other minimum IFR altitudes guarantee obstruction clearance in nonmountainous areas by providing at least 1,000 ft. of vertical distance from the highest obstruction 4 NM either side of the center of the airway to be flown.

   a. In mountainous areas, 2,000 ft. of vertical distance is provided.

5. Routes designed to serve aircraft operating from 18,000 ft. MSL up to and including FL 450 are referred to as jet routes or "J" routes.

10.2 VFR-ON-TOP (Questions 14-27a)

1. VFR-on-top operations can be conducted only after a pilot has received a VFR-on-top clearance to operate in VFR conditions.

NOTE: The pilot must request a VFR-on-top clearance.

2. VFR-on-top must comply with the appropriate VFR cruising altitudes as prescribed in FAR 91.159, which is based upon magnetic courses.

    a. 000° through 179° -- odd 1,000 ft. plus 500 ft.
    b. 180° through 359° -- even 1,000 ft. plus 500 ft.

3. VFR-on-top must be conducted at an altitude above the minimum IFR altitude.

4. VFR-on-top is conducted such that both VFR and IFR rules apply.

5. A clearance "to VFR-on-top" is authorization to fly through cloud layers to VFR conditions on top.

6. VFR-on-top operations are specifically prohibited in Class A airspace.

7. In VFR-on-top clearances, you must provide the same reports to ATC that are required for any other IFR flight, and you must adhere to any ATC clearances.

10.3 IFR EN ROUTE CHART INTERPRETATION (Questions 28-59)

1. The FAA knowledge test questions in this module are wide ranging. They are best prepared for by studying the legends for En Route Low-Altitude Charts.

    a. Legend 25 is presented below.

    b. Legends 23 and 24 are presented in color on pages 428 and 429.

    c. Some questions require application of previously covered topics such as interpretation of VOR indicators.

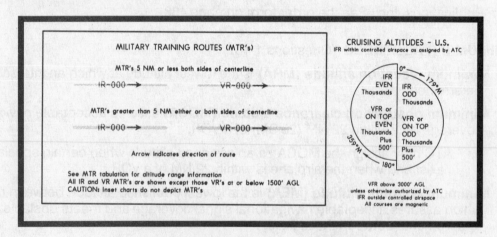

Legend 25 -- IFR En Route Low Altitude (U.S.)

10.1 Minimum IFR Altitudes

1.
4429. What is the definition of MEA?

A— The lowest published altitude which meets obstacle clearance requirements and assures acceptable navigational signal coverage.
B— The lowest published altitude which meets obstacle requirements, assures acceptable navigational signal coverage, two-way radio communications, and provides adequate radar coverage.
C— An altitude which meets obstacle clearance requirements, assures acceptable navigation signal coverage, two-way radio communications, adequate radar coverage, and accurate DME mileage.

Answer (A) is correct (4429). *(AIM P/C Glossary)*
The minimum en route altitude (MEA) is the lowest published altitude between radio fixes which assures acceptable navigational signal coverage and meets the obstacle clearance requirements between those fixes.
Answer (B) is incorrect because, by definition, the MEA does not assure either two-way radio communications or adequate radar coverage. Answer (C) is incorrect because, by definition, the MEA is the lowest published, not any, altitude that meets obstacle clearance requirements and assures acceptable navigation signal coverage. It does not provide for either two-way radio communications or adequate radar coverage.

2.
4435. Reception of signals from an off-airway radio facility may be inadequate to identify the fix at the designated MEA. In this case, which altitude is designated for the fix?

A— MRA.
B— MCA.
C— MOCA.

Answer (A) is correct (4435). *(AIM P/C Glossary)*
MRA (minimum reception altitude) is the lowest altitude at which an intersection can be determined. It is the altitude assigned for a fix when the MEA will not provide adequate reception of an off-airway radio facility (NAVAID) identifying the fix.
Answer (B) is incorrect because MCA (minimum crossing altitude) is the lowest altitude at a fix at which an aircraft must cross when proceeding in the direction of a higher MEA. Answer (C) is incorrect because the MOCA (minimum obstruction clearance altitude) is the lowest published altitude in effect between radio fixes on VOR airways, off-airway routes, or route segments which meets obstacle clearance requirements for the entire route segment and which assures acceptable navigation signal coverage only within 22 NM of a VOR.

3.
4544. Reception of signals from a radio facility, located off the airway being flown, may be inadequate at the designated MEA to identify the fix. In this case, which altitude is designated for the fix?

A— MOCA.
B— MRA.
C— MCA.

Answer (B) is correct (4544). *(AIM P/C Glossary)*
MRA (minimum reception altitude) is the lowest altitude at which an intersection can be determined. It is the altitude assigned for a fix when the MEA will not provide adequate reception of an off-airway radio facility (NAVAID) identifying the fix.
Answer (A) is incorrect because the MOCA (minimum obstruction clearance altitude) is the lowest published altitude in effect between radio fixes on VOR airways, off-airway routes, or route segments which meets obstacle clearance requirements for the entire route segment and which assures acceptable navigation signal coverage only within 22 NM of a VOR. Answer (C) is incorrect because MCA (minimum crossing altitude) is the lowest altitude at a fix at which an aircraft must cross when proceeding in the direction of a higher MEA.

4.
4545. ATC may assign the MOCA when certain special conditions exist, and when within

A— 22 NM of a VOR.
B— 25 NM of a VOR.
C— 30 NM of a VOR.

Answer (A) is correct (4545). *(AIM P/C Glossary)*
MOCA (minimum obstruction clearance altitude) is the lowest published altitude in effect between radio fixes on VOR airways, off-airway routes, or route segments which meets obstacle clearance requirements for the entire route segment and which assures acceptable navigational signal coverage only within 22 NM of a VOR. Thus, ATC may assign the MOCA as an assigned altitude, but only within 22 NM of a VOR.
Answer (B) is incorrect because the MOCA provides acceptable navigational signal coverage only within 25 SM, not 25 NM, of a VOR. Answer (C) is incorrect because ATC may assign the MOCA as an assigned altitude only within 22 NM, not 30 NM.

5.
4547. Acceptable navigational signal coverage at the MOCA is assured for a distance from the VOR of only

A— 12 NM.
B— 22 NM.
C— 25 NM.

Answer (B) is correct (4547). *(AIM P/C Glossary)*
MOCA (minimum obstruction clearance altitude) is the lowest published altitude in effect between radio fixes on VOR airways, off-airway routes, or route segments which meets obstacle clearance requirements for the entire route segment and which assures acceptable navigational signal coverage only within 22 NM of a VOR. Thus, ATC may assign the MOCA as an assigned altitude, but only within 22 NM of a VOR.
Answer (A) is incorrect because acceptable navigational signal coverage at the MOCA is assured for a distance from the VOR of 22 NM, not 12 NM. Answer (C) is incorrect because acceptable navigational signal coverage at the MOCA is assured for a distance from the VOR of 22 NM, not 25 NM.

6.
4546. Which aeronautical chart depicts Military Training Routes (MTR) above 1,500 feet?

A— IFR Planning Chart.
B— IFR Low Altitude En Route Chart.
C— IFR High Altitude En Route Chart.

Answer (B) is correct (4546). *(AIM Para 3-5-2)*
IFR En Route Low-Altitude Charts depict all IFR and VFR MTRs (IR and VR routes) that accommodate operations above 1,500 ft. AGL.
Answer (A) is incorrect because the U.S. IFR/VFR Planning Chart does not depict MTRs. The DOD Area Planning Chart depicts all MTRs, not only those above 1,500 ft. AGL. Answer (C) is incorrect because IFR En Route High-Altitude Charts cover altitudes at and above 18,000 ft. MSL; generally, MTRs are established below 10,000 ft. MSL.

7.
4432. The altitude that provides acceptable navigational signal coverage for the route, and meets obstacle clearance requirements is the minimum:

A— obstacle clearance altitude.
B— reception altitude.
C— enroute altitude.

8.
4436. Which condition is guaranteed for all of the following altitude limits: MAA, MCA, MRA, MOCA, and MEA? (Non-mountainous area.)

A— Adequate navigation signals.
B— Adequate communications.
C— 1,000-foot obstacle clearance.

9.
4437. If no MCA is specified, what is the lowest altitude for crossing a radio fix, beyond which a higher minimum applies?

A— The MEA at which the fix is approached.
B— The MRA at which the fix is approached.
C— The MOCA for the route segment beyond the fix.

10.
4765. In the case of operations over an area designated as a mountainous area, no person may operate an aircraft under IFR below 2,000 feet above the highest obstacle within a horizontal distance of

A— 3 SM from the course flown.
B— 4 SM from the course flown.
C— 4 NM from the course flown.

11.
4541. In the case of operations over an area designated as a mountainous area where no other minimum altitude is prescribed, no person may operate an aircraft under IFR below an altitude of

A— 500 feet above the highest obstacle.
B— 1,000 feet above the highest obstacle.
C— 2,000 feet above the highest obstacle.

Answer (C) is correct (4432). *(AIM P/C Glossary)*
The MEA (minimum en route altitude) is the lowest published altitude between radio fixes which assures acceptable navigational signal coverage and meets obstacle clearance requirements between those fixes.
Answer (A) is incorrect because the MOCA (minimum obstruction clearance altitude) only guarantees acceptable navigational signal coverage and meets obstacle clearance requirements when within 22 NM of a NAVAID, not along an entire route that takes the aircraft more than 22 NM from a NAVAID. Answer (B) is incorrect because the MRA (minimum reception altitude) is the lowest altitude at which an intersection can be identified. It is usually higher than the MEA.

Answer (C) is correct (4436). *(AIM P/C Glossary)*
The MAA, MCA, MRA, MOCA, and MEA meet the minimum obstacle clearance requirements. In non-mountainous areas, 1,000 ft. above the highest obstacle is guaranteed within a horizontal distance of 4 NM from the course to be flown.
Answer (A) is incorrect because the MOCA assures acceptable navigational signals only within 22 NM of a VOR. Answer (B) is incorrect because the minimum IFR altitudes do not guarantee adequate communications coverage.

Answer (A) is correct (4437). *(FAR 91.177)*
If no MCA (minimum crossing altitude) is specified, the lowest altitude for crossing a radio fix beyond which a higher minimum IFR altitude exists is the MEA at which the fix is approached. A climb must be initiated to a higher minimum immediately after passing the point beyond which that minimum altitude applies.
Answer (B) is incorrect because, if a higher minimum altitude exists after the fix and a higher altitude is needed to identify a fix, usually an MCA, not an MRA, is established at that fix. Answer (C) is incorrect because, if there is no MCA, the higher minimum altitude does not apply until immediately after passing the fix.

Answer (C) is correct (4765). *(FAR 91.177)*
In the case of operations over an area designated as a mountainous area where no other minimum altitude is prescribed, no person may operate an aircraft under IFR below 2,000 ft. above the highest obstacle within a horizontal distance of 4 NM from the course to be flown.
Answer (A) is incorrect because the horizontal distance is 4 NM, not 3 SM, from the course flown. Answer (B) is incorrect because the horizontal distance is 4 NM, not SM, from the course flown.

Answer (C) is correct (4541). *(FAR 91.177)*
In the case of operations over an area designated as a mountainous area where no other minimum altitude is prescribed, no person may operate an aircraft under IFR below 2,000 ft. above the highest obstacle within a horizontal distance of 4 NM from the course to be flown.
Answer (A) is incorrect because no person may operate an aircraft under IFR below an altitude of 2,000 ft., not 500 ft., above the highest obstacle in a mountainous area. Answer (B) is incorrect because no person may operate an aircraft under IFR below an altitude of 1,000 ft. above the highest obstacle in a nonmountainous, not mountainous, area.

12.
4542. MEA is an altitude which assures

A— obstacle clearance, accurate navigational signals from more than one VORTAC, and accurate DME mileage.
B— a 1,000-foot obstacle clearance within 2 miles of an airway and assures accurate DME mileage.
C— acceptable navigational signal coverage and meets obstruction clearance requirements.

13.
4485. Unless otherwise specified on the chart, the minimum en route altitude along a jet route is

A— 18,000 feet MSL.
B— 24,000 feet MSL.
C— 10,000 feet MSL.

10.2 VFR-on-Top

14.
4633. Under which of the following circumstances will ATC issue a VFR restriction to an IFR flight?

A— Whenever the pilot reports the loss of any navigational aid.
B— When it is necessary to provide separation between IFR and special VFR traffic.
C— When the pilot requests it.

15.
4430. What altitude may a pilot select upon receiving a VFR-on-Top clearance?

A— Any altitude at least 1,000 feet above the meteorological condition.
B— Any appropriate VFR altitude at or above the MEA in VFR weather conditions.
C— Any VFR altitude appropriate for the direction of flight at least 1,000 feet above the meteorological condition.

Answer (C) is correct (4542). *(AIM P/C Glossary)*
The minimum en route altitude (MEA) is the lowest published altitude between radio fixes which assures acceptable navigational signal coverage and meets the obstacle clearance requirements between those fixes.
Answer (A) is incorrect because only one VORTAC is needed at a time to provide acceptable coverage, and DME is not a required navigational signal. Answer (B) is incorrect because the clearance is within 4 NM, not 2 mi., and there is no assurance of DME coverage.

Answer (A) is correct (4485). *(FAR 71.603)*
Each designated jet route consists of a direct course for navigating from 18,000 ft. MSL up to and including FL 450 between the navigational aids and intersections specified for that route. Thus, the MEA along a jet route is 18,000 ft. MSL.
Answer (B) is incorrect because 24,000 ft. MSL (FL 240) is the minimum altitude at which DME is required when navigating by VOR, not the MEA for a jet route. Answer (C) is incorrect because 10,000 ft. MSL is the minimum altitude at which aircraft are required to operate the transponder on Mode C, not the MEA for a jet route.

Answer (C) is correct (4633). *(AIM Para 4-4-7)*
VFR-on-top is an ATC authorization for an IFR aircraft to operate in VFR conditions at any appropriate VFR altitude. ATC may not authorize VFR-on-top operations unless the pilot requests the clearance to operate in VFR conditions.
Answer (A) is incorrect because a pilot would report only a malfunction of navigation equipment, not a loss of any navigational aid, to ATC. Answer (B) is incorrect because special VFR traffic would be found near an airport in Class B, C, or D airspace or Class E airspace designated for an airport that is currently experiencing IMC. Thus, ATC would not issue a VFR restriction to an IFR flight.

Answer (B) is correct (4430). *(AIM Para 4-4-7)*
When operating in VMC with an ATC authorization to "maintain VFR-on-top/maintain VFR conditions," pilots on IFR flight plans are required to

1. Fly at the appropriate VFR altitude;
2. Comply with the VFR visibility and distance from clouds criteria; and
3. Comply with instrument flight rules that are applicable to the flight, i.e., minimum IFR altitudes, position reporting, course to be flown, adherence to ATC clearances, etc.

Answer (A) is incorrect because, after receiving a VFR-on-top clearance, the pilot may select any appropriate VFR altitude at or above the minimum IFR altitude in VMC, not only 1,000 ft. above the meteorological condition. This may be above, below, between layers, or in areas where there is no meteorological obscuration. Answer (C) is incorrect because, after receiving a VFR-on-top clearance, the pilot may select any appropriate VFR altitude at or above the minimum IFR altitude in VMC, not only 1,000 ft. above the meteorological condition. This may be above, below, between layers, or in areas where there is no meteorological obscuration.

16.
4449. Which rules apply to the pilot in command when operating on a VFR-on-Top clearance?

A— VFR only.
B— VFR and IFR.
C— VFR when "in the clear" and IFR when "in the clouds."

17.
4451. Which ATC clearance should instrument-rated pilots request in order to climb through a cloud layer or an area of reduced visibility and then continue the flight VFR?

A— To VFR on Top.
B— Special VFR to VFR Over-the-Top.
C— VFR Over-the-Top.

18.
4450. When can a VFR-on-Top clearance be assigned by ATC?

A— Only upon request of the pilot when conditions are indicated to be suitable.
B— Any time suitable conditions exist and ATC wishes to expedite traffic flow.
C— When VFR conditions exist, but there is a layer of clouds below the MEA.

19.
4452. When on a VFR-on-Top clearance, the cruising altitude is based on

A— true course.
B— magnetic course.
C— magnetic heading.

20.
4431. When must a pilot fly at a cardinal altitude plus 500 feet on an IFR flight plan?

A— When flying above 18,000 feet in VFR conditions.
B— When flying in VFR conditions above clouds.
C— When assigned a VFR-on-Top clearance.

Answer (B) is correct (4449). *(AIM Para 4-4-7)*
When operating in VMC with an ATC authorization to "maintain VFR-on-top/maintain VFR conditions," pilots on IFR flight plans are required to

1. Fly at the appropriate VFR altitude;
2. Comply with the VFR visibility and distance from clouds criteria; and
3. Comply with instrument flight rules that are applicable to the flight, i.e., minimum IFR altitudes, position reporting, course to be flown, adherence to ATC clearances, etc.

Answer (A) is incorrect because an ATC clearance to operate VFR-on-top does not imply cancellation of the IFR flight plan. Answer (C) is incorrect because a VFR-on-top clearance is issued when the pilot is in VMC and must remain in VMC unless the VFR-on-top clearance is canceled. It does not allow a pilot to fly in IMC.

Answer (A) is correct (4451). *(AIM Para 4-4-7)*
Pilots desiring to climb through a cloud, haze, smoke, or other meteorological formation and then either cancel their IFR flight plan or operate VFR-on-top may request an ATC clearance to climb to VFR-on-top.
Answer (B) is incorrect because a special VFR clearance is issued only in Class B, C, or D airspace or Class E airspace designated for an airport, and the pilot must remain clear of clouds, not climb through them. Answer (C) is incorrect because it is VFR-on-top, not VFR-over-the-top.

Answer (A) is correct (4450). *(AIM Para 4-4-7)*
ATC may assign a VFR-on-top clearance only when the pilot requests such a clearance, and the flight must be conducted in VFR weather conditions.
Answer (B) is incorrect because ATC can issue a VFR-on-top clearance only upon a pilot's, not ATC's, request. Answer (C) is incorrect because ATC can issue a VFR-on-top clearance only upon a pilot's request; clearance is not based only on the meteorological conditions.

Answer (B) is correct (4452). *(FAR 91.159)*
While operating under a VFR-on-top clearance, you must fly at the appropriate VFR altitude, which is based on magnetic course.
Answer (A) is incorrect because VFR cruising altitudes are based on magnetic, not true, course. Answer (C) is incorrect because VFR cruising altitudes are based on magnetic course, not heading.

Answer (C) is correct (4431). *(AIM Para 4-4-7)*
VFR-on-top clearances are flown at VFR altitudes, which are even or odd thousand-foot intervals plus 500 ft. This is in contrast to IFR altitudes that are at even or odd thousand-foot intervals. Cardinal altitude means 1,000-ft. intervals, e.g., 3,000, 4,000, etc.
Answer (A) is incorrect because VFR-on-top is not permitted in Class A airspace, which is from 18,000 ft. MSL to and including FL 600. Answer (B) is incorrect because a pilot on an IFR flight plan uses VFR altitudes only when assigned a VFR-on-top clearance.

21.
4447. Where are VFR-on-Top operations prohibited?

A— In Class A airspace.
B— During off-airways direct flights.
C— When flying through Class B airspace.

Answer (A) is correct (4447). *(AIM Para 4-4-7)*
ATC will not authorize VFR or VFR-on-top operations in Class A airspace.
Answer (B) is incorrect because VFR-on-top operations during off-airway direct flights are not prohibited. Answer (C) is incorrect because VFR-on-top operations within Class B airspace are permitted.

22.
4433. You have filed an IFR flight plan with a VFR-on-Top clearance in lieu of an assigned altitude. If you receive this clearance and fly a course of 180°, at what altitude should you fly? (Assume VFR conditions.)

A— Any IFR altitude which will enable you to remain in VFR conditions.
B— An odd thousand-foot MSL altitude plus 500 feet.
C— An even thousand-foot MSL altitude plus 500 feet.

Answer (C) is correct (4433). *(FAR 91.159)*
When operating in VMC with a VFR-on-top clearance, you must fly at the appropriate VFR cruising altitude. On a magnetic course of 180° through 359°, an even thousand-foot MSL altitude plus 500 ft. must be flown.
Answer (A) is incorrect because, on VFR-on-top, one uses VFR, not IFR, altitudes. Answer (B) is incorrect because odd thousand-foot altitudes plus 500 ft. are for a magnetic course of 0° through 179°, not 180°.

23.
4457. What minimums must be considered in selecting an altitude when operating with a VFR-on-Top clearance?

A— At least 500 feet above the lowest MEA, or appropriate MOCA, and at least 1,000 feet above the existing meteorological condition.
B— At least 1,000 feet above the lowest MEA, appropriate MOCA, or existing meteorological condition.
C— Minimum IFR altitude, minimum distance from clouds, and visibility appropriate to altitude selected.

Answer (C) is correct (4457). *(AIM Para 4-4-7)*
When operating in VMC with an ATC authorization to "maintain VFR-on-top/maintain VFR conditions," pilots on IFR flight plans are required to

1. Fly at the appropriate VFR altitude;
2. Comply with the VFR visibility and distance from clouds criteria; and
3. Comply with instrument flight rules that are applicable to the flight, i.e., minimum IFR altitudes, position reporting, course to be flown, adherence to ATC clearances, etc.

Answer (A) is incorrect because you must be at or above, not a specified distance from, the minimum IFR altitude, and while on a VFR-on-top clearance, you may operate above, below, or between layers of, not only above, the existing meteorological condition. Answer (B) is incorrect because you must be at or above, not a specified distance from, the minimum IFR altitude, and while on a VFR-on-top clearance, you may operate above, below, or between layers of, not only above, the existing meteorological condition.

24.
4543. If, while in Class E airspace, a clearance is received to "maintain VFR conditions on top," the pilot should maintain a VFR cruising altitude based on the direction of the

A— true course.
B— magnetic heading.
C— magnetic course.

Answer (C) is correct (4543). *(FAR 91.159)*
While operating under a VFR-on-top clearance, you must fly at the appropriate VFR cruising altitude, which is based on magnetic course.
Answer (A) is incorrect because VFR cruising altitudes are based on magnetic, not true, course. Answer (B) is incorrect because VFR cruising altitudes are based on magnetic course, not heading.

25.
4453. In which airspace is VFR-on-Top operation prohibited?

A— Class B airspace.
B— Class E airspace.
C— Class A airspace.

Answer (C) is correct (4453). *(AIM Para 4-4-7)*
ATC will not authorize VFR or VFR-on-top operations in Class A airspace.
Answer (A) is incorrect because VFR-on-top operations are permitted, not prohibited, in Class B airspace. Answer (B) is incorrect because VFR-on-top operations are permitted, not prohibited, in Class E airspace.

26.
4454. What cruising altitude is appropriate for VFR on Top on a westbound flight below 18,000 feet?

A— Even thousand-foot levels.
B— Even thousand-foot levels plus 500 feet, but not below MEA.
C— Odd thousand-foot levels plus 500 feet, but not below MEA.

27.
4455. What reports are required of a flight operating on an IFR clearance specifying VFR on Top in a nonradar environment?

A— The same reports that are required for any IFR flight.
B— All normal IFR reports except vacating altitudes.
C— Only the reporting of any unforecast weather.

27a.
4643. When operating under IFR with a VFR-On-Top clearance, what altitude should be maintained?

A— An IFR cruising altitude appropriate to the magnetic course being flown.
B— A VFR cruising altitude appropriate to the magnetic course being flown and as restricted by ATC.
C— The last IFR altitude assigned by ATC.

10.3 IFR En Route Chart Interpretation

28.
4493. (Refer to figure 87 on page 440.) Where is the VOR COP when flying east on V306 from Daisetta to Lake Charles?

A— 50 NM east of DAS.
B— 40 NM east of DAS.
C— 30 NM east of DAS.

29.
4494. (Refer to figure 87 on page 440.) At STRUT intersection headed eastbound, ATC instructs you to hold west on the 10 DME fix west of LCH on V306, standard turns. What entry procedure is recommended?

A— Direct.
B— Teardrop.
C— Parallel.

Answer (B) is correct (4454). *(FAR 91.159)*
When operating in VMC with a VFR-on-top clearance, you must fly at the appropriate VFR cruising altitude but not below the minimum IFR altitude (e.g., MEA). On a magnetic course of 180° through 359° (i.e., westbound), an even thousand-foot MSL altitude plus 500 ft. must be flown.
Answer (A) is incorrect because an even thousand-foot level is an IFR, not VFR, cruising altitude for a westbound flight. VFR-on-top clearances must maintain VFR altitudes. Answer (C) is incorrect because an odd thousand-foot level plus 500 ft. is for eastbound, not westbound, flight or a magnetic course from 0° to 179°.

Answer (A) is correct (4455). *(AIM Para 4-4-7)*
When on a VFR-on-top clearance, you must comply with instrument flight rules that are applicable to the flight, e.g., minimum flight altitudes, position reporting, radio communications, course to be flown, adherence to ATC communications, etc.
Answer (B) is incorrect because all normal IFR reports are required when operating on a VFR-on-top clearance. You should advise ATC prior to any altitude change to ensure the exchange of accurate traffic information. Answer (C) is incorrect because all IFR reports, not only unforecast weather, must be made while operating on a VFR-on-top clearance.

Answer (B) is correct (4643). *(AIM Para 4-4-7)*
When operating in VMC with an ATC authorization to "maintain VFR-on-top/maintain VFR conditions," pilots on IFR flights plans are required to

1. Fly at the appropriate VFR altitude;
2. Comply with the VFR visibility and distance from clouds criteria; and
3. Comply with instrument flight rules that are applicable to the flight, i.e., minimum IFR altitudes, position reporting, course to be flown, adherence to ATC clearances, etc.

Answer (A) is incorrect because pilots operating with a VFR-on-top clearance should maintain a VFR, not an IFR, cruising altitude appropriate to the magnetic course being flown. Answer (C) is incorrect because pilots operating with a VFR-on-top clearance should maintain a VFR, not an IFR, cruising altitude.

Answer (C) is correct (4493). *(AIM Para 5-3-6)*
On Fig. 87, when flying east on V306 from Daisetta to Lake Charles, the VOR changeover point (COP) is indicated by the symbol "⌠," and the mileages are given to each VORTAC station. The COP is 30 NM east of Daisetta and 50 NM west of Lake Charles.
Answer (A) is incorrect because the COP is 50 NM west, not east, of Lake Charles, not DAS. Answer (B) is incorrect because 40 NM is the midway point, not the prescribed COP.

Answer (A) is correct (4494). *(AIM Para 5-3-7)*
You are instructed to hold west at the 10 DME fix west of LCH VORTAC on V306. Since you are at STRUT int., flying eastbound on V306, you should make a direct entry to a heading of 265°. Since the direction of turn was not specified, you should make right turns, which is a standard holding pattern.
Answer (B) is incorrect because a teardrop entry may be used if you are instructed to hold east, not west, of the 10 DME fix. Answer (C) is incorrect because a parallel entry may be used if you are instructed to hold east, not west, of the 10 DME fix.

30.
4496. (Refer to figure 87 on page 440.) What is indicated by the localizer course symbol at Jefferson County Airport?

A— A published LDA localizer course.
B— A published ILS localizer course, which has an additional navigation function.
C— A published SDF localizer course.

Answer (B) is correct (4496). *(ACL)*
When a localizer course symbol is shown on a low altitude en route chart, this indicates that the published ILS localizer has a navigation function in addition to course guidance. The localizer at Jefferson County airport, which is located near the center of Fig. 87, is used to define PORTZ and MARSA intersections. See Legend 23 on page 428.
Answer (A) is incorrect because ILS course symbols, not LDA, are shown as depicted to indicate an additional navigation function. Answer (C) is incorrect because ILS course symbols, not SDF, are shown as depicted to indicate an additional navigation function.

31.
4497. (Refer to figure 87 on page 440.) Which VHF frequencies, other than 121.5, can be used to receive De Ridder FSS in the Lake Charles area?

A— 122.1, 126.4.
B— 123.6, 122.65.
C— 122.2, 122.3.

Answer (C) is correct (4497). *(ACL)*
The Lake Charles VORTAC communication box is located in the upper right of Fig. 87. The available frequencies are shown above the box, and the controlling FSS (De Ridder) is shown below the box. All FSSs normally use frequency 122.2 and emergency 121.5, which are not shown. Note the thin line box indicates that other frequencies at the controlling FSS are available; however, altitude and terrain may determine their reception. On top of the box is frequency 122.3. Thus, you can receive De Ridder FSS on the VHF frequencies (other than 121.5) of 122.2 and 122.3.
Answer (A) is incorrect because neither 122.1 nor 126.4 is an available frequency to receive De Ridder FSS. Answer (B) is incorrect because 123.6 and 122.65 are not available frequencies to receive De Ridder FSS.

32.
4498. (Refer to figure 87 on page 440.) Why is the localizer back course at Jefferson County Airport depicted?

A— The back course is not aligned with a runway.
B— The back course has a glide slope.
C— The back course has an additional navigation function.

Answer (C) is correct (4498). *(ACL)*
Jefferson County Airport in Beaumont, TX is located near the center of Fig. 87. The extended localizer course symbol shown there applies to this question. This symbol indicates that there is a published ILS localizer course with an additional navigation function. The arrow is further identified (on the chart) as the back course. The back course is used to identify both PORTZ and MARSA intersections. See Legend 23 on page 428.
Answer (A) is incorrect because the back course symbol suggests an ILS localizer front course, which is always aligned with the runway. Answer (B) is incorrect because a LOC back course never has a glide slope.

33.
4499. (Refer to figure 87 on page 440.) Where is the VOR changeover point on V20 between Beaumont and Hobby?

A— Halfway point.
B— MOCKS intersection.
C— Anahuac Beacon.

Answer (A) is correct (4499). *(AIM Para 5-3-6)*
In Fig. 87, V20 connects Beaumont (BPT) VORTAC and Hobby (HUB) VORTAC. Note that HUB VORTAC is west of Ellington VOR and is not shown on the chart. The changeover point (COP) is located midway between BPT and HUB, which is 34 NM. When the COP is **not** located at the midway point, the symbol " ⌐ " is used, and the mileage to each NAVAID is given (see Legend 24 on page 429).
Answer (B) is incorrect because MOCKS INT is 25 NM from BPT, and the halfway point is 34 NM. Answer (C) is incorrect because Anahuac Beacon is not on the airway.

34.
4495. (Refer to figure 87 on page 440 and figure 88 below.) What is your position with reference to FALSE intersection (V222) if your VOR receivers indicate as shown?

A— South of V222 and east of FALSE intersection.
B— North of V222 and east of FALSE intersection.
C— South of V222 and west of FALSE intersection.

Answer (A) is correct (4495). *(IFH Chap VIII)*
Note: In this edition of the test, Fig. 88 was not updated; thus VOR No. 2 incorrectly shows an OBS setting of 139 instead of 142.
Your No. 1 VOR (Fig. 88) is tuned to the BPT VORTAC, Fig. 87, with an OBS setting of 264. If you are flying outbound (FROM) BPT on V222 (R-264), a right deflection indicates that V222 is to the right of your location. Thus, you are to the south of V222. Your No. 2 VOR is tuned to the DAS VORTAC with an OBS setting of 142. If you are flying outbound (FROM) DAS on R-142, a right deflection would mean that R-142 is to the right of your location. Thus, you are to the east of R-142. FALSE INT is the intersection of V222 (BPT R-264) and DAS R-142; you are presently to the south of V222 and east of FALSE INT.
Answer (B) is incorrect because to be north of V222 would be indicated by a left, not right, CDI deflection in the No. 1 VOR. Answer (C) is incorrect because to be north of V222 and west of FALSE INT would be indicated by a left, not right, CDI deflection on both No. 1 and No. 2 VORs.

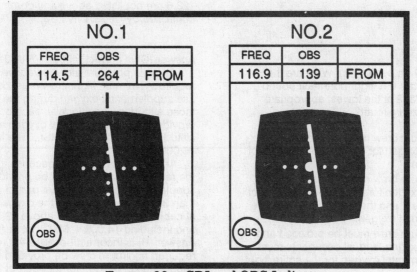

FIGURE 88.—CDI and OBS Indicators.

35.
4500. (Refer to figure 87 on page 440.) While holding at the 10 DME fix east of LCH for an ILS approach to RWY 15 at Lake Charles Muni Airport, ATC advises you to expect clearance for the approach at 1015. At 1000 you experience two-way radio communications failure. Which procedure should be followed?

A— Squawk 7600 and listen on the LOM frequency for instructions from ATC. If no instructions are received, start your approach at 1015.
B— Squawk 7700 for 1 minute, then 7600. After 1 minute, descend to the minimum final approach fix altitude. Start your approach at 1015.
C— Squawk 7600; plan to begin your approach at 1015.

Answer (C) is correct (4500). *(AIM Para 6-4-1)*
Upon radio failure, the transponder should be set to 7600. Since the expected clearance for the approach was 1015, you should plan to begin your approach at 1015.
Answer (A) is incorrect because there is no LOM shown on the chart at Lake Charles Muni. Answer (B) is incorrect because you should not squawk 7700 unless you are in an emergency situation, and you should hold at your altitude until the time necessary to begin your approach at 1015.

36.
4501. (Refer to figure 89 on page 441.) When flying from Milford Municipal to Bryce Canyon via V235 and V293, what minimum altitude should you be at when crossing Cedar City VOR?

A— 11,400 feet.
B— 12,000 feet.
C— 13,000 feet.

37.
4502. (Refer to figure 89 on page 441.) What VHF frequencies are available for communications with Cedar City FSS?

A— 123.6, 121.5, 108.6, and 112.8.
B— 122.2, 121.5, 122.6, and 112.1.
C— 122.2, 121.5, 122.0, and 123.6.

38.
4503. (Refer to figure 89 on page 441.) What are the oxygen requirements for an IFR flight northeast bound from Bryce Canyon on V382 at the lowest appropriate altitude in an unpressurized aircraft?

A— The required minimum crew must be provided and use supplemental oxygen for that part of the flight of more than 30 minutes.
B— The required minimum crew must be provided and use supplemental oxygen for that part of the flight of more than 30 minutes, and the passengers must be provided supplemental oxygen.
C— The required minimum crew must be provided and use supplemental oxygen, and all occupants must be provided supplemental oxygen for the entire flight above 15,000 feet.

39.
4505. In the event of two-way radio communications failure while operating on an IFR clearance in VFR conditions, the pilot should continue

A— by the route assigned in the last ATC clearance received.
B— the flight under VFR and land as soon as practical.
C— the flight by the most direct route to the fix specified in the last clearance.

Answer (B) is correct (4501). *(ACL)*
In Fig. 89, CDC VOR has a flag with an "X" inside to indicate an MCA (minimum crossing altitude). The MCA is indicated above the CDC communication box. When flying east on V293 to Bryce Canyon, you must cross CDC at a minimum altitude of 12,000 ft. (V293 12000E).
Answer (A) is incorrect because 11,400 ft. is the MCA when flying south on V235. Answer (C) is incorrect because 13,000 ft. is the MEA for V293 east of CDC.

Answer (B) is correct (4502). *(ACL)*
Cedar City communication box (left center of Fig. 89) is a shadow box, which indicates an FSS. On top of the box is frequency 122.6. Additionally, VHF frequencies 122.2 and 121.5 are available at all FSSs. Frequency 122.1 is used by pilots to contact Cedar City FSS in the vicinity of Milford (MLF), and the FSS would transmit (pilots receive) on the MLF VORTAC frequency 112.1.
Answer (A) is incorrect because 123.6 is not listed above any communication boxes controlled by Cedar City FSS and both CDC and BCE VORTACs are underlined, which means there is no voice on that frequency. Answer (C) is incorrect because 122.0 and 123.6 are not listed above any communication boxes controlled by Cedar City FSS.

Answer (C) is correct (4503). *(FAR 91.211)*
At cabin pressure altitudes above 14,000 ft. MSL, the required minimum flight crew must be provided with and use supplemental oxygen during the entire flight time at those altitudes. Additionally, each occupant must be provided with supplemental oxygen at cabin pressure altitudes above 15,000 ft. MSL. The MEA for V382 is 16,000 ft. MSL.
Answer (A) is incorrect because the requirement that the required minimum crew be provided with and use supplemental oxygen for that part of the flight of more than 30 minutes describes the oxygen requirements when at cabin pressure altitudes above 12,500 ft. MSL up to and including 14,000 ft. MSL, not at 16,000 ft. MSL. Answer (B) is incorrect because the requirement that the required minimum crew be provided with and use supplemental oxygen for that part of the flight of more than 30 minutes describes the oxygen requirements when at cabin pressure altitudes above 12,500 ft. MSL up to and including 14,000 ft. MSL, not at 16,000 ft. MSL.

Answer (B) is correct (4505). *(FAR 91.185)*
If two-way radio communications fail while operating in VFR conditions, or if VFR conditions are encountered after the failure, each pilot shall continue the flight under VFR and land as soon as practicable.
Answer (A) is incorrect because, if the failure occurs in IFR, not VFR, conditions, and VFR conditions are not encountered after the failure, each pilot shall continue the flight by the route assigned in the last ATC clearance received. Answer (C) is incorrect because one continues the last route assigned by ATC if in IFR, not the most direct route to the next fix.

40.
4504. On what frequency should you obtain En Route Flight Advisory Service below FL 180?

A— 122.1T/112.8R.
B— 123.6.
C— 122.0.

Answer (C) is correct (4504). *(AIM Para 7-1-4)*
En Route Flight Advisory Service (EFAS) is a service specifically designed to provide en route aircraft with timely and meaningful weather advisories pertinent to the type of flight intended, route of flight, and altitude. EFAS is normally available from 6:00 a.m. to 10:00 p.m. EFAS provides communications capabilities for aircraft flying at 5,000 ft. AGL to 17,500 ft. MSL on a common frequency of 122.0 MHz.
Answer (A) is incorrect because 122.1T/112.8R is an example of communicating with an FSS through a VOR, not the EFAS frequency below FL 180. Answer (B) is incorrect because you would use 122.0, not 123.6, to contact EFAS below FL 180.

41.
4506. (Refer to figure 89 on page 441.) What is the ARTCC discrete frequency at the COP on V208 southwest bound from HVE to PGA VOR/DME?

A— 122.1.
B— 122.4.
C— 133.6.

Answer (C) is correct (4506). *(ACL)*
The COP on V208 southwest bound to PGA VOR/DME from HVE VORTAC is indicated by the symbol " ∫ ", and the mileages are given to each VOR station. The COP is 61 NM northeast of PGA and 35 NM southwest of HVE. Notice the ragged line (see Legend 24 on page 429) south of HVE VORTAC, which is the symbol that divides Salt Lake City ARTCC to the north and Denver ARTCC to the south. Thus, the COP is in Salt Lake City ARTCC airspace. To the right of HVE VORTAC is a box indicating that Salt Lake City ARTCC uses an RCO at Hanksville on a discrete frequency of 133.6.
Answer (A) is incorrect because 122.1 is shown above the communications boxes at MLF, HVE, and PGA VORs and is used for communicating with FSSs, not the ARTCC. Answer (B) is incorrect because 122.4 is shown in the remote communications outlet (RCO) boxes at Bullfrog Basin and Cal Black Memorial Airports and is used for communicating with Cedar City FSS, not the ARTCC.

42.
4508. (Refer to figure 89 on page 441.) What type airspace exists above Bryce Canyon Airport from the surface to 1,200 feet AGL?

A— Class D.
B— Class E.
C— Class G.

Answer (C) is correct (4508). *(ACL, AIM Para 3-2-6)*
Bryce Canyon Airport symbol is brown in color, which means it does not have a published IAP. The airport is not indicated to be in Class B or C airspace but does lie below a federal airway (the white area to either side of and along V8). Federal airways are Class E airspace and, unless otherwise specified, extend upward from 1,200 ft. AGL to, but not including, 18,000 ft. MSL. Bryce Canyon is not a Class D airport (indicated by D following the airport name). Class E surface areas are not shown on En Route Low-Altitude Charts. However, since Bryce Canyon has no IAP, we can assume that no Class E surface area is associated with the airport. Therefore, Class G airspace extends from the surface upward to 1,200 ft. AGL, the floor of the federal airway.
Answer (A) is incorrect because Class D airports are indicated by a D following the airport name. Answer (B) is incorrect because federal airways normally extend upward from 1,200 ft. AGL, not from the surface.

43.
4507. (Refer to figure 89 on page 441 and figure 90 below.) What is your relationship to the airway while en route from BCE VORTAC to HVE VORTAC on V8?

A— Left of course on V8.
B— Left of course on V382.
C— Right of course on V8.

Answer (A) is correct (4507). *(IFH Chap VIII)*
Your No. 1 VOR (Fig. 90) is tuned to the BCE VORTAC with a OBS setting of 033° FROM the station. This is the course for V382, which is north of V8 in Fig. 89. The CDI is deflected to the left, which indicates you are to the right of V382. Your No. 2 VOR is tuned to the HVE VORTAC with an OBS setting of 046° TO the station, which is the inbound course on V8. The CDI is deflected to the right, which means you are to the left of course on V8. Thus, you are located to the right of V382 and to the left of V8 while en route from BCE VORTAC to HVE VORTAC.
Answer (B) is incorrect because, if you were left of V382, you would have a right, not left, CDI deflection on NAV No. 1. Answer (C) is incorrect because, if you were right of V8, you would have a left, not right, CDI deflection on NAV No. 2.

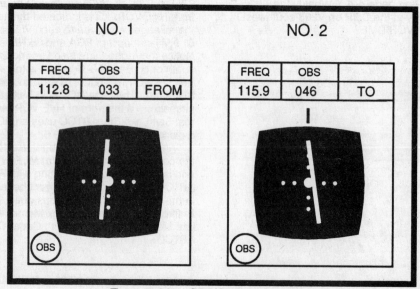

FIGURE 90.—CDI/OBS Indicators.

44.
4510. (Refer to figure 91 on page 442.) What are the two limiting cruising altitudes useable on V343 for a VFR-on-Top flight from DBS VORTAC to RANEY intersection?

A— 14,500 and 16,500 feet.
B— 15,000 and 17,000 feet.
C— 15,500 and 17,500 feet.

Answer (C) is correct (4510). *(FAR 91.159)*
In Fig. 91, a flight from DBS VORTAC to RANEY intersection on V343 has an MEA of 15,000 ft. A flight with a clearance of VFR-on-top will operate at appropriate VFR cruising altitudes, at or above the minimum IFR altitude. On a magnetic course of 008°, you must be at an odd thousand-foot altitude plus 500 ft. Thus, a VFR-on-top flight is limited to only 15,500 ft. and 17,500 ft. You cannot operate VFR in Class A airspace, i.e., 18,000 ft. MSL to FL 600.
Answer (A) is incorrect because the appropriate VFR-on-top altitudes for a magnetic course of 008° are odd, not even, thousand-foot altitudes plus 500 ft. Also, 14,500 ft. is below the MEA. Answer (B) is incorrect because VFR-on-top altitudes are cardinal (1,000, 2,000, etc.) plus 500 ft.

45.
4511. (Refer to figure 91 on page 442.) What should be the approximate elapsed time from BZN VOR to DBS VORTAC, if the wind is 24 knots from 260° and your intended TAS is 185 knots? (VAR 17 °E.)

A— 33 minutes.
B— 37 minutes.
C— 39 minutes.

Answer (C) is correct (4511). *(PHAK Chap 8)*
First convert your wind from 260° true to 243° magnetic because of the 17°E variation. Then place the 243 below the true index on the wind side of your flight computer and mark the wind speed of 24 kt. up from the grommet (center hole). Then place your magnetic course of 186° under the true index. Next, slide the scale so that the pencil mark is on the 185-kt. TAS and note that the grommet is at 171 kt., which is the groundspeed.
On the computer side, put 171 kt. on the outer scale under the true index. Locate 111 NM on the outer scale and read the time below on the inner scale, which is approximately 39 min.
Answer (A) is incorrect because 33 min. is the approximate time going north from DBS VORTAC to BZN VOR, not from BZN VOR to DBS VORTAC. Answer (B) is incorrect because 37 min. is the approximate time from BZN VOR to DBS VORTAC using the wind direction of 260°, not the magnetic wind direction of 243°.

46.
4514. (Refer to figure 91 on page 442.) Southbound on V257, at what time should you arrive at DBS VORTAC if you crossed over CPN VORTAC at 0850 and over DIVID intersection at 0854?

A— 0939.
B— 0943.
C— 0947.

Answer (B) is correct (4514). *(PHAK Chap 8)*
CPN VORTAC is on the left side of the chart about 1½ in. down from the top. Going south on V257, DIVID INT is 9 NM from CPN VORTAC. Use your flight computer to determine the groundspeed. Locate 9 on the outer scale and place 4 on the minute scale under the 9. The groundspeed is read over the index, which is 135 kt.
From DIVID to DLN VORTAC is 39 NM; then from DLN VORTAC to DBS VORTAC is 71 NM, or a total of 110 NM. To determine the time, place 135 kt. over the index of your flight computer and locate 110 NM on the outer scale; the time is read below on the minute scale, which is 49 min. from DIVID INT to DBS VORTAC. Thus, your ETA at DBS VORTAC is 0943 (0854 + 49).
Answer (A) is incorrect because the 49 min. is added to the time you crossed DIVID INT (0854), not the time you crossed CPN VORTAC (0850). Answer (C) is incorrect because the distance from CPN VORTAC to DIVID INT (9 NM) must be subtracted from the 48 NM between CPN VORTAC and DLN VORTAC.

47.
4509. (Refer to figure 91 on page 442.) What is the minimum crossing altitude at DBS VORTAC for a northbound IFR flight on V257?

A— 7,500 feet.
B— 8,600 feet.
C— 11,100 feet.

Answer (B) is correct (4509). *(ACL)*
DBS VORTAC is at the center of the large compass rose in the lower left of Fig. 91. At DBS VORTAC, there is a flag with an "X" inside that indicates an MCA. The MCA is indicated next to the VORTAC symbol. When flying north on V257, you must cross DBS VORTAC at a minimum altitude of 8,600 ft. (V21-257 8600N).
Answer (A) is incorrect because 7,500 ft. is the MEA on V257 south of DBS VORTAC. Answer (C) is incorrect because 11,100 ft. is the MOCA on V21-257 northwest of DBS VORTAC.

48.
4513. (Refer to figure 91 on page 442.) What are the oxygen requirements for an IFR flight eastbound on V520 from DBS VORTAC in an unpressurized aircraft at the MEA?

A— The required minimum crew must be provided and use supplemental oxygen for that part of the flight of more than 30 minutes.
B— The required minimum crew must be provided and use supplemental oxygen for that part of the flight of more than 30 minutes, and the passengers must be provided supplemental oxygen.
C— The required minimum crew must be provided and use supplemental oxygen.

49.
4515. (Refer to figure 91 on page 442.) What is the function of the Great Falls RCO (Yellowstone vicinity)?

A— Long range communications outlet for Great Falls Center.
B— Remote communications outlet for Great Falls FSS.
C— Satellite remote controlled by Salt Lake Center with limited service.

Answer (C) is correct (4513). *(FAR 91.211)*
On Fig. 91, when going eastbound from DBS VORTAC on V520, the MEA is 15,000 ft. MSL. At cabin pressure altitudes above 14,000 ft. MSL, the flight crew must be provided and use supplemental oxygen for the entire flight. At cabin pressure altitudes above 15,000 ft. MSL, the passengers must be provided with supplemental oxygen.

Answer (A) is incorrect because the required minimum crew must be provided and use supplemental oxygen for that part of the flight of more than 30 min. at cabin pressure altitudes above 12,500 ft. MSL up to and including 14,000 ft. MSL. Answer (B) is incorrect because the required minimum crew must be provided and use supplemental oxygen at all times, not only that part of the flight of more than 30 min., at cabin pressure altitudes above 14,000 ft. MSL. Passengers must be provided supplemental oxygen at cabin pressure altitudes above, not at, 15,000 ft. MSL.

Answer (B) is correct (4515). *(ACL)*
The Great Falls RCO communication box is located in the center of the chart, in Fig. 91, just above the DBS VORTAC box. An arrow points to a symbol ⊙, which indicates an FSS remote communications outlet (see Legend 23 on page 428). Thus, Great Falls RCO is a remote communications outlet for Great Falls FSS on 122.45 MHz.

Answer (A) is incorrect because the center for that area is Salt Lake City, not Great Falls, as indicated by the ARTCC RCO box above the Great Falls RCO box. Answer (C) is incorrect because Great Falls RCO is just an antenna site for an FSS that extends the communication range for the controlling FSS (e.g., Great Falls FSS), not ARTCC (e.g., Salt Lake Center).

50.
4516. (Refer to figure 91 on page 442.) Where should you change VOR frequencies when en route from DBS VORTAC to JAC VOR/DME on V520?

A— 35 NM from DBS VORTAC.
B— 60 NM from DBS VORTAC.
C— 60 NM from JAC VOR/DME.

Answer (B) is correct (4516). *(AIM Para 5-3-6)*
When flying from DBS VORTAC to JAC VOR/DME on V520 (Fig. 91), notice that very close to the JAC VOR/DME is a VOR changeover point symbol (∫), which is 60 NM from the DBS VORTAC.
Answer (A) is incorrect because, in this case, the changeover point (COP) is not located at the midway point; the COP is marked by the symbol " ∫ ", and mileage is given to the VORs. Answer (C) is incorrect because the COP is located 10 NM, not 60 NM, from JAC VOR/DME.

51.
4512. (Refer to figure 91 on page 442.) What lighting is indicated on the chart for Jackson Hole Airport?

A— Lights on prior request.
B— No lighting available.
C— Pilot controlled lighting.

Answer (C) is correct (4512). *(ACL)*
The Jackson Hole Airport is located at the lower right of Fig. 91. The "L" indicates that Jackson Hole Airport has night lighting. The circle indicates pilot-controlled lighting.
Answer (A) is incorrect because an asterisk would indicate lighting on request or in operation for only part of the night. Answer (B) is incorrect because, if no lighting were available, there would be a "–" after the airport elevation.

52.
4517. (Refer to figure 91 on page 442.) What is the minimum crossing altitude at SABAT intersection when eastbound from DBS VORTAC on V298?

A— 8,300 feet.
B— 11,100 feet.
C— 13,000 feet.

Answer (B) is correct (4517). *(ACL)*
SABAT INT is located east of DBS VORTAC on V298 at the lower middle area in Fig. 91. There is a flag with an "X" in it which indicates an MCA at SABAT. Underneath the SABAT is the MCA, which is 11,100 ft. when eastbound on V298 (V298 11100E).
Answer (A) is incorrect because 8,300 ft. is the MOCA between DBS VORTAC and SABAT INT (*8300). Answer (C) is incorrect because 13,000 ft. is the MEA when eastbound on V298 between DBS VORTAC and SABAT INT.

53.
4325. (Refer to figure 58 on page 355.) On which frequencies could you communicate with the Montgomery County FSS while on the ground at College Station?

A— 122.65, 122.2, 122.1, 113.3.
B— 122.65, 122.2.
C— 118.5, 122.65, 122.2.

54.
4326. (Refer to figure 58 on page 355.) Which indications on the VOR receivers and DME at the Easterwood Field VOR receiver checkpoint would meet the regulatory requirement for this flight?

VOR No. 1	TO/FROM	VOR No. 2	TO/FROM	DME
A— 097°	FROM	101°	FROM	3.3
B— 097°	TO	096°	TO	3.2
C— 277°	FROM	280°	FROM	3.3

Answer (B) is correct (4325). *(A/FD)*
Fig. 58 is an excerpt from an *A/FD* for Easterwood Field located at College Station, TX. Locate the **Communications** heading for information on frequencies. There is a College Station RCO to communicate with the Montgomery County FSS on frequencies 122.65 and 122.2 only.
Answer (A) is incorrect because 122.1 is not available at College Station to contact the Montgomery County FSS. College Station VORTAC operates on frequency 113.3, but under **Radio Aids to Navigation**, the "W" after VORTAC means that no voice is transmitted on this frequency. Answer (C) is incorrect because 118.5 is the tower/CTAF, not FSS, frequency.

Answer (A) is correct (4326). *(FAR 91.171)*
The bottom portion of Fig. 58 lists the VOR receiver checkpoints. Locate College Station (Easterwood Field) to determine that the checkpoint is on the ground (on west edge of parking ramp), the azimuth from the VORTAC is 097° (i.e., R-097), and the distance is 3.2 NM from the VORTAC. On the R-097, you want the CDI needle centered with an OBS setting of 097° FROM or 277° TO the station, with the acceptable error of ±4°. Thus, the acceptable VOR indications are 097° FROM and 101° FROM the station.
Answer (B) is incorrect because the magnetic azimuth (i.e., radial) from the station at the ground checkpoint is 097°, which results in a FROM, not TO, indication with the OBS set to 097°. Answer (C) is incorrect because the magnetic azimuth (i.e., radial) from the station at the ground checkpoint is 097°, which results in a TO, not FROM, indication with the OBS set to 277°.

140   **TEXAS**

COLLEGE STATION
EASTERWOOD FLD   (CLL)   3 SW   UTC–6(–5DT)   30°35'18"N 96°21'49"W   HOUSTON
  320   B   S4   FUEL 100LL, JET A   OX 2   ARFF Index A   H-2K, 5B, L-17A
  RWY 16-34: H7000X150 (ASPH–GRVD)   S-70, D-90, DT-150   MIRL   IAP
    RWY 16: VASI(V4R)—GA 3.0°TCH 51'. Tree.   RWY 34: MALSR.
  RWY 10-28: H5160X150 (CONC)   S-27, D-50, DT-87   MIRL
    RWY 10: VASI(V4L)—GA 3.0°TCH 50'. Tree.   RWY 28: REIL VASI(V4L)—GA 3.0° TCH 54'. Tree.
  RWY 04-22: H5149X150 (CONC)   S-27, D-50, DT-87
    RWY 04: Tree.   RWY 22: Tree.
  AIRPORT REMARKS: Attended 1200-0500Z‡. CAUTION: deer on rwys. CAUTION: Rwy 10-28 taxiway B and taxiway E
    have uneven surfaces. Birds on and in vicinity of arpt. MIRL Rwy 10-28 preset medium ints when twr clsd, to
    increase ints and ACTIVATE MIRL Rwy 16–34 and MALSR Rwy 34—CTAF. CLOSED to unscheduled air carrier
    ops with more than 30 passenger seats except 24 hours PPR call, arpt manager 409–845-4811. Rwy 04–22
    day VFR ops only. Itinerant acft park North of twr, overnight parking fee. Ldg fee scheduled FAR 135 and all FAR
    121 ops. For fuel after hours PPR call 409–845-4811/823 –0690 or ctc Texas A and M University police
    409–845-2345; late ngt fee. Rwy 16–34 grvd except south 200'. Rwy 04–22 deteriorating and vegetation
    growing through cracks. NOTE: See SPECIAL NOTICE—Simultaneous Operations on Intersecting Runways.
  COMMUNICATIONS: CTAF 118.5   ATIS 126.85 (1200-0400Z‡)   UNICOM 122.95
    MONTGOMERY COUNTY FSS (CXO) TF 1–800–WX–BRIEF. NOTAM FILE CLL.
    COLLEGE STATION RCO 122.65 122.2 (MONTGOMERY COUNTY FSS).
  ®HOUSTON CENTER APP/DEP CON: 120.4
    TOWER: 118.5 (1200-0400Z‡) (VFR only)   GND CON: 121.7
  RADIO AIDS TO NAVIGATION: NOTAM FILE CLL. VHF/DF ctc FSS
    COLLEGE STATION (L) VORTACW 113.3   CLL   Chan 80   30°36'17"N 96°25'13"W   100° 3.1 NM to fld.
    370/08E. HIWAS.
    ROWDY NDB (LOM) 260   CL   30°29'36"N 96°20'16"W   341° 5.9 NM to fld.
    ILS 111.7 I-CLL Rwy 34 LOM ROWDY NDB. ILS unmonitored when twr closed.

COLLEGE STATION   30°36'17"N 96°25'13"W   NOTAM FILE CLL.   HOUSTON
  (L) VORTACW 113.3   CLL   Chan 80   100° 3.1 NM to Easterwood Fld. 370/08E. HIWAS.   H-2K, 5B, L-17A
  RCO 122.65 122.2 (MONTGOMERY COUNTY FSS)

VOR RECEIVER CHECK   259

TEXAS

VOR RECEIVER CHECK POINTS

Facility Name (Arpt Name)	Freq/Ident	Type Check Pt. Gnd. AB/ALT	Azimuth from Fac. Mag	Dist. from Fac. N.M.	Check Point Description
Abilene (Abilene Regional)	113.7/ABI	A/2800	047	10.1	Over silos in center of Ft Phantom Lake.
Alice (Alice International)	114.5/ALI	G	270	0.5	On twy N of hangar.
Amarillo (Amarillo Internationl)	117.2/AMA	G	210	4.5	On east runup pad Rwy 22.
Austin (Robert Mueller Muni)	114.6/AUS	G	118	0.6	On runup area on twy to Rwy 31L.
Beaumont (Jefferson County)	114.5/BPT	G	310	1.0	On runup area for Rwy 12.
Big Spring (Big Spring McMahon-Wrinkle)	114.3/BGS	A/3500	107	10.5	Over red and white water tank.
Borger (Hutchinson Co)	108.6/BGD	G	175	6.7	On intersecting twy in front of terminal.
Brownsville (Brownsville/South Padre Island Intl)	116.3/BRO	G	248	3.2	On NE corner of parking ramp.
Brownwood (Brownwood Muni)	108.6/BWD	A/2600	169	6.2	Over rotating bcn.
Childress (Childress Muni)	117.6/CDS	G	353	3.7	At intersection of edge of ramp at center twy.
College Station (Easterwood Field)	113.3/CLL	G	097	3.2	On W edge of parking ramp.
Corpus Christi (Corpus Christi Intl)	115.5/CRP	A/1100	187	7.5	Over grain elevator.
Corpus Christi (San Patricio County)	115.5/CRP	A/1000	318	9.5	Over rotating beacon on arpt.
Daisetta (Liberty Muni)	116.9/DAS	A/1200	195	7.5	Over hangar S of arpt.
Dalhart (Dalhart Muni)	112.0/DHT	G	170	3.9	On SE corner of main ramp.
Eagle Lake (Eagle Lake)	116.4/ELA	A/1200	180	4.5	Over water tank 0.4 NM SW

FIGURE 58.—Excerpts from Airport/Facility Directory.

55.
4327. (Refer to figure 59 on page 436 and figure 60 on page 357.) What are the operating hours (local standard time) of the Houston EFAS?

A— 0600 to 2200.
B— 0700 to 2300.
C— 1800 to 1000.

Answer (A) is correct (4327). *(AIM Para 7-1-4)*
EFAS is specifically designed to provide en route aircraft with timely and meaningful weather advisories pertinent to the type of flight intended, route of flight, and altitude. EFAS is provided by specialists in selected AFSSs/FSSs controlling multiple RCOs covering a large geographic area.
The bottom of Fig. 60 shows the EFAS outlets and indicates that the Houston EFAS is operated by Montgomery Co. FSS. The hours of operation are from 1200Z to 0400Z. Convert Z time to local time by subtracting 6 hr. as indicated in the time conversion in the first line of the *A/FD*. Thus the hours of operation (local standard time) are from 0600 to 2200.
Answer (B) is incorrect because, to convert Z time to local standard time, you must subtract 6 hr., not 5 hr. Answer (C) is incorrect because to convert Z time to local standard time you must subtract, not add, 6 hr.

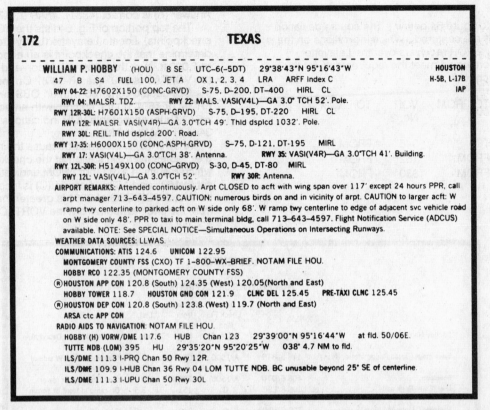

172   **TEXAS**

WILLIAM P. HOBBY   (HOU)   8 SE   UTC-6(-5DT)   29°38'43"N 95°16'43"W   **HOUSTON**
  47   B   S4   FUEL 100, JET A   OX 1, 2, 3, 4   LRA   ARFF Index C   H-5B, L-17B
  RWY 04-22: H7602X150 (CONC-GRVD)   S-75, D-200, DT-400   HIRL   CL   IAP
    RWY 04: MALSR. TDZ.   RWY 22: MALS. VASI(V4L)—GA 3.0° TCH 52'. Pole.
  RWY 12R-30L: H7601X150 (ASPH-GRVD)   S-75, D-195, DT-220   HIRL   CL
    RWY 12R: MALSR. VASI(V4R)—GA 3.0°TCH 49'. Thld dsplcd 1032'. Pole.
    RWY 30L: REIL. Thld dsplcd 200'. Road.
  RWY 17-35: H6000X150 (CONC-ASPH-GRVD)   S-75, D-121, DT-195   MIRL
    RWY 17: VASI(V4L)—GA 3.0°TCH 38'. Antenna.   RWY 35: VASI(V4R)—GA 3.0°TCH 41'. Building.
  RWY 12L-30R: H5149X100 (CONC-GRVD)   S-30, D-45, DT-80   MIRL
    RWY 12L: VASI(V4L)—GA 3.0°TCH 52'.   RWY 30R: Antenna.
  AIRPORT REMARKS: Attended continuously. Arpt CLOSED to acft with wing span over 117' except 24 hours PPR, call
    arpt manager 713-643-4597. CAUTION: numerous birds on and in vicinity of arpt. CAUTION to larger acft: W
    ramp twy centerline to parked acft on W side only 68'. W ramp twy centerline to edge of adjacent svc vehicle road
    on W side only 48'. PPR to taxi to main terminal bldg, call 713-643-4597. Flight Notification Service (ADCUS)
    available. NOTE: See SPECIAL NOTICE—Simultaneous Operations on Intersecting Runways.
  WEATHER DATA SOURCES: LLWAS.
  COMMUNICATIONS: ATIS 124.6   UNICOM 122.95
    MONTGOMERY COUNTY FSS (CXO) TF 1-800-WX-BRIEF. NOTAM FILE HOU.
    HOBBY RCO 122.35 (MONTGOMERY COUNTY FSS)
  Ⓡ HOUSTON APP CON 120.8 (South) 124.35 (West) 120.05(North and East)
    HOBBY TOWER 118.7   HOUSTON GND CON 121.9   CLNC DEL 125.45   PRE-TAXI CLNC 125.45
  Ⓡ HOUSTON DEP CON 120.8 (South) 123.8 (West) 119.7 (North and East)
    ARSA ctc APP CON
  RADIO AIDS TO NAVIGATION: NOTAM FILE HOU.
    HOBBY (H) VORW/DME 117.6   HUB   Chan 123   29°39'00"N 95°16'44"W   at fld. 50/06E.
    TUTTE NDB (LOM) 395   HU   29°35'20"N 95°20'25"W   038° 4.7 NM to fld.
    ILS/DME 111.3 I-PRQ Chan 50 Rwy 12R.
    ILS/DME 109.9 I-HUB Chan 36 Rwy 04 LOM TUTTE NDB. BC unusable beyond 25° SE of centerline.
    ILS/DME 111.3 I-UPU Chan 50 Rwy 30L

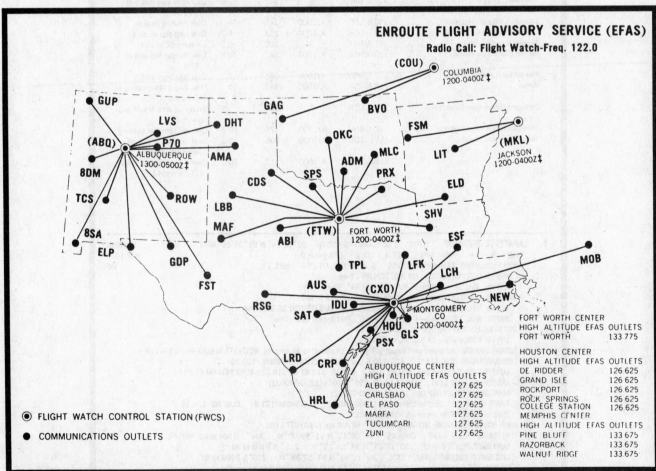

FIGURE 60.—Airport/Facilty Directory and Enroute Flight Advisory Service (EFAS).

56.

4337. (Refer to figure 64 below.) The course deviation indicator (CDI) are centered. Which indications on the No. 1 and No. 2 VOR receivers over the Lafayette Regional Airport would meet the requirements for the VOR receiver check?

VOR No. 1	TO/FROM	VOR No. 2	TO/FROM
A— 162°	TO	346°	FROM
B— 160°	FROM	162°	FROM
C— 341°	FROM	330°	FROM

Answer (A) is correct (4337). *(FAR 91.171)*
The top portion of Fig. 64 lists the VOR receiver checkpoints. Locate Lafayette (Lafayette Regional) to determine that the checkpoint is an airborne checkpoint at 1,000 ft. over the rotating beacon and the azimuth from the VORTAC is 340° (i.e., R-340). On the R-340, you want the CDI needle centered with an OBS setting of 340° FROM or 160° TO the station, with an acceptable error of ±6°. Thus, acceptable VOR indications are 162° TO and 346° FROM the station.

Answer (B) is incorrect because the magnetic azimuth (i.e., radial) from the station at the checkpoint is 340°, which results in a TO, not FROM, indication with the OBS set to 160° and 162°. Answer (C) is incorrect because the No. 2 VOR OBS of 330° is greater than 6° difference from the 340° azimuth from the VORTAC.

LOUISIANA

VOR RECEIVER CHECK POINTS

Facility Name (Arpt Name)	Freq/Ident	Type Check Pt. Gnd. AB/ALT	Azimuth from Fac. Mag	Dist. from Fac. N.M.	Check Point Description
Baton Rouge (Baton Rouge Metro, Ryan)	116.5/BTR	A/1500	063	7.7	Over water tank W side of arpt.
Downtown	108.6/DTN	A/1500	290	10	Over white water tower.
Esler (Esler Regional)	108.8/ESF	G	151	3.5	On ramp in front of admin bldg.
Hammond (Hammond Muni)	109.6/HMU	G	342	.6	On twy W side app end Rwy 18.
Lafayette (Lafayette Regional)	110.8/LFT	A/1000	340	25	Over rotating beacon.
Lake Charles (Lake Charles Muni)	113.4/LCH	A/1000	253	6.2	Over rotg bcn on atct.
Monroe (Monroe Muni)	117.2/MLU	G	209	0.9	On ramp SE of atct.
Natchez (Concordia Parish)	110.0/HEZ	A/1000	247	10.5	Over hangar NW end of field.
New Orleans (Lakefront)	113.2/MSY	A/1000	081	7.7	Over lakefront atct.
Ruston	112.8/RSN	A/2000	343	14	Over hwy & RR crossing at Dubash.
Shreveport (Shreveport Downtown)	108.6/DTN	G	307	.5	On runup area N side of rwy 14.
Shreveport (Shreveport Regional)	117.4/SHV	A/1200	175	19.3	Over old terminal building.
Tibby (Thibodaux Muni)	112.0/TBD	A/1000	006	5.0	Over railroad bridge off apch end rwy 26.
	112.0/TBD	A/1000	117	10.0	Over intersection of rwys 17-35 and 12-30.

§ **LAFAYETTE REGIONAL** (LFT) 2 SE GMT–6(–5DT) 30°12'14"N 91°59'16"W   HOUSTON
    42 B S4 FUEL 100LL, JET A OX 1 CFR Index B   H-4F, L-17C
    RWY 03-21: H7651X150 (ASPH-GRVD) S-75, D-170, DT-290 HIRL   IAP
      RWY 03: REIL. VASI(V4L)—GA 3.0°TCH 35'. Tree.
      RWY 21: MALSR. VASI(V4L)—GA 3.0°TCH 44'. Tree.
    RWY 10-28: H5401X150 (ASPH) S-85, D-110, DT-175 MIRL
      RWY 10: REIL (out of svc indefinitely). VASI(V4L)—GA 3.0° TCH 35.33'. Tree.
      RWY 28: REIL. VASI(V4L)—GA 3.0° TCH 55'. Thld dsplcd 202'. Tree.
    RWY 01-19: H5069X150 (ASPH) S-25, D-45
      RWY 01: VASI(V4R)—GA 3.0°TCH 50'. Tree.
    AIRPORT REMARKS: Attended continuously. Rwy 01-19 closed to air carriers. ACTIVATE MALSR Rwy 21—118.5.
    COMMUNICATIONS: CTAF 118.5   ATIS 120.5 Opr 1200-0500Z‡   UNICOM 122.95
      LAFAYETTE FSS (LFT) on arpt. 122.35, 122.2, 122.1R, 110.8T LD 318-233-4952 NOTAM FILE LFT.
    ® APP/DEP CON 121.1 (011°-190°) 124.0 (191°-010°) (1200-0400Z‡)
      HOUSTON CENTER APP/DEP CON 133.65 (0400-1200Z‡)
      TOWER 118.5, 121.35 (Helicopter ops) (1200-0400Z‡)   GND CON 121.8   CLNC DEL 125.55
      STAGE III ctc APP CON within 25 NM below 7000'
    RADIO AIDS TO NAVIGATION: NOTAM FILE LFT. VHF/DF ctc LAFAYETTE FSS
      (L) VORTAC 110.8 LFT Chan 45 30°08'45"N 91°59'00"W 344°3.0 NM to fld. 40/06E
      LAFFS NDB (LOM) 375 LF 30°17'21"N 91°54'29"W 215° 5.8 NM to fld
      LAKE MARTIN NDB (MHW) 362 LKM 30°11'33"N 91°52'58"W 270°5.2 NM to fld
      ILS/DME 109.5 I-LFT Chan 32 Rwy 21 LOM LAFFS NDB. Unmonitored when twr clsd.
      ASR

FIGURE 64.—Excerpt from Airport/Facility Directory (LFT).

57.
4336. (Refer to figure 65 on page 437.) Which point would be the appropriate VOR COP on V552 from the LFT to the TBD VORTACs?

A— CLYNT intersection.
B— HATCH intersection.
C— 34 DME from the LFT VORTAC.

Answer (C) is correct (4336). *(AIM Para 5-3-6)*
    The changeover point (COP) is located midway between the navigation facilities for straight route segments, unless the COP symbol (∫) is depicted on the route, in which case the indicated location is the COP. Since no COP symbol appears on V552 from LFT VORTAC (middle left) to TBD VORTAC (lower right), in Fig. 65, the COP is at the midway point. Since the leg is 68 NM, the COP would be at 34 DME from LFT VORTAC.
    Answer (A) is incorrect because CLYNT INT is only about 1/4, not 1/2, the distance from LFT to TBD VORTACs. Answer (B) is incorrect because HATCH INT is 5 NM before the COP at 34 NM (i.e., midway point between the LFT and TBD VORTACs).

58.
4338. (Refer to figure 65 on page 437 and figure 66 below.) What is your position relative to GRICE intersection?

A— Right of V552 and approaching GRICE intersection.
B— Right of V552 and past GRICE intersection.
C— Left of V552 and approaching GRICE intersection.

Answer (A) is correct (4338). *(IFH Chap VIII)*
    GRICE INT is located at the lower middle portion of Fig. 65 along V552; it is the intersection of V552 and the localizer course to Harry P. Williams Mem. Airport. Your No. 1 VOR (Fig. 66) is tuned to the TBD VORTAC with an OBS setting of 116° TO the station. If you are flying toward TBD VORTAC on V552 (R-296), a left CDI deflection indicates that you are to the right of V552. Your No. 2 VOR is tuned to the I-PTN localizer course. If you are flying inbound on the localizer, a left CDI needle deflection indicates that you are to the right of the localizer course. Thus, you are right of V552 and approaching GRICE INT.
    Answer (B) is incorrect because, if you were past GRICE INT, you would be to the left of the localizer; thus, the CDI needle would have a right, not left, deflection. Answer (C) is incorrect because, if you were to the left of V552, the CDI needle would have a right, not left, deflection.

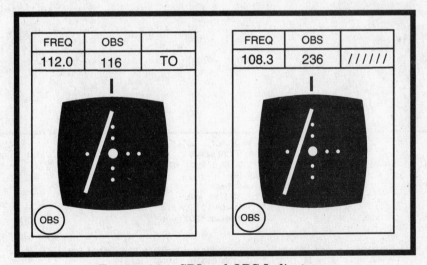

FIGURE 66.—CDI and OBS Indicators.

59.
4339. (Refer to figure 65 on page 437 and figure 67 below.) What is the significance of the symbol at GRICE intersection?

A— It signifies a localizer-only approach is available at Harry P. Williams Memorial.
B— The localizer has an additional navigation function.
C— GRICE intersection also serves as the FAF for the ILS approach procedure to Harry P. Williams Memorial.

Answer (B) is correct (4339). *(ACL)*
The large localizer symbol from Harry P. Williams Memorial to GRICE INT (Fig. 65) indicates that the localizer has a navigation function in addition to course guidance. In this case, the localizer's navigational function is to identify GRICE INT.
Answer (A) is incorrect because the localizer symbol indicates the availability of an ILS, not an LOC only, approach. Answer (C) is incorrect because GRICE INT is identified by the localizer course. The FAF on an ILS is the interception of the glide slope, not an intersection.

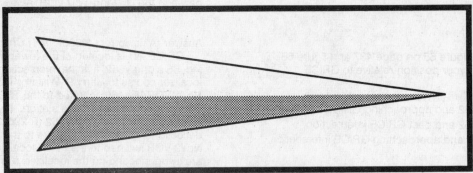

FIGURE 67.—Localizer Symbol.

END OF CHAPTER

CHAPTER ELEVEN
IFR FLIGHTS

This chapter contains 96 FAA test questions and answers regarding eight IFR flights and an explanation of each answer. The individual trips within this chapter are listed above, followed in parentheses by the number of corresponding questions from the FAA knowledge test and the page on which the trip begins.

CAUTION: The **sole purpose** of this book is to expedite your passing the FAA instrument rating knowledge test. Accordingly, all extraneous material (i.e., topics or regulations not directly tested on the FAA knowledge test) is omitted, even though much more information and knowledge are necessary to fly safely. This additional material is presented in *Instrument Pilot Flight Maneuvers and Practical Test Prep*, *Pilot Handbook*, *Aviation Weather and Weather Services*, and *FAR/AIM*, available from Gleim Publications, Inc. See the order form on page 488.

Note that there are two helicopter trips in the FAA instrument rating test bank. We do not believe it is appropriate to ask helicopter questions on the instrument rating (airplane) knowledge test. However, nine of the questions included in these two helicopter trips are generic to IFR flight, i.e., could apply to you in an airplane. Examples are questions regarding en route charts and the *A/FD*. These questions will appear in other chapters as appropriate, e.g., IFR En Route.

The following provides you with a list of the eight IFR trips. The departure and destination airports are listed, followed by the question numbers that relate to that trip.

1. Grand Junction, CO to Durango, CO (Questions 1-7)
2. Medford, OR to Eugene, OR (Questions 8-18)
3. Yakima, WA to Portland, OR (Questions 19-33)
4. Santa Barbara, CA to Paso Robles, CA (Questions 34-43)
5. Hot Springs, AR to Dallas, TX (Questions 44-53)
6. Big Spring, TX to Dallas, TX (Questions 54-65)
7. W. Milford, NJ to Windsor Locks, CT (Questions 66-79)
8. Helena, MT to Billings, MT (Questions 80-93)

Each trip provides you with the following types of data:

1. Partially completed IFR flight plan
2. Aircraft model and equipment status sheet
3. Partially completed flight log
4. DPs and STARs
5. Appropriate *Airport/Facility Directory* excerpts
6. Instrument approach chart(s)
7. En route low-altitude chart

The general sequence of questions includes

1.   Equipment code to put in block 3 of your IFR flight plan

AIRCRAFT EQUIPMENT SUFFIXES

Suffix	Aircraft Equipment Suffixes
	NO DME
/X	No transponder
/T	Transponder with no Mode C
/U	Transponder with Mode C
	DME
/D	No transponder
/B	Transponder with no Mode C
/A	Transponder with Mode C
	TACAN ONLY
/M	No transponder
/N	Transponder with no Mode C
/P	Transponder with Mode C
	AREA NAVIGATION (RNAV)
/Y	LORAN, VOR/DME, or INS with no transponder
/C	LORAN, VOR/DME, or INS, transponder with no Mode C
/I	LORAN, VOR/DME, or INS, transponder with Mode C
	ADVANCED RNAV WITH TRANSPONDER AND MODE C (If an aircraft is unable to operate with a transponder and/or Mode C, it will revert to the appropriate code listed above under Area Navigation.)
/E	Flight Management System (FMS) with en route, terminal, and approach capability. Equipment requirements are: (a) Dual FMS which meets the specifications of AC 25-15, Approval of Flight Management Systems in Transport Category Airplanes; AC 20-129, Airworthiness Approval of Vertical Navigation (VNAV) Systems for use in the U.S. NAS and Alaska; AC 20-130A, Airworthiness Approval of Navigation or Flight Management Systems Integrating Multiple Navigation Sensors; or equivalent criteria as approved by Flight Standards. (b) A flight director and autopilot control system capable of following the lateral and vertical FMS flight path. (c) At least dual inertial reference units (IRU's). (d) A database containing the waypoints and speed/altitude constraints for the route and/or procedure to be flown that is automatically loaded into the FMS flight plan. (e) An electronic map. (U.S. and U.S. territories only unless otherwise authorized.)
/F	A single FMS with en route, terminal, and approach capability that meets the equipment requirements of /E, (a) through (d), above. (U.S. and U.S. territories only unless otherwise authorized.)
/G	Global Positioning System (GPS)/Global Navigation Satellite System (GNSS) equipped aircraft with en route and terminal capability
/R	Required Navigational Performance (Denotes capability to operate in RNP designated airspace and routes)
/W	Reduced Vertical Separation Minima (RVSM)

LEGEND 26.—Aircraft Equipment Suffixes.

2.   Calibrated airspeed (CAS) to maintain true airspeed (TAS) indicated in the flight plan

    a.   On your flight computer, put air temperature (given in question) over the flight altitude (given in the IFR flight plan). Then on the outer scale find TAS; CAS is on the inner scale.

3.   Time to complete the flight (time en route for block 10 of the IFR flight plan)

    a.   This question requires you to complete the flight log, which involves wind triangle computations (on your manual or electronic flight computer).

4. Interpretation of ADF, VOR, RMI, HSI, and GS/LOC indicators to determine position relative to a position specified on a particular approach, DP, STAR, or en route chart

   a. These interpretations are covered in Chapter 3, Navigation Systems.

5. Interpretation of appropriate procedures, minimum altitude, and other restrictions on instrument approach charts

   a. See the instrument approach chart legends (on pages 192 through 202) in Chapter 6, Holding and Instrument Approaches.

6. Interpretation of appropriate procedures, minimum altitude, and other restrictions on low-altitude en route charts

   a. See the IFR en route chart legends. Legend 25 appears on page 338 in Chapter 10, IFR En Route. Legends 23 and 24 are provided in color on pages 428 and 429.

7. Interpretation of DPs and STARs

   a. A careful reading of the DP or STAR usually provides the correct answer, especially in conjunction with the DP/STAR legend reproduced on page 203 in Chapter 6.

QUESTIONS AND ANSWER EXPLANATIONS

All the FAA questions from the instrument rating knowledge test relating to IFR flights are reproduced on the following pages. To the immediate right of each question are the correct answer and answer explanation. You should cover these answers and answer explanations with the Gleim bookmark (provided at the end of the book) while responding to the questions. The first line of each answer explanation gives the FAA question number and the citation of the authoritative source for the answer. Refer to the general discussion in the Introduction on how to take the FAA knowledge test.

Remember that the questions from the FAA instrument rating knowledge test bank have been reordered by topic, and the topics have been organized into a meaningful sequence. The first line of the answer explanation gives the FAA question number and the citation of the authoritative source for the answer.

11.1 GJT to DRO

Questions 1 through 7 pertain to an IFR flight from Walker Field, Grand Junction, Colorado to Durango-La Plata County Airport, Durango, Colorado, and return to Grand Junction.

The route of flight is given in block 8 on the flight plan portion of Figs. 21 and 21A on pages 366 and 367. Information which pertains to your aircraft is given on the bottom portion of Figs. 21 and 21A. The partially completed flight planning log is given in Figs. 22 and 22A on pages 368 and 369.

The figures provided for this flight are listed below and are grouped together after the sequence of questions, except for Fig. 24, which is provided in color on page 430. Note that not all are needed to answer these seven questions.

Fig.	Page	
21	366	Flight Plan and Aircraft Information (GJT-DRO)
21A	367	Flight Plan and Aircraft Information (DRO-GJT)
22	368	Flight Planning Log (GJT-DRO)
22A	369	Flight Planning Log (DRO-GJT)
23	370	Grand Junction Nine Departure (NOS)
24	430	En Route Low-Altitude Chart Segment
25	371	ILS/DME RWY 2 (DRO) (NOS)
26	372	ILS RWY 11 (GJT) (NOS)

11.1 GJT to DRO

1.
4260. (Refer to figures 21, 22, and 24 on pages 366, 368, and 430.) (Refer to FD excerpt below, and use the wind entry closest to the flight planned altitude.) Determine the time to be entered in block 10 of the flight from GJT to DRO.

Route of flight	Figure 21
Flight log & MAG VAR	Figure 22
En route chart	Figure 24

FT	12,000	18,000
FNM	2408–05	2208–21

A— 1 hour 08 minutes.
B— 1 hour 03 minutes.
C— 58 minutes.

Answer (A) is correct (4260). *(IFH Chap XIII)*
Complete the flight log for GJT to DRO (Fig. 22). Note that the wind has been interpolated for you from the figures for 12,000 and 18,000 ft. Calculate groundspeed for the cruise portion of the trip using the wind side of the flight computer. Remember to convert wind direction to magnetic direction first; i.e., 230° – 14° E var. = 216° at 8 kt. Then compute ETE for each leg.

	Distance	MC	Wind (Mag)	Ground-speed	Time
HERRM INT.	X	151°G	216/8G	X	:24:00G
MANCA INT.	75	151°G	216/8G	172	:26:10
Approach and Landing	X	92°G	216/8G	X	:18:30G
					1:08:40

G = Given

Answer (B) is incorrect because an ETE of 1 hr. 3 min. requires a TAS of 223 kt., not 175 kt. Answer (C) is incorrect because an ETE of 58 min. requires a TAS of approximately 293 kt., not 175 kt.

2.
4259. (Refer to figures 21, 21A, 22, 22A, 23, 25, and 26 on pages 366 through 372 and figure 24 on page 430.) After departing GJT and arriving at Durango Co., La Plata Co. Airport, you are unable to land because of weather. How long can you hold over DRO before departing for return flight to the alternate, Grand Junction Co., Walker Field Airport?

Total useable fuel on board, 68 gallons.
Average fuel consumption 15 GPH.
Wind and velocity at 16,000, 2308–16°.

A— 1 hour 33 minutes.
B— 1 hour 37 minutes.
C— 1 hour 42 minutes.

Answer (A) is correct (4259). *(IFH Chap XIII)*
To solve this problem, you must calculate times en route and fuel consumption for both trips, GJT-DRO and DRO-GJT, add 45 min. reserve, and subtract the total fuel used from 68 gal.

First, complete the flight log for each trip (Figs. 22 and 22A). Calculate groundspeed for the cruise portions of each trip using the wind side of the flight computer. Remember to convert wind direction to magnetic direction first; i.e., 230° – 14°E var. = 216° at 8 kt. Then compute ETE for each leg and fuel consumption for each trip using the slide rule side of the computer.

GJT to DRO

	Distance	MC	Ground-speed	Time	Fuel (gal.)
HERRM INT.	X	X	X	:24:00G	6.0
MANCA INT.	75	151°	172	:26:10	6.5
Approach and Landing	X	X	X	:18:30G	4.6
G = Given				1:08:40	17.1

DRO to GJT

	Distance	MC	Ground-speed	Time	Fuel (gal.)
MANCA INT.	X	X	X	:14:30G	3.6
HERRM INT.	75	333°	177	:25:21	6.3
JNC	35	331°	177	:11:52	3.0
Approach and Landing	X	X	X	12:00G	3.0
G = Given				1:03:43	15.9

	Fuel (gal.)
GJT-DRO	17.1
DRO-GJT	15.9
45 min. reserve	11.3
Total	44.3

With 68 gal. usable fuel, 23.7 gal. (68 – 44.3) would be available to hold at DRO. At 15-GPH fuel consumption, this would be approximately 1 hr. 34 min. of fuel.

Answer (B) is incorrect because to be able to hold for 1 hr. 37 min. would require an average fuel consumption of approximately 14.8 GPH, not 15 GPH. Answer (C) is incorrect because to be able to hold for 1 hr. 42 min. would require an average fuel consumption of approximately 14.5 GPH, not 15 GPH

3.
4265. (Refer to figures 21, 22, and 24 on pages 366, 368, and 430, respectively.) What fuel would be consumed on the flight between Grand Junction Co. and Durango, Co. if the average fuel consumption is 15 GPH?

A— 17 gallons.
B— 20 gallons.
C— 25 gallons.

Answer (A) is correct (4265). (IFH Chap XIII)
Complete the flight log by computing the fuel consumption at 15 GPH.

	Time	Fuel (gal.)
HERRM INT.	:24:00G	6.0
MANCA INT.	:26:10	6.5
Approach and landing	:18:30G	4.6
Total	1:08:40	17.1

G = Given

Answer (B) is incorrect because 20 gal. of fuel would require an average fuel consumption of 17.5 GPH, not 15 GPH. Answer (C) is incorrect because 25 gal. of fuel would require an average fuel consumption of approximately 22 GPH, not 15 GPH.

4.
4261. (Refer to figure 24 on page 430.) Proceeding southbound on V187, (vicinity of Cortez VOR) contact is lost with Denver Center. You should attempt to contact Denver Center on:

A— 133.425 MHz.
B— 122.1 MHz and receive on 108.4 MHz.
C— 122.35 MHz.

Answer (A) is correct (4261). (ACL)
To the northwest of the Cortez VOR and south of Dove Creek VORTAC is a box with serrated edges. This box shows the frequency for Denver Center in the Cortez VOR area as 133.425.
Answer (B) is incorrect because 122.1 is not shown on the chart, and 108.4 is the frequency for the Cortez VOR, not Denver Center. Additionally, 108.4 is underlined, indicating that the VOR has no voice capability (i.e., that there would be nothing to receive on 108.4). Answer (C) is incorrect because 122.35 is the frequency you would use to contact Denver Flight Service when in the vicinity of the Durango VOR, not Denver Center.

5.
4262. (Refer to figure 22 on page 368 and figure 24 on page 430.) For planning purposes, what would be the highest MEA on V187 between Grand Junction, Walker Airport, and Durango, La Plata Co. Airport?

A— 12,000 feet.
B— 15,000 feet.
C— 16,000 feet.

Answer (B) is correct (4262). (ACL)
The highest MEA along the route is 15,000 ft. MSL along V187 between HERRM INT. and MANCA INT.
Answer (A) is incorrect because 12,000 ft. MSL is the MEA between JNC and HERRM INT., but is not the highest. Answer (C) is incorrect because 16,000 ft. MSL is not an MEA along any part of this route.

6.
4263. (Refer to figure 24 on page 430.) At what point should a VOR changeover be made from JNC VOR to MANCA intersection southbound on V187?

A— 36 NM south of JNC.
B— 52 NM south of JNC.
C— 74 NM south of JNC.

Answer (B) is correct (4263). (AIM Para 5-3-6)
The VOR changeover point is depicted on V187, south of HERRM INT and depicts the mileage between the VORTAC stations. It shows the COP as being 52 NM south of JNC.
Answer (A) is incorrect because the COP is depicted as 52 NM, not 36 NM, south of JNC. Answer (C) is incorrect because the COP is depicted as 52 NM, not 74 NM, south of JNC.

7.
4264. (Refer to figure 24 on page 430.) What is the MOCA between JNC and MANCA intersection on V187?

A— 10,900 feet MSL.
B— 12,000 feet MSL.
C— 13,700 feet MSL.

Answer (C) is correct (4264). (ACL)
The MOCA (minimum obstruction clearance altitude) appears with an asterisk under the MEA on V187. It is 13,700 ft. MSL.
Answer (A) is incorrect because 10,900 ft. MSL is the MEA, not MOCA, between MANCA and RIZAL intersections. Answer (B) is incorrect because 12,000 ft. MSL is the MEA, not MOCA, between JNC and HERRM INT.

FIGURE 21.—Flight Plan and Aircraft Information.

Form Approved: OMB No. 2120-0034						

U.S. DEPARTMENT OF TRANSPORTATION
FEDERAL AVIATION ADMINISTRATION

FLIGHT PLAN

(FAA USE ONLY) ☐ PILOT BRIEFING ☐ VNR TIME STARTED SPECIALIST INITIALS

☐ STOPOVER

1. TYPE	2. AIRCRAFT IDENTIFICATION	3. AIRCRAFT TYPE/ SPECIAL EQUIPMENT	4. TRUE AIRSPEED	5. DEPARTURE POINT	6. DEPARTURE TIME		7. CRUISING ALTITUDE
VFR					PROPOSED (Z)	ACTUAL (Z)	
X IFR	N 123RC	T210N/	175 KTS	DRO			16,000
DVFR							

8. ROUTE OF FLIGHT

V211, MANCA, V187, HERRM, V187, JNC

9. DESTINATION (Name of airport and city)	10. EST. TIME ENROUTE		11. REMARKS
	HOURS	MINUTES	
GJT			

12. FUEL ON BOARD		13. ALTERNATE AIRPORT(S)	14. PILOT'S NAME, ADDRESS & TELEPHONE NUMBER & AIRCRAFT HOME BASE	15. NUMBER ABOARD
HOURS	MINUTES			
			17. DESTINATION CONTACT/TELEPHONE (OPTIONAL)	2

16. COLOR OF AIRCRAFT
RED/WHITE/BLUE

CIVIL AIRCRAFT PILOTS. FAR Part 91 requires you file an IFR flight plan to operate under instrument flight rules in controlled airspace. Failure to file could result in a civil penalty not to exceed $1,000 for each violation (Section 901 of the Federal Aviation Act of 1958, as amended). Filing of a VFR flight plan is recommended as a good operating practice. See also Part 99 for requirements concerning DVFR flight plans.

FAA Form 7233-1 (8-82)   CLOSE VFR FLIGHT PLAN WITH _____ FSS ON ARRIVAL

AIRCRAFT INFORMATION

MAKE Cessna   MODEL T210N

N 123RC   Vso 58 ___

AIRCRAFT EQUIPMENT/STATUS**

**NOTE: X= OPERATIVE INOP= INOPERATIVE N/A= NOT APPLICABLE
TRANSPONDER: X (MODE C) X ILS: (LOCALIZER) X (GLIDE SLOPE) X
VOR NO. 1 X (NO. 2) X ADF: X RNAV: X
VERTICAL PATH COMPUTER: N/A DME: X
MARKER BEACON: X (AUDIO) X (VISUAL) X

FIGURE 21A.—Flight Plan and Aircraft Information.

FLIGHT LOG

GRAND JUNCTION (GJT) TO WALKER FIELD, DURANGO (DRO)

CHECK POINTS		ROUTE	COURSE	WIND	SPEED-KTS		DIST	TIME		FUEL	
FROM	TO	ALTITUDE		TEMP	TAS	GS	NM	LEG	TOT	LEG	TOT
GJT	JNC	JNC9,JNC CLIMB		230 08				✕			
	HERRM	V187 15,000	151°		175			:24:0			
	MANCA	V187	151°								
APPROACH & LANDING		V211 DESCENT	092°					:18:30			
	DRO										

OTHER DATA:

NOTE: TAKEOFF RUNWAY 29.
MAG. VAR. 14° E.

FLIGHT SUMMARY

TIME	FUEL (LBS)	
		EN ROUTE
		RESERVE
		MISSED APPR.
		TOTAL

FIGURE 22.—Flight Planning Log.

FLIGHT LOG

DURANGO (DRO) TO GRAND JUNCTION, WALKER FIELD (GJT)

| CHECK POINTS | | ROUTE | COURSE | WIND | SPEED-KTS | | DIST | TIME | | FUEL | |
FROM	TO	ALTITUDE		TEMP	TAS	GS	NM	LEG	TOT	LEG	TOT
DRO	MANCA	V211 CLIMB	272°	230 08				:14:30			
	HERRM	V187 16.000	333°		174						
	JNC	V187	331°								
APPROACH & LANDING		DESCENT						:12:00			
	GJT										

OTHER DATA:
NOTE: MAG. VAR. 14° E.

FLIGHT SUMMARY

TIME	FUEL (LBS)	
		EN ROUTE
		RESERVE
		MISSED APPR.
		TOTAL

FIGURE 22A.—Flight Planning Log.

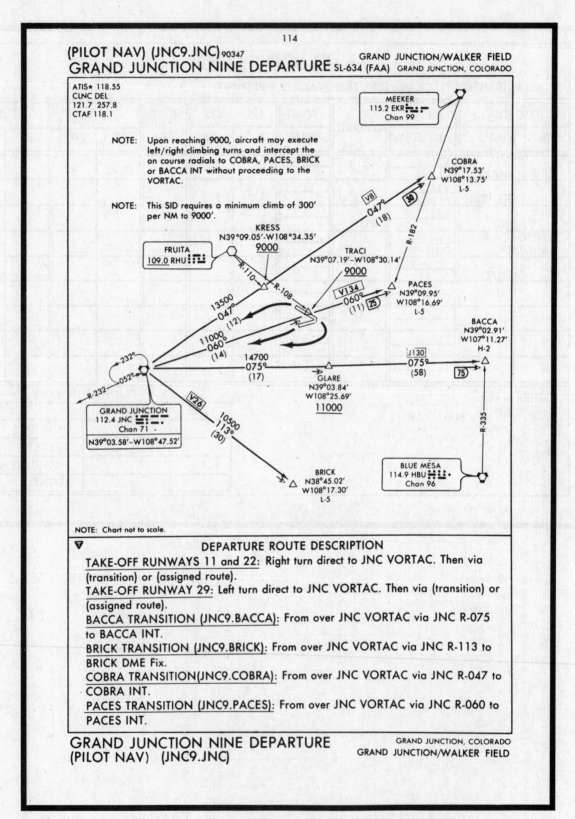

FIGURE 23.— Grand Junction Nine Departure (JNC9.JNC).

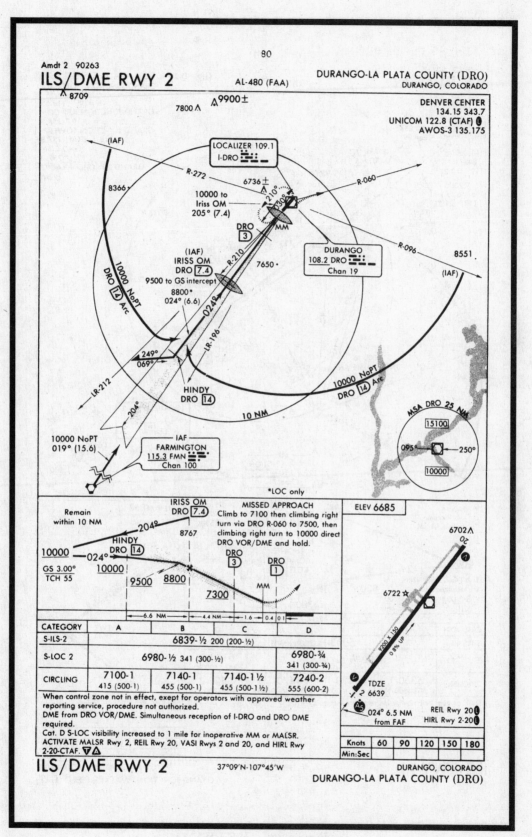

FIGURE 25.—ILS/DME RWY 2.

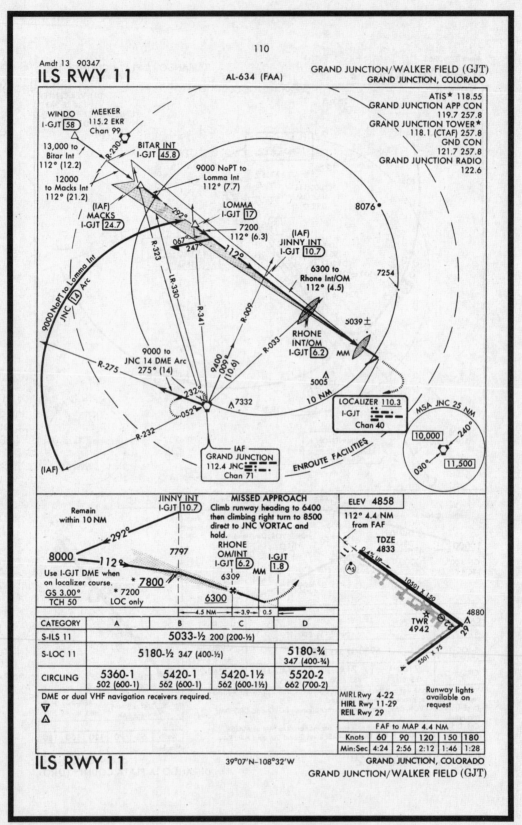

FIGURE 26.— ILS RWY 11.

11.2 MFR to EUG

Questions 8 through 18 pertain to an IFR flight from Medford-Jackson County Airport, Medford, Oregon to the Mahlon Sweet Field, Eugene, Oregon.

The route of flight is given in block 8 on the flight plan portion of Fig. 27 on page 377. Information which pertains to your aircraft is given on the bottom portion of Fig. 27. The partially completed flight planning log is given in Fig. 28 on page 378.

The figures provided for this flight are listed below and are grouped together after the sequence of questions, except for Fig. 31, which is provided in color on page 431.

11.2 MFR to EUG

8.
4266. (Refer to figure 27 on page 377.) What aircraft equipment code should be entered in block 3 of the flight plan?

A— T.
B— U.
C— A.

Answer (C) is correct (4266). *(AIM Para 5-1-7)*
In block 3 of the flight plan, you enter the designation of the aircraft followed by a slash (/) and a letter for the equipment code. The bottom portion of Fig. 27 indicates you have a transponder with Mode C and DME, which requires code A. (See Legend 26 on page 362.)
Answer (A) is incorrect because T indicates only a transponder with no encoding capability and no DME. Answer (B) is incorrect because U indicates a transponder with encoding capability but no DME.

9.
4267. (Refer to figures 27 and 28 on pages 377 and 378.) What CAS must be used to maintain the filed TAS at the flight planned altitude if the outside air temperature is −5 °C?

A— 134 KCAS.
B— 139 KCAS.
C— 142 KCAS.

Answer (B) is correct (4267). *(Fl Comp)*
In the center of the computer side of your flight computer, on the right side, put the air temperature of −5°C over the altitude of 8,000 ft. (given in block 7 of the flight plan). On the outer scale, find TAS of 155 (from block 4), which is over calibrated airspeed (CAS) on the inner scale of 139 KCAS.
Answer (A) is incorrect because maintaining 134 KCAS would result in a TAS of 150 kt., not 155 kt. Answer (C) is incorrect because maintaining 142 KCAS would result in a TAS of 158 kt., not 155 kt.

10.
4268. (Refer to figures 27, 28, 29, and 30 on pages 377 through 380 and figure 31 on page 431.) (Refer to the FD excerpt below, and use the wind entry closest to the flight planned altitude.) Determine the time to be entered in block 10 of the flight plan.

Route of flight . . . . Figures 27, 28, 29, 30, & 31
Flight log & MAG VAR . . . . Figure 28
GNATS ONE DEPARTURE
  and Excerpt from AFD . . . . Figure 30

FT	3000	6000	9000
OTH	0507	2006+03	2215–05

A— 1 hour 10 minutes.
B— 1 hour 15 minutes.
C— 1 hour 20 minutes.

11.
4269. (Refer to figure 30 on page 380.) During the arc portion of the instrument departure procedure (GNATS1.MOURN), a left crosswind is encountered. Where should the bearing pointer of an RMI be referenced relative to the wing tip to compensate for wind drift and maintain the 15 DME arc?

A— Behind the right wing tip reference point.
B— On the right wing tip reference point.
C— Behind the left wing tip reference point.

12.
4270. (Refer to figure 30 on page 380.) Using an average ground speed of 120 knots, what minimum rate of climb must be maintained to meet the required climb rate (feet per NM) to 4,100 feet as specified on the instrument departure procedure?

A— 400 feet per minute.
B— 500 feet per minute.
C— 800 feet per minute.

Answer (C) is correct (4268). *(IFH Chap XIII)*
To determine the estimated time en route to be entered in block 10, you must complete the flight planning log in Fig. 28.

Compute the distance from MERLI intersection to MOURN intersection. First, compute the distance traveled on the OED 15 DME from R-251 (MERLI) to R-333. The number of degrees of the arc is 82° (333 – 251). Use the following general rule to find the distance traveled on the arc:

$$\text{Dist. of arc} = \frac{\# \text{ of deg.} \times DME \text{ arc}}{60}$$

$$\text{Dist. of arc} = \frac{82 \times 15}{60} = 20.5 \; NM$$

Next, add the 16 NM on R-333 from the 15 DME arc to MOURN, which is 36.5 (20.5 + 16). Given an average groundspeed of 135 kt., the time is 16 min. 13 sec.

For the next three legs, you need to compute the wind triangle on either your flight computer or your electronic computer to determine the groundspeed as given in the table below.

Remember that winds are given in true direction and must be converted to magnetic. Fig. 28 shows a variation of 20°E. Use the wind at 9,000 ft. because that is closest to the flight planned altitude of 8,000 ft. 220° – 20°E var. = 200° at 15 kt.

	Distance	MC	Wind (Mag)	Ground-speed	Time
MERLI INT.	X	X	X	X	:11:00G
MOURN INT.	37	X	X	135G	:16:13
RBG VOR	19	287°	200/15	153	:07:26
OTH VORTAC	38	272°	200/15	149	:15:12
EUG VORTAC	59	026°	200/15	170	:20:50
Approach and Landing	X	X	X	X	:10:00G
					1:20:41

G = Given

Answer (A) is incorrect because an ETE of 1 hr. 10 min. requires a TAS of approximately 200 kt., not 155 kt. Answer (B) is incorrect because an ETE of 1 hr. 15 min. requires a TAS of 180 kt., not 155 kt.

Answer (A) is correct (4269). *(IFH Chap VII)*
Normally when flying a DME arc, the RMI needle will point exactly to 090° or 270° in wind-free conditions. Given a crosswind from the left, you will have to make a correction to the left, which will mean that the needle is behind the right wing while on an arc to the right.

Answer (B) is incorrect because it will be on the right wing tip only when there is no wind. Answer (C) is incorrect because the VOR is to the right and the RMI points directly to the VOR.

Answer (C) is correct (4270). *(ACL)*
The instrument departure procedure in Fig. 30 has a note which indicates a minimum climb of 400 ft. per NM to 4,100 ft. To convert this to a rate of climb (fpm), use Legend 16 on page 204. Find the 400 ft. per NM column on the left margin and move right to the 120-kt. ground speed column to determine a rate of climb of 800 fpm.

Answer (A) is incorrect because a 400 fpm rate of climb at an average ground speed of 120 kt. would result in a climb rate of 200 ft. per NM, not 400 ft. per NM. Answer (B) is incorrect because a 500 fpm rate of climb at an average ground speed of 120 kt. would result in a climb rate of 250 ft. per NM, not 400 ft. per NM.

13.
4271. (Refer to figure 30 on page 380.) Which restriction to the use of the OED VORTAC would be applicable to the (GNATS1.MOURN) departure?

A— R-333 beyond 30 NM below 6,500 feet.
B— R-210 beyond 35 NM below 8,500 feet.
C— R-251 within 15 NM below 6,100 feet.

Answer (A) is correct (4271). *(ACL)*
On Fig. 30, in the *A/FD* under the **Radio Aids to Navigation** for the OED VORTAC, the VORTAC is listed as being unusable in certain segments. For example, it indicates that radials 280° to 345° are not usable below 6,500 ft. beyond 30 NM. This includes R-333.
Answer (B) is incorrect because there is no restriction to R-210. Answer (C) is incorrect because the restriction to R-251 is beyond 25 NM, not within 15 NM.

14.
4273. (Refer to figures 27 and 30 on pages 377 and 380.) To which maximum service volume distance from the OED VORTAC should you expect to receive adequate signal coverage for navigation at the flight planned altitude?

A— 100 NM.
B— 80 NM.
C— 40 NM.

Answer (C) is correct (4273). *(AIM Para 1-1-8)*
The flight plan in Fig. 27 shows a planned altitude of 8,000 ft. OED VORTAC is an H-type (high altitude) VORTAC as indicated in the *A/FD* in Fig. 30 by (H) ABVORTAC in the first line of **Radio Aids to Navigation**. For such VORTACs, the altitude and range boundaries are from 1,000 ft. AGL up to and including 14,500 ft. AGL at distances out to 40 NM.
Answer (A) is incorrect because 100 NM applies to 14,500 ft. AGL up to 18,000 ft. AGL, and from 45,000 ft. AGL up to 60,000 ft. AGL. Answer (B) is incorrect because 80 NM is not given as a range for VORs.

15.
4272. (Refer to figure 30 on page 380 and figure 30A below.) What is your position relative to GNATS intersection and the instrument departure routing?

A— On departure course and past GNATS.
B— Right of departure course and past GNATS.
C— Left of departure course and have not passed GNATS.

Answer (B) is correct (4272). *(IFH Chap VII)*
On the RMI, the fat needle is tuned to the OED VOR (113.6). The tail of the needle is on 224°, which means that the airplane is on R-224. Accordingly, the airplane is past GNATS (which is on R-216). The thin needle is tuned to the VIOLE LMM (356). The tail of the needle is on 280°, which means that the airplane is on the 280° MB FROM. Thus, the airplane is to the right of the departure course (which is the 270° MB FROM).
Answer (A) is incorrect because the ADF needle indicates the 280° MB FROM, which is right of, not on, the departure course. Answer (C) is incorrect because the ADF needle indicates the 280° MB FROM, which is right, not left, of the departure course, and the VOR needle indicates R-224, which is past, not approaching, GNATS.

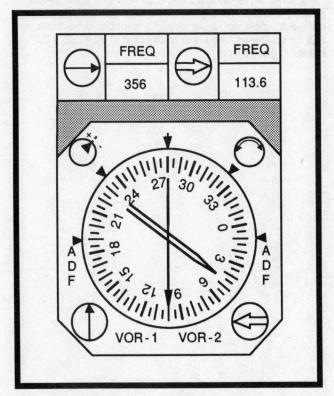

FIGURE 30A.—RMI Indicator.

16.
4274. (Refer to figure 29 on page 379.) What is the TDZ elevation for RWY 16 on Eugene/Mahlon Sweet Field?

A— 363 feet MSL.
B— 365 feet MSL.
C— 396 feet MSL.

17.
4275. (Refer to figure 29 on page 379.) What are the hours of operation (local standard time) of the control tower at Eugene/Mahlon Sweet Field?

A— 0800 - 2300.
B— 0600 - 0000.
C— 0700 - 0100.

18.
4276. (Refer to figure 29 on page 379.) Using a groundspeed of 90 knots on the ILS final approach course, what rate of descent should be used as a reference to maintain the ILS glide slope?

A— 415 feet per minute.
B— 480 feet per minute.
C— 555 feet per minute.

Answer (A) is correct (4274). *(ACL)*
On the IAP chart, the TDZE is shown in the airport diagram near the approach end of the landing runway. The TDZE for RWY 16 at EUG is 363 ft.
Answer (B) is incorrect because 365 ft. MSL is the airport elevation. Answer (C) is incorrect because 396 ft. MSL is the height of an obstacle to the right of the approach end of RWY 16.

Answer (B) is correct (4275). *(IFH Chap X)*
The hours of operation of the control tower at Eugene/Mahlon Sweet Field are listed on Fig. 29 in the *A/FD* under Eugene tower. It operates from 1400Z to 0800Z. To convert to local standard time, use the conversion code on the first line of the *A/FD*: GMT-8(-7DT). This means that, to adjust Greenwich mean time (GMT) to local standard time, you subtract 8 hr., which is 0600 - 0000.
Answer (A) is incorrect because 0800 - 2300 are not related hours at this airport. Answer (C) is incorrect because 0700 - 0100 are the hours of operation converted to daylight, not standard, time. Note the symbol (‡) indicates that, during periods of daylight saving time, effective hours will be 1 hr. earlier than shown (i.e., standard time).

Answer (B) is correct (4276). *(IFH Chap X)*
The profile view of the NOS chart shows a glide slope (GS) angle of 3.00°. Legend 21 on page 199 gives rates of descent based on various glide slope angles and groundspeeds. Find the 3.0° glide slope at the left margin and move right to the 90-kt. groundspeed column to determine a rate of descent of 480 fpm.
Answer (A) is incorrect because 415 fpm is the rate of descent required for a glide slope between 2.5° and 3.0°, not a 3.0° glide slope. Answer (C) is incorrect because 555 fpm is the required rate of descent at 90 kt. on a 3.5°, not 3.0°, glide slope.

U.S. DEPARTMENT OF TRANSPORTATION FEDERAL AVIATION ADMINISTRATION **FLIGHT PLAN**	(FAA USE ONLY) ☐ PILOT BRIEFING ☐ VNR ☐ STOPOVER			TIME STARTED	SPECIALIST INITIALS

Form Approved: OMB No. 2120-0034

1. TYPE	2. AIRCRAFT IDENTIFICATION	3. AIRCRAFT TYPE/ SPECIAL EQUIPMENT	4. TRUE AIRSPEED	5. DEPARTURE POINT	6. DEPARTURE TIME PROPOSED (Z) / ACTUAL (Z)	7. CRUISING ALTITUDE
VFR / X IFR / DVFR	N132SM	C 182/	155 KTS	MFR		8,000

8. ROUTE OF FLIGHT

GNATS 1, MOURN, V121 EUG

9. DESTINATION (Name of airport and city)
MAHLON/SWEET FIELD, EUGENE, OR.

10. EST. TIME ENROUTE HOURS / MINUTES

11. REMARKS INSTRUMENT TRAINING FLIGHT

12. FUEL ON BOARD HOURS / MINUTES

13. ALTERNATE AIRPORT(S)

14. PILOT'S NAME, ADDRESS & TELEPHONE NUMBER & AIRCRAFT HOME BASE

15. NUMBER ABOARD

17. DESTINATION CONTACT/TELEPHONE (OPTIONAL) N/R

16. COLOR OF AIRCRAFT

CIVIL AIRCRAFT PILOTS. FAR Part 91 requires you file an IFR flight plan to operate under instrument flight rules in controlled airspace. Failure to file could result in a civil penalty not to exceed $1,000 for each violation (Section 901 of the Federal Aviation Act of 1958, as amended). Filing of a VFR flight plan is recommended as a good operating practice. See also Part 99 for requirements concerning DVFR flight plans.

FAA Form 7233-1 (8-82)   CLOSE VFR FLIGHT PLAN WITH _____ FSS ON ARRIVAL

AIRCRAFT INFORMATION

MAKE CESSNA   MODEL 182

N 132SM   Vso 57

AIRCRAFT EQUIPMENT/STATUS**

**NOTE: X= OPERATIVE   INOP= INOPERATIVE   N/A= NOT APPLICABLE
TRANSPONDER: X (MODE C) X ILS: (LOCALIZER) X (GLIDE SLOPE) N/A
VOR NO. 1 X (NO. 2) X ADF: X RNAV: N/A
VERTICAL PATH COMPUTER: NA DME: X
MARKER BEACON: (AUDIO) INOP (VISUAL) Inop.

FIGURE 27.—Flight Plan and Aircraft Information.

FLIGHT LOG

MEDFORD - JACKSON CO. AIRPORT TO HAHLON/SWEET FIELD, EUGENE, OR.

CHECK POINTS		ROUTE		WIND	SPEED-KTS		DIST	TIME		FUEL	
FROM	TO	ALTITUDE	COURSE	TEMP	TAS	GS	NM	LEG	TOT	LEG	TOT
MFR	MERLI	GNATS 1 CLIMB	270°		155			:11:0			
	MOURN	V121 8000	333°			AVER. 135					
	RBG	V121 8000	287°								
	OTH	V121 8000	272°								
	EUG	APPROACH DESCENT	026°								
APPROACH & LANDING								:10:0			
	SWEET FIELD										

OTHER DATA:
  NOTE:

  MAG. VAR. 20° E.
  AVERAGE G.S. 135 KTS. FOR GNATS 1
  DEPARTURE CLIMB.

FLIGHT SUMMARY		
TIME	FUEL (LB)	
		EN ROUTE
		RESERVE
		MISSED APPR.
		TOTAL

FIGURE 28.—Flight Planning Log.

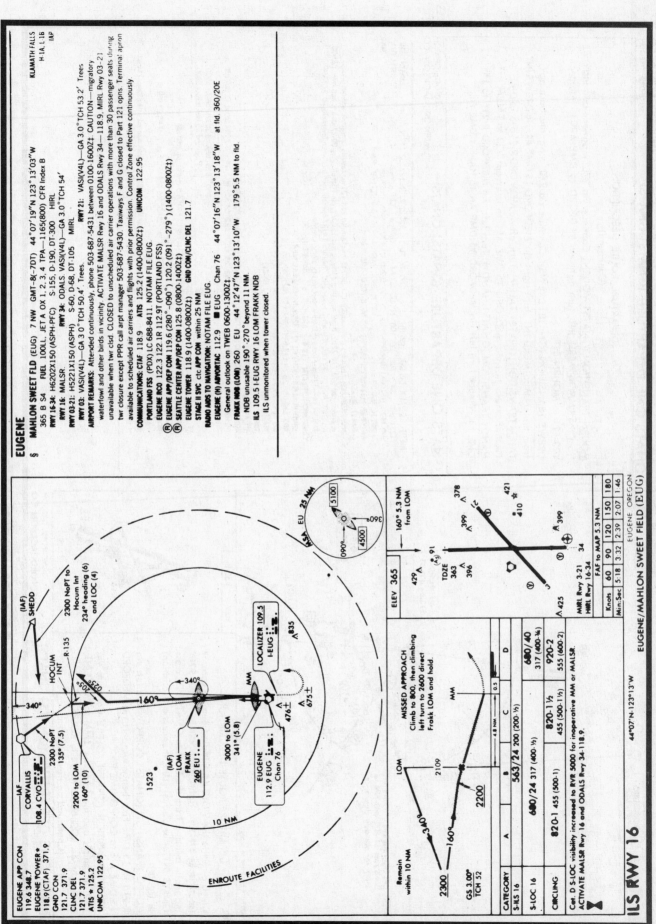

FIGURE 29.—ILS RWY 16 (EUG) and Excerpt from Airport/Facility Directory.

GNATS ONE DEPARTURE (GNATS1.GNATS)

MEDFORD-JACKSON CO
MEDFORD, OREGON

DEPARTURE ROUTE DESCRIPTION
(Continued)

MOURN TRANSITION (GNATS1.MOURN): Continue via 270° magnetic bearing from the LMM to MERLI INT, turn right via MEDFORD 15 DME ARC to intercept V23-121 to MOURN INT.

DREWS TRANSITION (GNATS1.DREWS): Continue via 270° magnetic bearing from the LMM to MERLI INT, turn right via MEDFORD 15 DME ARC to DREWS INT.

TALEM TRANSITION (GNATS1.TALEM): Turn left via MEDFORD R-216 to 15 DME Fix thence turn left via MEDFORD 15 DME ARC to Intercept V23 to TALEM INT.

HANDY TRANSITION (GNATS1.HANDY): Turn left via MEDFORD R-216 to 15 DME Fix, thence turn left via MEDFORD 15 DME Arc to HANDY DME Fix.

GNATS ONE DEPARTURE (GNATS1.GNATS)

MEDFORD, OREGON
MEDFORD-JACKSON CO

§ **MEDFORD-JACKSON CO** (MFR) 3 N GMT–8(–7DT) 42°22'21"N 122°52'17"W **KLAMATH FALLS** H-1A, L-1A
1331 B S4 FUEL 80, 100, 100LL, JET A1 + OX 1, 3 CFR Index B IAP
RWY 14-32: H6700X150 (ASPH-PFC) S-200, D-200, DT-400 HIRL 5% up S
RWY 09-27: H3145X150 (ASPH) S-50, D-70, DT-108 MIRL
RWY 14: MALSR. Trees. RWY 32: REIL. VASI(V4L)—GA 3.0°TCH 49'. Road.
RWY 27: Road.
AIRPORT REMARKS: Attended continuously. CLOSED to unscheduled Part 121 air carriers operation, without prior approval, call 503-776-7222. Night refueling delay sunset-1500Z‡, ctc TOWER. Rwy 09-27 clsd to acft over 12,500 lbs GWT. Rwy 09/27 CLOSED when tower clsd. Rwy lgts 14/32 operate med ints when tower closed. ACTIVATE MALSR 14—119.4. Flocks of large waterfowl in vicinity Nov-May
COMMUNICATIONS: CTAF 119.4 ATIS 125.75 UNICOM 122.95
NORTH BEND FSS (OTH) LC 773-3256. NOTAM FILE MFR.
RCO 122.65 122.1R 113.6T (NORTH BEND FSS)
APP CON 124.3 (1400-0800Z‡) DEP CON 124.3 (1400-0800Z‡)
SEATTLE CENTER APP/DEP CON 125.3 (0800-1400Z‡)
TOWER 119.4 (1400-0800Z‡) GND CON 121.7
VFR ADVSY SVC ctc TOWER
RADIO AIDS TO NAVIGATION: NOTAM FILE OTH. VHF/DF ctc Medford TOWER
(M) ABVORTAC 113.6 ■ OED Chan 83 42°28'47"N 122°54'43"W 146° 6.1 NM to fld. 2080/19E
    VORTAC unusable:
        160°-165° beyond 35 NM below 8900' 280°-345° beyond 30 NM below 6500'
        198°-205° beyond 35 NM below 8500' 345°-360° beyond 35 NM below 6800'
        250°-280° beyond 25 NM below 6100'
PUMIE NDB (LOM) 373 MF 42°27'04"N 122°54'44"W 140° 4.5 NM to fld. NOTAM FILE MFR
    LOM unusable 150°-165° and 260°-265° beyond 5 miles.
VIOLE NDB (LMM) 356 FR 42°23'22"N 122°52'47"W 140° 0.5 NM to fld. NOTAM FILE MFR
    LMM unusable 305°-335° beyond 10 NM, all altitudes
ILS/DME 110.3 I-MFR Chan 40 Rwy 14 LOM PUMIE NDB. LMM VIOLE NDB. ILS unmonitored when tower closed.
    Localizer unusable inside threshold.

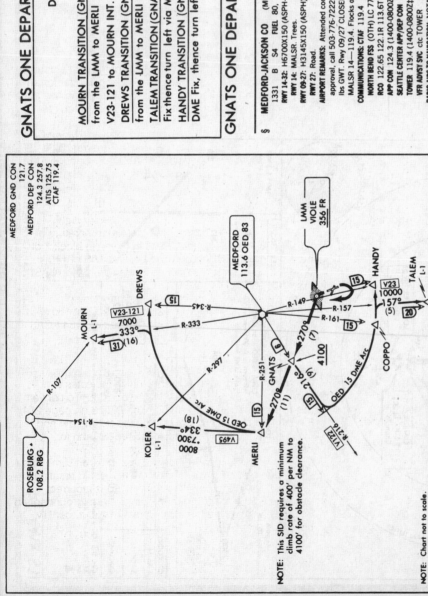

MEDFORD GND CON 121.7
MEDFORD DEP CON 124.3 257.8
ATIS 125.75
CTAF 119.4

ROSEBURG
108.2 RBG

MEDFORD 113.6 OED 83

LMM
VIOLE
356 FR

DREWS

MOURN
L-1

V23-121
7000
333°
[31] (16)

R-345

[15]

R-333

R-107

R-154

KOLER
L-1
8000
*7300
334°
(18)
V495

MERLI
[15] 270°
(11)

R-251

R-297

GNATS [6]
270°
(9) 4100

R-216
(6)

OED 15 DME Arc

V-172

270°
(7)

R-149

R-157

R-161

HANDY
[15]

[15]

[15]

V23
10000
157°
(5)

COPPO

TALEM
L-1

[20]

ELEV 1331

NOTE: This SID requires a minimum climb rate of 400' per NM to 4100' for obstacle clearance.

NOTE: Chart not to scale.

DEPARTURE ROUTE DESCRIPTION

▶ Climb direct to the VIOLE ILS Middle Compass Locator (south take-off turn right), then climb on the 270° magnetic bearing from the LMM to GNATS INT, cross GNATS INT at or above 4100; thence via (transition) or (route).

COPPO TRANSITION (GNATS1.COPPO): Turn left via R-216 to 15 DME Fix, thence turn left via MEDFORD 15 DME Arc to COPPO DME Fix.

KOLER TRANSITION (GNATS1.KOLER): Continue via 270° magnetic bearing from the LMM to MERLI INT, turn right via ROSEBURG R-154 to KOLER INT.
(Continued on next page)

MEDFORD, OREGON
MEDFORD-JACKSON CO

FIGURE 30.—GNATS One Departure and Excerpt from Airport/Facility Directory.

GNATS ONE DEPARTURE (GNATS1.GNATS)

11.3 YKM to PDX

Questions 19 through 33 pertain to an IFR flight from Yakima Air Terminal, Yakima, Washington to the Portland International Airport, Portland, Oregon.

The route of flight is given in block 8 on the flight plan portion of Fig. 44 on page 385. Information which pertains to your aircraft is given on the bottom portion of Fig. 44. The partially completed flight planning log is given in Fig. 45 on page 386.

The figures provided for this flight are listed below and are grouped together after the sequence of questions, except for Fig. 47, which is provided in color on page 434.

11.3 YKM to PDX

19.
4300. (Refer to figure 44 on page 385.) What aircraft equipment code should be entered in block 3 of the flight plan?

A— A.
B— C.
C— I.

Answer (C) is correct (4300). *(AIM Para 5-1-7)*
In block 3 of the flight plan, you enter the designation of the aircraft followed by a slash (/) and a letter for an equipment mode. Fig. 44 indicates the airplane has a transponder with Mode C and RNAV, which requires code I. (See Legend 26 on page 362.)
Answer (A) is incorrect because A means Mode C trans-ponder and DME, but no RNAV. Answer (B) is incorrect because C indicates RNAV and a transponder with no altitude encoding capability.

20.
4301. (Refer to figure 44 on page 385.) What CAS must be used to maintain the filed TAS at the flight planned altitude if the outside air temperature is +5 °C?

A— 147 KCAS.
B— 150 KCAS.
C— 154 KCAS.

Answer (A) is correct (4301). *(Fl Comp)*
In the center of the slide rule side of your flight computer, on the right side, put the air temperature of +5°C over the altitude of 12,000 ft. (given in block 7 of the flight plan). On the outer scale, find TAS of 180 kt. (from block 4), which is over calibrated airspeed (CAS) on the inner scale of 147 KCAS.
Answer (B) is incorrect because maintaining 150 KCAS would result in a TAS of 185 kt., not 180 kt. Answer (C) is incorrect because maintaining 154 KCAS would result in a TAS of 190 kt., not 180 kt.

21.
4303. (Refer to figure 46 on page 387.) Using an average groundspeed of 140 knots, what minimum indicated rate of climb must be maintained to meet the required climb rate (feet per NM) to 6,300 feet as specified on the instrument departure procedure?

A— 350 feet per minute.
B— 583 feet per minute.
C— 816 feet per minute.

Answer (C) is correct (4303). *(ACL)*
The DP in Fig. 46 has a note which indicates a minimum climb of 350 ft. per NM to 6,300 ft. To convert this to a rate of climb (fpm), use Legend 16 on page 204. Find the 350 ft. per NM column on the left margin and move right to the 140-kt. groundspeed column to determine a rate of climb of 816 fpm.
Answer (A) is incorrect because a 350 fpm climb rate at a groundspeed of 60 kt., not 140 kt., would result in a climb rate of 350 ft. per NM. Answer (B) is incorrect because a 583 fpm climb rate at an average groundspeed of 140 kt. would result in a climb rate of 250 ft. per NM, not 350 ft. per NM.

22.
4302. (Refer to figures 44, 45, and 46 on pages 385 through 387 and figure 47 on page 434.) Determine the time to be entered in block 10 of the flight plan. (Refer to the FD excerpt below, and use the wind entry closest to the flight planned altitude.)

Route of flight . . . . Figures 44, 45, 46, and 47
Flight log & MAG VAR . . . . Figure 45
GROMO TWO DEPARTURE
  and Excerpt from AFD . . . . Figure 46

FT	3000	6000	9000	12000
YKM	1615	1926+12	2032+08	2035+05

A— 54 minutes.
B— 1 hour 02 minutes.
C— 1 hour 07 minutes.

Answer (B) is correct (4302). *(IFH Chap XIII)*
  To determine estimated time en route to be entered in block 10, you must complete the flight planning log in Fig. 45. Using the wind side of your flight computer, determine groundspeeds as given in the table below.
  Remember that winds are given in true direction and must be converted to magnetic. Fig. 45 indicates a variation of 20°E. 200° – 20°E var. = 180° at 35 kt.
  The distance from BTG VORTAC to PDX is not given. It may be estimated at 10 NM by comparing it to other airway segments of similar length.

	Distance	MC	Wind (Mag)	Ground-speed	Time
HITCH INT	X	X	X	X	:10:00G
VOR COP	37	206°	180/35	148	:15:00
BTG VORTAC	53	234°	180/35	157	:20:15
PDX	10	160°	180/35	147	:04:05
Approach and Landing	X	X	X	X	:13:00G
					1:02:20

G = Given

  Answer (A) is incorrect because an ETE of 54 min. requires a TAS of 220 kt., not 180 kt. Answer (C) is incorrect because an ETE of 1 hr. 7 min. requires a TAS of approximately 165 kt., not 180 kt.

23.
4304. (Refer to figure 46 on page 387 and figure 48 below.) What is your position relative to the 9 DME ARC and the 206° radial of the instrument departure procedure?

A— On the 9 DME arc and approaching R-206.
B— Outside the 9 DME arc and past R-206.
C— Inside the 9 DME arc and approaching R-206.

Answer (A) is correct (4304). *(IFH Chap VII)*
  The HSI shows that you are currently on a 130° heading, thus flying in a southeasterly direction. The OBS selector is set on R-206, and a left deflection is indicated. This means you are west and north of R-206. (If you were flying out the R-206 with a left deflection, you would turn left to intercept.) You are approaching R-206 because you are flying in a southeasterly direction. The DME indicates 9 NM out, so you are on the 9 DME arc.
  Answer (B) is incorrect because you are on, not outside, the arc and approaching, not past, R-206. Answer (C) is incorrect because you are on, not inside, the arc.

NAV - 1

FREQ	N.M.	KNOTS	MIN
116.0	9.0	7	////

FIGURE 48.—CDI — NAV 1.

24.
4305. (Refer to figure 46 on page 387.) What are the hours of operation (local time) of the ATIS for the Yakima Air Terminal when daylight savings time is in effect?

A— 0500 to 2100 local.
B— 0600 to 2200 local.
C— 0700 to 2300 local.

25.
4645. (Refer to figure 47 on page 434.) En route on V112 from BTG VORTAC to LTJ VORTAC, the minimum altitude crossing Gymme intersection is

A— 6,400 feet.
B— 6,500 feet.
C— 7,000 feet.

26.
4646. (Refer to figure 47 on page 434.) When en route on V448 from YKM VORTAC to BTG VORTAC, what minimum navigation equipment is required to identify ANGOO intersection?

A— One VOR receiver.
B— One VOR receiver and DME.
C— Two VOR receivers.

27.
4647. (Refer to figure 47 on page 434.) En route on V468 from BTG VORTAC to YKM VORTAC, the minimum altitude at TROTS intersection is

A— 7,100 feet.
B— 10,000 feet.
C— 11,500 feet.

28.
4306. (Refer to figure 49 on page 388.) What determines the MAP on the LOC/DME RWY 21 approach at Portland International Airport?

A— I-GPO 1.2 DME.
B— 5.8 NM from ROBOT FAF.
C— 160 radial of BTG VORTAC.

Answer (B) is correct (4305). *(ACL)*
The hours of operation of the ATIS at Yakima Air Terminal are listed on Fig. 46 in the *A/FD* on the **Communications** line at ATIS. It operates from 1400Z to 0600Z. Note that the ‡ symbol indicates that, during periods of daylight saving time, effective hours of operation are 1 hr. earlier than those shown (i.e., standard time). For example, the ATIS will begin operation at 6:00 a.m. local time, regardless of whether daylight saving time is in effect. Thus, you should always use the standard conversion; e.g., GMT-8 = 0600-2200 local.
Answer (A) is incorrect because you must subtract 8 hr., not 9 hr., from Zulu to convert to local time. Answer (C) is incorrect because you must always use the standard, not daylight, conversion.

Answer (C) is correct (4645). *(FAR 91.177)*
When no minimum crossing altitude (MCA) is specified, e.g., at GYMME intersection, the intersection may be crossed at or above the preceding MEA. Since the MEA along V112 eastbound is 7,000 ft., GYMME may be crossed no lower than 7,000 ft.
Answer (A) is incorrect because 6,400 ft. is the MOCA, not the MEA, along V112. Answer (B) is incorrect because 6,500 ft. is the MEA west of GYMME when westbound, not eastbound.

Answer (A) is correct (4646). *(IFH VIII)*
To identify ANGOO INT, only one VOR receiver is required. It is important to establish yourself on V448 and maintain heading while you orient yourself to LTJ VORTAC R-330. Your position checks and tuning will need to be done quickly and accurately.
Answer (B) is incorrect because, since ANGOO INT can be determined by cross radials, only one VOR receiver is required; a DME is not. Answer (C) is incorrect because only one VOR receiver, not two, is required to identify ANGOO INT.

Answer (C) is correct (4647). *(FAR 91.177)*
TROTS intersection (45 NM northeast of BTG VORTAC on V468 in Fig. 47) shows a minimum crossing altitude (MCA) of 11,500 ft. when northeastbound on V468.
Answer (A) is incorrect because 7,100 ft. is the MOCA along V468, not the MCA at TROTS. Answer (B) is incorrect because 10,000 ft. is the MEA before TROTS, not the MCA at TROTS.

Answer (A) is correct (4306). *(ACL)*
The MAP on the LOC/DME RWY 21 approach is the 1.2 DME fix on the localizer (I-GPO).
Answer (B) is incorrect because, while the MAP is located 5.8 NM from ROBOT FAF, the MAP is the 1.2 DME fix on the localizer. Answer (C) is incorrect because the 160 radial of BTG VORTAC is part of the missed approach procedure, not the missed approach point (MAP).

29.
4307. (Refer to figures 44 and 49 on pages 385 and 388.) What is the MDA and visibility criteria for a straight-in LOC/DME RWY 21 approach at Portland International?

A— 1,100 ft. MSL; visibility 1 SM.
B— 680 ft. MSL; visibility 1 SM.
C— 680 ft. MSL; visibility 1 NM.

Answer (B) is correct (4307). *(ACL)*
Refer to Fig. 44 to determine the aircraft category. V_{S0} is 77 kt.; thus, 1.3 V_{S0} is 100.1 kt., which puts the airplane in Category B. The minimums for the LOC/DME RWY 21 approach, Category B, are 680 ft. MSL and one statute mile visibility.
Answer (A) is incorrect because 1,100 ft. MSL is the minimum altitude after crossing ROBOT FAF, but before reaching the 4 DME fix on the localizer. Answer (C) is incorrect because visibility minimums are given in statute miles, not nautical miles.

30.
4308. (Refer to figure 49 on page 388.) When conducting the LOC/DME RWY 21 approach at PDX, what is the Minimum Safe Altitude (MSA) while maneuvering between the BTG VORTAC and CREAK intersection?

A— 3,400 feet MSL.
B— 5,700 feet MSL.
C— 6,100 feet MSL.

Answer (C) is correct (4308). *(ACL)*
The circle in the lower right corner of the plan view of the LOC/DME RWY 21 approach into PDX indicates that the minimum safe sector altitudes for this approach are based on the BTG VORTAC. The circle also indicates that the minimum safe sector altitude in the area between the 310° and 120° radials in a clockwise direction is 6,100 ft. MSL (note that the 310° and 120° radials are the reciprocals of the 130° and 300° inbound courses shown on the plan view, respectively). Because CREAK intersection lies in this area, the minimum safe altitude for maneuvering between BTG VORTAC and CREAK intersection is 6,100 ft. MSL.
Remember, MSA altitudes are for emergency use only and may differ from published minimum altitudes on the IAP chart.
Answer (A) is incorrect because 3,400 ft. MSL is the minimum safe sector altitude in the area between the 120° and 330° radials in a clockwise direction. CREAK intersection, which is defined by the intersection of the 054° radial of the BTG VORTAC and the localizer, is not in this area. Answer (B) is incorrect because 5,700 ft. MSL is the minimum altitude for flying the charted feeder route, not maneuvering, between BTG VORTAC and CREAK intersection.

31.
4309. (Refer to figure 49 on page 388.) You have been cleared to the CREAK intersection via the BTG 054° radial at 7,000 ft. Approaching CREAK, you are cleared for the LOC/DME RWY 21 approach to PDX. Descent to procedure turn altitude should not begin prior to

A— completion of the procedure turn, and established on the localizer.
B— intercepting the glide slope.
C— CREAK outbound.

Answer (C) is correct (4309). *(ACL)*
CREAK intersection is an initial approach fix, identified by the letters IAF. It is the fix at which the procedure turn should begin. Because you were cleared to CREAK intersection at an altitude of 7,000 ft., you should remain at that altitude until you reach the intersection. Since you have been cleared for the approach, you may then turn to the northeast and track the localizer outbound (the first portion of the procedure turn) while descending to the minimum procedure turn altitude of 5,700 ft. MSL.
Answer (A) is incorrect because you should be at the procedure turn altitude (5,700 ft. MSL) at or before the completion of the procedure turn. Descent to the first step-down fix minimum altitude (not the procedure turn altitude) should begin after completion of the procedure turn and when established on the localizer (if you are past CREAK intersection). Answer (B) is incorrect because the LOC/DME RWY 21 approach has no glide slope. Additionally, descent to the procedure turn altitude may begin after crossing CREAK intersection.

32.
4310. (Refer to figure 49 on page 388.) With a ground speed of 120 knots, approximately what minimum rate of descent will be required between I-GPO 7 DME fix (ROBOT) and the I-GPO 4 DME fix?

A— 1,200 fpm.
B— 500 fpm.
C— 800 fpm.

Answer (C) is correct (4310). *(ACL)*
The LOC/DME RWY 21 approach chart does not provide descent angle information, so you must calculate the required rate of descent. From the chart, you can see that the 7 DME fix and the 4 DME fix off I-GPO are 3 NM apart. If your ground speed is 120 kt., you will cover 2 NM every minute. Thus, it will take you 1.5 minutes to cover 3 NM. The minimum altitude at ROBOT is 2,300 ft. MSL, and the minimum altitude at the 4 DME fix is 1,100 ft. MSL, a difference of 1,200 ft. Therefore, you must lose 1,200 ft. of altitude in 1.5 minutes, which requires a descent rate of 800 fpm ($1,200 \div 1.5 = 800$).
Answer (A) is incorrect because a 1,200 fpm descent rate would be required if your ground speed were 180 kt., not 120 kt. Answer (B) is incorrect because a 500 fpm descent rate would be required if your ground speed were 75 kt., not 120 kt.

33.
4311. (Refer to figure 49 on page 388.) What is the usable runway length for landing on runway 21 at PDX?

A— 7,900 ft.
B— 7,000 ft.
C— 5,957 ft.

Answer (C) is correct (4311). *(ACL)*

In the upper right corner of the airport diagram, there is a notation that says "Rwy 21 ldg 5957′." This notation signifies that the runway length available for landing is 5,957 ft.; the remainder of the 7,000 ft. runway length is a displaced threshold.

Answer (A) is incorrect because 7,900 ft. is not a runway length or runway length available for landing at Portland International (PDX). Answer (B) is incorrect because 7,000 ft. is the total length of runway 21, not the runway length available for landing.

Form Approved: OMB No. 2120-0034

U.S. DEPARTMENT OF TRANSPORTATION
FEDERAL AVIATION ADMINISTRATION
FLIGHT PLAN

(FAA USE ONLY) ☐ PILOT BRIEFING ☐ VNR ☐ STOPOVER | TIME STARTED | SPECIALIST INITIALS

1. TYPE	2. AIRCRAFT IDENTIFICATION	3. AIRCRAFT TYPE/ SPECIAL EQUIPMENT	4. TRUE AIRSPEED	5. DEPARTURE POINT	6. DEPARTURE TIME PROPOSED (Z)	ACTUAL (Z)	7. CRUISING ALTITUDE
VFR X IFR DVFR	N3678A	PA31/	180 KTS	YKM			12000

8. ROUTE OF FLIGHT
GROMO 2, HITCH, V468 BTG, DIRECT

9. DESTINATION (Name of airport and city)	10. EST. TIME ENROUTE HOURS	MINUTES	11. REMARKS
PORTLAND INTL. AIRPORT PDX			INSTRUMENT TRAINING FLIGHT

12. FUEL ON BOARD HOURS	MINUTES	13. ALTERNATE AIRPORT(S)	14. PILOT'S NAME, ADDRESS & TELEPHONE NUMBER & AIRCRAFT HOME BASE / 17. DESTINATION CONTACT/TELEPHONE (OPTIONAL)	15. NUMBER ABOARD
		N/A		2

16. COLOR OF AIRCRAFT
GOLD/WHITE

CIVIL AIRCRAFT PILOTS. FAR Part 91 requires you file an IFR flight plan to operate under instrument flight rules in controlled airspace. Failure to file could result in a civil penalty not to exceed $1,000 for each violation (Section 901 of the Federal Aviation Act of 1958, as amended). Filing of a VFR flight plan is recommended as a good operating practice. See also Part 99 for requirements concerning DVFR flight plans.

FAA Form 7233-1 (8-82) CLOSE VFR FLIGHT PLAN WITH ______________ FSS ON ARRIVAL

AIRCRAFT INFORMATION

MAKE Piper MODEL PA-31

N 3678A Vso 77

AIRCRAFT EQUIPMENT/STATUS**

**NOTE: X= OPERATIVE INOP= INOPERATIVE N/A= NOT APPLICABLE
TRANSPONDER: X (MODE C) X ILS: (LOCALIZER) X (GLIDE SLOPE) X
VOR NO. 1 X (NO. 2) X ADF: X RNAV: X
VERTICAL PATH COMPUTER: N/A DME: X
MARKER BEACON: X (AUDIO) INOP (VISUAL) X

FIGURE 44.—Flight Plan and Aircraft Information.

FLIGHT LOG

YAKIMA AIR TERMINAL TO PORTLAND, INTL.

| CHECK POINTS | | ROUTE | COURSE | WIND | SPEED-KTS | | DIST | TIME | | FUEL | |
FROM	TO	ALTITUDE		TEMP	TAS	GS	NM	LEG	TOT	LEG	TOT
YKM	HITCH	GROMO 2 CLIMB	206°					:10.			
	VOR C.O.P.	V468 12,000	206°		180						
	BTG	V468 12,000	234°								
	PDX	DIRECT	160°								
APPROACH & LANDING								:13.			
	PDX AIRPORT										

OTHER DATA:
    NOTE: MAG. VAR. 20° E.

FLIGHT SUMMARY

TIME	FUEL (LB)	
		EN ROUTE
		RESERVE
		MISSED APPR.
		TOTAL

FIGURE 45.—Flight Planning Log.

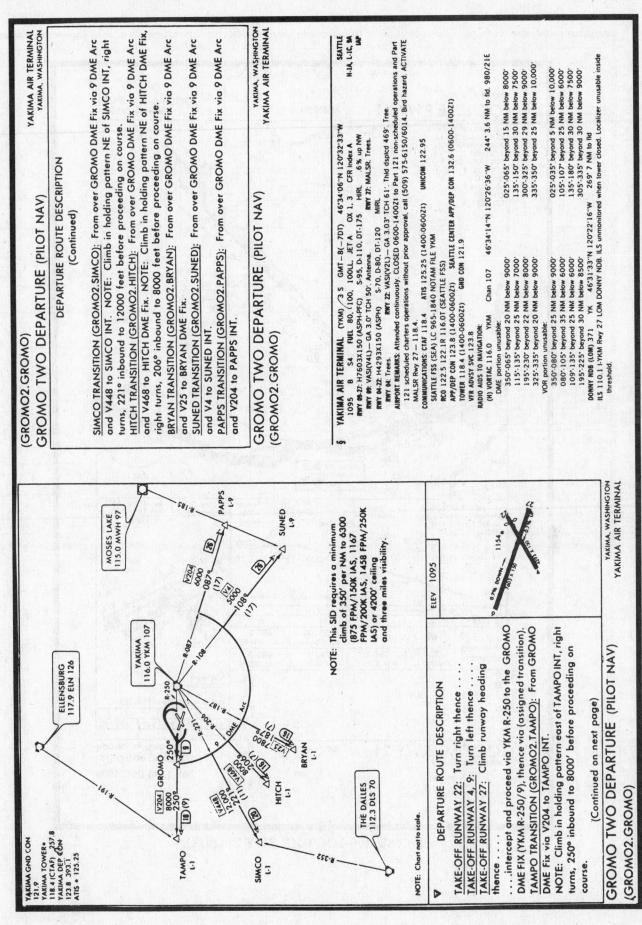

FIGURE 46.—GROMO Two Departure and Excerpt from Airport/Facility Directory.

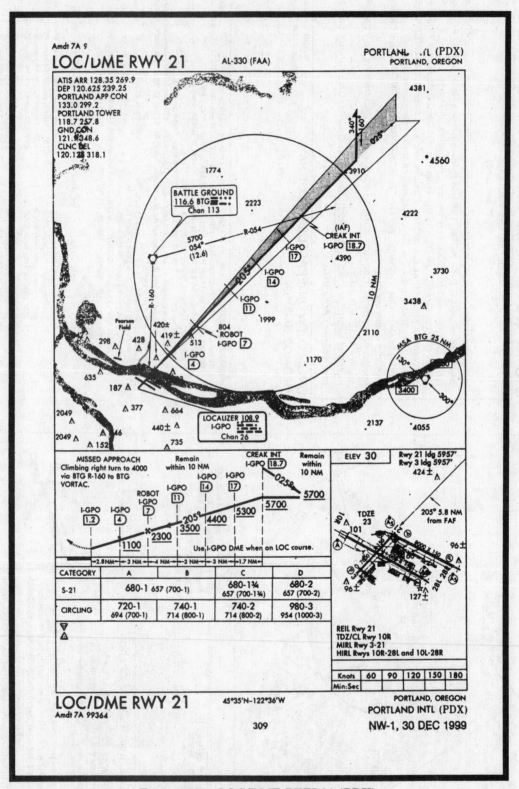

FIGURE 49.—LOC/DME RWY 21 (PDX).

11.4 SBA to PRB

Questions 34 through 43 pertain to an IFR flight from Santa Barbara Municipal Airport, Santa Barbara, California to the Paso Robles Municipal Airport, Paso Robles, California.

The route of flight is given in block 8 on the flight plan portion of Fig. 50 on page 392. Information which pertains to your aircraft is given on the bottom portion of Fig. 50. The partially completed flight planning log is given in Fig. 51 on page 393.

The figures provided for this flight are listed below and are grouped together after the sequence of questions, except for Fig. 53, which is provided in color on page 435.

11.4 SBA to PRB

34.
4315. (Refer to figure 52 on page 394 and 54 below.) What is the aircraft's position relative to the HABUT intersection? (The VOR-2 is tuned to 116.5.)

A— South of the localizer and past the GVO R-163.
B— North of the localizer and approaching the GVO R-163.
C— South of the localizer and approaching the GVO R-163.

Answer (B) is correct (4315). *(IFH Chap VII)*

On the RMI (Fig. 54), VOR-2 is tuned to 116.5, which is the GVO VORTAC, and the tail indicates that the airplane is on R-130, which means it is to the east of HABUT INT. The VOR is tuned to 110.3, which is the localizer, and you are flying outbound on the front course (our heading is 240 as shown by the RMI). This means there is a reverse sensing indicated, and the airplane is to the north or right of the localizer as flying outbound.

Answer (A) is incorrect because, when you are flying outbound on the front course, there is reverse sensing, so you are north, not south, of the localizer. Since you are on R-130 from GVO, you are approaching, not past, R-163. Answer (C) is incorrect because, when you are flying outbound on the front course, there is reverse sensing, so you are north, not south, of the localizer.

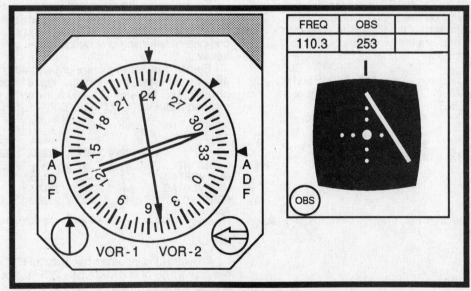

FIGURE 54.—RMI and CDI Indicators.

35.
4316. (Refer to figure 52 on page 394.) Using an average ground speed of 100 knots, what minimum rate of climb would meet the required minimum climb rate per NM as specified by the instrument departure procedure?

A— 425 feet per minute.
B— 580 feet per minute.
C— 642 feet per minute.

Answer (C) is correct (4316). *(ACL)*
The DP on Fig. 52 has a note which indicates a minimum climb rate of 385 ft. per NM to 6,000 ft. To convert this to a rate of climb (fpm), use Legend 16 on page 204. Since 385 ft. per NM is not listed on the left margin, use 350 and 400 and interpolate between them. Move right to the 100-kt. ground speed column to see a rate of climb between 583 and 667 fpm, but closer to 667. By interpolation, the minimum rate of climb required would be 642 fpm.
Answer (A) is incorrect because a 425 fpm climb rate at an average ground speed of 100 kt. would result in a climb rate of 255 ft. per NM, not 385 ft. per NM. Answer (B) is incorrect because a 580 fpm climb rate at an average ground speed of 100 kt. would result in a climb rate of approximately 350 ft. per NM, not 385 ft. per NM.

36.
4312. (Refer to figure 50 on page 392.) What aircraft equipment code should be entered in block 3 of the flight plan?

A— I.
B— T.
C— U.

Answer (A) is correct (4312). *(AIM Para 5-1-7)*
In block 3 of the flight plan, you enter the designation of the aircraft followed by a slash (/) and a letter for the equipment code. Fig. 50 indicates the airplane has a transponder with Mode C and RNAV, which requires Code I. (See Legend 26 on page 362.)
Answer (B) is incorrect because a T indicates only a transponder with no Mode C. Answer (C) is incorrect because a U indicates a transponder with Mode C, but no DME.

37.
4313. (Refer to figure 50 on page 392.) What CAS must be used to maintain the filed TAS at the flight planned altitude? (Temperature 0 °C.)

A— 136 KCAS.
B— 140 KCAS.
C— 147 KCAS.

Answer (B) is correct (4313). *(FI Comp)*
In the center of the slide rule side of your flight computer, on the right side, put the air temperature of 0°C over the altitude of 8,000 ft. (given in block 7 of flight plan). On the outer scale, find TAS of 158 kt. (from block 4), which is over CAS on the inner scale of 140 KCAS.
Answer (A) is incorrect because maintaining 136 KCAS would result in a TAS of 154 kt., not 158 kt. Answer (C) is incorrect because maintaining 147 KCAS would result in a TAS of 168 kt., not 158 kt.

38.
4314. (Refer to figures 50, 51, and 52 on pages 392 through 394 and figure 53 on page 435.) Determine the time to be entered in block 10 of the flight plan. (Refer to the FD excerpt below, and use the wind entry closest to the flight planned altitude.)

Route of flight . . . . Figures 50, 51, 52, and 53
Flight log and MAG VAR . . . . Figure 51
HABUT ONE DEPARTURE
  and Excerpt from AFD . . . . Figure 52

FT	3000	6000	9000
SBA	0610	2115+05	2525+00

A— 43 minutes.
B— 46 minutes.
C— 51 minutes.

Answer (C) is correct (4314). *(IFH Chap XIII)*
To determine the estimated time en route to be entered in block 10, you must complete the flight planning log in Fig. 51. Using the wind side of your flight computer, determine groundspeeds as given in the table below.
Remember that winds are given in true direction and must be converted to magnetic. Fig. 51 shows a variation of 16°E. Use the wind at 9,000 ft. (which is closest to the planned altitude of 8,000 ft.): 250° – 16°E var. = 234° at 25 kt.

	Distance	MC	Wind (Mag)	Ground-speed	Time
HABUT INT	X	X	X	X	:08:00G
GVO VORTAC	6.4	343°	234/25	164	:02:20
MSO VORTAC	54	307°	234/25	149	:21:45
PRB VORTAC	26	358°	234/25	171	:09:07
Approach and Landing	X	X	X	X	:10:00G
					:51:12

G = Given

Answer (A) is incorrect because an ETE of 43 min. requires a TAS of approximately 205 kt., not 158 kt. Answer (B) is incorrect because an ETE of 46 min. requires a TAS of approximately 185 kt., not 158 kt.

39.
4317. (Refer to figure 53 on page 435.) Where is the VOR COP on V27 between the GVO and MQO VORTACs?

A— 20 DME from GVO VORTAC.
B— 20 DME from MQO VORTAC.
C— 30 DME from SBA VORTAC.

Answer (A) is correct (4317). *(ACL)*
When going north from GVO VORTAC to MQO VORTAC, there is a VOR changeover point (COP) 20 NM northwest of GVO VORTAC and 34 NM southeast of MQO VORTAC.
Answer (B) is incorrect because the COP is 20 NM from GVO, not MQO. Answer (C) is incorrect because SBA is Santa Barbara localizer, which is not on V27.

40.
4318. (Refer to figure 53 on page 435.) What service is indicated by the inverse "H" symbol in the radio aids to navigation box for PRB VORTAC?

A— VOR with TACAN compatible DME.
B— Availability of HIWAS.
C— En Route Flight Advisory Service available.

Answer (B) is correct (4318). *(ACL)*
See also Legend 23 on page 428. The inverse "H" symbol in the upper right corner of the VOR communication box indicates the availability of HIWAS (Hazardous Inflight Weather Advisory Service).
Answer (A) is incorrect because the VORTAC symbol itself indicates TACAN-compatible DME. Answer (C) is incorrect because En Route Flight Advisory Service (Flight Watch) is available nationwide on 122.0.

41.
4319. (Refer to figure 55 on page 395.) Using an average ground speed of 90 knots, what constant rate of descent from 2,400 feet MSL at the 6 DME fix would enable the aircraft to arrive at 2,000 feet MSL at the FAF?

A— 200 feet per minute.
B— 400 feet per minute.
C— 600 feet per minute.

Answer (A) is correct (4319). *(ACL)*
The profile view of the IAP chart shows the distance from the 6 DME fix to the FAF to be 3 NM. At 90 kt. (1½ NM per min.), this distance would be traveled in 2 min. To descend from 2,400 ft. to 2,000 ft. (400 ft.) in 2 min. would require a descent rate of 200 fpm.
Answer (B) is incorrect because 400 fpm would require an average ground speed of 180 kt., not 90 kt. Answer (C) is incorrect because 600 fpm would require an average ground speed of 270 kt., not 90 kt.

42.
4320. (Refer to figure 55 on page 395.) As a guide in making range corrections, how many degrees of relative bearing change should be used for each one-half-mile deviation from the desired arc?

A— 2° to 3°.
B— 5° maximum.
C— 10° to 20°.

Answer (C) is correct (4320). *(IFH Chap VIII)*
As a guide in making corrections when tracking DME arcs, turn 10° to 20° toward the arc for each ½ NM that you are off the desired arc.
Answer (A) is incorrect because 10° to 20° corrections, not 2° to 3°, should be made for each ½-NM deviation. Answer (B) is incorrect because there is no maximum; the amount of correction should be proportional to the amount of error.

43.
4321. (Refer to figure 55 on page 395.) Under which condition should a missed approach procedure be initiated if the runway environment (Paso Robles Municipal Airport) is not in sight?

A— After descending to 1,440 feet MSL.
B— After descent to 1,440 feet or reaching the 1 NM DME, whichever occurs first.
C— When you reach the established missed approach point and determine the visibility is less than 1 mile.

Answer (C) is correct (4321). *(FAR 91.175)*
The missed approach point is the point prescribed in each instrument approach procedure at which a missed approach procedure shall be executed if the required visual reference has not been sighted or the flight visibility is less than visibility prescribed in the IAP. The MAP for VOR/DME-B is the PRB VORTAC. Thus, when you reach the VORTAC and you determine the visibility is less than 1 SM, you must execute the missed approach procedure.
Answer (A) is incorrect because the MAP is PRB VORTAC, not arrival at the MDA. Answer (B) is incorrect because the MAP is PRB VORTAC, not arrival at the MDA or the 1 DME fix.

43a.
0601-331. (Refer to figure 55 on page 395.) Under which condition should a missed approach procedure be initiated if the runway environment (Paso Robles Municipal Airport) is not in sight?

A— When you reach the established missed approach point and determine the visibility is less than 1/2 mile.
B— After descent to 1,440 feet or reaching the 1 NM DME, whichever occurs first.
C— After descending to 1,440 feet MSL.

Answer (A) is correct (0601-331). *(FAR 91.175)*
The missed approach point is the point prescribed in each instrument approach procedure at which a missed approach procedure shall be executed if the required visual reference has not been sighted or the flight visibility is less than visibility prescribed in the IAP. The MAP for VOR/DME-B is the PRB VORTAC. Thus, when you reach the VORTAC and you determine the visibility is less than 1/2 SM, which is below the visibility minimum of 1 SM, you must execute the missed approach procedure.
Answer (B) is incorrect because the MAP is PRB VORTAC, not arrival at the MDA or the 1 DME fix. Answer (C) is incorrect because the MAP is PRB VORTAC, not arrival at the MDA.

Form Approved: OMB No.2120-0034

U.S. DEPARTMENT OF TRANSPORTATION FEDERAL AVIATION ADMINISTRATION **FLIGHT PLAN**	(FAA USE ONLY) ☐PILOT BRIEFING ☐VNR ☐ STOPOVER		TIME STARTED	SPECIALIST INITIALS

1 TYPE	2 AIRCRAFT IDENTIFICATION	3 AIRCRAFT TYPE/ SPECIAL EQUIPMENT	4 TRUE AIRSPEED	5 DEPARTURE POINT	6 DEPARTURE TIME		7 CRUISING ALTITUDE
VFR / X IFR / DVFR	N2468	A36/	158	SBA	PROPOSED (Z)	ACTUAL (Z)	8000

8 ROUTE OF FLIGHT

HABUTI GVO, V27 MQO, V113 PRB

9 DESTINATION (Name of airport and city)	10 EST TIME ENROUTE		11 REMARKS
PASO ROBLES MUNI PRB	HOURS	MINUTES	IFR TRAINING FLIGHT

12 FUEL ON BOARD		13 ALTERNATE AIRPORT(S)	14 PILOTS NAME, ADDRESS & TELEPHONE NUMBER & AIRCRAFT HOME BASE	15 NUMBER ABOARD
HOURS	MINUTES	N/R	17 DESTINATION CONTACT/TELEPHONE (OPTIONAL)	2

16 COLOR OF AIRCRAFT	CIVIL AIRCRAFT PILOTS. FAR Part 91 requires you file an IFR flight plan to operate under instrument flight rules in controlled airspace. Failure to file could result in a civil penalty not to exceed $1,000 for each violation (Section 901 of the Federal Aviation Act of 1958. as amended; Filing of a VFR flight plan is recommended as a good operating practice. See also Part 99 for requirements concerning DVFR flight plans.
GOLD/WHITE	

FAA Form 7233-1 (8-82)   CLOSE VFR FLIGHT PLAN WITH _____ FSS ON ARRIVAL

AIRCRAFT INFORMATION

MAKE Beechcraft   MODEL A-36

N 2468   Vso 52

AIRCRAFT EQUIPMENT/STATUS**

**NOTE: X= OPERATIVE   INOP= INOPERATIVE   N/A= NOT APPLICABLE
TRANSPONDER: X (MODE C) X ILS: (LOCALIZER) X (GLIDE SLOPE) X
VOR NO.1 X (NO 2) X ADF: X RNAV: X
VERTICAL PATH COMPUTER: NA DME: X
MARKER BEACON: X (AUDIO) X (VISUAL) Inop.

FIGURE 50.—Flight Plan and Aircraft Information.

FLIGHT LOG

SANTA BARBARA MUNI TO PASO ROBLES MUNI

| CHECK POINTS | | ROUTE | COURSE | WIND | SPEED-KTS | | DIST | TIME | | FUEL | |
FROM	TO	ALTITUDE		TEMP	TAS	GS	NM	LEG	TOT	LEG	TOT
SBA	HABUT	HABUT 1 CLIMB	253°					:08:00			
	GVO	163°R 8000	343°		158						
	MQO	V27 8000	306°								
	PRB	V113	358°								
APPROACH & LANDING		DESCENT						:10:00			
	PRB AIRPORT										

OTHER DATA:
NOTE: MAG. VAR. 16° E.

FLIGHT SUMMARY

TIME	FUEL (LBS)	
		EN ROUTE
		RESERVE
		MISSED APPR.
		TOTAL

FIGURE 51.—Flight Planning Log.

HABUT ONE DEPARTURE (HABUT1.GVO)

SANTA BARBARA MUNI
SANTA BARBARA, CALIFORNIA

SANTA BARBARA MUNI GND CON
121.7
SANTA BARBARA TOWER *
119.7 242.4
SANTA BARBARA DEP CON
120.55 321.4
ATIS * 125.1

GAVIOTA
116.5 GVO 112
L-3

SANTA BARBARA
114.9 SBA 96

LOCALIZER
110.3 I-SBA 40

R-249

6000

6000
253°
(13)

Aprx dist
fr T/off area

343°
(6.4)

073°   R-163

HABUT
INT

NOTE: IFR departure Rwys 33L/R
not authorized.

NOTE: Chart not to scale

DEPARTURE ROUTE DESCRIPTION

TAKE-OFF RUNWAY 7: Maintain runway heading to at
least 650', then turn right, thence intercept and climb
westbound via I-SBA localizer west course to HABUT INT,
thence via GVO R-163 to GVO VORTAC. Cross SBA R-249
at or above 6000'.

TAKE-OFF RUNWAY 15: Maintain runway heading to at
least 310', then turn right, thence intercept and climb
westbound via I-SBA localizer west course to HABUT INT,
thence via GVO R-163 to GVO VORTAC. Cross SBA R-249
at or above 6000'.

(Continued on next page)

HABUT ONE DEPARTURE (HABUT1.GVO)

SANTA BARBARA, CALIFORNIA
SANTA BARBARA MUNI

HABUT ONE DEPARTURE (HABUT1.GVO)

SANTA BARBARA MUNI
SANTA BARBARA, CALIFORNIA

DEPARTURE ROUTE DESCRIPTION
(Continued)

TAKE-OFF RUNWAY 25: Climb westbound via I-SBA localizer west course to HABUT
INT, thence via GVO R-163 to GVO VORTAC. Cross SBA R-249 at or above 6000'.

HABUT ONE DEPARTURE (HABUT1.GVO)

SANTA BARBARA, CALIFORNIA
SANTA BARBARA MUNI

§ **SANTA BARBARA MUNI**   (SBA)   7 W   GMT–8(–7DT)   34°25'34"N 119°50'22"W   **LOS ANGELES**
   10   B   S4   FUEL 80, 100, 100LL, JET A   OX 1, 2, 3, 4   TPA—See Remarks   **H-2F, L-3B**
   CFR Index C   **IAP**
RWY 07-25: H6049X150 (ASPH-GRVD)   S-110, D-160, DT-245   HIRL
   RWY 07: MALSR. Tree. Rgt tfc.   RWY 25: VASI(V4L)—GA 3.0° TCH 46'. Thld dsplcd 324'. Road.
   RWY 15R-33L: H4183X100 (ASPH)   S-48, D-63, DT-100   MIRL
   RWY 15R: REIL. Pole.   RWY 33L: Road. Rgt tfc.
RWY 15L-33R: H4179X75 (ASPH)   S-35, D-41, DT-63
   RWY 15L: Thld dsplcd 225'. Tree.   RWY 33R: Pole. Rgt tfc.
AIRPORT REMARKS: Attended 1330-0600‡. Fee after hours. Numerous flocks of birds on and in vicinity of arpt.
   TPA—1000(990) small acft, 1500(1490) large acft. Pure jet touch/go or low approaches prohibited.
COMMUNICATIONS: CTAF 119.7   ATIS 125.1 (1430-060002‡)   UNICOM 122.95
® APP CON 125.4 (1430-060002‡)   ® DEP CON 120.55 (1430-060002‡)
® LOS ANGELES CENTER APP/DEP CON 128.05 (0600-1430‡)
TOWER 119.7 (1430-060002‡)   GND CON 121.7
VFR ADVSY SVC. ctc TOWER
RADIO AIDS TO NAVIGATION: NOTAM FILE SBA. VHF/DF ctc SANTA BARBARA FSS
   (H) ABVORTAC 114.9   ■ SBA   Chan 96   34°30'34"N 119°46'12"W   198° 5.6 NM to fld. 3620/16E.
   GAVIOTA (L) VORTAC 116.5   GVO   Chan 112   34°31'53"N 120°05'24"W   099° 14.0 NM to fld. 2620/16E
   ILS/DME 110.3 I-SBA Chan 40 Rwy 07

ELEV 10

25
158
103
158
33L 33R
4179 X 75
4183 X 100
6049 X 150

NOTE: This departure requires
a minimum climb rate of
385' per NM to 6000

CALIFORNIA

VOR RECEIVER CHECK POINTS

Facility Name (Arpt Name)	Freq/Ident	Type Check Pt. Gnd. AB/ALT	Azimuth from Fac. Mag	Dist. from Fac. N.M.	Check Point Description
Sacramento (Sacramento Executive)	115.2/SAC	A/1000	015		Over apch end rwy 02.
Salinas (Salinas Muni)	117.3/SNS	G	247		0.4 NM on Compass rose.
Santa Ana (John Wayne Airport/Orange County)	109.4/SNA	G	186		On runup pad rwy 01R.
Santa Barbara	114.9/SBA	A/2000	277	11	Over Lake Cachuma Dam spillway.
Santa Barbara (Santa Barbara Muni)	114.9/SBA	G	200	5.9	On runup area end rwy 15.

FIGURE 52.—HABUT One Departure and Excerpt from Airport/Facility Directory.

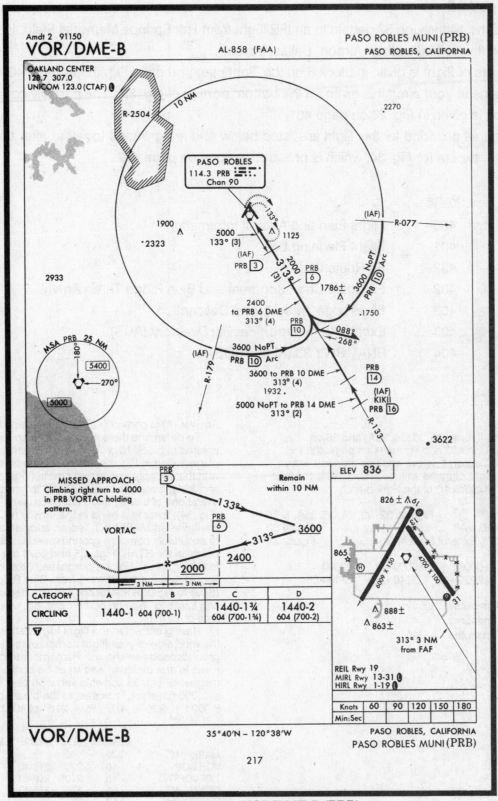

FIGURE 55.—VOR/DME-B (PRB).

11.5 HOT to ADS

Questions 44 through 53 pertain to an IFR flight from Hot Springs Memorial Field, Hot Springs, Arkansas to the Dallas/Addison Airport, Dallas, Texas.

The route of flight is given in block 8 on the flight plan portion of Fig. 32 on page 400. Information which pertains to your aircraft is given on the bottom portion of Fig. 32. The partially completed flight planning log is given in Fig. 33 on page 401.

The figures provided for this flight are listed below and are grouped together after the sequence of questions, except for Fig. 34, which is provided in color on page 432.

11.5 HOT to ADS

44.
4279. (Refer to figures 32, 33, 35, 35A, and 36 on pages 400 through 403 and figure 34 on page 432.) (Refer to the FD excerpt below, and use the wind entry closest to the flight planned altitude.) Determine the time to be entered in block 10 of the flight plan.

Route of flight . . . . Figures 32, 33, 34, 35, 35A, & 36
Flight log & MAG VAR . . . . Figure 33
RNAV RWY 33 & Excerpt from AFD . . . . Figure 36

FT	3000	6000	9000	12000
DAL	2027	2239+13	2240+08	2248+05

A— 1 hour 35 minutes.
B— 1 hour 41 minutes.
C— 1 hour 46 minutes.

Answer (A) is correct (4279). *(IFH Chap XIII)*
To determine the estimated time en route to be entered in block 10, you must complete the flight planning log in Fig. 33. As you compare the flight log with the en route and arrival charts (Figs. 34, 35, and 35A), it will become apparent to you that some alterations of the flight log are necessary. On V573 (Fig. 34), there is a bend in the airway (COP) 10 NM southwest of MARKI INT., so an additional leg is required to accurately compute groundspeeds. Also, the check points in the STAR (Figs. 35 and 35A) are not labeled well in the flight log. For the purposes of this question, you should assume that the leg from Blue Ridge VORTAC (BUJ) to WEDER intersection is included in the "Approach and Landing" portion of the flight log, which has a given time of 10 min.

Having corrected the flight log as shown below, use the wind side of your flight computer to determine groundspeeds as shown. Remember that winds are given in true direction and must be converted to magnetic. Fig. 33 shows a variation of 4°E. Use the wind at 9,000 ft. (which is closest to the planned altitude of 8,000 ft.): 220° − 4°E var. = 216° at 40 kt.

	Distance	MC	Wind (Mag)	Ground-speed	Time
MARKI INT	X	X	X	X	:12:00G
VOR COP	10	221°	216/40	140	:04:17
TXK VORTAC	45	210°	216/40	140	:19:17
CONNY INT	61	272°	216/40	154	:23:46
BUJ VORTAC	59	239°	216/40	142	:24:56
Approach and Landing	X	X	X	X	:10:00G
					1:34:16

G = Given

Answer (B) is incorrect because an ETE of 1 hr. 41 min. requires a TAS of approximately 165 kt., not 180 kt.
Answer (C) is incorrect because an ETE of 1 hr. 46 min. requires a TAS of approximately 160 kt., not 180 kt.

45.
4277. (Refer to figure 32 on page 400.) What aircraft equipment code should be entered in block 3 of the flight plan?

A— A.
B— C.
C— I.

Answer (C) is correct (4277). *(AIM Para 5-1-7)*
In block 3 of the flight plan, you enter the designation of the aircraft followed by a slash (/) and a letter for the equipment code. Fig. 32 indicates a transponder with Mode C and RNAV. Thus, Code I is required. (See Legend 26 on page 362.)
Answer (A) is incorrect because A indicates DME and transponder with Mode C, but no RNAV. Answer (B) is incorrect because C indicates RNAV and transponder, but with no Mode C.

46.
4278. (Refer to figure 32 on page 400.) What CAS must be used to maintain the filed TAS at the flight planned altitude if the outside air temperature is +8 °C?

A— 154 KCAS.
B— 157 KCAS.
C— 163 KCAS.

Answer (B) is correct (4278). *(Fl Comp)*
In the center of the slide rule side of your flight computer, on the right side, put the air temperature of +8°C over the altitude of 8,000 ft. (see block 7 of the flight plan in Fig. 32). On the outer scale, find TAS of 180 (from block 4), which is over calibrated airspeed on the inner scale of 157 KCAS.
Answer (A) is incorrect because maintaining 154 KCAS would result in a TAS of 176 kt., not 180 kt. Answer (C) is incorrect because maintaining 163 KCAS would result in a TAS of 187 kt., not 180 kt.

47.
4280. (Refer to figure 34 on page 432 and figure 34A below.) At which altitude and location on V573 would you expect the navigational signal of the HOT VOR/DME to be unreliable?

A— 3,000 feet at APINE intersection.
B— 2,600 feet at MARKI intersection.
C— 4,000 feet at ELMMO intersection.

Answer (A) is correct (4280). *(ACL)*
The *A/FD* in Fig. 34A, under **Radio Aids to Navigation**, does not indicate that the HOT VOR/DME is unusable in any quadrants. APINE intersection is 26 NM from HOT, which means that the MEA, not MOCA, is the lowest altitude that assures acceptable navigational signals. The MEA at APINE is 3,500 ft., therefore 3,000 ft. is 500 ft. below the minimum required to receive acceptable navigational signals.
Answer (B) is incorrect because MARKI is 21 NM from HOT VOR/DME, and the MOCA is 2,600 ft. The MOCA assures acceptable navigation signals within 22 NM of the VOR. Answer (C) is incorrect because the MEA at ELMMO is 4,000 ft., which assures acceptable navigation signals and meets obstacle clearance requirements.

ARKANSAS

HOT SPRINGS
   MEMORIAL FLD (HOT)   3 SW   UTC–6(–5DT)   34°28′41″N 93°05′46″W   **MEMPHIS**
   540   B   S4   FUEL 100LL, JET A   ARFF Index Ltd.   H-4G, L-14E
   RWY 05-23: H6595X150 (ASPH-GRVD)   S-75, D-125, DT-210, DDT-400.   HIRL   0.6% up NE   IAP
      RWY 05: MALSR. Tree.   RWY 23: REIL. Thld dsplcd 490′. Tree.
   RWY 13-31: H4099X150 (ASPH)   S-28, D-36, DT-63   MIRL
      RWY 13: REIL. Road/Trees.   RWY 31: Pole.
   AIRPORT REMARKS: Attended 1130-0400Z‡. CLOSED to unscheduled air carrier ops with more than 30 passenger
      seats except PPR, call arpt manager 501–624-3306. Last 500′ Rwy 05 CLOSED to takeoffs. Rwy 13-31 fair
      with extensive loose grvl-pavement debris. ACTIVATE HIRL Rwy 05–23 and MALSR Rwy 05—CTAF. Rwy 23 REIL
      out of svc indefinitely. Control Zone effective 1200–0400Z‡.
   COMMUNICATIONS: CTAF/UNICOM 123.0
      JONESBORO FSS (JBR) TF 1–800–WX–BRIEF. NOTAM FILE HOT.
      HOT SPRINGS RCO 122.1R 110.0T (LITTLE ROCK FSS)
      MEMPHIS CENTER APP/DEP CON: 118.85
   RADIO AIDS TO NAVIGATION: NOTAM FILE HOT.
      HOT SPRINGS (L) VOR/DME 110.0   HOT   Chan 37   34°28′43″N 93°05′26″W   at fld. 530/4E.
      HOSSY NDB (HW/LOM) 385   HO   34°25′21″N 93°11′22″W   050° 5.7 NM to fld.
      ILS/DME 111.5 I-HOT Chan 52 Rwy 05 LOM HOSSY NDB. Unmonitored.

FIGURE 34A.—Airport/Facility Directory (HOT).

48.
4281. (Refer to figure 35 on page 402 and figure 37 below). What is your position relative to the CONNY intersection on the BUJ.BUJ3 transition?

A— Left of the TXK R-272 and approaching the BUJ R-059°.
B— Left of the TXK R-266 and past the BUJ R-065.
C— Right of the TXK R-270 and approaching the BUJ R-245.

Answer (A) is correct (4281). *(IFH Chap VIII)*

Refer to Figs. 35 and 35A and note that this is actually the TXK.BUJ3 transition (to the BUJ.BUJ3 arrival). In Fig. 37, NAV 1 (an HSI) is tuned to 114.9 (BUJ VORTAC) and set to 239°. Since the bar is deflected to the northwest, you are southeast of the BUJ R-059, and thus approaching it (note the 270° heading). NAV 2 (an RMI) has the fat needle tuned to 116.3 (TXK VORTAC). The tail of the needle indicates R-270, which is south of R-272 and thus to the left.

Answer (B) is incorrect because the R-270 of TXK is right not left of the TXK R-266 and you are on, not past, the BUJ R-065. Answer (C) is incorrect because you are on, not right of, the R-270 of TXK and approaching R-244 of LIT, not BUJ.

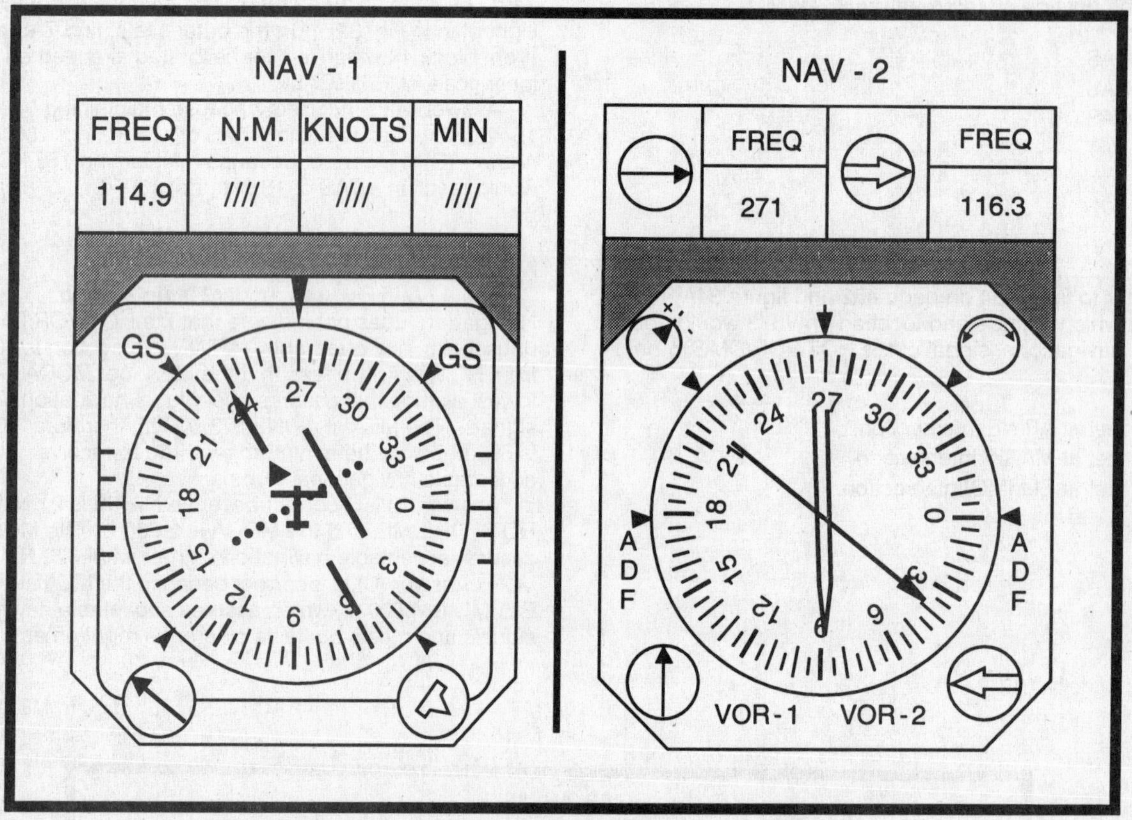

FIGURE 37.—CDI and RMI — NAV 1 and NAV 2.

49.
4282. (Refer to figure 36A on page 404.) Under which condition should the missed approach procedure for the VOR/DME RNAV RWY 33 approach be initiated?

A— Immediately upon reaching the 5.0 DME from the FAF.
B— When passage of the MAP way point is shown on the ambiguity indicator.
C— After the MDA is reached and 1.8 DME fix from the MAP way point.

Answer (B) is correct (4282). *(FAR 91.175)*

The missed approach point (MAP) is the point prescribed in each instrument approach procedure at which a missed approach procedure shall be executed if the required visual reference has not been sighted. The MAP on the RNAV RWY 33 approach is arrival at the indicated MAP way point. Passage of the MAP way point is shown on the ambiguity indicator (TO-FROM flag).

Answer (A) is incorrect because the FAF is identified as 5.0 DME from the MAP, not vice versa. Answer (C) is incorrect because 1.8 DME from the MAP way point is where you would arrive at MDA, assuming a 2.85° glide path.

50.
4283. (Refer to figures 32 on page 400, 36 on page 403, and 36A on page 404.) What is the MDA and visibility criteria respectively for the S-33 approach procedure?

A— 1,240 feet MSL; 1 SM.
B— 1,280 feet MSL; 1 and ¼ SM.
C— 1,300 feet MSL; 1 SM.

Answer (A) is correct (4283). *(ACL)*
Refer to Fig. 32 to determine the aircraft category. V$_{so}$ is 74 kt.; thus 1.3 V$_{so}$ is 96.2 kt., which puts the airplane in Category B (91-120). The minimums for the straight-in RWY 33 approach, Category B, are 1,240 ft. MSL and 1 SM on the approach chart (Fig. 36A).
Answer (B) is incorrect because 1,280 ft. is the MDA for circling Category D on the approach chart, and 1¼ SM is not an applicable minimum. Answer (C) is incorrect because 1,300 ft. and 1 SM are the minimums for using the Dallas Love Field altimeter setting.

51.
4285. (Refer to figure 36A on page 404.) What is the minimum number of way points required for the complete RNAV RWY 33 approach procedure including the IAF's and missed approach procedure?

A— One way point.
B— Two way points.
C— Three way points.

Answer (B) is correct (4285). *(ACL)*
Two way points are given for the RNAV RWY 33 approach: ADDIS and the MAP.
Answer (A) is incorrect because the MAP is a way point (as shown by the box) even though it has no way point star. Answer (C) is incorrect because the FAF is not a way point; it is a DME fix off of the MAP way point.

52.
4286. (Refer to figures 35 and 35A on pages 402 and 403.) At which point does the BUJ.BUJ3 arrival begin?

A— At the TXK VORTAC.
B— At BOGAR intersection.
C— At the BUJ VORTAC.

Answer (C) is correct (4286). *(ACL)*
The arrival, in contrast to the transition, begins over the BUJ VORTAC as explained in the written description in Fig. 35A.
Answer (A) is incorrect because the Texarkana transition, TXK BUJ8, begins over the TXK VORTAC. Answer (B) is incorrect because BOGAR INT does not appear on the BUJ.BUJ3 arrival chart.

53.
4287. (Refer to figure 34 on page 432.) For planning purposes, what is the highest useable altitude for an IFR flight on V573 from the HOT VORTAC to the TXK VORTAC?

A— 16,000 feet MSL.
B— 14,500 feet MSL.
C— 13,999 feet MSL.

Answer (A) is correct (4287). *(AIM Para 3-2-6)*
The VOR airway system consists of airways designated from 1,200 ft. AGL up to, but not including, 18,000 ft. MSL. Flying on V573 from HOT to TXK is a generally westerly course which requires an even-thousands altitude. Thus, 16,000 ft. MSL is the highest usable altitude.
Answer (B) is incorrect because 14,500 ft. MSL is a VFR, not IFR, cruising altitude from 180° to 359°. Answer (C) is incorrect because IFR altitudes are even or odd thousands of feet.

53a.
0601-292. (Refer to figure 36A on page 404.) What is the MDA and visibility criteria, respectively, for the S 33 approach procedure?

A— 1,240 feet MSL; 1/2 SM.
B— 1,240 feet MSL; 1 SM.
C— 1,280 feet MSL; 1 and 1/4 SM.

Answer (B) is correct (0601-292). *(ACL)*
The MDA and visibility criteria are found in the minimums section of the RNAV RWY 33 approach chart. The straight-in (S-33) MDA and visibility criteria for Category A and B aircraft are 1,240 ft. MSL and 1 SM, respectively (note that the question does not specify the aircraft category).
Answer (A) is incorrect because the minimum visibility is not shown to be 1/2 SM for any category of aircraft using the straight-in RNAV RWY 33 approach into ADS. Answer (C) is incorrect because 1,280 ft. MSL is the MDA for a circling approach, not a straight-in approach, and because the minimum visibility is not shown to be 1 and 1/4 SM for any category of aircraft using the straight-in RNAV RWY 33 approach into ADS.

Form Approved: OMB No.2120-0034

U.S. DEPARTMENT OF TRANSPORTATION FEDERAL AVIATION ADMINISTRATION **FLIGHT PLAN**	(FAA USE ONLY) ☐PILOT BRIEFING ☐STOPOVER	☐VNR	TIME STARTED	SPECIALIST INITIALS

1 TYPE VFR / IFR X / DVFR	2 AIRCRAFT IDENTIFICATION N4078A	3 AIRCRAFT TYPE/ SPECIAL EQUIPMENT PA 31/	4 TRUE AIRSPEED 180	5 DEPARTURE POINT HOT	6 DEPARTURE TIME PROPOSED (Z) / ACTUAL (Z)	7 CRUISING ALTITUDE 8,000

8 ROUTE OF FLIGHT

HOT V573, TXK, TXK.BUJ3

9 DESTINATION (Name of airport and city) DALLAS ADDISON AIRPORT DALLAS, TX	10 EST TIME ENROUTE HOURS / MINUTES	11 REMARKS

12 FUEL ON BOARD HOURS / MINUTES	13 ALTERNATE AIRPORT(S) N/A	14 PILOTS NAME, ADDRESS & TELEPHONE NUMBER & AIRCRAFT HOME BASE 17 DESTINATION CONTACT/TELEPHONE (OPTIONAL)	15 NUMBER ABOARD 2

16 COLOR OF AIRCRAFT TAN/WHITE	CIVIL AIRCRAFT PILOTS. FAR Part 91 requires you file an IFR flight plan to operate under instrument flight rules in controlled airspace. Failure to file could result in a civil penalty not to exceed $1,000 for each violation (Section 901 of the Federal Aviation Act of 1958. as amended; Filing of a VFR flight plan is recommended as a good operating practice. See also Part 99 for requirements concerning DVFR flight plans.

FAA Form 7233-1 (8-82)   CLOSE VFR FLIGHT PLAN WITH _____ FSS ON ARRIVAL

AIRCRAFT INFORMATION

MAKE Piper   MODEL PA-31

N 4078A   Vso 74

AIRCRAFT EQUIPMENT/STATUS**

**NOTE: X= OPERATIVE   INOP= INOPERATIVE   N/A= NOT APPLICABLE
TRANSPONDER: X (MODE C) X ILS: (LOCALIZER) X (GLIDE SLOPE) X
VOR NO.1 X (NO 2) X ADF: X RNAV: X
VERTICAL PATH COMPUTER: NA DME: X
MARKER BEACON: X (AUDIO) X (VISUAL) X

FIGURE 32.—Flight Plan and Aircraft Information.

FLIGHT LOG

HOT SPRINGS, MEMORIAL FIELD TO DALLAS, ADDISON, TX..

CHECK POINTS		ROUTE	COURSE	WIND	SPEED-KTS		DIST	TIME		FUEL	
FROM	TO	ALTITUDE		TEMP	TAS	GS	NM	LEG	TOT	LEG	TOT
HOT	MARKI	V573 CLIMB	221°					:12:00			
	TXK	V573 8000	210°	180							
TXK	BUJ3	BUJ3 8000	272°								
BUJ3		BUJ3 DESCENT	239°								
APPROACH & LANDING								:10:00			
	DALLAS ADDISON										

OTHER DATA:
    NOTE: MAG. VAR. 4° E.

FLIGHT SUMMARY

TIME	FUEL (LBS)	
		EN ROUTE
		RESERVE
		MISSED APPR.
		TOTAL

FIGURE 33.—Flight Planning Log.

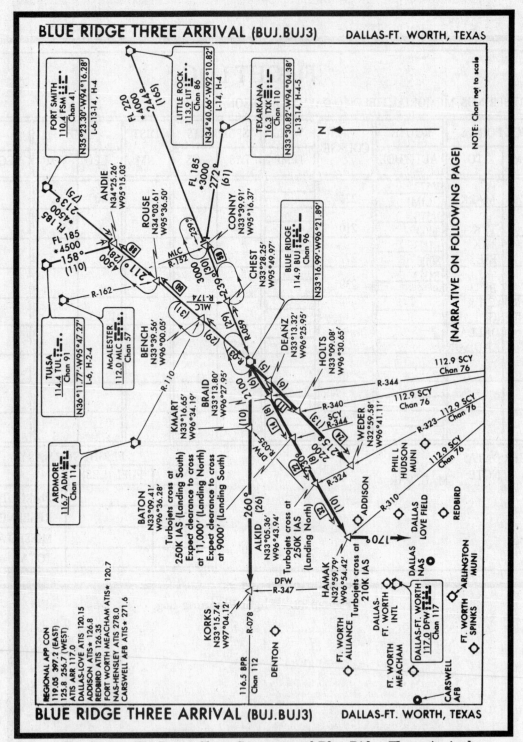

FIGURE 35.—En Route Chart Segment and Blue Ridge Three Arrival.

91094

SL-6039 (FAA)

BLUE RIDGE THREE ARRIVAL (BUJ.BUJ3)   DALLAS-FT. WORTH, TEXAS

ARRIVAL DESCRIPTION

FORT SMITH TRANSITION (FSM.BUJ3): From over FSM VORTAC via FSM R-213 and BUJ R-031 to BUJ VORTAC. Thence . . . .

LITTLE ROCK TRANSITION (LIT.BUJ3): From over LIT VORTAC via LIT R-244 and BUJ R-059 to BUJ VORTAC. Thence . . . .

TEXARKANA TRANSITION (TXK.BUJ3): From over TXK VORTAC via TXK R-272 and BUJ R-059 to BUJ VORTAC. Thence . . . .

TULSA TRANSITION (TUL.BUJ3): From over TUL VORTAC via TUL R-158 and BUJ R-031 to BUJ VORTAC. Thence . . . .

TURBOJETS LANDING DALLAS-FT WORTH INTL: (Landing South): From over BUJ VORTAC via BUJ R-230 to HAMAK INT. Expect vectors at BATON INT. (Landing North): From over BUJ VORTAC via BUJ R-230 to HAMAK INT, thence heading 170° for vector to final approach course.

NON-TURBOJETS LANDING DALLAS-FT WORTH INTL: (Landing South): From over BUJ VORTAC via BUJ R-230 to HAMAK INT. Expect vectors at BATON INT. (Landing North): From over BUJ VORTAC via BUJ R-215 to WEDER INT. Expect vectors to final approach course.

ALL AIRCRAFT LANDING DALLAS-LOVE FIELD, ADDISON, REDBIRD, NAS DALLAS, and PHIL L. HUDSON: (Landing South/North): From over BUJ VORTAC via BUJ R-215 to WEDER INT. Expect vectors to final approach course.

ALL AIRCRAFT LANDING MEACHAM, CARSWELL AFB, ALLIANCE, ARLINGTON, DENTON and FT. WORTH SPINKS: (Landing South/North): From over BUJ VORTAC via BUJ R-260 to KORKS INT. Expect vectors to final approach course.

FIGURE 35A.—Blue Ridge Three Arrival Description.

TEXAS   145

DALLAS

ADDISON   (ADS)   9 N   UTC−6(−5DT)   32°58'06"N 96°50'10"W   **DALLAS-FT. WORTH**

643   B   S4   FUEL 100LL, JET A   **H-2K, 4F, 5B, L-13C, A**

IAP

RWY 15-33: H7201X100 (ASPH)   S-80, D-100, DT-160   MIRL

   RWY 15: MALSR. VASI(V4R)—GA 3.0°TCH 51'. Thld dsplcd 980'. Ground.

   RWY 33: REIL. Thld dsplcd 468'. Road.

AIRPORT REMARKS: Attended continuously. Numerous flocks of birds on and in vicinity of arpt. Use extreme care: numerous 200' AGL buildings within 1 mile East, and South of arpt, transmission towers and water tanks West of arpt. Rwy 33 REIL out of svc indefinitely. ACTIVATE MALSR Rwy 15—CTAF. Rwy limited to maximum gross weight 120,000 pounds. Control Zone effective 1200-0400Z‡.

WEATHER DATA SOURCES: LAWRS

COMMUNICATIONS: CTAF 121.1   ATIS 126.8 (1200-0400Z‡)   UNICOM 122.95

   FORT WORTH FSS (FTW) TF 1−800−WX−BRIEF. NOTAM FILE ADS.

Ⓡ REGIONAL APP CON 123.9   Ⓡ REGIONAL DEP CON 124.3

   TOWER 121.1 (1200-0400Z‡)   GND CON 121.6   CLNC DEL 119.55

RADIO AIDS TO NAVIGATION: NOTAM FILE DAL.

   LOVE (L) VORW/DME 114.3   LUE   Chan 90   32°50'51"N 96°51'42"W   002° 7.4 NM to fld. 490/08E.

   BRONS NDB (LOM) 407   AD   33°02'40"N 96°52'13"W   153° 4.9 NM to fld.

   ILS/DME 110.1 I-ADS Chan 38 Rwy 15. LOM BRONS NDB. Unmonitored when tower closed.

   ILS 110.1 I-TBQ Rwy 33 LOC only. Unmonitored when twr clsd.

FIGURE 36.—Excerpt from Airport/Facility Directory.

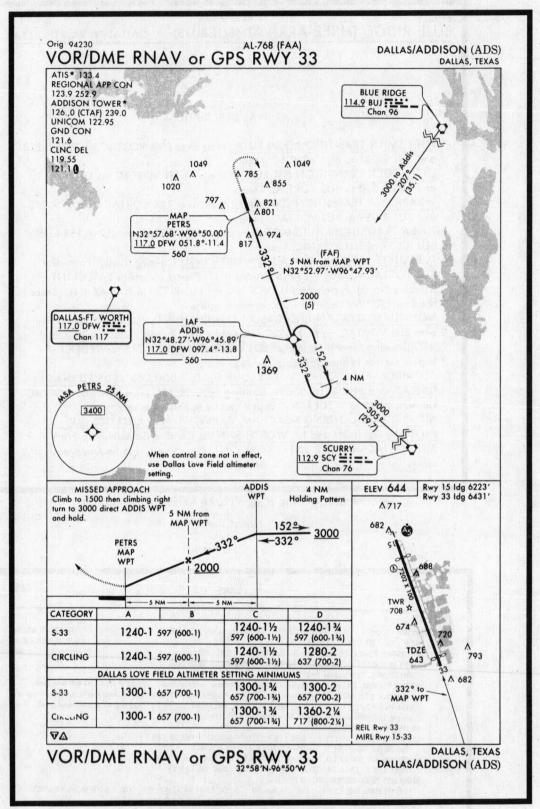

FIGURE 36A.—RNAV RWY 33 (ADS).

11.6 21XS to DFW

Questions 54 through 65 pertain to an IFR flight from Big Spring McMahon-Wrinkle Airport, Big Spring, Texas to the Dallas-Ft. Worth International Airport, Dallas-Ft. Worth, Texas.

The route of flight is given in block 8 on the flight plan portion of Fig. 38 on page 409. Information which pertains to your aircraft is given on the bottom portion of Fig. 38. The partially completed flight planning log is given in Fig. 39 on page 410.

The figures provided for this flight are listed below and are grouped together after the sequence of questions, except for Fig. 40, which is provided in color on page 433.

Fig.	Page	
38	409	Flight Plan and Aircraft Information
39	410	Flight Log and Excerpt from *Airport/Facility Directory* (21 XS)
40	433	En Route Chart Segment
41	411	ACTON Two Arrival
41A	412	ACTON Two Arrival Description
42	412	ILS-1 RWY 36L, Dallas-Fort Worth Intl. (*A/FD* Excerpt)
42A	413	ILS-1 RWY 36L (DFW) (NOS)

11.6 21XS to DFW

54.
4288. (Refer to figure 38 on page 409.) What aircraft equipment code should be entered in block 3 of the flight plan?

A— C.
B— I.
C— A.

Answer (B) is correct (4288). *(AIM Para 5-1-7)*
In block 3 of the flight plan, you enter the designation of the aircraft followed by a slash (/) and a letter for the equipment code. Fig. 38 indicates there is a transponder with Mode C and RNAV. Thus, you need Code I. (See Legend 26 on page 362.)
Answer (A) is incorrect because C indicates RNAV and transponder, but with no Mode C. Answer (C) is incorrect because A indicates DME and transponder with Mode C, but no RNAV.

55.
4289. (Refer to figure 38 on page 409.) What CAS must be used to maintain the filed TAS at the flight planned altitude if the outside air temperature is +05 °C?

A— 129 KCAS.
B— 133 KCAS.
C— 139 KCAS.

Answer (A) is correct (4289). *(Fl Comp)*
In the center of the slide rule side of your flight computer, on the right side, put the air temperature of +5°C over the altitude of 11,000 ft. (from block 7 of the flight plan, Fig. 38). On the outer scale, find TAS of 156 (from block 4), which is over calibrated airspeed on the inner scale of 129 KCAS.
Answer (B) is incorrect because maintaining 133 KCAS would result in a TAS of 161 kt., not 156 kt. Answer (C) is incorrect because maintaining 139 KCAS would result in a TAS of 168 kt., not 156 kt.

Chapter 11: IFR Flights

4290. (Refer to figures 38, 39, and 41 on pages 409 through 411 and figure 40 on page 433.) (Refer to the FD excerpt below, and use the wind entry closest to the flight planned altitude.) Determine the time to be entered in block 10 of the flight plan.

Route of flight . . . . Figures 38, 39, and 40
Flight log & MAG VAR . . . . Figure 39
ACTON TWO ARRIVAL . . . . Figure 41

FT	3000	6000	9000	12000
ABI		2033+13	2141+13	2142+05

A— 1 hour 24 minutes.
B— 1 hour 26 minutes.
C— 1 hour 31 minutes.

57.

4291. (Refer to figure 40 on page 433.) For planning purposes, what is the highest useable altitude for an IFR flight on V16 from the BGS VORTAC to ABI VORTAC?

A— 17,000 feet MSL.
B— 18,000 feet MSL.
C— 6,500 feet MSL.

58.

4292. (Refer to figures 41 and 41A on pages 411 and 412.) At which point does the AQN.AQN2 arrival begin?

A— ABI VORTAC.
B— ACTON VORTAC.
C— CREEK intersection.

59.

4293. (Refer to figures 41 and 41A on pages 411 and 412.) Which frequency would you anticipate using to contact Regional Approach Control? (ACTON TWO ARRIVAL).

A— 119.05.
B— 124.15.
C— 125.8.

Answer (C) is correct (4290). *(IFH Chap XIII)*
To determine the estimated time en route to be entered in block 10, you must complete the flight planning log in Fig. 39. Using the wind side of your flight computer, determine groundspeeds as shown in the table below.

Remember that winds are given in true direction and must be converted to magnetic. Fig. 39 shows a variation of 11 E. Use the wind at 12,000 ft. (which is closest to the planned altitude of 11,000 ft.): 210 − 11 E var. = 199 at 42 kt.

	Distance	MC	Wind (Mag)	Ground-speed	Time
BGS VORTAC	X	X	X	X	:06:00G
LORAN INT	42	075°	199/42	176	:14:19
ABI VORTAC	40	076°	199/42	175	:13:43
COTTN INT	63	087°	199/42	167	:22:38
AQN VORTAC	50	075°	199/42	176	:17:03
CREEK INT	32	040°	199/42	194	:09:54
Approach and Landing	X	X	X	X	:08:00G
					1:31:37

G = Given

Answer (A) is incorrect because an ETE of 1 hr. 24 min. requires a TAS of 175 kt., not 156 kt. Answer (B) is incorrect because an ETE of 1 hr. 26 min. requires a TAS of 170 kt., not 156 kt.

Answer (A) is correct (4291). *(AIM Para 3-2-6)*
The VOR airway system consists of airways designated from 1,200 ft. AGL up to, but not including, 18,000 ft. MSL.
Answer (B) is incorrect because Victor airways go up through 17,999 ft. but do not include 18,000 ft. Answer (C) is incorrect because 6,500 ft. is the MRA at LORAN intersection.

Answer (B) is correct (4292). *(ACL)*
The arrival, in contrast to the transition, begins over the AQN VORTAC, as explained in the written description in Fig. 41A.
Answer (A) is incorrect because the ABI VORTAC is the beginning of the Abilene transition. Answer (C) is incorrect because CREEK intersection is part, not the beginning, of the AQN.AQN2 arrival.

Answer (C) is correct (4293). *(ACL)*
The upper left-hand corner of the STAR chart (Fig. 41) shows the pertinent frequencies to be used. Since aircraft using this arrival are approaching from the west, the appropriate approach frequency is 125.8.
Answer (A) is incorrect because 119.05 is for aircraft approaching from an easterly direction. Answer (B) is incorrect because 124.15 is the DFW tower, not regional approach control, frequency for aircraft approaching from the west.

60.
4294. (Refer to figures 41 and 41A on pages 411 and 412.) On which heading should you plan to depart CREEK intersection?

A— 010°.
B— 040°.
C— 350°.

Answer (C) is correct (4294). *(ACL)*
Presumably, you should assume that you are flying a jet aircraft since non-jet aircraft (such as the C-402 in this flight) do not fly to CREEK INT (refer to Fig. 41A). The turbojet arrival indicates that you should maintain a heading of 350° after CREEK. Non-turbojet aircraft will proceed from AQN VORTAC via AQN R-040 to CREEK INT and should expect radar vectors at BRYAR INT (i.e., before CREEK INT).
Answer (A) is incorrect because 010° is not an applicable heading in this STAR. Answer (B) is incorrect because 040° is the course from AQN to CREEK INT, not after CREEK INT.

61.
4295. (Refer to figures 41, 42, and 42A on pages 411 through 413.) Approaching DFW from Abilene, which frequencies should you expect to use for regional approach control, control tower, and ground control respectively?

A— 119.05; 126.55; 121.65.
B— 119.05; 124.15; 121.8.
C— 125.8; 124.15; 121.8.

Answer (C) is correct (4295). *(A/FD)*
Refer to the **Communications** section of the *A/FD* in Fig. 42. Since the ACTON two arrival approaches from the west, approach control uses 125.8 or 132.1, tower uses 124.15, and ground uses 121.65 or 121.8.
Answer (A) is incorrect because 119.05 is for approach control from the east, not west, and 126.55 is for tower from the east, not west. Answer (B) is incorrect because 119.05 is for approach control from the east, not west.

62.
4296. (Refer to figure 42A on page 413.) Which navigational information and services would be available to the pilot when using the localizer frequency?

A— Localizer and glide slope, DME, TACAN with no voice capability.
B— Localizer information only, ATIS and DME are available.
C— Localizer and glide slope, DME, and no voice capability.

Answer (C) is correct (4296). *(ACL)*
ILS RWY 36L is an ILS (localizer and glide slope). On the NOS chart, a channel number indicates DME. The line under the I-BXN frequency 111.9 means no voice capability.
Answer (A) is incorrect because there is no TACAN indicated in the IAP chart. TACAN is the military version of VOR/DME. Answer (B) is incorrect because it is an ILS approach with glide slope.

63.
4297. (Refer to figures 42 and 42A on pages 412 and 413.) What is the difference in elevation (in feet MSL) between the airport elevation and the TDZE for RWY 36L?

A— 15 feet.
B— 18 feet.
C— 22 feet.

Answer (A) is correct (4297). *(ACL)*
The airport elevation (603 ft.) is shown in the upper left corner of the airport diagram, and the TDZE (588 ft.) is shown to the left of the approach end of RWY 36L. The difference between the two is 15 ft. (603 – 588).
Answer (B) is incorrect because 603 – 588 = 15 ft., not 18 ft. Answer (C) is incorrect because 22 ft. is the difference between airport elevation and the TDZE for RWY 36R, not RWY 36L.

64.
4298. (Refer to figure 42A on page 413.) What rate of descent should you plan to use initially to establish the glidepath for the ILS RWY 36L approach? (Use 120 knots ground speed.)

A— 425 feet per minute.
B— 530 feet per minute.
C— 635 feet per minute.

65.
4299. (Refer to figure 42A on page 413 and figure 43 below.) What is your position relative to CHAAR intersection? The aircraft is level at 3,000 feet MSL.

A— Right of the localizer course approaching CHAAR intersection and approaching the glide slope.
B— Left of the localizer course approaching CHAAR intersection and below the glide slope.
C— Right of the localizer course, past CHAAR intersection and above the glide slope.

Answer (C) is correct (4298). *(ACL)*
The profile view of the IAP chart (Fig. 42A) shows a glide slope angle of 3.00°. Legend 21 on page 199 gives rates of descent based on various glide slope angles and ground speeds. Find the 3.0° on the left margin and move right to the 120-kt. ground speed column to determine a rate of descent of 635 fpm.
Answer (A) is incorrect because 425 fpm is the required rate of descent at 120-kt. ground speed on a 2.0°, not 3.0°, glide slope. Answer (B) is incorrect because 530 fpm is the required rate of descent at 120-kt. ground speed on a 2.5°, not 3.0°, glide slope.

Answer (A) is correct (4299). *(IFH Chap VIII)*
NAV-1 (111.9) is on the I-BXN localizer indicating right of course because of the left deviation. Also, you are outside (approaching) CHAAR intersection since the DME readout is 7.5 DME (CHAAR is 7.2 DME). The glide slope is 3,000 ft. MSL at CHAAR, and thus you are beneath and approaching the glide slope. On NAV-2, the ADF frequency 233 does not appear on the approach chart. The VOR (114.3) is LOVE VOR, indicating R-230, and CHAAR is R-233, which confirms you are south of CHAAR position.
Answer (B) is incorrect because the left localizer deviation means right, not left, of course. Answer (C) is incorrect because you are below, not above, the glide slope and have not passed CHAAR intersection.

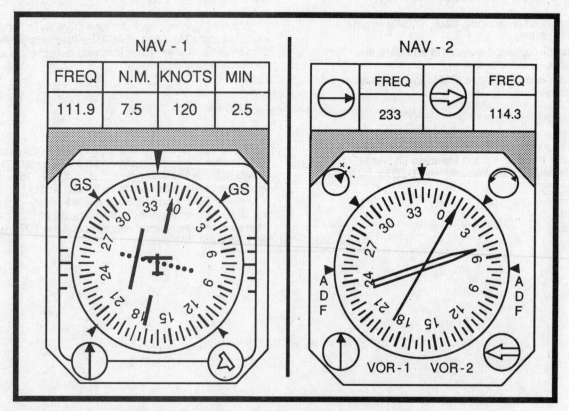

FIGURE 43.—CDI and RMI — NAV 1 and NAV 2.

Form Approved: OMB No.2120-0034

U.S. DEPARTMENT OF TRANSPORTATION FEDERAL AVIATION ADMINISTRATION **FLIGHT PLAN**	(FAA USE ONLY)	☐ PILOT BRIEFING ☐ STOPOVER	☐ VNR	TIME STARTED	SPECIALIST INITIALS

1 TYPE	2 AIRCRAFT IDENTIFICATION	3 AIRCRAFT TYPE/ SPECIAL EQUIPMENT	4 TRUE AIRSPEED	5 DEPARTURE POINT	6 DEPARTURE TIME		7 CRUISING ALTITUDE
					PROPOSED (Z)	ACTUAL (Z)	
X IFR	N4321P	C402/	156	BGS			110

8 ROUTE OF FLIGHT

DIRECT BGS, V16 ABI, ABI.AQN2

9 DESTINATION (Name of airport and city) DALLAS FT. WORTH DFW

10 EST TIME ENROUTE — HOURS — MINUTES

11 REMARKS

12 FUEL ON BOARD — HOURS — MINUTES

13 ALTERNATE AIRPORT(S) N/A

14 PILOTS NAME, ADDRESS & TELEPHONE NUMBER & AIRCRAFT HOME BASE

17 DESTINATION CONTACT/TELEPHONE (OPTIONAL)

15 NUMBER ABOARD 2

16 COLOR OF AIRCRAFT RED/BLUE/WHITE

CIVIL AIRCRAFT PILOTS. FAR Part 91 requires you file an IFR flight plan to operate under instrument flight rules in controlled airspace. Failure to file could result in a civil penalty not to exceed $1,000 for each violation (Section 901 of the Federal Aviation Act of 1958. as amended; Filing of a VFR flight plan is recommended as a good operating practice. See also Part 99 for requirements concerning DVFR flight plans.

FAA Form 7233-1 (8-82)   CLOSE VFR FLIGHT PLAN WITH _____ FSS ON ARRIVAL

AIRCRAFT INFORMATION

MAKE Cessna   MODEL 402C

N 4321P   Vso 71

AIRCRAFT EQUIPMENT/STATUS**

**NOTE: X= OPERATIVE   INOP= INOPERATIVE   N/A= NOT APPLICABLE
TRANSPONDER: X (MODE C) X ILS: (LOCALIZER) X (GLIDE SLOPE) X
VOR NO.1 X (NO 2) X ADF: X RNAV: X
VERTICAL PATH COMPUTER: NA DME: X
MARKER BEACON: X (AUDIO) X (VISUAL) X

FIGURE 38.—Flight Plan and Aircraft Information.

FLIGHT LOG

BIG SPRING McMAHON-WRINKLE TO DALLAS FT. WORTH (DFW)

CHECK POINTS		ROUTE	COURSE	WIND	SPEED-KTS		DIST	TIME		FUEL	
FROM	TO	ALTITUDE		TEMP	TAS	GS	NM	LEG	TOT	LEG	TOT
21XS	BGS	DIRECT CLIMB	DIRECT					:06:0			
	LORAN	V16 11,000	075°								
	ABI	V16 11,000	076°		156						
	COTTN	DIRECT 11,000	087°								
	AQN	AQN2	075°								
	CREEK	AQN2	040°								
APPROACH & LANDING		RADAR VEC-DESCENT						:08:0			
	DFW AIRPORT										

OTHER DATA:
NOTE: MAG. VAR. 11° E.
(STAR) ACTON TWO ARRIVAL (AQN2)

FLIGHT SUMMARY

TIME	FUEL (LB)	
		EN ROUTE
		RESERVE
		MISSED APPR.
		TOTAL

BIG SPRING McMAHON-WRINKLE   (21XS) 2SW UTC-6(-5DT).
  32°12'45"N101°31"17"W
  2572 B S4FUEL 100LL, JET A
  RWY 17-35: H8803X100 (ASPH-CONC) S-44, D-62, DDT-101 MIRL
    RWY 17:SSALS.PVASI(ASPH)-GA3.0°TCH 41'.
  RWY 06-24:H4600X75(ASPH) MIRL
    RWY 24:PVASI(PSIL)-GA3.55°TCH31'. P-line.
  AIRPORT REMARKS: Attended 1400-2300Z . For fuel after hours call 915-263-3958. ACTIVATE MIRL Rwy 06-24
    and Rwy 17-35, SSALS Rwy 17 and PVASI Rwy 17 and 24-CTAF.
  COMMUNICATIONS:CTAF/UNICOM 122.8
    SAN ANGELOSFSS (SJT) TF 1-800-WX-BRIEF. NOTAM FILE SJT.
    RCO 122.4(SAN ANGELOFSS)
    FORT WORTH CENTER APP/DEP CON 133.7
  RADIO AIDS TO NAVIGATION: NOTAM FILE SJT.
    (L) VORTACW 144.3 BGS Chan 90 32°23'08"N 101°10.5NM to fld. 2670/11E.

DALLAS-FT. WORTH
H-21, 5A, L-13A, 15B
IAP

EXCERPT FROM AIRPORT/FACILITY DIRECTORY (21 XS)

FIGURE 39.—Flight Log and Excerpt from Airport/Facility Directory (21 XS).

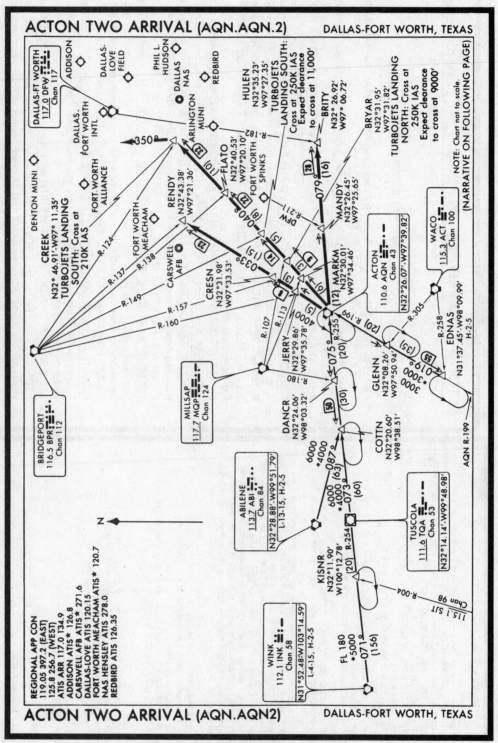

FIGURE 41.—ACTON Two Arrival.

ACTON TWO ARRIVAL (AQN.AQN2)   DALLAS-FORT WORTH, TEXAS

ARRIVAL DESCRIPTION

ABILENE TRANSITION (ABI.AQN2): From over ABI VORTAC via ABI R-087 and AQN R-255 to AQN VORTAC. Thence . . . .

EDNAS TRANSITION (EDNAS.AQN2): From over EDNAS INT via AQN R-199 to AQN VORTAC. Thence . . . .

WINK TRANSITION (INK.AQN2): From over INK VORTAC via INK R-071, TQA R-254, TQA R-073 and AQN R-255 to AQN VORTAC. Thence . . . .

TURBOJETS LANDING DALLAS-FT. WORTH INTL, MEACHAM, CARSWELL AFB, DENTON, ALLIANCE: (Landing South): From over AQN VORTAC via AQN R-040 to CREEK INT, thence heading 350° for vector to final approach course. (Landing North): From over AQN VORTAC via AQN R-040 to CREEK INT. Expect vectors at BRYAR INT.

NON-TURBOJETS LANDING DALLAS-FT. WORTH INTL, MEACHAM, CARSWELL AFB, DENTON, ALLIANCE: (Landing South): From over AQN VORTAC via AQN R-033 to RENDY INT. Expect vectors to final approach course. (Landing North): From over AQN VORTAC via AQN R-040 to CREEK INT. Expect vector at BRYAR INT.

TURBOJETS LANDING DALLAS-LOVE FIELD and ADDISON: (Landing South): From over AQN VORTAC via AQN R-040 to CREEK INT, thence heading 350° for vector to final approach course. (Landing North): From over AQN VORTAC via AQN R-079 to BRITY INT. Expect vector to final approach course.

NON-TURBOJETS LANDING DALLAS-LOVE FIELD and ADDISON: (Landing South/North): From over AQN VORTAC via AQN R-079 to BRITY INT. Expect vector to final approach course.

ALL AIRCRAFT LANDING FORT WORTH SPINKS, ARLINGTON, NAS DALLAS, REDBIRD, and PHIL L. HUDSON: (Landing South/North): From over AQN VORTAC via AQN R-079 to BRITY INT. Expect vectors to final approach course.

FIGURE 41A.—ACTON Two Arrival Description.

TEXAS

DALLAS-FORT WORTH INTL   (DFW)   12 NW   UTC-6(-5DT)32°53'47"N 97°02'28"W   DALLAS-FT. WORTH
603   B   FUEL 100LL, JET A   OX 1, 3   LRA   ARFF Index E   H-2K, 4F, 5B, L-13C, A
RWY 17L-35R: H11,388X150 (CONC-GRVD)   S-120, D-200, DT-600, DDT-850   HIRL CL   IAP
  RWY 17L: ALSF2. TDZ.   RWY 35R: MALSR. TDZ.
RWY 17R-35L: H11,388X200 (CONC-GRVD)   S-120, D-200, DT-600, DDT-850   HIRL CL
  RWY 17R: MALSR. TDZ.   RWY 35L: TDZ. VASI(V6L).
RWY 18R-36L: H11,388X150(CONC-GRVD)   S-120, D-200, DT-600, DDT-850   HIRL CL
  RWY 18R: ALSF2. TDZ   RWY 36L: MALSR. TDZ
RWY 18L-36R: H11,387X200 (CONC-GRVD)   S-120, D-200, DT-600, DDT-850   HIRL CL
  RWY 18L: MALSR. TDZ.   RWY 36R: TDZ. VASI(V6L).
RWY 13R-31L: H9300X150(CONC-GRVD)   S-120, D-220, DT-600, DDT-850   HIRL CL
  RWY 13R: TDZ.   RWY 31L: TDZ.
RWY 13L-31R: H9000X200 (CONC-GRVD)   S-120, D-200, DT-600, DDT-850   HIRL CL   0.5% up NW
  RWY 13L: TDZ. VASI(V6L)—Upper GA 3.25° TCH 93'. Lower GA 3.0° TCH 47'.   RWY 31R: MALSR. TDZ.
RWY 18S-36S: H4000X100 (CONC)
AIRPORT REMARKS: Attended continuously. Rwy 18S-36S CLOSED indefinitely. Arpt under construction, men and equipment in movement areas. Partial outages of arpt lgt circuits will occur daily. Prior Permission Required from arpt ops for General Aviation acft to proceed to airline terminal gate except to General Aviation Facility. Rwy 18S-36S located on taxiway G, 4000' long 100' wide restricted to prop acft 12,500 lbs. & below and stol acft daylight VFR plus IFR departures. Prior permission required from the primary tenant airlines to operate within central terminal area, CAUTION: proper minimum clearance may not be maintained within the central terminal area. Landing fee. Helipad H1 on apt 104X104 (CONC) Heliport located at Twy G and Twy 24 intersection, daylight VFR. Clearways 500X1000 each end Rwy 17L-35R, Rwy 17R-35L, Rwy 18L-36R and Rwy 18R-36L.
Flight Notification Service (ADCUS) available.
WEATHER DATA SOURCES: LLWAS.
COMMUNICATIONS: ATIS 117.0 134.9 (ARR) 135.5 (DEP)   UNICOM 122.95
FORT WORTH FSS (FTW) LC 429-6434, TF 1-800-WX-BRIEF. NOTAM FILE DFW
®REGIONAL APP CON 119.05(E) 119.4(E) 125.8(W) 132.1(W)
®REGIONAL DEP CON 118.55 (E) 124.25 (WEST) 127.75 (NORTH-SOUTH)
REGIONAL TOWER 126.55 (E) 124.15 (W)   GND CON 121.65 133.15(E) 121.8 (W)   CLNC DEL 128.25 127.5
TCA: See VFR Terminal Area chart.
RADIO AIDS TO NAVIGATION: NOTAM FILE DFW.
(H) VORTACW 117.0   DFW   Chan 117   32°51'57"N 97°01'40"W   at fld. 560/08E.
  VOR Portion unusable 045°-050' all altitudes and distances, 350°-100' beyond 30 NM below 2100'.
ISSUE NDB (LOM) 233   PK   32°47'35"N 97°01'49"W   348°-6.2 NM to fld.
JIFFY NDB (LOM) 219   FL   32°59'44"N 97°01'46"W   179° 6.0 NM to fld.
ILS/DME 109.5 I-LWN Chan 32 Rwy 13R.
ILS/DME 109.1 I-FLQ Chan 28 Rwy 17L. LOM JIFFY NDB.
ILS 111.5 I-JHZ Rwy 17R. LOM JIFFY NDB.
ILS 111.3 I-CIX Rwy 18L.
ILS/DME 111.9 I-VYN Chan 56 Rwy 18R.
ILS 110.9 I-RRA Rwy 31R.
ILS/DME 109.1 I-PKQ Chan 28 Rwy 35R. LOM ISSUE NDB.
ILS/DME 111.9 I-BXN Chan 56 Rwy 36L.

FIGURE 42.—ILS-1 RWY 36L, Dallas-Fort Worth Intl.

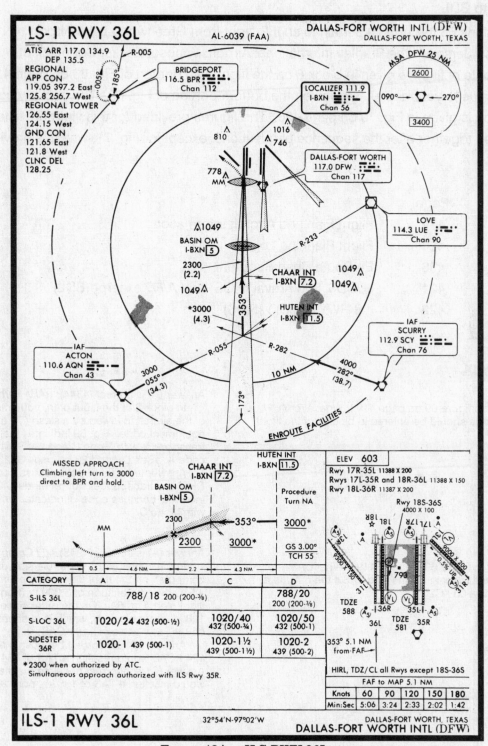

FIGURE 42A.—ILS RWY 36L.

11.7 4N1 to BDL

Questions 66 through 79 pertain to an IFR flight from Greenwood Lake Airport (4N1), West Milford, New Jersey to the Bradley International Airport, Windsor Locks, Connecticut.

The route of flight is given in block 8 on the flight plan portion of Fig. 69 on page 419. Information which pertains to your aircraft is given on the bottom portion of Fig. 69. The partially completed flight planning log is given in Fig. 70 on page 420. The figures provided for this flight are listed below and are grouped together after the sequence of questions, except for Fig. 71, which is provided in color on page 438.

11.7 4N1 to BDL

66.
4344. (Refer to figure 69 on page 419.) What aircraft equipment code should be entered in block 3 of the flight plan?

A— A.
B— B.
C— U.

Answer (A) is correct (4344). *(AIM Para 5-1-7)*
In block 3 of the flight plan, you enter the designation of the aircraft followed by a slash (/) and a letter for the equipment code. Fig. 69 indicates that you have a transponder with Mode C and DME, which requires code A. (See Legend 26 on page 362.)
Answer (B) is incorrect because code B indicates DME and transponder but no Mode C. Answer (C) is incorrect because code U indicates only a transponder with Mode C.

67.
4345. (Refer to figure 69 on page 419.) What CAS should be used to maintain the filed TAS if the outside air temperature is +05 °C?

A— 119 KCAS.
B— 124 KCAS.
C— 126 KCAS.

Answer (A) is correct (4345). *(Fl Comp)*
In the center of the slide rule side of your flight computer, on the right side, put the air temperature of +5°C over the altitude of 5,000 ft. (from block 7 of the flight plan, Fig. 69). On the outer scale, find TAS of 128 kt. (from block 4), which is over calibrated airspeed on the inner scale of 119 KCAS.
Answer (B) is incorrect because maintaining 124 KCAS would result in a TAS of 134 kt., not 128 kt. Answer (C) is incorrect because maintaining 126 KCAS would result in a TAS of 136 kt., not 128 kt.

68.

4346. (Refer to figures 69, 70, and 72 on pages 419 through 421 and figure 71 on page 438.) Determine the time to be entered in block 10 of the flight plan. (Refer to the FD excerpt below, and use the wind entry closest to the flight planned altitude.)

Route of flight .... Figures 69, 70, and 71
Flight log and MAG VAR .... Figure 70
JUDDS TWO ARRIVAL
  and Excerpt from AFD .... Figure 72

FT	3000	6000	9000
BDL	3320	3425+05	3430+00

A— 1 hour 14 minutes.
B— 58 minutes.
C— 50 minutes.

Answer (B) is correct (4346). *(IFH Chap XIII)*
    To determine the estimated time en route to be entered in block 10, you must complete the flight planning log in Fig. 70. Using the wind side of your flight computer, determine groundspeeds as shown in the table below. The arrow in Fig. 71 points to the departure airport.
    Remember that winds are given in true direction and must be converted to magnetic. Fig. 70 shows a variation of 14°W. Use the wind at 6,000 ft. (which is closest to the planned altitude of 5,000 ft.): 340° + 14°W var. = 354° at 25 kt.

	Distance	MC	Wind (Mag)	Ground-speed	Time
SHAFF INT	X	X	X	X	:08:00G
HELON INT	24	029°	354/25	107	:13:27
IGN VORTAC	21	102°	354/25	134	:09:24
VOR COP	15	112°	354/25	138	:06:31
JUDDS INT	17	100°	354/25	133	:07:40
BRISS INT	6	057°	354/25	115	:03:07
Approach and Landing	X	X	X	X	:12:00G
					1:00:09

G = Given

    Answer (A) is incorrect because an ETE of 1 hr. 14 min. requires a TAS of approximately 95 kt., not 128 kt. Answer (C) is incorrect because an ETE of 50 min. requires a TAS of 170 kt., not 128 kt.

69.

4347. (Refer to figure 71 on page 438 and figure 71A below.) What is your position relative to the FLOSI intersection northbound on V213 airway?

A— West of V213 and approaching the FLOSI intersection.
B— East of V213 and approaching the FLOSI intersection.
C— West of V213 and past the FLOSI intersection.

Answer (A) is correct (4347). *(IFH Chap VII)*
    VOR-1 is tuned to IGN VORTAC (117.6) with an OBS setting of 265°. The FROM indication and right needle deflection indicates you are south of the IGN R-265 and thus approaching it. VOR-2 is tuned to SAX VORTAC (115.7) with an OBS setting of 029°. The FROM indication and right needle deflection indicates you are to the left or west of the SAX R-029.
    Answer (B) is incorrect because a left, not right, needle deflection in VOR-2 would indicate right or east of the V213. Answer (C) is incorrect because a left, not right, needle deflection in VOR-1 would indicate that you have passed FLOSI intersection.

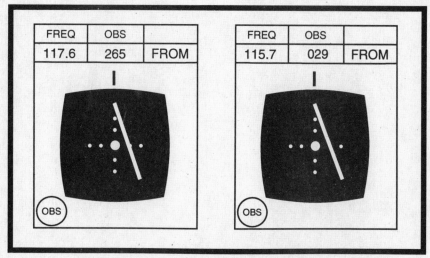

FIGURE 71A.—CDI and OBS Indicators.

70.
4348. (Refer to figure 70 on page 420 and figure 71 on page 438.) Which VORTAC navigational facility along the proposed route of flight could provide you with HIWAS information?

A— SPARTA VORTAC.
B— HUGUENOT VORTAC.
C— KINGSTON VORTAC.

71.
4349. (Refer to figure 72 on page 421.) At which location or condition does the IGN.JUDDS2 arrival begin?

A— JUDDS intersection.
B— IGN VORTAC.
C— BRISS intersection.

72.
4350. (Refer to figure 72 on page 421.) How many precision approach procedures are published for Bradley International Airport?

A— One.
B— Three.
C— Four.

Answer (C) is correct (4348). (ACL)
The Kingston VORTAC (IGN) communication box contains a small square with a white H in the upper right-hand corner indicating availability of HIWAS.
Answer (A) is incorrect because the Sparta (SAX) VORTAC communication box has no small square with an H. Answer (B) is incorrect because the Huguenot VORTAC communication box has no small square with an H.

Answer (B) is correct (4349). (ACL)
The IGN.JUDDS2 arrival on Fig. 72 indicates "from over Kingston VORTAC via R-112 ...." Thus, the JUDDS2 arrival begins over the Kingston (IGN) VORTAC.
Answer (A) is incorrect because the JUDDS INT is in the middle of the arrival route. Answer (C) is incorrect because the BRISS INT is in the middle of the arrival route.

Answer (B) is correct (4350). (A/FD)
To determine the number of precision approaches at Bradley International Airport, check the appropriate Airport/Facility Directory, which is reproduced in Fig. 72. At the end of the A/FD, note ILS/DMEs for RWY 6, RWY 33, and RWY 24.
Answer (A) is incorrect because there are three, not one, ILSs. Answer (C) is incorrect because there are three, not four, ILSs.

73.
4351. (Refer to figure 73 on page 422.) What is the minimum altitude at which you should intercept the glide slope on the ILS RWY 6 approach procedure?

A— 3,000 feet MSL.
B— 1,800 feet MSL.
C— 1,690 feet MSL.

74.
4352. (Refer to figure 73 on page 422.) At which indication or occurrence should you initiate the published missed approach procedure for the ILS RWY 6 approach provided the runway environment is not in sight?

A— When reaching 374 feet MSL indicated altitude.
B— When 3 minutes (at 90 knots ground speed) have expired or reaching 374 feet MSL, whichever occurs first.
C— Upon reaching 374 feet AGL.

75.
4353. (Refer to figure 73 on page 422.) Which sequence of marker beacon indicator lights, and their respective codes, will you receive on the ILS RWY 6 approach procedure to the MAP?

A— Blue – alternate dots and dashes; amber – dashes.
B— Amber – alternate dots and dashes; blue – dashes.
C— Blue – dashes; amber – alternate dots and dashes.

76.
4354. (Refer to figure 73 on page 422.) Using an average groundspeed of 90 knots on the final approach segment, what rate of descent should be used initially to establish the glidepath for the ILS RWY 6 approach procedure?

A— 395 feet per minute.
B— 480 feet per minute.
C— 555 feet per minute.

Answer (B) is correct (4351). *(ACL)*
In the profile section of the IAP chart, there is an 1800 with a lightning bolt pointing to the glide slope. This is the glide slope intercept altitude and final approach fix for precision approaches. Thus, here, one should not intercept below 1,800 ft. MSL.
Answer (A) is incorrect because 3,000 ft. MSL is the minimum altitude in the holding pattern at PENNA INT. Answer (C) is incorrect because 1,690 ft. MSL is the altitude at which you will cross CHUPP LOM when descending on the glide slope.

Answer (A) is correct (4352). *(ACL)*
When flying the ILS RWY 6 approach, you should execute a missed approach when you have reached the decision height of 374 ft. MSL.
Answer (B) is incorrect because the ILS is a precision approach and timing is only for the backup localizer approach. Answer (C) is incorrect because the decision height is 374 ft. MSL, not AGL.

Answer (C) is correct (4353). *(AIM Para 1-1-9)*
The outer marker is identified with continuous dashes at the rate of two dashes per sec. and a blue marker beacon light. The middle marker is identified with alternate dots and dashes keyed at the rate of 95 dot/dash combinations per minute and an amber marker beacon light. Note that the inner marker, which is identified with continuous dots at the rate of six dots per sec. and a white marker beacon light, is crossed after (not before) the MAP.
Answer (A) is incorrect because the outer marker has dashes, not dots and dashes, and the middle marker has dots and dashes, not just dashes. Answer (B) is incorrect because the outer marker is blue with dashes, and the middle marker is amber with dots and dashes, not vice versa.

Answer (B) is correct (4354). *(ACL)*
The profile view of the IAP chart shows a glide slope angle of 3.00°. Legend 21 on page 199 gives rates of descent based on various glide slope angles and groundspeeds. Find the 3.0° angle of descent on the left margin and move right to the 90-kt. groundspeed column to determine a rate of descent of 480 fpm.
Answer (A) is incorrect because 395 fpm is the required rate of descent at a groundspeed of 75 kt., not 90 kt. Answer (C) is incorrect because 555 fpm is the required rate of descent at a groundspeed of 105 kt., not 90 kt.

77.
4355. (Refer to figure 73 on page 422.) What is the touchdown zone elevation for RWY 6?

A— 174 feet MSL.
B— 200 feet AGL.
C— 270 feet MSL.

78.
4356. (Refer to figure 73 on page 422.) After passing the OM, Bradley Approach Control advises you that the MM on the ILS RWY 6 approach is inoperative. Under these circumstances, what adjustments, if any, are required to be made to the DH and visibility?

A— DH 424/24.
B— No adjustments are required.
C— DH 374/24.

79.
4357. (Refer to figure 73 on page 422.) Which runway and landing environment lighting is available for approach and landing on RWY 6 at Bradley International?

A— HIRL, REIL, and VASI.
B— HIRL and VASI.
C— ALSF2 and HIRL.

Answer (A) is correct (4355). *(ACL)*
The IAP chart shows the TDZE in the airport diagram near the approach end of the landing runway. The TDZE is 174 ft. MSL.
Answer (B) is incorrect because 200 ft. AGL is the HAT (height above touchdown) at the DH on the ILS. Answer (C) is incorrect because 270 ft. MSL is the height of an obstruction near the approach end of RWY 6.

Answer (B) is correct (4356). *(ACL)*
Refer to Legend 22 on page 200, Inoperative Components or Visual Aids Table. Since the MM is not listed in the table, no adjustments are required.
Answer (A) is incorrect because no adjustments are required due to an inoperative MM. Answer (C) is incorrect because no adjustments are required due to an inoperative MM.

Answer (C) is correct (4357). *(ACL)*
The airport diagram in Fig. 73 has a circle enclosing the letter "A," with a dot above it, near the approach end of RWY 6. Legend 19 on page 201 indicates that this means ALSF-2 approach lighting. Information listed at the bottom left corner of the airport diagram (Fig. 73) indicates that RWY 6-24 has high-intensity runway lights (HIRL).
Answer (A) is incorrect because REIL and VASI are not indicated for RWY 6. Answer (B) is incorrect because VASI is not indicated for RWY 6.

FIGURE 69.—Flight Plan and Aircraft Information.

FLIGHT LOG

GREENWOOD LAKE (4N1) TO BRADLEY INTL. (BDL)

| CHECK POINTS | | ROUTE | COURSE | WIND | SPEED-KTS | | DIST | TIME | | FUEL | |
FROM	TO	ALTITUDE		TEMP	TAS	GS	NM	LEG	TOT	LEG	TOT
4N1	SHAFF	DIRECT CLIMB	350°					:08:0			
	HELON	V213 5000	029°		128						
	IGN	V58 5000	102°								
		JUDDS2	112°								
	JUDDS	JUDDS2	100°								
	BRISS	JUDDS2	057°								
APPROACH & LANDING								:12:0			
	BDL INTL										

OTHER DATA:
NOTE: MAG. VAR. 14° W.

FLIGHT SUMMARY

TIME	FUEL (LB)	
		EN ROUTE
		RESERVE
		MISSED APPR.
		TOTAL

FIGURE 70.—Flight Planning Log.

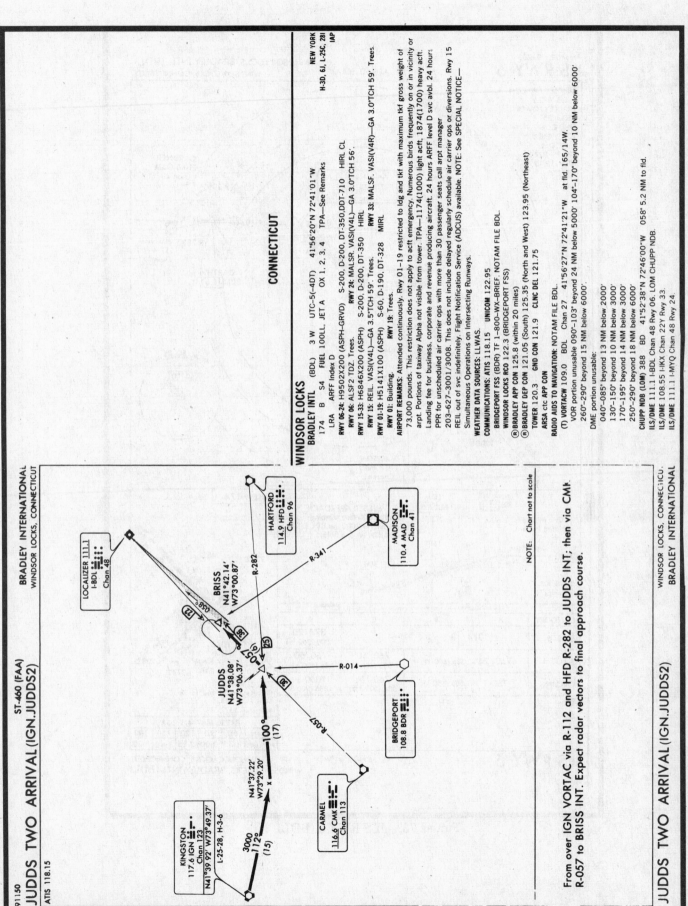

FIGURE 72.— JUDDS TWO ARRIVAL.

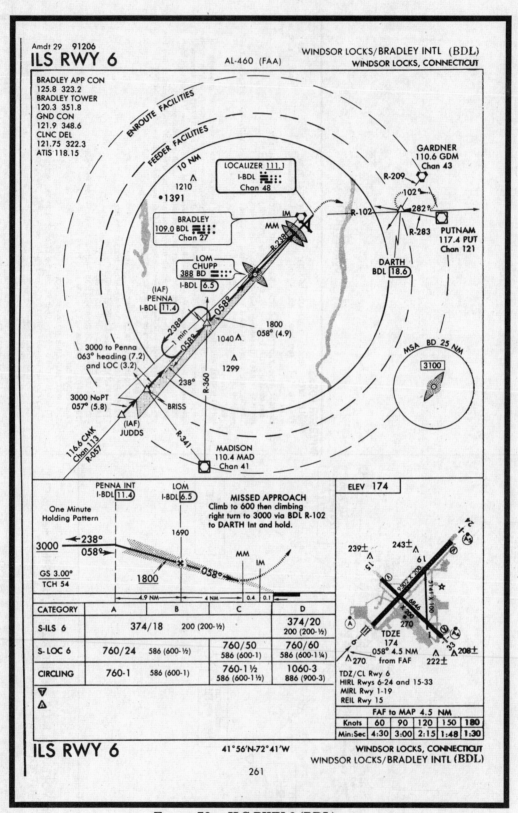

FIGURE 73.—ILS RWY 6 (BDL).

11.8 HLN to BIL

Questions 80 through 93 pertain to an IFR flight from Helena Regional Airport, Helena, Montana to the Billings Logan International Airport, Billings, Montana.

The route of flight is given in block 8 on the flight plan portion of Fig. 74 on page 443. Information which pertains to your aircraft is given on the bottom portion of Fig. 74. The partially completed flight planning log is given in Fig. 75 on page 444.

The figures provided for this flight are listed below and are grouped together after the sequence of questions, except for Fig. 78, which is provided in color on page 439.

Fig.	Page	
74	443	Flight Plan and Aircraft Information
75	444	Flight Planning Log
76	445	VOR Indications and Excerpts from *Airport/Facility Directory* (HLN)
77	446	STAKK Two Departure
78	439	En Route Chart Segment
80	447	VOR/DME RWY 27R and *Airport/Facility Directory* (BIL)

11.8 HLN to BIL

80.
4358. (Refer to figure 74 on page 443.) What aircraft equipment code should be entered in block 3 of the flight plan?

A— T.
B— U.
C— A.

Answer (C) is correct (4358). *(AIM Para 5-1-7)*
In block 3 of the flight plan, you enter the designation of the aircraft followed by a slash (/) and a letter for the equipment code. Fig. 74 indicates that you have a DME and transponder with Mode C, which requires code A. (See Legend 26 on page 362.)
Answer (A) is incorrect because T indicates only a transponder with no Mode C. Answer (B) is incorrect because U indicates only a transponder with Mode C.

81.
4359. (Refer to figure 74 on page 443.) What CAS should be used to maintain the filed TAS at the flight planned altitude if the outside air temperature is +5 °C?

A— 129 KCAS.
B— 133 KCAS.
C— 139 KCAS.

Answer (B) is correct (4359). *(Fl Comp)*
In the center of the slide rule side of your flight computer, on the right side, put the air temperature of +5°C over the altitude of 11,000 ft. (from block 7 of the flight plan, Fig. 74). On the outer scale, find TAS of 160 (from block 4), which is over calibrated airspeed on the inner scale of 133 KCAS.
Answer (A) is incorrect because maintaining 129 KCAS would result in a TAS of 156 kt., not 133 kt. Answer (C) is incorrect because maintaining 139 KCAS would result in a TAS of 168 kt., not 133 kt.

82.
4360. (Refer to figures 74, 75, 76, and 77 on pages 443 through 446 and figure 78 on page 439.) Determine the time to be entered in block 10 of the flight plan. (Refer to the FD excerpt below, and use the wind entry closest to the flight planned altitude.)

Route of flight . . . . Figures 74, 75, 76, 77, and 78
Flight log & MAG VAR . . . . Figure 75
VOR indications
   and Excerpts from AFD . . . . Figure 76

FT	6000	9000	12000	18000
BIL	2414	2422+11	2324+05	2126−11

A— 1 hour 15 minutes.
B— 1 hour 20 minutes.
C— 1 hour 25 minutes.

83.
4361. (Refer to figure 77 on page 446.) At which point does the basic instrument departure procedure terminate?

A— When Helena Departure Control establishes radar contact.
B— At STAKK intersection.
C— Over the BOZEMAN VOR.

84.
4362. (Refer to figure 76 on page 445.) Which indication would be an acceptable accuracy check of both VOR receivers when the aircraft is located on the VOR receiver checkpoint at the Helena Regional Airport?

A— A.
B— B.
C— C.

84a.
0601-614. (Refer to figure 78 on page 439.) When eastbound on V86 between Whitehall and Livingston, the minimum altitude that you should cross BZN is

A— 9,300 feet.
B— 10,400 feet.
C— 8,500 feet.

Answer (C) is correct (4360). *(IFH Chap XIII)*
To determine the estimated time en route to be entered in block 10, you must complete the flight planning log in Fig. 75. Using the wind side of your flight computer, determine groundspeeds as shown in the table below.
Remember that winds are given in true direction and must be converted to magnetic. Fig. 75 shows a variation of 18°E. Use the wind at 12,000 ft. (which is closest to the planned altitude of 11,000 ft.): 230° − 18°E var. = 212° at 24 kt.

	Distance	MC	Wind (Mag)	Ground-speed	Time
VESTS INT	X	X	X	X	:15:00G
BZN VOR/DME	44	140°	212/24	151	:17:29
VOR COP VORTAC	13	110°	212/24	163	:04:47
LVM VORTAC	20	063°	212/24	180	:06:40
REEPO INT	39	067°	212/24	179	:13:04
BIL VORTAC	38	069°	212/24	178	:12:49
Approach and Landing	X	X	X	X	:15:00G
					1:24:49

G = Given

Answer (A) is incorrect because an ETE of 1 hr. 15 min. requires a TAS of 195 kt., not 160 kt. Answer (B) is incorrect because an ETE of 1 hr. 20 min. requires a TAS of 175 kt., not 160 kt.

Answer (B) is correct (4361). *(ACL)*
On the STAKK Two Departure in Fig. 77, the departure route description at the bottom indicates that, for takeoffs from RWY 9 and RWY 27, you should climb eastbound on HLN R-087 to cross STAKK INT at or above 10,200 ft. "Thence via transition."
Answer (A) is incorrect because Helena Departure Control will establish contact shortly after you get off the runway. Answer (C) is incorrect because the BOZEMAN VOR is the end of the BOZEMAN transition, not the basic DP.

Answer (C) is correct (4362). *(ACL)*
To determine the VOR receiver checkpoint at the Helena Regional Airport, consult the VOR receiver check table on Fig. 76. The checkpoint is on TWY (taxiway) E, midway between TWY C and RWY 27, and is on R-237 of Helena VORTAC. Thus, the RMI should show the tails of both needles on 237°, ± 4°.
Answer (A) is incorrect because R-180 ±4° would be the expected indication when using a VOT, not a ground VOR checkpoint. Answer (B) is incorrect because the tail, not the head, of the RMI needle indicates the radial.

Answer (A) is correct (0601-614). *(ACL)*
On Fig. 78, the Bozeman (BZN) VOR/DME has a flag with an X, indicating a minimum crossing altitude (MCA). Near the center of the page, above the BZN VOR/DME communications box, is MCA V86-365 9300 SE. Thus, the minimum crossing altitude over the BZN VOR/DME for a flight southeast bound on V86 is 9,300 ft. MSL.
Answer (B) is incorrect because 10,400 ft. MSL is the MEA on V86-365 between BZN and LVM, not the MCA at BZN VOR/DME. Answer (C) is incorrect because 8,500 ft. MSL is the MEA on V86 prior to BZN VOR/DME. The MEA is not the MCA when an MCA is specified.

85.
4363. (Refer to figure 77 on page 446.) At which minimum altitude should you cross the STAKK intersection?

A— 6,500 feet MSL.
B— 1,400 feet MSL.
C— 10,200 feet MSL.

86.
4364. (Refer to figure 77 on page 446.) Using an average ground speed of 140 knots, what minimum rate of climb would meet the required minimum climb rate per NM as specified on the instrument departure procedure?

A— 350 feet per minute.
B— 475 feet per minute.
C— 700 feet per minute.

87.
4365. (Refer to figures 76 and 77 on pages 445 and 446.) Which en route low altitude navigation chart would cover the proposed routing at the BOZEMAN VORTAC?

A—L-2.
B—L-7.
C—L-9.

88.
4366. (Refer to figure 78 on page 439.) What is the maximum altitude that you may flight plan an IFR flight on V-86 EASTBOUND between BOZEMAN and BILLINGS VORTACs?

A— 14,500 feet MSL.
B— 17,000 feet MSL.
C— 18,000 feet MSL.

89.
4370. (Refer to figure 78 on page 439.) What is the minimum crossing altitude over the BOZEMAN VORTAC for a flight southeast bound on V86?

A— 8,500 feet MSL.
B— 9,300 feet MSL.
C— 9,700 feet MSL.

Answer (C) is correct (4363). *(ACL)*
On the STAKK Two Departure (Fig. 77), the departure route description for either runway states, "Cross STAKK at or above 10,200'." Thus, the minimum altitude at which you should cross the STAKK INT is 10,200 ft. MSL.
Answer (A) is incorrect because 6,500 ft. MSL is not a pertinent altitude in this DP. Answer (B) is incorrect because 1,400 ft. MSL is not a pertinent altitude in this DP.

Answer (C) is correct (4364). *(ACL)*
On Fig. 77 on the DP, the note to the left indicates a minimum climb rate of 300 ft. per NM. To convert this to a climb rate (fpm), use Legend 16 on page 204. Find the required climb rate of 300 ft. per NM on the left margin and move right to the 140-kt. ground speed column to determine a rate of climb of 700 fpm.
Answer (A) is incorrect because a 350 fpm climb rate at an average ground speed of 140 kt. would result in a climb rate of less than 200 ft. per NM, not 300 ft. per NM. Answer (B) is incorrect because a 475 fpm climb rate at an average ground speed of 140 kt. would result in a climb rate of approximately 200 ft. per NM, not 300 ft. per NM.

Answer (C) is correct (4365). *(ACL)*
On Fig. 77, Bozeman VOR/DME is in the planview in the lower right corner. Below the frequency box, the notation L-9 is the number of the appropriate en route low-altitude navigation chart.
Answer (A) is incorrect because Bozeman VOR/DME is found on L-9, not L-2. Answer (B) is incorrect because Bozeman VOR/DME is found on L-9, not L-7.

Answer (B) is correct (4366). *(ACL)*
Victor airways consist of altitudes from 1,200 ft. AGL up to, but not including, 18,000 ft. MSL. The jet route is from 18,000 ft. MSL through FL 450. Thus, the maximum altitude on an airway is 17,000 ft. MSL because IFR flight is conducted at cardinal altitudes, odd numbers for eastbound and even for westbound.
Answer (A) is incorrect because 14,500 ft. MSL (i.e., thousand-foot plus 500 ft.) is a VFR, not IFR, cruising altitude. Answer (C) is incorrect because Victor airways extend up to, but do not include, 18,000 ft. MSL. Jet routes begin at 18,000 ft. MSL (FL 180).

Answer (B) is correct (4370). *(ACL)*
On Fig. 78, the Bozeman (BZN) VOR/DME (it is not a VORTAC) has a flag with an X, indicating a minimum crossing altitude (MCA). Near the center of the page, above the BZN VOR/DME communications box, is MCA V86-365 9300 SE. Thus, the minimum crossing altitude over the BZN VOR/DME for a flight southeast bound on V86 is 9,300 ft. MSL.
Answer (A) is incorrect because 8,500 ft. MSL is the MEA on V86 prior to BZN VOR/DME. The MEA is not the MCA when an MCA is specified. Answer (C) is incorrect because 9,700 ft. MSL is the MEA on V365, not the MCA at BZN VOR/DME.

90.
4367. (Refer to figure 78 on page 439 and figure 79 below.) What is your position relative to the VOR COP southeast bound on V86 between the BOZEMAN and LIVINGSTON VORTACs? The No. 1 VOR is tuned to 116.1 and the No. 2 VOR is tuned to 112.2.

A— Past the LVM R-246 and west of the BZN R-110.
B— Approaching the LVM R-246 and west of the BZN R-110.
C— Past the LVM R-246 and east of the BZN R-110.

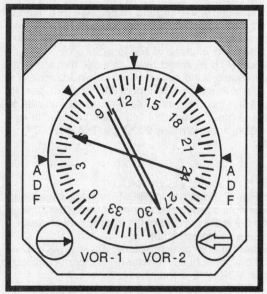

FIGURE 79.—RMI Indicator.

91.
4371. (Refer to figure 80 on page 447.) What is the TDZE for landing on RWY 27R?

A— 3,649 feet MSL.
B— 3,514 feet MSL.
C— 3,450 feet MSL.

92.
4368. (Refer to figures 74 and 80 on pages 443 and 447.) Which aircraft approach category should be used for a circling approach for a landing on RWY 27?

A— A.
B— B.
C— C.

93.
4369. (Refer to figure 80 on page 447.) How many initial approach fixes serve the VOR/DME RWY 27R (Billings Logan) approach procedure?

A— Three.
B— Four.
C— Five.

Answer (C) is correct (4367). *(IFH Chap VII)*
The tail of an RMI indicates the radial. You are on a 130° heading, so you are southeast bound. VOR-2 indicates R-105 of BZN (112.2). VOR-1 indicates on R-239 of LVM (116.1). Because you are on R-105 of BZN, you are to the east of BZN R-110. Because you are on R-239 of LVM, you have passed the LVM R-246.
Answer (A) is incorrect because you are east, not west, of the BZN R-110. Answer (B) is incorrect because you are past, not approaching, the LVM R-246, and east, not west, of the BZN R-110.

Answer (B) is correct (4371). *(ACL)*
On the IAP chart, the TDZE is depicted in the airport diagram near the approach end of the landing runway (RWY 27R) as 3,514 ft. MSL.
Answer (A) is incorrect because 3,649 ft. MSL is the airport elevation, not the TDZE. Answer (C) is incorrect because 3,450 ft. MSL is not a relevant altitude at an airport with a 3,649 ft. MSL elevation.

Answer (B) is correct (4368). *(ACL)*
Approach categories are based upon 1.3 V_{so} and weight. Fig. 74 indicates V_{so} of the Cessna 310 is 72. Using the general rule, 1.3 V_{so} is 93.6, which is Category B (91 to 120 kt.).
Answer (A) is incorrect because Category A is for approach speeds less than 91 kt. Answer (C) is incorrect because Category C is for approach speeds from 121 to 140 kt.

Answer (B) is correct (4369). *(ACL)*
Initial approach fixes are indicated by the designation "(IAF)" on instrument approach charts (Fig. 80). Note that there is an IAF at the 16 DME arc at R-157 INT and also at the R-040 INT. The Billings VORTAC is also indicated as an IAF, as is MUSTY INT.
Answer (A) is incorrect because the VOR/DME RWY 27R approach has four, not three, IAFs. Answer (C) is incorrect because the VOR/DME RWY 27R approach has four, not five, IAFs.

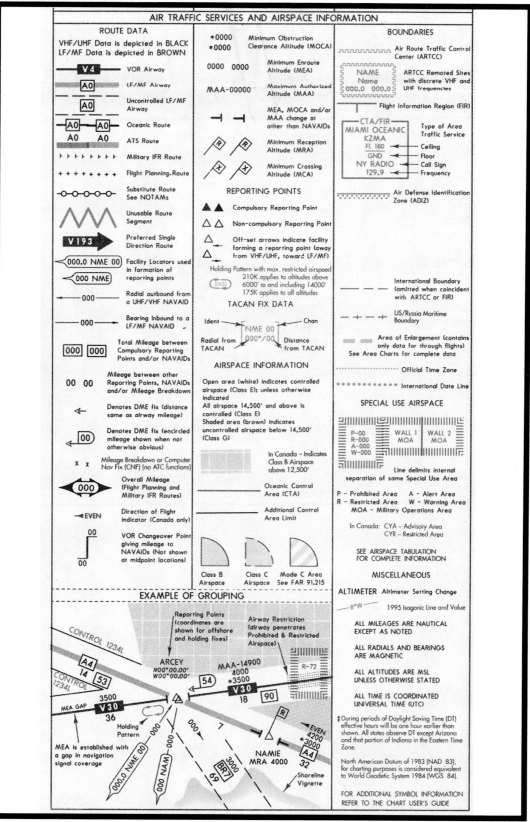

LEGEND 24.—IFR En Route Low Altitude (U.S.).

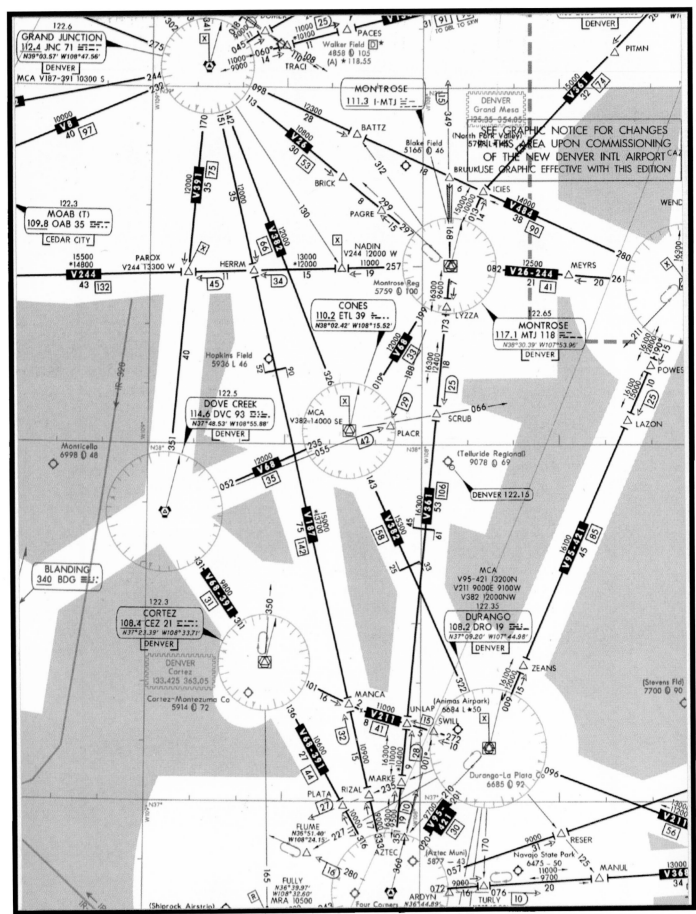

FIGURE 24.—En Route Low-Altitude Chart Segment.

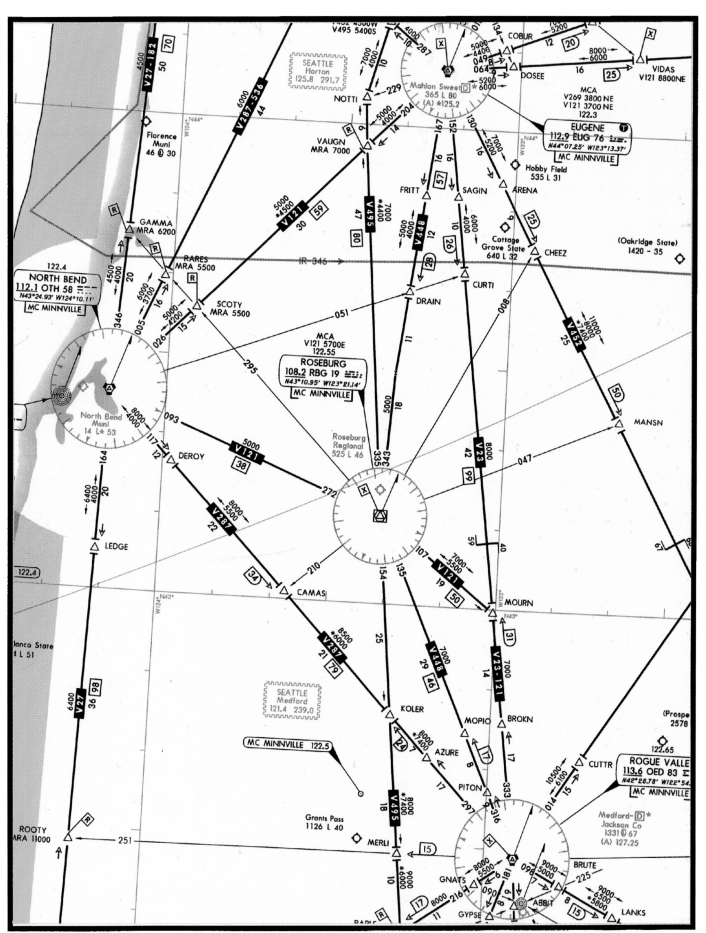

FIGURE 31.—En Route Low-Altitude Chart Segment.

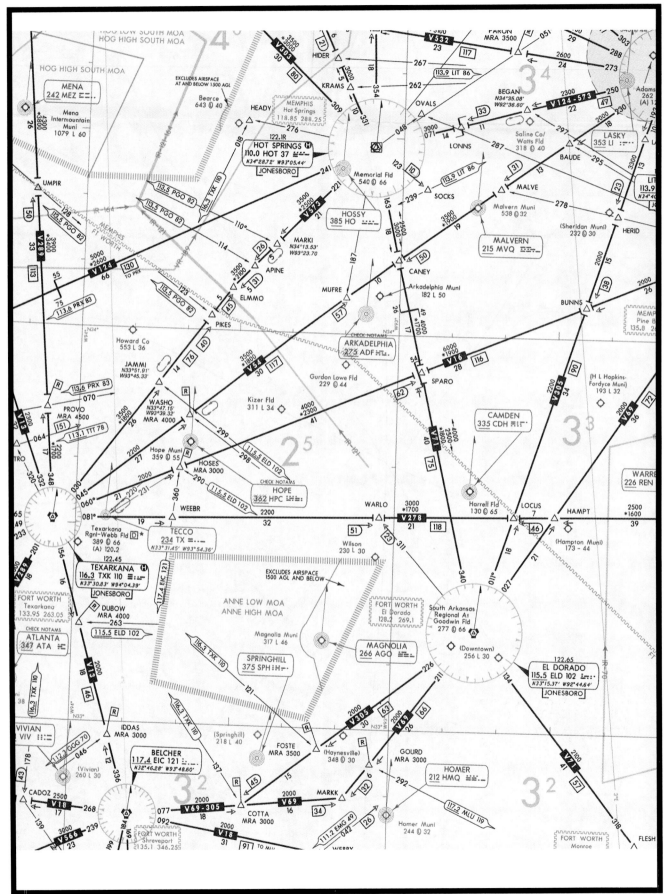

FIGURE 34.—En Route Chart.

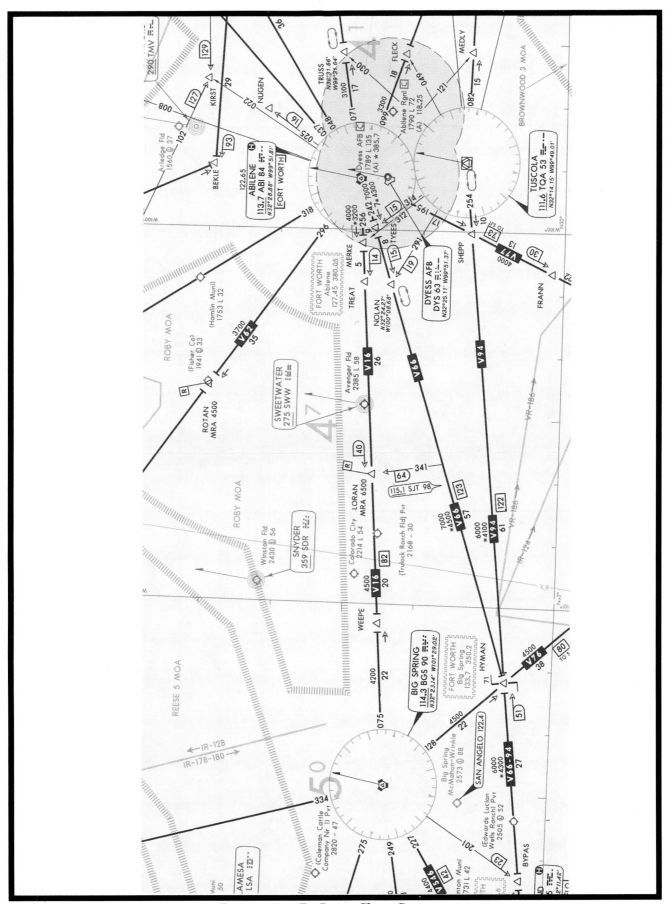

FIGURE 40.—En Route Chart Segment.

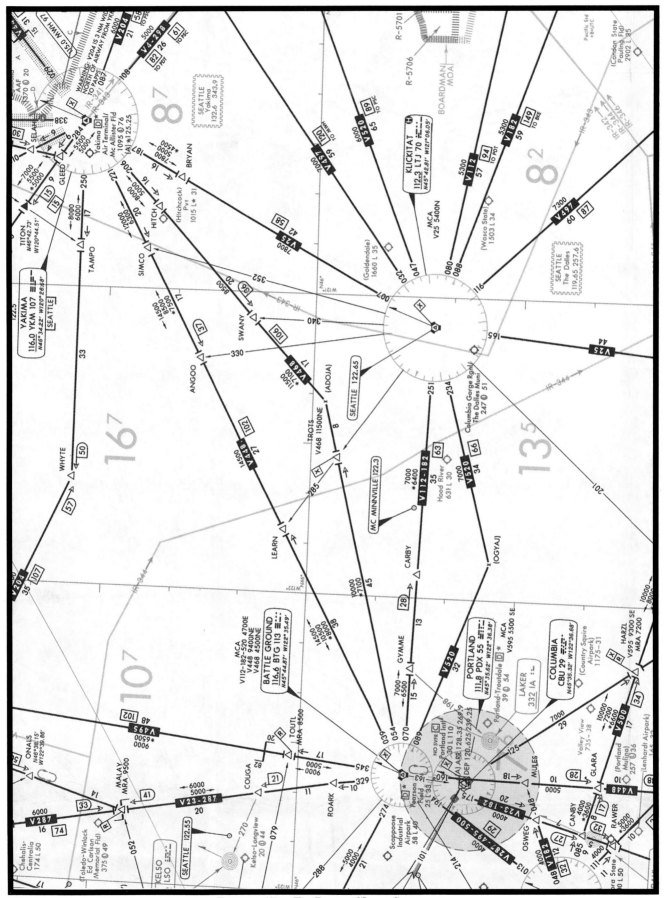

FIGURE 47.—En Route Chart Segment.

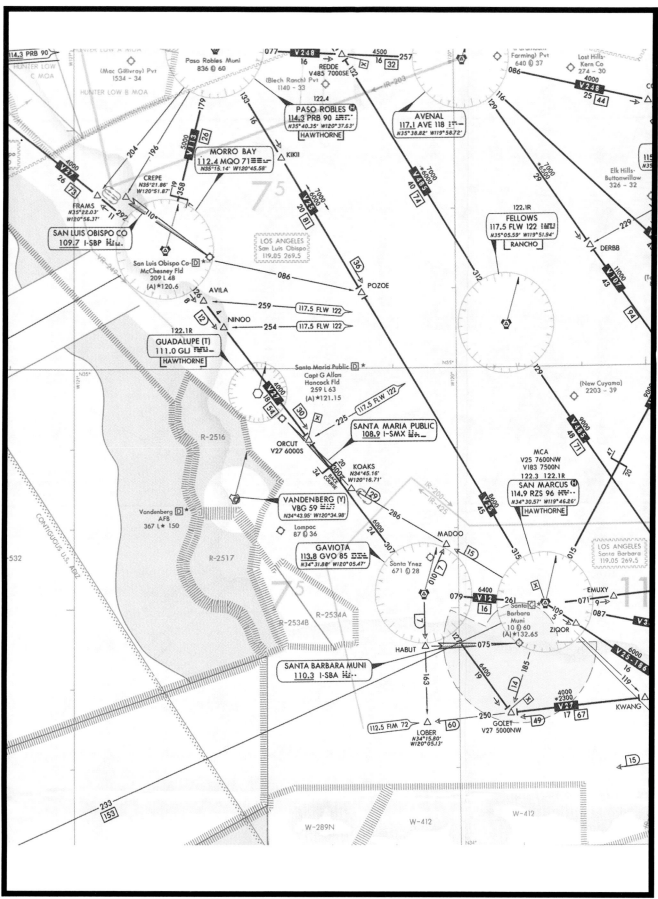

FIGURE 53.—En Route Chart Segment.

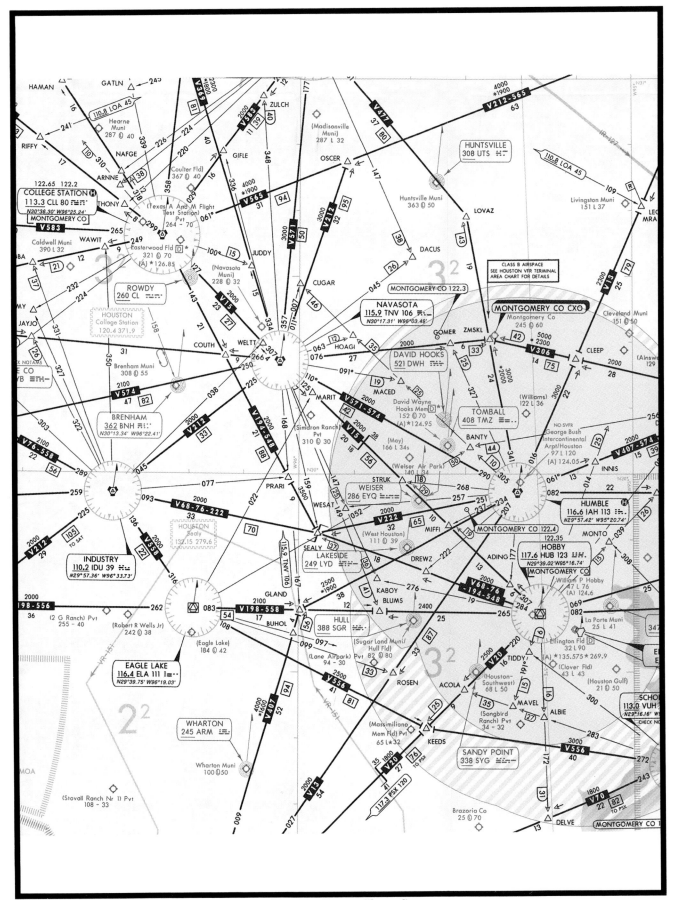

FIGURE 59.—En Route Chart Segment.

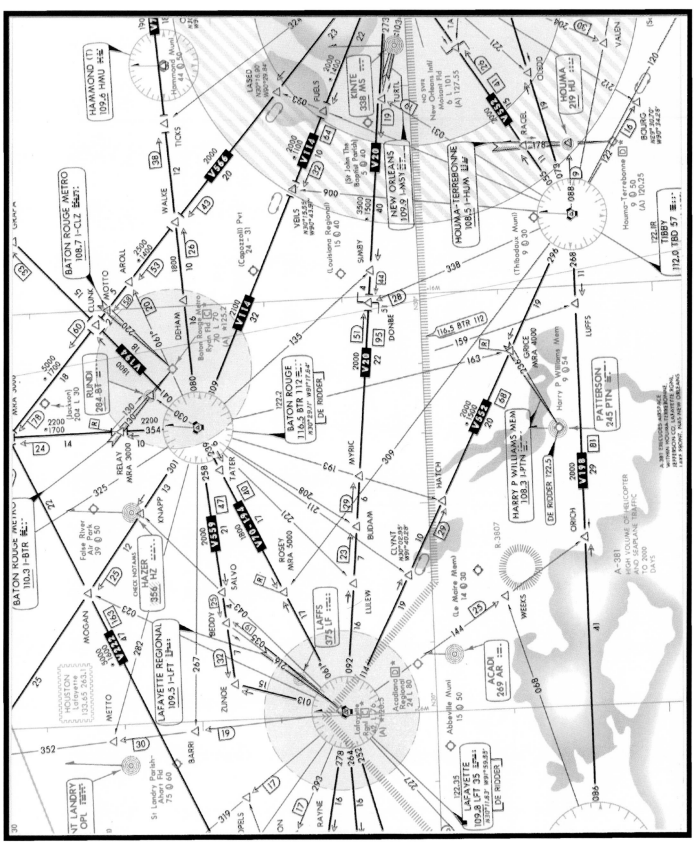

FIGURE 65.—En Route Chart Segment.

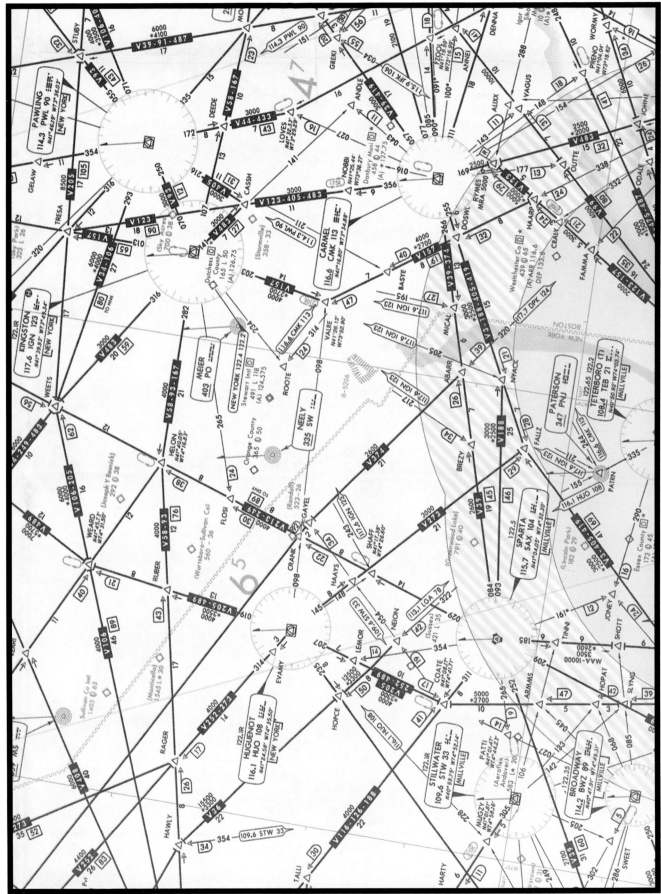

FIGURE 71.—En Route Chart Segment.

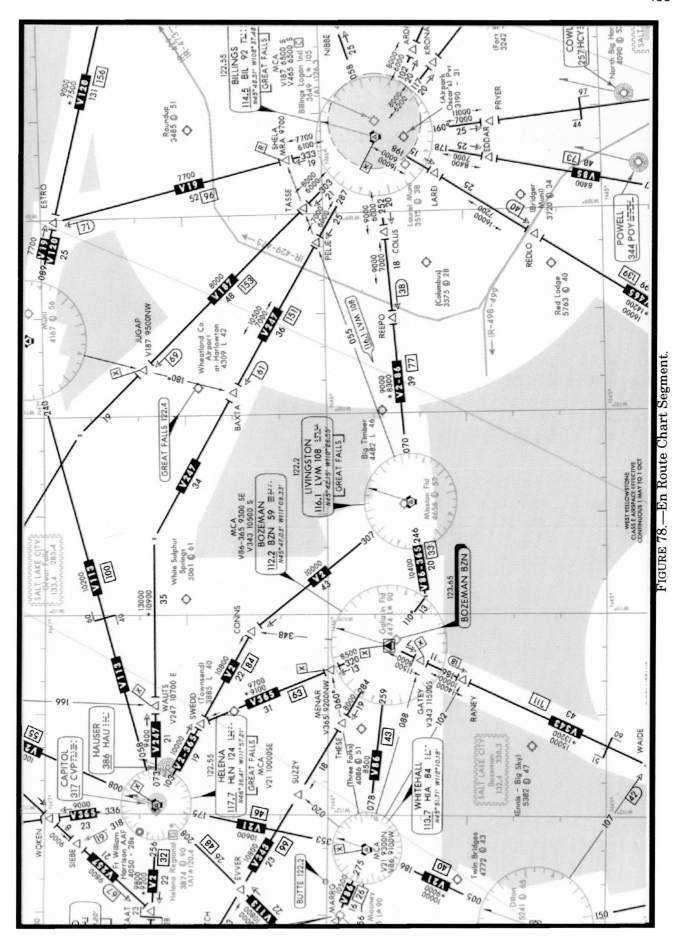

FIGURE 78.—En Route Chart Segment.

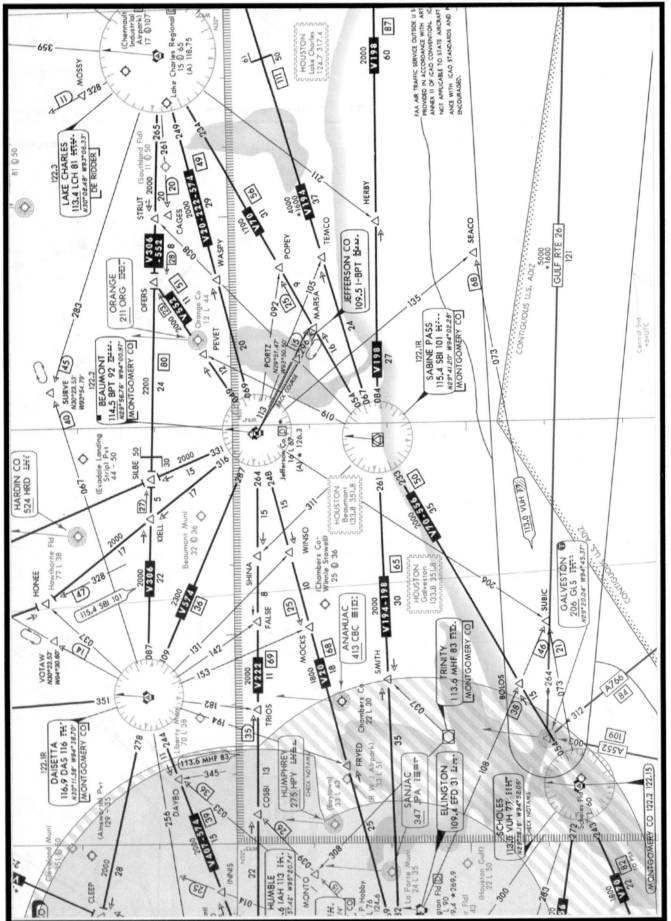

FIGURE 87.—En Route Chart Segment.

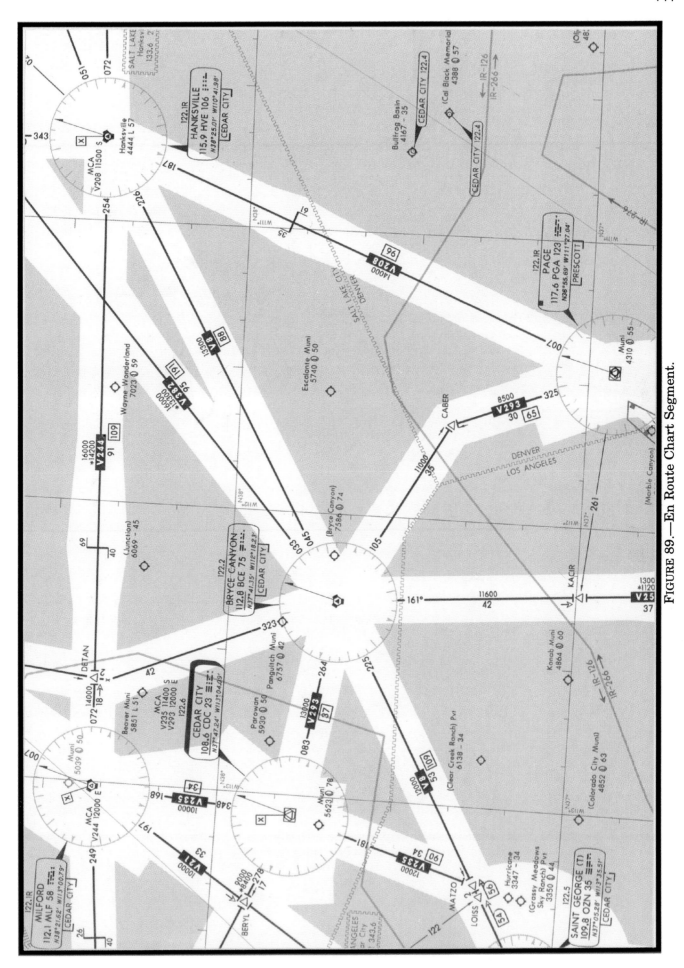

FIGURE 89.—En Route Chart Segment.

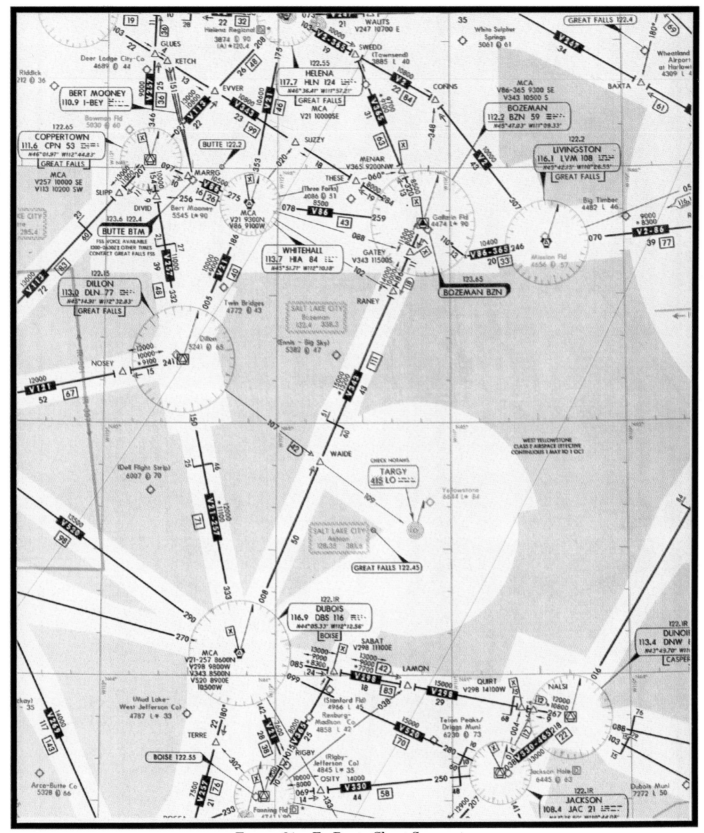

FIGURE 91.—En Route Chart Segment.

| | | | | Form Approved: OMB No. 2120-0034 | | | |

U.S. DEPARTMENT OF TRANSPORTATION
FEDERAL AVIATION ADMINISTRATION
FLIGHT PLAN

(FAA USE ONLY) ☐ PILOT BRIEFING ☐ VNR TIME STARTED SPECIALIST INITIALS
☐ STOPOVER

1. TYPE	2. AIRCRAFT IDENTIFICATION	3. AIRCRAFT TYPE/ SPECIAL EQUIPMENT	4. TRUE AIRSPEED	5. DEPARTURE POINT	6. DEPARTURE TIME		7. CRUISING ALTITUDE
VFR					PROPOSED (Z)	ACTUAL (Z)	
X IFR DVFR	N242T	C310/	160 KTS	HLN			11000

8. ROUTE OF FLIGHT
STAKK2, V365 BZN, V86

9. DESTINATION (Name of airport and city)	10. EST. TIME ENROUTE		11. REMARKS
LOGAN INTL. AIRPORT (BIL)	HOURS	MINUTES	

12. FUEL ON BOARD		13. ALTERNATE AIRPORT(S)	14. PILOT'S NAME, ADDRESS & TELEPHONE NUMBER & AIRCRAFT HOME BASE	15. NUMBER ABOARD
HOURS	MINUTES		17. DESTINATION CONTACT/TELEPHONE (OPTIONAL)	
		N/A		2

16. COLOR OF AIRCRAFT
RED/BLACK/WHITE

CIVIL AIRCRAFT PILOTS. FAR Part 91 requires you file an IFR flight plan to operate under instrument flight rules in controlled airspace. Failure to file could result in a civil penalty not to exceed $1,000 for each violation (Section 901 of the Federal Aviation Act of 1958, as amended). Filing of a VFR flight plan is recommended as a good operating practice. See also Part 99 for requirements concerning DVFR flight plans.

FAA Form 7233-1 (8-82)   CLOSE VFR FLIGHT PLAN WITH _____ FSS ON ARRIVAL

AIRCRAFT INFORMATION

MAKE Cessna   MODEL   310R

N 242T   Vso 72

AIRCRAFT EQUIPMENT/STATUS**

**NOTE: X= OPERATIVE   INOP= INOPERATIVE   N/A= NOT APPLICABLE
TRANSPONDER: X (MODE C) X ILS: (LOCALIZER) X (GLIDE SLOPE) INOP
VOR NO. 1 X (NO. 2) X ADF: X RNAV: N/A
VERTICAL PATH COMPUTER: N/A DME: X
MARKER BEACON: X (AUDIO) X (VISUAL) X

FIGURE 74.—Flight Plan and Aircraft Information.

FLIGHT LOG

HELENA REGIONAL AIRPORT TO BILLINGS LOGAN INTL.

CHECK POINTS		ROUTE	COURSE	WIND	SPEED-KTS		DIST	TIME		FUEL	
FROM	TO	ALTITUDE		TEMP	TAS	GS	NM	LEG	TOT	LEG	TOT
HLN	VESTS	STAKK2 CLIMB	103°					:15:0			
	BZN	V365 11000	140°		160						
	LVM	V86 11000	110° /063°								
	REEPO	V86 11000	067°								
	BIL	V86	069°								
APPROACH & LANDING	LOGAN INTL							:15:0			

OTHER DATA:
NOTE: MAG. VAR. 18° E.

FLIGHT SUMMARY

TIME	FUEL (LB)	
		EN ROUTE
		RESERVE
		MISSED APPR.
		TOTAL

FIGURE 75.—Flight Planning Log.

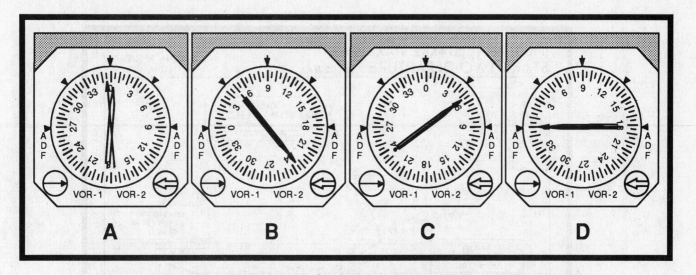

HELENA REGIONAL   (HLN)   2 NE   UTC–7(–6DT)   46°36′25″N 111°58′55″W   GREAT FALLS
    3873   B   S4   FUEL 100LL, JET A   OX 1,3   AOE   ARFF Index B   H-1C, L-9B
RWY 09–27: H9000X150 (ASPH-PFC)   S-100, D-160, DT-250   HIRL   IAP
    RWY 09: VASI(V4L)—GA 3.0°TCH 45′. Ground.   RWY 27: MALSR. VASI(V4L)—GA 3.0°TCH 55′. Rgt tfc.
RWY 05–23: H4599X75 (ASPH-PFC)   S-21, D-30
    RWY 05: Road.   RWY 23: Fence. Rgt tfc.
RWY 16–34: H2979X75 (ASPH)   S-21, D-30   MIRL
    RWY 34: Ground. Rgt tfc.
AIRPORT REMARKS: Attended 1200-0800Z‡. East 2400′ Taxiway C and first 900′ Rwy 27 not visible from tower.
    Prior permission for unscheduled FAR 121 operations, Call 406-442-2821. AOE, 1 hour prior notice required,
    phone 449-1569 1500-0000Z‡, 0000-1500Z‡ 449-1024. Twys A;B; high speed and C (between A and D)
    not available for air carrier use by acft with greater than 30 passenger seats. Rwy 16-34 and Rwy 05-23 (except
    between Rwy 09-27 and Twy D) not available for air carrier use by acft with greater than 30 passenger seats.
    When tower closed, ACTIVATE HIRL Rwy 09-27 and MALSR Rwy 27—CTAF, when twr closed MIRL Rwy 16-34
    are off. Ldg fee for all acft over 12,500 lbs. NOTE: See SPECIAL NOTICE—Simultaneous Operations on
    Intersecting Runways.
COMMUNICATIONS: CTAF 118.3   ATIS 120.4 (Mon-Fri 1300-0700Z‡, Sat-Sun 1300-0500Z‡)
    UNICOM 122.95
    GREAT FALLS FSS (GTF) TF 1-800-WX-BRIEF. NOTAM FILE HLN.
    RCO 122.2 122.1R 117.7T (GREAT FALLS FSS)
    APP/DEP CON 119.5 (Mon-Fri 1300-0700Z‡, Sat-Sun 1300-0500Z‡)
    SALT LAKE CENTER APP/DEP CON 133.4 (Mon-Fri 0700-1300Z‡, Sat-Sun 0500-1300Z‡)
    TOWER 118.3 (Mon-Fri 1300-0700Z‡, Sat-Sun 1300-0500Z‡)   GND CON 121.9
RADIO AIDS TO NAVIGATION: NOTAM FILE HLN.
    (H) VORTAC 117.7   HLN   Chan 124   46°36′25″N 111°57′10″W   254° 1.2 NM to fld. 3810/16E.
        VORTAC unusable:
            006°-090° beyond 25 NM below 11,000′   091°-120° beyond 20 NM below 16,000′
            121°-240° beyond 25 NM below 10,000′   355°-006° beyond 15 NM below 17,500′
            241°-320° beyond 25 NM below 10,000′
CAPITOL NDB (HW) 317   CVP   46°36′24″N 111°56′11″W   254° 1.9 NM to fld.
    NDB unmonitored when tower closed.
HAUSER NDB (MHW) 386   HAU   46°34′08″N 111°45′26″W   268° 9.6 NM to fld.
ILS 110.1 I-HLN Rwy 27 ILS unmonitored when tower closed.

VOR RECEIVER CHECK

Facility Name (Arpt Name)	Freq/Ident	Type Check Pt. Gnd. AB/ALT	Azimuth from Fac. Mag	Dist. from Fac. N.M.	Check Point Description
Helena (Helena Regional)	117.7/HLN	G	237	0.7	On Twy E midway between Twy C and Rwy 27.
Kalispell (Glacier Park Intl)	108.4/FCA	A/4000	316	6.4	Over apch end Rwy 29.
Lewistown (Lewistown Muni)	112.0/LWT	A/5200	072	5.4	Over apch end Rwy 07.
Livingston	116.1/LVM	A/6500	234	5.5	Over northern most radio twr NE of city.
Miles City (Frank Wiley Field)	112.1/MLS	G	036	4.2	On twy leading to Rwy 30.
Missoula (Missoula Intl)	112.8/MSO	G	340	0.6	On edge of ramp in front of Admin Building.

FIGURE 76.— VOR Indications and Excerpts from Airport/Facility Directory (HLN).

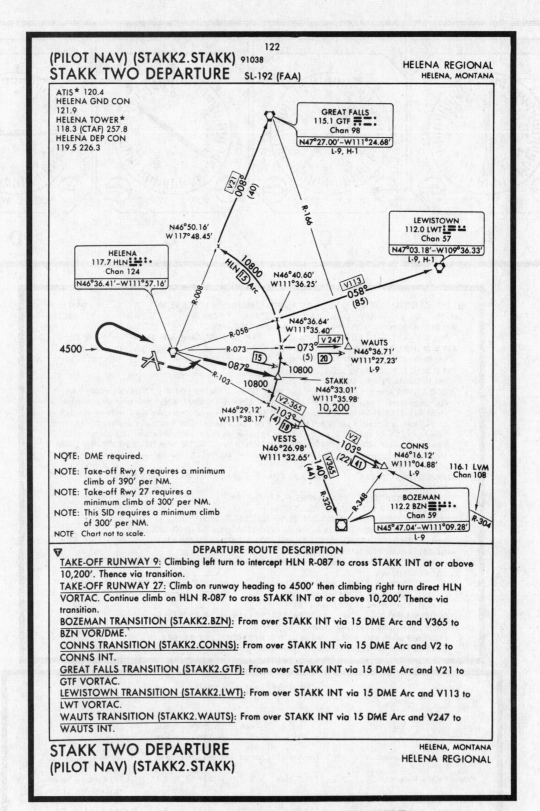

FIGURE 77.— STAKK TWO DEPARTURE.

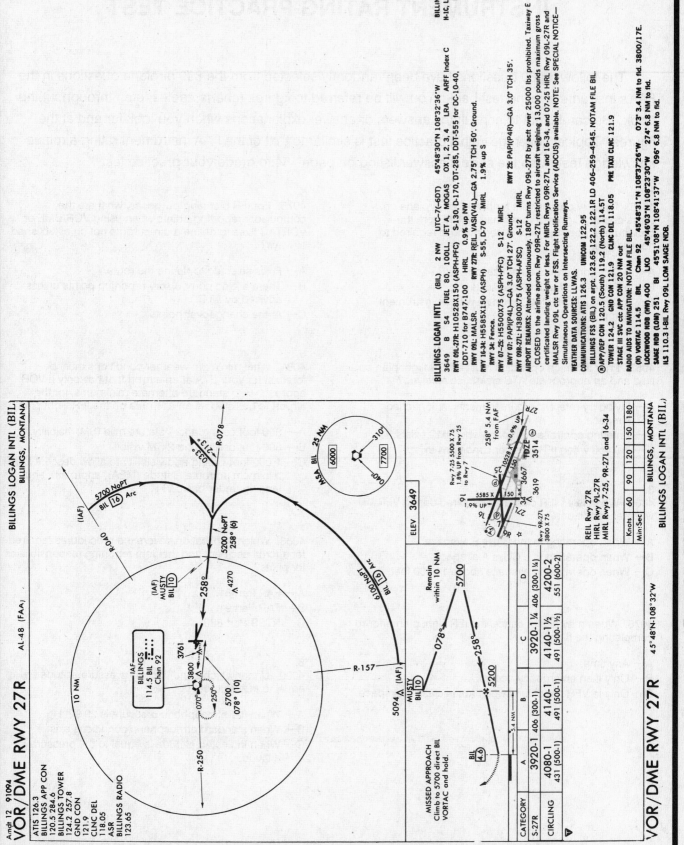

FIGURE 80.—VOR/DME RWY 27R and Airport/Facility Directory (BIL).

APPENDIX A
INSTRUMENT RATING PRACTICE TEST

The following 60 questions have been randomly selected from the 899 airplane questions in the FAA's instrument rating test bank. You will be referred to figures (charts, tables, etc.) throughout this book. Be careful not to consult the answers or answer explanations when you look for and at the figures. Topical coverage in this practice test is similar to that of the FAA instrument rating-airplane knowledge test. Use the correct answer listing on page 454 to grade your practice test.

1.
4035. To carry passengers for hire in an airplane on cross-country flights of more than 50 NM from the departure airport, the pilot in command is required to hold at least

A— a Category II pilot authorization.
B— a First-Class Medical certificate.
C— a Commercial Pilot Certificate with an instrument rating.

2.
4063. Prior to which operation must an IFR flight plan be filed and an appropriate ATC clearance received?

A— Flying by reference to instruments in controlled airspace.
B— Entering controlled airspace when IMC exists.
C— Takeoff when IFR weather conditions exist.

3.
4066. When is an IFR clearance required during VFR weather conditions?

A— When operating in the Class E airspace.
B— When operating in a Class A airspace.
C— When operating in airspace above 14,500 feet.

4.
4076. When may a pilot cancel the IFR flight plan prior to completing the flight?

A— Any time.
B— Only if an emergency occurs.
C— Only in VFR conditions when not in class A airspace.

5.
4078. For IFR planning purposes, what are the compulsory reporting points when using VOR/DME or VORTAC fixes to define a direct route not on established airways?

A— Fixes selected to define the route.
B— There are no compulsory reporting points unless advised by ATC.
C— At the changeover points.

6.
4081. What minimum weather conditions must be forecast for your ETA at an airport that has only a VOR approach with standard alternate minimums, for the airport to be listed as an alternate on the IFR flight plan?

A— 800-foot ceiling and 1 statute mile (SM) visibility.
B— 800-foot ceiling and 2 SM visibility.
C— 1,000-foot ceiling and visibility to allow descent from minimum en route altitude (MEA), approach, and landing under basic VFR.

7.
4088. Which publication covers the procedures required for aircraft accident and incident reporting responsibilities for pilots?

A— FAR Part 61.
B— FAR Part 91.
C— NTSB Part 830.

8.
4090. Under which condition will pressure altitude be equal to true altitude?

A— When the atmospheric pressure is 29.92" Hg.
B— When standard atmospheric conditions exist.
C— When indicated altitude is equal to the pressure altitude.

9.
4108. Which force, in the Northern Hemisphere, acts at a right angle to the wind and deflects it to the right until parallel to the isobars?

A— Centrifugal.
B— Pressure gradient.
C— Coriolis.

10.
4118. What type clouds can be expected when an unstable air mass is forced to ascend a mountain slope?

A— Layered clouds with little vertical development.
B— Stratified clouds with considerable associated turbulence.
C— Clouds with extensive vertical development.

11.
4130. Standing lenticular clouds, in mountainous areas, indicate

A— an inversion.
B— unstable air.
C— turbulence.

12.
4161. Which precipitation type normally indicates freezing rain at higher altitudes?

A— Snow.
B— Hail.
C— Ice pellets.

13.
4167. What situation is most conducive to the formation of radiation fog?

A— Warm, moist air over low, flatland areas on clear, calm nights.
B— Moist, tropical air moving over cold, offshore water.
C— The movement of cold air over much warmer water.

14.
4193. (Refer to figure 2 on page 318.) What approximate wind direction, speed, and temperature (relative to ISA) should a pilot expect when planning for a flight over ALB at FL 270?

A— 270° magnetic at 97 knots; ISA –4 °C.
B— 260° true at 110 knots; ISA +5 °C.
C— 275° true at 97 knots; ISA +4 °C.

15.
4217. (Refer to figure 18, SFC-400MB, on page 323.) The 24-Hour Low Level Significant Weather Prog at 12Z indicates that southwestern West Virginia will likely experience

A— ceilings less than 1,000 feet, visibility less than 3 miles.
B— clear sky and visibility greater than 6 miles.
C— ceilings 1,000 to 3,000 feet and visibility 3 to 5 miles.

16.
4234. (Refer to figure 8 on page 313.) What weather conditions are depicted in the area indicated by arrow E on the Radar Summary Chart?

A— Highest echo tops 30,000 feet MSL, weak to moderate echoes, thunderstorms and rain showers, and cell movement toward northwest at 15 knots.
B— Echo bases 29,000 to 30,000 feet MSL, strong echoes, rain showers increasing in intensity, and area movement toward northwest at 15 knots.
C— Thundershowers decreasing in intensity; area movement toward northwest at 15 knots; echo bases 30,000 feet MSL.

17.
4241. The Hazardous Inflight Weather Advisory Service (HIWAS) is a continuous broadcast over selected VORs of

A— SIGMETs, CONVECTIVE SIGMETs, AIRMETs, Severe Weather Forecast Alerts (AWW), and Center Weather Advisories.
B— SIGMETs, CONVECTIVE SIGMETs, AIRMETs, Wind Shear Advisories, and Severe Weather Forecast Alerts (AWW).
C— Wind Shear Advisories, Radar Weather Reports, SIGMETs, CONVECTIVE SIGMETs, AIRMETs, and Center Weather Advisories (CWA).

18.
4249. (Refer to figure 12 on page 334.) What is the approximate wind direction and velocity at CVG at 34,000 feet (see arrow A)?

A— 040°/35 knots.
B— 097°/40 knots.
C— 230°/35 knots.

19.
4312. (Refer to figure 50 on page 392.) What aircraft equipment code should be entered in block 3 of the flight plan?

A— I.
B— T.
C— U.

20.
4313. (Refer to figure 50 on page 392.) What CAS must be used to maintain the filed TAS at the flight planned altitude? (Temperature 0 °C.)

A— 136 KCAS.
B— 140 KCAS.
C— 147 KCAS.

21.
4314. (Refer to figures 50, 51, and 52 on pages 392 through 394 and figure 53 on page 435.) Determine the time to be entered in block 10 of the flight plan. (Refer to the FD excerpt below, and use the wind entry closest to the flight planned altitude.)

Route of flight . . . . Figures 50, 51, 52, and 53
Flight log and MAG VAR . . . . Figure 51
HABUT ONE DEPARTURE
  and Excerpt from AFD . . . . Figure 52

FT	3000	6000	9000
SBA	0610	2115+05	2525+00

A— 43 minutes.
B— 46 minutes.
C— 51 minutes.

22.
4315. (Refer to figure 52 on page 394 and figure 54 on page 389.) What is the aircraft's position relative to the HABUT intersection? (The VOR-2 is tuned to 116.5.)

A— South of the localizer and past the GVO R-163.
B— North of the localizer and approaching the GVO R-163.
C— South of the localizer and approaching the GVO R-163.

23.
4316. (Refer to figure 52 on page 394.) Using an average groundspeed of 100 knots, what minimum rate of climb would meet the required minimum climb rate per NM as specified by the instrument departure procedure?

A— 425 feet per minute.
B— 580 feet per minute.
C— 642 feet per minute.

24.
4318. (Refer to figure 53 on page 435.) What service is indicated by the inverse "H" symbol in the radio aids to navigation box for PRB VORTAC?

A— VOR with TACAN compatible DME.
B— Availability of HIWAS.
C— En Route Flight Advisory Service available.

25.
4320. (Refer to figure 55 on page 395.) As a guide in making range corrections, how many degrees of relative bearing change should be used for each one-half-mile deviation from the desired arc?

A— 2° to 3°.
B— 5° maximum.
C— 10° to 20°.

26.
4321. (Refer to figure 55 on page 395.) Under which condition should a missed approach procedure be initiated if the runway environment (Paso Robles Municipal Airport) is not in sight?

A— After descending to 1,440 feet MSL.
B— After descent to 1,440 feet or reaching the 1 NM DME, whichever occurs first.
C— When you reach the established missed approach point and determine the visibility is less than 1 mile.

27.
4339. (Refer to figure 65 on page 437 and figure 67 on page 360.) What is the significance of the symbol at GRICE intersection?

A— It signifies a localizer-only approach is available at Harry P. Williams Memorial.
B— The localizer has an additional navigation function.
C— GRICE intersection also serves as the FAF for the ILS approach procedure to Harry P. Williams Memorial.

28.
4410. What indication should a pilot receive when a VOR station is undergoing maintenance and may be considered unreliable?

A— No coded identification, but possible navigation indications.
B— Coded identification, but no navigation indications.
C— A voice recording on the VOR frequency announcing that the VOR is out of service for maintenance.

29.
4419. Which procedure applies to instrument departure procedures?

A— Instrument departure clearances will not be issued unless requested by the pilot.
B— The pilot in command must accept an instrument departure procedure when issued by ATC.
C— If an instrument departure procedure is accepted, the pilot must possess at least a textual description.

30.
4437. If no MCA is specified, what is the lowest altitude for crossing a radio fix, beyond which a higher minimum applies?

A— The MEA at which the fix is approached.
B— The MRA at which the fix is approached.
C— The MOCA for the route segment beyond the fix.

31.
4452. When on a VFR-on-Top clearance, the cruising altitude is based on

A— true course.
B— magnetic course.
C— magnetic heading.

32.
4463. Which procedure should you follow if you experience two-way communications failure while holding at a holding fix with an EFC time? (The holding fix is not the same as the approach fix.)

A— Depart the holding fix to arrive at the approach fix as close as possible to the EFC time.
B— Depart the holding fix at the EFC time.
C— Proceed immediately to the approach fix and hold until EFC.

33.
4494. (Refer to figure 87 on page 440.) At STRUT intersection headed eastbound, ATC instructs you to hold west on the 10 DME fix west of LCH on V306, standard turns. What entry procedure is recommended?

A— Direct.
B— Teardrop.
C— Parallel.

34.
4505. In the event of two-way radio communications failure while operating on an IFR clearance in VFR conditions, the pilot should continue

A— by the route assigned in the last ATC clearance received.
B— the flight under VFR and land as soon as practical.
C— the flight by the most direct route to the fix specified in the last clearance.

35.
4515. (Refer to figure 91 on page 442.) What is the function of the Great Falls RCO (Yellowstone vicinity)?

A— Long range communications outlet for Great Falls Center.
B— Remote communications outlet for Great Falls FSS.
C— Satellite remote controlled by Salt Lake Center with limited service.

36.
4530. (Refer to figure 93 on page 178.) What is the maximum altitude that Class G airspace will exist? (Does not include airspace less than 1,500 feet AGL.)

A— 18,000 feet MSL.
B— 14,500 feet MSL.
C— 14,000 feet MSL.

37.
4558. (Refer to figure 95 on page 102.) On which radial is the aircraft as indicated by the No. 1 NAV?

A— R-175.
B— R-165.
C— R-345.

38.
4566. (Refer to figures 96 and 97 on pages 110 and 111.) To which aircraft position does HSI presentation "D" correspond?

A— 1.
B— 10.
C— 2.

39.
4593. (Refer to figure 105 on page 82.) If the magnetic heading shown for airplane 3 is maintained, which ADF illustration would indicate the airplane is on the 120° magnetic bearing TO the station?

A— 4.
B— 5.
C— 8.

40.
4603. (Refer to figure 108 on page 91.) Where should the bearing pointer be located relative to the wingtip reference to maintain the 16 DME range in a left-hand arc with a left crosswind component?

A— Ahead of the left wingtip reference for the VOR-2.
B— Ahead of the right wingtip reference for the VOR-1.
C— Behind the left wingtip reference for the VOR-2.

41.

4612. (Refer to figure 113 on page 225.) You receive this ATC clearance:

"...CLEARED TO THE XYZ VORTAC. HOLD NORTH ON THE THREE SIX ZERO RADIAL, LEFT TURNS..."

What is the recommended procedure to enter the holding pattern.

A— Parallel only.
B— Direct only.
C— Teardrop only.

42.

4637. When making an instrument approach at the selected alternate airport, what landing minimums apply?

A— Standard alternate minimums (600-2 or 800-2).
B— The IFR alternate minimums listed for that airport.
C— The landing minimums published for the type of procedure selected.

43.

4655. (Refer to figure 124 on page 243.) What options are available concerning the teardrop course reversal for LOC RWY 35 approach to Duncan/Halliburton Field?

A— If a course reversal is required, only the teardrop can be executed.
B— The point where the turn is begun and the type and rate of turn are optional.
C— A normal procedure turn may be made if the 10 DME limit is not exceeded.

44.

4659. (Refer to figure 126 on page 254.) What landing minimums apply for a 14 CFR Part 91 operator at Dothan, AL using a category C aircraft during a circling LOC 31 approach at 120 knots? (DME available.)

A— MDA 860 feet MSL and visibility 2 SM.
B— MDA 860 feet MSL and visibility 1 and ½ SM.
C— MDA 720 feet MSL and visibility 3/4 SM.

45.

4680. (Refer to figure 129 on page 237.) What indication should you get when it is time to turn inbound while in the procedure turn at LABER?

A— 4 DME miles from LABER.
B— 10 DME miles from the MAP.
C— 12 DME miles from LIT VORTAC.

46.

4707. What wind condition prolongs the hazards of wake turbulence on a landing runway for the longest period of time?

A— Direct headwind.
B— Direct tailwind.
C— Light quartering tailwind.

47.

4737. When may you obtain a contact approach?

A— ATC may assign a contact approach if VFR conditions exist or you report the runway in sight and are clear of clouds.
B— ATC may assign a contact approach if you are below the clouds and the visibility is at least 1 mile.
C— ATC will assign a contact approach only upon request if the reported visibility is at least 1 mile.

48.

4748. To remain on the ILS glidepath, the rate of descent must be

A— decreased if the airspeed is increased.
B— decreased if the groundspeed is increased.
C— increased if the groundspeed is increased.

49.

4771. Assume this clearance is received:

"CLEARED FOR ILS RUNWAY 07 LEFT APPROACH, SIDE-STEP TO RUNWAY 07 RIGHT."

When would the pilot be expected to commence the side-step maneuver?

A— As soon as possible after the runway environment is in sight.
B— Any time after becoming aligned with the final approach course of Runway 07 left, and after passing the final approach fix.
C— After reaching the circling minimums for Runway 07 right.

50.

4789. (Refer to figure 136 on page 159.) Which illustration would a pilot observe if the aircraft is "slightly high" (3.2°) on the glidepath?

A— 8.
B— 9.
C— 11.

51.
4797. (Refer to figure 138 on page 154.) What night operations, if any, are authorized between the approach end of the runway and the threshold lights?

A— No aircraft operations are permitted short of the threshold lights.
B— Only taxi operations are permitted in the area short of the threshold lights.
C— Taxi and takeoff operations are permitted, providing the takeoff operations are toward the visible green threshold lights.

52.
4817. Which use of cockpit lighting is correct for night flight?

A— Reducing the interior lighting intensity to a minimum level.
B— The use of regular white light, such as a flashlight, will not impair night adaptation.
C— Coloration shown on maps is least affected by the use of direct red lighting.

53.
4824. (Refer to figures 139 and 140 on page 211.) Which displacement from the localizer and glide slope at the 1.9 NM point is indicated?

A— 710 feet to the left of the localizer centerline and 140 feet below the glide slope.
B— 710 feet to the right of the localizer centerline and 140 feet above the glide slope.
C— 430 feet to the right of the localizer centerline and 28 feet above the glide slope.

54.
4836. What instruments are considered supporting bank instruments during a straight, stabilized climb at a constant rate?

A— Attitude indicator and turn coordinator.
B— Heading indicator and attitude indicator.
C— Heading indicator and turn coordinator.

55.
4874. Which instrument is considered primary for power as the airspeed reaches the desired value during change of airspeed in a level turn?

A— Airspeed indicator.
B— Attitude indicator.
C— Altimeter.

56.
4891. What should be the indication on the magnetic compass as you roll into a standard rate turn to the right from a westerly heading in the Northern Hemisphere?

A— The compass will initially show a turn in the opposite direction, then turn to a northerly indication but lagging behind the actual heading of the aircraft.
B— The compass will remain on a westerly heading for a short time, then gradually catch up to the actual heading of the aircraft.
C— The compass will indicate the approximate correct magnetic heading if the roll into the turn is smooth.

57.
4899. The three conditions which determine pitch attitude required to maintain level flight are

A— flightpath, wind velocity, and angle of attack.
B— airspeed, air density, and aircraft weight.
C— relative wind, pressure altitude, and vertical lift component.

58.
4900. Errors in both pitch and bank indication on an attitude indicator are usually at a maximum as the aircraft rolls out of a

A— 180° turn.
B— 270° turn.
C— 360° turn.

59.
4910. The local altimeter setting should be used by all pilots in a particular area, primarily to provide for

A— the cancellation of altimeter error due to nonstandard temperatures aloft.
B— better vertical separation of aircraft.
C— more accurate terrain clearance in mountainous areas.

60.
4932. (Refer to figure 144 on page 50.) Which illustration indicates a coordinated turn?

A— 3.
B— 1.
C— 2.

For additional practice tests, use *FAA Test Prep* software. Call (800) 87-GLEIM or use the order form at the back of this book to obtain your copy of this software. The advantage of this software is that you cannot cheat (yourself) when taking practice tests. You can make up as many tests as you desire, and you can also have the software rearrange the question sequence and answer order. The questions on each test are randomly selected from the FAA's actual test questions so that the coverage of topics (weather, FARs, etc.) is the same as on the actual FAA test.

PRACTICE TEST LIST OF ANSWERS

Q. #	Answer	Page	Q. #	Answer	Page	Q. #	Answer	Page	Q. #	Answer	Page
1.	C	125	16.	A	314	31.	B	343	46.	C	160
2.	B	138	17.	A	308	32.	B	175	47.	C	207
3.	B	129	18.	C	335	33.	A	345	48.	C	215
4.	C	166	19.	A	390	34.	B	348	49.	A	219
5.	A	171	20.	B	390	35.	B	352	50.	B	159
6.	B	134	21.	C	390	36.	B	179	51.	C	154
7.	C	142	22.	B	389	37.	C	102	52.	A	267
8.	B	36	23.	C	390	38.	C	109	53.	B	210
9.	C	277	24.	B	391	39.	B	83	54.	A	58
10.	C	280	25.	C	391	40.	A	91	55.	A	61
11.	C	286	26.	C	391	41.	C	225	56.	C	26
12.	C	289	27.	B	360	42.	C	229	57.	B	54
13.	A	283	28.	A	98	43.	A	242	58.	A	41
14.	C	317	29.	C	261	44.	B	252	59.	B	30
15.	A	322	30.	A	341	45.	A	236	60.	A	50

APPENDIX B
INTERPOLATION

The following tutorial appeared in the FAA's *Pilot Handbook of Aeronautical Knowledge*.

Interpolation is required in questions found in the following three modules:

Chapter 9 - Aviation Weather Services

Module 9.8, Winds and Temperatures Aloft Forecast (page 317)

Chapter 11 - IFR Flights

Module 11.1, GJT to DRO (page 364)
Module 11.4, SBA to PRB (page 389)

A. To interpolate means to compute intermediate values between a series of given values.

1. In many instances when performance is critical, an accurate determination of the performance values is the only acceptable means to enhance safe flight.

2. Guessing to determine these values should be avoided.

B. Interpolation is simple to perform if the method is understood. The following are examples of how to interpolate or accurately determine the intermediate values between a series of given values.

C. The numbers in column A range from 10 to 30, and the numbers in column B range from 50 to 100. Determine the intermediate numerical value in column B that would correspond with an intermediate value of 20 placed in column A.

A	B
10	50
20	X = Unknown
30	100

1. It can be visualized that 20 is halfway between 10 and 30; therefore, the corresponding value of the unknown number in column B would be halfway between 50 and 100, or 75.

D. Many interpolation problems are more difficult to visualize than the preceding example; therefore, a systematic method must be used to determine the required intermediate value. The following describes one method that can be used.

1. The numbers in Column A range from 10 to 30 with intermediate values of 15, 20, and 25. Determine the intermediate numerical value in column B that would correspond with 15 in column A.

A	B
10	50
15	
20	
25	
30	100

2. First, in column A, determine the relationship of 15 to the range between 10 and 30 as follows:

$$\frac{15 - 10}{30 - 10} = \frac{5}{20} \text{ or } 1/4$$

a. It should be noted that 15 is 1/4 of the range between 10 and 30.

3. Now determine 1/4 of the range of column B between 50 and 100 as follows:

$$100 - 50 = 50$$
$$1/4 \text{ of } 50 = 12.5$$

a. The answer 12.5 represents the number of units, but to arrive at the correct value, 12.5 must be added to the lower number in column B as follows:

$$50 + 12.5 = 62.5$$

4. The interpolation has been completed, and 62.5 is the actual value which is 1/4 of the range of column B.

E. Another method of interpolation is shown below:

1. Using the same numbers as in the previous example, a proportion problem based on the relationship of the number can be set up.

Proportion: $\dfrac{5}{20} = \dfrac{X}{50}$

$$20X = 250$$
$$X = 12.5$$

a. The answer 12.5 must be added to 50 to arrive at the actual value of 62.5.

F. The following example illustrates the use of interpolation applied to a problem dealing with one aspect of airplane performance:

Temperature (°F)	Takeoff Distance (ft)
70	1,173
80	1,356

1. If a distance of 1,173 feet is required for takeoff when the temperature is 70°F and 1,356 feet is required at 80°F, what distance is required when the temperature is 75°F? The solution to the problem can be determined as follows:

$$\frac{5}{10} = \frac{X}{183}$$
$$10X = 915$$
$$X = 91.5$$

a. The answer 91.5 must be added to 1,173 to arrive at the actual value of 1,264.5 ft.

FAA LISTING OF
SUBJECT MATTER KNOWLEDGE CODES

The next five pages reprint the FAA's subject matter codes relating to the instrument rating knowledge test. These are the codes that will appear on your Airman Knowledge Test Report. See the illustration on page 10. Check the Gleim website for any FAA changes to these codes at www.gleim.com/Aviation/Updates/smke-600.html. Your test report will list the subject matter code of each question answered incorrectly. The total number of questions answered incorrectly may differ from the number of subject matter codes shown on the test report since you may have missed more than one question in a certain subject matter code.

When you receive your Airman Knowledge Test Report, you can trace the subject matter codes listed on it to the next five pages to find out the topics with which you had difficulty. You should discuss your knowledge test results with your CFII.

Additionally, you should cross-reference the subject knowledge codes on your Airman Knowledge Test Report to our listing of FAA instrument rating test question numbers beginning on page 462. Determine which Gleim study units you need to review.

The publications listed in the following pages contain study material you need to be familiar with when preparing for the instrument rating knowledge test. All of these publications can be purchased through U.S. Government bookstores, commercial aviation supply houses, or industry organizations.

14 CFR part 61—Certification: Pilots, Flight Instructors, and Ground Instructors

A20	General
A21	Aircraft Ratings and Pilot Authorizations
A22	Student Pilots
A23	Private Pilots
A24	Commercial Pilots
A25	Airline Transport Pilots
A26	Flight Instructors
A27	Ground Instructors
A29	Recreational Pilot

14 CFR part 91—General Operating and Flight Rules

B07	General
B08	Flight Rules - General
B09	Visual Flight Rules
B10	Instrument Flight Rules
B11	Equipment, Instrument, and Certificate Requirements
B12	Special Flight Operations
B13	Maintenance, Preventive Maintenance, and Alterations
B14	Large and Turbine-powered Multiengine Airplanes
B15	Additional Equipment and Operating Requirements for Large and Transport Category Aircraft
B16	Appendix A - Category II Operations: Manual, Instruments, Equipment, and Maintenance
B17	Foreign Aircraft Operations and Operations of U.S.-Registered Civil Aircraft Outside of the U.S.

14 CFR part 97—Standard Instrument Approach Procedures

B97	General

NTSB 830—Rules Pertaining to the Notification and Reporting of Aircraft Accidents or Incidents and Overdue Aircraft, and Preservation of Aircraft Wreckage, Mail, Cargo, and Records

G10	General
G11	Initial Notification of Aircraft Accidents, Incidents, and Overdue Aircraft
G12	Preservation of Aircraft Wreckage, Mail, Cargo, and Records
G13	Reporting of Aircraft Accidents, Incidents, and Overdue Aircraft

AC 61-23—Pilot's Handbook of Aeronautical Knowledge

H300	Forces Acting on the Airplane in Flight
H301	Turning Tendency (Torque Effect)
H302	Airplane Stability
H303	Loads and Load Factors
H304	Airplane Structure
H305	Flight Control Systems
H306	Electrical System
H307	Engine Operation
H308	Propeller
H309	Starting the Engine
H310	Exhaust Gas Temperature Gauge
H311	Aircraft Documents, Maintenance, and Inspections
H312	The Pitot-Static System and Associated Instruments
H313	Gyroscopic Flight Instruments
H314	Magnetic Compass
H315	Weight Control
H316	Balance, Stability, and Center of Gravity

H317	Airplane Performance	H531	Integrated Flight Instruction
H318	Observations	H532	Attitude Flying
H319	Service Outlets	H533	Straight-and-level Flight
H320	Weather Briefings	H534	Turns
H321	Nature of the Atmosphere	H535	Climbs
H322	The Cause of Atmospheric Circulation	H536	Descents
H323	Moisture and Temperature	H538	Slow Flight
H324	Air Masses and Fronts	H539	Stalls
H325	Aviation Weather Reports, Forecasts, and Weather Charts	H540	Spins
H326	Types of Airports	H541	Spin Procedures
H327	Sources for Airport Data	H542	Aircraft Limitations
H328	Airport Markings and Signs	H543	Weight and Balance Requirements
H329	Airport Lighting	H545	Maneuvering by Reference to Ground Objects
H330	Wind Direction Indicators	H546	Performance Maneuvers
H331	Radio Communications	H548	Airport Traffic Patterns and Operations
H332	Air Traffic Services	H549	Normal Approach and Landing
H333	Wake Turbulence	H550	Crosswind Approach and Landing
H334	Collision Avoidance	H551	Short-field Approach and Landing
H335	Controlled Airspace	H552	Soft-field Approach and Landing
H336	Uncontrolled Airspace	H553	Power-off Accuracy Approaches
H337	Special Use Airspace	H554	Faulty Approaches and Landings
H338	Other Airspace Areas	H555	Final Approaches
H339	Aeronautical Charts	H556	Roundout (Flare)
H340	Latitude and Longitude	H557	Touchdown
H341	Effect of Wind	H559	Basic Instrument Training
H342	Basic Calculations	H560	Basic Instrument Flight
H343	Pilotage	H561	Use of Navigation Systems
H344	Dead Reckoning	H562	Use of Radar Services
H345	Flight Planning	H564	Night Vision
H346	Charting the Course	H565	Night Illusions
H347	Filing a VFR Flight Plan	H566	Pilot Equipment
H348	Radio Navigation	H567	Airplane Equipment and Lighting
H349	Obtaining a Medical Certificate	H568	Airport and Navigation Lighting Aids
H350	Health Factors Affecting Pilot Performance	H569	Preparation and Preflight
H351	Environmental Factors Which Affect Pilot Performance	H570	Starting, Taxiing, and Runup
		H571	Takeoff and Climb

FAA-H-8083—Airplane Flying Handbook

		H572	Orientation and Navigation
H501	Choosing a Flight School	H573	Approaches and Landing
H502	Instructor/Student Relationship	H574	Night Emergencies
H503	Role of the FAA	H576	VOR Navigation
H504	Flight Standards District Offices (FSDO's)	H577	VOR/DME RNAV
H505	Study Habits	H578	LORAN-C Navigation
H506	Study Materials	H579	Global Positioning System (GPS)
H507	Collision Avoidance	H580	Radar Services
H509	Pilot Assessment	H582	Systems and Equipment Malfunctions
H510	Preflight Preparation and Flight Planning	H583	Emergency Approaches and Landings (Actual)
H511	Airplane Preflight Inspection	H585	Airplane Systems
H512	Minimum Equipment Lists (MEL's) and Operations with Inoperative Equipment	H586	Pressurized Airplanes
		H587	Oxygen Systems
H513	Cockpit Management	H588	Physiological Altitude Limits
H514	Use of Checklists	H589	Regulatory Requirements
H515	Ground Operations	H591	Multiengine Performance Characteristics
H516	Taxiing	H592	The Critical Engine
H517	Taxi Clearances at Airports with an Operating Control Tower	H593	Vmc for Certification
		H594	Performance
H518	Before Takeoff Check	H595	Factors in Takeoff Planning
H519	After-landing	H596	Accelerates/Stop Distance
H520	Postflight	H597	Propeller Feathering
H522	Terms and Definitions	H598	Use of Trim Tabs
H523	Prior to Takeoff	H599	Preflight Preparation
H524	Normal Takeoff	H600	Checklist
H525	Crosswind Takeoff	H601	Taxiing
H526	Short-field Takeoff and Climb	H602	Normal Takeoffs
H527	Soft-field Takeoff and Climb	H603	Crosswind Takeoffs
H528	Rejected Takeoff	H604	Short-field or Obstacle Clearance Takeoff
H529	Noise Abatement	H605	Stalls

H606   Emergency Descent
H607   Approaches and Landings
H608   Crosswind Landings
H609   Short-field Landing
H610   Go-around Procedure
H611   Engine Inoperative Emergencies
H612   Engine Inoperative Procedures
H613   Vmc Demonstrations
H614   Engine Failure Before Lift-off (Rejected Takeoff)
H615   Engine Failure After Lift-off
H616   Engine Failure En Route
H617   Engine Inoperative Approach and Landing
H618   Types of Decisions
H619   Effectiveness of ADM

FAA-H-8083-15—Instrument Flying Handbook

Human Factors

H800   Sensory Systems
H801   Spatial Disorientation
H802   Optical Illusions
H803   Physiological and Psychological Factors
H804   Medical Factors
H805   Aeronautical Decision Making
H806   Crew/Cockpit Resource Management

Aerodynamics

H807   Basic Aerodynamics

Flight Instruments

H808   Pitot Static
H809   Compass
H810   Gyroscopic
H811   Flight Director
H812   Systems Preflight

Airplane Attitude Instrument Flying

H813   Fundamental Skills

Airplane Basic Flight Maneuvers

H814   Straight-and-level Flight
H815   Straight Climbs and Descents
H816   Turns
H817   Approach to Stall
H818   Unusual Attitude Recoveries
H819   Instrument Takeoff
H820   Instrument Flight Patterns

Helicopter Attitude Instrument Flying

H821   Instrument Flight
H822   Straight-and-level
H823   Straight Climbs
H824   Straight Descents
H825   Turns
H826   Unusual Attitude Recoveries
H827   Emergencies
H828   Instrument Takeoff

Navigation Systems

H829   Basic Radio Principles
H830   Nondirectional Beacon (NDB)
H831   Very High Frequency Omnidirectional Range (VOR)
H832   Distance Measuring Equipment (DME)
H833   Area Navigation (RNAV)
H834   Long Range Navigation (LORAN)
H835   Global Positioning System (GPS)

H836   Inertia Navigation System (INS)
H837   Instrument Landing System (ILS)
H838   Microwave Landing System (MLS)
H839   Flight Management Systems (FMS)
H840   Head-up Display (HUD)
H841   Radar Navigation (Ground Based)

National Airspace System

H842   IFR Enroute Charts
H843   U.S. Terminal Procedures Publications
H844   Instrument Approach Procedures

Air Traffic Control Systems

H845   Communications Equipment
H846   Communications Procedures
H847   Communications Facilities

IFR Flight

H848   Planning
H849   Clearances
H850   Departures
H851   Enroute
H852   Holding
H853   Arrival
H854   Approaches
H855   Flying Experience
H856   Weather Conditions
H857   Conducting an IFR Flight

Emergency Operations

H858   Unforecast Adverse Weather
H859   Aircraft System Malfunction
H860   Communication/Navigation System Malfunction
H861   Loss of Situational Awareness

Glossary

H862   Glossary

AC 61-27—Instrument Flying Handbook

I01   Training Considerations
I02   Instrument Flying: Coping with Illusions in Flight
I03   Aerodynamic Factors Related to Instrument Flying
I04   Basic Flight Instruments
I05   Attitude Instrument Flying — Airplanes
I06   Attitude Instrument Flying — Helicopters
I07   Electronic Aids to Instrument Flying
I08   Using the Navigation Instruments
I09   Radio Communications Facilities and Equipment
I10   The Federal Airways System and Controlled Airspace
I11   Air Traffic Control
I12   ATC Operations and Procedures
I13   Flight Planning
I14   Appendix: Instrument Instructor Lesson Guide — Airplanes
I15   Segment of En Route Low Altitude Chart

AC 00-6—Aviation Weather

I20	The Earth's Atmosphere
I21	Temperature
I22	Atmospheric Pressure and Altimetry
I23	Wind
I24	Moisture, Cloud Formation, and Precipitation
I25	Stable and Unstable Air
I26	Clouds
I27	Air Masses and Fronts
I28	Turbulence
I29	Icing
I30	Thunderstorms
I31	Common IFR Producers
I32	High Altitude Weather
I33	Arctic Weather
I34	Tropical Weather
I35	Soaring Weather
I36	Glossary of Weather Terms

AC 00-45—Aviation Weather Services

I54	The Aviation Weather Service Program
I55	Aviation Routine Weather Report (METAR)
I56	Pilot and Radar Reports, Satellite Pictures, and Radiosonde Additional Data (RADATs)
I57	Aviation Weather Forecasts
I58	Surface Analysis Chart
I59	Weather Depiction Chart
I60	Radar Summary Chart
I61	Constant Pressure Analysis Charts
I62	Composite Moisture Stability Chart
I63	Winds and Temperatures Aloft Chart
I64	Significant Weather Prognostic Charts
I65	Convective Outlook Chart
I66	Volcanic Ash Advisory Center Products
I67	Turbulence Locations, Conversion and Density Altitude Tables, Contractions and Acronyms, Station Identifiers, WSR-88D Sites, and Internet Addresses

AIM—Aeronautical Information Manual

J01	Air Navigation Radio Aids
J02	Radar Services and Procedures
J03	Airport Lighting Aids
J04	Air Navigation and Obstruction Lighting
J05	Airport Marking Aids and Signs
J06	Airspace — General
J07	Class G Airspace
J08	Controlled Airspace
J09	Special Use Airspace
J10	Other Airspace Areas
J11	Service Available to Pilots
J12	Radio Communications Phraseology and Techniques
J13	Airport Operations
J14	ATC Clearance/Separations
J15	Preflight
J16	Departure Procedures
J17	En Route Procedures
J18	Arrival Procedures
J19	Pilot/Controller Roles and Responsibilities
J20	National Security and Interception Procedures
J21	Emergency Procedures — General
J22	Emergency Services Available to Pilots
J23	Distress and Urgency Procedures
J24	Two-Way Radio Communications Failure
J25	Meteorology
J26	Altimeter Setting Procedures
J27	Wake Turbulence
J28	Bird Hazards, and Flight Over National Refuges, Parks, and Forests
J29	Potential Flight Hazards
J30	Safety, Accident, and Hazard Reports
J31	Fitness for Flight
J32	Type of Charts Available
J33	Pilot Controller Glossary

Other Documents

J34	Airport/Facility Directory
J35	En Route Low Altitude Chart
J36	En Route High Altitude Chart
J37	Sectional Chart
J39	Terminal Area Chart
J40	Instrument Departure Procedure Chart
J41	Standard Terminal Arrival (STAR) Chart
J42	Instrument Approach Procedures
J43	Helicopter Route Chart

ADDITIONAL ADVISORY CIRCULARS

K01	AC 00-24, Thunderstorms
K02	AC 00-30, Atmospheric Turbulence Avoidance
K03	AC 00-34, Aircraft Ground Handling and Servicing
K04	AC 00-54, Pilot Wind Shear Guide
K05	AC 00-55, Announcement of Availability: FAA Order 8130.21A
K06	AC 43-4, Corrosion Control for Aircraft
K11	AC 20-34, Prevention of Retractable Landing Gear Failures
K12	AC 20-32, Carbon Monoxide (CO) Contamination in Aircraft — Detection and Prevention
K13	AC 20-43, Aircraft Fuel Control
K20	AC 20-103, Aircraft Engine Crankshaft Failure
K23	AC 20-121, Airworthiness Approval of Airborne Loran-C Navigation Systems for Use in the U.S. National Airspace System
K26	AC 20-138, Airworthiness Approval of Global Positioning System (GPS) Navigation Equipment for Use as a VFR and IFR Supplemental Navigation System
K40	AC 25-4, Inertial Navigation Systems (INS)
K45	AC 39-7, Airworthiness Directives
K46	AC 43-9, Maintenance Records
K47	AC 43.9-1, Instructions for Completion of FAA Form 337
K48	AC 43-11, Reciprocating Engine Overhaul Terminology and Standards
K49	AC 43.13-1, Acceptable Methods, Techniques, and Practices - Aircraft Inspection and Repair
K50	AC 43.13-2, Acceptable Methods, Techniques, and Practices - Aircraft Alterations
K80	AC 60-4, Pilot's Spatial Disorientation
L05	AC 60-22, Aeronautical Decision Making
L10	AC 61-67, Stall Spin Awareness Training
L15	AC 61-107, Operations of Aircraft at Altitudes Above 25,000 Feet MSL and/or MACH numbers (Mmo) Greater Than .75
L25	FAA-G-8082-11, Inspection Authorization Knowledge Test Guide
L34	AC 90-48, Pilots' Role in Collision Avoidance
L42	AC 90-87, Helicopter Dynamic Rollover
L44	AC 90-94, Guidelines for Using Global Positioning System Equipment for IFR En Route and Terminal Operations and for Nonprecision Instrument Approaches in the U.S. National Airspace System

L45   AC 90-95, Unanticipated Right Yaw in Helicopters
L50   AC 91-6, Water, Slush, and Snow on the Runway
L52   AC 91-13, Cold Weather Operation of Aircraft
L53   AC 91-14, Altimeter Setting Sources
L57   AC 91-43, Unreliable Airspeed Indications
L59   AC 91-46, Gyroscopic Instruments — Good Operating
      Practices
L61   AC 91-50, Importance of Transponder Operation and
      Altitude Reporting
L62   AC 91-51, Effect of Icing on Aircraft Control and
      Airplane Deice and Anti-Ice Systems
L70   AC 91-67, Minimum Equipment Requirements for
      General Aviation Operations Under FAR Part 91
L80   AC 103-4, Hazard Associated with Sublimation of Solid
      Carbon Dioxide (Dry Ice) Aboard Aircraft
L90   AC 105-2, Sport Parachute Jumping
M01   AC 120-12, Private Carriage Versus Common Carriage
      of Persons or Property
M02   AC 120-27, Aircraft Weight and Balance Control
M08   AC 120-58, Pilot Guide for Large Aircraft Ground Deicing
M13   AC 121-195-1, Operational Landing Distances for Wet
      Runways; Transport Category Airplanes
M35   AC 135-17, Pilot Guide — Small Aircraft Ground Deicing
M51   AC 20-117, Hazards Following Ground Deicing and Ground
      Operations in Conditions Conducive to Aircraft Icing
M52   AC 00-2, Advisory Circular Checklist

FAA Accident Prevention Program Bulletins

V01   FAA-P-8740-2, Density Altitude
V02   FAA-P-8740-5, Weight and Balance
V03   FAA-P-8740-12, Thunderstorms
V04   FAA-P-8740-19, Flying Light Twins Safely
V05   FAA-P-8740-23, Planning your Takeoff
V06   FAA-P-8740-24, Tips on Winter Flying
V07   FAA-P-8740-25, Always Leave Yourself an Out
V08   FAA-P-8740-30, How to Obtain a Good Weather
      Briefing
V09   FAA-P-8740-40, Wind Shear
V10   FAA-P-8740-41, Medical Facts for Pilots
V11   FAA-P-8740-44, Impossible Turns
V12   FAA-P-8740-48, On Landings, Part I
V13   FAA-P-8740-49, On Landings, Part II
V14   FAA-P-8740-50, On Landings, Part III
V15   FAA-P-8740-51, How to Avoid a Midair Collision
V16   FAA-P-8740-52, The Silent Emergency

NOTE: AC 00-2, Advisory Circular Checklist, transmits the
status of all FAA advisory circulars (AC's), as well as FAA
internal publications and miscellaneous flight information, such
as Aeronautical Information Manual, Airport/Facility Directory,
knowledge test guides, practical test standards, and other
material directly related to a certificate or rating. To obtain a
free copy of AC 00-2, send your request to:

U.S. Department of Transportation
Subsequent Distribution Office, SVC-121.23
Ardmore East Business Center
3341 Q 75th Ave.
Landover, MD 20785

CROSS-REFERENCES TO THE FAA KNOWLEDGE TEST QUESTION NUMBERS

Pages 462 through 468 contain the FAA question numbers from the instrument pilot knowledge test bank. The questions are numbered 4001 to 0601-944. To the right of each FAA question number*, we have added the FAA's subject matter knowledge code. To the right of the subject matter knowledge code, we have listed our answer and our chapter and question number. For example, the FAA's question 4002 is cross-referenced to the FAA's subject matter knowledge code A24, "FAR Part 61, Commercial Pilots." The correct answer is C, and the question appears with answer explanations in our book under 4-19, which means it is reproduced in Chapter 4 as question 19. Non-airplane questions (omitted from this book) are indicated as NA.

The first line of each of our answer explanations in Chapters 1 through 11 contains

1. The correct answer
2. The FAA question number
3. A reference for the answer explanation, e.g., *FTH Chap 1*. If this reference is not practical, use the following chart to identify the subject matter knowledge code to determine which reference is appropriate for the question.

Thus, our question numbers are cross-referenced throughout this book to the FAA question numbers, and these seven pages cross-reference the FAA question numbers back to this book.

FAA		GLEIM		FAA		GLEIM		FAA		GLEIM	
Q. No.	Subject Code	Answer	Chap/ Q. No.	Q. No.	Subject Code	Answer	Chap/ Q. No.	Q. No.	Subject Code	Answer	Chap/ Q. No.
4001	A20	A	4-7	4027	A20	A	4-8	4053	B11	C	4-72
4002	A24	C	4-19	4028	A20	C	4-20	4054	B10	A	4-60
4003	B08	C	4-25	4029	A20	B	4-21	4055	B11	C	4-69
4004	B07	A	4-23	4030	A20	NA		4056	I05	B	1-20
4005	B10	B	4-46	4031	A20	B	4-1	4057	B11	C	4-71b
4006	B10	C	4-68	4032	B10	B	4-45	4058	J15	C	5-54
4007	B11	B	4-80	4033	B08	C	4-24	4059	J15	B	5-50
4008	A20	A	4-5	4034	A20	C	4-18	4060	J15	A	5-51
4009	A20	B	4-4	4035	A20	C	4-17	4061	J15	A	5-52
4010	A20	B	4-3	4036	B10	C	4-58	4062	B10	C	4-35
4011	B08	A	4-26	4037	B11	B	4-76	4063	B10	B	4-66
4012	A20	A	4-9	4038	B11	A	4-77	4064	B10	A	4-65
4013	A20	A	4-12	4039	B07	C	4-22	4065	B10	C	4-64
4014	A20	B	4-11	4040	B10	NA		4066	B10	B	4-34
4015	A20	A	4-14	4041	B10	NA		4067	B10	B	4-36
4016	A20	NA		4042	B11	C	4-75	4068	B10	C	4-63
4017	A20	A	4-13	4043	B11	A	4-71a	4069	I07	A	5-55
4018	A20	NA		4044	B10	B	4-59	4070	J34	B	6-151
4019	A20	NA		4045	B11	C	4-74	4071	J15	B	5-82
4020	A20	A	4-15	4046	B10	A	4-57	4072	J15	C	5-45
4021	A20	B	4-6	4047	B13	C	4-81	4073	J15	B	5-48
4022	A20	NA		4048	B10	A	4-61	4074	J15	A	5-47
4023	A20	A	4-10	4049	B13	C	4-82	4075	J15	C	5-46
4024	A20	C	4-33	4050	B11	A	4-70	4076	J15	C	5-53
4025	A20	B	4-2	4051	B11	C	4-71	4077	J15	A	5-95
4026	A20	B	4-16	4052	B11	C	4-73	4078	J15	A	5-71

*In June 2001, the FAA test bank was released without the familiar four-digit FAA question numbers. We identified all of the new questions and added them to the end of our cross-reference chart using our own question numbering system. The first four digits of this code refer to the month and year the question first appeared. The remaining digits identify the question number used in that particular FAA test bank release.

FAA Q. No.	Subject Code	GLEIM Answer	Chap/Q. No.	FAA Q. No.	Subject Code	GLEIM Answer	Chap/Q. No.	FAA Q. No.	Subject Code	GLEIM Answer	Chap/Q. No.
4079	J34	C	5-41	4135	I30	C	8-75	4191	I63	C	9-44
4080	J06	C	5-39	4136	I27	A	8-12	4192	I63	C	9-36
4081	B10	B	4-50	4137	I30	C	8-15	4193	I63	C	9-35
4082	B10	C	4-47	4138	I28	C	8-76	4194	I63	A	9-37
4083	B10	C	4-51	4139	I28	C	8-74	4195	I61	C	9-58
4084	B10	NA		4140	I28	A	8-13	4196	I55	A	9-10
4085	B10	A	4-53	4141	I27	C	8-61	4197	I65	A	9-56
4086	B10	C	4-52	4142	I57	A	8-60	4198	I56	A	9-13
4087	B10	A	4-54	4143	I30	B	8-59	4199	I63	B	9-38
4088	G10	C	4-83	4144	I30	A	8-58	4200	I21	A	8-30
4089	I22	A	1-43	4145	I30	B	8-57	4201	I57	C	9-33
4090	I22	B	1-42	4146	I30	C	8-56	4202	I55	C	9-8
4091	I22	C	1-46	4147	I30	B	8-55	4203	I57	A	9-9
4092	I31	A	8-63	4148	I30	C	8-54	4204	I57	C	9-27
4093	I22	B	1-45	4149	I28	A	8-53	4205	I55	C	9-7
4094	I21	C	8-32	4150	I28	C	8-72	4206	I59	B	9-16
4095	I21	C	9-39	4151	I29	C	8-70	4207	I59	B	9-15
4096	I21	A	8-1	4152	I29	C	8-64	4208	I59	C	9-14
4097	I20	C	8-7	4153	I29	B	8-67	4209	I58	C	9-61
4098	I27	C	8-22	4154	I20	C	8-9	4210	I67	A	8-73
4099	I24	C	8-69	4155	I32	C	8-8	4211	I64	A	9-48
4100	I29	C	8-45	4156	I31	A	8-41	4212	I64	C	9-47
4101	I24	A	8-44	4157	I26	C	8-52	4213	I64	A	9-46
4102	I24	A	8-68	4158	I27	C	8-6	4214	I64	C	9-45
4103	I24	B	8-42	4159	I24	B	8-23	4215	I65	B	9-62
4104	I24	A	8-43	4160	I30	B	2-65	4216	I64	B	9-52
4105	I23	B	8-5	4161	I24	C	8-66	4217	I64	A	9-51
4106	I23	B	8-4	4162	I32	C	8-40	4218	I64	A	9-50
4107	I23	B	8-3	4163	I31	B	8-39	4219	I64	A	9-49
4108	I23	C	8-2	4164	I31	A	8-38	4220	I56	C	9-12
4109	I22	B	1-44	4165	I31	A	8-37	4221	I64	C	9-70
4110	I22	B	1-37	4166	I31	C	8-36	4222	I64	C	9-69
4111	I22	A	1-29	4167	I31	A	8-34	4223	I64	B	9-67
4112	I21	A	8-35	4168	I32	B	8-10	4224	I64	B	9-68
4113	I21	B	8-71	4169	I31	C	8-33	4225	I64	C	9-66
4114	I21	A	8-29	4170	I57	B	9-32	4226	I57	B	9-60
4115	I25	C	8-21	4171	I29	C	8-65	4227	I20	C	8-11
4116	I27	A	8-20	4172	I63	A	9-40	4228	I43	C	9-26
4117	I27	B	8-19	4173	I61	B	9-59	4229	I64	B	9-71
4118	I25	C	8-18	4174	I60	A	9-24	4230	I60	C	9-17
4119	I27	C	8-17	4175	I64	A	9-63	4231	I60	B	9-20
4120	I27	C	8-27	4176	I57	C	9-31	4232	I60	C	9-19
4121	I25	B	8-26	4177	I57	A	9-30	4233	I60	B	9-18
4122	I25	B	8-25	4178	I57	B	9-29	4234	I60	A	9-21
4123	I25	C	8-24	4179	I57	C	9-34	4235	I60	B	9-25
4124	I25	A	8-28	4180	I57	A	9-28	4236	I60	A	9-23
4125	I21	A	8-31	4181	I57	B	9-3	4237	I60	A	9-22
4126	I30	A	8-62	4182	I56	B	9-11	4238	I23	C	8-77
4127	I27	A	8-14	4183	I57	A	9-4	4239	I65	C	9-53
4128	I27	B	8-16	4184	I56	C	9-57	4240	I65	C	9-54
4129	I28	B	8-51	4185	I57	C	9-65	4241	I54	A	9-6
4130	I28	C	8-50	4186	I57	C	9-64	4242	I64	B	9-71a
4131	I26	B	8-49	4187	I57	C	9-2	4243	I64	C	9-72
4132	I28	B	8-48	4188	I63	B	9-42	4244	I64	C	9-73
4133	I29	B	8-47	4189	I63	C	9-41	4245	I64	C	9-71b
4134	I26	C	8-46	4190	I63	B	9-43	4246	I63	A	9-76

FAA Q. No.	FAA Subject Code	GLEIM Answer	GLEIM Chap/Q. No.	FAA Q. No.	FAA Subject Code	GLEIM Answer	GLEIM Chap/Q. No.	FAA Q. No.	FAA Subject Code	GLEIM Answer	GLEIM Chap/Q. No.
4247	I63	C	9-77	4303	J40	C	11-21	4359	H342	B	11-81
4248	I65	A	9-55	4304	J40	A	11-23	4360	H342	C	11-82
4249	I63	C	9-78	4305	J34	B	11-24	4361	J40	B	11-83
4250	I63	B	9-79	4306	J42	A	11-28	4362	J01	C	11-84
4251	J25	C	8-80	4307	J42	B	11-29	4363	J40	C	11-85
4252	J25	C	8-79	4308	I10	C	11-30	4364	J40	C	11-86
4253	J25	C	8-78	4309	J42	C	11-31	4365	J34	C	11-87
4254	J25	C	8-85	4310	J42	C	11-32	4366	J35	B	11-88
4255	J25	C	8-81	4311	J42	C	11-33	4367	J35	C	11-90
4256	J25	C	8-82	4312	J15	A	11-36	4368	J42	B	11-92
4257	J25	A	8-83	4313	H342	B	11-37	4369	J42	B	11-93
4258	J25	B	8-84	4314	H342	C	11-38	4370	J35	B	11-89
4259	H342	A	11-2	4315	J40	B	11-34	4371	J42	B	11-91
4260	H342	A	11-1	4316	J40	C	11-35	4372	J01	A	4-62
4261	J17	A	11-4	4317	J35	A	11-39	4373	J02	B	5-36
4262	J35	B	11-5	4318	J35	B	11-40	4374	J24	A	5-91a
4263	J35	B	11-6	4319	J42	A	11-41	4375	J08	B	4-30
4264	J35	C	11-7	4320	H832	C	11-42	4376	J01	C	3-40
4265	H342	A	11-3	4321	J42	C	11-43	4377	J01	B	3-38
4266	J15	C	11-8	4322	J15	NA		4378	J01	B	3-34
4267	H342	B	11-9	4323	H342	NA		4379	J12	C	5-86
4268	H342	C	11-10	4324	H342	NA		4380	J14	B	5-69
4269	H832	A	11-11	4325	J34	B	10-53	4381	J21	A	4-29
4270	H342	C	11-12	4326	J01	A	10-54	4382	J01	A	3-42
4271	J40	A	11-13	4327	J34	A	10-55	4383	J01	B	3-36
4272	J40	B	11-15	4328	J42	NA		4384	J01	B	3-37
4273	J01	C	11-14	4329	J08	NA		4385	J01	C	3-43
4274	J42	A	11-16	4330	J42	NA		4386	J01	C	3-39
4275	J34	B	11-17	4331	J42	C	6-138	4387	J01	C	3-41
4276	J42	B	11-18	4332	J42	C	6-137	4388	J01	C	3-32
4277	J15	C	11-45	4333	J15	NA		4389	J01	A	3-33
4278	H342	B	11-46	4334	H342	NA		4390	J11	B	5-72
4279	H342	A	11-44	4335	H342	NA		4391	J01	A	3-35
4280	J35	A	11-47	4336	J35	C	10-57	4392	J14	B	5-63
4281	J41	A	11-48	4337	J34	A	10-56	4393	J14	C	5-67
4282	H833	B	11-49	4338	J35	A	10-58	4394	J16	B	5-61
4283	H833	A	11-50	4339	J35	B	10-59	4395	J14	B	5-56
4284	K26	A	3-84	4340	J42	NA		4396	J14	B	5-57
4285	J42	B	11-51	4341	J42	NA		4397	J01	A	3-1
4286	J41	C	11-52	4342	J34	NA		4398	J14	C	5-60
4287	J35	A	11-53	4343	J42	NA		4399	J01	B	3-4
4288	J15	B	11-54	4344	J15	A	11-66	4400	J01	C	3-50
4289	H342	A	11-55	4345	H342	A	11-67	4401	J33	B	6-11
4290	H342	C	11-56	4346	H342	B	11-68	4402	J26	C	1-22
4291	J35	A	11-57	4347	J35	A	11-69	4403	J11	B	5-42
4292	J41	B	11-58	4348	J35	C	11-70	4404	J11	A	5-43
4293	J41	C	11-59	4349	J41	B	11-71	4405	J15	B	5-38
4294	J41	C	11-60	4350	J34	B	11-72	4406	J15	B	5-40
4295	J18	C	11-61	4351	J42	B	11-73	4407	J14	A	4-27
4296	J42	C	11-62	4352	J42	A	11-74	4408	J03	B	5-44
4297	J42	A	11-63	4353	J01	C	11-75	4409	J08	C	5-78
4298	J42	C	11-64	4354	J42	B	11-76	4410	J01	A	3-44
4299	J42	A	11-65	4355	J42	A	11-77	4411	J01	C	3-45
4300	J15	C	11-19	4356	J42	B	11-78	4412	J01	C	3-47
4301	H342	A	11-20	4357	J42	C	11-79	4413	J01	B	3-5
4302	H342	B	11-22	4358	J15	C	11-80	4414	J16	B	5-58

FAA		GLEIM		FAA		GLEIM		FAA		GLEIM	
Q. No.	Subject Code	Answer	Chap/ Q. No.	Q. No.	Subject Code	Answer	Chap/ Q. No.	Q. No.	Subject Code	Answer	Chap/ Q. No.
4415	J11	C	5-84	4471	J19	C	5-37	4527	J08	B	5-102
4416	J11	B	5-85	4472	H832	B	3-2	4528	J08	B	5-103
4417	J15	C	6-148	4473	J08	A	5-97	4529	J08	C	5-104
4418	J40	C	6-149	4474	J08	B	5-99	4530	J06	B	5-105
4419	J16	C	6-150	4475	J07	A	5-96	4531	J08	B	5-106
4420	J16	B	5-66	4476	J08	C	5-98	4532	J08	C	5-107
4421	J11	A	5-73	4477	H808	A	1-34	4533	J08	C	5-108
4422	J33	A	5-76	4478	H808	A	1-33	4534	J05	B	5-9
4423	J33	B	5-75	4479	H808	B	1-31	4535	J05	B	5-10
4424	J33	C	5-77	4480	J26	C	1-30	4536	J05	A	5-11
4425	B07	NA		4481	J26	C	1-41	4537	J05	B	5-12
4426	J08	C	4-31	4482	J26	C	1-36	4538	J13	C	5-65
4427	J08	C	4-67	4483	H808	C	1-27	4539	J08	A	5-109
4428	B08	NA		4484	H808	B	1-26	4540	J18	B	6-89
4429	J33	A	10-1	4485	J17	A	10-13	4541	B08	C	10-11
4430	J19	B	10-15	4486	J16	B	5-59	4542	J33	C	10-12
4431	J19	C	10-20	4487	H832	B	3-3	4543	B08	C	10-24
4432	J33	C	10-7	4488	J40	C	6-139	4544	J33	B	10-3
4433	J06	C	10-22	4489	J40	A	6-140	4545	J33	A	10-4
4434	J09	B	5-100	4490	J40	B	6-141	4546	J10	B	10-6
4435	J33	A	10-2	4491	J40	A	6-142	4547	J33	B	10-5
4436	J06	C	10-8	4492	J40	C	6-143	4548	H831	C	3-48
4437	J33	A	10-9	4493	J35	C	10-28	4549	H831	C	3-51
4438	J08	A	4-79	4494	J17	A	10-29	4550	H831	C	3-52
4439	J08	C	4-78	4495	J17	A	10-34	4551	H831	C	3-53
4440	J08	A	4-32	4496	J35	B	10-30	4552	H576	B	3-54
4441	B08	A	5-34	4497	J35	C	10-31	4553	I08	B	3-55
4442	J14	C	6-144	4498	J35	C	10-32	4554	H831	C	3-56
4443	J14	B	5-62	4499	J35	A	10-33	4555	J14	C	5-68
4444	J14	C	1-38	4500	J24	C	10-35	4556	H831	C	3-57
4445	J26	C	1-40	4501	J35	B	10-36	4557	H576	A	3-60
4446	J26	B	1-39	4502	J35	B	10-37	4558	H831	C	3-61
4447	J08	A	10-21	4503	B11	C	10-38	4559	H831	B	3-62
4448	B08	C	5-92	4504	J35	C	10-40	4560	H831	C	3-63
4449	J14	B	10-16	4505	B10	B	10-39	4561	H831	A	3-64
4450	J14	A	10-18	4506	J35	C	10-41	4562	H831	C	3-65
4451	J14	A	10-17	4507	J35	A	10-43	4563	H831	A	3-75
4452	J14	B	10-19	4508	J35	C	10-42	4564	H831	B	3-76
4453	J14	C	10-25	4509	J35	B	10-47	4565	H831	C	3-77
4454	J14	B	10-26	4510	J35	C	10-44	4566	H831	C	3-78
4455	J14	A	10-27	4511	H342	C	10-45	4567	H831	C	3-79
4456	B07	B	5-70	4512	J03	C	10-51	4568	H831	A	3-80
4457	J14	C	10-23	4513	B11	C	10-48	4569	H831	B	3-82
4458	J14	A	5-64	4514	H342	B	10-46	4570	H831	B	3-81
4459	B08	C	5-93	4515	J35	B	10-49	4571	H831	C	3-83
4460	J17	A	5-94	4516	J35	B	10-50	4572	H831	C	3-70
4461	J14	A	4-28	4517	J35	B	10-52	4573	H831	B	3-71
4462	J21	B	5-87	4518	B09	B	4-38	4574	H831	C	3-72
4463	J21	B	5-88	4519	B09	A	4-37	4575	H831	A	3-67
4464	J24	A	5-89	4520	B09	C	4-42	4576	H831	C	3-68
4465	J24	A	5-91	4521	B09	B	4-43	4577	H831	C	3-69
4466	J24	A	5-90	4522	B09	C	4-40	4578	H830	B	3-7
4467	J25	C	9-1	4523	B09	A	4-41	4579	H831	B	3-22
4468	J25	A	9-5	4524	B09	B	4-39	4580	H831	B	3-23
4469	J08	C	5-83	4525	B09	C	4-44	4581	H831	A	3-24
4470	J16	C	6-84	4526	J08	B	5-101	4582	H831	B	3-25

FAA Q. No.	Subject Code	GLEIM Answer	Chap/Q. No.	FAA Q. No.	Subject Code	GLEIM Answer	Chap/Q. No.	FAA Q. No.	Subject Code	GLEIM Answer	Chap/Q. No.
4583	H830	C	3-18	4640	J18	B	6-147	4697	B97	NA	
4584	H830	A	3-19	4641	J18	C	6-92	4698	J17	A	6-121
4585	H830	B	3-21	4642	J42	B	6-125	4699	J17	C	6-122
4586	H830	B	3-20	4643	J14	B	10-27a	4700	J42	C	6-123
4587	H831	A	3-29	4644	J14	NA		4701	B97	C	6-124
4588	H831	C	3-30	4645	J35	C	11-25	4702	J01	A	6-10
4589	H831	A	3-31	4646	J35	A	11-26	4703	J01	A	6-8
4590	H831	C	3-28	4647	J35	C	11-27	4704	J01	B	6-9
4591	H830	C	3-8	4648	J42	B	6-127	4705	J01	B	6-7
4592	H830	C	3-9	4649	J42	A	6-128	4706	B10	B	6-36
4593	H830	B	3-10	4650	J42	B	6-129	4707	J27	C	5-30
4594	H830	A	3-11	4651	J42	B	6-130	4708	J27	C	5-31
4595	H830	B	3-12	4652	J42	C	6-131	4709	J27	B	5-32
4596	H830	A	3-13	4653	J42	B	6-102	4710	J27	C	5-33
4597	H830	B	3-14	4654	J42	B	6-101	4711	J18	C	6-50
4598	H830	C	3-15	4655	J42	A	6-118	4712	J18	C	6-3a
4599	H830	A	3-16	4656	J42	A	6-119	4713	B10	NA	
4600	H830	C	3-17	4657	B97	B	6-132	4714	J18	A	6-95
4601	H831	B	3-59	4658	J18	C	6-133	4715	J18	A	6-81
4602	H831	B	3-26	4659	J42	B	6-134	4716	B10	A	6-13
4603	H831	A	3-27	4660	J33	C	6-135	4717	J18	B	6-83
4604	I08	B	3-58	4661	J42	A	6-136	4718	J18	A	6-2
4605	J17	B	5-74	4662	J42	A	6-96	4719	B10	C	4-48
4606	H831	A	3-66	4663	J01	B	3-46	4720	K04	B	6-40
4607	H831	C	3-73	4664	J01	A	6-33	4721	I10	B	6-41
4608	H831	C	3-74	4665	J01	C	3-6	4722	J42	NA	
4609	J17	B	6-62	4666	H831	B	3-49	4723	J42	NA	
4610	J17	A	6-69	4667	J18	A	6-16	4724	B97	NA	
4611	J17	B	6-70	4668	J17	C	6-80	4725	J19	C	5-81
4612	J17	C	6-71	4669	B97	A	6-20	4726	J18	B	5-80
4613	J17	B	6-72	4670	J18	A	6-93	4727	K04	C	6-45
4614	J17	C	6-65	4671	J18	A	6-86	4728	J18	C	6-51
4615	J17	C	6-66	4672	J18	A	6-90	4729	J01	C	6-25
4616	J17	A	6-67	4673	B97	NA		4730	J01	C	6-27
4617	J17	B	6-63	4674	J01	C	6-97	4731	J42	A	6-29
4618	J17	C	6-61	4675	J17	A	6-98	4732	J01	A	6-30
4619	J17	B	6-68	4676	B97	NA		4733	J42	B	6-31
4620	J17	C	6-60	4677	J42	B	6-99	4734	J18	A	6-91
4621	J17	C	6-74	4678	J18	A	6-100	4735	J18	C	6-4
4622	J17	B	6-75	4679	B97	NA		4736	J19	A	6-5
4623	J17	A	6-76	4680	I10	A	6-103	4737	J18	C	6-6
4624	J17	A	6-73	4681	J17	C	6-104	4738	V14	B	5-8
4625	J17	C	6-77	4682	J42	A	6-105	4739	K04	B	6-44
4626	J17	B	6-78	4683	J42	C	6-106	4740	J18	B	6-54
4627	J18	B	6-57	4684	J42	C	6-107	4741	J18	C	6-49
4628	J18	B	6-58	4685	H837	B	6-108	4742	J01	B	6-32
4629	J18	C	6-59	4686	J42	A	6-109	4743	J18	C	6-1
4630	B10	A	4-49	4687	J42	B	6-110	4744	J18	A	6-18
4631	J18	C	6-17	4688	J42	A	6-111	4745	K04	C	6-38
4632	J18	B	6-88	4689	J42	A	6-112	4746	J18	C	6-82
4633	J19	C	10-14	4690	J42	A	6-114	4747	J01	B	6-26
4634	J14	C	5-35	4691	B97	C	6-113	4748	K04	C	6-39
4635	J42	B	6-126	4692	J18	B	6-28	4749	J18	C	6-94
4636	J42	A	6-85	4693	J42	B	6-116	4750	J18	A	6-3
4637	B10	C	6-87	4694	J42	A	6-117	4751	J18	C	6-145
4638	J16	B	6-146	4695	J42	A	6-115	4752	J01	C	6-37
4639	J15	A	3-50a	4696	J42	B	6-120	4753	J01	B	6-21

FAA			GLEIM	FAA			GLEIM	FAA			GLEIM
Q. No.	Subject Code	Answer	Chap/ Q. No.	Q. No.	Subject Code	Answer	Chap/ Q. No.	Q. No.	Subject Code	Answer	Chap/ Q. No.
4754	B10	C	6-15	4810	J31	C	7-5	4866	H816	B	2-37
4755	K04	A	6-46	4811	J31	C	7-6	4867	H818	A	2-55
4756	H815	B	6-42	4812	J31	B	7-14	4868	H807	B	2-3
4757	J18	C	6-43	4813	J31	B	7-7	4869	H813	C	2-39
4758	J11	B	5-79	4814	J31	C	7-3	4870	H807	C	2-1
4759	B10	A	6-12	4815	J31	C	7-4	4871	H814	C	2-40
4760	B10	B	4-55	4816	J31	B	7-2	4872	H816	C	2-50
4761	B10	C	5-49	4817	J31	A	7-13	4873	H818	B	2-57
4762	B10	C	6-14	4818	J31	A	7-15	4874	H816	A	2-51
4763	B10	A	6-19	4819	J31	C	7-16	4875	H818	B	2-58
4764	J01	B	6-35	4820	H814	B	2-25	4876	H813	C	2-24
4765	B10	C	10-10	4821	L57	A	1-15	4877	H809	C	1-2
4766	J17	A	6-64	4822	J18	C	6-52	4878	H816	B	2-11
4767	J17	A	6-79	4823	J18	A	6-53	4879	H808	C	1-19
4768	J17	B	6-56	4824	H837	B	6-22	4880	H812	C	1-23
4769	B10	C	4-56	4825	H837	C	6-23	4881	L59	C	1-47
4770	J01	B	6-34	4826	H837	A	6-24	4882	L59	B	1-62
4771	J18	A	6-55	4827	H809	C	1-50	4883	L59	A	1-63
4772	K04	B	6-47	4828	H809	A	1-51	4884	H807	C	2-52
4773	H837	A	6-48	4829	H809	C	1-52	4885	H812	A	1-49
4774	J03	B	5-14	4830	L57	C	1-13	4886	H314	C	1-3
4775	J03	B	5-15	4831	H812	B	1-68	4887	H314	A	1-4
4776	J03	C	5-18	4832	H814	A	2-42	4888	H314	B	1-5
4777	J03	A	5-19	4833	H816	A	2-12	4889	H809	C	1-6
4778	J03	A	5-16	4834	H812	C	1-1	4890	H314	A	1-7
4779	J03	C	5-17	4835	H812	A	1-54	4891	H314	C	1-8
4780	J03	A	5-20	4836	H815	A	2-36	4892	H314	B	1-9
4781	J03	B	5-13	4837	H815	A	2-43	4893	H314	C	1-10
4782	J03	C	5-21	4838	H816	B	2-44	4894	H314	B	1-11
4783	J03	B	5-22	4839	H810	A	1-65	4895	H810	C	2-15
4784	J03	C	5-23	4840	H813	C	2-34	4896	H810	A	2-16
4785	J03	A	5-24	4841	H822	NA		4897	H810	B	2-17
4786	J03	B	5-25	4842	H812	C	1-53	4898	H807	C	2-18
4787	J03	C	5-26	4843	H807	A	2-2	4899	H807	B	2-21
4788	J03	A	5-27	4844	H807	B	2-10	4900	H810	A	1-59
4789	J03	B	5-28	4845	H815	A	2-53	4901	H810	B	1-56
4790	J03	C	5-29	4846	H828	NA		4902	H810	B	1-48
4791	J05	B	5-1	4847	H810	A	1-64	4903	H810	A	2-20
4792	J05	B	5-2	4848	H815	C	2-49	4904	H807	C	2-13
4793	J05	B	5-3	4849	H827	NA		4905	H807	C	2-14
4794	J05	A	5-6	4850	H816	A	2-45	4906	H815	A	2-22
4795	J03	C	5-5	4851	H816	C	2-46	4907	H815	A	2-23
4796	J03	A	5-4	4852	H827	NA		4908	I04	C	1-17
4797	J05	C	5-7	4853	H815	B	2-48	4909	H808	A	1-12
4798	J01	B	6-152	4854	L57	A	1-14	4910	H312	B	1-25
4799	J01	A	6-153	4855	H813	B	2-32	4911	H808	B	1-35
4800	J01	NA		4856	H816	A	1-66	4912	H808	B	1-32
4801	J01	C	6-154	4857	H810	C	1-58	4913	H808	C	1-16
4802	H800	A	7-8	4858	H816	A	2-47	4914	H807	B	2-19
4803	J31	A	7-17	4859	H813	C	2-33	4915	H807	B	2-4
4804	J31	A	7-18	4860	H810	B	1-57	4916	H303	B	2-66
4805	J31	A	7-9	4861	I04	C	1-55	4917	K04	B	2-67
4806	J31	C	7-12	4862	H813	B	2-31	4918	H810	A	1-61
4807	J31	A	7-10	4863	H814	C	2-35	4919	H810	C	1-60
4808	J31	B	7-11	4864	H810	A	1-21	4920	H814	C	2-41
4809	J31	B	7-1	4865	H814	C	2-38	4921	H816	C	1-67

FAA		GLEIM		FAA		GLEIM		FAA		GLEIM	
Q. No.	Subject Code	Answer	Chap/ Q. No.	Q. No.	Subject Code	Answer	Chap/ Q. No.	Q. No.	Subject Code	Answer	Chap/ Q. No.
4922	H808	B	1-28	0601-835	H814	NA	2-23a	0601-937	H758	NA	
4923	H808	B	1-24	0601-836	H822	NA		0601-940	H758	NA	
4924	H815	C	2-26	0601-851	H825	C	2-12a	0601-942	H758	NA	
4925	H815	B	2-27	0601-855	H823	NA		0601-944	H758	NA	
4926	H815	B	2-28	0601-857	H823	NA		0601-948	H758	NA	
4927	H818	C	2-59	0601-859	H825	NA		0601-961	H823	NA	
4928	H815	C	2-29	0601-862	H821	NA		0601-963	H824	NA	
4929	H815	A	2-30	0601-866	H703	NA		0601-964	H859	A	1-18a
4930	H312	B	1-18	0601-873	H825	NA		0601-973	J37	NA	
4931	H814	A	2-5	0601-878	H825	NA		0601-979	H822	NA	
4932	H814	A	2-6	0601-884	H821	NA		0601-985	H824	NA	
4933	H814	B	2-8	0601-888	H825	NA		0601-993	H758	NA	
4934	I04	B	2-7	0601-890	H821	NA		0601-995	H758	NA	
4935	H814	C	2-9	0601-892	H816	B	2-12c	0601-997	H758	NA	
4936	H818	B	2-54	0601-895	H821	NA		0601-999	H516	NA	
4937	H818	A	2-60	0601-897	H822	NA		0601-1001	H758	NA	
4938	H818	B	2-56	0601-899	H822	NA		0601-1006	H826	NA	
4939	H818	B	2-61	0601-902	H825	NA		0601-1008	H826	NA	
4940	H818	C	2-62	0601-905	H703	NA		0601-1010	H826	NA	
4941	H818	A	2-63	0601-907	H821	NA		1001-1	J05	B	5-12a
4942	H826	B	2-64	0601-911	H822	NA		1001-2	J05	A	5-12b
0601-292	H833	B	11-53a	0601-913	H825	NA		1001-3	J05	C	5-12c
0601-331	J42	A	11-43a	0601-917	H825	NA		1001-4	J05	B	5-12d
0601-614	H842	A	11-84a	0601-921	H822	NA		1001-758	J01	B	3-85
0601-767	H824	NA		0601-933	H758	NA		1001-760	J01	B	3-86
0601-772	B10	B	4-56a	0601-935	H758	NA		1001-762	J01	C	3-87

ABBREVIATIONS AND ACRONYMS IN
INSTRUMENT PILOT FAA WRITTEN EXAM

A/FD	*Airport/Facility Directory*
AC	Severe Weather Outlook Chart
AC	Advisory Circular
AC	convective outlook
AC Form	Airman Certification Form (i.e., AC Form 8080-2)
ADF	automatic direction finder
ADIZ	Air Defense Identification Zone
AGL	above ground level
AI	attitude indicator
AIM	*Aeronautical Information Manual*
AIRMET	airman's meteorological information
ALS	approach light systems
ALT	altimeter
AME	aviation medical examiner
ARTCC	Air Route Traffic Control Center
ASI	airspeed indicator
ASR	airport surveillance radar
ATC	air traffic control
ATIS	Automatic Terminal Information Service
CAS	calibrated airspeed
CAT	clear air turbulence
CDI	course deviation indicator
CFII	certificated flight instructor -- instrument
COP	changeover point
CTAF	common traffic advisory frequency
DH	decision height
DME	distance measuring equipment
DP	departure procedure
DUATS	Direct User Access Terminal System
EFAS	En Route Flight Advisory Service
EFC	expected further clearance
ELT	emergency locator transmitter
ETA	estimated time of arrival
ETE	estimated time en route
FA	area forecast
FAA	Federal Aviation Administration
FAF	final approach fix
FAR	Federal Aviation Regulation
FBO	fixed-base operator
FD	winds and temperatures aloft forecast
FDC NOTAM	Flight Data Center Notice to Airmen
FL	flight level
FSDO	Flight Standards District Office
FSS	Flight Service Station
GPH	gallons per hour
GS	glide slope or groundspeed
HAA	height above airport
HAT	height above touchdown
Hg	mercury
HI	heading indicator
HIRL	high-intensity runway lights
HSI	horizontal situation indicator
IAF	initial approach fix
IAP	instrument approach procedure
IAS	indicated airspeed
ICAO	International Civil Aviation Organization
IFR	instrument flight rules
IGI	instrument ground instructor
ILS	instrument landing system
IM	inner marker
IMC	instrument meteorological conditions
INT	intersection
ISA	international standard atmosphere
KCAS	knots calibrated airspeed
LAA	Local Airport Advisory
LDA	localizer-type directional aid
LF	low frequency
LMM	middle compass locator
LOC	localizer
LOM	outer compass locator
LORAN	long range navigation
MAA	maximum authorized altitude
MAP	missed approach point
Mb	millibar
MB	magnetic bearing
MCA	minimum crossing altitude
MDA	minimum descent altitude
MEA	minimum en route altitude
METAR	aviation routine weather report
MH	magnetic heading
MHA	minimum holding altitude
MIRL	medium-intensity runway lights
MLS	microwave landing system
MM	middle marker
MOA	Military Operations Area
MOCA	minimum obstruction clearance altitude
MP	manifold pressure
MRA	minimum reception altitude
MSA	minimum safe altitude
MSL	mean sea level
NAVAID	navigational aid
NDB	nondirectional radio beacon
NoPT	no procedure turn
NOTAM	Notice to Airmen
NTSB	National Transportation Safety Board
OAT	outside air temperature
OBS	omnibearing selector
OM	outer marker
PAPI	precision approach path indicator
PAR	precision approach radar
PIC	pilot in command
PIREP	pilot weather report
PTS	Practical Test Standards
RAIL	runway alignment indicator lights
RB	relative bearing
REIL	runway end identifier lights
RIC	remote indicating compass
RMI	radio magnetic indicator
RNAV	area navigation
RPM	revolutions per minute (tachometer)
RVR	runway visual range
SDF	simplified directional facility
SIAP	standard instrument approach procedure
SIGMET	significant meteorological information
STAR	standard terminal arrival route
SVFR	special VFR
T&SI	turn-and-slip indicator
TACAN	tactical air navigation
TAF	terminal aerodrome forecast
TAS	true airspeed
TC	turn coordinator
TDZ	touchdown zone
TDZE	touchdown zone elevation
TWEB	Transcribed Weather Broadcast
UTC	Coordinated Universal Time
VASI	visual approach slope indicator
VDP	visual descent point
VFR	visual flight rules
VHF	very high frequency
VMC	visual meteorological conditions
VOR	VHF omnidirectional range
VORTAC	collocated VOR and TACAN
VOT	VOR test facility
VSI	vertical speed indicator
Z	Zulu or UTC time

470

INDEX OF LEGENDS AND FIGURES

FOR CHOOSING GLEIM

We dedicate ourselves to providing pilots with knowledge transfer systems, enabling them to pass the FAA knowledge (written) tests and FAA practical (flight) tests. We solicit your feedback. Use the last page in this book to make notes as you use *Instrument Pilot FAA Written Exam* and other Gleim products. Tear out the page and mail it to us when convenient. Alternatively, e-mail (irvin@gleim.com) or FAX (352-375-6940) your feedback to us.

GLEIM'S E-MAIL UPDATE SERVICE

update@gleim.com

Your message to Gleim must include (in the subject or body) the acronym for your book or software, followed by the edition-printing for books and version for software. The edition-printing is indicated on the book's spine and at the bottom right corner of the cover. The software version is indicated on the CD-ROM label.

	Written Exam		Flight Maneuvers
	Book	Software	Book
Private Pilot	PPWE	FAATP PPWE	PPFM
Instrument Pilot	IPWE	FAATP IPWE	IPFM
Commercial Pilot	CPWE	FAATP CPWE	CPFM
Flight/Ground Instructor	FIGI	FAATP FIGI	FIFM
Fundamentals of Instructing	FOI	FAATP FOI	
Airline Transport Pilot	ATP	FAATP ATP	
Flight Engineer	FEWE	FAATP FEWE	

	Reference Book
Pilot Handbook	PH
Aviation Weather and Weather Services	AWWS
Private Pilot Syllabus and Logbook	PPSYL
Instrument Pilot Syllabus	IPSYL
Commercial Pilot Syllabus	CPSYL
FAR/AIM	FARAIM

E
X
A
M
P
L
E

For *Instrument Pilot FAA Written Exam,* seventh edition-sixth printing:

> To: update@gleim.com
> From: your e-mail address
> Subject: IPWE 7-6

For *FAA Test Prep* software, Instrument Pilot, version 4.0:

> To: update@gleim.com
> From: your e-mail address
> Subject: FAATP IP 4-0

IT
ONLY
TAKES
A
MINUTE

If you do not have e-mail, have a friend send e-mail to us and print our response for you.

INSTRUCTOR AUTHORIZATION FORM
INSTRUMENT RATING KNOWLEDGE TEST

Name: _____

    I certify that I have reviewed the above individual's preparation for the FAA Instrument Rating -- Airplane knowledge test [covering the topics specified in FAR 61.65(b)(1) through (10)] using the *Instrument Pilot FAA Written Exam* book and/or software by Irvin N. Gleim and find him/her competent to pass the knowledge test.

_____ _____ _____ _____ _____
Signed   Date   Name   CFI Number Expiration Date

AUTHOR'S RECOMMENDATION

The Experimental Aircraft Association, Inc. is a very successful and effective nonprofit organization that represents and serves those of us interested in flying, in general, and in sport aviation, in particular. I personally invite you to enjoy becoming a member. Visit their web site at http://www.eaa.org.

$40 for a 1-year membership
$56 for a 1-year membership (international)
$23 per year for individuals under 19 years old
Family membership available for $50 per year

> Membership includes the monthly magazine *Sport Aviation*.

Write to: EAA Aviation Center
P.O. Box 3086
Oshkosh, Wisconsin 54903-3086

Or call: (920) 426-4800
(800) 564-6322

The annual EAA Oshkosh AirVenture is an unbelievable aviation spectacular with over 12,000 airplanes at one airport! Virtually everything aviation-oriented you can imagine! Plan to spend at least 1 day (not everything can be seen in a day) in Oshkosh (100 miles northwest of Milwaukee).

Convention dates: 2002 -- July 23 through July 29
2003 -- July 29 through August 4

The annual Sun 'n Fun EAA Fly-In is also highly recommended. It is held at the Lakeland, FL (KLAL) airport (between Orlando and Tampa). Visit the Sun 'n Fun web site at http://www.sun-n-fun.org.

Convention dates: 2002 -- April 7 through April 13
2003 -- April 6 through April 12

BE-A-PILOT: INTRODUCTORY FLIGHT

Be-A-Pilot is an industry-sponsored marketing program designed to inspire people to "Stop dreaming, start flying." Be-A-Pilot has sought flight schools to participate in the program and offers a $49 introductory flight certificate that can be redeemed at a participating flight school.

The goal of this program is to encourage people to experience their dreams of flying through an introductory flight and to begin taking flying lessons.

For more information, you can visit the Be-A-Pilot home page at http://www.beapilot.com or call 1-888-BE-A-PILOT.

AIRCRAFT OWNERS AND PILOTS ASSOCIATION

AOPA is the largest, most influential aviation association in the world, with more than 370,000 members--half of all pilots in the United States. AOPA's most important contribution to the world's most accessible, safest, least expensive, friendliest, easiest-to-use general aviation environment is their lobbying on our behalf at the federal, state, and local levels. AOPA also provides legal services, advice, and other assistance to the aviation community.

We recommend that you become an AOPA member, which costs only $39 annually. To join, call 1-800-USA-AOPA or visit the AOPA Web site www.aopa.org.

AN OVERVIEW OF GLEIM'S *FAA TEST PREP* SOFTWARE FOR WINDOWS

Gleim's *FAA Test Prep for Windows*™ contains many of the same features found in earlier versions. However, we have simplified the study process by incorporating the outlines and figures from our books into the new software. Everything you need to study for any of the FAA knowledge tests will be contained in one unique, easy-to-use program. Below are some of the enhancements you will find with our new study software.

USE GLEIM'S *FAA TEST PREP* --
A POWERFUL TOOL IN THE
GLEIM KNOWLEDGE TRANSFER SYSTEM

Give yourself the competitive edge! Because all of the FAA's "written" tests have been converted to computer testing, Gleim has developed software specifically designed to prepare you for the computerized pilot knowledge test.

➡ *FAATP* emulates the computer testing vendor of your choice -- CATS, LaserGrade, or AvTEST. You will be completely familiar with the computer testing system you will be using.

➡ *FAATP* has two interactive modes: "Study" and "Test." Study mode permits you to select questions from specific sources, e.g., Gleim modules, questions that you missed from the last session, etc. You can also determine the order of the questions (Gleim or random), and you can randomize the order of the answer choices for each question.

➡ *FAATP* precludes you from looking at the answers before you commit to an answer and provides the actual testing environment. This is a major difference from the book.

➡ *FAATP* contains the well-known Gleim answer explanations which are intuitively appealing and easy to understand.

➡ *FAATP* maintains a history of your proficiency in each topic. This enables you to focus your study only on topics that need additional study.

➡ *FAATP* is the most versatile and complete software available.

Index

━━ PILOT KNOWLEDGE TEST (WRITTEN EXAM) BOOKS AND SOFTWARE ━━

Before pilots take their FAA knowledge tests, they want to understand the answer to every FAA test question. Gleim's *FAA Written Exam* books and *FAA Test Prep* software have set the standard in FAA knowledge test preparation. Gleim's easy-to-use format helps pilots learn and understand exactly what they need to know to pass. Each chapter includes a study outline, actual FAA questions, and answer explanations. Gleim's *FAA Test Prep* provides standard FAA tests under simulated exam conditions. Additional information can be found in our reference books.

Books

- *Private Pilot FAA Written Exam*
- *Instrument Pilot FAA Written Exam*
- *Commercial Pilot FAA Written Exam*
- *Flight/Ground Instructor FAA Written Exam*
- *Fundamentals of Instructing FAA Written Exam*
- *Airline Transport Pilot FAA Written Exam*
- *Flight Engineer FAA Written Exam*

Software

- *Private Pilot FAA Test Prep*
- *Instrument Pilot FAA Test Prep*
- *Commercial Pilot FAA Test Prep*
- *Flight/Ground Instructor FAA Test Prep* (includes *Fundamentals of Instructing*)
- *Airline Transport Pilot FAA Test Prep*
- *Flight Engineer FAA Test Prep*

━━ REFERENCE AND FLIGHT MANEUVERS/PRACTICAL TEST PREP BOOKS ━━

Pilot Handbook - A complete ground school text using an outline format with diagrams. This book augments and enhances Gleim's *FAA Written Exam* books in preparing pilots for the private, commercial, and flight instructor certificates and the instrument rating. A complete, organized, and detailed text makes it useful and saves time. It also contains a special section on flight reviews.

Aviation Weather and Weather Services - A complete rewrite of the FAA's *Aviation Weather* (AC 00-6A) and *Aviation Weather Services* (AC 00-45E) into a single, easy-to-understand book complete with maps, diagrams, charts, and pictures. Pilots can learn and understand the subject matter more easily and effectively with this book.

FAR/AIM - The purpose of this book is to consolidate the common parts of Title 14 of the Code of Federal Regulations (14 CFR) [formerly known as the *Federal Aviation Regulations* (FAR)] and the *Aeronautical Information Manual* (AIM) into one easy-to-use reference book. Gleim's **FAR/AIM** resets the standard with a better presentation, easier-to-read type, improved indexes, and full-color figures. Included are Parts 1,43, 61, 67, 71, 73, 91, 97, 103, 105, 119, Appendices I and J of 121, 135, 137, 141, and 142.

Gleim's *Flight Maneuvers* books are designed to simplify and facilitate flight training and will help pilots prepare for the FAA practical test. Each task, objective, concept, requirement, etc. in the FAA Practical Test Standards is explained, analyzed, illustrated, and interpreted so pilots will gain practical test proficiency as quickly as possible. The actual FAA Practical Tests Standards are included.

- *Private Pilot Flight Maneuvers and Practical Test Prep*
- *Instrument Pilot Flight Maneuvers and Practical Test Prep*
- *Commercial Pilot Flight Maneuvers and Practical Test Prep*
- *Flight Instructor Flight Maneuvers and Practical Test Prep*

━━ PILOT KITS ━━

Gleim's Pilot Kits provide everything a pilot needs to complete his/her training, except an airplane, local charts, and a flight instructor. Each kit contains the easiest, most effective, and least expensive pilot training materials available.

Private Pilot Kit   *Instrument Pilot Kit*   *Commercial Pilot Kit*   *Instrument/Commercial Pilot Kit*

━━ ONLINE REFRESHER COURSES ━━

Flight Instructor Refresher Course is the first FAA-approved online CFI renewal program. Gleim's FIRC contains all of the lessons and tests required to renew your CFI certificate. Visit www.gleim.com/firc to try Lesson 1 FREE and begin your renewal today.

Private Pilot Refresher Course is a recurrent ground training course designed to increase pilot knowledge and safety. Gleim's PPRC is designed to meet the ground school requirement for the flight review. It also satisfies the "safety meeting" requirement for the FAA's Pilot Proficiency Award Program (Wings Program). Visit www.gleim.com/pprc to try Lesson 1 FREE.

| Gleim Publications, Inc.
P.O. Box 12848
Gainesville, FL 32604 | TOLL FREE:
LOCAL:
FAX:
INTERNET:
E-MAIL: | (800) 87-GLEIM/(800) 874-5346
(352) 375-0772
(888) 375-6940 (toll free)
http://www.gleim.com
sales@gleim.com | Customer service is available:
8:00 a.m. - 7:00 p.m., Mon. - Fri.
9:00 a.m. - 2:00 p.m., Saturday
Please have your credit card ready or
save time by ordering online! |

Gleim's *PRIVATE PILOT KIT*
Includes everything you need to pass the FAA pilot knowledge (written) test and FAA practical test.
Our price is far lower than similarly equipped kits found elsewhere . . . . $119.95 _____

Gleim's *INSTRUMENT PILOT KIT*
Everything you need, just like our Private Pilot Kit. With CD-ROM . . . . $114.95 _____

Gleim's *COMMERCIAL PILOT KIT*
Everything you need to prepare for your commercial certificate. With CD-ROM . . . . $94.95 _____

SPECIAL COMBO: *INSTRUMENT/COMMERCIAL KIT* . . . . $189.95 _____

KNOWLEDGE TEST

	Books	Software*	Book/Software	Audios**	Book/Software*/ Audios**	
Private/Recreational Pilot	☐ @ $15.95	☐ @ $49.95	☐ @ $58.95	☐ @ $60	☐ @ $106.95	_____
Instrument Pilot	☐ @ $18.95	☐ @ $59.95	☐ @ $70.95	☐ @ $60	☐ @ $117.95	_____
Commercial Pilot	☐ @ $14.95	☐ @ $59.95	☐ @ $66.95	**Please select audio format.**		_____
Fundamentals of Instructing	☐ @ $12.95	☐ } both for		☐ CDs ☐ Cassettes		_____
Flight/Ground Instructor	☐ @ $14.95	☐ } $59.95	☐ @ $66.95			_____
Airline Transport Pilot	☐ @ $26.95	☐ @ $59.95	☐ @ $77.95			_____
Flight Engineer	☐ @ $26.95	☐ @ $59.95	☐ @ $77.95			_____

*CD-ROM (Windows) includes all questions, figures, charts, and outlines for each of the pilot knowledge tests.

REFERENCE AND FLIGHT MANEUVERS/PRACTICAL TEST PREP BOOKS

FAR/AIM	$15.95	_____
Aviation Weather and Weather Services	22.95	_____
Pilot Handbook	13.95	_____
Private Pilot Flight Maneuvers and Practical Test Prep	16.95	_____
Instrument Pilot Flight Maneuvers and Practical Test Prep	18.95	_____
Commercial Pilot Flight Maneuvers and Practical Test Prep	14.95	_____
Flight Instructor Flight Maneuvers and Practical Test Prep	17.95	_____

OTHER BOOKS AND ACCESSORIES

Private Pilot Syllabus and Logbook	$ 9.95	_____
Instrument Pilot Syllabus	14.95	_____
Commercial Pilot Syllabus	14.95	_____
Flight Computer	9.95	_____
Navigational Plotter	5.95	_____
Flight Bag	29.95	_____

Shipping (nonrefundable): **First item = $5; each additional item = $1** $_____

Add applicable sales tax for shipments within the State of Florida.

Please FAX, e-mail, or write for additional charges for outside the 48 contiguous United States. **TOTAL** $_____

Printed 11/01. Prices subject to change without notice.

1. We process and ship orders daily, within one business day over 98.8% of the time. Call by noon for same-day service!
2. Please PHOTOCOPY this order form for others.
3. No CODs. Orders from individuals must be prepaid. Library and company orders may be purchased on account.
4. Gleim Publications, Inc. guarantees the immediate refund of all resalable texts and unopened software and audios if returned within 30 days. Applies only to items purchased direct from Gleim Publications, Inc. Our shipping charge is nonrefundable.
5. Components of specially priced package deals are nonreturnable.

NAME (please print) _____

ADDRESS _____ Apt. _____
(street address required for UPS)

_____

CITY _____ STATE _____ ZIP _____

_____ MC/VISA/DISC _____ Check/M.O.   Daytime
Telephone (____)_____

Credit Card No. _____ - _____ - _____ - _____

Exp. ____/____   Signature _____
Mo./Yr.

Please forward your suggestions, corrections, and comments concerning typographical errors, etc., to **Irvin N. Gleim • c/o Gleim Publications, Inc. • P.O. Box 12848 • University Station • Gainesville, Florida • 32604**. Please include your name and address on the back of this page so we can properly thank you for your interest. Also, please refer to both the page number and the FAA question number for each item.

1. _____

2. _____

3. _____

4. _____

5. _____

6. _____

7. _____

8. _____

9. _____

We need your help identifying which questions the FAA is pretesting (but not grading - see page 4). After you take your exam, please e-mail, fax, or mail us a description of these questions so we can anticipate their future use by the FAA.

10. _____

11. _____

12. _____

13. _____

14. _____

15. _____

16. _____

17. _____

| Remember for superior service: | Mail, e-mail, or fax questions about our books or software. |
| | Telephone questions about orders, prices, shipments, or payments. |

Name: _____

Address: _____

City/State/Zip: _____

Telephone: Home: _____   Work: _____   FAX: _____

E-mail _____

GLEIM BOOKMARK

Dr. Gleim's Recommendation: Cover the answers and explanations in your book with this bookmark to make sure you do NOT cheat yourself. The answers will not be alongside the questions when you take your exam. Use our test prep software, flight maneuvers/ practical test prep books, audio lectures, and online programs to complete your training.

FAA TEST PREP SOFTWARE

CD-ROM version for Windows 95, Windows 98, and Windows NT. Outlines, figures, and questions are integrated in our new interface.

Private thru ATP available.

> **If you don't have it - GET IT!**
> *FAA Test Prep* software will enhance your effectiveness in passing your FAA Knowledge Test.

FLIGHT MANEUVERS / PRACTCAL TEST PREP BOOKS

These books are designed to replace or enhance the FAA Practical Test Standards reprints. Gleim integrates the FAA books, advisory circulars, FARs, Practical Test Standards, etc., into one easy-to-use text. In addition to being complete, each book is well organized and structured to focus on exactly what you need to know and do to pass your FAA practical test.

ONLINE LEARNING TOOLS

Gleim currently offers the following programs for aviation online learning:

Non-airplane Question and Answer Service

Go to: www.gleim.com/Aviation/nonairplane/
All non-airplane questions are listed by certificate & rating.

Flight Instructor Refresher Course (FIRC)

CFIs can renew their certificates at their convenience by using Gleim's online FIRC. Visit www.gleim.com/firc/ and try Lesson One for FREE.

Private Pilot Refresher Course (PPRC)

PPRC is a recurrent ground training course designed to increase your knowledge and abilities while preparing you for your flight review. Visit www.gleim.com/pprc/ and try Lesson One for FREE.

(800) 87-GLEIM • www.gleim.com

GLEIM BOOKMARK

Dr. Gleim's Recommendation: Cover the answers and explanations in your book with this bookmark to make sure you do NOT cheat yourself. The answers will not be alongside the questions when you take your exam. Use our test prep software, flight maneuvers/ practical test prep books, audio lectures, and online programs to complete your training.

FAA TEST PREP SOFTWARE

CD-ROM version for Windows 95, Windows 98, and Windows NT. Outlines, figures, and questions are integrated in our new interface.

Private thru ATP available.

> **If you don't have it - GET IT!**
> *FAA Test Prep* software will enhance your effectiveness in passing your FAA Knowledge Test.

FLIGHT MANEUVERS / PRACTCAL TEST PREP BOOKS

These books are designed to replace or enhance the FAA Practical Test Standards reprints. Gleim integrates the FAA books, advisory circulars, FARs, Practical Test Standards, etc., into one easy-to-use text. In addition to being complete, each book is well organized and structured to focus on exactly what you need to know and do to pass your FAA practical test.

ONLINE LEARNING TOOLS

Gleim currently offers the following programs for aviation online learning:

Non-airplane Question and Answer Service

Go to: www.gleim.com/Aviation/nonairplane/
All non-airplane questions are listed by certificate & rating.

Flight Instructor Refresher Course (FIRC)

CFIs can renew their certificates at their convenience by using Gleim's online FIRC. Visit www.gleim.com/firc/ and try Lesson One for FREE.

Private Pilot Refresher Course (PPRC)

PPRC is a recurrent ground training course designed to increase your knowledge and abilities while preparing you for your flight review. Visit www.gleim.com/pprc/ and try Lesson One for FREE.

(800) 87-GLEIM • www.gleim.com